W9-COX-966

Twin City Tales

It is a special pleasure to present Lindsay Jones's Twin City Tales as the third volume in our series Mesoamerican Worlds. Jones's original study of the symbolic, architectural, and historical relationships between Tula and Chichén Itzá reflects the labor and insights of a new generation of historians of religions working in the field of Mesoamerican cultures. The formation of Jones's vision took place, in part, under the influence of the Mesoamerican Archive at the University of Colorado–Boulder, and his rich interpretive voice extends the lessons of his teachers in entirely new directions. The discussion of the Toltec and Maya cities is expanded and depended in this finely illustrated volume.

DAVÍD CARRASCO AND EDUARDO MATOS MOCTEZUMA

Mesoamerican Worlds: From the Olmecs to the Danzantes

Twin City Tales:

A Hermeneutical Reassessment of Tula and Chichén Itzá

Lindsay Jones

Photographs by Lawrence G. Desmond

UNIVERSITY PRESS OF COLORADO

Published by the University Press of Colorado
P. O. Box 849
Niwot, Colorado 80544

The University Press of Colorado is a cooperative publishing enterprise supported, in part, by Adams State College, Colorado State University, Fort Lewis College, Mesa State College, Metropolitan State College of Denver, University of Colorado, University of Northern Colorado, University of Southern Colorado, and Western State College of Colorado.

Library of Congress Cataloging-in-Publication Data

Jones, Lindsay, 1954–
Twin City Tales : a hermeneutical reassessment of Tula and Chichén Itzá / Lindsay Jones ; photographs by Lawrence G. Desmond.
p. cm.
Includes bibliographical references and index.
ISBN 0-87081-403-6 (cloth : alk. paper)
1. Tula Site (Tula de Allende, Mexico) 2. Chichén Itzá Site (Mexico) 3. Indian architecture—Mexico. 4. Indians of Mexico—Religion. 5. indian of Mexico—Antiquities. I. Title.
F1219.1.T8J66 1995
972'.46—dc20 95-12731
CIP

This book was set in ITC Usherwood.

The paper used in this publication meets the minimum requirements of the American National Standard for Information Sciences—Permanence of Paper for Printed Library Materials. ANSI Z39.48–1948
∞

10 9 8 7 6 5 4 3 2 1

To Professora Alicia Alfaro Villamil, for opening her home and my way to Mexico

Contents

Preface

One Sunday night in the fall of 1987, I found myself sitting in the back of a huge fortress-like cathedral in Cuernavaca, Morelos, Mexico, immediately under the arch that held up the rear balcony. The upright portion of that arch protruded slightly from the wall, and at its base was a stone relief of an angel, some 3 feet high, hands folded toward the altar.

Inside the cathedral in Cuernavaca, Morelos, Mexico. (Photo courtesy of Anupama G. Mande.)

The place was hot and packed full when the priest made his dramatic entrance. Dressed in elaborate vestments and swinging his incense decanter, he led a very formal procession to the altar and then, to the oddly appropriate background music of mariachi guitars, the celebration of the Eucharist began. More memorable than the actual mass, however, was a little Mexican boy, perhaps three years old, who wandered in the aisle in front of me and who became fascinated with the modest carving of the angel, which was, conveniently enough, precisely his height. Seemingly oblivious to the meticulously choreographed mass with its music, vestments, scriptural readings, and holy sacraments, this little boy spent the hour in the side aisle involved, instead, in a very animated exchange with this same-sized stone angel. He paced in front of her, a diligent if unintimidating sentry, guarding the praying stone cherub. Yet, at each pass, he paused, confronted the angel, nose to nose, put his hands all over her, interrogated her, and then stepped back, impatient and fully expectant, so it seemed, of a response.[1]

This encounter between an inquisitive child and a 350-year-old stone angel, a ritual-architectural event of compelling simplicity, a hermeneutical conversation in which a human being questioned an architectural monument and then listened for its answer, provides the image that sustains this project. Overstuffed with outlines, distinctions and disclaimers, abstractions and methodologies, critical

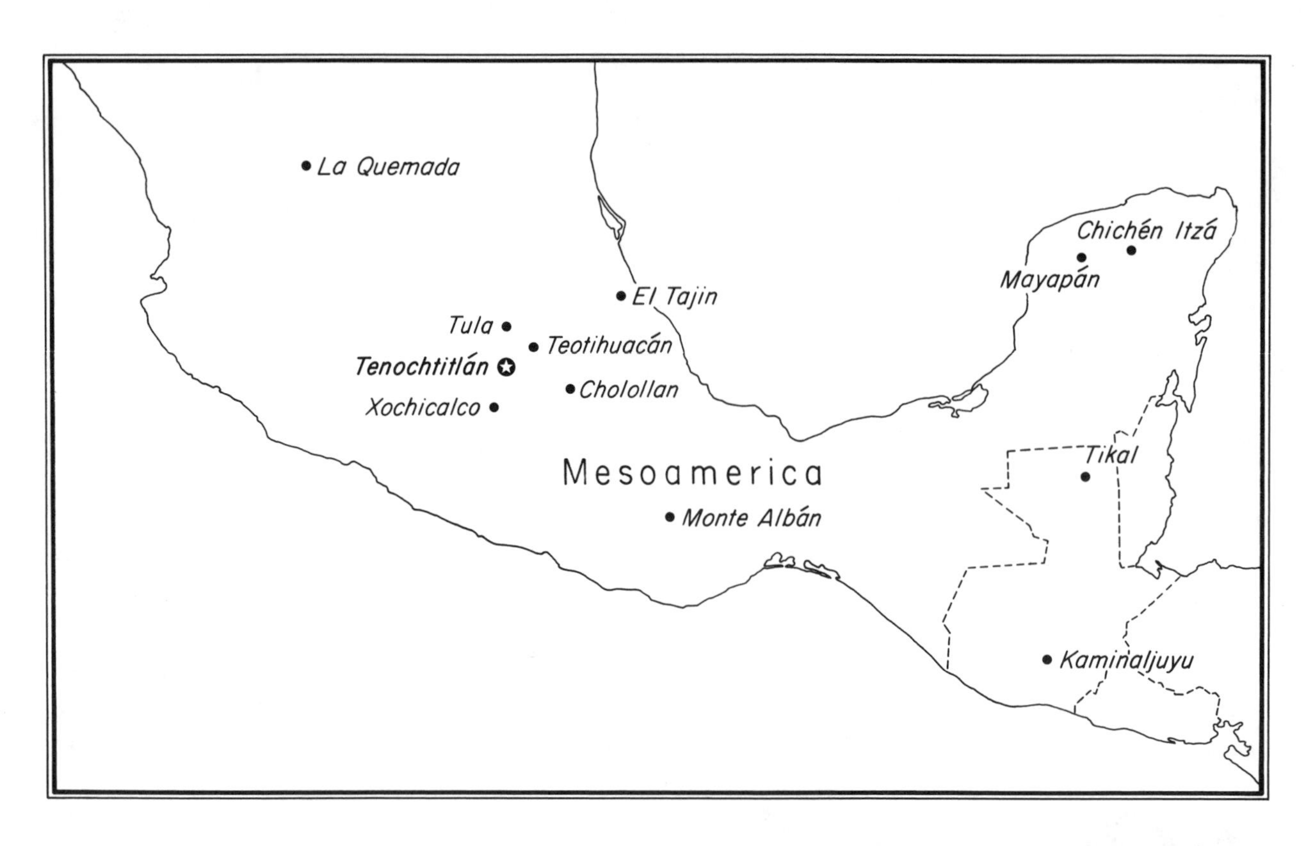

Mesoamerica. (Reprinted from *Quetzacoatl and the Irony of Empire* by Davíd Carrasco. Copyright ©1982 by the University of Chicago Press.)

reviews and recommendations, in the end, my work aspires to nothing more complicated than this: to engage, as that young Mexican did, the ancient monuments of Mesoamerica in conversation, to question and speak to them, and to listen for their answers.

Notes

1. A version of this paragraph appeared in Lindsay Jones, "The Hermeneutics of Sacred Architecture: A Reassessment of the Similitude Between Tula, Hidalgo and Chichén Itzá, Yucatán; Part I, *History of Religions* 32 (February 1993): 207.

Acknowledgments

This book, at least in its early drafts, was written on the roll, the work of a transient with a pencil and a truckload of books. Consequently, its strengths, weaknesses, and idiosyncrasies owe equally to people and places. From the first place, the University of Colorado at Boulder, I must thank David Carrasco (currently at Princeton University), who contributed generously to every stage of the process. He provided not only the initial stimulus with respect to the matters of sacred space but also a continuing demonstration of the wealth of possibilities that come with juxtaposing the historical phenomena of ancient Mesoamerica and methodologies of the history of religions. Annual pilgrimages over the past decade to the marvelous summer seminars that he orchestrated at the Mesoamerican Archive and Research Project in Boulder provided me direct access to an abundance of ideas and scholars that would have been otherwise unimaginable. In that context, the counsels of Anthony Aveni, in very direct ways, and of Charles Long, in less direct but equally important ways, have been particularly important for this project.

From the next place, The University of Chicago, where I drafted critical reviews of the literature contained in the first two chapters, I am most indebted to Joseph Kitagawa for my aspirations to methodological self-consciousness and to "significant organization." Mircea Eliade, who originally allured me to the south side of the city, provides my archetype for creative and comparative morphological hermeneutics. My teachers Frank Reynolds and Wendy Doniger exposed me to a broad range of myths and traditions that have enlivened the comparative enterprise. And Lawrence Sullivan (currently at Harvard University), who served as the advisor to the Ph.D. dissertation from which this book grew, provided the critical and encouraging response that gave me confidence to write with freedom and candor, particularly in the final sections.

The most important places for this project are, of course, scattered between south Texas and the Petén rain forest. A halting fourteen-month sojourn into and around Mexico provided me the rare opportunity to compose most of the text outside, in the shadows of the very ruins I aspired to understand. The largely theoretical and cross-culturally comparative third chapter was crafted mainly in the cheap and wonderful hotels and cafes of Cholula, Puebla, at the base of Mesoamerica's most massive pyramidal ruin. Deliberately mimicking the trajectory of the problem of Mexican Tula and Maya Chichén Itzá relatedness, the various portions now in the fourth chapter (which deals with more specific sites) were conceived and written along the roadways and ruins from Central Mexico, to the Veracruzan-Tabascan Gulf Coast, and into Chiapas and the Yucatán Peninsula. In every instance, the pre-Columbian monuments proved themselves worthy and indefatigable conversation partners, my most kind teachers, beckoning, challenging, encouraging, perplexing, inexhaustible.

Finally, from the Ohio State University, where I have rewritten every sentence, merged and slashed whole chapters, I thank my colleagues in the Division of Comparative Studies in the Humanities, particularly Marilyn Waldman, Sabra Webber, and Gary Ebersole (currently at The University of Chicago). Their combined influences have reinforced the suspicion that grew throughout this project that the academic literature concerning Tula and Chichén Itzá is actually much more instructive as a mirror on our Western processes of constructing knowledge than as a lens into the mindsets of indigenous Mesoamerican peoples. Those colleagues have, however, contributed less to the formulation of this manuscript than to a set of awarenesses as to just how different it would be were I to begin completely anew.

Also, I thank Lawrence Desmond not only for the original photographs that he contributed to this book but also for his counsel in selecting and locating many of the others; his generous efforts have significantly enhanced my own. And, from the University Press of Colorado, I am much indebted to editors Gail Reitenbach and Jody Berman for their skill and patience in smoothing my sometimes-tedious writing style.

Able, then, to fault my teachers and colleagues only for not insisting more strongly that I heed their advice, I accept full responsibility for the shortcomings of this project. It was, for all that I now wish were different, my best at the time.

Twin City Tales

Reconstruction drawing of main plaza of Chichén Itzá, with the Sacred Cenote in the foreground. (Tatiana Proskouriakoff, *An Album of Maya Architecture.*)

Introduction

The Similitude Between Tula and Chichén Itzá as a Problem in the History of Religions

> Chichén Itzá, then, is a very fine site . . . in which, as the old men of the Indians say, three Lords who were brothers ruled . . . They were devoted worshippers of their god; and so they erected many and magnificent buildings, and especially one, which was the largest [i.e., the Castillo]. . . . This building had around it, and still has today, many other well built and large buildings. . . . From the court in front of these stages a wide and handsome causeway runs, as far as a well [i.e., the Sacred Cenote] which is about two stones' throw off. Into this well they have had, and then had, the custom of throwing men alive as a sacrifice to the gods in times of drought, and they believed that they did not die though they never saw them again. They also threw into it a great many other things, like precious stones and things which they prized. And so if this country had possessed gold, it would be this well that would have the greater part of it, so great was the devotion which the Indians showed for it.
>
> *Bishop Diego de Landa, 1566*[1]

Something extra because of something missing, an accident of nature, the architecture of supernature, as though a giant cork had been drawn out of the earth and discarded — Chichén's Sacred Cenote is an exactly cylindrical shaft, 150 feet across, 60 feet from ground level down to the water, and another 40 feet from the water's surface to the perpetually filling bottom. The dank sinkhole has served variously as a place of pilgrimage, of human sacrifice, of nostalgia, of tourism, of life, petition, death, and new life. It is religious architecture found not made, sanctified and sanctifying, axis mundi and omphalos, the quintessence of sacred space.

The so-called Sacred Cenote, once controlled by the pre-Columbian Itzá, superabundant with meanings and endlessly revalorized since then, is the force that perpetuates Chichén Itzá's insuperable allure and prestige among Mesoamerican sites. By geological reckoning, the Sacred Cenote is simply an exceptionally deep and round version of the fairly common natural wells that result with the collapse of cavities formed by groundwater in the

Frenchman Désiré Charnay accompanied his nineteenth-century wood engraving of the Sacred Cenote at Chichén Itzá with the following musings: "The desolation of the *aguado,* its walls shrouded with brambles, shrubs, and lianas, the sombre forest beyond, but above all the lugubrious associations attaching to it, fill the imagination with indescribable melancholy." (Désiré Charnay, *Ancient Cities of the New World.*)

porous limestone; it is, from this view, just one of many such sources of open water on a shelf-flat Yucatán Peninsula that is virtually devoid of lakes and streams. For the traditional Maya, the Sacred Cenote is home to the *chacs,* the temperamental gods of rain; it is for them a mouth, a womb, an opening out and an entrance into the subterranean netherworld of dark water, ultimately tapped to the sea; it is a point of sacred access at which their petitions have the best chance of being heard and at which their debts can be most expediently settled. And, according to the storiological conventions of early (and not so early) Mesoamericanist scholars, the Sacred Well of Chichén Itzá marks the final destination of a Toltec invasion of Yucatán some thousand years ago, the place where the peerless Toltec warriors from Central Mexico, led by Quetzalcoatl, the Lord of the Feathered Serpent, consummated their conquest of the effete, "over-civilized" Yucatán Maya. Quetzalcoatl and his mighty Toltec warriors, so the old story goes, thrashed the gentle Yucatecan Maya and then constructed (or forced the Maya to construct) the "many and magnificent buildings" that, even in ruin, so impressed Bishop Landa in the sixteenth century. The fabulous city of Chichén Itzá was born, according to this familiar rehearsal, via the awkward synthesis of Toltec might and Maya finesse. In these

EL CASTILLO OF CHICHEN-ITZA.

Charnay's *Ancient Cities of the New World: Being Travels and Explorations in Mexico and Central America from 1857–1882* is amply illustrated with wood engravings made from his own original photographs. This one depicts the Castillo pyramid at Chichén Itzá, atop which Charnay made his headquarters in 1882. (Désiré Charnay, *Ancient Cities of the New World*.)

accounts, the wrecked old buildings are the remains of a new Toltec capital at Chichén Itzá, a facsimile modeled after the conquerors' former home base at Tula, Hidalgo, made grander and more potent than the original by tethering itself to the most revered spot in Yucatán, the Sacred Cenote.

Extracted initially from poetic native traditions and colonial period texts, this exciting script of Toltec marauding, victory, and coerced synthesis at the Sacred Cenote has been sustained, most of all, for better than a hundred years, by the uncanny likeness between the respective architectures of Tula, Hidalgo, on the

Charnay places these two images, which he labels respectively "Toltec Column in the Castillo" and "Toltec Column at Tula," side by side and explains, "These shafts [on the Castillo in Chichén Itzá] are an almost exact reproduction of a Toltec column we unearthed at Tula. . . . It could not be the result of mere accident." (Désiré Charnay, *Ancient Cities of the New World.*)

Central Mexican altiplano, and Chichén Itzá, Yucatán, some 800 straight-line miles to the east in the Northern Maya Lowlands. Arriving in the ruined City of the Sacred Well in 1882, just months after having visited Tula, French explorer Désiré Charnay was perhaps the first to be struck by what he termed a sense of déjà vu, a sense of having already experienced the plaza of North Chichén even before arriving in Yucatán. Never shy of hyperbole, Charnay described his experience of paramnesia as he stood before the giant Castillo pyramid-temple of Chichén Itzá:

> It was in this temple [that is, the Castillo pyramid] that the striking analogy between the sculptures and the bas-reliefs of the [Central Mexican] plateaux with those of Chichén was first revealed to us . . . the balustrade on the grand staircase consists of a plumed serpent like those forming the outer wall of the temple

DOOR-POSTS IN THE CASTILLO, CHICHEN-ITZA.

As further evidence of his theory that the Toltecs were responsible for building the monuments of Chichén Itzá, Charnay identified these carvings on the doorposts of the Castillo as "caryatides," all of whom "represent long-bearded men whose type is identical with those of the Tula relief, as may be seen by the most superficial comparison of the two." (Désiré Charnay, *Ancient Cities of the New World*.)

> in Mexico. . . . Further, the two columns of the temple facade furnish a still more striking example: the bases represent two serpents' heads, whilst the shafts were ornamented with feathers, proving that the temple was dedicated to Cukulcan (Quetzalcoatl). These shafts are almost an exact reproduction of a Toltec column we unearthed at Tula. . . . The two columns are found three hundred leagues from each other, separated by an interval of several centuries; but if, as we firmly believe, the Tula column is Toltec, the other must be so too, for it could not be the result of mere accident.[2]

Though most of Charnay's extravagant theories were dismissed as speedily as he concocted them, he was, in one regard anyway, on the mark. There is, most assuredly, a remarkable resemblance between the respective ruins of Tula and Chichén Itzá. In Charnay's wake, scholars would be arguing for decades that the uncanny similitude in architectures — the leitmotif of this entire book — issues not only in the unmistakable serpent columns and balustrades, but also in a full range of architectural features that are manifest at Chichén Itzá, at Tula, and, so it appeared, nowhere in between. The principal public plaza in the northern sector of the Yucatán capital, for instance, the so-called Gran Nivelación or "Toltec" Chichén Itzá, while bigger, more complex, and more eclectic than its Central Mexican counterpart, adheres to the same general approach to architectural space that characterizes the main plaza of Tula. The two distant plazas share the same 17 degrees east of north orientation. They have the same basic articulation of pyramid-lofted temples above wide-open, rectangular amphitheatric courtyards.

Moreover, and even more strikingly, whole buildings find mirroring counterparts: both plazas, for instance, feature large I-shaped ball courts, which in each case are associated with similarly positioned *tzompantlis* (or skull racks). Each site has a number of corresponding tribunes, daises, or "dance platforms." The exceedingly unusual colonnaded halls of Tula's Palacio Quemado (or Burnt Palace), which feature large interior spaces that are very unusual in Mesoamerican architecture, find even more spacious counterparts in the Group of a Thousand Columns at Chichén Itzá. And Tula's so-called Pyramid of Quetzalcoatl, in the most stunning full-building identity of all, finds its near-perfect analogue in North Chichén's magnificent Temple of the Warriors.

The parallels between the respective architectural sculpture of Tula and Chichén Itzá are equally dramatic: both sites, as so impressed Charnay, are graced with numerous instances of paired serpent columns at the doorways of major buildings and, along the stairways, with similarly paired balustrades formed of downflying serpents; this redundant motif was long considered the very signature of "Toltec" culture and its legendary patron Quetzalcoatl. Both Tula and Chichén Itzá are similarly well endowed with several pairs, rows, and clusters of elaborately clad anthropomorphic statues of varying sizes, which were termed *Atlanteans* because they appear as stone men who support lintels or tables on their upstretched arms. And, nearly as notorious as the stone feathered serpents, the singularly distinctive *chacmool* statues, reclining humanoid figures with awkwardly craned necks and bowls held over their stomachs, rare anywhere else in ancient Mesoamerica, are found in abundance at these two sites. Furthermore, there is a near interchangeability between much of the two sites' architectural decoration: the friezes and columns of Chichén Itzá, for instance, are embellished with bas-reliefs of jaguars and regally dressed warriors in procession and with gorily veristic images of ocelots and eagles devouring human hearts — all graphically militaristic themes that are (according to conventional assessments) atypical of the Yucatán Maya zone but virtually interchangeable with the decoration at Tula.

Top, the most startling parallel on the scale of full buildings is the similarity between the so-called Pyramid of Quetzalcoatl at Tula and *below,* the Temple of the Warriors at Chichén Itzá. The respective colonnaded halls adjacent to both of these structures, because they are quite rare elsewhere in pre-Columbian architecture, have provided yet another sign of the special relationship between Tula and Chichén Itzá. (Photos by Lawrence G. Desmond.)

Top, the Great Ball Court at Chichén Itzá, which is the largest in all Mesoamerica, and *below,* Ball Court II at Tula Grande, which is the second largest. These two huge I-shaped ball courts are exceedingly similar not only in form but also in their configurations with respect to other surrounding structures. (Top photo by Lawrence G. Desmond. Bottom photo by the author.)

These carved stone images of plumed serpents at the entrance to the Upper Temple of the Jaguars are one of several sets that remain intact at Chichén Itzá. Though only one such serpent-column portal survives today at Tula, doorjambs and stairway balustrades fashioned like downflying feathered snakes have been, since Charnay's era, among the paramount indicators of the special similitude between Tula and Chichén Itzá. (Photo by William M. Ferguson, courtesy of the University of Texas, Austin.)

Top, Atlantean Altar in the Temple of the Warriors at Chichén Itzá. *Below,* Atlantean figure from Tula Grande in Museo Jorge R. Acosta, adjacent to the site. Similar caryatid figures of varying sizes, usually with upstretched arms that support tables, benches, corbeled vaults, or lintels, remain intact throughout Chichén Itzá. Several sets of these so-called Atlantean statues, also of varying sizes, were likewise found at Tula. Today only the four huge warrior figures atop Pyramid B, which probably supported roof beams for the Quetzalcoatl temple, remain in situ. These humanoid sculptural supports, which are uniquely prevalent at Tula and Chichén Itzá, have been among the strongest signs of a special link between the two cities. (*Top,* Carnegie Institution of Washington photo, courtesy of Peabody Museum, Harvard University. *Bottom,* photo by the author.)

The unique abundance of these awkwardly reclining *chacmool* statues, fourteen of which have been found at Chichén Itzá and twelve at Tula, has long been among the strongest evidences of a special relationship between the two cities. *Top,* this one, among the best extant examples at Chichén Itzá, was buried within the so-called Platform of the Eagles until Augustus Le Plongeon (re)discovered it in 1875. *Below,* at Tula, the most well-preserved *chacmool* statue was found in the Palacio Quemado. (*Top* photo by Augustus Le Plongeon. *Bottom* photo by Lawrence G. Desmond.)

Much of the iconography of marching jaguars, snakes, and eagles devouring humans is virtually identical at Tula and Chichén Itzá. For instance, *top,* the east facade of Pyramid B at Tula is decorated with profile images of jaguars and coyotes, which are positioned above relief panels that depict eagles with human hearts in their mouths and a figure that may be Tlahuizcalpantecuhtli, a form of Quetzalcoatl as Venus, the Morning Star or Lord of the Dawn. *Below,* the so-called Platform of the Eagles, among several examples in the great plaza of North Chichén Itzá, is decorated with very similar images of cats, birds, and snakes. (Photos by Lawrence G. Desmond.)

In short, for all the other uncertainties associated with the two sets of ruins, the most casual tourist, even now, visiting one site after the other, reexperiences, as Charnay had in the nineteenth century, a strange sense of connectedness between these two far-spaced architectural spaces. Moreover, among the more scholarly ranks, no generation of Middle Americanists since the emergence of the field has declined to offer its own characteristic set of solutions to the apparent mystery and anomaly of the sister-city coincidence. Between the amateur and academic assays of the problem — most (but not all) of which build upon the notion of a "Toltec Conquest of the Yucatán Maya" — there are literally dozens of creative versions of the play of pre-Columbian forces and events that might have accounted for the preternatural similitude between Tula and Chichén Itzá.[3]

The infamous sister-city semblance, then, may at first seem the burnt-over district of Mesoamerican studies, a tired old problem, already worked from every angle. Yet, because this terrain has never been surveyed from the perspective of hermeneutics and the comparative history of religions — and because developments from within the Mesoamerican field have, of late, seriously challenged both the typecast actors and the chronological script in the captivating old story of a "Toltec Conquest" — the aged problem of the resemblance in Tula's and Chichén Itzá's architectures is, if timorously in flux at the moment (had I only known), nonetheless pregnant for reassessment.

Agenda: Suspicion and Recovery

One way in which a historian of religions emerging from the *Religionswissenschaft* tradition of Joachim Wach, Mircea Eliade, and others might imagine making a special contribution to this timeworn debate would be by insisting, as Eliade so often did, on the autonomy and "irreducibility" of religion.[4] In that case, then (increasingly unfashionable as this point of view has become), where ethnohistorians, archaeologists, anthropologists, and art historians had presumably attended with some thoroughness to the social, cultural, economic, political, and perhaps even artistic dimensions of the infamous "Toltec Conquest of Yucatán," it would become the special project of the historian of religions to reveal and interpret the previously neglected, "specifically religious" dimensions of that notorious historical episode. Where other disciplinary perspectives had "reduced" the religious components of the circumstance to something else (for instance, social or economic processes), the historian of religions, by insisting on a nonreductionist approach, would retrieve and respect what was intrinsically, "irreducibly religious" about the religions of the ancient Maya and Mexican peoples. The contribution would be, in other words, primarily in the spirit of *the creative hermeneutics of retrieval* (or of *recovery*).[5]

If enthusiasm for this version of the historian of religions' task may be on the wane (though it has not yet vanished altogether), a second, equally, or perhaps more important, sort of contribution comes to the fore. Beyond providing a more nuanced interpretation of the ostensibly religious significance of the events of the pre-Columbian past, historians of religions (because they are, for the most part, "outsiders" to this long-running debate) are likewise well placed to bring a more critically suspicious attitude to the conventional ways in which those supposed events have been presented (or constructed).[6] Particularly in relation to this specific problem, as one applies more and harder scrutiny to the library of different explanations of the apparent resemblance between Tula and Chichén Itzá — most of which present themselves as "historical reconstructions" of the infamous adventurings of the Toltecs in

Yucatán — the presumably empirical object of our attentions becomes not more clear but more elusive. I will wager, in fact, that this most infamous circumstance in the annals of ancient Mesoamerica — the so-termed "Toltec Conquest" — was *not* an event (or even a sequence of events) that had ever happened in any plain historical sense. That is to say, even with the most magically fortuitous placement in pre-Columbian Yucatán, we would never have witnessed the sorts of battles and confrontations between the native Toltec and Maya peoples that have become familiar from the historiographical accounts. At that point, then, historians of religions have a second sort of contribution to make to the reassessment of the old problem of Tula–Chichén Itzá, a contribution that belongs more to the realm of *the hermeneutics of suspicion*.[7]

As I engage the dusty old matter of the paired pre-Columbian plazas from the perspective of a historian of religions,[8] I will then endeavor to make two quite distinct (though overlapping) sorts of contributions to the indefatigable debate. The first two chapters, which traffic more heavily in the history of ideas and the politics of knowledge, belong largely to the so-called hermeneutics of suspicion. They work to survey and expose the unexamined presuppositions that have sustained the enduring polemic. I am, however, unwilling to abandon entirely the hermeneutics of recovery (or, perhaps better termed, "the hermeneutics of replenishment") in favor of the sort of "diagnostic hermeneutic" that is dedicated primarily to laying bare the abuses, prejudices, and distortions of previous (and our own) generations of scholars.[9] Thus, the final and longer two chapters, which strive to avoid the pitfalls mapped out in the discussion that precedes them, embrace the more constructive and heuristic sort of approach that will enable me to launch my own alternative hypotheses regarding the resemblance of these two architectures. Exposing deceptions and stemming prejudices are only preliminary moves. In this case anyway, although they are always interpenetrating, the hermeneutics of suspicion pave the way for a hermeneutic of retrieval. A detailed table of contents, introductory statements of agenda in each chapter, and the periodic summary sections are designed to mark the way (though advanced reviewers have convinced me that virtually no one will be equally interested in all parts of this project).

Chapter 1 — "Dramas of Polarity" — a primer to the long intellectual history of the Tula–Chichén Itzá problem, begins by locating the twin-city debate with respect to the more general issue of Mesoamerican unity and a centuries-old tendency to polarize inordinately the character and pre-Columbian accomplishments of Maya versus Central Mexican peoples. Relying on the eccentric reflections of Désiré Charnay as a kind of rhetorical benchmark, the history of storytelling about the respective sites of Tula and Chichén Itzá, and about their mysterious linkage, is tracked to the present and still very tenuous academic state of the art. The basic thesis here is that, for all the eulogies to cool "objectivity" that grace the files of Mesoamericanist scholarship, the very fragmentary records concerning connections between Tula and Chichén Itzá have typically been filled out imaginatively (though hardly dispassionately) into a number of variations on the spellbinding drama of a Maya-Mexican confrontation. In critical retrospect, then, the conventionalized archaeo-historical scripts, which in their most unsubtle versions feature battles and alliances between stereotyped native protagonists, while not wholly fictive, do not seem to represent empirical pre-Hispanic conquests so much as, if you will, Western "conquests of the imagination." Thus, in light of recent advances in historical research, together with heightened sensitivities regarding the insidiousness of Eurocentric views of American Indians, the time is right for reopening the problem.

Chapter 2 — "Insignificant Organization" — which is similarly committed to a long, wide perspective on the twin-city issue, concerns itself with the various ways in which Middle Americanists have studied (and, especially, *organized* and *compared*) the enormous diversity of ancient Mesoamerican buildings and monuments. The first portion of this somewhat more general chapter, in a search after methodological allies and adversaries, explores the relative presuppositions that have undergirded five major approaches to pre-Columbian architecture, namely those of nineteenth-century antiquarianism, traditional archaeology, "new archaeology," art history, and ethnohistory. The second portion of the chapter, which searches for the most useful means of comparing specific pre-Columbian architectures, cuts back across much of the same academic literature, this time in terms of such common principles of organization as the formal appearances of buildings, construction techniques, ages, supposed functions, geographical locations, the cultural status of the builders, or the historical relatedness of some building to earlier and later works of art and architecture. The central conclusion here is that, while each of these schemes may succeed in imposing a measure of manageable order on the vast heterogeneity of pre-Columbian monuments, none qualifies as the sort of "significant organization" that most comparative historians of religions would find compelling or even satisfactory.

Chapter 3 — "Significant Alternatives" — acts on the discontents expressed in the previous chapter. In its attempt to lay the groundwork for an alternative, very different sort of reassessment of the architectural similitude between Tula and Chichén Itzá, this two-part discussion is by far the most theoretical and constructively methodological. The first portion, providing the pivotal concept that will inform the rest of the project, argues for an alternative approach to the religious architectures of Mesoamerica and elsewhere that requires constituting specific interpretations, not in terms of static, timeless buildings, but rather in terms of ceremonial occasions — or, as I will call them, ritual-architectural events — that is, circumstances that subsume the work of architecture, the human participants, and the ritual occasion that brings them together. The second portion of the chapter operationalizes the concept of a ritual-architectural event as an alternative principle of organization that might serve to compare specific historical architectural cases, not at the level of commonalities in building, but rather at the more rewarding level of ceremonial occasions in which buildings are key participants. These efforts eventuate in a tripartite *framework of ritual-architectural priorities,* the various heuristic elements of which are illustrated by a sweeping range of cross-cultural and Mesoamerican examples.

Chapter 4 — "Deceptions in Form" — the last and longest, enliststhe concept of so-called ritual-architectural events and the spectrum of heuristic options developed in the previous chapter to launch an alternative set of interpretive conclusions regarding Tula, Chichén Itzá, and why they look so much alike. This alternative and iconoclastic position avoids as completely as possible the insidious paradigm of Maya-Mexican polarity and argues that we needn't rely on the apocryphal "Toltec Conquest" to explain the architectural commonalities. The specific historical and hermeneutical hypotheses are not easily summarized, but the arching argument is that Mesoamericanists have largely been seduced, or deceived, by the superficial formal resemblance between these two plazas. When the comparison between Tula and Chichén Itzá is reformulated in terms of "ritual-architectural events," instead of focusing on mirroring buildings and architectural decorations, we come to appreciate just how profoundly different the respective religio-architectural priorities of these two pre-Columbian cities actually were.

Many will not be convinced. The apparent resemblance between the ruins of Tula and Chichén Itzá is, from the perspective of some contemporary Mesoamericanists, an insoluble problem. For others, it is a false problem that has already received far more attention than it is due. And, from the perspective of many non-Mesoamericanists, the endurance of the problem seems only to instantiate how idiosyncratic obscurities can come to dominate the attentions of a field's specialists. I would argue to the contrary, however, that reassessing the supposed special resemblance, and even more the complex history of the debate surrounding that resemblance, raises manifold and very important issues not only for Mesoamericanists but also for comparative students of religion and art working in other historical contexts.

For instance, engaging the venerable Tula–Chichén Itzá problem, unlike a more tightly circumscribed topic (one site or one building, for instance), by its geographical spread draws us into dialogue with peoples and traditions from an exceedingly wide swath of Mesoamerica. The specific historical problems regarding the movements and dispositions, not to mention the religious orientations, of various pre-Columbian populations are enormous. Moreover, by its distinguished heritage of debate, the Tula–Chichén Itzá problem forces us to confront the methodological supposals and insights of each generation of Americanists since the field emerged (and even before there was a professional field). Likewise, as a case study in the ways in which predominantly Western explorers and scholars have imagined the native peoples of the Americas, this problem leads us into a whole wad of hotly contested theoretical (and even moral) issues involving colonialism, the implications of constituting "others" as objects of study, and the "constructedness" of the so-called archaeo-historical "reconstructions" that have played such prominent roles in the debates about these two cities.

Furthermore, as a problem in the general history of religions (or, to circumscribe the field somewhat, the general history of sacred architecture), the absence of contemporaneous written texts for either site (except for the Maya glyphs at Chichén Itzá) makes the controversy over Tula–Chichén Itzá similitude an apt test case for exploring the special potentialities and limitations of *nonliterary* modes of human expression, especially architecture, as "data" for historians of religions. Moreover, regarding the general hermeneutics of sacred architecture, the "deceptions in form" that operate so prominently in this debate expose the inadequacy of imagining that specific building types will always (and to everyone) carry the same sorts of religious meanings and significances. We are thus challenged, as are all students of sacred architecture, to do a much better job of finding methodological strategies that respect the autonomy and superabundance of architectural forms, that is, the way in which even the apparently simplest buildings invariably both transcend and subvert the deliberate intentions of their designers. The incredibly complex succession of different ceremonial occasions in which these millennium-old structures have participated, and the wildly diversified interpretations that the staid old stones have engendered (that is, the intricate "ritual-architectural reception histories" of these monuments) forces us to acknowledge the endlessly flexible interactions between buildings, rituals, and religious meanings. And, furthermore, were these matters not theoretically challenging enough, because the semblance of Tula and Chichén Itzá architectures is explicitly a matter of comparison, this reassessment must, of necessity, engage the fundamental problems of significant organization, generalization, and comparative method with which historians of religions are especially preoccupied.

In other words, the fascinating and *specific* circumstance of Tula-Chichén architectural similitude, recently revitalized in itself, is a wonderful, worthy topic of consideration because it caricatures so many important issues in the *general* interpretation both of indigenous peoples and of sacred architecture. Thus, throughout this project, as I thrash through the idiosyncrasies and sometimes tedious details regarding this pair of pre-Columbian ruins, it is, in the end, with respect to these larger theoretical, methodological, and comparative problems that this reassessment has its best chance of making an important contribution.

Notes

1. *Landa's Relación de las Cosas de Yucatán,* trans. and ed. with nn. Alfred M. Tozzer, Papers of the Peabody Museum of Archaeology and Ethnology, vol. 18 (Cambridge, Mass.: Harvard University, 1941). References to the direct translation of Bishop Landa's sixteenth-century manuscript, the most important work on Maya life in the late pre-Conquest period, will be cited as Landa, *Relación*. References to Tozzer's footnotes to Landa's text, considerably more voluminous than the manuscript itself, will be cited as Tozzer/Landa. These specific remarks on Chichén Itzá are from Landa, *Relación,* 177–82.

2. Désiré Charnay, *Les Anciennes Villes du Nouveau Monde. Voyages d'Explorations au Mexique et dans l'Amérique Central, 1857–1882* (Paris: Hachette, 1885); trans. from French by J. Gonino and Helen S. Conant as *The Ancient Cities of the New World: Being Voyages and Explorations in Mexico and Central America from 1857–1882* (London: Chapman, 1887; New York: Harper Brothers, 1887). All citations are from the English translation, referred to as Charnay, *Ancient Cities.* For this particular quotation, see ibid., 341–43.

3. By far the most thorough treatment of the problem of the similitude between Tula and Chichén Itzá is Alfred M. Tozzer, *Chichén Itzá and Its Cenote of Sacrifice: A Comparative Study of Contemporaneous Maya and Toltec,* Memoirs of the Peabody Museum, vols. 11 and 12 (Cambridge, Mass.: Harvard University, 1957). References to this work will be cited as Tozzer, *Chichén and Cenote.* By way of demonstrating the far fame of the problem, note that, already in the mid-1950s, Tozzer (ibid., 266, n. 39) was able to generate a list (which he considered incomplete) of some thirty scholars who had addressed the architectural similarities between Tula and Chichén Itzá, most of whom will appear elsewhere in the course of this work, and all of whom are indebted either directly or indirectly to Désiré Charnay: Daniel Brinton, 1868, 1887; A. Garcia y Cubas, 1873; D. Reynolds, 1904; Eduard Seler, 1909; Herbert Spinden, 1913; Walter Lehmann, 1922, 1938; Sylvanus Morley, 1931; Earl Morris, Jean Charlot, Ann Axtel Morris, 1931; Sigvald Linné, 1934, 1942; Eric Thompson, 1934, 1941; Alfonso Caso, 1940, 1941; Jorge Acosta, 1940, 1941; Enrique Palacios, 1941, 1945; Wigberto Jiménez Moreno, 1941; Ignacio Marquina, 1941, 1951; Gordon Ekholm, 1941; Alberto Ruz Lhuiller, 1945; D. E. Wray, 1945; Eduardo Noguera, 1946; J. A. Vivo, 1946; José Pijoán, 1946; Hugo Moedano Koer, 1947; R. B. Weitzel, 1947; Pedro Armillas, 1950; Karl Ruppert, 1952; and Gordon Willey, 1953. Since that time, and currently, virtually every synthesis of Mesoamerican culture history includes at least perfunctory remarks on the architectural parallels between Tula and Chichén Itzá.

4. Regarding the "irreducibility of religion" and the task of *Religionswissenschaft,* see, for instance, Joachim Wach, *Introduction to the History of Religions,* eds., Joseph M. Kitagawa and Gregory D. Alles (New York: Macmillan Publishing Company, 1988); and Mircea Eliade, *The Quest: History and Meaning in Religion* (Chicago: University of Chicago Press, 1969).

5. Regarding "creative hermeneutics," see ibid. Giles Gunn, *The Culture of Criticism and the Criticism of Culture* (New York: Oxford University Press, 1987), 194–95, contrasts "the hermeneutics of suspicion," which involves interpretation "in order not to be deceived" (as pursued, for instance, by Karl

Marx, Sigmund Freud, and Friedrich Nietzsche) and "the hermeneutics of restoration," which involves interpretation in order to be replenished (as pursued, for instance, by Martin Heidegger, Gabreil Marcel, Hans-Georg Gadamer, and Paul Ricouer).

6. While Americanists have, most definitely, always been very interested in the indigenous religions of this area, David Carrasco deserves credit as the first historian of religions to bring the characteristic questions of *Religionswissenschaft* to bear on the specific historical materials of Mesoamerica in a sustained fashion.

7. Also regarding the so-called hermeneutics of suspicion, see Paul Ricouer, *Interpretation Theory: Discourse and the Surplus of Meaning* (Fort Worth: Texas Christian University Press, 1976).

8. By alluding to "the perspective of a historian of religions" I do *not* want to imply that there is at this point any unified history of religions method, though there may still be a generally shared set of concerns.

9. Gunn, *The Culture of Criticism and the Criticism of Culture,* 95, writes: "If [the hermeneutic of suspicion] is chiefly concerned with complicating our methods of reading, [the hermeneutics of restoration] is more interested in refining our understanding of what is read and how it can be applied." While Gunn is almost strictly concerned with the interpretation of written texts, in this project I am principally concerned with interpreting nonliterary architectural forms of expression (a problem that is addressed in Chapter 3). Nonetheless, I concur with his assessment (ibid.) that it would be lamentable in the extreme to abandon fully the later in favor of the former, as many contemporary critics are apparently willing to do.

A color version of this painting by H. M. Herget accompanied an article by Sylvanus G. Morley entitled "Yucatán, Home of the Gifted Maya" in the November 1936 issue of *National Geographic Magazine.* The imaginative if lurid caption read as follows: "A Human Sacrifice Is Hurled Into the Sacred Well [at Chichén Itzá]: Young girls were flung into the pit at daybreak in times of drought or other national crises to intercede with the gods on behalf of the Itzá tribe. If they survived the 80-foot plunge, they were hauled out at noon and questioned as to what the gods had in store. If the maidens failed to reappear, it was considered an evil omen; rocks were thrown into the well, and onlookers fled with loud lamentations. The sinister place is a natural hole in the limestone, 180 feet across." (*National Geographic Magazine* {November 1936}: 623.)

Chapter One

Dramas of Polarity:
A Historical Review of the Tula–Chichén Itzá Problem

The Maya were never colonizers like the Toltecs and Aztecs. Movements into the Maya area by Mexican peoples were not uncommon. The most famous was the general trek of Mexicans into Yucatán during the last period of Maya history, bringing new styles of architecture as well as countless objects of new types.

Alfred M. Tozzer, 1934[1]

Never has the Spenglerian theme of "raw man" conquering effete "over civilized man" been so well illustrated as in the Toltec conquest of the Maya.

Victor W. von Hagen, 1948[2]

Agenda: Mesoamerican and Intellectual History

Alfred Marston Tozzer (1877–1954) dominated Maya studies from the early decades of this century until, and even after, his death. The dominant concern of that incomparably prodigious career was with the cultural history of Yucatán and its capital city, Chichén Itzá, and, more specifically, with the problematic relationship between the indigenous Maya of Yucatán and the "Toltecs" of Central Mexico, a problem that he reckoned as the most significant in Middle American studies — for Tozzer, "the difference between Maya and Toltec in the total record is the great determinant."[3]

Tozzer was present at Chichén Itzá as early as 1904, when Edward H. Thompson undertook his daring (and, in retrospect, highly destructive) operation to dredge artifacts from the Sacred Cenote.[4] Then, over the next half century, Tozzer acquainted himself with virtually all the relevant ethnohistorical texts (he was responsible for the magnificently annotated translation of Bishop Landa's *Relación de las Cosas de Yucatán* on which every student of the Maya relies),[5] with the ethnography of present-day Maya (he was the first "serious student" to live for a time with the Lancandon Indians on the borderlands of Guatemala and Mexico, collecting myths and observing ceremonies),[6] and with the excavationary projects of every archaeologist who worked at Chichén Itzá during those fifty years.[7] The synthesis of this lifetime of ethnohistorical, ethnographical, and archaeological Maya research — ever with an eye to Chichén Itzá and the indomitable "Maya-Toltec problem" — appears in the posthumously published, two-volume tour de force, *Chichén Itzá and Its Cenote of Sacrifice: A Comparative Study of Contemporaneous Maya and Toltec* (1957). Eric Thompson's praise for this grand opus is appropriate:

> Tozzer was a great teacher, and these volumes reveal the excellent qualities which enabled him to digest, abstract, and then expound general progress in his profession. Presentation of the complex material is lucid, straightforward, and excellently arranged; the stream of knowledge flows, like Arethusa, shepherding the bright fountains of duly annotated quotation or paraphrase . . . a veritable *enciclopedia maya-tolteca*.[8]

In short then, Tozzer set the standard. The common wisdoms about the history of Chichén Itzá and the supposed Toltec intrusion into Yucatán, have been, since the 1930s, when he begins publishing on the respective Maya and Toltec aspects of Chichén Itzá, in large part, the wisdoms of Alfred Tozzer.[9] Even now, amid a flurry of major challenges to the traditional chronologies and stereotypes in the "Toltec" Chichén Itzá story, Tozzer's work, not simply the voice of outmoded conventions, "remains the basic descriptive text on the archaeological and ethnohistoric data pertaining to this great pre-Columbian city."[10]

Tozzer's work on the so-termed Mexicanization of Yucatán, it would seem, constitutes the obvious starting point for understanding and chronicling the theoretical literature on Chichén Itzá, the seminal point of departure for mapping the rough road to the state-of-the-art regarding the remarkable, if puzzling, similitude between the architectures of Tula, Hidalgo, and Chichén Itzá, Yucatán. Nevertheless, this first chapter, despite undertaking precisely that task, begins elsewhere and earlier; it wants a longer and wider view of the problem. The basic thesis here is that Tozzer's massive synthesis — the Tozzer paradigm of the Tula-Chichén relationship if you will — for all its originality and endurance, is a reflection of prejudices and paradigms about the pre-Columbian Maya and about the Central Mexicans that evolved far in advance of Tozzer's era. In fact, the radical polarization of all that is "Maya" over against all that is "Toltec" (or Central Mexican) — the interpretive frame through which Tozzer sifts all of the data regarding Chichén Itzá — has roots that can be traced clear back to the initial encounters between Europeans and native Mesoamericans.

While the development of antipodean images for the peoples of Central Mexico and the Mayaland is a slowly evolving process, there are conflicted assessments and deep ambivalences about native Mesoamericans from the very beginning.[11] The seeds of this Maya-Mexican polarity — that is, the Western imagination of two contradistinctive sorts of Indians that will come to figure so largely in conventional explanations of Tula-Chichén relatedness — are, in other words, sown virtually as early as the initial European "discovery" of America. The diary of Columbus's first voyage, for instance, is filled with references to "the gentle, beautiful, and friendly people on the island of Hispanola who seemed eminently ready to accept the truths of Christianity"; yet, almost immediately, disputes arise as to the nature of the Indians and their position on the spectrum of animals to humans.[12] Where one school of thought, epitomized for instance by Vasco de Quiriguá, held that the Indians were living in a "Golden Age" that had already come and gone in Europe, other Spaniards were dubious that the natives were even humans, much less potential Christians. In the apt phrasing of

Alfred Marston Tozzer with Lacandon Maya in Chiapas, Mexico, 1904. Tozzer's *Chichén Itzá and Its Cenote of Sacrifice: A Comparative Study of Contemporaneous Maya and Toltec*, published posthumously in 1957, integrates a massive quantity of ethnographic, ethnohistoric, art historical, and archaeological material concerning the Maya. This massive volume continues to provide the foundational text for studying the problem of the similitude between Tula and Chichén Itzá. (Courtesy of Peabody Museum, Harvard University.)

Lewis Hanke, "there developed during the first half century of Spanish action in America a kind polarity between two extremes — what might be called the 'dirty dog' and the 'noble savage' schools of thought — although there were many different and more subtle shades of opinion in between."[13]

With the continued adventurings of Spanish conquistadors and friars in the New World, the array of ambivalent and contradictory characterizations of Native Americans and their culture grew more and more elaborate. Coming ashore with Cortés at the Yucatecan Maya port of Campeche in 1517, Bernal Díaz del Castillo, for instance, was simultaneously dazzled by the shimmering pyramids, which he compared favorably to those of "el Gran Cairo," and repulsed by the hideousness of the elaborate serpents and "idols" that were painted on their walls.[14] Masterfully manipulating every communiqué from New Spain to his own advantage, Cortés himself similarly conjoined very contradictory images of the Indians: his letters to Charles V, on the one hand, express awe and admiration for the majestic cities of the Aztecs, a rhetorical stratagem that emphasizes both the splendid potential of this new frontier and his own prowess in conquering so formidable an enemy; yet, on the other hand, Cortés discommends the Indians for their heathen sacrifices, idolotry, sodomy, and general depravity, and so legitimates his slaughter of these somewhat-less-than-humans.[15]

The writings of Franciscan Fray Bernardino de Sahagún, Dominican Fray Diego Durán, and virtually all of the sixteenth-century friars who worked closely with the native peoples in the New Spain — documents that continue to be foundational in our understandings of pre-Columbian life — if more reflective than the conquistadors' brusque accounts, similarly evince ambivalent feelings of commingled admiration and disgust for the Indians. The polar images of the Indians in early Spanish America crystalize in the famous Valladolid debate in 1550 between Bartolomé de las Casas, arch-defender of the intrinsic humanity and potential Christianity of the Indians, and his opponent, Juan Ginés de Sepulveda, a Renaissance scholar who argues via Aristotle that the Indians are by nature slaves.[16] And, similarily contradistinct images of the Indians likewise emerge from the hostile dialogues in the 1560s between Bishop Landa and Bishop Toral over the appropriate status, treatment, and conversion strategy for the Yucatecan natives; in this case, conflicting perceptions of the Indian divide over whether they are responsible moral beings who should be held accountable for their idolatrous digressions, as Landa believes, or, in Toral's condescendingly sympathetic view, "pure, innocent victims" from whom very little could be expected.[17] It is clear, then, even in the scantiest review of the colonial literature, that the early European discourse on Native Americans is wadded with all sorts of radically contradictory images and constructions of the Indian that issue not simply from empirical observations of indigenous life but from the Spaniards' ulterior motives and from their freewheeling analogies to Egyptians, Persians, Muslims, Greeks, and Romans.[18]

In the past hundred years, the emergence of a more professional strain of Americanist scholarship, by its dedication to empirical research methods, puts the study of pre-Columbian peoples on a more "scientifically" respectable course (a shift in perspective that will be examined in some detail momentarily). Yet, for all their dedication to "objectivity" and "pure description" (and, thus, to a more nuanced set of Eurocentric prejudices), these pioneering scholars (Tozzer among them) are only partially successful in extricating themselves from the obvious biases and excesses of the early Spaniards. In fact, it was largely due to these deliberately academic efforts (a review of the specifics is forthcoming) that these antithesizing stereotypes of the Indian were, in the late nineteenth century, systematically correlated with the respective regions of Central Mexico and Yucatán and then, in the early twentieth century, explicitly enlisted in explanations of the "Mexicanization" of Chichén Itzá.[19] University training, in other words, proves to be a very imperfect antidote to ethnocentric biases. In hindsight, every author's claim to have effaced personal history and simply come forward with "the facts" about the personalities and events of Yucatán's pre-Hispanic past appears naive or, in some cases, completely absurd. Even where the methodological ideal is, as Tozzer understands his agenda, "straightforward historical reconstruction,"[20] invariably, the stories of Tula and Chichén Itzá have been molded by powerful, if silent, forces and counterforces that have very little to do with the actual historical evolution of those sites.

This opening survey of ideas (itself a contribution to the storytelling about Tula and Chichén Itzá) aims to retrieve a few of those silent forces that have molded the conventional explanations of sister-city relatedness. Specifically, this review of the literature explores the possibility that the Tula-Chichén narrative that we have become accustomed to hearing — that is, the story of the so-called Toltec Conquest of the Maya — is *not,* after all, a faithful accounting of the events as they happened so much as it is the manifestation of a pervasive Western tendency to cast various images of the American Indian into diametrical opposition with one another, the manifestation of a paradigm of polarity, if you will, wherein two radically opposed images of "Indianness" are correlated respectively with the natives of Central Mexico and the Maya natives of Yucatán, and then pushed into collision with one another. Extrapolating from the apparent (if imaginary) contrast between Maya and Mexican peoples, the conventionalized story of Mexican Toltec warriors bashing the gentle, intellectual Yucatecan Maya and subsequently establishing their religio-military capital at the mouth of Chichén's Sacred Cenote, explores what *might* transpire (rather than what *did* transpire) in confrontations between "noble savage" and "savage savage," between "Indian scribe" and "Indian warrior," between native priests and heathen brutes, between primitive victims and primitive attackers. The story of the "Toltec Conquest," moreover, provides Western commentators a forum for reflecting as well on more generalized confrontations between families and unmarried men, between rural mentalities and urban mentalities, between sedentary cultures and mobile cultures, and even between democratic and totalitarian governments. In short, then, to exercise a more rigorous hermeneutic of suspicion, the infamous story of a confrontation between Toltecs and Maya at Chichén Itzá depicts a collision not of two historical peoples but of two idealized images (or sets of images) of the American Indian. The historical peoples and geography of pre-Columbian Mesoamerica provide a skeleton, but fertile Western imaginations flesh out the body and set it in motion.

In other words, to circle back to Tozzer's massive contribution (and to the specifically architectural dimensions of our current problem), the dean of early Maya studies inherited and embellished rather than invented the broad-stroking distinction between the presumed gentle, sublime, artistic, and intellectual natives of southern and eastern Middle America versus the imagined totalitarian, ferocious, and human-sacrificing Central Mexican Aztecs and their predecessors, the Toltecs. Where these antilogical stereotypes had been simmering virtually since the earliest arrival of Europeans in

America (and perhaps even in the pre-Columbian Mesoamericans' vision of themselves), Tozzer plays a decisive role in attaching them to the architectural ruins of Tula and Chichén Itzá. For Tozzer, the specialness and uniqueness of Chichén Itzá was in its being (or at least being perceived as) the swirling confluence of these two great pre-Columbian streams, the point, the sinkhole, the square mile of Middle America where native sublimity and ferociousness had intersected. Tozzer, a paragon of level-headedness, a model of cautious reserve and determination by careful evidence, is, nonetheless, swept, perhaps more than anyone, into the biethnic drama, the mythology of confrontation between a pristine, otherworldly Maya and bloodthirsty Toltec warriors — an irresistible story of conquest, of unlikely partnership, of mongrel toughness and success, of an imperfect but expedient synthesis that is "Toltec" Chichén Itzá. And, were the pivotal role of art and architecture in the phenomenon of Chichén Itzá ever in doubt, this vision of dramatic Maya-Toltec collision and admixing is sustained, above all, for Tozzer (and for a host of scholars who follow in his wake), by the remarkable similitude between the artistic forms of Tula and of Chichén Itzá.

Thus, to state the thesis of the chapter another way, the problems of Mesoamerican history, that is, the journalistic questions regarding who, what, when, where, and why, questions that remain so elusive for these two sites (particularly for Chichén Itzá) are frustratingly — and excitingly — ensnarled with the methodological problems of Western intellectual history, that is, with the questions regarding who said what about Tula and Chichén Itzá and why.[21] Orienting oneself in the Tula–Chichén Itzá problem, and advancing the cause, depends, then, upon appreciating both the Mesoamerican historical and the intellectual historical problems and, even more, their inextricability. In other words, one must, at every juncture, be wary of the motives and preconceptions of those nonscholars and scholars alike who nurture and flesh out the very skeletal Mesoamerican historical record, breathe life into it, set it back on its feet, and become enthralled by the antics of their (re)creation.

To that end, the chapter is organized as a prologue and two main sections. The prologue adopts nineteenth-century French expeditionary Désiré Charnay (rather than Tozzer) as the unlikely hero — or perhaps mascot — who marks, not the beginning of the problem, but a century-past benchmark wherein the startlingly special relationship between the architecture of Tula and Chichén Itzá is explicitly recognized, perhaps for the first time, and, thus, sets the initiative to explain it in motion. If typically credited as the earliest to spot the Tula–Chichén Itzá similitude, Charnay is, in fact, unoriginal and wrong about nearly every aspect of the problem. His vain flounderings, nevertheless, caricature the interpenetrability of intellectual, methodological problems with specific historical ones, and, by his game approach, he participates in the juvenescence of each of the important controversies that have sustained the Tula–Chichén Itzá problem. Accordingly, his work functions as an apt benchmark, a ground level from which a complex of relevant issues may be traced downward along their historical roots and upward toward the present academic state of the art. Following a short comment on Charnay, then, I will track through: (1) a set of issues dealing with the general problem of Maya–Central Mexican relatedness and with the progressive appreciation of Mesoamerica's essential unity, and (2) a second set dealing with the more specific historical problems related to: (a) Tula, (b) Chichén Itzá, and (c) the connections between Tula and Chichén Itzá.

Désiré Charnay: A Fractured Benchmark

> Only partially correct in his ideas, [Charnay] must be given credit for being one of the first to point out the strong Mexican influence at Chichén.
>
> *Alfred M. Tozzer, 1957*[22]

In the 1860s — when studies of ancient Mexico in the United States were still strangled by Lewis Henry Morgan's unilinear evolution and disappreciation of "barbaric" pre-Columbian civilization and before the great English scholar Alfred P. Maudslay, the German, Eduard Seler, and his Mexican counterpart, Francisco del Paso y Troncosco, had initiated a rigorously "scientific" approach to ancient Mexico — the French, already endowed with a long enthusiasm for pre-Hispanic civilization, found an opportunity in the reign of Napoleon III and the French intervention in Mexico.[23] In imitation of the researches that Napoleon I had promoted in Egypt, Napoleon III, about 1860, initiated the Commission Scientifique du Mexique to study the region's geography, history, linguistics, and archaeology.[24] Major ethnohistorical contributors — C. E. Brasseur de Bourbourg, J.M.A. Aubin, and architectural historian E. Viollet-le-Duc — were among the commission's distinguished ranks, but it is a later adjunct to this French initiative — Claude Joseph Désiré Charnay — who bore the weightiest significance for the Tula–Chichén Itzá problem.

Désiré Charnay (1828–1915), after studying at the Lycée Charlemange in Paris, goes to Germany, England, and then, in 1850, to the United States to teach school in New Orleans.[25] Inspired, as were nearly all the Maya aficionados of that era, by the journals of John Lloyd Stephens,[26] Charnay wrangled the sponsorship of Napoleon III's commission to echo Stephens with his own explorations of the Yucatán and, in 1858–60, made the first of his three expeditions to Mexico.[27] Amid a paucity of resources and a heap of logistical problems (a civil war among them), this initial expedition visited and made the first photographs of several major sites, Chichén Itzá included. Considered the most significant achievement of his distinguished photographic career, Charnay's images — "an eloquent summation of his efforts at scientific objectivity and the magnitude of his personal awe"[28] — were published together with a curious racist-diffusionist interpretation of Mexican architecture by Viollet-le-Duc as *Cités et Ruines Américaines* (1862–63).[29]

The modest celebrity from this publication earned Charnay more well-financed French expeditions to Madagascar (1863), to Chile and Argentina (1875), to Java (1878), and to Australia (1878–79).[30] In 1880–82, by now an explorer of renown, Charnay launched a second, more ambitious expedition to Mexico. Unsated by the strictly photographic triumphs of his original trek, Charnay, twenty-two years later, returned to Mesoamerica with redoubled expectations and, in his own words, "better prepared in every way: with additional knowledge, backed by influential supporters, and the aid of numerous documents which I had collected."[31]

The main fruit of this blossoming from photo-documentarian to antiquarian idealogue is Charnay's unflagging conviction that Toltec civilization was the fountainhead of all the high cultures of Mexico and Central America. Relying primarily on documentary sources,[32] Charnay fashioned a reconstruction of pre-Hispanic history that is, as he said, "beautifully simple": in contradistinction to antiquarian ruminations of transoceanic diffusion and antediluvian antiquity for the ruins, all of the Central American monuments from the Valley of Mexico to Yucatán and Guatemala are, according to Charnay, of Toltec origin, and all are relatively modern, the oldest being no more than eight centuries old.[33]

Désiré Charnay (1828–1915), frontispiece to *Ancient Cities of the New World,* 1887.

Tracking his omnipotent Toltecs from their homeland in Central Mexico to the peninsula of Yucatán — the breadth of his travels exceeds considerably those of Stephens — Charnay enlists excavation, site measurements, artifacts, and mold-making, along with his photography, as means of retrieving the lifestyles, patterns of migration, and cultural accomplishments of (what he reckons to be) this most energetic of ancient American peoples. A review of his own maraudings as well as those of his beloved Toltecs appears in his opus, *Les Anciennes Villes du Nouveau Monde* (1885), a windy treatise that sums up his entire Mexican career to date. A substantially condensed English version appeared two years later. In 1881 Charnay returned to Mexico for the third and last time; this final expedition was brief and anticlimactic.[34]

In his orientation, style, goals, and method, Désiré Charnay was truly a "man-in-between,"[35] astraddle the eras of Romanticism and Positivism, on the border of what Gordon Willey calls the "speculative period" and the "descriptive-classifying period" of Americanist archaeology.[36] The contradictions in his work are fascinating and, at times, laughable. On the one hand, he is a luxuriant amateur, a swashbuckling individualist who looses his rapine on the facts of Mesoamerican history as well as its physical remains; on the other hand, he declares his allegiance to pragmatic science and the pure "objectivity" to which the young methods of photography — "which can not be wrong" — and on-site excavation are the perfect servants.[37] He craves the respect of the academic establishment but apes the travelogue style of Stephens, spicing his theoretical expositions with salacious anecdotes about the rape of fair Mexican maidens, icon-worshipping prostitutes, and the antics of a dog he had brought along on the expedition.[38] He pleads the motives of modern, disinterested science for his expeditioning — "to re-establish the historical truth" — but espouses with equal commitment the causes of French nationalism and expansionism: "it was France's duty to rouse Mexico from its numbness."[39] He requires that "a sound study of American civilization should put aside preconceived opinions and commentaries"[40] but is tellingly unsubtle about his own forenotions, writing in advance of even seeing Teotihuacán: "I look forward to bringing to light a house, that I may prove Teotihuacán to have been as much a Toltec city as Tula."[41]

Charnay is modern in eschewing the futile search after "first origins," and rants against fantastic scenarios of global diffusion and antediluvian antiquity for the ruins;[42] but then he perpetuates equally bizarre racial stereotypes — "it is an accepted fact that a high state of civilization can be developed only in temperate regions"[43] — and is flagrant in his ethnocentric photo-documentation of dehumanized "racial types."[44] With a laudable command of both the documentary sources and the archaeological features across Mexico and Yucatán, Charnay stands at the edge of critical source analysis and ethnographic analogy and, besides his photographic triumphs, he is a pioneer in excavating technique.[45] Yet, the speed with which he pounces on archaeological "confirmation" of the Spanish chronicles is, at points, comical.[46] In sum, Charnay's work, refreshingly robust and disturbingly unselfconscious, is a dizzying medley of insights and abominations. To read Charnay requires equally rigorous hermeneutics of suspicion and retrieval.

Not surprisingly, Charnay's nervy contradictoriness has landed him in a fraternity of disrepute that includes the likes of Brasseur de Bourbourg, Count Waldeck, and the irascible Augustus Le Plongeon. Charnay did not enjoy the respect of his contemporaries: Teobert Maler (1880s), for instance, gloated about "the

Désiré Charnay on the march in Mexico in the 1880s. (Charnay, *Ancient Cities of the New World.*)

great failure of Désiré Charnay, which with great resources and noice [sic] has done nothing! [In Paris, they] are laughing at Mr. Charnay";[47] and F. A. Ober (1884) dispraised the single-mindedness of *Les Anciennes Villes du Nouveau Monde,* saying, "[Charnay] has ingeniously twisted every discovery into a 'proof' of his pet [Toltec] theory, which unfortunate manner of working vitiates all the labor heretofore done."[48] Likewise, any retrospective praise of Charnay has been, at best, highly qualified: David Adamson's assessment (1975) epitomizes the typical short shrift: "Charnay was the nineteenth century's equivalent of those intrepid impresarios of the remote or primitive who lead television teams into the jungles or mountains";[49] and Ignacio Bernal's commendation (1980) is characteristically backhanded: "[Charnay's] conclusions may be based on false premises, but for the first time the Maya and the Mexico of Central Mexico were seen as a unity, and their joint territories as a superzone."[50] Leo Deuel (1967), more generous in his assessment, applauds Charnay's commonsensical conclusions of an indigenous and relatively recent origin for the ruins and says, "though modern archaeologists are wont to consider his writings somewhat 'extravagant,' they have been forced to tacitly accept some of his deductions, foremost his identification of Tula in the state of Hidalgo with Tula [that is, Tollan] of the Toltecs."[51] Furthermore, in reference to the issue that wins him a kind of de facto paternity for the Tula–Chichén Itzá problem (and thus for the present project), Deuel finds that Charnay "was probably the first to observe the close resemblances between Tula and Chichén Itzá in the Maya territory, nearly a thousand miles away."[52] Even Tozzer, the eventual doyen of the "Mexicanization" or "Toltecization" problem, grudgingly concedes that "only partially right in his ideas, [Charnay] must be given credit for being one of the first to point out the strong Mexican influence at Chichén."[53]

Assuredly, to don a mantle in defense of Désiré Charnay would be an exercise in frustration. Yet, for all his failings — actually *because* of those failings — Charnay is an appropriate lens into the Tula–Chichén Itzá problem. His insouciant manipulations and prejudices (not wholly without insight) are a flag to the inextricability of intellectual history and (re)constructed Mesoamerican history, to the dependency of viable interpretation on sound methodology, to the necessity of rigorous self-reflexivity, and to the power of external forces on the evolution of ideas about these two sites. Politicized interests and prejudices, of course, intrude on every academic controversy. But in the case of this particular problem, and more particularly still, with respect to the study of Mesoamerica's most notoriously controversial site, Chichén Itzá, the force of pet theories (like Charnay's pan-Toltec postulate), professional reputations, funding requests, popularizing exaggerations, Mexican nationalism, and tourist dollars has been truly exceptional. And nowhere is this more evident than in Charnay's transparent maneuverings. By the ease with which he succumbs to the temptation to twist and patch the fragmentary historical record for the sake of coherence, good drama, and self-aggrandizement — a temptation that in more subtle guises will taunt every era of debate about the Tula–Chichén Itzá connection — Charnay caricatures the measure of control that such external forces have exercised. His free-wheeling presence (and occasional perspicacity) can serve us in the next sections as a rhetorical device to initiate reviews of the general problem of Maya-Mexican relatedness and the more specific historical controversies about Tula and Chichén Itzá; yet, even more, his methodological indiscretion serves as a constant reminder — a warning of sorts — of our own boundedness and distance from the native Mesoamericans of a millennium past.

The General Problem: Maya-Mexican Interrelatedness

> These remains [found at Tula, Hidalgo] are priceless in every respect because of their analogy and intimate connection with all those we shall subsequently discover forming the first links in the chain of evidence respecting our theory of the unity of American civilization, which it is our object to prove in the course of this work.
>
> *Désiré Charnay, 1887*[54]

> The Maya and Nahuatl [that is, Central Mexican] stocks were distinct in origin, different in character, only similar by reason of that general similarity which of necessity arose from the two nations being subject to like surroundings, and nearly in the same stage of progress.
>
> *Daniel Brinton, 1881*[55]

Mesoamerica is a bow tie–shaped area, squeezed in the middle by the Isthmus of Tehuantepec, the Maya zone to the southeast and Central Mexico to the northeast. More than a hundred years ago, Charnay and another pioneering Americanist, Daniel Brinton, were vigorously debating the nature of the relatedness between the two halves, between the peoples of Yucatán (the Maya) and their counterparts in the Valley of Mexico (the Nahua, the Aztecs, and their predecessors, the Toltecs and Teotihuacános — collectively the Central Mexicans).[56] Charnay (1885), albeit on bogus grounds, stressed Maya-Mexican commonality, and, with characteristic superconfidence, argued for the sweeping cultural unity of Middle America. Brinton (1881), ever at odds with Charnay and spokesman for the more conventional opinion of their era, stressed disunity and polarized the Maya and Mexican stocks. Alfred P. Maudslay (1889), the voice of impartiality, stated the quandary that remains, as yet, unresolved: "it is still a matter of dispute . . . whether the Mayas derived their culture from the Nahuas, or the Nahuas from the Mayas, or whether both inherited it from the Toltecs, or again, whether the Toltecs are not altogether mythical."[57]

The Tula–Chichén Itzá problem, the controversy about the relationship between a major site in Central Mexico and another on the other half of the bow tie (that is, in the Maya zone), is a subspecies of the more general problem of Maya-Mexican interrelatedness and, ultimately, the even broader issue of the simultaneous diversity and unity of all Mesoamerica.[58] To the indomitable question, what is the relationship between the Maya Indians and the Central Mexican Indians? (and more specifically, what is the relationship between their respective religions, arts, and architectures?), historically, there have been three characteristic sorts of answers: (1) they are *not* related; (2) they are related by virtue of common ancestry; and (3) they are related by virtue of ongoing, inter-regional interaction. By way of laying the background, charting the frames of references from which scholars have excogitated on the similitude between Tula and Chichén, these three, roughly chronological classes of response to the question of Maya-Mexican relatedness will be treated successively as: (1) a paradigm of polarity, (2) a fascination with "mother cultures," and (3) arguments for the mobility and perpetual interactivity of ancient Mesoamericans.

Two Indians: A Paradigm of Polarity

> Into the bright and joyous religion of the early Maya, whose beneficent gods ask only offerings of fruit, flowers, prayers and incense . . . was infused the black, cruel, gloomy religion of Mexico, with its bloodthirsty priests and its savage, obscene deities demanding hecatombs of human sacrifice.
>
> *Thomas Gann, 1924*[59]

One powerful strain of Americanist studies has forever treated the Maya and the Mexicans, or Nahua (including Teotihuacános, Toltecs, and Aztecs), as two discrete entities, the former perceived as more antique, more sophisticated and artistic, and in all important ways more sympathetic. Beginning as early as European contact with Middle America, Spanish friars attribute a beauty, serenity, and positive sense of awe to the Maya ruins but consider the monuments of Central Mexico impressive principally for their brutish massiveness.[60] In things religious the polarity is particularly drastic: the Maya are astronomer-priests, worshippers of time, contemplative intellectuals, "the Greeks of the New World" whose benign purity is eventually contaminated by sanguinary Toltec Mexican warriors who bring with them the vile practices of human sacrifice, cannibalism, idolatry, and sodomy. The two are not only different, they are opposites.[61]

This perception of the Maya and the Mexicans as two culturally differentiated groups is made explicit at least by the writings of Pedro Sánchez de Aguilar (about 1635) and attains near-canonical status by the nineteenth century.[62] Guillermo Dupaix, for instance, after surveying pre-Columbian ruins from Mexico City to Palenque (at the west edge of the Maya area) in 1804, concluded that Maya architecture is as distinct from the Zapotec or Aztec styles as it is from the Gothic, Arabic, Chinese, or Carthaginian;[63] and Count Frederic Waldeck, carousing Mexico only a short time later, similarly found no semblance between the presumably Maya religion, hieroglyphs, and architecture of Palenque and their Mexican, "Toltec" counterparts.[64] The influential works of Manuel Orozco y Berra, *Historia Antiqua y de la Conquista de Mexico* (1880), and Hubert Howe Bancroft, *The Native Races of the Pacific States* (1886), likewise define the Maya and the Central Mexicans as two culturally differentiated groups;[65] Brinton writes in 1881 that "the Maya and Nahuatl stocks were distinct in origin, different in character";[66] and Antonio Peñafiel, in three enormous folio volumes, *Monumentos de Artes Antiguo Mexicano* (1890), holds that the Maya and Mexican cultures were completely independent, no more indebted to one another than to Egypt.[67]

The insistence on the autonomy, independence, and isolation of the Maya not only from the Old World but from the rest of the New World continues to flourish in the twentieth century, finding its hyperbolic expression and most influential supporter in the energetic person of Sylvanus Morley, who was director of the Maya research program of the Carnegie Institution of Washington (CIW) from its beginning in 1913 until 1929 (The incomparably influential CIW program was, not incidentally, headquartered at Chichén Itzá.) Morley vigorously promoted the notion that the entire Maya story, from 3000 B.C.E. forward, developed within the confines of the Yucatán Peninsula, "practically without influences from the outside," and that any Mexican influence occurred late and was of slight duration.[68] Certainly a capable and pioneering Maya researcher of major significance, particularly in epigraphical problems, Morley was, nonetheless, most of all preoccupied (and successful) in bringing the fabulous cultural accomplishments of the ancient Maya to public consciousness. He not only studied the Maya, he promoted them. Formulating his ecstatic opinion of the Classic Maya largely in the teens, and then promulgating his vision until its climactic exposition in the immensely popular *The Ancient Maya* (1946), Morley spared no superlative in praising their excellence, beneficence, and absolutely self-initiated ascent to cultural perfection.[69] For Morley, the Classic Maya were the "Greeks of the New World," and, "by implication the Toltecs and the Aztecs were the Romans who did no more than crudely copy the culture of the Maya. Just as the Greeks were the sources of European civilization, so the Maya were the cultural innovators and intellectual superiors of all indigenous American peoples."[70] The romanticization (and Maya-Mexican polarization) snowballs as others, even less stayed by the facts (like Morley's contemporary Thomas Gann), wax ad infinitum about the Maya as "joyous, peaceful, care-free, art-loving children of nature" who persist in a kind of socio-intellectual utopia, contaminated only by the overspill of repugnant practices from Central Mexico.[71] Gann, for instance, holds that human sacrifice and "quasi-ceremonial religious cannibalism [were among] the many evil practices introduced among the Maya by the Mexicans."[72]

Center, Sylvanus Morley, consummate host as well as archaeologist, conducting one of his countless personal tours through the Great Ball Court at Chichén Itzá. A master at public relations, Morley seized every opportunity to promulgate his view that the ancient Maya were the "Greeks of the New World." He argued that the "almost complete isolation" of the Yucatán Peninsula provided an ideal "laboratory case" for the intensive study of America's premier aboriginal civilization. Subsequent research would dismantle Morley's depiction of the Maya as an autonomous and isolated special case. (Photo by Luis Marden, courtesy of George Stuart.)

Despite a load of dissenting evidence against their isolationism — much of which Morley himself was definitely aware[73] — this vision of the Maya as a disconnected special case, more refined and affable in all regards than their Central Mexican brethren, has proved tremendously resilient, particularly in the more popular literature. Moreover, the radical polarization of Maya and Mexican was nowhere more piquant, even among first-rate scholars, than in the assessment of their respective arts and architectures. Art historian Donald Robertson, for instance, perpetuates the notion of a singular and isolated Maya architecture: "the Maya, living behind mountain barriers, isolated by the sea and difficult swampy jungle terrain, were separated from the rest of Mexico, free to work out their own destiny uninterrupted by constant invasions. Their isolation was comparable to that of Egypt, and they were able to develop local architectural styles of a thousand year duration."[74] George Vaillant, in the thirties, enjoined the standard practice of explaining the diversity in Mesoamerican art by posing an extreme antithesis between Maya and Central Mexican: "Maya art is the aesthetic of a gentle people, whereas Nahua art is the product of a more austere and warlike folk."[75] And, forty years later, this basic polarity between two kinds of pre-Hispanic art persisted particularly in the more popular literature on ancient Mesoamerica. Consider, for instance, the assessment of Frank Waters: "[the art and architecture] of the Maya is expressed in a style opulent, elaborate and decorative . . . that of the Nahuas . . . seems its direct antithesis. With its geometrical arrangement of pyramids, temples and palaces, its architecture is dedicated to the austere and the abstract.[76]

Eric Thompson, perhaps the most influential of all in this regard, embellishes the Maya-Mexican distinction in art with psychological and even moral dimensions, presenting an antipodean formulation that exceeds even Morley's. Thompson maintained that Mexican culture was "morally weaker . . . with lower standards" than the Maya; consequently, where Mexican architecture is "restless . . . showy but unstable" and characterized by "incredible stiffness . . . depressing monotony," by contrast, according to Thompson, Maya art and architecture "conveys a message of calm assurance . . . moderation, orderliness, and dignity."[77]

Besides making this radical contradistinction between their religions, psychologies, and arts, Eric Thompson is generally credited with another major dimension of the Maya-Mexican polarity that weighs heavily on the Tula-Chichén problem, namely, two antithetical attitudes toward urbanism and centralized political authority. In Thompson's scheme, while the Central Mexicans are totalitarian, empire-building militarists who operate out of "true cities," the peaceful, intellectual Maya are indifferent to large-scale political integration and, thus, reserve their monumental construction efforts for "ceremonial centers" or "vacant cities" that are occupied only periodically for festivals and pilgrimages.[78] This complex issue of Maya nonurbanism, or "semi-urbanism" — another self-fertilizing stereotype that is not seriously challenged until the 1970s — likewise has a history that stretches deep into the structure of Mesoamerican scholarship. Charnay, again stumbling upon some insight, is the litmus of the antiquity of the "Maya city" issue; he concludes that the Maya had a peculiar brand of urbanism that distinguished them to an extent from Central Mexico and absolutely from the cities of Europe:

> Yucatán had centers rather than cities; for the groups of dwellings and palaces we find resemble in no way our cities of the present day, although they are continually compared to Spanish places, notably Seville, by the conquerors. . . . [The Maya centers] consist everywhere of temples and palaces, either of the reigning prince or caciques, of public edifices scattered about, apparently at random, covering a vast area, with cemented roads and gardens intervening.[79]

These paired stereotypes of Mexican urbanism versus Maya nonurbanism that were just taking flight in the nineteenth century would later be concretized during the Carnegie Institution's domination of Maya studies in the form of pat (if dubious) distinctions between Maya "ceremonial centers" versus Mexican "true cities," dispersed Maya versus compacted Mexican settlement patterns, and random Maya as opposed to systematic Mexican spatial orientations. These tenuous distinctions, then, would provide the interpretive categories for explaining the seeming anomaly of Chichén Itzá's dense-packed layout as "an experiment in urbanism . . . that seems to have been new to the Maya" or, more tellingly still, as "a Mexican city in the non-urban Maya zone."[80]

The rise and fall of these antipodean images of Maya and Mexican urbanism, and of the consequent interpretation of "Toltec Maya" Chichén Itzá as some sort of urban aberration, deserve brief review. In the mid-nineteenth century, Lewis Henry Morgan and Adolph Bandelier mounted an offensive against what they took to be an apocryphal Aztec urbanism, arguing that the great pre-Columbian cities of the Aztecs existed only in the self-aggrandizing fables of the conquistadors.[81] Morgan's estimable influence notwithstanding, the existence of "cities" in ancient Central Mexico (in the sense of large permanent concentrations of population that are socially stratified and functionally diversified) has been forever taken for granted. In the 1960s, William Sanders's long-term studies of pre-Hispanic Mexican settlement systems and Rene Millon's companion study of Teotihuacán and its residential patterns confirmed the ubiquity of a genuinely metropolitan pattern in the Basin of Mexico. Currently, Davíd

Carrasco, insisting upon the urban character of pre-Hispanic Mexico in a whole series of publications, is heading exploration into the specifically religious implications of the "traditional urbanism" that characterized this area.[82]

The intellectual history regarding the "Maya city" is considerably more disputatious; three broad pulses are evident.[83] The first, which is evident in the works of nearly all the early European and American Mayanists — Waldeck, Stephens, Maudslay, Maler, Holmes, Bodwitch, and Edward Thompson — is a simple, nontechnical presumption that the Maya were an urban people. This group assumes, as Bishop Landa had in the sixteenth century, that the monumental architectural ruins of Yucatán denote former nuclei of large, socially stratified populations with all the attendant functions of government, trade, and manufacture that the Old World model of the city typically implies.[84]

The second pulse is composed of scholars who are dubious that the Maya sites were ever loci of residential or political centralization. Charnay participates in this skepticism; Cyrus Thomas (1899) deems Copan a "sacred city . . . probably a religious center"; and Thomas Joyce (1927), after a survey of their "town-planning," concludes that the Maya sites were probably "ceremonial centers" rather than cities.[85] However, the very wide currency of the ceremonial center model can be traced to a succession of Eric Thompson's popular works, beginning in 1927 and culminating in *The Rise and Fall of Maya Civilization* (1954).[86] Thompson contended that the Maya, as swidden agriculturalists, could not possibly have maintained populous permanent settlements; accordingly, the Classic Maya sites had been only temple and palace precincts — essentially "vacant cities" — inhabited only by a priestly aristocracy and its retinue, who were supported by a lowly, agrarian peasantry living in scattered farmsteads at some distance from the centers of the elite.[87] Furthermore, Thompson maintained that the various Classic Maya centers were not politically integrated, nor were they combative; rather, they constituted a "loose confederation of autonomous city states" that evinced happy fidelity to their credo, "live and let live."[88]

Marshall Becker, part of the third pulse that reasserts that the Maya were a truly urban people, argues convincingly that Thompson's "priest-peasant," "vacant city" model "derived more from [Thompson's exposure to] English social structure and Bolshevik history than from archaeological evidence" and, moreover, that the verdure of the vacant city notion among Western commentators owed more to their growing disdain for urbanization than to anything intrinsic in Maya civilization.[89] Nevertheless, this happy characterization of the pastoral Maya — particularly in contrast to the "morally inferior," megalomaniacal, oppidan Mexicans — is embraced as the reigning paradigm for most of four decades.

The Carnegie Mayanists, the voice of orthodoxy that fed (and fed off of) Tozzer's exposition of the Maya-Toltec problem, embraced Thompson's model of Maya ceremonial centers with disturbing alacrity. Thus, with respect specifically to the Tula–Chichén Itzá problem, an issue seemingly tailor-made for the Maya center versus Mexican city dichotomy, the Carnegie party line considered Tula (like Teotihuacán and Tenochtitlán) a stellar participant in a Central Mexican tradition of compacted, residential, and, thus, fully urban centers that functioned as the seats of politically, or at least economically, integrated "empires" of considerable breadth. By contrast, the Classic Maya were pictured as ambiguously semi-urban, a highly diffused agrarian population who gathered periodically at ritual centers that were otherwise essentially vacant. In the imaginations of the Carnegie Americanists, centralized authority and regional political integration were neither realities nor aspirations for the ancient Maya.

Accordingly, the melodramatic story of the Toltec invasion and conquest of Chichén — the so-called "Mexicanization" of Yucatán — became seriously entangled with the images of a totalitarian Mexican urbanism that spread, almost like an infectious disease, into the villatic Maya Lowlands. For instance, Brainerd's 1956 revision of Morley's *The Ancient Maya* demonstrated the victory of the vacant city model by excising Morley's original notion of the Classic Maya "city" (a vestige of the first pulse) and then replacing it with the notion of intermittently occupied "ceremonial centers" (the party line of the second pulse).[90] Moreover, in his own synthesis, *Maya Civilization* (1956), Brainerd went ever further to conclude, consonant with the then-prevailing consensus, that, "with little question 'city-life' in Yucatán must have been introduced through Mexican influence."[91]

From this vantage, Postclassic Chichén Itzá, anomalous among other reasons for its seemingly atypical (that is, "non-Maya") dense-packed urban character, was taken as "an incomplete transition" between these two disparate organizational patterns, the bastard offspring that resulted when the bucolic Yucatán Maya were raped by the displaced, roving Toltec urbanites. In turn, Chichén Itzá's younger sibling, Mayapán (presumed the next great capital of Yucatán, some 60 miles west and 200 years later than Chichén Itzá), seemed to represent the wholesale materialization of the centralized pattern of Mexican urbanism now transplanted and full-blown in Yucatán. Thus, Mayapán, this last and most degenerate of Maya centers, dispraised by every scholarly critic, was, ironically enough, (mis)labeled as the first truly urban form in the Maya zone, in H.E.D. Pollock's words, "the first great Maya city."[92]

For that tremendously resilient and prestigious strain of Middle American studies, which for several generations held that the pre-Columbian Maya and Mexicans were discrete, even opposite peoples (this group explained the diversity of Mesoamerica by shoving all cases toward polar extremes), the Maya/Mexican phenomenon of "Toltec" Chichén Itzá was the most exciting and melodramatic of circumstances: the intersection, the crossing, the collision of two modes of human existence. The controversy over Mesoamerican urbanism added yet one more dimension to the already captivating (if imaginal) scenario wherein the marauding Toltecs bully and bash the introspective Maya. The thoroughgoing acceptance of the contrast between Maya ceremonial centers and Mexican cities, albeit suspect in the extreme, spiced the "Mexicanization" drama more still as a classic confrontation between urban and rural mentalities and even, as Thompson would have us believe, between "secularism" and religion.[93] These glib images of opposition, at once understating the unity and reducing the diversity of Mesoamerica, nonetheless provided considerable theatrical appeal. Even more satisfying (to its proponents anyway), the paired Maya-Mexican opposition provided a framework of heuristic coherence for explaining the pre-Hispanic history of the area. Not surprisingly then, these mismated images have had great staying power. The next two sections, emphasizing (more appropriately, I think) the oneness of pre-Columbian Mesoamerican peoples, will chart a series of reservations with and challenges to the so-termed "paradigm of Maya-Mexican polarity" but never its wholesale abandonment.

Mother Cultures: Unity via Common Ancestry

> The great mistake of explorers is that they have studied each palace, each ruin separately without

> troubling themselves as to whether they had not a common bond, and whether the civilizations they represented were not interrelated and sprung from one common source.
>
> *Désiré Charnay, 1887*[94]

If there has been an untoward tendency by one stream of Mesoamericanists — for decades, the mainstream of Mesoamerican studies — to polarize inordinately the collective psychologies, religions, and cultural accomplishments of the Maya and the Mexicans, Charnay (among others) errs in the opposite direction, arguing for the complete homogeneity of ancient Middle America. His sweeping spirit and fanatical attribution of every cultural accomplishment to a superrace of Toltecs makes pan-American uniformity a cause célèbre — "our theory of the unity of American civilization, which it is our object to prove in the course of this work."[95] Moreover, again earning a kind of paternity for the current project, Charnay's strongest "proof" for the homogeneity of pre-Hispanic culture is a sameness in the surviving architecture, a commonality that he traces ultimately to a "Toltec house" at Tula, Hidalgo. In Charnay's eyes, the basic form of this prototypical Toltec house persists across the Mexican, Maya, and, in fact, all ancient American zones:

> the American mounds . . . were built on one plan without intermission . . . the hieroglyph *calli* (or house) is the outline of the Toltec palace and temple, the foundation of his architecture, which never varies, and which we shall find in all monuments, whether we travel north or south, on the plateau or in the lowlands; so that had everything else been destroyed we might nevertheless pronounce with safety that all the monuments in North America were of Toltec origin.[96]

Impressed by Charnay's unusually inclusive vision, Ignacio Bernal, a latter-day champion of Mesoamerican unity, deems him the earliest to include the joint territories of the Maya and Mexican in a superzone.[97] Actually, however, Charnay, as usual, has a number of important predecessors and, of course, an even stronger congregation of successors. His impetuous explanation of unity on the basis of pan-Toltec domination participates in the first of two sorts of positive responses to the query of Maya-Mexican relatedness; the former argues for Mesoamerican unity on the basis of a common heritage, the latter, on the basis of continuing interactions between the respective areas of Middle America.

With respect to claims of a shared cultural parentage, an indefatigable fascination with "mother cultures" and vanished superpeoples (exemplified in North America by visions of the fantastic "Mound Builders"[98]) has engendered a kind of revolving priority among the cultures of Mesoamerica. Owing particularly to their prestige in the Aztec documentary sources, the "Toltecs" are acclaimed, not only by Charnay, but by a host of antiquarians, as the original super-genitors of Middle America.[99] Given the gushing assessment of the Maya, it is not surprising that they too should enjoy, particularly in the nineteenth century, a consensual tenure as not simply the eldest of Middle American cultures but also the wellspring of all others.[100] With the broader perspective and improved chronology of twentieth-century archaeology, unqualified Maya primacy falters until, beginning in the 1940s, above the protests of Morley and Thompson, the newly discovered Olmec civilization is lauded by Caso, Covarrubias, Noguera, and Stirling as the true and original disseminator of Mesoamerican high culture.[101]

In each of these scenarios, the observed unities, continuities, and parallels between various regions of Middle America (Central Mexico and northern Yucatán included) could be explained, albeit lamely, by a kind of spoked diffusion from a hub of maternal, generative excellence. Alternatively, however, there is a more likely (if less dramatic) set of explanations for the perceived unity of Mesoamerica, which argues for the possibility that all variations of pre-Hispanic civilization derive from a modest, though wide-flung cultural substratum. Despite its lack of histrionic appeal, this notion of unspectacular but widely shared cultural beginnings, in fact, provides a far more plausible accounting of Middle American unity than any of the claims to a grand Toltec, Maya, or even Olmec "mother culture." The discernment of a less regionalized cultural stage to which the Maya and Mexican alike are indebted — variously termed "Archaic," "pre-Classic," "Village Formative," or "Basic," among other titles — has been cumulative and unrelenting.[102]

As early as 1861, Brasseur de Bourbourg, for instance, theorized the existence in Mexico of a culture prior to that of the Aztecs and Toltecs; around the turn of the century, Bishop Plancarte and Zelia Nuttall likewise speculated about an "archaic" Mexican culture; and, in the early teens, Manuel Gamio, Franz Boas, and Tozzer each archaeologically documented a culture that preceded that of the Classic in the Valley of Mexico.[103] In 1917, Herbert Spinden present a bold and controversial "Archaic Hypothesis" that explained the unity of the region in terms of a homogenous and widespread culture based on maize agriculture and sedentary village life that underlies the more spectacular developments of both Middle America and the Central Andes.[104] Taking the reins of the Carnegie Maya project from Morley in 1929, Alfred Kidder, perhaps the most important scholar of all in this regard, espoused Paul Kirchhoff's famous conception of "Mesoamerica" as "a region whose inhabitants, both the very old immigrants and the relatively recent ones, were united by a common history that set them apart as a unit from other tribes of the Continent,"[105] and then redirected the Carnegie research program to net considerable data on a pan-Mesoamerican Preclassic horizon.[106] By the forties, the material remains of this shared anterior cultural horizon were documented in Central Mexico by George Vaillant, in the Guatemalan Highlands by E. M. Shook, and in Yucatán by Brainerd. Moreover, Kidder, Julian Stewart, Gordon Willey, and William Strong each reechoed Spinden's "Archaic Hypothesis" with revised theories of an original, geographically widespread, technologically uniform cultural era that would have encompassed both the Central Mexican and Maya areas.[107]

Since that mid-century flurry of interest, there has been continual debate as to the chronology and characterization of the earliest phases of Mesoamerican culture; specifically, knowledge as to both the religious complexion of the proto-Mesoamericans and the earliest emergence of a characteristically ceremonial architecture remains very incomplete and controversial.[108] Yet, by now, there is nearly unanimous assent that the Maya and Mexicans are, at least ultimately, siblings of a mutual cultural parentage. Michael Coe, for instance, articulates the current consensus that the peoples of Yucatán and Central Mexico were not, after all, disconnected and isolated from one another but, instead, were similarly inheritors of a shared cultural tradition: "From such profound similarities one can only conclude that Mesoamerican peoples must have shared a common cultural origin so far back in time that it may never be brought to light by archaeology."[109] If rather more bland than the old stories of familial descent from a wondrous mother culture, this tempered acknowledgment that there is a significant fraternity between Maya and Mexican will, nonetheless, prove crucial for a realistic understanding of the relatedness between Tula and Chichén Itzá.

Mobility and Interaction: Unity via Ongoing Relations

> The fact is that the Maya of both highlands and lowlands have never been isolated from the rest of Mesoamerica, and that Mexican influences have sporadically guided the course of Maya cultural history since very early times.
>
> *Michael Coe, 1984*[110]

The case for Mesoamerican unity on the basis of shared cultural parentage is reinforced by a second, more live set of positive responses to the question of Maya-Mexican interrelatedness, one that explains commonalities in terms of dynamic processes of cross-regional interaction — conquests, migrations, pilgrimage, and, above all, long-distance trade. This recognition, still tentative, of the fabulous mobility and interactivity of ancient Mesoamericans, the Maya included, comes as an even stiffer challenge to the old paradigm of Maya-Mexican polarity.

Tozzer and Morley (mis)characterize the Maya — in contrast to the mobile and expansionist Mexicans — as politically complacent, "sedentary," "remarkably fixed and conservative," "content to remain very much in one place . . . , their custom was not to send out colonies to distant parts of the country."[111] Moreover, effecting a kind of self-fulfillment of their assessment of Maya immobility, these scholars intentionally telescope the energies of the Carnegie project on the Maya Lowland area because it constitutes, in their eyes, a kind of closed laboratory for observing the stay-at-home Maya. Brainerd, Eric Thompson, and Strong each condemn that narrow perspective.[112] And, following Morley's tenure, the next Carnegie helmsman, Alfred Kidder, initiated an expanded agenda that included, in addition to a deeper look into the "Archaic" era, a geographical stretch to investigate transregional interactions between the Highland, Central, and Northern Maya; between the Maya and Central Mexico; and wider still, between Middle and South America.[113] Progress in this sphere continues steadily — it is precisely this sort of inquiry at which the more systems-oriented "new archaeologists" who come to dominate the field in the 1960s excel — so that the redefined Maya that emerge at present are anything but flat-footed and eremitical.[114]

Morley's simplistic and geographically circumscribed reconstruction of Maya culture history — that is, the notion that Maya civilization begins in the Petén Southern Lowland region, expands in an attenuated form to northern Yucatán, and then is invaded and squelched by marauding Toltecs from Central Mexico[115] — has been supplanted by a labyrinthine drama of superlocal integration wherein, at least by the Classic period, there are flourishing trade networks that criss-cross not only the Southern and Northern Maya Lowlands but the entire breadth of Maya and Mexican Mesoamerica. The conception of the Maya as myopic isolationists, or even as swidden farmers whose agricultural production was aimed primarily at local consumption, has been thoroughly undermined by a legion of studies of pre-Hispanic commercial processes. A mutually beneficial "symbiosis" between the Mexican Highlands and the Maya Lowlands is even more well documented — nothing is being investigated so energetically as long-distance trade — and, at present, no one contests the necessity of viewing Maya economics as an active part of the total "Mesoamerican interaction sphere."[116] Moreover, this energetic Maya mercantile traffic was coupled in a great many cases by religiously motivated pilgrimage travel; the far fame of Cozumel and Chichén Itzá as pilgrimage centers had been known since Landa's time, but the extension and formative power of Maya pilgrimage-trade networks is only recently being appreciated.[117]

Furthermore, to rattle the polarizing stereotypes even harder, the same sorts of wide-angle studies that reveal the extreme mobility of the pre-Columbian Maya similarly dislodge Thompson's entrenched model of Maya nonurbanism. (This is the third pulse in the "Maya city" debate discussed earlier.) Beginning in the 1950s, the then-novel techniques of regional and settlement pattern archaeology employed by Gordon Willey and William Bullard laid a foundation for exploring a number of important new hypotheses about the Maya's participation in large cultural processes such as urban genesis and state formation.[118] Then, as part of the University of Pennsylvania's Tikal Project (1956–1970) — "the most ambitious and costly Maya field program ever mounted"[119] — huge peripheral settlement surveys by Haviland and Dennis Puleston landed a coup de grâce to the vacant city model. They established, seemingly irrefutably, that Maya centers were *not* just sporadically occupied ceremonial centers but were essentially pre-industrial cities in their range of functions and in many aspects of their form and, moreover, that Maya urbanization was a result of local emergences, not a "foreign" mode of integration forcibly imposed by Central Mexicans.[120] In Haviland's explanation, the Maya cities were (as Charnay had recognized) "of a different sort than the urban centers of Mexico," but rather than seeing them as extreme antitheses, "it is more realistic to think in terms of a continuum, with heavily populated centers at one end and centers inhabited by fewer people at the other."[121] Accordingly, the compact, supposedly "Mexican" articulation of Chichén Itzá (and even of Mayapán, the so-called first great Maya city), rather than being atypical and unprecedented, was likely the dynamic outgrowth of an indigenous Maya tradition of urbanism.[122] Thus, contrary to the old image of the Maya as villatic patsies to the commercial exploitations of Central Mexicans, these iconclastic studies suggest that, in all probability, the socially complex and militarily proficient cities of the Maya were aggressive, valued, and formidable partners in pre-Columbian long-distance trade.

Broadly speaking, where older (re)constructions of Maya-Mexican relatedness relied primarily on the more abrupt (and often apocryphal) mechanisms of migration and conquest, subsequent assessments accentuate the possibility of abiding, gradually evolving cross-regional relations (that is, *processes* rather than events). The old paradigm of polarity held that, while there may have been a very early Maya influence in Central Mexico (the coarse Mexicans had, after all, gotten a measure of refinement from somewhere), in the main, Mexicans were the aggressors in a one-way movement into a passive Maya zone, and, thus, Mexican encroachment was coercive and destructive. Moreover, prevailing opinions long held that the Mexican intrusions into the Mayaland had come in two distinct waves: one, in the Classic period, emanating from Teotihuacán and aimed almost exclusively at the Guatemalan Highlands, and a second, in the Postclassic, supposedly emanating from Tula, Hidalgo, and converging upon Chichén Itzá.[123] The long (and continuing) debate regarding the nature and extent of this earlier wave of Teotihuacán-based "Mexicanization" suggests a number of tentative amendments to the old unidirectional model: interaction was probably not simply west to east;[124] mutual trade rather military coercion was probably the most important mechanism;[125] and Teotihuacán influence, instead of being confined to the Guatemalan Highlands, apparently intruded upon virtually the whole of the Maya zone.[126] Likewise, there is a parallel (and even more well-documented) set of amendments suggesting that the later wave of so-called Toltec Mexicanization (which, according to the old party line, emanated from Postclassic Tula and headed straight for northern Yucatán) was also much broader and more collaborative than previously assumed. (Because this later wave of Central Mexican influences, invariably hung up with the notion of a Toltec Conquest of the Maya, bears directly on the Tula–Chichén Itzá problem, it will be treated in more specific historical detail later.)

In any case, like the old conceptions of Maya economic independence and rural complacence, the notion of two eccentric and distinct waves of "Mexicanization" has also proven unacceptable in virtually every respect. The movement was not simply one-way. Besides the demonstration of Maya contact at Teotihuacán, there are, for instance, dramatic (if puzzling) evidences of Maya influence in the murals at Cacaxtl, Tlaxcala, and in the statuary at Xochicaclo, Morelos, both in the Central Highlands of Mexico.[127] Nor can we any longer believe that the Mexican incursion was restricted to two specific trajectories; instead, it seems to have affected virtually all of the Maya area in an almost continuous fashion. And, perhaps most important in resolving the Tula-Chichén problem (as argued in Chapter 4), rather than being simply submissive and resigned to Mexican encroachment, the pre-Columbian Maya are now emerging from the archaeo-historical record as a progressive, cosmopolitan, urban people, wise to the ways of the world as well as the otherworld, an "outward-looking population" who, in all probability, actively courted the transference of, if not people, certainly ideas from Central Mexico.[128]

The General Problem Summarized

The general problem that has, at every turn, conditioned the explanation of the architectural similitude between Tula and Chichén Itzá is the polarization of the Maya and the Central Mexican Indians. Confronted with the manifold diversity of Middle American peoples and ruins, in wildly different states of preservation and disrepair, the broad-stroking solution has all too often been an expedient bipartitioning of "Maya" versus "Mexican." Perhaps this tendency for positing two antithetical types of Indians can be traced to the sixteenth-century Spanish confrontations with a belligerent and formidable indigenous population in Central Mexico in contrast to the already depleted, militarily less-imposing Yucatán Maya; or, perhaps, the imagined polarization derives from the stark ecological contrast between the hard, sun-baked Mexican plateau and the "mist-enshrouded" jungles of the Maya Lowlands. Perhaps the constructed Maya-Mexican duality is an expression of Westerners' deeply conflicted ambivalences about American Indians (and about themselves); or, perhaps, given the inimical defamation of the Itzás and Mexicans as "foreigners" in the Yucatán Maya ethnohistorical sources (particularly, *The Books of Chilam Balam*), it is even possible that there is a fundamental polarity in the way that indigenous Mesoamericans defined themselves. There simply are no easy explanations for these pervasive imaginings of Maya-Mexican polarity.[129] Yet, for whatever complex reasons, amateur and professional Americanists alike (notable exceptions notwithstanding), at least until recently, have invariably assessed the Maya with a sympathy inordinately greater than that afforded their pre-Columbian Central Mexican counterparts.[130] And, moreover, once the "Maya" and the "Mexican" respectively are constituted as distinct entities, constructed as objects of study and fascination, those imaginal categories, in an important sense, take on lives of their own that are quite independent of the character and activities of any historical, indigenous American peoples.

The architectural ruins of Chichén Itzá, majestically dilapidated even when the Spaniards first encountered them, provide a particularly evocative stimulus for Western imaginings about the Mesoamerican past. Totally devoid of contemporaneous texts (the glyphic inscriptions withstanding), ironically enough, the wrecked old buildings of Chichén provide both a rare window into pre-Columbian life and, at other times, an open invitation for the exercise of a whole set of Eurocentric prejudices and preconceptions about non-Western peoples. Where that double role may apply to all indigenous ruins, Chichén Itzá is made uniquely evocative by the seeming contradiction of its unmistakably "Mexican-looking" architecture deep within the Maya zone, a peculiarity that all investigators from Charnay forward feel compelled to address. With such rich architectural remains and so little firm historical information to stay their creative (re)construction efforts, Chichén Itzá offers researchers the perfect stage to play out this particular set of oppositional stereotypes, that is, to choreograph the spark-flying drama of a head-on Maya-Mexican collision. Historical conquests and "conquests of the imagination" merge. The story of Chichén Itzá and its Mexican Tula connection holds its audience by pitting a savage Mexican Toltec antagonist against a priestly Maya protagonist and then watching the melodrama unfold.

The whole contrariety on which this spellbinding confrontational saga is based has, however, begun to unravel. The conventionalized polarization of Mesoamerica, and with it the romanticization of the Maya, have not simply been revised but thoroughly shredded. Serving almost as a manifesto of the new view, Linda Schele and Mary Miller's *The Blood of Kings: Dynasty and Ritual in Maya Art* (1986), companion volume to a much-discussed traveling roadshow of Maya art, synthesizes an alternative vision of the Maya that, intentionally no doubt, subverts the old stereotypes with a set of shocking reversals.[131] The ramifications of this new outlook are elaborated more fully in Schele and David Freidel's *A Forest of Kings: The Untold Story of the Ancient Maya* (1990).[132] In their iconoclastic view, Morley and Thompson's characterization of Classic Maya religion as "the chaste worship of a celestial pantheon with a tendency toward monotheism" (and, thus, the very antithesis of the heart-ripping Mexican Aztecs)[133] is dynamited by a vision of Maya spirituality that is, as Norman Hammond notes, "if dark and unlovely, eminently more characteristically Mesoamerica.[134] Four elements in the new-fashioned view of Classic Maya religion and art — all impossible in the older, euphoric, special-case vision of the Lowlanders — are outstanding: (1) the Maya religion of this amended vision is preponderantly and unabashedly political — "the great programs of Maya art, inscriptions and architecture known today were commissioned by Maya kings to memorialize themselves and to insure their place in history";[135] (2) these re-imagined Maya have an intense fascination with death, the dead, and particularly with ancestor worship;[136] (3) they rely heavily on mind-altering drugs; and (4) the most piquant emphasis in Schele and Miller's volume, this version of Maya spirituality gives center place to human blood obtained in auto- and human sacrifice. Their revamped alternative, based primarily on new (and certainly more successful) readings of Maya iconography and epigraphy, provides a vision of Maya ritual that is, if less prodigal, at least as sanguinary to that of the Aztecs:

> Blood was the mortar of ancient Maya ritual life. The Maya let blood on every important occasion in the life of the individual and in the life of the community. It was the substance offered by kings and other nobility to seal ceremonial events . . . the purpose of art was to document the bloodlines of the Classic Maya kings . . . bloodlines dominated the determination of legitimate rule.[137]

There is, of course, the very real danger of simply replacing one ultraistic view of the Maya with its mirror opposite and thus playing in a new way into the same old polarization of images of the American Indian. We should not be so easily seduced. Nevertheless, this wholesale revision of Maya ritual and art, together with the fundamental amendments to the paradigm of polarity discussed earlier, has cast a new paradigm of Maya-Mexican interrelatedness. In the current view, ancient Mesoamerica remains diversified to be sure, but there is no simple bilateral polarity in its liquid, rippling body. Moreover, it appears that Mesoamerica was, at an important spiritual level, an integrated whole.[138]

The prevailing consensus for Mesoamerican unity (a realization of cultural integrality that has nothing to do with Charnay's theory of pan-Toltec domination) has a drastic impact on the conventional story of a black and white confrontation at Chichén Itzá. While these archaeo-historical controversies are less than definitively resolved (nor will they be resolved by this work), the cumulative effect of all these reconsiderations is devastating for the historical viability of the wonderful old story of the "Toltec Conquest" of Chichén Itzá. The familiar plot of a face-to-face confrontation between two diametrically opposed types of Indians alongside Chichén's Sacred Cenote has lost its ring of credibility and truth. The archetypes and images that for so long sustained the chess game of pre-Columbian historical (re)construction have been undercut. The victimized protagonists in Tozzer's drama of Tula and Chichén Itzá had been well played by the peaceful, introspective Maya of Morley, Gann, and Thompson, but the politically astute, blood-obsessed Maya of Schele, Miller, and Freidel cannot be easily accommodated as stand-ins.[139] The old script no longer makes sense.

Even before considering the historical particulars of the two sites, we have been given a new starting point, a new frame of reference from which to interpret the similitude between Tula, Hidalgo, and Chichén Itzá, Yucatán. The dynamic Maya-Mexican interrelatedness ensures that in their merger at Chichén Itzá, however foreign the actors were to one another, they were not absolutely unfamiliar. However radical the political and religious innovations of Chichén's florescence, they were not entirely unprecedented. And, however bizarre the art and architecture of Tula might have appeared to the indigenous Yucatecans, they were not wholly disorienting.

The Historical Problem: A Post-Paradigm Pause

> The whole question of Toltec influence and Chichén Itzá needs to be reopened and investigated.
>
> *Kenneth Brown, 1985*[140]

Aiming for the reputability of modern science, Charnay's stated objective was to disentangle the strict history of the New World from its "traditions, pre-historic legends, language and religion . . . to re-establish the historical truth."[141] In this regard, he was a dismal failure. In his characteristically reckless way, Charnay was, however, successful in gallivanting through the three major historical controversies that remain foundational to the Tula–Chichén Itzá problem: (1) the historicity of the mythical Tollan and its relationship to the site of Tula, Hidalgo, (2) Chichén Itzá's historical relationship to the rest of the Maya Lowlands, and (3) the historical phenomenon that interlocks Tula and Chichén Itzá, or the so-called Mexicanization of Yucatán. And, thus, the musings of the intrepid Frenchman are enlisted once again as the flawed benchmark that enables "a long view" of the problem.

Tracking these three controversies, and therefore still concerned more with the history of ideas about Tula and Chichén Itzá than with the actual histories of the two sites, this final portion of the first chapter, if amused by Charnay's overconfident and tawdry reconstructions, must admit that the ten decades of scholarship since Charnay's work have definitely settled almost none of the key historical debates. Still the basic journalistic questions — who? what? when? and why? — concerning Tula and, even more concerning Chichén Itzá, remain among the most controversial in the field, and the historical mechanism that joins the two cities and breeds the famous similitude in architectures persists like an insoluble algebraic equation with too many variables on either side.

The continuing confusion regarding the historical relationship between the twin cities has not, however, been for lack of effort. Mesoamericanists for decades embrace "historical reconstruction" as the end-all of Middle American studies and thus work ceaselessly to craft plausible and appealing scenarios of the pre-Columbian past.[142] Yet, even where the best academic intentions prevail, the considerable slack in the historical record has usually been cinched up with quick analogies to the rise and fall of Old World empires and with other Eurocentric archetypes of historical reconstruction — barbarians, rustics, prophets, priests, peasants, and kings. The narrative explanations that result from these imaginative efforts may express and satisfy Western sensibilities, but they are worlds away from the perspectives of the pre-Hispanic peoples they claim to describe. The extent to which supposed *re*constructions of ancient events at Tula and Chichén Itzá are interfused with the *constructions* of the modern West becomes increasingly (and disturbingly) more evident, the overlap between textbooks and storybooks, between scholars and raconteurs, increasingly more difficult to deny. Moreover, particularly in the case of this problem, a critical survey of the debate's history shows every new *re*vision, *re*working, and *re*assessment ensnarled with old prejudices and mistakes. There are no clean slates (nor can we claim any exception for our own *re*considerations).

And yet, for all the tenuousness of the "historical reconstruction" project (an approach that, if out of favor in some fields, is actually making a comeback in Mesoamericanist studies rather than disappearing), there is reason for optimism. Progress on several academic fronts has radically altered and enhanced our understandings regarding both "what happened" in pre-Columbian Mesoamerica and why scholars have tended to write about what happened in the ways they have. Together, these new perspectives, many inconceivable two decades ago, are forcing a major reconsideration of the timeworn prejudices behind the inordinate polarization of Maya and Mexican peoples and thus providing, if not a higher, certainly a new point of departure into the mystery of "Toltec" Chichén Itzá. With that in mind, consider in turn the status of academic ideas — first about Tula, then about Chichén Itzá, and then about the connectedness between the two.

Tula Chronology: Toltecs of Myth and History

> On examining the monuments at Tula, we are filled with admiration for the marvelous building capacity of the people who erected them.
>
> *Désiré Charnay, 1887*[143]

By now it can be said with assurance that Tula, Hidalgo, was the capital of a historical Toltec empire of major proportions in the tenth through twelfth centuries C.E., the locus of a distinct politico-cultural florescence after Teotihuacán and in advance of the great Aztec Tenochtitlán. The discernment of this impressive

Tula-based empire — the most potent and well-integrated polity of its era — was, however, forestalled for generations by confusion between the events of literal history and those of the quasihistorical traditions of the Aztec documentary sources. While there are no extant written sources contemporaneous with the physical remains of Tula, the Toltecs are prominently featured and treated with the greatest respect and admiration in a whole spectrum of Aztec sources.[144] The *Florentine Codex,* for instance, eulogizes "Tollan" as the fabulous, primordial city of the equally fabulous "Toltecs," the place where cotton grows in colors, surplus corn stokes the fire, and priest-king Topiltzin Quetzalcoatl presides with perfect justice and insight over the indefatigable Toltecas, or *Tlanquacemilhuime,* "they that crook the knee all day without ever tiring."[145]

If abundant, the Aztecs' effusive praises of the marvelous Toltecs, along with their marvelous lord Quetzalcoatl and their marvelous city of Tollan, are likewise historically ambiguous in the extreme. Accordingly, two aspects of the "Tollan problem"[146] (perhaps the most notorious and well documented scrimmage in the history of Mexican archaeology) would need some measure of resolution before Tula, Hidalgo, was given its due: first, there had to be some disentanglement of the historical Toltecs from the imaginal Toltecs of myth and legend, and, second, there had to be some resolution of the equally prolonged confusion as to which, if either, of the Central Mexican archaeological sites of San Juan Teotihuacán or Tula, Hidalgo, is the historical correlate to the paradisical Tollan of tradition.

Retrieving a clear record of Toltec identity and activity is complicated immensely by the pre-Columbian enthusiasm for deliberately "falsified" genealogies, fantastic claims of ethnic purity, networks of strategic marriage, and masks of hereditary authority.[147] Pre-Columbians, in other words, were exceedingly adept "manipulators of remembered history."[148] Prestigious pedigrees, contrived or otherwise, were the paramount tools of pre-Hispanic statecraft, the strategy of choice for distinguishing legitimate from illegitimate authority. Bastards, upstarts, and usurpers of power each dedicated themselves to the compensatory fabrication of ethnic purity and familial relatedness to the fabulous Toltecs.[149] The Aztecs were, of course, the most drastic manifestation of the "urge to reconstruct Toltec power," but innumerable Mexican and Maya constituencies — that of Chichén Itzá included — wove themselves into the prestigious Toltec heritage in ways that, to the befuddlement of modern scholars, disregarded entirely our strictures between myth and history.

Charnay, characteristically untroubled by their impossibly magnificent resume, easily believed that the traditional raves about the Toltecs all referred to actual historical adventures. Moreover, in another brush with genuine academic respectability, Charnay elevated Tula, Hidalgo, into an unabashed equation with the paradisical Tollan (a position that became archaeological orthodoxy some half century later). Owing to a very literal reading of the Spanish histories, Charnay believed, contrary to most of his Americanist contemporaries, that Tula was the original and paramount capital of his super-Toltecs, the corporeal referent of the Tollan of the Aztec manuscripts, and that Teotihuacán (the more obvious and more widely accepted correlate to Tollan) was but a second Toltec center, posterior to and modeled after the earlier Tula.[150] Oblivious that he had miscalculated Tula's chronology by several centuries, Charnay attempted to confirm his bookish theory that Tula had been the authentic pivot of Toltec globetrotting by conducting the first "systematic" excavations at Tula during the late summer of

1880.[151] The "Atlantean" figures that he unearthed and named, the serpent columns, the great ball court, and the warrior and animal figures in the frieze decoration — all of which he recognized from elsewhere in Middle America (particularly from Chichén Itzá) — for him clinched the case for Tula as the preeminent historical Toltec capital.[152]

Chronological atrocities notwithstanding, Charnay deserves some credit as a prophetic voice in the din over the Tollan-Tula-Teotihuacán triumvirate and the eventual scholarly equation of Tollan with Tula.[153] Charnay's generous assessment of Tula was, however, due less to his excavations than to his participation in the timeworn tendency to interpret Aztec legends of the marvelous Toltecs in an uncritical, very matter-of-fact fashion. His was an old position rather than a new one. Fray Bernardino de Sahagún, for instance, along with his indigenous informants and nearly all the colonial-era chroniclers — preeminently Ixtlilxochitl, Veytia, and Francisco Javier Clavijero (Charnay's three principal documentary authorities) — believed quite literally that the Toltecs had created Central American civilization and that the wellspring of their migrations, the miraculous Tollan, was located at Tula.[154] And most of Charnay's near predecessors in the nineteenth century (for instance, José Ramírez, William Prescott, Brasseur de Bourbourg, Orozoco y Berra, and "scores of other writers"[155]) drew on these chronicles to perpetuate the notion of Toltec preeminence.

There are ruminations among these authors that ethnohistorical allusions to the "Toltecs" might also refer in a generic sense to "architects" and "artificers," but, in the main, for them, the prehistory of Mexico was essentially a record of Toltecs adventuring out from their base at Tula.[156] Prescott (1843), for instance, something of a pan-Toltecist himself, concluded on the basis of Sahagún and Ixtlilxochitl that "the Toltecs . . . the true fountainheads of the civilization which distinguishes this part of the continent in later times . . . established their capital at Tula north of the Mexican Valley" and from there won sway over the remotest borders of Central America.[157] Apparently influenced by the same sources, Brantz Mayer, secretary to the American Legation in Mexico (1841–42), considered Tula "the headquarters of a parent stock" that eventually penetrated into the Valley of Mexico and perhaps Yucatán.[158] And Antonio Garcia Cubas, commissioned in 1873 by the Sociedad Mexicana de Geografía y Estadística to visit and report on Tula, similarly accepted without question Ixtlilxochitl's account of Toltec kings dispersing from Tula to Yucatán and Guatemala.[159]

The first to mount a systematic challenge to this literal historical interpretation of the textual references to the Toltecs was Charnay's nemesis and contemporary, Daniel Brinton (1890).[160] Unnerved particularly by the discrepancy between the lofty images of Tollan in the documentary sources and puny archaeological remains that Charnay uncovered at the site of Tula, Hidalgo, Brinton proposed an alternative that is extreme in the opposite direction.[161] Brinton denied entirely the facticity of the Toltecs' florescence, claiming instead that

> the story of the city of Tula [that is, the Tollan of tradition] and its inhabitants, the Toltecs, as currently related in ancient Mexican history, is a myth, not history . . . the Toltec "empire" is a baseless fable. What gave them their singular fame in later legend was partly the tendency of the human mind to glorify the "good old times" and to merge ancestors into divinities, and especially the significance of the name Tula [i.e., Tollan], "the Place in the Sun," leading to the confounding and identification of a half-forgotten legend with the ever-living light and darkness of the gods, Quetzalcoatl and Tezcatlipoca.[162]

Daniel G. Brinton (1837–99), professor of American linguistics and archaeology at the University of Pennsylvania, and a vehement critic of Désiré Charnay. (Courtesy of the America Philosophical Society.)

Otto Stoll (1886), concurring with Brinton that the Toltecs "reside among the fairies," elaborated on the transhistorical significances of the term "Toltec" as "artificer" and "trader" to argue that the Toltec legends simply refer to "foreign mechanics or peddlers" and not to any particular nationality.[163]

The skeptical attitude of Brinton and Stoll (again not all that original) marks an important advance in the Tollan problem, because it set the quest for Toltec history on a more modest, realistic course and, even more importantly, because it initiated a more profound appreciation of the autonomous career of the transhistorical Quetzalcoatl-Toltec-Tollan paradigm. For Brinton and Stoll, it is the *idea* of the Toltecs rather than their historical exploits that is most significant. They suspect (as becomes ever more piquant in light of the revisionist view of Mesoamerica as a unified, "liquid rippling body") that what was trafficking across pre-Columbian Middle America — for example, between Tula and Chichén Itzá — were less likely discrete national peoples than ideological paradigms and religio-aesthetic ideas. Unfortunately, however, by posing this either/or antithesis between myth and history, their appreciation of the transhistoricity of the famous Toltecs necessarily (though inappropriately) strips Tula, Hidalgo, of any real historical significance.

This disappreciation of Tula's historic importance dropped lower still with subsequent excavation of far more spectacular remains some 30 miles to the southeast at San Juan Teotihuacán. The text-based view of Tula's preeminence that reigned from Sahagún through Charnay was flatly rejected by a growing archaeological community that found the fabulous ruins of Teotihuacán — immeasurably more impressive than those at Tula — to be an eminently closer match to the Tollan of tradition. Bishop Francisco Plancarte (1911) is typically considered the earliest to propose that Teotihuacán, not Tula, is the Tollan of the ancient sources; but it was Manuel Gamio, the leading Mexican archaeologist of the teens and twenties, who combined his prestige with his excitement over the excavations of Teotihuacán to canonize the Teotihuacán-Tollan equation.[164] Charnay's extravagant claims to have found the legendary Tollan in the relatively meager ruins of Tula were discounted by the archaeological establishment as so many amateurish ravings, and the seemingly obvious correlation between Mexico's most megatherian ruins (Teotihuacán) and its most esteemed antique people (the Toltecs) was entrenched ever deeper in the literature. The immense fascination with Teotihuacán shoved Tula into the shadows. In 1941 (ironically, on the verge of the collapse of this temporary consensus), Enrique Palacios articulated the Tollan-as-Teotihuacán dogma: he quoted Sahagún about the "great buildings, the very strong and rich city with its vigorous and intelligent people . . . Tulla [or Tollan] is its name . . ." and then concluded that "this is, of course, the metropolis Teotihuacán."[165]

At this point, then, equating Tula with the great capital of the Toltecs, was considered a naive mistake; Tula's prestige was thoroughly usurped by Teotihuacán. Throughout the early decades of the twentieth century, most scholars subscribed to an (over)simple two-stage chronology for Central Mexico wherein the "Toltecs" of Teotihuacán are the only significant cultural antecedents to the Aztecs of Tenochtitlán, while the history of Tula, Hidalgo (and, thus, of the actual historical Toltecs), is a virtual blank.[166] It took conjoined advances in archaeology and ethnohistory before Tula was appreciated as an interim and great capital in its own right.[167] Beginning in 1931, George Vaillant and Sigvald Linné found a hitherto unknown ceramic type in the Valley of Mexico (named "Mazapan" by Vaillant), that postdates that of Teotihuacán but predates that of the Aztecs. As part of what turned out to be a twenty-year Mexican-sponsored archaeological project at Tula (1940–60), the first systematic excavations since Charnay, Jorge Acosta found the same ware in the Hidalgo ruins and concluded that the bearers of this so-called Mazapan culture had erected the buildings of Tula. Acosta's discovery demanded, in other words — and this was a major change — that the chronological succession of Teotihuacán and Tenochtitlán be pried open to give Tula its rightful place in between.[168]

Vaillant was the first to come forward with a substantially revised historical scheme to match the new archaeological data, an impressive bit of historical-archaeological jockeying that is recorded in the original edition of his renowned synthesis, *The Aztecs of Mexico* (1944). His provisional scheme distinguishes between two kinds of Toltecs: the "Classic Toltecs of Teotihuacán," who are followed by the "Dynastic Toltecs" (or "Toltecs-Chichimecs"), which included the Mazapan culture and its occupation at Tula, Hidalgo.[169]

The currency of Vaillant's ingenious reconstruction was short-lived as Acosta's archaeology revealed a Tula of unsuspected refinement and sophistication.[170] Moreover, at roughly the same time and even more significantly, Wigberto Jiménez Moreno (1941) delivered a revolutionary re-reading of the documentary sources (based particularly on Central Mexican place-names), which seemed to confirm that Tula, Hidalgo, not Teotihuacán, was the Tollan of tradition.[171] In 1941, the Mesa Redonda de la Sociedad Mexicana de Antropología reconsidered the Tollan problem in light of the dramatic new archaeological and textual findings and, on the weight of evidence presented by Jiménez Moreno, Alfonso Caso, Vaillant, and Acosta, undersigned a new orthodoxy (which in part vindicate Charnay). This roundtable committee, in a stroke of historical (re)construction by decree, proclaimed that Tula, Hidalgo — not Teotihuacán — was the home of the Toltecs after all. Tula was, in other words, deemed the historical correlate to the lauded Tollan of the documentary sources and the capital city of a major empire that followed that of the "Teotihuacános" (as the occupants of Teotihuacán are now known) and preceded that of the Aztecs. Pedro Armillas then fashioned that consensus into an archaeological-historical framework that is still generally accepted today.[172]

While there were refutations to the specific historical conclusions of the 1941 watershed (Kirchhoff, Chadwick, and Séjourné were among the most important dissenters[173]), Tula's historical status as the seat of a distinct and important Toltec empire was never again seriously threatened. Furthermore, while there was, appropriately enough, smoldering discontent with a simple one-to-one correlation of Tula and Tollan,[174] blanket dismissals of the Tula-based Toltec empire as simply imaginary or as an apotheosis (as Brinton had argued) evolved into a more reasonable separation of the "*historical Toltecs*" of Tula and the "*mythical Toltecs*" of tradition.[175] This more subtle take on the relations between myth and history culminate in book-length treatments of the symbolic, transhistorical Toltec tradition by Nigel Davies (1977, 1980) and Davíd Carrasco (1982).[176]

Heightened sensitivities about the complex play of Toltec myth and history notwithstanding, the unraveling of Tula's historical particulars proceeds ever so slowly. The mainline syntheses of the 1960s and early 1970s continue to be resigned to summarizing Tula's rise and fall in terms of the Quetzalcoatl myth cycle (much as Brinton had), adding to that a perfunctory endorsement of the orthodox Tula-Tollan correlation and a lament about the opacity of the historical specifics.[177] By far the most ambitious (re)construction of the diachronic succession of events in this orphic period comes in Davies's pioneering volumes, *The Toltecs Until the Fall of Tula* (1977) and *The Toltec Heritage: From the Fall of Tula to the Rise of Tenochtitlán* (1980). He too gives qualified endorsement to the correlation of Tula and Tollan but then parlays the ethnohistorical record into a singularly detailed (if controversial) interpretation of Toltec chronology. Unfortunately, in his mission to distill the "strictly historical" career of the Toltecs from the documentary sources, Davies has had all too few collaborators, competitors, or similarly well-versed critics.[178]

On the archaeological front, efforts at retrieving Tula's past have been more collaborative. Two major initiatives, the Proyecto Tula of the Mexican Instituto Nacional de Antropología e Historia (INAH) under the direction of Eduardo Matos Moctezuma and the University of Missouri, Columbia Tula Archaeological Project (UMC), directed by Richard Diehl, cooperated for more than a decade, beginning in 1968, to re-examine Tula.[179] Where Acosta's major project (likewise sponsored by INAH) had been patented traditional archaeology (aspiring, in other words, to develop a site chronology via ceramic stratigraphy and excavation of large public architecture), the goals and methods of Matos and Diehl were textbook "new archaeology."[180] Adopting a cultural materialist orientation, Matos and Diehl were eminently concerned with the "daily lives of ordinary people in the city" and with social, economic, and political processes. Tula's state religion, along with its large-scaled public art and architecture, were, for them, ancillary concerns.

This latest, more sophisticated archaeological sweep demanded that the traditional picture of Tula, still based largely on ethnohistorical evidence, be revised on several salient points. The amended Tula chronology (not radically different from Acosta's assessment) holds that the first major occupation of the Tula ridge was in the Corral phase (800–900 C.E.), and that Tula's peak was in the Tollan phase (950–1100 C.E.), after which the city declined rapidly, thus implying that Tula was not a causal factor in Teotihuacán's collapse.[181] Settlement and residential studies showed that Tula had a peak population of thirty to forty thousand (far less than either Teotihuacán or Tenochtitlán), a somewhat slack grid orientation, and a pattern of residential clusters around shared courtyards that acted as social microcosms within the larger urban society.[182] Moreover, while Tula continues to be understood as predominantly an agricultural society, the new archaeologists likewise documented a vital nonagrarian economy based on craft specialization and an extensive interregional exchange network of luxury and utilitarian products and suggested that Tula had a government-controlled trading cadre similar to the famed Aztec *pocheteca*.[183] Apparently, however, Tula never had anything like the economic security or the preeminence in long-distance trade enjoyed before by Teotihuacán and after by Tenochtitlán. Tula's socio-economic situation was always more tenuous.

In reference to the indomitable question about a Toltec "empire," Diehl concluded (fairly unoriginally) that Tula, even at its apex, was only the strongest of several competing urban centers, that it enjoyed a short-lived commercial and military hegemony over the entire Valley of Mexico, and that, to a lesser extent, it impinged upon societies from the southwestern United States to northern Central America. Diehl also argued, however, that Tula's rapid decline after only a century or two of relative prosperity is a sign that the Toltec state was never well integrated.[184] Furthermore, the dominant materialist line concluded, in consonance with the old sweeping stereotypes of Central Mexicans, that Tula, like Teotihuacán and Tenochtitlán, was essentially the manifestation of an unslackable and brutal ambition. Diehl, for instance, surmised that "the Toltecs were imperialists motivated by economic goals which they attempted to achieve through a combination of political and military means, and their brief but spectacular career as an imperial power set the pattern for later Aztec ventures along the same lines."[185]

Finally, with respect to the fall of Tula, the traditional, ethnohistorically based account describes a subterfuge perpetrated by the dark and delusory Tezcatlipoca against a trusting Quetzalcoatl (who were ostensibly surrogates for warring factions within Tula), and Acosta's discovery of fire and destruction in every building he excavated in Tula Grande seemed to verify the conventional view that the death of the city came in a sudden and overwhelming cataclysm.[186] The later, wider-scale INAH and UMC investigations, however, revealed that the peripheries of Tula were abandoned *before* the city's central core and that Tula's decline was a long process rather than a spasmodic catastrophe.[187] Furthermore, the newer view argues that Tula remained in Aztec times "quite an important place" and that "perhaps it even enjoyed a privileged position, due to its sanctity and prestige."[188]

In sum then, the blustery ebb and flow of ideas about Tula, Hidalgo, over the past hundred years hardly inspire historiographic confidence. (And this is the straightforward side of the Tula-Chichén problem!) Yet, given that there are no contemporaneous texts and that the very existence of a major Tula-based Toltec empire was in doubt until the 1940s, the progress has been impressive. There are, at this point, sufficient data from which to venture considerable hypotheses about the fundamental religious and architectural priorities at Tula. At the same time, even the most basic historical issues of Tula's rise and fall — not to mention its relationship to Chichén Itzá — remain frustratingly sketchy.[189] Ironically, whereas three weeks' digging at the site imbued Charnay with the superconfidence that he had found the wellspring of Mesoamerican culture, a century later even the most authoritative versions of the history of Tula must be is framed between a proviso that all (re)constructions are tentative and an addendum that much more study is needed.

Chichén Chronology: Empires and Overlaps

> Perhaps the most misunderstood aspect of the [Lowland Maya] Postclassic period is its chronology.
>
> *Arlen Chase and Diane Chase, 1985*[190]

On the eastern end of the Tula–Chichén Itzá connection, the snarl of pre-Hispanic peoples and events in the Northern Maya Lowlands, while providing grist for even more magniloquent theorizing than Central Mexican history, has proven at least as confounding. The arcana of Yucatán pre-Columbian chronology deflated even Charnay's hauteur. Admitting a certain bafflement and lamenting the paucity of historicity in the documents, Charnay posed his reconstruction of Chichén Itzá history with uncharacteristic trepidation. For Charnay, Chichén Itzá was, of course, preeminently the work of Toltecs from Tula — his discovery of the spectacular Tula-Chichén coincidence in architectures was, for him, definitive proof of what he had already suspected. Beyond that, however, he mentions the mysterious Itzá people but leaves open who they may have been; he recognizes two distinct periods of occupation but falls short of differentiating between "Old Chichén" and "New Chichén"; and he believes that Yucatán was eventually racked by incessant warfare and fragmentation, forcing the inhabitants of Chichén Itzá to migrate south, but he hazards no historical details.[191]

Admittedly, Charnay contributed little that was original (or correct) to the cipher of Northern Lowland chronology. But, here again, he does deserve credit for disassociating himself from the likes of Del Río, Dupaix, Lord Kingsbourgh, Brasseur de Bourbourg, Waldeck, and Le Plongeon, all of whom attributed a much-exaggerated antiquity to the monuments of Yucatán and Guatemala and variously proposed that the builders had been Egyptians, Phoenicians, Scandinavians, refugees from Atlantis, or some other mysteriously vanished stock of superhumans.[192] Furthermore, Charnay appropriately rejected the popular nineteenth-century supposal that Maya civilization had preceded, perhaps by several millennia, that of Central Mexico, a notion that persisted well into the twentieth century.[193] Instead, Charnay followed Prescott, Stephens, and

Catherwood in their conjoined abnegation of extreme antiquity and nonindigenous origins for the Yucatec monuments. All of these scholars agreed that no Maya ruin is liable to be more than a thousand years old, a position that (albeit unknowingly) reverts to the original opinion of Bishop Landa.[194]

By the start of this century, the claims of fantastic antiquity for the Maya were generally discarded. An equally untoward prejudice, however, emerged in the radical bifurcation between the cultural accomplishments of the Southern Maya Lowlands (the Petén basin and rainforests of Guatemala and southern Mexico) and those of the Northern Maya Lowlands (the low limestone plain of the Yucatán Peninsula, which, of course, includes Chichén Itzá).[195] Proclamations by Maudslay (1879–1915), Spinden (1913, 1917), Joyce (1914, 1927), and others that the stelae-rich Petén area held the artistic and cultural culmination of the Maya presaged a disproportionate concentration on that area. Moreover, and even more influential in subsequent theorizing about the Maya, in the teens, Sylvanus Morley (as noted earlier) began fifty years of soapboxing that would virtually canonize the polarizing stereotypes of the Southern Lowlands as the heartland of the oldest, the best, and the "real" Maya, while the flatlands to the north — including Chichén Itzá and, not incidentally, the most obvious signs of "Mexicanization" — were dispraised as later and less in all important respects.[196]

The dean of hieroglyphic decipherment, Morley (in an era before sophisticated stratigraphy or radiocarbon dating) seized upon the abundance of inscribed stelae in the Petén to develop a solid and detailed, if controversial, chronology for that area.[197] Inconveniently, the Northern Lowlands are almost wholly devoid of stelae with initial series dates. Consequently, Morley retreated to the chronicles (particularly, *The Books of the Chilam Balam* and the manuscripts of Landa and Lizana) to construct a Yucatán chronology that is, at best, seriously flawed.[198] The fruit of his efforts is a creative (re)construction scenario in which Maya civilization peaks first and highest in the Petén Lowlands, the so-called Old Empire (317–987 C.E.); then, following a mysterious and total collapse, Petén Maya refugees migrate into the Northern Lowlands and instigate a moderately successful renaissance, termed the "New Empire" (987–1200 C.E.), with Chichén Itzá as the premier capital.[199]

Morley's exciting two-stage story of the Maya, including his explanation of Chichén Itzá as a moderately successful attempt at reclaiming the former greatness of the southern Maya cities, gained a wide and enduring following. Particularly among more popular audiences, his (re)construction of the events at Chichén enjoyed considerably wider currency than, for instance, Tozzer's convoluted five-stage scheme for the site's history. In fact, Morley's deft scheme persists as regular fare in the tourist literature, and, ironically enough, variations on this rendition of pre-Columbian history continue even now to be favored by many indigenous Maya guides at Chichén Itzá![200]

In any case, at the opening of Morley's enduring two-empire saga, during the era of the so-termed Old Empire (which is eventually termed the "Classic" Maya period), Chichén Itzá is on an undistinguished par with a number of other modest Yucatec centers: "[Chichén Itzá was] a provisional settlement of the Old Empire, far removed from the great centers of cultural inspiration in the south . . . analogous to the Roman towns in Britain during the first and second centuries of the Christian era . . . a faint reflection of the higher order flourishing at the same time in the heart of the Old Empire to the South."[201] Morley's version continues by describing how the backward northern periphery is eventually "Mayanized" by two waves of

Carnegie Institution headquarters in the Chichén Itzá hacienda, early 1920s. *From left to right,* Edward H. Thompson, A. Munro Amsden, Earl Morris, Ann Axtel Morris, and Sylvanus Morley. Morley had argued successfully that Chichén Itzá, as the preeminent city-state of the "League of Mayapán" and capital of the "New Maya Empire," was the most appropriate location for the headquarters of the massive Carnegie Institution research project. If based on dubious historical (re)construction, the site selection nonetheless proved fortuitous. (Photo by Jerome O. Kilmartin, courtesy of George Stuart.)

migration from the declining Old Empire (waves that, in his estimation, correspond to the controversial "Small Descent" and "Great Descent" of Lizana's seventeenth-century history): the first, less numerous and slightly earlier migration comes along the east coast of the Yucatán Peninsula (416–623 C.E.); and the second, larger migration, itself composed of several different waves, proceeds along the west coast (475–623 C.E.).[202] Toward the end of this first era (about 692 C.E.), Chichén Itzá is supposedly abandoned by the Itzá (who are, according to Morley, simply Old Empire Maya who had recently colonized the site). He ventures no explanation for their desertion of Chichén but believes that these Itzá moved to Chakanputun on the southwestern coast of Yucatán.[203] During their two-and-a-half-century hiatus at Chakanputun, the Itzá join company with a group of wandering Central Mexicans (Morley does not call them Toltecs) under a leader named Kukulcán (a Maya name for Quetzalcoatl). Then, in what Morley considers to be a final wave of the "Great Descent," an Itzá-Mexican coalition from Chakanputun led by Kukulcán-Quetzalcoatl returns to Chichén Itzá. It is this hybrid contingent of Old Empire Maya (or Itzás) and renegade Central Mexicans that builds the "Mexican"-looking portion of Chichén Itzá (that which comes to be called "Toltec" Chichén Itzá or "New Chichén"), fashioning the site for the first time into a truly powerful capital and the locus of the Maya renaissance, which Morley terms the "Second" or "New Empire."[204] (Having developed this scheme in advance of the "resolution" of the Tollan problem, Morley says nothing specifically about either Toltecs or Tula, Hidalgo.)

Morley's influential and resilient scheme, in other words, reduces the Northern Lowlands of Yucatán to a kind of vanilla backdrop for the maraudings of outsiders, first from the Petén and later from Mexico. Yucatán is portrayed as a passive zone whose cultural accomplishments — preeminently, the great Chichén Itzá — are, unlike the forgetive south, almost strictly the result of foreign intervention, first by other Maya groups and then by Central Mexicans.

Adopted originally as a working hypothesis, the Old Empire/New Empire formulation became virtual dogma in the teens. The two-empire scheme served as the convenient framework of coherence with which Morley maneuvered the Carnegie Institution of Washington (CIW) to launch its first two major projects in the Maya zone, one at Uaxactún in the Petén south, as a representative center of the Old Empire, and the other at Chichén Itzá in the north, as the most representative New Empire site.[205] The massive CIW initiative, the results of which permeate all subsequent thinking about the Maya, excavated at Chichén Itzá from 1924 to 1933 (and then in the general area for another two decades); yet, even before serious digging began, Yucatecan Chichén was prefigured as a secondary or derivative phenomenon, a hybridized Maya-Mexican facsimile of the truly great and "pure" Maya sites to the south.[206] Moreover, as, ironically enough, the CIW work subsequently revealed a picture of Yucatán very different from that of Morley's preconceived imagination, demonstrating incontestably that the Northern Lowlands were hardly the runt of Maya civilization after all, he, nonetheless, persevered with his by-now-familiar old scheme, pampering his chimerical Old and New Empires to their consummate exposition in *The Ancient Maya* (1946), a synthesis of unprecedented popularity.[207]

Among the first inklings that northern Yucatán had been slighted came with the "discovery" of Cobá. Piqued by Stephens's advertence to a lost city in Quintana Roo, some 60 miles east of Chichén Itzá, Thomas Gann, in 1926, became the first European to actually find this model-busting site.[208] Following Gann's initial reconnaissance, the CIW exhumed a settlement that was startling in several respects.[209] There was a profusion of inscribed stelae that, besides doubling the number then known in the north, bore dates as old as those in the Petén centers. Moreover, there was a ball court at Cobá, but no other "Mexican" features, thus controverting the conventional belief that the ball game was belatedly introduced by Mexican invaders. Furthermore, the impressive public architecture and an extensive system of causeways that radiate from Cobá bespoke its subsequent acknowledgement as one of the largest and most powerful of the Maya centers. In all these respects, particularly in its surprisingly antique stelae dates, Cobá closely resembled the "Old Empire" Petén sites, and thus, according to then-current ideas, ought not to have been in northeastern Yucatán.[210] And so, the two-empire scheme was generally discarded (at least by professional Americanists), and it now seems likely that Cobá, just east of Chichén Itzá, was seat to a contemporaneous, competing, and wholly indigenous northern Maya "empire" that never fell under the sway of its more famous neighbor.[211]

Improved ethnohistorical research, beginning in the 1930s, similarly helped to redress the disparagement of the Northern Lowlands. Re-readings of the same sources on which Morley had relied, this time by Ralph Roys and Eric

Dinner at Carnegie headquarters in the hacienda at Chichén Itzá, early 1920s. *Clockwise from the head of the table,* Morley, Ann Axtel Morris, Earl Morris, Jerome O. Kilmartin, and A. Munro Amsden. (Photo by Jerome O. Kilmartin, courtesy of George Stuart.)

Thompson, spawned a considerably longer Yucatecan sequence, thus affording a far more flattering picture of the indigenous northern Maya during the era of the southern Petén florescence.[212] Roys and Thompson's exegetical efforts dovetailed with an increasing fund of local archaeological knowledge collected through the forties and fifties, particularly ceramic data, to yield a refreshed appreciation of the autonomy and uniqueness of Northern Lowland Maya culture.[213] George Brainerd aired the revised interpretation in his own synthesis, *Maya Civilization* (1954), and in his heavily revised edition of Morley's *Ancient Maya* (1956):

> the evidence all points to an indigenous cultural development in Northern Yucatán more or less parallel to that of the Petén, but certainly not entirely provincial thereto. The New Empire culture of Northern Yucatán is better explained as a local cultural development than as a blaze from a torch of Maya culture borne from the collapsing southern ruins by a group of survivors who colonized and ruled the north.[214]

However, while Brainerd and his contemporaries (Tozzer and Eric Thompson included) freed Yucatec culture from its status of total dependency and unoriginality, they continued to preserve the old two-empire polarity in an equally stigmatizing dichotomy between what is now termed the "Classic Maya Stage," which peaked in the Southern Lowlands (still considered the apex of Maya civilization), and the so-called Post Classic Stage, the degenerate and violent age that manifested itself in Chichén Itzá and the Northern Lowlands after the collapse in the south.[215] This new contradistinction, albeit somewhat more nuanced, was, in the broad strokes, not really so different from the harsh antithesis of the Old Empire/New Empire model. In the revised (re)constructive script, honed from the 1950s into the 1980s,[216] the story of the pre-Columbian Lowland Maya has not two, but three, successive and quite distinct artistic-cultural climaxes: (1) the *Late Classic climax* (roughly corresponding to Morley's Old Empire) in the Petén south, wherein the Maya attain their zenith of peace, prosperity, and intellectual sublimity; (2) following the "collapse" of the Petén centers, the *Terminal Classic climax* in central Yucatán, an indigenous northern Maya florescence, less spectacular than its southern counterpart but nonetheless distinguished for the finely decorated Puuc architecture of Uxmal, Kabah, Sayil, and Labná, a cluster of major sites some 70 miles southwest of Chichén Itzá (the more modest and presumably more antique portion of Chichén Itzá — so-called Old Chichén — is likewise considered a peripheral manifestation of this indigenous Puuc Maya florescence); and (3) an *Early Postclassic, foreign-born climax,* which begins with a strong influx of militarily expert but morally degenerate Toltecs (by now presumed to have originated in Tula, Hidalgo), who conceive the more glamorous portion of Chichén Itzá (that is, "Toltec" Chichén Itzá or "New Chichén") and transform the modest site into the preeminent governmental center of Yucatán.[217]

In short — and these glib stereotypes are perpetrated in virtually every archaeological synthesis from the 1950s through the early 1980s — following indigenous (and relatively peaceful) Maya florescences in the Petén south and Puuc north respectively during the Classic period, Postclassic Yucatán became the stage for the quintessential enactment of the drama of Maya-Mexican polarity. In this widely circulated rendition of pre-Columbian events, the fabric of indigenous Maya civilization, if somewhat tattered in its northern manifestation, was ripped wide open by renegade Tula Toltec militarists whose antipodean, foreign orientation eventuates in the unprecedented aberration that is "Toltec" Chichén Itzá.

However (since the mid-1980s), among the most live debates in Mesoamerican studies, both the fascinating spectacle of a Maya-Mexican confrontation and the "non-Maya" character of "Toltec" Chichén Itzá are being seriously challenged by a major reorientation in both the approach to and the vision of Lowland Maya culture history, particularly in the Postclassic north. The so-termed Postclassic era (that is, post-800 C.E.) — so long dispraised for decline, decadence, depopulation, "the breakdown of the closely integrated, religiously centered cultures of the Classic Stage, an increase in militarism, [and] the adaption of human sacrifice,"[218] all presumably the deleterious consequences of an influx of Tula Toltecs — is, for the first time, being affirmed as a period of native Maya creativity in its own right.[219] Furthermore, in consonance with the more general appreciation of the interrelatedness and mobility of Mesoamericans, the conventional "linear succession model" (that is, the notion of three consecutive Lowland climaxes that are, to an extent, separated by cultural gaps) has been rejected in favor of a more holistic view. The entirety of the Maya Lowlands is viewed now as a "totality," a relatively unified area that encompasses a number of competing and cooperating "interaction spheres."[220] Yet, rather than abandon the conventional conception of three Maya climaxes entirely, there is a fresh appreciation of their interrelatedness and, particularly, to use the vogue terminology, their "overlaps" in time.[221] Given this majorly revised outlook — an outlook that, among other things, mitigates considerably both the old northern-southern and Maya-Mexican polarities — currently competing views on

Chichén Itzá's history can be summarized in terms of three sorts of "overlaps": (1) the general overlap between the climaxes of the Northern Lowlands (including Chichén Itzá) and that of the Southern Lowlands; (2) the overlap between the two northern climaxes, that is, between the Puuc tradition and the "Toltec" Chichén Itzá tradition; and (3) most specifically, the overlap within the site itself between "Old Chichén" (or "Maya Chichén") and "New Chichén" (or "Toltec Chichén"). I will consider each in turn.

First, with respect to Chichén Itzá's relation to the early Southern Lowland climax, virtually all the old (and not so old) (re)construction schemes radically polarize the otherworldly, pure Petén Maya of the south against the militaristic and exploitative "Toltec Maya" of Chichén, the bastard offspring of a coerced union of Mexican and Yucatecan stocks. The new consensus, however — and this is a profound shift — stresses the continuity rather than disjunction between the northern and southern Maya areas.[222] The so-called collapse of the southern centers (the traditional endpoint of the Classic Maya period) now seems not to have been nearly so complete as once thought, thus implying a considerable overlap in time between the decline of the Petén centers and the rise of the Puuc and "Toltec Chichén" florescences. Moreover, the contradistinction in religio-cultural orientations has similarly been muted considerably. Currently, the southern Maya (as noted earlier) are imagined as "darker and more characteristically Mesoamerican" than originally presumed, and it now appears that the real potency behind Chichén Itzá's success was pragmatic political and commercial acumen rather than sheer military superiority; that is to say, Chichén Itzá was more like the southern Maya centers than originally presumed.[223] The cultural continuities between Chichén Itzá and the Petén centers are now considered so strong that the "significant disjunction" (that is, the transition from Classic to Postclassic Lowland history) occurs *not* with the "collapse" of Classic Maya civilization in the south before Chichén Itzá's florescence but rather with the demise of Chichén Itzá itself.[224] Thus, amazingly, in 1986, Chichén Itzá was lifted out of the stigmatized Postclassic era and resituated along with the beloved Petén Maya in the Classic period. With this major turning point in the history of the Tula–Chichén Itzá problem, even the "Toltec" portion of Chichén Itzá is no longer dismissed as a foreign, Mexican aberration in the Mayaland but, instead, is now applauded as an integral portion of a genuinely indigenous Classic Maya city![225]

Next, the debate regarding the second sort of "overlap" — Chichén Itzá's relationship to the other northern Maya climax, the Puuc florescence centered to the southwest at Uxmal — is likewise currently regarded as "one of the most burning matters in late Maya prehistory."[226] The older views hold that the magnificent Puuc architecture (including "Old Chichén"), typically considered the "most beautiful" in Mesoamerica, was the wholly indigenous accomplishment of the Yucatec Maya that immediately preceded the Toltec invasion of Yucatán. By contrast, "Toltec" Chichén Itzá architecture is considered the slightly later, hybrid expression of native Maya craftsmen who were coerced by the crass tastes of conquering Mexican architects. In other words, by convention, Puuc and "Toltec" Chichén Itzá architectures succeed one another in time without overlap and, in terms of aesthetic character, are at the extreme poles of the Mesoamerican continuum, representing respectively the best and worst in pre-Columbian tastes.[227]

While recent studies do little to moderate the aesthetic antithesis between the Puuc and "Toltec" styles — Western artistic standards notwithstanding, the two styles really are profoundly different[228] — some Mayanists now hold that the two artistic climaxes were actually expressions of a single indigenous northern Maya florescence, a position that essentially cancels the historical viability of a Maya-Mexican confrontational drama.[229] Moreover, virtually all archaeologists now concur that, rather than pan-peninsular successors, the Puuc and the "Toltec" were regional and, to some extent, coexistent stylistic variations, the hot controversy becoming the extent of the overlap.[230] The irrefutability of at least some contemporaneity between the Puuc and "Toltec" styles is, among other things, more controverting evidence to the old notion of a Chichén Itzá–based "empire" that enjoyed total and unchallenged hegemony over the whole of Yucatán. In other words, Uxmal to the southwest joined Cobá to the east as relatively near, contemporaneous, and major competitors to "Toltec" Chichén Itzá domination.

Third and finally, the controversy about Puuc-"Toltec" overlap crystallizes within the single site of Chichén Itzá. The traditional view (specifically that of Tozzer) holds that the ancient city has essentially two adjacent halves: (1) "Old Chichén," which was built by indigenous Yucatán Maya in the Terminal Classic and belongs at least tangentially to the Puuc tradition, and (2) the more famous "New Chichén" or "Toltec Chichén," the supposedly foreign portion of the site, built by "Toltecs" or "Toltec-Maya" in the Early Postclassic, which resembles Tula, Hidalgo, and has spawned all the controversy.[231] However, the new consensus for at least partial overlap of the Puuc and "Toltec" traditions similarly implies that "Old Chichén" and "New Chichén" were *not* successors but, to some important extent, contemporaries.

At once the most thoroughgoing and radical discussant of this problem, Charles Lincoln challenges the conventional assessment of "Old Chichén" and "New Chichén" as consecutive stages, arguing instead for complete contemporaneity of the two halves, that is, "total overlap."[232] Relying on the archaeological evidence, particularly the ceramic data (or, more properly, the lack thereof), Lincoln rejects the historical (re)construction that Tozzer had formulated primarily on the basis of ethnohistorical and art historical interpretations. Because the original Chichén Itzá excavations by the Carnegie Project and Mexico's INAH neglected (and, in fact, largely destroyed) the ceramics that could have established a sound chronology for the site — they pursued "goals with a more public than academic orientation"[233] — Lincoln contends that there is *not* firm evidence after all for the entrenched opinion of Tozzer (and nearly everyone) that the "Toltec Chichén" architecture (that is, the Tula-like portion) was constructed later than the Puuc-style portion of the city. Moreover, notable instances of an interpenetration of the two styles, both in single buildings and in the site as a whole, speak strongly for their contemporaneity. Accordingly, Lincoln argues that "Old Maya Chichén" and "New Toltec Chichén" are not differentiated by time nor by the ethnicity of their builders; rather, the two halves of the site represent differences in function and social status: "The expression of power at Chichén Itzá takes two different forms corresponding to two contrasting types of architectural context — one appears to be public and the other private."[234] Thus, Lincoln concludes, in diametric opposition to Tozzer, that

> Chichén Itzá is best interpreted as an integrated whole community, considering both the overall site plan and the organization of individual architectural groups. The settlement pattern and the architecture provide no evidence of ethnic heterogeneity at the site. Rather, the picture is one of a highly stratified and internally complex political society that was *probably* ethnically uniform and Maya.[235]

Lincoln's radical advocacy for total Puuc-"Toltec" overlap and a wholly unified Maya Chichén Itzá has won only limited support. Most archaeologists will currently accept that the whole of Chichén Itzá now deserves to be classed as an essentially Classic Maya site and that its two distinct sections do overlap significantly — though not totally — both in time and in terms of the ethnicity of their builders. Few critical scholars are, however, willing to abandon fully the tenacious idea of two phases and two peoples at Chichén Itzá. The prevailing opinion holds, in other words, for a partial rather than total overlap of "Old Maya" and "New Toltec Chichén."

The flap over Lincoln's excitingly iconoclastic hypothesis, if inconclusive, provides an apt point of departure for the final section of this chapter. The so-called overlap controversy (actually a whole set of controversies) displays once again the snug grip of conventionalized explanations and the mixed motives that have worked over the Tula-Chichén problem. At Chichén Itzá, tourist dollars, professional reputations, resilient and suspect stereotypes, archaeological methodologies, and genuine intellectual curiosities swirl against a veritable logjam of problems in historical reconstruction. Despite the new flurry of attention and a willingness to part with the fabled Maya-Mexican fracas, scholars continue to rearrange giant blocks of time, artistic styles, and supposed ethnic influences into a mosaic of Yucatán culture history that remains considerably more tenuous than its Central Mexican counterpart. Our misunderstandings of Chichén Itzá are still more serious than those of Tula, Hidalgo. Most perplexingly (and intriguingly) of all is the very real possibility that the most histrionically appealing and infamous episode of Yucatán pre-Columbian historiography, the phenomenon that sustained Alfred Tozzer's enthusiasm for a half century — the Toltec invasion and the so-called Mexicanization of Yucatán — in fact, never happened. The concluding section of this chapter attempts to understand how this apparently apocryphal idea could have been born and how it could thrive with such health and vitality for generations.

The Tula-Chichén Connection: The "Mexicanization" of Yucatán

> Into this rather easygoing [Yucatán Maya] milieu came the Toltecs, with such catalytic effect over Mesoamerica that stories concerning them were almost universally encountered by the Spanish five hundred years later. In Yucatán the Toltec conquest changed the Maya way of life considerably more than did the Spanish.
>
> *George Brainerd, 1956*[236]

"Mexicanization," when applied to the glamorous confrontational drama between the Toltecs and the Maya at Chichén Itzá, is an obvious and telling misnomer. (The "Mexica," the preeminent third of the Aztec triple alliance, did not enjoy their moment in the Mesoamerican sun until some three centuries after the presumed Toltec conquest of Yucatán.) Yet, anachronisms notwithstanding, the ill-known Toltecs are fleshed out with the megalomaniacal ferocity of their Aztec (or Mexica) descendants and, so the story goes, unleashed onto the Yucatán stage against the effete and virtually defenseless Maya.

The familiar old plot is as implausible as it is appealing, both fetching and farfetched. Yet, where the respective succession of events in Tula, and even more in Chichén Itzá, is already highly confused, attempting to synchronize the histories of those two cities produces a grating of imperfectly meshing gears so irritatingly abrasive that historians have been willing to hazard almost any adjustment to tune the Mexican-Yucatán historical mechanism. In this initiative, the polarization of Maya and Mexican has proven their most effective tool. Because the so-called Mexicanization of Yucatán and, more specifically, the appearance of multiple ethnicities and turnovers in rulership at Chichén Itzá are historical circumstances of fabulous complexity, virtually all imperfectly retrieved, the paradigm of Maya-Mexican polarity has operated as the fundamental heuristic framework, the best stratagem for smoothing the contours of very incomplete, craggy historical record. Accuracy has, very often, been sacrificed to narrative coherence.

The number of alternative historical (re)constructions — for decades virtually synonymous with the number of scholars who chose to address the phenomenon of Tula–Chichén Itzá similitude and the "Mexicanization" of Yucatán (most of whom relied on a basic opposition between Maya and Mexican peoples) — is truly mind-boggling. In this brief review, the morass of proposed "Mexicanization" scenarios, many simply disposable idiosyncrasies, are arranged in roughly chronological order and then divided in half, even more roughly, as participants in one of two sorts of manifestations of the polarity paradigm: the first set of historical (re)constructions considers the Maya and the Mexicans as fundamentally different and irreconcilably at odds; the second set agrees that the Maya and the Mexicans (including the Itzá) are fundamentally different but explains the "Mexicanization" of Yucatán as an occasion for the two entities to capitalize on their respective attributes and to join somehow into a mutually beneficial symbiosis. In short, the two storiological options involve "Mexicanization" as irreconcilable polarity versus "Mexicanization" as symbiotic polarity.

Irreconcilable Polarity: Toltecs Versus Maya

As usual Charnay negotiated the declivitous historical landscape with dauntless confidence, entertaining no doubt that Toltecs from Tula, under the leadership of Quetzalcoatl, had marched east, established a capital at Chichén Itzá, and then spread themselves and their culture across the breadth of Yucatán. However, even Charnay's streamlined, ethnohistorically based reconstruction exposes major ambiguities that undermine the conventional image of Yucatán's smooth and complete inundation under a tidal wave of "Mexicanization" or, slightly more appropriately, "Toltecization." First, even Charnay, the consummate aficionado of all things Toltec, felt compelled to accept the traditional account of Tula's tragic demise, that is, the story wherein Quetzalcoatl, the great priest-king of the Toltecs, is tricked and disgraced by his nemesis, Tezcatlipoca, and then banished from the splendid Toltec capital. Thus, even Charnay described the Quetzalcoatl-led Toltec diaspora from Tula as a flight of desperation: "after years of warfare, followed by calamitous inundations, tempests, droughts, famine and pestilence, the Toltecs, greatly reduced in numbers dispersed."[237] In this version, the victorious maraudings of the Toltecs over the Yucatecan Maya are initiated by default rather than as an extension of their empire. And second, besides the irony that the peerless Toltec conquerors are actually on the lam in Yucatán, Charnay likewise anticipated the interminable controversy over the number and nature of Central Mexican incursions into Yucatán by imagining at least two distinct waves of "Mexicanization." He writes:

> [Quetzalcoatl] had traveled thither [from Tula into Yucatán] with a branch of the Toltecs, which advancing from the west to east, had taken Tabasco on their way and occupied the peninsula earlier than a second branch, which entered the country by a southern route, under the command of their chief Tutulxiu, and became the rival and enemy of the first, whose reigning family were the Cocomes.[238]

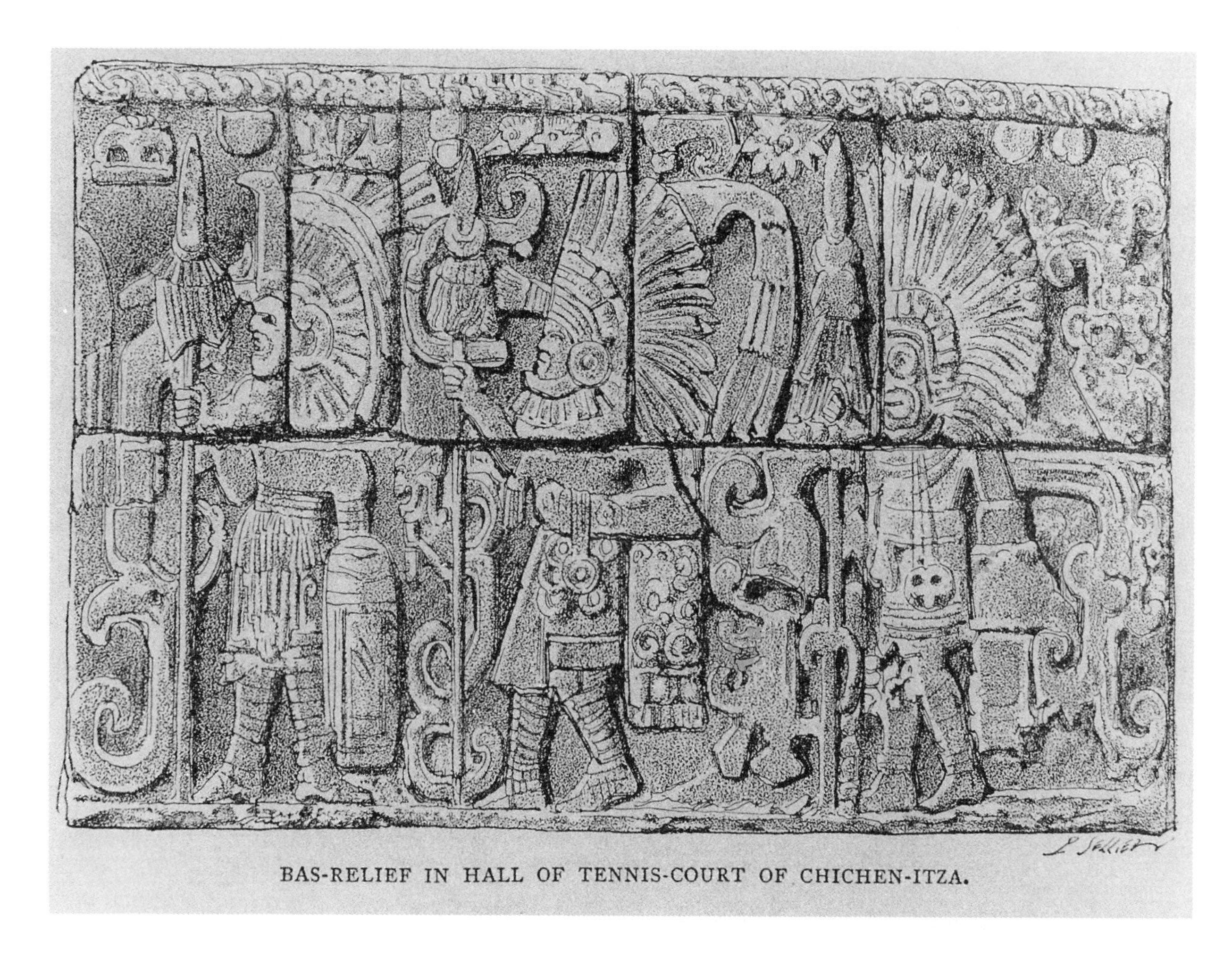

Relief sculpture in the small structure that overlooks Chichén Itzá's Great Ball Court from the north, sometimes called the Temple of the Bearded Man. Consistent with his theory that the great priest-king Quetzalcoatl led a Toltec incursion from Tula into Yucatán, Charnay glibly interpreted this carving as the Lord of the Feathered Serpent commemorating his victory over Tezcatlipoca, Lord of the Smoking Mirror, in a "foot-ball match which probably took place at Tula." No serious scholar any longer shares that opinion. (Désiré Charnay, *Ancient Cities of the New World.*)

By pleading a Toltec origin for the ruins of Yucatán (and of the Mayaland generally) Charnay was advancing a familiar case. His two most direct debts, the traditional histories of Ixtlilxochitl (early 1500s) and Mariano Veytia (mid-1700s), both describe a Toltec diaspora and subsequent conquest of the Maya area. The former maintains that the Toltecs, upon the breakup of their Central Mexican empire, headed across the Isthmus of Tehuantepec and established themselves over the entire Maya area;[239] similarly, Veytia says, "there can be little doubt that some of these people [the Toltecs] established themselves in Yucatán" — an assertion that Charnay finds "confirmed at every step."[240] Prior to Charnay, Prescott (1843) and Catherwood (1844) similarly relied on these sources to come to essentially the same conclusion; in the latter's words, "the Toltecs, it is supposed, went to the south and

Relief sculpture in the Temple of the Bearded Man. Besides noting the strong parallels between the respective iconography of eagles and jaguars at Tula and Chichén Itzá, Charnay argued that all the human figures in the carvings of this section of Chichén Itzá "have the usual type of the Toltec of the high plateaux." The matter of Toltec (or Central Mexican) "ethnic types" in the art of Chichén Itzá would remain a topic of academic debate for decades. (Désiré Charnay, *Ancient Cities of the New World.*)

east, taking possession of Central America and Yucatán. . . . At all events, it is probable that the Toltecs and their descendants erected the buildings that we have been considering."[241] And in 1882, Brinton, somewhat less disputatious in this regard, augmented the case for the "Mexicanization" of Yucatán by translating testimony from a seventeenth-century lawsuit at Valladolid (20 miles east of Chichén Itzá) in which the interested parties claimed that their ancestors came from Mexico to found cities in Yucatán and to build the great temples of Chichén Itzá.[242] In short, the general consensus of nineteenth-century scholars and native Yucatecans alike supported the notion of a kind of steamrolling movement of peoples and culture from Central Mexico into the peninsula.[243]

The blanketing "Mexicanization" (or "Toltecization") of Yucatán was, however, even in this early period, by no means an undisputed fact. Lopez de Cogolludo, in 1688, had denied emphatically the assertion by Sanchez de Aguilar (about 1635) that "Mexicans" (by which they meant Toltecs) were responsible for the mighty ruins of Uxmal, Chichén Itzá, and other Yucatán sites.[244] At least as early as Count Waldeck (1838), there was a constituency that interpreted architectural parallels between Central Mexico and the peninsula as evidence that the really important movement was a "reverse" migration whereby the inhabitants of Yucatán were actually the sources rather than the victims of Toltec and Aztec civilization (an important minority position that continues to be reasserted in various forms even now).[245] And, in the interest of thoroughly independent cultural evolutions, William Henry Holmes (1897), an arch-conservative against diffusion, recognized an atypicality about Chichén Itzá but wholly denied the influence of Mexicans along with that of Egyptians, Assyrians, and Chaldeans. Holmes argued that "the builders of Chichén were Maya stock, but, dwelling in the midst of a unique environment and much isolated from the other branches of the family, there had grown up wide distinctions between their art and that of other sections."[246]

Holmes was perhaps the last to deny that Chichén Itzá shows any special indebtedness to Central Mexico — the debate is always over the nature of the Tula-Chichén connection rather than its existence — and, generally speaking, by the 1910s, it was granted that Mexicans (though confusedly traced to Teotihuacán and Tenochtitlán rather than Tula[247]) were the protagonists in a movement that was principally one way. As Tozzer would eventually argue, because "identical Mexican warriors are found [in the art] at both Tula and Chichén, but almost no Maya appear at Tula . . . the movement was all in one direction, from west to east."[248]

Still, the Mayanists of Tozzer's era were justifiably loath to accept the simplistic notion that the great Chichén Itzá represents the wholesale translocation of Mexican religion, architecture, and culture into Yucatán. To the contrary, Morley (and later Eric Thompson) maintained that the essential process had been a "Mayanization" of wayward Mexicans rather than the "Mexicanization" of Yucatán Maya. In Morley's (re)construction, several groups of closely related Mexican peoples move into the southwest part of the peninsula. Morley contended that these dislocated Mexicans "become completely Mayanized in speech and perhaps even culture" before moving north and establishing Maya-Mexican dynasties at the three leading cities of a prosperous Yucatecan confederacy called the "League of Mayapán": the "Mayanized Mexican" followers of Quetzalcoatl-Kukulcán settle at Chichén Itzá, the Cocoms at Mayapán, and the Xiu at Uxmal.[249] Proskouriakoff (now considered a key precursor for Puuc-"Toltec" overlap) excised the suspect notion of a League of Mayapán but likewise suspected a kind of transitional, acculturative period of Mexican-Maya interaction before the migration crystallize in the so-called Toltec florescence at Chichén Itzá: "it is possible that Toltec immigrants were in the country for some time before they established themselves as a dominant group at Chichén Itzá or that they settled for a time in some peripheral location where they were in contact with the people of Yucatán."[250] And Sigvald Linné (1942), retrieving an old idea of John Lloyd Stephens and dissipating the Mexicans' eastward charge even more, divined an indirect link between Tula and Chichén Itzá: "the happiest solution would perhaps be that of finding, if possible, an intermediary between Tula and Chichén Itzá which could be made responsible, wholly or in part, for the Mexican infiltration of Yucatán."[251] Similarly resistant to the idea of Central Mexicans bettering the Maya, Herbert Spinden (1910s and 1920s) made a last-ditch effort both to preserve Maya primacy and to explain the striking parallels between Tula and Chichén by presenting a sort of rebound theory, which concedes that there was, at some late date, a Mexican "invasion" of Yucatán, "but complications arise from the fact that much of the early Nahua[that is, Central Mexican] culture was itself derived at an earlier date from Maya sources and still retained traces of its origin at the time of its reversion to Yucatán."[252]

Even after the notion of Maya primacy died,[253] apologia for this sort of reverse, or east-to-west, movement from Chichén Itzá to Tula continued to emerge right to the present.[254] By far the most significant is the iconoclastic contention of art historian George Kubler (1961) that "Toltec" Chichén Itzá is the original and Tula the copy.[255] Kubler, in other words, solves the problem of the similitude between the two sets of ruins by arguing that Tula is nothing more than "a frontier garrison or colonial outpost of Chichén Itzá at the edge of the then-civilized world."[256] Typically dismissed as an eccentric (and nonarchaeological) polemic for "backward" migration, Kubler's hypothesis is actually both exceptional and prophetic, first, because he moves outside the standard two-actor paradigm of Maya-Mexican polarity and draws the whole of Mesoamerica into his "Toltec" Chichén Itzá drama and, second, because he anticipates the current consensus that "Toltec" Chichén Itzá is an essentially indigenous Maya phenomenon. In short, Kubler, emphasizing particularly that the repertoire of "Toltec Chichén" architecture includes many forms and techniques that have no counterparts in Tula and thus could not have been modeled after the Hidalgo capital, concludes: (1) that "Toltec Chichén" constitutes a "renaissance of Classic *Maya* art," (2) that "Toltec Chichén" architecture is more cosmopolitan than to lead only to comparison with Tula, and (3) that the cosmopolitanism of "Toltec Chichén" owes to an eclectic incorporation of foreign themes from the Petén, Oaxaca, and Teotihuacán as well as from Tula.[257] Kubler's foray into historical reconstruction may be ill-fated (particularly his over-modest assessment of Tula is no longer viable), but his unique perspective persists as an important alternative and continues to illumine the Tula-Chichén problem in productive and original ways.[258]

Yet, if the mainstream was always for an east-rolling "Mexicanization" of Yucatán,[259] the 1940s and 1950s witnessed a free-for-all debate regarding the number of Mexican invasions, the origin and trajectory of the principals, and whether the incursions had been peaceful migrations, military conquests, religious crusades, or commercial forays — a brawl for coherence that culminated in Tozzer's gargantuan study of the "contemporaneous Maya and Toltec" (1957).[260] Uniquely equipped by his lifetime association with

Chichén Itzá, Tozzer amassed every sort of conceivable reference to the Tula-Chichén issue before presenting his own elaborate five-stage historical (re)construction.[261] Ironically, while typically considered the gospel on the Toltec-Maya problem, Tozzer's solution had a number of idiosyncrasies that were never widely accepted. According to him, Chichén Itzá (or Uucil-Abnal as it may have been called at that time) was originally occupied by indigenous Yucatán Maya, a stage that Tozzer terms Chichén I (600–948 C.E.). In the "first" or "great Mexican period" (Chichén II, 948–1145 C.E.), the native Maya were overwhelmed by the nonviolent penetration of Toltecs from Tula who, perhaps led by Kukulcán I (that is, Quetzalcoatl), built the Tula-like architecture and fashioned Chichén Itzá into the preeminent city in the territory.

Tozzer is atypical in concluding that the intense similitude between Tula and Chichén that arose in this period "could only have come from direct connection between the two sites"; he insists, in other words, that there was no significant stopover or intermediary as Morley and Proskouriakoff had contended.[262] Furthermore, while Tozzer ascribed essentially all of Chichén's gory iconography of war and human sacrifice to the foreign Mexican invaders, he differed from most of his contemporaries in his assessment that the so-called Toltec invasion (for Tozzer, only the first of three waves of "Mexicanization" into Chichén Itzá) was, "in all probability a generally peaceful one . . . a nonviolent conquest."[263] In the Tozzer scheme, after 200 years of hegemony, the Toltec overlords abandoned Chichén Itzá (about 1150 C.E.), whereupon there is a brief Maya resurgence (an era termed Chichén III B'). According to Tozzer, about 1224–44 C.E., the Itzá, themselves "somewhat Mayanized Mexicans" from the Gulf Coast community of Chakanputun, apparently led by Kukulcán II (that is, a new leader who had taken Quetzalcoatl-Kukulcán's name), make their maiden entry into Chichén Itzá and re-establish Mexican supremacy; Tozzer terms this Mexican renaissance Chichén III B'' or the "second Mexican period." In so-termed Chichén IV, the Itzá are beset with great difficulty and eventually (in 1451) are deposed by the treachery of a rival Maya leader named Hunac Ceel and his army of Mexican mercenaries from Tabasco. Ingeniously enough then, Tozzer actually envisions the "Mexicanization" of Yucatán in terms of three distinct waves: the first by Toltecs from Tula, the second by Itzás (or "Mayanized Mexicans") from the Gulf Coast, and the third by Mexican mercenaries from Tabasco.[264] Between these successive Mexican invasions into Chichén, the indigenous Maya make modest and short-lived recoveries. Finally, in the last stretch of Tozzer's scheme, termed Chichén V, the once-great city peters out into obscurity; most of the remaining Itzá go south, and the Spanish win control of Yucatán.[265]

Tozzer's brisk "Virginia reel of alternating Maya and Mexican regimes,"[266] besides being the most ambitious full-length (re)construction of Chichén Itzá's history, marks a zenith in other respects as well. Bifurcating all of Chichén's art and architecture into Maya and Mexican camps, and searching desperately for archaeological correlates to the very ambiguous ethnohistorical traditions, Tozzer relies particularly on the dubious assumption that a predominance of Mexican or "Toltec ethnic figures" in a building's artistic decoration is evidence that the Toltecs were in control when it was erected and that, similarly, an abundance of "Maya ethnic figures" marks a Maya resurgence.[267] He himself is nowise certain about the convoluted rotational scheme. Eric Thompson concludes flatly that "it doesn't make sense."[268] And, in its particulars, Tozzer's grand arrangement at no time enjoyed a

The Great Ball Court at Chichén Itzá, which is very similar to Ball Court II at Tula Grande. (Photo by William M. Ferguson, courtesy of the University of Texas, Austin.)

strong following among professional or amateur Americanists.[269] Tozzer's scheme is, however, the quintessence of antagonistic Maya-Mexican polarity. His elaborate story of Chichén Itzá is a confrontational saga of two oil-and-water entities, two fundamentally and irreconcilably contrary sorts of Indians who pass the baton of authority back and forth but who never merge or cooperate in any important fashion.

By contrast, the (re)constructions of the "Mexicanization" phenomenon after Tozzer's efforts, in the main, while likewise espousing the two-culture antithesis, feature accommodation and synthesis between Maya and Mexican constituencies rather than wholesale antagonism. Instead of the irreconcilable differences between two pre-Columbian ethnicities that Tozzer had imagined, subsequent theorists attempt to explain the success of "Toltec" Chichén Itzá in terms of a more symbiotic Maya-Mexican polarity, a pairing of contrasting entities whose respective strengths and weaknesses interlock, and thus somehow complete one another, resulting in a synthetic admixture more potent than either of its individual parts.

Relief carvings on a wall of the Great Ball Court, beneath one of the circular rings. Alfred Tozzer interpreted these scenes as a stylized depiction of the victory of "Toltec ethnic types" over "Maya ethnic types," who were subsequently sacrificed and decapitated. Interpreted in that fashion, these carvings seemed to Tozzer irrefutable archaeological confirmation of the story of the "Toltec conquest of the Maya" with which he was already familiar from the ethnohistorical sources. (Photo by William M. Ferguson, courtesy of the University of Texas, Austin.)

Symbiotic Polarity: Admixing Itzá

> It has never been satisfactorily explained just who the Itzá were.
>
> *Ralph Roys, 1933*[270]

Unfortunately, Tozzer's and virtually every attempt to reconstruct the history of "Toltec" Chichén Itzá is doomed by the conjoined unavoidability and impenetrability of that most maligned and elusive of pre-Columbian peoples — the Itzá. The Itzá people, the least well-understood (and, consequently most versatile) players in the "Mexicanization" story, appear at times to be allied with the Toltecs, yet, at other times, to be quite distinct from the Toltecs. Traditional Yucatecan accounts typically depict the Itzá as a second major group of interlopers or "foreigners" who, in some manner of alliance with the Toltecs, conquered and ruled as the great lords of "Toltec" Chichén Itzá. Their precise historical identity is, however, always murky.

Proposed solutions to the enigmatic identity of Itzá — from where and whence they came to Chichén and their relationship to the Toltecs —

invariably key on two bits of ethnohistorical arcana. First are the deprecatory references, presumably to the Itzá as the usurping lords of Chichén Itzá, in the quasihistorical, native Yucatecan *Books of Chilam Balam*: "They sit crookedly on their thrones; crookedly in carnal sin . . . They are the unrestrained lewd ones of the night, the rouges of the world. They twist their necks, they wink their eyes, they slaver at the mouth, at the rulers of the land, lord. Behold when they come, there is no truth in the words of the foreigners to the land."[271] The second, equally ambiguous bit of evidence is Bishop Landa's oft-quoted account of confusion among the sixteenth-century Maya themselves as to the actual relationship between the invading Itzá and the similarly intruding Toltecs under Kukulcán-Quetzalcoatl: "It is the judgement of the Indians that with the Itzás who settled Chichén Itzá there reigned a great lord named Kukulcán, and the principal building [that is, the Castillo] shows this to be the truth as it is called Kukulcán, and they say he entered from the west, but they differ as to whether he entered before or after the Itzá or with them."[272]

Several generations of scholars capitalized on these ambiguous references to the Itzá to interject them as a kind of wild card with which to fill out their hypothetical (re)constructions of Chichén Itzá history, and thus, with almost comically protean versatility, the Itzá have been attributed all manner of nationality and disposition. On the conservative side this time, Charnay cites a number of traditional textual references to the Itzá but abstains with respect to their specific identity.[273] Similarly tentative, Edward H. Thompson notes that, already by the 1910s, "about the word Itzá enough has been written to fill a volume," and so, he opts not to add to the heap of conjecture.[274] Within the context of Maya-Mexican polarity, in the early twentieth century the lines of controversy on this issue are drawn between a prevailing consensus, led by Morley and Barrera Vasquez, which holds that the Itzá were thoroughly Maya (that is, "Old Empire" people from the Southern Lowlands who introduced Maya culture into Yucatán),[275] and a significant minority, which takes the antilogical position that the Itzá were full-blooded Mexicans. Spinden, for instance, says that "the Itzá themselves were Toltec."[276] Advocates of the extremes notwithstanding, the more respectable opinion, since the 1930s, locates the Itzá homeland in the Gulf Coast hinterland between the major Mexican zone to the west and the Mayaland to the east. In this view, the original Itzá sit, as it were, on the knot of the bow tie of Mesoamerica. Accordingly, in keeping with the paradigm of Maya-Mexican bifurcation, the Itzá traditionally join the fray not as an equal and autonomous third party but rather are invariably classed — and this is where the notion of symbiotic polarity blossoms — as either "Mayanized Mexicans" or "Mexicanized Maya."

Roys and Tozzer, in somewhat different ways, each argue for the first option (the Itzá as "Mayanized Mexicans") and for scenarios that disconnect the Itzá entirely from the Tula Toltecs; they, in other words, afford the Itzá virtually no responsibility for "Toltec" Chichén Itzá's great success. Roys, working from the ethnohistorical sources, points out both Maya and Mexican cultural affinities among the Itzá and is perhaps the earliest to suggest the possibility of a Gulf Coast origin. Roys, however, concurs with Tozzer that the Itzá did *not* bring the "Toltec" culture to Chichén Itzá but simply arrived there later (perhaps 1224–44 C.E.), that is, *after* the great period of Tula Toltec domination at Chichén when there was already a pronounced degeneration of culture.[277] Thus, both Tozzer and Roys, while tacitly acknowledging that the Itzá were, to an extent, hybrid Mayanized Mexicans, see them as at most latecomers and scavenging opportunists, a kind of asterisk to the great two-culture confrontational drama of Chichén Itzá. This little and late assessment of the Itzá survives as a minority position into the 1980s, finding its most faithful advocate in Michael D. Coe.[278]

By contrast, George Brainerd and, even more, Eric Thompson credit the Itzá with a far more important role in Chichén Itzá's ascent to domination of Yucatán. For them, the Itzá are "Mexicanized Maya," that is, Chontal Maya who, by virtue of prolonged interaction, particularly trading relationships emanating from their Gulf Coast homeland, had absorbed considerable Central Mexican traits.[279] Relying particularly on the ceramic data, and working to reconcile the ethnohistorical accounts in a different way, they place the Itzá arrival at Chichén some two and a half centuries earlier than Roys had (that is, a katun earlier, or 968–987 C.E.), thus elevating the Itzá from the role of latecoming squatters to that of indispensable participants in the "great Mexican period" at Chichén Itzá.[280] They contend that the Itzá, in fact, preceded the Toltecs in conquering Chichén Itzá and laid the essential groundwork without which no "Toltec" Chichén Itzá would have been possible.

Thompson, whose solution to the Itzá and "Mexicanization" problems evolves over several decades, is by far the most exuberant in testing schemes that depend, not on simple Maya-Mexican antagonism, but rather on the idea of a genuinely symbiotic relationship. His two major alternative (re)constructions — 1954 and 1970 respectively — are tremendously influential. In the earlier synthesis, Thompson explains that the Itzá established themselves at Chichén Itzá well in advance of the Mexican Toltecs and the Feathered Serpent cult, possibly in the year 918 C.E. (presumably the "Great Descent" of the traditional sources), and then enjoyed some sixty years of pre-Toltec autonomy before Kukulcán-Quetzalcoatl and a slim force of followers arrived from Mexico (though not strictly from Tula). Thompson correlates this second, smaller but more intense wave of "Mexicanization" with the "Little Descent" of the sources.[281] The cultural and architectural accomplishments of the pre-Toltec Itzá period were, according to Thompson, quite modest and only somewhat inconsistent with native Yucatán patterns.[282] However, the fresh injection of more purely Mexican blood and devotedness to the Feathered Serpent into Chichén Itzá sparked a building boom of "Toltec," Tula-like architecture, and, moreover, precipitated "a complete reorientation of life . . . a shift from the old pacific and essentially introvert position of moderation to the militant and extrovert attitude of the belligerent Mexicans."[283] Yet, ending his version of the story more happily, Thompson contends that this abrupt "Mexicanization" of Yucatán was superficial and short-lived. The Feathered Serpent fervor quickly cooled, and the foreign interlopers gradually acceded to the more refined speech and outlook of the Yucatán Maya, retaining only the boast of their descent from Mexican warriors.[284]

In other words, Thompson's early (re)construction scheme describes a kind of one-two punch with two successive and very different modes of "Mexicanization" at Chichén Itzá. Both, however, entail actual bicultural syntheses rather than Tozzer's model of Maya-Mexican rotational authority. Thompson's first mode of "Mexicanization" begins with a prolonged and apparently mutually beneficial commercial and even intermarital melding of Itzá Maya and Central Mexicans in the Gulf Coast region and then culminates when the partially Mexicanized Itzá seize Chichén away from their Yucatecan Maya brethren. The second, more drastic Mexicanizing coup de grâce begins as an abrupt, coercive invasion by a small Toltec militia direct from Mexico to Chichén and culminates in a Toltec-Itzá collusion that effects a spectacular, if unsavory and short-lived, florescence. With this second wave of foreigners, "Toltec" Chichén Itzá becomes, in other words, a somewhat more motley hybrid of pure Mexican Toltecs, partially Mexicanized Itzá, and indigenous Yucatec Maya.[285]

Thompson's fascination with the possibility that the extravagant success of "Toltec" Chichén Itzá eventuated from a productive symbiosis of the drastically contrasting Maya and Mexican peoples intensified as he recast his outline of Yucatán history and, in 1970, presented his seminal Putun hypothesis.[286] A watershed in the study of the Itzá, Thompson's Putun theory is an elaboration rather than a denegation of his earlier scheme, and thus, rather than controverting the two modes of "Mexicanization," throws them into yet higher relief. Armed with hitherto neglected colonial-period documents (particularly the Paxbolon papers),[287] an alternative interpretation of the battle scenes in the murals at Chichén Itzá,[288] and an iconoclastic new reading of key portions of *The Book of the Chilam Balam of Chumayel,* Thompson argues for a thorough reconsideration of the presumed "Mexican conquest" of Chichén Itzá. Thompson's new solution to the problem places the Itzá in an even more decisive role. Refining and concretizing his initial suspicions that the Itzá were a branch of the Putun Maya (or Chontal Maya as he called them earlier) based in that interjacent Gulf Coast region, Thompson again contends that they had already settled at Chichén Itzá when the features that stem from Tula were introduced. The revolutionary portion of this revamped proposal is Thompson's reckoning that the Putun Maya (that is, the Itzá), so long relegated to supporting roles, were, in fact, fabulously accomplished warrior-merchants who had "established an 'Empire' which can be postulated with considerably more certainty than the proposed Teotihuacán and Olmec 'Empires.'"[289]

According to Thompson's amended script, during the Early Classic period, the Putun Itzá lived modestly on the Gulf Coast of Tabasco, deeply involved with their Mexican-speaking neighbors but only peripherally participants in the great advances in art, architecture, and astronomy in the Southern Maya Lowlands. In the Late Classic (850–950 C.E.), however, they parlayed their fortuitous "between" position on the coast and their supereminence as sea-traders into dominance of an immense commercial network that encompassed all sides of the Yucatán Peninsula as well as the Usumacinta and Grijalva riverways. Besides their maritime triumphs, Thompson considers that the Putun Itzá penetrated inland from a beachhead at Pole, across from the island of Cozumel (one more supposed correlate to the "Great Descent" of tradition), and conquered a number of Yucatecan centers, preeminently Chichén Itzá (918 C.E.). Under Putun Itzá domination — the Tula Toltecs still had not entered the Yucatecan scene according to this rendition — Chichén Itzá became a distinguished regional capital that apparently shared power with Chakanputun and, perhaps, Potonchan, both on the Gulf Coast, as the preeminent foci of the giant Putun empire.

Thus, as in Thompson's earlier (re)construction, the first wave of "Mexicanization" was an evolving process wherein the Putun Itzá Maya interacted and absorbed from the Central Mexicans the decidedly "non-Maya" flair for unscrupulous commercial and military exploitation that would enable them to win mastery over the whole of Yucatán. Thompson, who continues to equate the "Mexicanization" of Yucatán with a kind of moral decay, maintains that the Putun Itzá overlords of this era were dedicated to a phallic cult and to "lewd, erotic practices," which were repugnant to the indigenous Yucatec Maya.[290] However, as in the earlier scheme, these Putun Itzá were indifferent to the famous Feathered Serpent religion and, in fact, for all their military and commercial potency, contributed very little in the realms of art and architecture at Chichén Itzá or anywhere else.[291]

In Thompson's updated scheme, the second wave of "Mexicanization" at Chichén Itzá — again correlated with the "Little Descent" of tradition — begins when Quetzalcoatl-Kukulcán and his Toltec retinue, ingloriously fleeing from their enemies at Tula, are welcomed into Tabasco by the flourishing and already strongly Mexicanized Putun Itzá (about 987 C.E.). Quetzalcoatl-Kukulcán and the Tula Toltec exiles are quickly ushered to Chichén Itzá by a second group of Putun Itzá, which was "more strongly influenced by Tula than the Putun Itzá invaders of A.D. 918."[292] (Recall that in Thompson's earlier [re]construction the Toltecs and Itzá first met at Chichén Itzá.)[293] This complementary union between the rich and powerful but disesteemed Putun Itzá and the prestigious but disenfranchised Tula Toltecs — the quintessence of symbiotic polarity — catapults Chichén Itzá to its zenith of temporal preeminence and, moreover, the fortuitous marriage between the corporeal resources of the Itzá and the transcorporeal vision of the Toltecs spawns the religio-architectural bravura of "Toltec" Chichén Itzá. With the sponsorship of their wealthy Putun Itzá backers, the Toltecs re-create a bigger and better version of that which they had lost at Tula. According to Thompson, the new alliance engineers "a kind of new Toltec empire" that singularly dominates Yucatán, promoting the cult of Kukulcán and the commercial interests of "Toltec" Chichén Itzá from Tabasco to Honduras.[294]

This compelling yarn of compensatory cooperation — still, in its broadest strokes a drama of Mexican might squashing the gentle Maya — was heralded as the new gospel and reiterated in virtually all of the general syntheses of the 1970s and 1980s. Joseph Ball, in particular, adopted and fleshed out Thompson's version of Yucatán culture history.[295] Yet, if Thompson's Putun hypothesis defined a new sort of benchmark that, for the first time, fetched the Gulf Coast peoples, specifically the Itzá, from backstage and gave them their due in the limelight, almost all critical Mayanists are skeptical about the neatness and extravagance of Thompson's claims for the Putun Itzá. A few scholars, notably Michael Coe, discount entirely the possibility of a Putun empire and continue to maintain, as Tozzer had, that the Itzá played no role in the florescence of "Toltec" Chichén Itzá but were simply a "wretched band of warriors" who settled as squatters in Chichén Itzá *after* the city had been abandoned by the Toltecs.[296]

Coe's holdout notwithstanding,[297] the more temperate (and more methodologically based) reservations about Thompson's Putun hypothesis fall into two groups. First are misgivings with Thompson's characteristic hyperbole that credits the Putun with virtually every major political coup for 800 years of Maya history. Art historian Arthur Miller, for instance, complains that the Putun "loom as supermen," when, in fact, they probably constituted several related, yet competitive Gulf Coast groups (all presumably hybrid Mexicanized Maya) rather than a single unified people.[298] And most archaeologists chide Thompson, like Tozzer, for an overreliance on the poetic, ambiguous ethnohistorical sources, and, thus, similarly dismiss the Putun models of Thompson and Ball as "quasi-historical sequences of events which offer felicitous, but somewhat simplistic, accounts of the arrival of foreign groups in northern Yucatán. . . . Because such reconstructions fail to clarify the

J. Eric S. Thompson (1898–1975) at Chichén Itzá. Thompson provided by far the most thoroughgoing (if suspiciously ingenious) narrative explanations of the "Mexicanization" of Chichén Itzá. (Courtesy of the Peabody Museum, Harvard University.)

archaeological record, we must assume that a far more complex series of events took place."[299] In Sabloff and Andrews V's cautioning terms, "we know next to nothing [archaeologically] about the Putun and their effect on the polities of Yucatán."[300]

Second are the related charges that Thompson mistakes generalized social processes for specific historical events, an accusation that testifies to Thompson's unwillingness to participate in the "new archaeological" methodological re-orientation that swept the Mesoamerican field beginning in the 1960s.[301] For instance, A. Andrews and Robles concede that Thompson's "migrations" and "invasions" may have some historical basis, but they argue that, instead of a singular event, the so-called Mexican conquest of Chichén Itzá "should be seen as the outcome of economic and political *processes* that were the result of competition over trade networks and foreign exploitation of the weakening political structure in the interior of northern Yucatán."[302] In the same spirit, Robert Carmack and, by now, most other scholars appreciate Thompson's assessment that the Gulf Coast was the intermediary, transitional frontier between the Mexican and Maya cultures, the staging area where the essential groundwork for the "Mexicanization" of the Mayaland was laid; but, rather than Thompson's vision of a momentous meeting between a specific group of Putun Itzá and a particular contingent of Tula Toltec renegades under Quetzalcoatl-Kukulcán, an alliance that in one fell swoop changed the face of Yucatán, Carmack prefers to tell the "Nahuatization" story in terms of two more generalized pulses or "types" of interactive forces: namely, the "Putun merchants" who were "Mexicanized Maya" interested in trade rather than imperial expansion, and the "Epi-Toltec warriors," elitist and exploitative militarists who fanned out from Tula to conquer in the interest of obtaining sacrificial victims and tribute.[303]

In any event, as a solution to the Tula–Chichén Itzá connection, more damning than either his oversimplification of the Putun component or his old-fashioned concern for specific historical events rather than general cultural processes (both quite likely intentional hyperbole), is Thompson's melodramatic typecasting of the Toltecs as flagitious bullies and the Yucatán Maya as tragic heroes. By self-admission "skating on very thin ice,"[304] Thompson's grand saga of the migration and re-seating of Tula's Quetzalcoatl-Kukulcán in Chichén Itzá is the last major production to feature the antithesizing stereotypes of Maya priest and Toltec warrior. Moreover, while Thompson tinkers with the notion of symbiotic polarity (a process that still may prove to be the key to the very eclectic phenomenon of "Toltec" Chichén Itzá) in a couple of very intriguing ways — first, in regard to the fortuitous mesh of Maya or Itzá otherworldliness and Mexican worldliness that vaults the Putun into commercial preeminence, and second, in regard to the equally fortuitous coalescence of Putun Itzá temporal power and Toltec prestige that manifests itself in the crassly spectacular "Toltec" Chichén Itzá — he nevertheless sticks to the end with his typecast actors. Throughout each of his ingenious "Mexicanization" scripts, the Maya and Mexicans alike remain stereotypical and contradistinct caricatures. Accordingly, neither Thompson's still-popular story nor the adjustments to its basic framework are any longer respectable ways of explaining the historical relationship between Tula and Chichén Itzá.

There is, then, as we aim toward a summary of the current status of the historical problem and a conclusion to this long review of ideas about the Tula-Chichén mystery, a kind of post-paradigm pause. Morley's, Tozzer's, and Thompson's overwrought stories and images of

Mexican warriors and Maya priests have been largely (though not completely) dismantled; yet, rebuilding has proven more difficult. The stage of archaeo-historical reconstruction (or perhaps simply *construction*) has been opened up to more and different players; an alternative, re-imagined cast of pre-Columbian actors has emerged, but, as yet, any satisfactorily coherent new script remains in its earliest drafts.

The Historical Problem Summarized

Wading through this seemingly endless swamp of misconceptions, corrections, and exasperations about the histories of Tula and Chichén Itzá, not to mention the circumstance of their unmistakable similitude, proves nothing so certainly as the difficulty with which Mesoamericanists have, in the last hundred years, transcended the cocksure (re)constructions of Désiré Charnay. On the western front, the ethnohistorical and, even more, archaeological reworkings of Tula since the 1970s have netted an impressive fund of new information about the local development of the Central Mexican capital. It is now possible to float a number of fresh hypotheses about the distinctive priorities of Tula's architecture and religion. Yet, there is still disappointingly little on this side of the equation that would clarify Tula's historical relationship to its mirroring counterpart in Yucatán.[305]

On the eastern end of the equation, where the inescapable specter of "Mexicanization" holds the Tula–Chichén Itzá problem closer to the fore, the progress has been, if mostly indirect, nonetheless, considerably greater. More significant than the defense or refutation of any specific Putun or Toltec adventurings has been the generalized reassessment of the Postclassic (or Terminal Classic) Yucatán ambience in which "Toltec" Chichén Itzá arose. The resilient and unsavory vision of the Postclassic as an era of "internal dryrot in Maya culture" has at last been soundly rejected. As the old prejudices soften, an energetic reassessment of the Postclassic has begun wherein "the period is not forced into the subsidiary posture of being merely 'Post'-something else. In fact, the Maya Postclassic may be viewed as a fresh start on a new and untried trajectory."[306]

This change in perspective is momentous, and — while the purveyors of this new vision of Postclassic Yucatán are wary not to repeat either the daring or the excesses of Charnay and Thompson and, thus, in the main, gingerly sidestep the specific riddle of Tula-Chichén relatedness — the current status of the historical phenomena of "Mexicanization" and "Toltec" Chichén Itzá may be summarized in terms of three crucial amendments that issue from their ambitious reclamation project.[307] In each case, the paradigm of Maya-Mexican polarity and its manifestation in the glamorous confrontational drama of Toltec hordes raining down on the "effete, over-civilized Maya" has been majorly challenged.

First, then, are challenges to the radical antithesis between the Postclassic Northern Lowlands (presumed to be a "secular," brutal, and Mexican-tainted epoch of artistic and moral decay) and the earlier, more sublime, and purely Maya florescence of the so-termed Classic Southern Lowlands. This enduring antithesis between the "real," pre-collapse Maya of the Southern Lowlands and the derivative, post-collapse Maya of the Northern Lowlands (including "Toltec" Chichén Itzá), while affording a kind of union of the presumed polarities between the "Old" and "New Maya Empires" and between the "pure Maya" and the "Mexicanized Maya," has proven to be one more historical fiction. The new consensus holds that the Maya "collapse" was not nearly so complete as once thought and that there was not, in fact, a drastic disjunction between the Classic and Postclassic Maya cultures.[308]

Moreover, in the wake of that realization, there has been a revival of the debate over the extent to which the daunting spectacle of "Toltec" Chichén Itzá represents the product of foreign versus indigenous forces. On the one side, A. Andrews and Robles espouse the familiar position that Gulf Coast Itzá and Highland Mexicans made a speedy and violent penetration into the interior of Yucatán and, thus, that the blossoming of "Toltec" Chichén Itzá (between 900 and 1200 C.E.) was almost exclusively the result of this foreign intrusion — "a disjunctive episode of substantial magnitude."[309] On the other side, David Freidel speaks for a growing number of scholars who generally believe that there was more communication and less actual influx of new populations into the Maya country.[310] They highlight the indigenous character of "Toltec" Chichén Itzá and believe that it demonstrates a significant contemporaneity and continuity both with the Puuc sites, also in the Northern Lowlands, as well as with a network of communities across the Southern Lowlands. Accordingly, this scholarly contingent argues for the previously unthinkable assertion that "Toltec" Chichén Itzá must be considered a full participant in indigenous Classic Maya civilization.[311]

The second set of crucial amendments includes closely related challenges to another manifestation of Maya-Mexican polarity, namely, the conventional linear succession model wherein an indigenous Yucatán Maya culture is blanketed and snuffed out by a pan-peninsular flood of "Mexicanized" authority controlled from the nonpareil capital of "Toltec" Chichén Itzá. This controversy explores whether the "Mexicanization" of Yucatán was pan-peninsular or regional, that is, total or partial. According to the traditional model, the Toltecs and Itzá moved in quickly, grabbing Chichén Itzá and with it political and economic supremacy of the entire peninsula: "so thorough was [Chichén Itzá's] control that civic construction virtually ceased elsewhere in northern Yucatán. All other Late Classic centers went into eclipse."[312] However, at present, rather than treat Postclassic Yucatán in terms of successive homogeneous cultures, the dominant alternative — that is, the overlap model — envisions a set of distinctive subregional cultures operating, at least to an extent, contemporaneously on the peninsula.[313] Accordingly, rather than the sole megalopolis of a well-integrated Yucatán jurisdiction (or the still older vision of Chichén Itzá as the preeminent third of the League of Mayapán),[314] "Toltec" Chichén Itzá emerges now as one of several major, competing polities, overlapping significantly with the Terminal Classic southern Maya sites and, quite likely, facing very substantial head-to-head competition from the indigenous northern Maya Puuc centers to the southwest and from Cobá, only 60 miles to the east.[315] To reiterate then, the new orthodoxy holds that "Toltec" Chichén Itzá was probably a largely indigenous Maya development after all and that the so-called Mexicanized reorientation of Yucatán was not nearly so drastic nor encompassing as once envisioned.

Third and finally are major challenges to the most flagrant expression of the paradigm of Maya-Mexican polarity, namely, the enduring and stigmatizing characterizations of the principals in the "Mexicanization" drama. The Yucatán Maya are now being appreciated not only as "darker and more characteristically Mesoamerican" but also as "more outward-looking" or "internationalizing."[316] Moreover, this revisionist image of native Yucatecans as worldly and capable entrepreneurs, in charge of their own destiny, rather than as the cowering subordinates or submissive pawns of external (specifically Mexican) forces, has revitalized the old controversy as to whether the "Mexicanization" of Yucatán was a process of alliance or invasion, that is, mutual cooperation or military coercion. Concentrating on the "Mexicanization" phenomenon in the Guatemalan Highlands rather than Yucatán, Kenneth Brown (1985) presents the most radical possibility. He argues that the innumerable references to "Toltec" migration and conquest in Maya ethnohistory (particularly in the Quiché myths) actually register remembrances of the great international trade alliance of the Middle Classic period between Teotihuacános and Maya (well before the ascendancy of either Tula or Chichén Itzá) and that the ballyhooed Postclassic invasion of both the Maya Lowlands and Highlands by "Toltecs" or "Toltecized" Maya — including the so-termed Toltec conquest of Chichén Itzá — in fact, never happened.[317] This startlingly iconoclastic view has gained few unqualified adherents. The historiographic tide is, nonetheless, steadily moving toward the possibility that the Maya were the instigators, or at least partners, rather than victims in the so-called Mexicanization process. Reticent about abandoning the whole wonderful saga of a Toltec conquest of the Maya, the conventional wisdom now holds that the migration and conquest traditions in the Guatemalan Quiché myths and the Yucatec *Books of Chilam Balam* were at least partly based in historical fact and that, at the very least, these documents evince that the Postclassic Maya had adopted the traditional Mexican (and thus presumably non-Maya) strategy of legitimating authority by demonstrating, even if artificially, connections with those most prestigious mythico-historical forebears, the Toltecs. The Maya willingness to participate in that characteristically Mexican means of validation — a ploy that is quintessentially manifest in "Toltec" Chichén Itzá — is, moreover, taken as evidence that the "Mexicanization" process was one of alliance rather than invasion, mutual cooperation rather than coercion, the transfer of ideas and political strategies rather than of peoples, or, in Freidel's words, "syncretic adoption rather than actual long-distance migration."[318]

In sum then — to the extent that summarizing these fluid debates is possible — these recently rejuvenated controversies are not simply refinements of some consensually accepted account of pre-Columbian history. These are not simply quibblings over minutiae. Instead, these controversies betray an uncertainty and dissension about the most major historical events and processes in the "Mexicanization" of Chichén Itzá, a kind of reopening of the historical as well as the general problem of Tula-Chichén similitude. Given these three paradigm-shaking amendments, all still subject to debate — (1) the indigenous Maya character of "Toltec" Chichén Itzá, (2) the limited and regional success of the "Mexican" reorientation of Yucatán, and (3) the outward-looking and enterprising participation of the indigenous Yucatán Maya — neither the old conventional explanation of Tula-Chichén similitude as the product of a west-to-east, Toltec-Itzá steamrolling of the passive Maya nor the minority argument for an east-to-west movement, wherein art forms originating at Chichén Itzá were exported to a colonial outpost at Tula, Hidalgo, now seems remotely possible. The archetypes and images of the pre-Columbian Maya and Mexicans, which for better than a century sustained the chess game of historical (re)construction, have been undercut.

Thus, while the Tula-Chichén controversy stands at something of a post-paradigm pause and the ground rules for the next rounds are still being laid out, the most appealing explanation of "Toltec" Chichén Itzá would seem to be a west-to-east movement (or transference of ideas) involving a number of parties (all of whom shared a fundamentally kindred Mesoamerican orientation), but a movement that is initiated from the Yucatán side rather than by the Tula Toltecs. In all likelihood, the

Toltec heritage — but probably not a Toltec people — was pulled east to Chichén Itzá by the indigenous Maya rather than pushed upon them by invading Central Mexicans.[319]

To anticipate the later hypothetical conclusions (and it is important to restate that this hermeneutical project is *not* primarily about solving the *historical* problem of Tula and Chichén Itzá relatedness), it now appears that some sort of constituency of the Putun Itzá Maya were the active, internationalizing agents who reached out and found in the architecture of Tula, Hidalgo — the Central Mexican capital of the Toltecs — the preeminent among *many* Mesoamerican models, the synthesis of which was intended to give their Chichén Itzá capital a singularly cosmopolitan allure and appeal. The most plausible historiographical option (an option that remains to be explored in Chapter 4) suggests, in other words, that the outward-looking, well-endowed Maya architects of Chichén Itzá aspired to re-create in their city the most appealing (and thus most legitimating) artistic forms from a whole series of distinguished indigenous capitals. In this case, then, the self-conscious imitation of Tula architecture at Chichén Itzá, fully consonant with pre-Columbian Mesoamerican practice, was, most probably, one major component — but only one resource among several — that was woven into a remarkably ambitious, eclectic project of religio-architectural synthesis, a project of making one from many.[320]

And so — if nostalgic for the "beautiful simplicity" of Charnay's pan-Toltecism, if unconfident of ever knowing precisely how the resemblance came to be, if called to mount a horse that won't stand still — the advances of late, nonetheless, make this an excitingly pregnant moment to delve once again, this time from the perspective of the history of religions, into the venerable old problem of Tula–Chichén Itzá similitude.

Notes

1. Alfred M. Tozzer, "Maya Research," *Maya Research* 1 (July 1934): 8.

2. Victor Wolfgang von Hagen, *Maya Explorer: John Lloyd Stephens and the Lost Cities of Central America and Yucatán* (Norman: University of Oklahoma Press, 1948), 220.

3. Herbert Joseph Spinden, "Alfred Marston Tozzer (1877–1954)," *National Academy of Sciences, Biographical Memoirs* 30 (1957): 383–97, has a concise (though not particularly complete) account of Tozzer's tremendous career and a bibliography of his publications. He emphasizes Tozzer's preoccupation with the "Maya-Toltec problem."

4. On Edward Thompson's dredging operation, see, for instance, Clemency Coggins and Orrin C. Shane III, eds. *Cenote of Sacrifice: Maya Treasures From the Sacred Well at Chichén Itzá* (Austin: University of Texas Press, 1984).

5. Tozzer's footnotes and syllabus are several times as long as the actual text of Landa's sixteenth-century manuscript and include remarks on virtually every aspect of Maya life.

6. On Tozzer's pioneering role in Maya ethnography, see Robert Brunhouse, *Sylvanus G. Morley and the World of the Ancient Maya* (Norman: University of Oklahoma Press, 1971), 29.

7. Tozzer, *Chichén and Cenote,* 270, says that he personally knew Augustus Le Plongeon (1826–1908) and all subsequent archaeologists working at Chichén, except for a few Mexican students toward the 1950s.

8. Eric Thompson, review of *Chichén and Cenote* by Alfred Tozzer, *American Journal of Archaeology* 63 (1959): 119–20. Following his effusive praise of Tozzer's work, Thompson expresses serious reservations about both the method and the consequent historical reconstruction expressed therein. Also, despite Thompson's praise for "excellent arrangement," Tozzer at many points seems to me to be overwhelmed by the avalanche of data he collects with respect to Chichén. *Chichén and Cenote,* for all its thoroughness, contains a confusing array of overlapping organizational schemes and a great deal of repetition, making it seem at times like a work in progress. Tozzer is largely relieved of this organizational burden in his massive annotating of Landa's *Relación,* each footnote being a unit unto itself, a circumstance that is better served by his encyclopedic knowledge.

9. Apparently the earliest article in which Tozzer addresses the Maya-Toltec problem head-on is Alfred Tozzer, "The Toltec Architect of Chichén Itzá," in *American Indian Life,* ed. Elsie Clews Parson (New York: B. W. Huebsch, 1922), 265–71; but the more important early article is idem, "Maya and Toltec Figures at Chichén Itzá," *Actes du XIII Congrès International des Américanistes New York, 1928* (1930) 155–64. Gordon Willey, keying in on the 1940 festschrift for Tozzer, to which every major Mayanist of the era contributed — *The Maya and Their Neighbors,* ed. Clarence L. Hay et al. (New York: Cooper Square Publishers, Inc., 1940) — notes that, rather than challenge Tozzer in regard to the Maya-Toltec problem, his students and colleagues were inclined to leave the problem of Tula Toltec influence in the Maya Lowlands to the master so that there is a notable (even suspicious) lack of alternative or dissenting opinions in this era; "in any event, the Toltec presence at Chichén Itzá could be considered as a solidly accepted datum on external influence into the Maya Lowlands as of 1940." Gordon Willey, "External Influences on the Lowland Maya: 1940 and 1975 Perspectives," *Social Process in Maya Prehistory: Studies in Honour of Sir Eric Thompson,* ed. Norman Hammond (London: Academic Press, 1977), 61. Given that general acceptance, it is somewhat puzzling that the voluminous footnotes in Tozzer's translation of Landa's *Relación,* completed in 1941, are replete with indirect allusions to the Maya-Toltec problem, but, perhaps because he compiled this material in advance of the "solution" to the Tollan problem, this volume never once mentions either Tula or Toltecs. (The sole reference to Toltec is in regard to Vaillant's idea of a "Toltec" period, ibid., 21.)

10. Charles E. Lincoln, "The Chronology of Chichén Itzá: A Review of the Literature," in *Late Lowland Maya Civilization: Classic to Postclassic,* ed., Jeremy A. Sabloff and E. Wyllys Andrews V (Albuquerque: University of New Mexico Press, 1986), 143. Lincoln, who is presenting a thoroughgoing alternative to Tozzer's framework for Chichén Itzá history, discusses Tozzer's basic premises and his tremendous influence on the ideas about Chichén Itzá. Ibid., 143–44.

11. The scholarly work on the problematic Western imagination of Native Americans is by now quite extensive. See, for instance, Lewis Hanke, *Aristotle and the American Indians* (Chicago: Henry Regenery Company, 1959); Lewis Hanke, *All Mankind Is One: A Study of the Disputation Between Bartolomé de las Casa and Juan Ginés de Sepulveda in 1550 on the Intellectual and Religious Capacity of the American Indian* (De Kalb: Northern Illinois: University Press, 1974); Edmundo O'Gorman, *The Invention of America* (Bloomington: Indiana University Press, 1961); Robert F. Berkhofer, *The White Man's Indian: Images of the American Indian From Columbus to the Present* (New York: Alfred A. Knopf, 1978); Raymond William Stedman, *Shadows of the Indian: Stereotypes in American Culture* (Norman: University of Oklahoma Press, 1982); Benjamin Keen, *The Aztec Image in Western Thought* (New Brunswick, N.J.: Rutgers University Press, 1971); Irene Sosa Vásquez, *Images of the Unspoked Maya: Silence and Discourse Concerning the New World Classic Maya Culture,* Ph.D. dissertation, Duke University, 1982; Tzvetan Todorov, *The Conquest of America: The Question of the Other,* trans. Richard Howard (New York: Harper & Row, 1985); Charles Long, *Significations: Signs, Symbols, and Images in the Interpretation of Religion* (Philadelphia: Fortress Press, 1986); and Inga Clendinnen, *Ambivalent Conquests: Maya and Spaniard in Yucatán 1517–1570* (Cambridge: Cambridge University Press, 1987).

12. See, for instance, Todorov, *The Conquest of America,* 1–50.

13. Hanke, *All Mankind Is One,* 9.

14. Clendinnen, *Ambivalent Conquests,* 6–9, discusses Bernal Diaz's ambivalent assessment of the natives and their cultural productions.

15. Todorov, *The Conquest of America,* 113, 127–28, 160, discusses Cortés's ambivalent and exploitative portrayal of the Indians. Cortés occasionally differentiates, for instance, between the Aztecs — whose intelligence, wealth, and civility supposedly far exceeded the native peoples he had encountered in the Caribbean — but it is difficult to see any systematic polarization in his relative assessments of the natives of Central Mexico and the Mayaland.

16. See Hanke, *All Mankind Is One,* 34, 140. Las Casas finds an even more vehement nemesis in royal officer and official historian Gonzalo Fernández de Oviedo y Valdes, a man for whom genocide and starting again seem the most expedient and appropriate solution to the "Indian problem." Ibid., 34, 145.

17. See, for instance, Clendinnen, *Ambivalent Conquests,* 84–126.

18. On the pervasive tendency to assess Native Americans by analog to other "heathen" peoples, see, for instance, Todorov, *The Conquest of America*, 108.

19. For a fuller exploration of the complex forces that eventually led to a correlation of these antithesizing stereotypes, respectively, with the Maya and Central Mexicans, see Lindsay Jones, "Conquests of the Imagination: Maya-Mexican Polarity and Story of Chichén Itzá, Yucatán," unpublished article.

20. On the methodological aspirations to straightforward "historical reconstruction" of Tozzer's generation of Mayanists, see, for instance, Alfred Kidder, "A Program for Maya Research," *Hispanic American Review* 17(1937): 160–69; and idem, "The Development of Maya Research," *Proceedings 2nd General Assembly, Pan American Institute of Geography and History* (1935), 218–25.

21. Clemency Coggins, "New Fire at Chichén Itzá," *Memorias del Primer Coloquio Internacional de Mayistas, 5–10 de Agosto de 1985* (Mexico, D.F.: Universidad Nacional Autonoma de Mexico, 1987), 426, for instance, comments on the elusiveness of the "journalistic questions" at Chichén Itzá. Coggins, ibid., 426–41, then provides what seem to her the most plausible answers.

22. Tozzer, *Chichén and Cenote*, 188.

23. Keen, *The Aztec Image in Western Thought*, has remarks on each of these nineteenth-century attitudes to pre-Hispanic Mexico. See particularly ibid., 411, 436.

24. See ibid., 436, and Ignacio Bernal, *A History of Mexican Archaeology: The Vanished Civilizations of Middle America*, trans. Ruth Malet (London: Thames and Hudson, Ltd., 1980), 107.

25. Keith Davis, *Désiré Charnay (1828–1915): Expeditionary Photographer* (Albuquerque: University of New Mexico Press, 1981), has studied Charnay particularly in regard to his contributions to photography, but en route provides a valuable resume of his life and travels. Peter Tompkins's popular work, *Mysteries of the Mexican Pyramids* (New York: Harper and Row, 1976), 141–64, has a whole flattering chapter on the career of Charnay.

26. Still among the finest descriptions of the Mesoamerican ruins are Stephens's accounts of his two pioneering journeys: John Lloyd Stephens, *Incidents of Travel in Central America, Chiapas and Yucatán*, 2 vols. (New York: Harper and Brothers, 1841; reprint, 2 vols., New York: Dover Publications, 1969); and idem, *Incidents of Travel in Yucatán*, 2 vols. (New York: Harper & Brothers, 1843; reprint, 2 vols., New York: Dover Publications, 1963). All references to these works will be to the Dover editions.

27. Davis, *Désiré Charnay: Expeditionary Photographer*, 12.

28. Ibid., 130.

29. With respect to *Cités et Ruines Americaines: Mitla, Palenqué, Izamal, Chichén Itzá, Uxmal, Receuilliés et Photographiées par Désiré Charnay Avec un Texte par M. Viollet-le-Duc* (Paris: Gides, 1862–63), it is interesting to compare the praise of Charnay's photography by Davis, *Désiré Charnay: Expeditionary Photographer*, 130, with the condemnation of Viollet-le-Duc's accompanying text by Keen, *The Aztec Image in Western Thought*, 437.

30. Davis, *Désiré Charnay: Expeditionary Photographer*, 164–65, assembles a thorough chronology of Charnay's travels.

31. Charnay, *Ancient Cities*, 1.

32. For "Toltec" history, Charnay relies particularly on the writing of Ixtlilxochitl, Veytia, Ramirez, and Clavijero; in the Maya area, Landa is his principal source. See Charnay, *Ancient Cities*, 12, 76–78.

33. Ibid., xii. With respect to Charnay's important and reasonable contention that the ruins of Middle America were of indigenous and relatively recent origin, Landa, Sahagún, and nearly all of the sixteenth- and seventeenth-century friars and soldiers had held the same belief. See Norman Hammond, "Lords of the Jungle: A Prosopography of Maya Archaeology," in *Civilization in the Ancient Americas: Essays in Honor of Gordon R. Willey*, ed. Richard M. Leventhal and Alan L. Kolata (Albuquerque: University of New Mexico Press, 1983), 6–8. Then, in the eighteenth and nineteenth centuries, there was a flood of wild speculation that explained the ruins via transoceanic diffusion or vanished races of antediluvian antiquity (for example, Del Río, Cabrera, Dupaix, Waldeck, and Le Plongeon). See Robert Wauchope, *Lost Tribes and Sunken Continents: Myth and Method in the Study of the American Indians* (Chicago: University of Chicago Press, 1962). In the reassertion of commonsensical conclusions, Charnay was preceded by Alexander von Humboldt (1799–1804), Franz Kugler (1842), John Lloyd Stephens (1841, 1843), Frederick Catherwood (1841), and William Prescott, author of the monumental *History of the Conquest of Mexico* (1845). Daniel G. Brinton, *Essays of an Americanist* (Philadelphia: Porter and Coates, 1890), 25, Charnay's contemporary, is also a strong advocate for the native and recent origin of the ruins; and the Peabody Museum of Archaeology

and Ethnology at Harvard under Roland B. Dixon in the early twentieth century became an "intellectual fortress for defending the independent development of indigenous American civilizations." See Wauchope, *Lost Tribes and Sunken Continents*, 22–23.

34. See Davis, *Désiré Charnay: Expeditionary Photographer*, 29–30.

35. In an entirely different context, Bernard E. Meland refers to the historian of religions as "'a many splendored thing' . . . really the man-in-between." Bernard E. Meland, "Theology and the Historian of Religions," *Journal of Religion* 41 (October 1961): 270–71.

36. Gordon R. Willey and Jeremy A. Sabloff, *A History of American Archaeology*, 2d ed. (San Francisco: W. H. Freeman and Company, 1980), chapters 2 and 3.

37. On photography, Charnay, *Ancient Cities*, 225, says, "it can not be wrong"; idem, *Cités et Ruines Américaines*, 11 (quoted by Davis, *Désiré Charnay: Expeditionary Photographer*, 101), says, "I wanted no one to be able to challenge the exactitude of my work. I therefore took photography as my witness." Davis, ibid., Chapter 3, has an excellent discussion on the alliance between photography and the positivistic ideal of "objectivity," which is addressed again in the next chapter relative to "Traditional Archaeology."

38. Charnay, *Ancient Cities*, xi, explains that he is, by design, a popularizer, giving his work "the dual form of a journal as well as a scientific account." On his dog, for instance, see ibid., 292.

39. On disinterested scientific motives, see Charnay, ibid., xii. On French nationalism, see Charnay, *Cités et Ruines Américaines*, 202–3; quoted by Davis, *Désiré Charnay: Expeditionary Photographer*, 21.

40. Charnay, *Ancient Cities*, xiii.

41. Ibid., 144.

42. On the futility of seeking "first origins," see ibid., xiii–xiv. On the rejection of diffusionism, see ibid., xvi, 306.

43. Ibid., 260.

44. On "racial types," Davis, *Désiré Charnay: Expeditionary Photographer*, 134–42, discusses Charnay as a participant in the common nineteenth-century practice of stripping natives bare and then artificially arranging them for the camera.

45. Charnay does some critical evaluation of the Spanish texts by considering the sources of information and special interests of the chroniclers, the context in which the texts were written, and the contradictions between various accounts. See, for example, Charnay, *Ancient Cities*, 76–78, 305, 312. In addition to his photographic pathfinding, Charnay made a number of other technical contributions; his Mexican excavations, however crude, preceded those of Schliemann at Troy (1871), Flinder-Petrie in Egypt (1883), and Sir Arthur Evans at Knossos (1894). See Davis, *Désiré Charnay: Expeditionary Photographer*, 33. Moreover, Charnay was the first to attempt dredging the Sacred Cenote at Chichén Itzá (see Charnay, *Ancient Cities*, 358), the first to employ mold-making or squeezes (see ibid., 341), and a pioneer in the use of tree-ring dates (see ibid., 292).

46. Examples of Charnay's shoestring "reconciliation" of texts and monuments include interpretations of serpent columns (ibid., 95), Toltec physiology (ibid., 97), ball courts (ibid., 111), stone rings (ibid., 145–46), and native "convents" (ibid., 331).

47. Englishman Teobert Maler was explicitly comparing his own more successful explorations in Mexico to Charnay's failures in a letter to Charles Bodwitch; quoted by David Grant Adamson, *The Ruins of Time: Four and a Half Centuries of Conquest and Discovery Among the Maya* (New York: Praeger Publishers, 1975), 193. Bodwitch's own dismissal of Charnay's efforts, expressed in a letter to Alfred Tozzer in 1910, was equally categorical: "I am afraid that is the way most of the Latin races prefer to work. They pick up what they can and then make up the rest out of their imagination"; quoted ibid., 192–93.

48. F. A. Ober, *Travels in Mexico* (San Francisco: J. Dewing and Company, 1884), 110; quoted by Davis, *Désiré Charnay: Expeditionary Photographer*, 30. Davis notes that in the same volume in which Ober casts these aspersions he uses at least eleven wood engravings from Charnay's photographs with no credit whatever. Ibid., 198. Charnay's reputation declined still further as he grew older, as evinced in 1910 when Mexican president Porfirio Díaz ignored him and selected Maudslay to represent the pioneers of Mexican archaeology. Ibid., 36.

49. Adamson, *Ruins of Time*, 193.

50. Bernal, *History of Mexican Archaeology*, 127.

51. Leo Deuel, *Conquistadors Without Swords: Archaeologists in the Americas* (New York: Schocken Books, 1967), 176–77. Deuel considers Charnay's "most important archaeological coup" his controversial discovery of wheeled toys in the Valley of Mexico.

52. Ibid., 176–77.

53. Tozzer, *Chichén and Cenote*, 188.

54. Charnay, *Ancient Cities*, 98.

55. Daniel G. Brinton, *The Names of the Gods in Kiché Myths, Central America* (Philadelphia: D. G. Brinton, 1881), 645.

56. There is a popular tendency to contrast Maya with Aztec; however, because "Maya" refers generally to a tremendous variety of peoples over thousands of years in a wide diversity of geographical climes — for instance, Petén Maya, Putun Maya, Puuc Maya, Chontal Maya, and Quiché Maya — and "Aztec" refers only to one late and spectacularly successful group, it is more appropriate to compare the Maya with the collective entity called the "Central Mexicans" (or simply "Mexicans").

57. Alfred P. Maudslay, "Archaeology," in *Biologia Centrali Americana*, eds. Frederic Ducane Godman and Osbert Savin (London: Porter and Dulau, 1889–1902), 1: 1–2. This classic work, five volumes in all (discussed more fully in Chapter 2), albeit published as a portion of a larger encyclopedia, will be referred to as Maudslay, *Archaeology*.

58. Within the problem of the general unity of Mesoamerica, there is the analogous problem of unity within the Maya area itself. Very briefly, there is an early period with roots as deep as Palacio (1576), del Río (1787), and John Lloyd Stephens (1840s) that progressively came to appreciate the cultural unity of the Maya. See Hammond, "Lords of the Jungle," 7–9. Through the era of Carnegie domination, the position that "the Maya area . . . shows throughout a greater degree of cultural homogeneity than does the Mexican mainland" was entrenched. See, for example, Brainerd, *Maya Civilization*, 23. But, currently, there is a major challenge to the notion of Maya homogeneity held by Brainerd, Morley, and Eric Thompson in favor of viewing the Maya as "a heterogeneous mosaic of sociocultural organizations." See David Freidel, "New Light on the Dark Age: A Summary of Major Themes," in *The Lowland Maya Postclassic*, ed. Arlen F. Chase and Prudence M. Rice (Austin: University of Texas Press, 1985), 285–309.

59. Thomas Gann, *In an Unknown Land* (1924; reprint, Freeport, N.Y.: Books for Libraries Press, 1971), 126. In this book Gann reflects upon his travels in Yucatán with Sylvanus Morley, an even stronger champion for the radical polarization of the Maya and Mexican cultures (see note 60); Gann, considerably less a scholar, simply echoes many of Morley's ideas.

60. Bernal, *History of Mexican Archaeology*, 45, 48, gives a number of plausible explanations for the disparity between the sympathy rendered the Maya and Mexicans by sixteenth-century friars. Bernal, himself a strong advocate for the unity of Mesoamerica, is exceedingly helpful in documenting changing attitudes about Maya-Mexican relatedness.

61. There is a recurrent problem in this section with the typecasting of the "Mexicans" as the antithesis of the "Maya" because, as Benjamin Keen's *The Aztec Image in Western Thought* so eloquently demonstrates, perceptions of pre-Hispanic Americans have fluctuated considerably over time; yet, with respect to Chichén Itzá and the way in which the story of the "Mexicanization" of Yucatán has been told, there is consistent reliance on the opposing images: brutal Toltec warriors and benign Maya intellectuals.

62. On Sánchez de Aguilar, see Bernal, *History of Mexican Archaeology*, 32–33.

63. Dupaix's report is eventually published in Lord Kingsborough's *Antiquities of Mexico* (1830–31); on Dupaix, see Robert Brunhouse, *In Search of the Maya: The First Archaeologists* (Albuquerque: University of New Mexico Press, 1973), 17–30, and Hammond, "Lords of the Jungle," 9–10.

64. See Brunhouse, *In Search of the Maya*, 72.

65. On Orozco y Berra and Bancroft, see respectively Bernal, *History of Mexican Archaeology*, 110 and 116–17.

66. Brinton, *The Names of Gods in Kiché Myths*, 645; quoted by Robert Carmack, *The Quiché Mayas of Utatlán* (Norman: University of Oklahoma Press, 1981), 31.

67. See Bernal, *History of Mexican Archaeology*, 153.

68. One of Morley's principal arguments in winning the support of the Carnegie Institution was his contention that the Lowland Maya were isolated and relatively free from outside influences, and, thus, formed "an ideal laboratory for the study of human history." See Brunhouse, *Sylvanus G. Morley*, 277.

69. No one in Maya studies generates more anecdotes than Sylvanus Morley; see Brunhouse, *Sylvanus G. Morley*, and Arthur J.O. Anderson, ed., *Morleyana: A Collection of Writings in Memoriam* (Sante Fe, N.M.: School of American Research and the Museum of New Mexico, 1950). Morley's own widely read synthesis, *The Ancient Maya* (Stanford, Calif.: Stanford University Press, 1946), appears in three later editions; one that is essentially the same

as the original appears in 1947, but two later editions are heavily revised. Idem, *The Ancient Maya,* 3d ed., rev. by George W. Brainerd (Stanford, Calif.: Stanford University Press, 1954), and Sylvanus Morley and George Brainerd, *The Ancient Maya,* 4th ed., rev. by Robert J. Sharer (Stanford, Calif.: Stanford University Press, 1983). Because the nature of the revisions bears directly on changing opinions about Chichén Itzá, references to the four editions of this book will be cited respectively as: Morley, *Ancient Maya,* 1st ed.; Morley, *Ancient Maya,* 2d ed.; Morley/Brainerd, *Ancient Maya;* and Morley/Brainerd/Sharer, *Ancient Maya.*

70. Brunhouse, *Sylvanus G. Morley,* 169, summarizing "Morley's gospel of his beloved Maya."

71. Gann, *In an Unknown Land,* 87.

72. Ibid., 126.

73. Two aspects of Morley's work in particular demonstrate that he formed his ideas early in his career and then refused to alter them even in the face of controverting evidence. The first deals with his "Old Empire"/"New Empire" scheme, which will be discussed later, and the second has to do with his conception of the isolated and autonomous Maya. In the mid-forties, Alfred Kidder discouraged Morley from publishing *Ancient Maya* because he found Morley's extravagant, judgmental praise of the Maya inappropriate and, more importantly, because he felt that Morley's failure to place the Maya in the broader framework of the other peoples of America displayed a lack of perspective. See Brunhouse, *Sylvanus G. Morley,* 313. Similarly, the most common criticism in the reviews of the original edition of *Ancient Maya* (1946) concerned Morley's continued insistence on the autonomy and isolation of Maya civilization and his neglect of cross-regional interactions. See, for instance, the following reviews; William D. Strong, *American Anthropologist* n.s., 49 (1947): 640–45; J. Eric S. Thompson, *New Mexican Quarterly Review* 17 (1947): 503–4; and George W. Brainerd, *American Antiquity* 14:2 (1948): 133–36. *Morleyana,* ed. Anderson, 83, has a full list of *Ancient Maya* reviews.

74. Donald Robertson, *Pre-Columbian Architecture* (New York: George Braziller, 1963), 14.

75. George Vaillant, *Artists and Craftsmen in Ancient Central America,* Guide Leaflet Series, no. 88 (New York: American Museum of Natural History, 1935), 20.

76. Frank Waters, *Mexico Mystique: The Coming Sixth World of Consciousness* (Chicago: Swallow Press, 1975), 79–80.

77. J. Eric S. Thompson, *The Rise and Fall of Maya Civilization* (Norman: University of Oklahoma Press, 1954; reprint, 1966), 111–15, 205. Arthur Miller, an art historian, excises most of the qualitative and pejorative language but nonetheless finds it helpful and appropriate to polarize Maya and Mexican art. Describing the mural art of the Classic period (particularly Maya Bonampak versus Mexican Teotihuacán), he holds that Maya murals are "narrative" (they tell stories or describe historical events) while Mexican murals are "presentational" with a timeless symbolic quality; Maya murals use color to create "stage-like space" while Mexican murals use color to deny a sense of space; and Maya murals are "curvilinear" with a soft roundness of the body line while Mexican murals are "angular" with rigid, standing frontal figures. Arthur G. Miller, "A Brief Outline of the Artistic Evidence for Classic Period Cultural Contact Between Maya Lowlands and Central Mexican Highlands," in *Middle Classic Mesoamerica,* ed. Esther Pasztory (New York: Columbia University Press, 1978), 63–67.

78. Marshall Joseph Becker, "Priests, Peasants, and Ceremonial Centers: The Intellectual History of a Model," in *Maya Archaeology and Ethnohistory,* ed. Gordon R. Willey and Norman Hammond (Austin: University of Texas Press, 1974), 3–20, has a very interesting discussion of the almost scandalous evolution of the notion of Maya "ceremonial centers" or "vacant cities," wherein the psychology and life experience of Eric Thompson are held largely responsible for the origin and perpetuation of the model. The article is a tremendous help, but I tend to believe that the model has somewhat deeper and more general roots and that Eric Thompson is not quite so unique as Becker portrays him.

79. Charnay, *Ancient Cities,* 326. It may be overly generous to assess Charnay as already toying with the notorious problem of ceremonial centers versus "true cities," but I think not.

80. See, for instance, H.E.D. Pollock, Introduction to H.E.D. Pollock et al., *Mayapán, Yucatán, Mexico,* Publication 619 (Washington: Carnegie Institution of Washington, 1962), 15, where he assesses both Chichén Itzá and Mayapán as atypically urban sites in the Maya region.

81. See Keen, *The Aztec Image in Western Thought,* Chapter 12.

82. See W. T. Sanders, J. R. Parsons, and M. H. Logan, "Summary and Conclusions," in *The Valley of Mexico,* ed. Eric R. Wolf (Albuquerque: University of New Mexico Press, 1976), 161–79; Rene Millon, *Urbanization at Teotihuacán, Mexico,* vol. 1, *The Teotihuacán Map* (Austin: University of Texas Press, 1971); and Davíd Carrasco, *Quetzalcoatl and the Irony of Empire: Myths and Prophecies in the Aztec Tradition* (Chicago: University of Chicago Press, 1982).

83. Becker, "Priests, Peasants and Ceremonial Centers," reviews the development of the major theories regarding the structure of ancient Maya society and, in an ancillary fashion, the nature of the "Maya city." I am indebted to Becker in this section, but I do *not* follow his periodization; *nor* does Becker discuss the polarization of models of Maya and Mexican urbanization with which I am particularly concerned.

84. See ibid., 4.

85. See Charnay, *Ancient Cities,* 326; Cyrus Thomas, "Maudslay's Archaeological Work in Central America," *American Anthropologist* 1:3 (1899): 552–61; and Thomas Joyce, *Maya and Mexican Art* (London: "The Studio" Ltd., 1927), 16–17.

86. Becker, "Priests, Peasants and Ceremonial Centers," 8–14, attributes the notion of Maya ceremonial centers or "vacant cities" almost exclusively to Eric Thompson's popular works. However, Becker himself mentions Cyrus Thomas as a possible precedent to Eric Thompson (ibid., 4–5), and I am inclined to believe that the idea of semi-urban Maya ceremonial centers has considerably deeper and more complicated origins. Charnay addressed it vaguely, as did Thomas Joyce (though it is possible that Joyce was influenced by Eric Thompson rather than the other way around), and Edward Herbert Thompson (definitely in advance of Eric Thompson) stated explicitly that the major Maya ruins were probably *not* residential cities as had been commonly believed but instead were sacred structures used for strictly religious purposes. See Edward Herbert Thompson, "Ancient Structures of Yucatán Not Communal Dwellings," *American Antiquarian Proceedings,* n.s. 8 (1892), 263; cited by Brunhouse, *In Search of the Maya,* 175–76.

87. Thompson, *Rise and Fall of Maya Civilization,* 48.

88. Ibid., 97–98.

89. Becker is exceedingly hard in his evaluation of the Eric Thompson who opened a wide chasm between his scholarly articles and the popular writing wherein the model of the Maya vacant city germinated and grew: "Thompson's scholarly works remained noncommittal regarding interpretations of [Maya] social structure. On the other hand, his popular works became more and more fanciful. Thompson never offered evidence, documentation, or tests of these concepts. . . . The ceremonial center concept was a conclusion regarding social relationships drawn from an undocumented assumption regarding the structure of a Maya site, and never tested." Becker, "Priests, Peasants and Ceremonial Centers," 12, 17.

90. Compare Morley's original introduction to Chapter 8, entitled "Cities and Architecture," which concurs with Landa that there were Maya towns and cities "even in the modern sense of the word" (Morley, *Ancient Maya,* 1st ed., 312), with Brainerd's revision of the same chapter, now simply entitled "Architecture": "there is no evidence thus far that the archaeological sites of the Classic stage are the ruins of cities and towns; there is on the other hand much evidence that they were religious centers to which the Maya resorted only for ceremonies." Morley/Brainerd, *Ancient Maya,* 261.

91. George W. Brainerd, *The Maya Civilization* (Los Angeles: Southwest Museum, 1954), 86, gives explicit credit to Eric Thompson on this point.

92. Pollock, Preface to Pollock et al., *Mayapán, Yucatán, Mexico,* 1.

93. Both the barbarian-versus-agriculturalist (or nomadic-versus-sedentary) scenario and the urban-versus-rural scenario involve exceedingly rich and complex stereotypes, and both are at play in the evolution of the Tula–Chichén Itzá problem. Relative to these sorts of archetypes for the reconstruction of history, see Nigel Davies, *The Toltec Heritage: From the Fall of Tula to the Rise of Tenochtitlán* (Norman: University of Oklahoma Press, 1980), Chapter 11, wherein he concludes that *the* fundamental issue in Mesoamerican history is the interaction between nomadic and sedentary peoples; and, in a more general discussion, Kenneth Frampton, "Labour, Work and Architecture," in *Meaning in Architecture,* eds. Charles Jencks and George Baird (New York: George Braziller, 1969), 151–70, argues that wherever urban forms have emerged there has been a tension between dispersed and compacted patterns of settlement; he builds his case by reference to Frank Lloyd Wright, Ebenezer Howard, and Marx and Engels. The issues involved are exciting and well worth pursuing.

94. Charnay, *Ancient Cities,* xiii.

95. Ibid., xxvii.

96. Charnay cites Guillemin Tarayre, *Archives de la Commission Scientifique du Mexique*, 378, 379, as his precedent in arguing that all of the public and ceremonial architecture of Mesoamerica evolved from the simple house form. Charnay, *Ancient Cities*, 80, 90. Some eighteen centuries earlier, Vitruvius had written that Roman temples derive from domestic prototypes, but whatever its origins, this reasonable claim that the elaboration of Mesoamerican religious architecture originates in simple domestic architecture has been repeated endlessly. See, for example: Edward Herbert Thompson, *People of the Serpent: Life and Adventure Among the Mayas* (Boston: Houghton Mifflin Co., 1932; reprint, New York: Capricorn Book, 1960), 230; Herbert J. Spinden, *A Study of Maya Art: Its Subject Matter and Historical Development* (Cambridge, Mass.: Peabody Museum, 1913; reprinted with new intro. and biblio. by J. Eric S. Thompson, New York: Dover Publications, 1975), 107, 132, 133; Morley/Brainerd, *Ancient Maya*, 310; Tozzer, *Chichén and Cenote*, 83, 84; Robert Wauchope, "Domestic Architecture of the Maya," in *The Maya and Their Neighbors*, ed. Clarence L. Hay et al. (New York: Appleton-Century, 1940), 240; Pál Kelemen, *Medieval American Art* (New York: Macmillan, 1943), 75; Victor W. von Hagen, *World of the Maya* (New York: New American Library, 1960), 51–53, 141; idem, *The Aztec: Man and Tribe* (New York: New American Library, 1958, 1961), 63, 135, 139, 151; Elizabeth P. Benson, *The Maya World* (New York: Thomas Y. Crowell, 1967), 38; Michael D. Coe, *The Maya*, 3d ed. (New York: Thames and Hudson, 1984), 34. The same claim is likewise oft-repeated for the Inca; see, for instance, G.H.S. Bushnell, *Ancient Arts of the Americas* (New York: Frederick A. Praeger, 1965), 212; and Victor W. von Hagen, *Realm of the Incas* (New York: New American Library, 1957, 1961), 50, 132. And, an interesting, if more eccentric, parallel on the same theme is Wolfe's claim that the great glass Miesan skyscrapers of Chicago and all of America have their original prototypes in the compound architecture of socialist worker housing of the 1920s in Europe. See Tom Wolfe, *From Bauhaus to Our House* (New York: Pocket Books, 1981), 61, 75.

97. Bernal, *History of Mexican Archaeology*, 126–27, gives Charnay first place in the recognition of Maya-Mexican unity. However, preceding Charnay, Stephens and Catherwood (Charnay's models) likewise did not observe any Maya versus Mexican distinction but rather emphasized the unity of the area as a whole. Stephens stressed particularly cultural homogeneity on the basis of hieroglyphic inscriptions. See von Hagen, *Maya Explorer: John Lloyd Stephens*, 195, 222, 231. And Catherwood stressed the continuity in architectural form, and was completely at ease using explanations of Aztec rituals to explain Yucatán temples. See Frederick Catherwood, *Views of Ancient Monuments in Central America, Chiapas, and Yucatán* (London: Owen Jones, 1844), the introduction of which is reprinted in Victor Wolfgang von Hagen, *Frederick Catherwood, Archt.* (New York: Oxford University Press, 1950), 119–44. The remainder of Catherwood's volume is his famous drawings. All citations to this work will refer to the 1950 reprinting.

98. With respect to the so-called Mound Builders, Brinton, *Essays of an Americanist*, 67, 82, mentions J. P. MacLean, *The Mound Builders* (Cincinnati, 1879), Chapter 7, and Thomas E. Pickett, *The Testimony of the Mounds* (Maysville, 1876), 9, 28.

99. Much balderdash has been written about the fabulous accomplishments of the Toltecs; the complex issue of mythical versus historical Toltecs, together with the prestige and manipulation of Toltec heritage, is addressed later in regard to the historical problem of Tula, Hidalgo. Perhaps the most prestigious proponent of Mesoamerican unity on the basis of Toltec primacy was Eduard Seler, writing in the 1910s. Synthesizing ethnographic, archaeological, and ethnohistorical materials in his commentaries on the Mexican codices, Seler points at many parallels in the religions of the Central Mexicans and the Maya; he explains the essential unity by sliding the Toltec era back and the Maya era forward and by arguing that the former enriched the Maya with a large variety of elements, such as hieroglyphs, stelae, and architecture. For comments on Seler's work in this regard, see Spinden, *Study of Maya Art*, 225 (he thinks Seler was "too subjective"); Tozzer, *Chichén and Cenote*, 25 (he gives a reference to a retrieval of Seler's position by Walter Lehmann in 1933); and Bernal, *History of Mexican Archaeology*, 151 (he considers that Seler's principal aim was to show Mesoamerica's essential unity).

100. For example, the two major syntheses of the early twentieth century, Thomas Joyce, *Mexican Archaeology: An Introduction to the Archaeology of the Mexican and Mayan Civilization of Pre-Spanish America* (London: Philip Lee Warner, 1914), and, even more, Herbert Spinden, *Ancient Civilizations of Mexico and Central America*, 3d ed. (New York:

American Museum of Natural History, 1928), continued to describe the Maya as the original fount of all Middle American civilization.

101. On the Olmec as the "mother culture" of Mesoamerica, see Michael D. Coe, "The Olmec Style and Its Distribution," *Handbook of Middle American Indians: Archaeology of Southern Mesoamerica*, 3: 739–75 (Austin: University of Texas Press, 1965); Bernal, *History of Mexican Archaeology*, 178–80; and Muriel Porter Weaver, *The Aztecs, Maya, and Their Predecessors: Archaeology of Mesoamerica* (New York: Seminar Press, 1972), 50–55, 89. As early as 1700, Don Carlos de Sigüenza Góngora had argued that a race of "Olmecs," originally from Atlantis, had preceded the Toltecs and built the monuments of Teotihuacán; Humboldt agreed. See Tompkins, *Mysteries of the Mexican Pyramids*, 35–36, 57, 81.

102. In 1934, Tozzer, "Maya Research," 6, argued that one of the most urgent areas of study should be the "Archaic" (though he refuses to endorse Spinden's Archaic Hypothesis). Tozzer, *Chichén and Cenote*, 253, n. 9, is helpful in collecting a myriad of names that have been used to refer to this antecedent archaeological period.

103. Tozzer is also helpful in tracing the progressive recognition of Middle American Archaic culture in the nineteenth and early twentieth centuries. See ibid., 9.

104. See Spinden, *Ancient Civilizations of Mexico*, 45–71.

105. Paul Kirchhoff, "Mesoamerica," *Acta Americana* 1:1 (1943): 92–107. Citations to this article will be from an English translation by Norman McQuown recently reprinted as Paul Kirchhoff, "Mesoamerica: Its Geographic Limits, Ethnic Composition and Cultural Character," in *Ancient Mesoamerica: Selected Readings*, ed. John A. Graham (Palo Alto, Calif.: Peek Publications, 1981), 1–10. Kirchhoff's classic conception of Mesoamerica as a distinct culture area is discussed in Chapter 2 relative to the organization of Mesoamerican architecture according to geography.

106. Kidder contributed to the appreciation of Mesoamerican unity in several ways: (1) by direct archaeological investigation of the Preclassic, (2) by retrieving Spinden's Archaic Hypothesis, (3) by disseminating Kirchhoff's concept of "Mesoamerica," and (4) by his strong concern for cross-regional relations. See Gordon R. Willey, "Alfred Vincent Kidder," *National Academy of Science, Biographical Memoirs* 39 (1967): 304–5, and Richard B. Woodbury, *Alfred V. Kidder* (New York: Columbia University Press, 1973), 65–67.

107. On Kidder's retrieval of Spinden's Archaic Hypothesis, see Willey, "Alfred Vincent Kidder," 305, and Woodbury, *Alfred V. Kidder*, 65. For the others, see Tozzer, *Chichén and Cenote*, 5.

108. The earliest dates for archaic Mesoamerican culture continue to be pushed back further and further; Richard MacNeisch, a journeyman on this problem, has established a tentative Archaic sequence running from 7500 B.C.E. to 2000 B.C.E. See Coe, *Maya*, 22, 169. The Archaic period is typically regarded as a village-farming culture, but there is also strong evidence of large-scale public, presumably ceremonial architecture even in this early era. See Weaver, *Aztecs, Maya, and Their Predecessors*, 36, 44–46, and Hammond, "Lords of the Jungle," 21–22. On the religion of this Archaic period, Brainerd, *Maya Civilization*, 13, 16, and Thompson, *Rise and Fall of Maya Civilization*, 246, 269, 270, for instance, both made some very general intimations about earth goddesses and figurine cults, but a much more recent discussion by Johanna Broda, "Templo Mayor as Ritual Space," in Johanna Broda, Davíd Carrasco, and Eduardo Matos Moctezuma, *The Great Temple of Tenochtitlán: Center and Periphery in the Aztec World* (Berkeley: University of California Press, 1987), discusses a stratum of pan-Mesoamerican popular religion in a far more helpful and thorough fashion.

109. Coe, *Maya*, 3.

110. Ibid., 41.

111. See Tozzer, "Maya Research," 8, and Morley, *Ancient Maya*, 1st ed., 46, 56–57. Morley uses Tozzer as his authority on this point, ibid., 20.

112. The reviews of Morley's *Ancient Maya* (1946) by Eric Thompson, W. D. Strong, and George Brainerd (see n. 73 of this chapter) criticize him for his neglect of cross-regional relations. Ironically, Morley, in his 1920 review of Herbert Spinden's *Ancient Civilizations of Mexico and Central America*, had criticized Spinden on the same grounds, for neglecting the interrelations between the different cultures. See Brunhouse, *Sylvanus G. Morley*, 161, 313.

113. See Woodbury, *Alfred V. Kidder*, 54–57.

114. The agenda of the "new archaeologists," particularly with respect to Mesoamerican ceremonial architecture, will be addressed in the next chapter.

115. Morley, *Ancient Maya*, 2d ed., 73.

116. The study of Mesoamerican trading systems has become a major sub-specialization, and there is

an immense fund of recent literature. For an expansive discussion that includes remarks on some of the older misconceptions and on the current hypotheses, particularly as they relate to the era and area of Chichén Itzá (and also for a helpful set of bibliographical references), see David Freidel, "Terminal Classic Lowland Maya: Successes, Failures, and Aftermaths," in *Late Lowland Maya Civilization,* ed. Sabloff and Andrews, 409–32.

117. Mesoamerican pilgrimage, particularly in regard to Chichén Itzá, is another tremendously rich and complex issue that will surface repeatedly through this project, particularly in Chapter 4. Landa, *Relación,* 109, makes the famous observation that the Maya "held Cozumel and the well at Chichén Itzá in the same veneration as we have for pilgrimages to Jerusalem and Rome, and so they used to visit these places and to offer presents there." Of the Carnegie-era Mayanists, Ralph Roys was exceptional in his willingness to appreciate pilgrimage as a specifically religious and genuinely influential force in the development of Maya culture. See, for example, Ralph L. Roys, Appendix B, "The Sacrificial Cenote at Chichén Itzá" in *The Book of the Chilam Balam of Chumayel,* trans. and ed. Ralph L. Roys, Publication 438 (Washington: Carnegie Institution of Washington, 1933); new ed., with intro. by J. Eric S. Thompson (Norman: University of Oklahoma Press, 1967), 173–76.

118. For an early synthesis of their work, see Gordon R. Willey and William R. Bullard, Jr., "Prehistoric Settlement Patterns in the Maya Lowlands," in *Handbook of Middle American Indians: Archaeology of Southern Mesoamerica,* 2: 360–77 (Austin: University of Texas Press, 1965). For remarks on the even earlier pioneers of settlement pattern archaeology (e.g., Ricketson, Wauchope, and Satterthwaite in the 1930s), see Becker, "Priests, Peasants and Ceremonial Centers," 8–22, and Hammond, "Lords of the Jungle," 22–30.

119. Gordon R. Willey, "Recent Researches and Perspectives in Mesoamerican Archaeology: An Introductory Commentary," in *Supplement to the Handbook of Middle American Indians,* 1: 17, and Hammond, "Lords of the Jungle," 26–28. Both locate the Tikal Project within the wider history of Maya studies.

120. See Christopher Jones, William R. Coe, and William A. Haviland, "Tikal: An Outline of Its Field Study (1956–1970) and a Project Bibliography," in *Supplement to the Handbook of Middle American Indians,* 1: 306–7. Ironically, this is a return to the original presumption of Landa and nearly all the early Mayanists that the Maya did have "true cities" in the sense of socially complex, multifunctional population centers. However, while the Tikal Project is taken as confirmation that Maya urbanism is a local development, the old notion that "city-life" was introduced by Mexicans is perpetuated by the Tikal Project's documentation of a very active relationship between Central Mexican Teotihuacán and Tikal, which may have been "the crucial factor in . . . a trend toward urbanism and, possibly, leading toward a first Maya Lowland 'state,' with Tikal as its capital." Willey, "External Influences on the Lowland Maya," 66.

121. William A. Haviland, "A New Population Estimate for Tikal, Guatemala," *American Antiquity* 34:4 (1969): 429, 432. Also see idem, "Tikal, Guatemala and Mesoamerican Urbanism," *World Archaeology* 2:2 (1970): 186–98, which is really the stronger article. The Tikal Project did not, however, lay the Maya city issue to rest; for example, Richard E. Diehl, *Tula: The Toltec Capital of Ancient Mexico* (New York: Thames and Hudson, 1983), 144, persisted in the old polarity by holding that "the Maya are not an urban people"; and Richard E. Blanton, "The Rise of Cities," in *Supplement to the Handbook of Middle American Indians,* 1: 392, rightly cautions against over-simple, cultural ecological theories of urban genesis, emphasizing that it is by no means a uniform phenomenon in different regions of Mesoamerica.

122. Mayapán (a Postclassic site in the Northern Lowlands) and Tikal (a Classic Maya site in the heart of the Southern Lowlands), in fact, turn out to have quite similar residential patterns. Moreover, Haviland, "Tikal and Mesoamerican Urbanism," argues that their differences are due not to contrasting mentalities but to contrasting terrains and the constraints of defense in Mayapán's volatile ambience.

123. For "a general stock-taking" of the shifting opinions concerning Mexican influence on the Maya, see Willey, "External Influences on the Lowland Maya," 57–75. For remarks on Teotihuacán influence at Tikal, see Jones, Coe, and Haviland, "Tikal," 296–312; Coe, *Maya,* 70–77; Clemency Coggins, "A New Order and the Role of the Calendar: Some Characteristics of the Middle Classic Period at Tikal," in *Maya Archaeology and Ethnohistory,* ed. Norman Hammond and Gordon Willey (Austin: University of Texas Press, 1979), 38–40; and Miller,

"Artistic Evidence for Classic Period Cultural Contact Between Maya Lowlands and Central Mexican Highlands," 63–70. For remarks on Teotihuacán's influence in the Northern Lowlands of Yucatán, see Coe, *Maya,* 77–81, and Andrews, "Dzibilchaltún," 325.

124. Regarding archaeological evidence of a "reverse" movement and substantial Maya contact at Teotihuacán in the Classic period, Norman Hammond, "Thrones of Blood," *Quarterly Review of Archaeology* 7 (June 1986): 9, for instance, discusses "the recent work of Evelyn Rattray in the Merchant's Barrio at Teotihuacán [that] has shown that there is substantial Maya contact during the Early Classic and the early Late Classic."

125. There has been an exceedingly wide range of opinions regarding the nature of the Teotihuacán-Kaminaljuyú cross-tie. For some of the older views, see, for instance, George Vaillant, "Patterns in Middle American Archaeology," in *Maya and Their Neighbors,* ed. Hay et al., 304. Vaillant was certain that it was not trade but rather "specific contact." Kidder (1940s) argued against a mass migration or slow diffusion of Mexicans into the area and believed instead that it was a small group of warlike adventurers, a position discussed by Robert Wauchope, "The Initiation of an Archaeologist," in *They Found the Buried Cities: Exploration and Excavation in the American Tropics,* ed. Robert Wauchope (Chicago: University of Chicago Press, 1965), 45. Tozzer, *Chichén and Cenote,* 12, argues for a trade relationship between Teotihuacán and Kaminaljuyú. More recently, Coe, *Maya,* 66–67, contends that it was a case of actual Teotihuacán hegemony over the Maya center. And Bushnell, *Ancient Arts of the Americas,* 304, argues that Kaminaljuyú art can be explained only by the actual presence of artificers from Teotihuacán.

126. The Tikal Project, for instance, provided a fresh set of evidence that shows major Classic-period Teotihuacán influences at Tikal, in the very heart of the Petén Southern Maya Lowlands, and, likewise, even in the Northern Lowlands of Yucatán at Acancéh, a possibility not even considered twenty years ago. For a whole series of relevant articles see *Highland-Lowland Interaction in Mesoamerica: Interdisciplinary Approaches,* A Conference at Dumarton Oaks, October 18th and 19th, 1980, ed. Arthur G. Miller (Washingon: Dumbarton Oaks Research Library and Collection, 1983).

127. For brief and inconclusive remarks on Maya influence at Cacaxtl, see Norman Hammond, *Ancient Maya Civilization* (New Brunswick, N.J.: Rutgers University Press, 1982), 263; Kenneth L. Brown, "Postclassic Relationships Between the Highland and Lowland Maya," in *The Lowland Maya Postclassic,* ed. Chase and Rice, 281; and Coe, *Maya,* 9. Also see George Kubler, "Eclecticism at Cacaxtla," in *Third Palenque Round Table, 1978,* vol. 5, pt. 2, ed. Merle Greene Robertson (Austin: University of Texas Press, 1980), 163–72. Spinden's seemingly bizarre notion of the "Mayanization of Mexico" (1917), may, at some point, prove prophetic. See Spinden, *Ancient Civilizations of Mexico,* 171–73. The advocates for a reverse migration of architectural forms from Chichén Itzá to Tula, preeminently George Kubler, will be discussed later in this chapter in relation to "The Tula-Chichén Connection."

128. Freidel, "New Light on the Dark Age," 285, concludes that the general inclination of Mayanists at present is to regard external influence in the Postclassic "in light of a more outward-looking indigenous population," though some "maintain the stance that the Lowland Maya were under severe acculturative pressures of an involuntary nature."

129. On the historical and theoretical forces that lead to the assignment of various stereotypes to the Maya and Mexicans, see Jones, "Conquests of the Imagination."

130. Of course, not all assessments of pre-Columbian Central Mexican culture have been negative. Keen, *The Aztec Image in Western Thought,* for instance, does a marvelous job of demonstrating that Western imaginations even of Central Mexicans alone have been deeply ambivalent and highly contradictory.

131. Linda Schele and Mary Ellen Miller, *The Blood of Kings: Dynasty and Ritual in Maya Art* (Ft. Worth, Texas: Kimball Art Museum, 1986).

132. Linda Schele and David Freidel, *A Forest of Kings: The Untold Story of the Ancient Maya* (New York: William Morrow and Company, 1990). This important and widely read work appeared after I had fashioned this argument and, thus, has not been fully integrated into the discussion.

133. Thompson, *Maya History and Religion,* 200.

134. Norman Hammond concludes his review of Schele and Miller's *Blood of Kings* by saying, "as the nature of the Maya otherworld and its relationship with humanity, especially with humanity's protagonists in the form of rulers, has been elucidated, so the verities of an earlier generation of scholars have been replaced by a view of Maya civilization which is darker and more disturbing, yet more

comprehensive and more compatible with what we know of human society in general." Hammond, "Thrones of Blood," 10. Hammond, "Lords of the Jungle," makes essentially the same remarks about the recent acknowledgment of "a darker, but more characteristically Mesoamerican relationship with the supernatural," here crediting particularly Clemency Coggins with the revisionist view of Classic Maya religion.

135. Schele and Miller, *Blood of Kings,* 9.

136. This is addressed more fully in Chapter 3 in "The Dead: Ancestral Bones and Stones."

137. Schele and Miller, *Blood of Kings,* 14.

138. Lest the case for Maya-Mexican integration swing too far in favor of pan-Mesoamerican unity, there is a contingent that continues to emphasize the uniqueness of the Maya; for instance, Henderson says, "all indications are that [the Maya] is a primary civilization. There is no convincing evidence that its development depended to a significant degree on influence from the highland civilizations of Mexico." John Henderson, *The World of the Ancient Maya* (Ithaca, N.Y.: Cornell University Press, 1981), 24.

139. Ironically, Tozzer, who worked so hard to polarize all that is Maya versus Mexican at Chichén Itzá, is unwittingly, by his thorough documentation of the geographical distribution of traits in *Chichén and Cenote,* a strong source for documenting the unity of Mesoamerica. Eric Thompson says, "many of the distributions serve only to emphasize the incontrovertible — the general unity of Middle American culture." Thompson, review of *Chichén and Cenote,* 119.

140. Kenneth L. Brown, "Postclassic Relationships Between the Highland and Lowland Maya," 280.

141. Charnay, *Ancient Cities,* Preface.

142. Chapter 2 will discuss the shifting goals of Mesoamerican studies, including an era in which "historical reconstruction" reigns supreme.

143. Charnay, *Ancient Cities,* 107.

144. Henry B. Nicholson, "Toplitzin Quetzalcoatl of Tollan: A Problem in Mesoamerican Ethnohistory," Ph.D. diss., Harvard University, 1957, still provides the most thorough survey of Aztec sources on the Toltecs.

145. Fray Bernardino de Sahagún, *Florentine Codex: General History of the Things of New Spain,* trans. Arthur J.O. Anderson and Charles Dibble, 2d rev. ed. (Sante Fe, N.M.: School of American Research and University of Utah, 1978), vol. 3.

146. There continues to be confusion over the usage of the terms *Tollan* and *Tula.* In this project, "Tollan" will always refer to the archetypal, mythical city and not to any specific historical site; "Tula" will always refer to the single site of Tula, Hidalgo (also known as Tollan Xicocotitlan).

147. On deliberately "falsified" genealogies, Davies, *Toltec Heritage,* Chapter 3, goes into great detail on the veracity and manipulation of genealogies in Central Mexico following the fall of Tula; Coe, *Maya,* 117, discusses manipulated genealogies in Yucatán. On strategic marriage, the Mixtecs contrive an extensive system of nuptial unions that eventually resulted in the entire aristocracy being a single family (ibid., 148–49). For more examples of strategic marriage in Mesoamerica, see Davies, *Toltec Heritage,* 239, 288, 292, 294, 338.

148. Harold Osborne, *Indians of the Andes: Aymaras and Quechuas* (London: Routledge and Kegan Paul, 1952), discusses the "selective manipulation of remembered history" in South America.

149. Throughout the history of Mesoamerica (the mestizo, Spanish/Indian experience of colonial and modern Mexico included), there is a fundamental problem with respect to the synthesis of heterogeneous ethnicities and peoples — a recurrent dynamic between mixed and pure. The ceaseless fascination with pedigrees and distinguished lines of descent may well be interpreted as a kind of search for a symbolic sort of "purity."

150. Charnay, *Ancient Cities,* Chapters 4 and 5. Eduardo Matos, director of major Instituto Nacional de Antropología e Historia (INAH) excavations at Tula in the 1970s, considers Charnay's reconnaissance and theorizing about Tula significant enough to have these two chapters translated into Spanish and used to introduce the two parts of his modern excavation reports. Eduardo Matos Montezuma, ed., *Proyecto Tula: Primero Parte* (Mexico: Instituto Nacional de Antropología e Historia, 1974), 17–26; and idem, *Proyecto Tula: Segunda Parte* (Mexico: Instituto Nacional de Antropología e Historia, 1976), 15–20.

151. Davis, *Désiré Charnay: Expeditionary Photographer,* 173–74, has a day-by-day account of Charnay's excavations at Tula in 1880.

152. Charnay, *Ancient Cities,* 93–103.

153. Deuel, *Conquistadors Without Swords,* 175–76, for instance, considers Charnay the first in the equation of Tollan and Tula; as usual, we will see that there are a number of precedents.

154. See Richard Diehl, "Tula," *Supplement to the Handbook of Middle American Indians,* 1: 277. Note that references to this summary article by Diehl (1981) and cited heretofore as Diehl, "Tula," should not be confused with Diehl's book-length treatment, entitled *Tula: The Toltec Capital of Ancient Mexico* (1983) and cited as Diehl, *Tula* (see n. 21). There are many changes and considerable progress in his ideas about the site between these two works.

155. On Manuel Orozco y Berra (1855), among the earliest to suggest a distinction between the Toltecs of Tula and those of Teotihuacán, see Bernal, *History of Mexican Archaeology,* 171. For Brasseur de Bourbourg's more extravagant ideas about the Toltecs (he visited Tula but placed Tollan somewhere in northern Europe), see Brunhouse, *In Search of the Maya,* 131–33. Brinton, *Essays of an Americanist,* 84, vehemently opposed to the literal historicity of the Toltec tradition, collects a list of his adversaries.

156. For instance, William H. Prescott, *History of the Conquest of Mexico* (New York: Harper and Brothers, 1843), 14, cited Sahagún and Torquemada for their recognition that "Toltec" became a synonym for "architect"; and Brasseur de Bourbourg, at the end of his career (around 1860), reversed his opinion and decided that the Toltecs had never existed at all and that the texts he had translated were allegory rather than history. See Wauchope, *Lost Tribes and Sunken Continents,* 47. Even Charnay, the arch voice for a literal historical interpretation of Toltec exploits, admitted that "Toltec" was also a generic label, "applied to every indigenous tribe that has left behind any monumental traces of its presence." Désiré Charnay, "The Ruins of Central America," *North America Review* 131 (1880): 131, 191. Also see Charnay, *Ancient Cities,* 83, where Charnay acknowledges Clavijero's notion that "Toltec" also means "architect" and "artificer." Deuel, *Conquistadors Without Swords,* 175, notes that throughout the nineteenth century, in the works of Humboldt, Prescott, Charnay, and others, the "magnificent Toltecs" rule supreme.

157. Prescott, *The Conquest of Mexico,* 14.

158. Brantz Mayer, *Mexico as It Was and as It Is* (New York, 1846); cited by Tozzer, *Chichén and Cenote,* 26.

159. Tozzer discusses the report of this commission. Ibid., 26.

160. Brinton, *Essays of an Americanist,* 100, cites Albert Gallatin (1845) as his sole precedent on this issue, but, because scholars had been discussing the transhistorical meanings of "Toltec" for 300 years, I would say that he somewhat overstates his originality.

161. Ibid., 85–87, 99.

162. Ibid., 83–85.

163. Otto Stoll, *Guatemala: Reisen und Schilderungen* (Leipzig, 1886), 408–9; discussed by Brinton, *Essays of an Americanist,* 100.

164. Nigel Davies, *The Toltecs Until the Fall of Tula* (Norman: University of Oklahoma Press, 1977), 30, and Tozzer, *Chichén and Cenote,* 256, both considered Plancarte (1911, 1923) to be the first to associate the Tollan of the ancient sources with Teotihuacán. I suspect that the identification, seemingly obvious, was presumed much earlier. The same sources also reflect on Gamio's equation of Teotihuacán and Tollan, as does Diehl, *Tula,* 28.

165. Enrique Juan Palacios, "Teotihuacán, los Toltecas y Tula," *Revista Mexicana de Estudios Antropológicos* 5 (1941): 113–34. See Tozzer, *Chichén and Cenote,* 256.

166. The obscurity of the history and site of Tula at the beginning of this century is evidenced in the fact that the most thoroughgoing survey of the era — William Henry Holmes, *Archaeological Studies Among the Ancient Cities of Mexico* (Chicago: Field Columbian Museum, 1895–97) — does not visit or even mention Tula, and Alfred Maudslay, another great positivistic scholar of that era, gives the Maya credit for building Tula. See Brunhouse, *Pursuit of Ancient Maya,* 43.

167. Bernal, *History of Mexican Archaeology,* 170–71; and Tozzer, *Chichén and Cenote,* 26–28, both have summary discussions of this phase of the Tollan problem. It is noteworthy with respect to the Tula–Chichén Itzá problem that Tozzer simply reviews the argument and does not voice a strong opinion on Tula history.

168. Jorge Acosta, "Exploraciones en Tula, Hidalgo, 1940," *Revista Mexicana de Estudios Antropológicos* 4 (1940): 172–94. Acosta, the principal excavator of Tula in this era, went on to publish countless articles about the site. Incidentally, despite the significance of Acosta's initial discovery, recent studies show that the dominant pottery of the "Tollan phase" at Tula is not Mazapan or Tula-Mazapan after all; instead, it is a continuation of the Coyotlatelco tradition. See Diehl, "Tula," 280; and Willey, "Recent Researches and Perspectives in Mesoamerican Archaeology," 16.

169. The original version of this classic, George C. Vaillant, *The Aztecs of Mexico: Origin, Rise, and Fall of the Aztec Nation* (New York: Doubleday, Durán and Co., 1944), was apparently written a few years earlier (he states explicitly that he works without the benefits of Jiménez Moreno's complete reinterpretation of the ethnographic sources that appears in 1941). See ibid., 282. In this 1944 edition, Chapter 3 is "Teotihuacán and the Classic Toltecs," and Chapter 4 is "The Chichimec Dynastic Toltecs" (that is, the Toltecs of Tula). In a postscript to the reprints of this edition in the 1950s, C. A. Burland apologizes for the outdatedness of this scheme (Vaillant had died in 1945). In George Vaillant, *The Aztecs of Mexico,* 2d ed., rev. Suzannah B. Vaillant (New York: Doubleday, Duran and Co., 1962), Vaillant's widow recrafts the scheme entirely to conform to the later orthodox separation of Teotihuacán and the Classic period (without any sort of Toltecs) from the Toltecs of Tula. (I see references to an even earlier edition of *Aztecs of Mexico* in 1941 by Garden City Press, for example, in Willey and Sabloff, *History of American Archaeology,* 299, which I cannot explain.)

170. Bernal, *History of Mexican Archaeology,* 184, expresses confidence that Vaillant, had he lived, would soon have altered his scheme.

171. Wigberto Jiménez Moreno, "Tula y los Toltecas según las Fuentes Históricas," *Revista Mexicana de Estudios Antropológicos* 5 (1941): 79–85. He explains that the Museo Nacional in Mexico City had identified Tula as the Tollan of the historical sources since 1934.

172. Pedro Armillas, "Teotihuacán, Tula y los Toltecas: Las culturas post-arcaicas y pre-Aztecas del centro de Mexico," *Revista de la Universidad Nacional de Argentina* 3 (1950): 37–70; cited by Diehl, *Tula,* 29.

173. Kirchhoff offers an alternative reading of the ethnohistorical evidence, focusing particularly on the multiplicity of calendars in Central Mexico, wherein Topiltzin Quetzalcoatl was the *last* rather than the first ruler of Tollan Tula (as Jiménez Moreno contends). Paul Kirchhoff, "Quetzalcoatl, Huemac ye el fin de Tula," *Cuadernos Americanos* 14 (1955): 163–96. Robert Chadwick, "Native Pre-Aztec History of Central Mexico," *Handbook of Middle American Indians: Archaeology of Northern Mesoamerica,* (Austin: University of Texas Press, 1971), 11: 474–504, presenting an iconoclastic reading of the *Codice Chimalpopoca,* contends that the "history" of Tula and the Toltecs that Jiménez Moreno has retrieved is actually a rehashing of events that transpired in Oaxaca and that were originally recorded in the Mixtec codices, and thus he concludes that the first Tollan was actually Teotihuacán, not Tula. And Laurette Séjourné, *Burning Water: Thought and Religion in Ancient Mexico* (Berkeley: Shambhala, 1976), 83–84, presents the most vociferous dissent to the Tula-Tollan correlation; she is certain that Teotihuacán was the original Tollan and berates Tula as "a second rate civic center which, except for a few remarkable sculptures, contains only crude copies of imported motifs and thus cannot possibly have been the cradle of a glorious civilization."

174. Most archaeologists continue to argue that even if Tula is the most explicit referent to the Tollan of tradition (as Jiménez Moreno held), there is, nonetheless, an important connection between Tollan and Teotihuacán. See, for example, Eric Wolf, *Sons of the Shaking Earth* (Chicago: University of Chicago Press, 1959), 257; or, more recently, Willey, "Recent Researches and Perspectives on Mesoamerican Archaeology," 16, who contends that "there is at least the possibility, considering the reverence and awe in which the name Toltec is held in the historical sources, that Teotihuacán may have been a still earlier Toltec capital, a more ancient Tollan."

175. As early as 1900, Eduard Seler had differentiated between the "historic Tula" and the Tula of ancient fable. See Davies, *Toltecs Until the Fall,* 30.

176. Davíd Carrasco, *Quetzalcoatl and the Irony of Empire: Myths and Prophecies in the Aztec Tradition* (Chicago: University of Chicago Press, 1982). Via the sensitive use of history of religions categories, Carrasco argues that the legendary traditions about the Toltecs arose originally at Teotihuacán (ibid., 126); that they contained "paradigms for spatial order, kingship, sanctity, priesthood, and major institutions of the city"; and that Quetzalcoatl, the ruler of Tollan, was, along with his myriad other meanings, a "symbol of sanctified authority" that contributed to the organization of a number of pre-Columbian capital cities, or "other Tollans" — Tula and Chichén Itzá among them. For Carrasco's discussion of Tollan's relationship to the physical site of Tula — an issue that "may never be settled in a strict, literal sense" — see ibid., 72–76. Davies, *Toltec Heritage,* 97, like Carrasco, is convinced that innumerable groups maneuvered to assume the Toltecs' prestigious mantle of urban legitimacy and that Tollan, rather than a specific city, is "first and foremost a concept, transferable from one metropolis to

another." Furthermore, Davies demonstrates that "Tollan" is but one of a host of transhistorical, universalized ideals to which the Central Mexicans adhere; for instance "Aztlan" and "Chicomoztoc" are concepts of remote, pristine order as much as geographical places (see ibid., 23–25, 97); "Xolotl" represents the concept of imperial authority more than any historical personae (see ibid., 98); and, most significantly, "Chichimec" is a romanticized appellation connoting something like "noble savage" or martially skilled, wandering rustic that, when paired with the urban Toltec pedigree, articulated a kind of "rags to riches" legend and thus endorsed the transition from nomadic to city life (see ibid., 86, 91, 238–40).

177. See, for instance, discussions of Tula in Robert McC. Adams, *The Evolution of Urban Society: Early Mesopotamia and Prehispanic Mexico* (Chicago: Aldine, 1966); Ignacio Bernal, "Evolución y alcance de las culturas Mesoamericanas," in *Esplendor del Mexico Antiguo,* ed. C. Cook de Leonard (Mexico, D.F.: Centro de Investigaciones Antropológicos de Mexico, 1959), 1: 97–126; Michael D. Coe, *Mexico* (New York: Praeger Publishers, 1962); William T. Sanders and Barbara Price, *Mesoamerica: The Evolution of Civilization* (New York: Random House, 1968); and Weaver, *Aztecs, Maya, and Their Predecessors.* Diehl, "Tula," 293, cites these works as exemplary of the deficiencies in Tula history.

178. In a sense, going out on a limb where no one can reach him, Nigel Davies's work on Tula is both exceedingly impressive and problematic because no other work approaches his level of detail. With respect to my project, two limitations are particularly acute: first, his only real division of Tula history is beginning, middle, and end (and he admits that the middle is poorly documented in the written sources and that the beginning and end are all mixed together); and second, being almost totally preoccupied with the reconstruction of large-scale events, he says very little (particularly in his earlier volume) about Toltec religion or the possible ritual usage of Tula's buildings.

179. The results of the INAH project are synthesized in the two-volume *Proyecto Tula,* ed. Eduardo Matos Moctezuma (1974, 1976), and in Juan Yadeún Angulo, *El Estado y la Ciudad: El Caso de Tula, Hgo* (Mexico: Instituto Nacional de Antropología e Historia, 1975). The results of the UMC Tula Project are synthesized in Diehl, *Tula.*

180. The different orientations of traditional archaeology and the "new archaeology" are addressed in Chapter 2, but for perfect examples of the goals and methods of the latter see Matos, *Proyecto Tula,* 1: 8, 10, 12; 2: 7–12; or Richard Diehl, ed., *Studies of Ancient Tollan: A Report of the University of Missouri Archaeological Project* (Columbia: University of Missouri, Columbia, 1974), 1; or idem, *Tula,* 97, 119, 140.

181. Diehl, "Tula," 293, had argued that Tula did not yet exist in the era of Teotihuacán. However, Eduardo Matos Moctezuma, "The Tula Chronology: A Revision," in *Middle Classic Mesoamerica, A.D. 400–700,* ed. Paszory, 172–77, explains how his excavations of Tula Chico, a plaza adjacent and anterior to Tula Grande (the famous plaza where Acosta worked) lead him to believe that the Tula area had been under Teotihuacán control. Diehl, *Tula,* 25, now believes that Tula was a minor village in Teotihuacán times.

182. On Tula's orientation scheme, in 1981, Diehl, "Tula," 29–94, said, "Tula lacks any evidence of planning beyond that involved in the Acropolis [Tula Grande]"; but, in 1983, Diehl, *Tula,* 15–16, entered new evidence that Tula is laid out on a grid plan with major avenues and uniform building orientations like other Mesoamerican centers. On residential clusters or neighborhoods, see ibid., 68–96. Incidentally, Charnay deserves some credit for preliminary investigations into Tula settlement patterns and house sites. See Charnay, *Ancient Cities,* Chapter 4. Weaver, *Aztecs, Maya, and Their Predecessors,* 34, reviewing Charnay's work, said in 1972, "our knowledge of settlement patterns and house sites [at Tula] has not progressed since that time."

183. See Diehl, "Tula," 288–90, and idem, *Tula,* 97–117.

184. Diehl, "Tula," 290, admitted that the archaeological data do not shed much light on the political structure of the Toltec state and that its boundaries are completely conjectural; in 1981, he opined that Tula, like Teotihuacán, was the only true urban center in the immediate area during its fluorescence (ibid., 294); but, in 1983, he adopted the position that Tula, even at its peak, was one of several competing cities (idem, *Tula,* 137–39). Virtually all recent syntheses agree that Tula was the capital city of an empire with military preeminence and a fair degree of politico-economic integration. For instance, Coe, *Mexico,* 138, and idem, *Maya,* 120, says that Tula "was certainly the administrative center of an

empire spanning from the Atlantic to the Pacific"; and Weaver, *Aztecs, Maya, and Their Predecessors,* 213, says, "Toltec expansion [from Tula] was a military operation coupled with intensive agriculture, and the beginning of confiscation of food surplus, which was later formalized as tribute payment." More specifically, Davies, *Toltecs Until the Fall of Tula,* 344, discusses the differences between his ethnohistorically based conclusions about the extent of the Toltec empire and those expressed by Lawrence H. Feldman, "Tollan in Hidalgo: Native Accounts of the Central Mexican Tolteca," in *Studies of Ancient Tollan,* ed. Diehl, 130–49.

185. Diehl, *Tula,* 140. Also see ibid., 118–139; and idem, "Tula," 294.

186. See, for instance, Coe, *Mexico,* 143.

187. See Diehl, *Tula,* 158–69. Davies, *Toltec Heritage,* 4, also holds that, though Tula may have declined fairly swiftly, it "did not fall in a day."

188. This is Davies's contention on the basis of ethnohistorical research (see Davies, *Toltecs Until the Fall of Tula,* 41–42), and Diehl finds archaeological data to bear it out (see Diehl, "Tula," 291).

189. Waters, *Mexico Mystique,* 61–66, has a brief account of the Toltecs of Tula that epitomizes both the frustrations with the historical contradictions and the typically negative assessment of the Toltecs' "semi-barbaric, transitional military culture."

190. Arlen Chase and Diane Chase, "Postclassic Temporal and Spatial Frames for the Lowland Maya: A Background," in *Lowland Maya Postclassic,* ed. Chase and Rice, 4. They discuss a number of the special problems that have made Postclassic dating particularly difficult. See ibid., 9–11.

191. Charnay, *Ancient Cities,* 327–34. Charnay admits that it is very difficult to date Chichén Itzá, but he believes that the city is fairly recent, that is, more recent than Izamal or Aké but older than Uxmal (see ibid., 327); in other words, his Yucatán chronology is essentially up for grabs.

192. In the main, these explorers take the accumulation of debris on the ruins as a sign of great antiquity; Edward Thompson deserves credit for rejecting that crude method of dating in the late nineteenth century. See Brunhouse, *In Search of the Maya,* 171.

193. For instance, in 1832, Alexandre Lenoir summarized the prevailing opinion that the Aztecs belonged to the twelfth century, the Toltecs to the sixth, while the Maya of Guatemala and Yucatán were "considerably more ancient." Bernal, *History of Mexican Archaeology,* 104. And Orozco y Berra (1880), while making some improvements in the chronology, continued to hold that the Maya are considerably older than any Central Mexican peoples. See ibid., 104, 110–12. In the 1910s, Joyce, *Mexican Archaeology;* idem, *Maya and Mexican Art;* Spinden, *Study of Maya Art;* and idem, *Ancient Civilizations of Mexico* perpetuated the notion of Maya primacy. They espoused chronologies that place Maya civilization well in advance of and largely responsible for Teotihuacán and the Toltecs.

194. Prescott apparently did believe that the Maya were more ancient than the Toltecs (see Bernal, *History of Mexican Archaeology,* 115), but he was a strong advocate generally for the relative modernity and indigenous origin of Middle American monuments. The relative modernity and antidiffusionist origin of the ruins were among Stephens's most emphatic claims. See, for instance, Stephens, *Incidents of Travel in Yucatán,* 1: 50, 53, 163, or 2: Chapter 24. Bernal, *History of Mexican Archaeology,* 123, sees Stephens as a forerunner in an opposing tendency to take the ruins for more recent than they are. An 1841 letter from Prescott to Stephens, interesting in itself, describes the coincidence between the former's ethnohistorically derived conclusions and the latter's on-sight investigations; Prescott: "your opinion as to the comparatively modern date of these remains [in Yucatán] agrees entirely with the conclusions I had come to from the much more inadequate sources of information, of course, than you possess." Von Hagen, *Maya Explorer: John Lloyd Stephens,* 192–93. For Catherwood's similar ideas on the age and origin of the monuments, see particularly Catherwood, *Views of Ancient Monuments,* 138–40; or von Hagen, *Frederick Catherwood, Archt.,* 94–95, 138–40.

195. The total Maya area is typically partitioned into three areas: the Northern Lowlands, the Southern Lowlands (or Central Maya area), and more southerly still, the Guatemalan Highlands. See, for instance, Morley, *Ancient Maya,* 2d ed., 3–16; or Thompson, *Rise and Fall of Maya Civilization,* 17–27.

196. Incidentally, Le Plongeon is quite unusual in believing that the "real" Maya had resided in Yucatán; he believed that Copán and Palenque were completely alien to Maya culture. See Brunhouse, *In Search of the Maya,* 149–56.

197. Sylvanus G. Morley, *The Inscriptions of Petén,* 5 vols., Publication 437 (Washington: Carnegie Institution of Washington, 1937–38), years in the making,

is Morley's most impressive academic contribution. Morley considered that initial series inscriptions on the stelae "by themselves alone provide a thoroughly reliable chronological framework for Old Empire [that is, Southern Lowland] history." Morley, *Ancient Maya,* 2d ed., 51.

198. Morley (ibid., 73) and Spinden, *Ancient Civilizations of Mexico,* 175, both express the same frustration with the lack of dated stelae in the Northern Lowlands as compared to the south. For Landa's brief and eccentric account of the history of Chichén Itzá, a story about three ruling brothers (which leads only to confusion), see Landa, *Relación,* 19–23.

199. The first origin of the notorious Old Empire/New Empire scheme continues to elude me, but it is clear that Morley came to it very early in his career and stubbornly held to it even in the face of controverting evidence. Morley presented this general scheme to the International Congress of Americanists in Washington as early as 1915 (see Brunhouse, *Sylvanus G. Morley,* 160), and its most full-blown exposition appears in 1946 in Morley, *Ancient Maya,* 1st ed., chapters 4–5. In 1924, Gann, *In an Unknown Land,* 89–97, gave a historical (re)construction of Yucatán that is simply a paraphrase of Morley's two-empire scheme — to which Gann subscribes "without a shadow of a doubt" (ibid., 226) — so the framework was definitely intact by that time. A. F. Chase and P. M. Rice, Introduction, *Lowland Maya Postclassic,* ed. Chase and Rice, 2–3, suggest a possible evolution of Morley's scheme.

200. Ironically, where tourists to Chichén Itzá often have the impression that the indigenous Maya guides are treating them to esoteric oral traditions regarding the site's history, many of these native raconteurs will freely acknowledge that Morley's *Ancient Maya* remains their most serviceable authority.

201. Morley, *Ancient Maya,* 2d ed., 73, 83.

202. Ibid., 76–81. Besides Bernardo de Lizana's *Historia de Yucatán* (1633), Morley worked from a number of references to the "Little and Great Descents" in *The Books of Chilam Balam.* Virtually every rendition of Yucatán culture history will work these two "descents" in one way or another.

203. Morley, *Ancient Maya,* 2d ed., 81–82.

204. Ibid., 50–97. Spinden, *Ancient Civilizations of Mexico,* 148–50, gives essentially the same rendition of events.

205. Brunhouse, *Sylvanus G. Morley,* 63–94, gives a full accounting of the political intrigues involved in Morley having his Chichén Itzá plan adopted by the CIW. Also see Bernal, *History of Mexican Archaeology,* 173.

206. Tozzer, *Chichén and Cenote,* 190, gives a concise account of the CIW work at Chichén Itzá. Brunhouse, *Sylvanus G. Morley,* 279–80, gives a somewhat wider overview of the CIW activities.

207. The reviews of Morley's *Ancient Maya* by Strong, Thompson, and particularly Brainerd (cited earlier in n. 73) all express serious reservations with the Old and New Empire scheme and with Morley's chronology. Brunhouse, *Sylvanus G. Morley,* 317, defends *Ancient Maya* by contending that it is a "work of art," an expression of Morley's enthusiasm and dedication that does not purport to be perfect scholarship.

208. It came out later that Teobert Maler had been to Cobá in the 1890s. Deuel, *Conquistadors Without Swords,* 295–99, recounts the significance of the Cobá discovery.

209. J. Eric S. Thompson, *Maya Archaeologist* (Norman: University of Oklahoma Press, 1963), 42–70, has a casual description of the CIW expeditions to Cobá.

210. Following these iconoclastic revelations about coeval Yucatán and Petén centers, even so laic an account as T. A. Willard's *The Lost Empires of the Itzáes and Mayas,* which bears the telling subtitle, *An American Civilization, Contemporary With Christ, Which Rivaled the Culture of Egypt* (Glendale, Calif.: Arthur H. Clark Company, 1933), disavows the two-empire scheme (see ibid., 25–26); yet Morley, who participated in the excavation at Cobá, did not. Thompson, *Maya Archaeologist,* 58, gives an account of his travels to Cobá with Morley.

211. See Anthony P. Andrews and Fernando Robles C., "Chichén Itzá and Cobá: An Itzá-Maya Standoff in Early Postclassic Yucatán," in *Lowland Maya Postclassic,* ed. Chase and Rice, 62–71.

212. Pierre Ventur, *Maya Ethnohistorian: The Ralph L. Roys Papers* (Nashville: Vanderbilt University, 1978), 76–81, discusses the endurance and productivity of Roys and Thompson's collaboration on the ethnohistorical sources: "hardly a fact of Maya culture is left unelaborated in the Roys-Thompson correspondence" (ibid., 79). With specific reference to their revisionist chronology of Yucatán, see Ralph L. Roys, Appendix C, *Chilam Balam of Chumayel,* ed. Roys, 177–81; and J. Eric S. Thompson, "A Survey of the Northern Maya Area," *American Antiquity* 11 (1945): 2–24. Thompson, *Maya Archaeologist,* 20–41, gives a more offhand discussion of his opinion

that the indigenous Yucatec Maya at Chichén Itzá (before "Mexicanization") represented a "regional divergence" from the southern Maya.

213. Besides Brainerd's important ceramic studies, the autonomy and independence of the Northern Lowlands in the Late Classic (roughly 600–1000 C.E.) is confirmed by Proskouriakoff, who documented a set of Yucatán art and sculpture styles that could not have derived from the Petén area. See Tatiana Proskouriakoff, *A Study of Classic Maya Sculpture,* Publication 593 (Washington: Carnegie Institution of Washington, 1950); and idem, "Some Non-Classic Traits in the Sculpture of Yucatán," in *The Civilizations of Ancient America,* ed. Sol Tax (Chicago: University of Chicago Press, 1951), 108–18. Andrews IV and Pollock, two more of the Carnegie troupe, isolated several distinct Yucatecan architectural styles (that is, the Río Bec, Chenes, and Puuc) that contrast sharply with both the Petén Maya to the south and the Toltec Maya that followed. For syntheses of years of work, see H.E.D. Pollock, "Architecture of the Maya Lowlands," *Handbook of Middle American Indians: Archaeology of Southern Mesoamerica* (Austin: University of Texas Press, 195) 2: 378–440, and E. Wyllys Andrews IV, "Archaeology and Prehistory in the Northern Maya Lowlands," *Handbook of Middle American Indians: Archaeology of Southern Mesoamerica* (Austin: University of Texas Press, 1965), 2: 288–330.

214. This quotation actually comes from Brainerd's 1948 review of Morley's *Ancient Maya,* 135. For more extended presentations of this alternative view of northern Yucatán history in the era of the so-called Old Empire, see Brainerd, *Maya Civilization,* 24–25, 80–81; and Brainerd/Morley, *Ancient Maya,* 57–99.

215. In Morley's original edition of *Ancient Maya* (1946) the chronological sections (chapters 4 and 5) are entitled "The Old Empire" and "The New Empire"; Brainerd's third and revised edition of this work (1956) reworks the chronology entirely as "The Classic Stage" and "The Post Classic Stage." The fourth edition, revised by Robert J. Sharer (1983), jettisoned Brainerd's evolutionary language and replaced "stage" with "period." The complicated origins and implications of applying the Preclassic, Classic, Postclassic categories to Mesoamerican civilization will be discussed in Chapter 2 in regard to the organization of Mesoamerican architecture by culture.

216. If Brainerd's *Maya Civilization* (1956) stands near the beginning of this "traditional" view of Lowland Maya chronology, the scheme finds a kind of endpoint in 1986 in Gordon Willey's "The Postclassic of the Maya Lowlands: A Preliminary Overview," in *Late Lowland Maya Civilization,* ed. Sabloff and Andrews V, 17–52, an article specifically intended to stand as "a benchmark against which the new interpretations [in this volume] might be compared."

217. Brainerd, *Maya Civilization,* 81–89.

218. Ibid., 80.

219. There are two major collections (respectively 1985 and 1986) that rely on a number of the same contributors, which aim specifically to redress the inordinate concentration on the Classic Maya of the Southern Lowlands by focusing on the era after 800 C.E. and to give equal consideration to the Northern Lowlands: *The Lowland Maya Postclassic,* ed. Chase and Rice; and *Late Lowland Maya Civilization,* ed. Sabloff and Andrews V, which concentrates even more on the problems relative to Chichén Itzá. The articles in these two important volumes, of course not all in agreement, are considered to constitute the "state of the art" for this project.

220. For instance, E. Wyllys Andrews V and Jeremy A. Sabloff, "Classic to Postclassic: A Summary Discussion," in *Late Lowland Maya Civilization,* ed. Sabloff and Andrews, 455–56, emphasize the necessity of looking at the "totality of developments in the [Southern and Northern] Maya Lowlands." Also see David A. Freidel, "Culture Areas and Interaction Spheres: Contrasting Approaches to the Emergence of Civilization in the Maya Lowlands," *American Antiquity* 44 (1979): 36–54.

221. With respect to the history of the current "overlap" controversy, Andrews and Sabloff, "Classic to Postclassic," 435–36, discuss a number of important earlier works that challenge the conventional linear succession model; Tatiana Proskouriakoff's work on Maya sculpture in the 1950s is particularly important.

222. The relationship between Chichén Itzá and the Petén centers is an aspect of the somewhat more general and, currently, very controversial debate about when and where to draw the line between the Classic and Postclassic Maya. The disjunction *after* Chichén Itzá, before Mayapán, is now considered more drastic than the conventional break between Chichén Itzá and the major Petén sites, thus, in effect, relocating Chichén Itzá in the Classic rather than Postclassic. See ibid., 434, 451–57.

223. For instance, David Freidel, "Terminal Classic Lowland Maya: Successes, Failures and Aftermaths," in *Late Lowland Maya Civilization,* ed. Sabloff and Andrews, 421–30, discusses "the most pressing issue in Lowland Maya archaeology . . . the relationship between the histories and evolutionary developments of the Northern and Southern Lowlands." Ibid., 421. Moving well beyond the old polarizing stereotypes, he offers a sensitive (and materialist) set of generalizations about the essential unity but notable differences between the Maya north and south; he concludes that where Southern Lowland public architecture and political religion were preeminently concerned with royal bloodlines and the transfer of power through "pure" lines of descent, the art and architecture of Northern Lowlanders suggest that they were less concerned with ruling lineages than with "the religious affirmation of political entities." Ibid., 423–25. Thus, Freidel implies that Chichén Itzá's success may have stemmed from its participation in this more pragmatic approach to political legitimation and integration rather than from simple military superiority, as the old stereotypes of militaristic Toltecs suggest.

224. See Andrews and Sabloff, "Classic to Postclassic," 435–36, where they mention important precedents to this alternative periodization of Lowland history, specifically in the 1960s by H.E.D. Pollock and E. W. Andrews IV.

225. I take 1986 as a significant date because *The Lowland Maya Postclassic,* ed. Chase and Rice (1985) continues to locate Chichén Itzá within the Early Postclassic, while the other major reassessment of the Maya Postclassic, *Late Lowland Maya Civilization,* ed. Sabloff and Andrews V (1986) relocates Chichén Itzá in the Terminal Classic period. Of course, it is a slow, evolving process that depends as much on the revaluation of the Petén Classic Maya as on the study of Chichén Itzá itself. As early as the 1950s, Rands documented "rather unexpected connections between the art of the Toltec period at Chichén Itzá and that of the late great period of the Classic centers to the south"; and Tozzer acknowledged (but never really came to terms with the fact that), "inferentially, this may indicate the approximate contemporaneity of the Chichén Itzá Toltec and the late Classic Maya." See R. L. Rands, "Artistic Connections Between the Chichén Itzá Toltec and the Classic Maya," *American Antiquity* 19 (1954): 281–82; discussed in Tozzer, *Chichén and Cenote,* 266, n. 48. Also from an art historical angle, Mary Miller's contention that the famous reclining *chacmool* figures, so prominent at Tula and Chichén Itzá (and few other places) are *not* of Central Mexican origin, as almost everyone since Charnay has presumed, but rather originated at Chichén, is one more argument for the indigenously Maya character of "Toltec" Chichén Itzá. Mary Ellen Miller, "A Re-examination of the Mesoamerican Chacmool," *Art Bulletin* 67 (March 1985): 7–17.

226. Jeremy Sabloff and E. Wyllys Andrews V, Introduction to *Late Lowland Maya Civilization,* ed. Sabloff and Andrews, 8.

227. The old view that the arrival of Toltecs (or Mexican-related groups) in Yucatán had brought an absolute end to the Puuc tradition (that is, no overlap) is present, for instance, in Morley/Brainerd, *Ancient Maya,* 77; and Weaver, *Aztecs, Maya, and Their Predecessors,* 227. R. E. Smith, *The Pottery of Mayapán,* Papers of the Peabody Museum of Archaeology and Ethnology, no. 66 (Cambridge: Harvard University, 1971) is sometimes taken as the definitive statement of the "sequential," "linear," or "no overlap" scheme.

228. The profound difference between Puuc and "Toltec" architectures, and the implication that they constitute two very distinct sorts of ritual contexts, are discussed at length in Chapter 4.

229. Ironically, the now-fashionable position that the Puuc climax and the "Toltec Chichén" climax were actually part of a single Northern Lowland florescence that was nearly as substantial as the earlier florescence in the Southern Lowlands constitutes an inadvertent sort of retrieval of Morley's bipartite Old and New Empire scheme. See Sabloff and Andrews, Introduction, 5; and idem, "Classic to Postclassic," 446.

230. Joseph W. Ball, "Ceramics, Culture History, and the Puuc Tradition: Some Alternative Possibilities," in *The Puuc: New Perspectives,* ed. Lawrence Mills (Pella, Iowa: Central College, 1979), 30–34, lays out the three basic options with respect to the relationship between the Puuc and "Toltec Chichén" styles: (1) the traditional model of sequential development (including Tozzer and R. E. Smith), (2) "partial overlap" (Andrews V and Sabloff), and (3) "total overlap" (Ball and Lincoln). Also see Joseph W. Ball, "The 1977 Central College Symposium on Puuc Archaeology: A Summary View," in *The Puuc: New Perspectives,* ed. Mills, 48–51; and Chase and Chase, "Postclassic Temporal and Spatial Frames," 11–13. Of these options, the mainstream position, at this

point, is for a partial overlap wherein various components of the Puuc and Toltec traditions overlap in varying durations; that is, the overlap is longest in the realm of ceramics and less in architecture and sculpture. See Andrews and Sabloff, "Classic to Postclassic," 446–49.

231. It is difficult to know the exact origin of the "Old Chichén"/"New Chichén" bifurcation. Edward H. Thompson, owner of the hacienda that included Chichén Itzá from the 1890s to the 1920s, takes credit for recognizing the antiquity and naming "Old Chichén Itzá" in his autobiography, *People of the Serpent,* 251. However, in advance of Thompson, Charnay, *Ancient Cities,* 328–34, had recognized two distinct styles at Chichén Itzá; and forty years before Charnay, Stephens, *Incidents of Travel in Yucatán,* 2: Chapter 17, had done likewise (though both Charnay and Stephens fell short of demarcating two stylistic periods). See Bernal, *History of Mexican Archaeology,* 122. In Tozzer's complex five-stage sequence for Chichén Itzá, this portion of the city is termed "Maya Chichén" or "Chichén I." See Tozzer, *Chichén and Cenote,* 13–15, 23. The Old Chichén/New Chichén designations are still standard in the tourist literature and continue to be plastered on signs around the site.

232. Lincoln, "The Chronology of Chichén Itzá," 141–98. This article is a tremendous help both in chronicling the academic debate over the history of Chichén Itzá and in articulating Lincoln's own position of total overlap. However, the greatest deficiency, from my perspective, is that Lincoln traces virtually every element of the older, "traditional view" of Chichén Itzá (particularly the polarization of Maya and Toltec elements there) to Alfred Tozzer; I have been arguing that, for all of Tozzer's influence and control, he was more a reflection of much older prejudices than an innovator. Lincoln abstains (at least in this article) from any possible historical connection between Chichén Itzá and Tula, Hidalgo.

233. Lincoln, "Chronology at Chichén Itzá," 142–43, argues repeatedly that "ceramic stratigraphy will ultimately prove the key to unraveling the sequence of development at Chichén Itzá" and that the current state of confusion on Chichén chronology owes largely to the nature of the previous work at the site: "[George] Vaillant's pioneering attempt to relate architectural and ceramic stratigraphy [1930s] remains the only one of its kind ever completed at the site." Ibid., 142. Also see ibid., 192–93, n. 4, for an interesting review of aborted attempts at studying the ceramics of Chichén Itzá.

234. Ibid., 153.

235. Ibid.

236. Morley/Brainerd, *Ancient Maya,* 79–80. I attribute the quote to Brainerd because it appears in his 1956 revision of Morley's *Ancient Maya* but not in the 1946 original.

237. Charnay, *Ancient Cities,* 125–26. Based on textual evidence of Veytia, Ixtlilxochitl, Clavijero, and Torquemada, Charnay knits together a confusing historical scenario of a fallen Tula and a Toltec diaspora in several directions, including Yucatán and Guatemala.

238. Ibid., 84–85. This presumably is Charnay's interpretation of the "greater and lesser descents," which are dragged into every reconstruction of the "Mexicanization" of Yucatán.

239. See Ixtlilxochitl, Fernando de Alva, *Obras Históricas* (Mexico: 1892). Prescott, *Conquest of Mexico,* 711, provides one of the earliest discussions of this portion of Ixtlilxochitl's work on the Toltec diaspora.

240. Veytia, *Historia Antiqua de Mexico;* quoted by Charnay, *Ancient Cities,* 81. Also on Veytia, see Bernal, *History of Mexican Archaeology,* 57–58.

241. Catherwood, *Views of Ancient Monuments,* 143–44. Catherwood confines his remarks on the Toltecs to a sole allusion to "the mysterious Toltecs," until the final pages of his work, where he abandons all tentativeness and flings out (on the basis of textual rather than archaeological data) a sweeping Toltec hypothesis. Also on the "Toltecization" of the Mayaland, see Prescott, *Conquest of Mexico,* 14, 711. These works undoubtedly influenced Charnay.

242. Daniel G. Brinton, ed., *The Maya Chronicles,* Library of Aboriginal American Literature, no. 1 (Philadelphia: D. G. Brinton, 1882), 116–18.

243. Juan Galindo (1831) presents another very politicized, nationalistic theory of the "Toltecization" of the Mayaland. See Brunhouse, *In Search of the Maya,* 36, 41–43.

244. Pedro Sánchez de Aguilar, "Informe contra idolorum cultores del obispado de Yucatán," in *Anales del Museo Nacional de Mexico,* period 1, vol. 6 (1982): 13–122 (originally written about 1635); and Diego López de Cogolludo, *Historia de Yucatán* (Madrid, 1688). Both are discussed in regard to the "Mexicanization" issue by Bernal, *History of Mexican Archaeology,* 32–33.

245. Jean Frederic Waldeck, *Voyage Pittoresque et Archéologique dans de Province d'Yucatán Pendant les Années 1834 et 1836* (Paris, 1838). Also see Prescott, *Conquest of Mexico*, 711.

246. Holmes, *Ancient Cities of Mexico*, 105; also see ibid., 120. With respect to diffusion and the Tula-Chichén problem, note that in the early 1950s, Gordon F. Ekholm and Robert Heine-Geldern seized upon the distinctive motifs and styles shared by Tula and Chichén Itzá as a particularly strong bit of evidence for *Asiatic* influences in the Americas. See Wauchope, *Lost Tribes and Sunken Continents*, 93–95, 119.

247. Given the muddle of Central Mexican chronology before the thirties — specifically the erroneous Toltec-Teotihuacán correlation and the disappreciation of Tula, Hidalgo — it is not surprising that Teotihuacános (that is, "Toltecs" supposedly from Teotihuacán rather than Tula) were considered the agents of "Mexicanization" in Yucatán and Guatemala. For instance, Spinden, *Ancient Civilizations of Mexico*, 169–75; Tozzer, "Maya Research," 11; and George Vaillant, "Hidden History," *Natural History* 33 (1933): 618–28, all labor under that misconception. (However, now, in the wake of considerable new evidence of Teotihuacán contact in all areas of the Mayaland, Yucatán included, those misconceptions may prove prophetic. See, in this chapter, "Mobility and Interaction: Unity via Ongoing Relations.") Others, like T. A. Willard (in less-than-rigorously academic work) mistakenly considered the Aztecs to be the agents of "Mexicanization" at Chichén Itzá: "Aztec soldiers marched clear around the rim of the Gulf of Mexico and through the jungle to Chichén Itzá, which was their final destination. Their influence is very evident in the buildings in newer Chichén Itzá." Theodore A. Willard, *The City of the Sacred Well* (New York: The Century Co., 1926), 217–18. To his credit, Willard substitutes "Toltecs" for "Aztecs" in his later work, for instance, idem, *The Lost Empires of the Itzáes and Mayas*, 33, 231. Reygadas Vertiz and Hermann Beyer are two others who, in the 1920s, argued that Mexican influence was Aztec rather than Teotihuacánoid (with Tula, Hidalgo, not yet a serious contender at that point). See Bernal, *History of Mexican Archaeology*, 170.

248. Tozzer, *Chichén and Cenote*, 148.

249. With respect to the so-called League of Mayapán, there are several references in *The Books of Chilam Balam* to a 200-year joint rulership of Yucatán by Chichén Itzá, Mayapán, and Uxmal. Brinton, *Maya Chronicles*, 88, seems to have been the first to call this the "League of Mayapán." Spinden, *Study of Maya Art*, 202; idem, *Ancient Civilizations of Mexico*, 149; Morley, *Ancient Maya*, 2d ed., 83–97, and virtually all Mayanists of that era considered the League to have existed from about 1000 to 1200 C.E. However, eventually, Brainerd's ceramic evidence and Roy's ethnohistorical evidence "proved" that the three cities were *not* contemporaneous and that the League of Mayapán was much later and much shorter — if it, in fact, existed at all. See Tozzer, *Chichén and Cenote*, 46–51. For some reason, in a broad new synthesis of the late Maya era, the term has been retrieved. See Chase and Rice, Introduction to *Lowland Maya Postclassic*, ed. Chase and Rice, 19, 25.

250. Proskouriakoff, *Classic Maya Sculpture*, 170; quoted by Tozzer, *Chichén and Cenote*, 165. The same section of Proskouriakoff's work is now cited repeatedly by advocates for "Toltec"-Puuc overlap as foreshadowing for their own position. See, for example, Andrews and Sabloff, "Classic to Postclassic," 435; and Lincoln, "Chronology of Chichén Itzá," 156. Morley, *Ancient Maya*, 2d ed., 88, had similarly argued for a transitional era.

251. Sigvald Linné, "Archaeological Researches at Teotihuacán, Mexico," *Ethnological Museum of Sweden Publication*, no. 1, n.s. (Stockholm, 1934); quoted by Tozzer, *Chichén and Cenote*, 165. As early as 1841, Stephens, *Incidents of Travel in Central America, Chiapas, and Yucatán*, vol. 2, had suggested a possible common origin for the Maya and Mexicans. See Brunhouse, *In Search of the Maya*, 103. Tozzer, *Chichén and Cenote*, 165, launched a vehement polemic against the supposed existence of "an original Tula [that is, Tollan]" somewhere in Tabasco that fed its culture to both Tula, Hidalgo, and Chichén Itzá.

252. Spinden, *Study of Maya Art*, 212. In Spinden's bizarre and convoluted (re)construction, Quetzalcoatl, one incredible human being, is born in Central Mexico, spends his impressionable youth in Yucatán, where he eventually conquers Chichén Itzá in 1191 C.E. (Quetzalcoatl is one and the same with Hunac Ceel in that episode), and then, at the late date of 1220 C.E., returns with the Itzá to found Tula, Hidalgo, in the image of Chichén Itzá. Spinden, *Ancient Civilizations of Mexico*, 149, 167–75. Joyce (1927), like Spinden a proponent of Maya primacy, held that the Feathered Serpent cult originated in the Maya zone (specifically Copán) and then moved

east to west to Central Mexico (that is, Teotihuacán). Joyce, *Maya and Mexican Art,* 44.

253. Willey, "External Influences on the Lowland Maya," 59, notes that Spinden was the last major scholar to hold to the idea of the Lowland Maya as the *"fons et origo,"* the essential creators of "civilization" (in the higher and refined sense of the term) for the rest of Mesoamerica.

254. For example, in regard to theories of "reverse," or east-to-west migration from Chichén Itzá to Tula, a small guidebook by José Díaz-Bolio, *Ruines de Chichén Itzá,* sold around Yucatán, perpetuates the theory that the Plumed Serpent cult originated among the Maya, traveled north to Mexico, and then was brought back to Yucatán in a more sophisticated form. Considerably newer and more thoroughgoing is the theory of Mexican archaeologist Roman Piña Chan, though he too cites only a couple of his antagonists (namely, Eric Thompson and Samuel Lothrop) and none of his precedents in arguing that the cult of Quetzalcoatl originated in Xochicalco but entered Tula, Hidalgo, only after flourishing in Chichén Itzá; the case is neither well documented nor convincing. Roman Piña Chan, *Chichén Itzá: La Ciudad de los Brujos del Agua* (Mexico: Fondo de Cultura Economica, 1980); also see idem, *Quetzalcoatl: Serpiente Esplumada* (Mexico: Fondo de Cultura Economica, 1977).

255. Kubler originally presented his iconoclastic hypothesis in George Kubler, "Chichén Itzá y Tula," *Estudios de Cultura Maya* 1 (1961): 47–79, but he sticks with the same formulation right through until the latest edition (1984) of his *Art and Architecture of Ancient America*. See ibid., 174–88. Methodologically, it is noteworthy that Kubler's approach to the Tula-Chichén problem is exactly consonant with his more general position that the first order of business for an art historian is to locate a work of art with respect to its historically related precedents and echoes; see Chapter 2 on "Organization by Tradition."

256. Ibid.

257. The direct and famous response to Kubler's heresy is Alberto Ruz Lhuillier, "Chichén Itzá y Tula: Commentaries a un ensayo," *Estudios de Cultura Maya* 2 (1962): 205–23. Reviewing the extreme positions of the day — namely, Jorge Acosta's opinion that Chichén Itzá was a thoroughly non-Maya, integral part of Tula Toltec culture and Kubler's antithetical opinion that Tula was simply a colonial outpost of Chichén — Ruz argues for the more conventional position that the relationship between the two is more complex, but that it is essentially a case of west-to-east, Tula-to-Chichén movement. Methodologically, it is ironic that Ruz especially criticizes Kubler for relying too exclusively on *formal* parallels (and not considering the ethnohistorical sources), because Kubler became the harshest critic against overreliance on strictly formal commonalities in Mesoamerican art. See the discussion of ethnographic analogy and the "principle of disjunction" in Chapter 2.

258. Kubler's perspective, particularly in regard to the cosmopolitan and eclectic character of "Toltec" Chichén Itzá, will become very important in the final third of Chapter 4.

259. It is noteworthy that Jiménez Moreno, "Tula y los Toltecs según las Fuentes Historicas," 81–82, took the standard line on the west-to-east Tula-Chichén connection but is atypical insofar as he uses the references to "Mexicanization" in the Yucatán chronicles and the archaeological documentation of "Toltec" features at Chichén Itzá (such as serpent columns and Atlanteans) to support his more central concern, namely, that the Tollan of tradition is, in fact, Tula, Hidalgo. Jiménez Moreno, ibid., 82, cited as his most important precedent, Walter Krickeberg, who in 1920 described a historical Toltec culture that went east to the Gulf Coast of Tabasco and then spread out in two directions — to Guatemala and Honduras and to northern Yucatán (that is, Chichén Itzá). Jiménez Moreno considered it important in this era (1941) to emphasize that the Mexican influence at Chichén Itzá was from Tula rather than from Teotihuacán.

260. Tozzer, *Chichén and Cenote,* 254–55, nn. 23, 24, 26, 27, has a helpful (though still very confusing) summary of some of the (re)constructions and periodizations for the era of "Toltec" Chichén Itzá that appeared in the forties and fifties; Andrews IV, Armillas, Bernal, Brainerd, Caso, Kroeber, Morley, Pollock, Spinden, Strong, Eric Thompson, and Willey all offer at least one scheme.

261. Tozzer was so preoccupied with presenting other people's theories of the Toltec-Maya problem that it is difficult to ferret out his own position; see ibid., 35, for one of the more succinct summaries of his own five-stage scheme.

262. Ibid., 27. Also see ibid., 148–54.

263. Tozzer considered and rejected the evidence that the Toltec incursion into Chichén Itzá was a violent conquest (ibid., 15–16) and then argued that, "in the same way, the [later and

lesser] Itzá penetration seems to have been unaccompanied by strife, but, on the other hand, there are no traces of welcome on the part of the native population" (ibid., 42) — that is, peaceful but, nonetheless, irreconcilable rather than symbiotic polarity. Morley, *Ancient Maya,* 1st ed., 84, abstained on the issue: "we are left in the dark . . . as to whether the Itzá-Mexican reoccupation of Chichén Itzá was peaceful or whether it was effected by conquest." Thompson, *Rise and Fall of Maya Civilization,* 116–38; Gordon Willey, "Archaeological Theories and Interpretation: New World," in *Anthropology Today: An Encyclopedic Inventory,* ed. A. L. Kroeber (Chicago: University of Chicago Press, 1953), 170–94; Pedro Armillas, "Fortalezas Mexicanas," *Cuadernos Americanos,* 5:5 (1948): 144–63; and Brainerd, *Maya Civilization,* 10, among others, all argued that Late Classic Yucatán and the coming of the Toltecs was a period of strife, warfare, and violent conquest.

264. Tozzer, *Chichén and Cenote,* 53, interprets a reference in *The Chilam Balam of Chumayel* — "three times it was, they say, that foreigners arrived" (*Chilam Balam of Chumayel,* ed. Roys, 84) — to refer to these three waves of "Mexicanization": (1) the bringers of Tula-Toltec culture, possibly under Kukulcán I; (2) the Itzá under Kukulcán II; and (3) the Mexican mercenaries from Tabasco. Countless authors tinker with this notion of Chichén Itzá as "thrice founded." See, for instance, von Hagen, *World of the Maya,* 160–63.

265. Tozzer, *Chichén and Cenote,* 20–64.

266. Eric Thompson, in his review of *Chichén and Cenote* (see n. 8 of this chapter) describes Tozzer's (re)construction of Chichén Itzá history as a "Virginia reel" that could not possibly be correct.

267. Tozzer, *Chichén and Cenote,* 36, 148, describes his reliance on this "ethnic distinction" between Maya and Toltecs in the art at Chichén Itzá. Thompson, review of *Chichén and Cenote,* 119, attacks this method of operating.

268. Ibid.

269. Lincoln, "Chronology of Chichén Itzá," 144, similarly notes that, for all of Tozzer's influence, "archaeologists were never entirely comfortable with this basically art historical reconstruction of events."

270. *Chilam Balam of Chumayel,* ed. Roys, 178.

271. Ibid., 169.

272. Landa, *Relación,* 22. This passage is quoted, for instance, by Tozzer, *Chichén and Cenote,* 37; Thompson, *Rise and Fall of Maya Civilization,* 118; idem, *Maya Archaeologist,* 23; Morley, *Ancient Maya,* 1st ed., 85; Morley/Brainerd, *Ancient Maya,* 80; and von Hagen, *World of the Maya,* 34. Robert Redfield notes that, even among the Maya peoples in the vicinity of Chichén Itzá in the 1930s, there was the recurrent idea that the Itzá were the wise protagonists in stories of the "Good Times" who still dwelled beneath the floors of the ruined cities and would someday return. See Robert Redfield and Alfonso Villa Rojas, *Chan Kom: A Maya Village* (Chicago: University of Chicago Press, 1934), 12; and Robert Redfield, *A Village That Chose Progress: Chan Kom Revisited* (Chicago: University of Chicago Press, 1950), 14.

273. See Charnay, *Ancient Cities,* 323–70.

274. See Thompson, *People of the Serpent,* 193–94. Edward Thompson's idiosyncratic (re)construction of Yucatán history features the Chanes (or "People of Serpent"), a light-skinned, mother culture sort of people who mysteriously landed on the Gulf Coast of Mexico; Chichén Itzá is originally built by the Ulmecas (one branch of the Chanes), and then later invaded by the Toltecs (another branch of the Chanes). See ibid., 20–21, 77–79. Gann, *In an Unknown Land,* 95, though with idiosyncrasies of his own, similarly considers that the Itzá were Chanes. These days there is little mention of the so-called Chanes.

275. A. Barrera Vasquez and S. G. Morley, *The Maya Chronicles,* Publication 585 (Washington: Carnegie Institution of Washington, 1949). Also, for instance, Holmes, *Ancient Cities of Mexico,* 122, implies that the Itzá were simply indigenous Yucatán Maya; Willard, *Lost Empires of the Itzáes and Mayas,* 25, equates the Itzá and "the original Maya"; and Morley, *Ancient Maya,* 1st and 2d eds., assumes that the Itzá were Old Empire Maya. Adrián Recinos, Introduction to *Popol Vuh: The Sacred Book of the Ancient Quiché Maya,* trans. Delia Goetz and Sylvanus G. Morley, from a translation of Adrián Recinos (Norman: University of Oklahoma, 1950), 67–68, generally subscribes to Morley's identification of the Itzá as Old Empire Maya, adding that the idea of a southern origin for the Itzá came originally from seventeenth-century historian Antonio de Herrera. Then Recinos suggests a more original correlation between the Itzá and the tyrannous and legendary Lords of Xibalbá (or the underworld) who figure so prominently in the myths of the *Popol Vuh.* (References to this work will be cited as Recinos, *Popol Vuh.*) M. Wells Jakeman, *The Origins and History of*

the Maya (Los Angeles: Research Publishing Co., 1945), similarly identifies the Itzá with the rulers of the Maya "Old Empire." Eric Thompson rejects that view, claiming instead that the Itzá were the people who introduced the "Mexican" culture at Chichén Itzá (see Thompson's review of Jakeman's book in *American Antiquity* 11 [January 1946]: 205–6) but Jakeman holds his ground in a rebuttal of his own: M. Wells Jakeman, "The Identity of the Itzá," *American Antiquity* 12 (1946): 127–30. Shuman's criticism of Thompson's position some thirty years later likewise returns explicitly to Barrera and Morley's contention that the Itzá were "a people with close cultural links to the Classic Maya." Malcolm K. Shuman, "Archaeology and Ethnohistory: The Case of the Lowland Maya," *Ethnohistory* 24 (Winter 1977): 10.

276. Herbert Joseph Spinden, *Maya Art and Civilization* (Indian Hills, Colo.: Falcon's Wing Press, 1957), 385, issues a direct challenge to Barrera Vasquez's and Morley's claims that the Itzá were Maya.

277. See *Chilam Balam of Chumayel*, ed. Roys; and Roys, "Literary Sources for the History of Mayapán," in Pollock et al., *Mayapán, Yucatán, Mexico*, 25–86. Tozzer, who was a close collaborator with Roys on this problem, concluded in the same vein that the Itzá were "a relatively unimportant Mexican [or more properly Mayanized Mexican] group who arrived in the city [of Chichén Itzá] a few years after it had been 'destroyed' about 1200." Tozzer, *Chichén and Cenote*, 1. Also see ibid., 36. With respect to the controversy over the identity of the Itzá, Tozzer collected the most important ethnohistorical sources and scholars' opinions (before 1941) in one huge footnote. See Tozzer/Landa, 20–22, n. 123.

278. Michael Coe's position with respect to Itzá is discussed in note 296 of this chapter.

279. See Eric Thompson, "A Co-ordination of the History of Chichén Itzá With Ceramic Sequences in Central Mexico," *Revista Mexicana de Estudios Antropológicos* 5 (1941): 97–109; idem, "A Survey of the Maya Area," 2–24; idem, *Rise and Fall of Maya Civilization*, 110–55; George Brainerd, *The Archaeological Ceramics of Yucatán*, University of California, Anthropological Records, vol. 19 (Berkeley, 1958). For a helpful summary, see H.E.D. Pollock, Introduction to Pollock et al., *Mayapán, Yucatán, Mexico*, 4.

280. Somewhat surprisingly, given that his ceramic studies are foundational for this revised view of the Itzá, Brainerd's more popular synthesis of Postclassic Yucatán culture history presents the simple model of a Mexican Toltec invasion of Yucatán and neglects even to mention the Itzá. Brainerd, *Maya Civilization*, 79–88.

281. See Thompson, *Rise and Fall of Maya Civilization*, 116–39, for his 1954 version of the "Mexicanization" of Yucatán.

282. According to Thompson's 1954 scheme, the most obvious architectural manifestation of this pre-Toltec, Itzá period at Chichén Itzá is the inner building of the Castillo, which, he says, is not pure Maya yet shows no evidence of Plumed Serpent rites. Ibid., 119.

283. Ibid., 120, 126.

284. Ibid., 133.

285. Among the more controversial dimensions of this scheme is Thompson's contention that the branch of the Itzá that first conquered Chichén Itzá, though significantly "Mexicanized," was wholly ambivalent toward Kukulcán/Quetzalcoatl and that the religion and imagery of the Feathered Serpent was brought to Chichén Itzá later by the small band of Toltecs who came directly from Mexico. By contrast, Tozzer went to great pains to demonstrate a close relationship between the Itzá and Kukulcán/Quetzalcoatl; "Kukulcán II" was, in fact, according to Tozzer, the one who led the Itzá to Chichén Itzá. Tozzer, *Chichén and Cenote*, 37.

286. See Thompson, *Maya History and Religion*, 3–47.

287. F. V. Scholes and R. L. Roys, *The Maya Chontal Indians of Acalan-Tixchel, A Contribution to the History and Ethnography of the Yucatán Peninsula*, Publication 560 (Washington: Carnegie Institution of Washington, 1948), that is, the Paxbolon papers, is the single most important document for Thompson's Putun hypothesis.

288. With respect to the battle scenes in the murals at Chichén Itzá, Tozzer had relied on differences in the regalia and physiognomy of the combatants to interpret them as conflicts between Toltec and Maya. Thompson, by contrast, argues that the ethnic identification on the murals and reliefs of Chichén has been greatly oversimplified and that, rather than Toltec versus Maya confrontations, they depict conflicts between a variety of different, somewhat Mexicanized, Putun Maya groups. Thompson, *Maya History and Religion*, 17–20. Later interpretations of these murals, specifically by Arthur Miller, will become very important in Chapter

4's discussion of ritual-architectural events in "Toltec" Chichén Itzá.

289. Thompson, *Maya History and Religion,* 45. Thompson himself notes the irony that he is proposing a kind of "New Empire" in the northern Maya area, after so many years as a front-line fighter against Morley's Old and New Empire scheme. Ibid., 46.

290. Ibid., 20–21.

291. Thompson's implication that there was a major disparity between the great corporeal strength of the Putun Itzá and their quite puny contribution in the realm of art and architecture poses a very important methodological problem for this project. The Putun Itzá emerge from Thompson's analysis as commercial geniuses who were either incapable or, more likely, uninterested in constructing monumental architecture. The fugitive Toltecs, on the other hand, almost without material resources, instigated perhaps the greatest building boom in Mesoamerican history. The historical veracity of this scenario aside, it well demonstrates the precariousness of launching an interpretation strictly on the basis of the architectural record; the limitations of architecture as data for the history of religions are discussed somewhat more fully in Chapter 3.

292. Thompson, *Maya History and Religion,* 24.

293. See Thompson, *Rise and Fall of Maya Civilization,* 119.

294. See Thompson, *Maya History and Religion,* 4–5.

295. Thompson's Putun hypothesis is advocated by, for instance, Weaver, *Aztecs, Maya, and Their Predecessors,* 195–228; Henderson, *World of the Ancient Maya,* 202–33; and Joseph W. Ball, "A Coordinate Approach to Northern Maya Prehistory: A.D. 700–1200," *American Antiquity* 39 (1974): 85–93. Significantly, scholars working on the other end of the Tula–Chichén Itzá connection similarly endorse Thompson's Putun hypothesis. Ethnohistorian Nigel Davies does not contribute anything original to the specific history of Chichén Itzá (he leaves that to Eric Thompson), but he does make a unique contribution to the Tula–Chichén Itzá problem by exploring the significance of the interjacent Gulf Coast area, "the crossroads where two worlds met . . . the Tabasco melting pot of Mesoamerica." Specifically, he considers that Tula and Chichén both had an *early* debt to this medial area (the Nonoalca left from Tabasco to go west to Tula, and the Itzá left from the same area to go east to Chichén) and, thus, that their similitude has far deeper roots than is generally appreciated. He concludes that "everything points to the contemporaneity of the two centers . . . [and to] a long continuity of contact rather than merely an early connection which later lost its vigor. . . . [It is] a trans-Mesoamerican cultural marriage." See Davies, *Toltecs Until the Fall of Tula,* 193, 200, 217–26. Later, in passing, Davies refers vaguely to "the extraordinary feat of [Tula] forming an apparent colony in Chichén." Ibid., 343–44, 417. Richard Diehl, archaeologist at Tula, is even more willing to accept Thompson's basic outline of events in Yucatán; however, his discussion of the Tula-Chichén problem is noteworthy because he says, on the one hand, that "the architectural and stylistic similarities between Tula and Chichén Itzá are so strong that they suggest a close and enduring relationship"; yet, on the other hand, he has been unable to find any Yucatán products at Tula, a contradiction that he explains by saying that the two centers "may have maintained an active trade which simply does not come to light in the archaeological record." See Diehl, *Tula,* 144–52.

296. Coe, *Maya,* 121–37. Coe's version of the events is very like that proposed by Tozzer. He holds that Topilitzin Quetzalcoatl (Kukulcán I) was exiled from Tula in 987 C.E., whereupon he, together with his force of "grim militarists," "wrests Yucatán from its rightful owners and established his capital at Chichén Itzá." (Thompson also believed that the Tula Toltecs arrived in Chichén Itzá in 987 C.E., though under the sponsorship of the Putun Itzá.) According to Coe, following their brutal takeover, the Toltecs rebuilt Chichén Itzá as a facsimile of Tula, instigated foreign religious practices — notably idolatry, religio-military orders, and human sacrifice — and fashioned the city into the supreme metropolis of a united Yucatán kingdom. For all their successes, around 1224 C.E. the Toltecs (for no reason that is apparent to Coe) abandoned Chichén Itzá and "they are heard of no more." Then, and only then, did the Itzá take the stage. In contrast to Thompson's virile Putun Itzá entrepreneurs, Coe defames the Itzá as transient derelicts led by a self-christened Kukulcán II, a "wretched band of warriors, [who] found their way up the coast and across to Chichén Itzá, where they settled as squatters in the desolate city in Katun 4 Ahau (A.D. 1224–44)." After a brief and uneventful tenure at Chichén Itzá, the Itzá, enamored of the Toltec heritage, built a shoddy imitation

of Toltec Chichén Itzá at Mayapán. Coe presents this (re)construction in the first edition of *Maya* (1966), that is, before Thompson's presentation of the Putun hypothesis, and reiterates it in the second (1980) and third (1984) editions.

297. Because Coe's *Maya* and Thompson's *Maya History and Religion* — still among the two most widely read general works on the Maya — present such widely disparate views of the history of the Itzá, Toltecs, and Chichén Itzá, the casual reader can only be bewildered. Charles Gallenkamp, *Maya: The Riddle and Rediscovery of a Lost Civilization,* 2d rev. ed. (New York: Penguin Books, 1981), 177–78, has a helpfully concise comparison of the two positions. Adamson, *Ruins of Time,* 43–44, notes the dispute between Thompson and Coe but dismisses it as "a fairly pedantic issue."

298. Arthur G. Miller, "Captains of the Itzás: Unpublished Mural Evidence From Chichén Itzá," in *Social Process in Maya Prehistory: Studies in Honour of Sir Eric Thompson,* ed. Norman Hammond (London: Academic Press, 1977), 222. Miller follows R.E.W. Adams in this assessment; see the next note. Similarly, Tatiana Proskouriakoff, "On Two Inscriptions at Chichén Itzá," in *Monographs and Papers in Maya Archaeology,* ed. William R. Bullard, Jr. (Cambridge, Mass.: Harvard University, 1970), suggests that the Itzá very possibly represent a military or political confederation of several groups rather than a single ethnic group.

299. Andrews and Robles, "Chichén Itzá and Cobá," 62. Similarly, R.E.W. Adams, "Maya Collapse: Transformation and Termination in the Ceramic Sequence at Altar de Sacrificios," in *The Classic Maya Collapse,* ed. T. P. Culbert (Albuquerque: University of New Mexico Press, 1973), 156–58, criticizes Thompson's overreliance on ethnohistorical sources and his failure to reconcile his argument with the archaeological data.

300. Sabloff and Andrews, Introduction to *Late Lowland Maya Civilization,* 9.

301. Thompson was decidedly old-fashioned insofar as he was never impressed by the vogue for social and cultural "processes" that has dominated Mesoamerican archaeology since the 1960s. The respective goals of traditional archaeology and the "new archaeology" are discussed in Chapter 2.

302. Andrews and Robles, "Chichén Itzá and Cobá," 64.

303. Carmack, who is primarily interested in explaining the very strong Mexican strain among the Highland Maya of Guatemala, argues that "Putun merchant" types were responsible for the first invasion of Chichén Itzá, but that "Epi-Toltec warrior" types were responsible for the second Chichén Itzá invasion as well as the Quiché empire of the Guatemalan Highlands. He also argues, against Thompson, that both groups were devoted to the Feathered Serpent religion. Carmack, *Quiché Mayas of Utatlán,* 43–51.

304. Thompson, *Maya History and Religion,* 48.

305. Summarizing the archaeological work at Tula, Richard Diehl (in 1981) admits that "the political relationships between Tula and Southern Mesoamerica, including Chichén Itzá, remain as poorly understood as ever." Diehl, "Tula," 291. Among the most important developments with regard specifically to the Tula–Chichén Itzá connection is Nigel Davies's very uncertain contention, on the basis of ethnohistorical evidence, that the original creative genius behind Tula's art, architecture, religion, and polity came from the Nonoalca, an ethnic group originating in the same general Gulf Coast region as the Itzá "founders" of Toltec Chichén Itzá. See Davies, *Toltecs Until the Fall of Tula,* 193, 200. The implications are explored in Chapter 4's "The Ritual-Architectural Events of Tula."

306. Chase and Rice, Preface to *Lowland Maya Postclassic,* ed. Chase and Rice, 2. Sabloff and Andrews, Introduction, similarly applaud the "wholesale changes" and long-overdue appreciation of the considerable creativity and vitality of the post–800 C.E. era in Maya development.

307. Freidel, "New Light on the Dark Age," 285–310, isolates these three general themes. With some shifts and twists, I follow his basic organization, but the emphases on challenges to Maya-Mexican polarity and the implications for "Toltec" Chichén Itzá are my own.

308. Henderson, *World of the Ancient Maya,* 202–4, is a good example of the attempt to appreciate the continuities between Classic and Postclassic Maya societies.

309. Andrews and Robles, "Chichén Itzá and Cobá," 65–67; discussed by Freidel, "New Light on the Dark Age," 287. They are concerned particularly with contrasting the "foreign" polity of Chichén Itzá with the indigenous Maya polity of Cobá, just 60 miles to the east.

310. Freidel, "New Light on the Dark Age," 288, cites Joseph Ball, Diane Chase, Arlen Chase, and Charles Lincoln as supporters of his position.

311. In his 1985 summary, Freidel emphasizes the overlap between "Toltec" Chichén Itzá and the Terminal Classic sites to the south, but he continues to speak of "Toltec" Chichén Itzá as an Early Postclassic site. See ibid., 288–93. However, as discussed earlier, the consensus view of *Late Lowland Maya Civilization,* ed. Sabloff and Andrews (1986), is that "Toltec" Chichén Itzá is more appropriately classed as Terminal Classic rather than as Early Postclassic.

312. Henderson, *World of the Ancient Maya,* 215. Among the many others who hold that Chichén Itzá enjoyed uncontested supremacy in Yucatán are Weaver, *Aztecs, Maya, and Their Predecessors,* 227; Carrasco, *Quetzalcoatl and the Irony of Empire,* 140–41; and Coe, *Maya,* 122.

313. The overlap issue was discussed somewhat more fully earlier in relation to Chichén Itzá chronology. For early summaries of the overlap model, see Ball, "Ceramics, Culture History, and the Puuc Tradition"; and idem, "Symposium on Puuc Archaeology." More recently, Chase and Chase, "Postclassic Temporal and Spatial Frames," 17–20, have been particularly concerned with redefining the Postclassic by advocating a model of "intensive and extensive regional variation." Also see Freidel, "New Light on the Dark Age," 304–8.

314. As discussed earlier, Brinton's (1882) — and then Spinden's (1928) and Morley's (1946) — conception of Chichén Itzá as a partner with Uxmal and Mayapán in the famed "League of Mayapán" was annulled when it was "proved" that the centers belonged to three different epochs. The new overlap model, in a very general sense, revives the possibility of some sort of "league" or confederation, particularly between Chichén and Uxmal.

315. Andrews and Robles, "Chichén Itzá and Cobá," are arguing that the leitmotif of Early Postclassic Yucatán (900–1200 C.E.) was a standoff between foreign-dominated Chichén Itzá and Cobá, with its basically indigenous polity.

316. For instance, Freidel, "New Light on the Dark Age," 287.

317. Kenneth Brown concludes, writing in 1985, that "the whole question of Toltec influence and Chichén Itzá needs to be reopened and investigated." Kenneth L. Brown, "Postclassic Relationships Between the Highland and Lowland Maya," 280.

318. Freidel, "New Light on the Dark Age," 299–304. In fact, of late, Schele and Miller, *Blood of Kings,* 9, suggest, on the basis of recent work at Copán by William Fash, that Middle Preclassic Maya seized upon Olmec imagery (to which they had no literal connection) as "the most effective expression of their newly emerging social structure" — that is to say, the early Maya were involved in a process of validation via contrived pedigrees very like the appeal to "Toltec" heritage at Chichén Itzá and elsewhere — thus, it is quite possible that the lords of "Toltec" Chichén Itzá were reviving an old Maya strategy rather than importing a Mexican one.

319. While, given the new ground rules, this seems to me the easiest, most reasonable scenario for the Tula-Chichén connection (and I will present the evidence and qualifications much more fully in Chapter 4; see especially the section entitled "Chichén as Active Receptor: A Historical Hypothesis"), I find no one else explicitly exploring this possibility with any thoroughness. Clemency Coggins, "New Fire at Chichén Itzá"; and idem, "A New Sun at Chichén Itzá" (also discussed more fully in Chapter 4) is probably the closest.

320. As noted, this possibility will be fleshed out in some detail in Chapter 4.

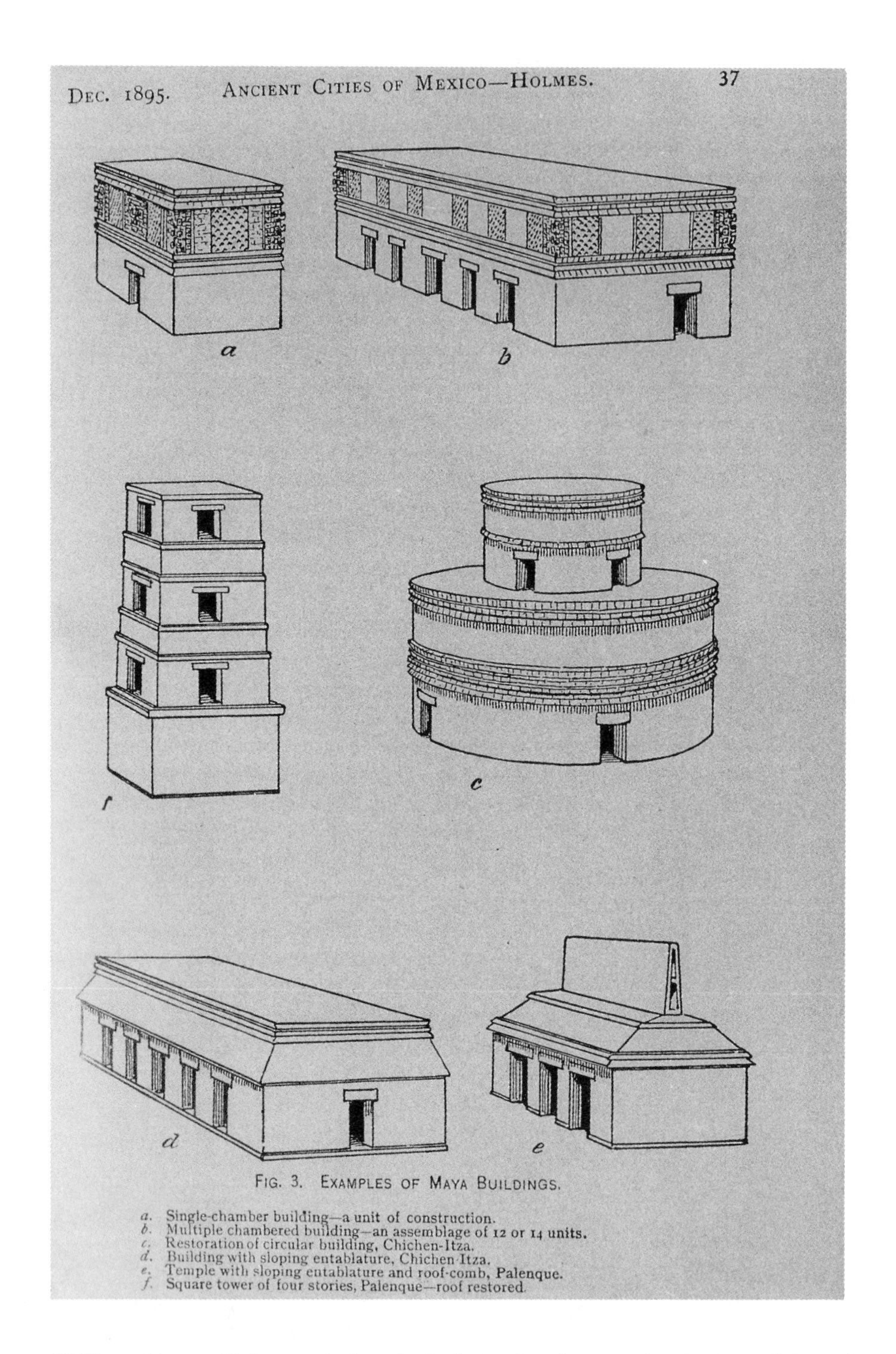

William Henry Holmes, *Archaeological Studies Among the Ancient Cities of Mexico* (1895–97), arranges his meticulous reconstruction drawings of Maya "building types" according to the following scheme: *a.* single-chamber building; *b.* multiple-chambered building; *c.* circular building, Chichén Itzá; *d.* building with sloping entablature, Chichén Itzá; *e.* temple with sloping entablature and roof comb, Palenque; and *f.* square tower of four stories, Palenque. (William H. Holmes, *Archaeological Studies Among the Ancient Cities of Mexico*.)

Chapter Two

Insignificant Organization: Reflections on the Study and Comparison of Mesoamerican Architecture

> In the case of the Maya, the art might almost be termed the concrete expression of the religion, since all the great monuments were apparently connected with religious practices and no minor object was too humble to receive decorations with religious significance. Clearly this wonderful art rose under the communal inspiration of a great religious awakening and was conserved by the persistence of ritual.
>
> *Herbert Spinden, 1913*[1]

Agenda: The Necessity of Generalization

Herbert Spinden well exemplifies the nearly unanimous tacit assumption of the past half-millennium: namely, that the splendorous pre-Columbian monuments of Mesoamerica are, as he says, "the concrete expression of the religion," massive buildings born of religious inspiration and "conserved by the persistence of ritual."[2] The nearly total consensus that "all the great monuments were apparently connected with religious practices" notwithstanding, disappointingly few historians of religions (students of *Religionswissenschaft* anyway) have embraced this area as their special concern.[3] The comparative methods and theoretical perspectives characteristic of historians of religions (to the extent that there is a shared set of methods and questions) have seldom been exercised in relation to the historical materials of ancient Mesoamerica, architectural or otherwise. And thus, coming to the field decidedly as an outsider, the historian of religions who is deeply concerned with the hermeneutical interpretation of religious meanings and with comparison cannot help but find the standard literature on pre-Columbian architecture at once fascinating and frustrating in the extreme.

Accordingly, where the preceding chapter explored the status of the specific, historical problem — that is, the uncanny similitude between the ruins of Tula and Chichén Itzá — this chapter takes aim at the more general, methodological problem concerning the ways in which scholars have (or might in the future) make sense of Mesoamerica's ostensibly religious architecture.[4] This section is a critical survey of past studies of pre-Columbian architecture, a reconnaissance of methodological adversaries and allies in my own interpretive mission. The simple premise here is that in order to understand and, even more, to compare religio-historical phenomena (including sacred architectures), scholars of every disciplinary perspective must adopt some principle of organization that, while respecting specific manifestations, drives beyond the idiosyncrasies and uniqueness of particular cases to some more manageable level of generality.[5] The interpretive generalizations regarding Mesoamerican buildings that serve archaeology, for instance, may prove inconsequential, unrewarding, or even distorting from the perspective of the history of religions (as they often do), but, in either case, some measure of generalization is unavoidable. Scholars of every theoretical orientation, albeit in very different ways and to very different ends, are compelled to utilize, however provisionally, some strategy of what G. van der Leeuw termed "significant organization."[6] Students of pre-Columbian architecture are certainly no exception. In fact, nowhere has the awkwardness of finding some sort of satisfying arrangement or heuristically rewarding classificatory scheme demonstrated itself more acutely than in the study of a Mesoamerican landscape that is literally strewn with thousands of pre-Hispanic buildings of all sizes and configurations, in all states of repair and disrepair, each with a convoluted and largely unknown story of its own.

By way of chronicling the struggle of Mesoamericanists for workable and significant principles to organize the plethora and diversity of ruined monuments (before looking ahead to my own alternative principles of organization), this chapter rummages through a hundred years of literature on pre-Columbian art and architecture, looking from a different angle at many of the older secondary sources enlisted in the previous chapter. By no stretch an annotated bibliography, nor a synopsis of state-of-the-art Mesoamericanist methodology, it persists in the longer view of the previous chapter by reflecting upon the methods and presuppositions of the foundational "great books" on Mesoamerican art and architecture.[7] A sweeping survey of currents and tendencies, it asks who has studied Mesoamerican architecture and how. It endeavors to map, from the perspective of a historian of religions, both the pitfalls and the promising points of departure.

Yet, because the study of Mesoamerican architecture has not evolved along anything like a straight line of progress, the arrangement of this chapter itself becomes a challenge in significant organization. The product of several tested and rejected *chronological* schemes, the chapter instead passes over the literature on pre-Columbian architecture two times in a *thematic* fashion. The first portion reviews four major streams of Mesoamerican scholarship — traditional archaeology, "new archaeology," art history, and ethnohistory — and considers the potentialities of each for contributing to the sort of hermeneutical, "eventful" approach to Mesoamerican sacred architecture that will be presented in the latter sections of this project. The second portion surveys the various classificatory schemes by which scholars of those four streams have variously attempted to tame the diversity of Mesoamerican architecture. Seven different principles of organization are identified: (1) form, what the buildings look like; (2) technique, how and of what they are made; (3) time, when they were built; (4) function, what transpired in the buildings; (5) geography, building locations and relationships to the natural environment; (6) culture, the evolutionary attainments of their builders; and (7) tradition, that is, organization in terms of chains of historically related buildings.[8]

Each of these alternatives, obvious though they seem, has been embraced, at one time or another, as the definitive criterion for comparing and understanding the plurality of Mesoamerican architecture. While this perusal of the secondary literature advances the specific comparison of the architectures of Tula and Chichén Itzá only in very indirect ways (and readers concerned strictly with those two sites might even pass this whole exercise by), it does bring to the fore the more general theoretical problem: namely, that the comparison and organization of Mesoamerican architecture has seldom been, from the perspective of a comparative history of religions, "significant organization."

Streams of Scholarship

> Second "Round Table" seminar [Mexico City, 1965]. There is also the anthropology professor, Jiménez Moreno, a specialist on Central America. He says some interesting things, but always stays on the descriptive and empirical level. Every time I tried to go further into interpretation and asked him what *meaning* all these religious facts could have, Moreno would agree with me, would seem delighted, but wouldn't continue the hermeneutic on that level. He would always go back to the "documents," to the "sources."
>
> *Mircea Eliade, 1965*[9]

Traditional Archaeology: Beyond Antiquarianism

> I do not know what temptations bedevil workers in other fields, but I can hardly believe that there open before physicists or chemists, biologists, or even psychologists, so many such alluring primrose paths, leading to scientific damnation, as there do to archeologists.
>
> *Alfred V. Kidder, 1937*[10]

The study of pre-Columbian American art and architecture, unlike the antique art of the Old World, has, from its inception as a professional academic enterprise, been dominated by archaeology and anthropology.[11] Around the turn of the century, the embryonic discipline of archaeology was the first strain of scholarship that worked vigorously and deliberately to constitute itself as a "legitimate" scientific enterprise, thoroughly disassociated from the nineteenth-century antiquarian fanaticism of Count Waldeck, Brasseur de Bourbourg, Doctor Le Plongeon, and Charnay.[12] That archaeological tutelage, which persists even now as the mainstream of Mesoamericanist scholarship, colors the orientation of the whole field and is thus largely responsible for both the affinities and the discontents that historians of religions (and others) feel in relation to the standard literature.

This ascent from causal inquisitiveness to scientific respectability depended from the earliest beginnings upon, as it were, "the play of the slash," or, more properly, two slashes.[13] The first is the slash between objective and subjective, the second between universal and particular (or between systematic and historical). The deft resolution of these two dichotomies — objective/subjective and universal/particular — albeit an imperfect resolution, forms the basis of the unwritten methodological charter that allowed the fledgling "professional" Americanists to distance themselves from their freewheeling predecessors.

In the case of the objective/subjective dichotomy, professionalism in archaeology and anthropology, from the outset, demanded a commitment to dispassionate and unadulterated objectivity.[14] A priori harangues about lost tribes, sunken continents, and ubiquitous Toltecs were drowned in a refrain of "let the facts speak."[15] Grand theorizing — in fact (presumably anyway), any theorizing — was jettisoned in favor of the meticulous collection of empirical data. From the end of the nineteenth century, armchair anthropologizing and premature speculation were counterpoised to a plea for specificity and the accumulation of "hard evidence." The untenability of "pure objectivity" notwithstanding, this policy has, in the last hundred years, engendered a stupendous cornucopia of "raw data" and ever more reliable chronological sequences. On this front, then, progress has been cumulative and unrelenting.

The slash between universal and particular has proven infinitely more problematic for Mesoamericanists. Turn-of-the-century rejection of grand theorizing on flimsy evidence was accompanied by an equally fervent disdain for the idiosyncratic catalogue of "specimens" and for excavation in the interest of filling out the curios collections in which antiquarians typically displayed their pre-Columbian treasures. If "scientific archaeology" had become, by 1900, "essentially . . . the study of objects,"[16] there was, from the earliest period, near-total unanimity that to be academically respectable, Americanist archaeology must transcend "mere description" in favor of a more synthetic, universalistic goal. The antiquarian tradition looked upon the architectural ruins of Middle America and their contexts as fascinating relics of an undifferentiated, "far away and long ago" past; antiquarians, according to the critique of their more academic heirs, stocked museum shelves but failed to fit the monuments and artifacts into any coherent, diachronic history. A scientific archaeology must do more.

Nevertheless, despite their deep discontent with the random display of artifacts, early Americanist scholars had great difficulty finding more academically reputable means of presenting their pre-Columbian discoveries. This vexing matter of "significantly organizing" an ever-mounting fund of empirical data — that is, finding some satisfactory resolution to the universal/particular problem — is never laid to rest. Where the rigor of the early positivists — Eduard Seler, Alfred Maudslay, William Holmes, and Franz Boas — did effectively slay the nemesis of premature theorizing and nonempirical speculation (a resolution of the objective/subjective problem), they were not nearly so successful in their initiative to move beyond the antiquarian, orderless collection and display of isolated relics (architectural monuments included) to some more generalized picture of pre-Hispanic life.

This interpretive deficiency did not, however, go unnoticed. From the teens through the forties, with the ideal of objective inquiry by then securely in place, Alfred V. Kidder spearheaded a movement in Americanist archaeology that focused on the slash between universal and particular. Targeting "historical particularism" (pejoratively described as the amassing of isolated facts and artifacts) as his methodological foil, Kidder argued that empirical rigor was only the first step. For him, the post-antiquarian legitimation of Americanist archaeology depended on "the transition from things, to what things mean"; excavationary finds could not simply be shelved and admired but instead must be interpreted just as written texts, that is, as "historical documents."[17] Moreover, particularistic archaeological discoveries about the indigenous peoples of the Americas were significant for Kidder to the extent that they opened the way to resolving larger questions. The professional archaeology to which he aspired would be, at its core, an interpretive, generalizing, synthetic enterprise — "a comprehensive comparative examination of the ways of mankind."[18] To be seduced by specialization, by "mere description," or by hyper-particularity (as he saw many of his colleagues doing) was, in his eyes, to fail in one's scientific mission. Kidder warned, for instance, in 1924, that

> we must be careful to hold ourselves to a proper balance between the detailed and the general. The details of archaeology are in themselves so interesting that it is fatally easy to become completely absorbed in them, and there is always the excuse that without close and accurate work one cannot arrive at trustworthy conclusions. The result is that too often one arrives at no conclusion at all.[19]

Most historians of religions (as well as anthropologists and archaeologists) would applaud Kidder's ambitious plea for synthetic conclusions. Even Boas, the scholar most tightly associated with "historical particularism," had considered that the analysis of particular entities was ultimately intended only as a means to understanding culture in general, its status and dynamics, its form and function, its general laws, and especially its "history."[20] Yet, where the positivistic solution to the objective/subjective tension eventuates in reams of empirical data about the pre-Columbian past, by contrast, the praiseworthy rhetoric on the slash between particular and universal, and the almost unanimous calls to transcend collection and description in favor of more satisfyingly general insights into ancient Mesoamerica, have been woefully unproductive.

There was, for decades (as subsequent Americanists would be forced to admit), no systematic interpretation of Mesoamerican archaeological finds (including architecture) from any point of view — cultural, religious, or otherwise. Herein lies the fundamental frustration (or perhaps potential) for the historian of religions in Mesoamerican studies (and the fundamental impediment to the sort of hermeneutical, "eventful" approach to pre-Columbian architecture advocated in the following chapters). In Joachim Wach's old formulation: the empirical, historical, or particularistic branch of Mesoamerican studies has thrived while the "systematic" or interpretive branch has, with irregular exceptions, starved.[21] Reconciliation of the empirical bonanza of architectural and other sorts of pre-Columbian remains unearthed in Mesoamerica with any systematic mode of interpretation simply does not (and cannot) happen within the confines of this early positivistic archaeology.[22] To paraphrase (and perhaps caricature) their detractors, traditional archaeologists dig up the buildings of Mesoamerica and lay before us a bounty of copious descriptions of those buildings' formal and constructional attributes, a meticulous charting of the geographical incidence of those attributes, and an impressive accuracy in dating; but nothing happens and no one lives in those descriptions. Loathe to compromise their "objectivity" and repeat the speculatory modes of their antiquarian predecessors, ruminations on the pre-Columbian usages, the native perceptions, let alone the religious meanings of those buildings are, for the positivistic archaeologists, largely out of bounds.[23]

With respect specifically to the study of Chichén Itzá — a perfect microcosm of the wider situation — the transition from antiquarianism to professional archaeology is personified in the stark contrast between the seminal figures of Edward Herbert Thompson and Alfred Tozzer. Thompson, resident curator of Chichén Itzá from 1885–1923, the "last of the great amateurs," was the undisputed expert on the site in his era.[24] While his unschooled assessments of the city's origins and antiquity were quite reasonable, Thompson was, nonetheless, unabashed in his romanticization and celebration of the impenetrable, "mist-enshrouded" history of Chichén. Disinclined to publish much himself,[25] Thompson's accomplishments are eulogized in T. A. Willard's none-too-rigorous *The City of the Sacred Well: Being a Narrative of the Discoveries and Excavations of Edward Herbert Thompson in the Ancient City of Chi-chen Itza . . .* (1926), wherein readers learn, for instance, that "there is not in all the world a metropolis living or dead more mysterious, more dowered with romance [than Chichén Itzá]. Its age, its origin, even the racial identity of its builders, are each and all sunk in mystery so profound that I doubt if we shall ever fathom them."[26]

Tozzer's style is very different, to say the least. In his tactful review of Willard's book (entitled "Architecture and Romance"), Tozzer does applaud the work as a needed popular contribution, but then he expresses his deep reservations about this sort of mystification of both archaeology and the ancient Maya. He explains that Thompson, whom he knew and respected, "belongs to the Romantic School of Archaeology — every human being thrown into the well was necessarily a virgin and every descent into a cavern was accompanied by an encounter with huge boa-constrictors, sometimes fourteen and fifteen feet long. Mauve-colored doves and sweet-smelling orchids meet one on every hand."[27] Thus, in the 1920s, when Tozzer took the reigns as the premier expert on Chichén Itzá and paved the way for the Carnegie Institution's major work there, he vehemently rejected the casual tone and romantic musings of Thompson and Willard, endeavoring, by contrast, to put the study of the ancient city on a more respectable, rigorously empirical foundation (a somewhat ironic claim given Tozzer's own creative imaginings of the Maya). Methodologically more cautious than innovative,[28] Tozzer's massive work on Chichén Itzá, while subtitled *A Comparative Study of Contemporaneous Maya and Toltec,* espoused a concept of comparison that was really only an encyclopedic file on the geographical distribution of cultural traits. Awe-inspiring as a tome of description and classification, it is, in Eric Thompson's apt assessment, "the approach of the teacher who wants to put everything on the blackboard — cram the boys with solid facts."[29] Thus, in short, with regard to Chichén Itzá and, in fact, Maya studies in general, Tozzer, and then Morley and the Carnegie Institution archaeologists, represent the mainstream of traditional archaeology, the group that confirms Mesoamerican studies' solid professional, "scientific" foundation, and the group that later draws fire for limitedness in interpretation and synthesis.[30]

In sum then, all of the claims to objectivity and "pure description" among this early generation of Mesoamericanists, of course, provide easy targets for the postmodern criticisms of the 1990s; their positivistic solution to the objectivity/subjectivity problem, while fruitful for several decades, is hardly fashionable now. Yet, closer to home, even within the deeper history of pre-Columbian studies (where this survey aims), and among Mesoamericanists who are similarly attached to these same positivistic presuppositions, there has long been a vigorous chorus of malcontent with the interpretive lethargy of traditional Mesoamerican archaeology. In the past half century, serious reservations issue particularly from three disciplinary fronts: (1) from within Mesoamerican archaeology itself, (2) from art history, and (3) from ethnohistory. (Historians of religion seldom even engage the area.) Because none of these three strains speaks with a unified or invariant voice, and because each has its own special interests, the energetic trialogue between "new archaeology," art history, and ethnohistory is a record of fragile alliances and resigned coexistences. Circling above the fray (with the special interests of a historian of religions), the following three sections consider in turn each of these constructive challenges to the conservative policies of post-antiquarian Middle American archaeology and, more specifically, the potential of each to contribute to a hermeneutical understanding of the religious architecture of Mesoamerica.

Edward Herbert Thompson, with his dredge at the Sacred Cenote in 1907. From 1885 to 1923, Thompson, "the last of the great amateurs," was the resident proprietor of the hacienda that encompassed the ruins of Chichén Itzá. Among his many exploratory projects, the most spectacular involved constructing this derrick with a hand windlass and a long boom that could be swung out over the cenote in order to lower a steel buck-scoop or bucket down to the subterranean floor of the well. Though they recovered an enormous fund of artifacts, along with some human bones and skulls, these rambunctious efforts were likewise lamentably destructive. (Carnegie Institution of Washington photo, courtesy of the Peabody Museum, Harvard University.)

At the rim of the Sacred Cenote. After several years of intermittent dredging for treasure with a derrick and steel buck-scoop, *left*, in 1909, Edward Thompson recruited Greek divers and a crew of Maya assistants to launch this diving expedition into the cenote. Thompson himself also donned a diving helmet and made the descent to the bottom of the well, hoping to retrieve objects that had eluded the dredging operation. (Courtesy of the Peabody Museum, Harvard University.)

"New Archaeology": Anthropological Goals

> Archaeology, in the service of anthropology, concerns itself necessarily with the nature and position of unique events in space and time but has for its ultimate purpose the discovery of regularities that are in a sense spaceless and timeless.
>
> *Gordon Willey and Philip Phillips, 1958*[31]

The most stinging dissatisfaction with the interpretive poverty of traditional Mesoamerican excavationary archaeology comes from within the discipline itself. In 1940, a notoriously critical review by Clyde Kluckhohn of the theoretical basis of Middle America archaeology dispraised the hollowness of gathering data but ignoring the potential for transempirical interpretation — an archaeology "which is on the intellectual level of stamp collecting."[32] His conclusion is blunt and irrefutable: "The very sophistication at the levels of method and technique (i.e., surveying,

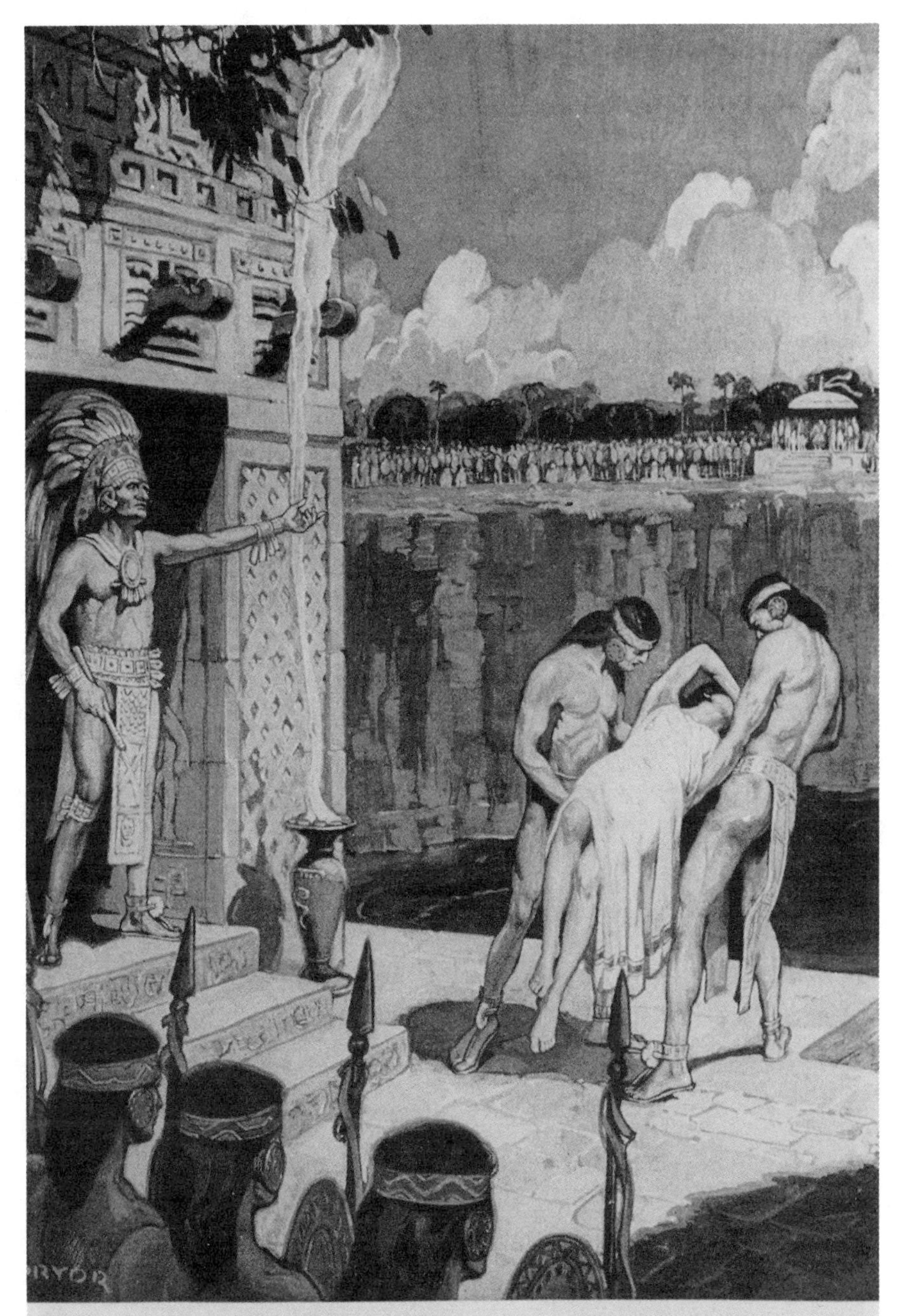

A last forward swing and the bride of Yum Chac hurtles far out over the well."

Antiquarian speculations regarding the religious practices of the pre-Columbian Maya are by no means confined to the nineteenth century. T. A. Willard, *The City of the Sacred Well* (1926), for instance, accompanies this imaginative rendering of human sacrifice at the Sacred Cenote of Chichén Itzá with the following incautious explanation: "A last forward swing and the bride of Yum Chac hurtles far out over the well." Present-day visitors to Yucatán can confirm that such interpretive liberties continue to be exercised on a daily basis. (T. A. Willard, *The City of the Sacred Well*.)

photographing, field cataloging and the like) makes the methodological and theoretical naïveté of Middle American studies stand out in shocking contrast. . . . Factual richness and conceptual poverty are a poor pair of hosts at an intellectual banquet."[33]

Kluckhohn's student, Walter W. Taylor, elaborated on his mentor's discontent with an archaeology obsessed with chronology and stalled at the level of "comparative chronicle."[34] Taking Kidder and the Carnegie Institution as his principal foils (and thus placing the study of Chichén Itzá at the very center of the controversy), Taylor lamented that, while Kidder talked a synthetic and expansively anthropological archaeology (Kidder had replaced Morley as the head of the Carnegie Maya project in 1929), he failed to deliver anything like a true "culture history" of the Maya.[35] Of the disappointing disparity between Kidder's methodological goals and the actual contribution his team was able to make through the fieldwork under his direction (a disparity that Kidder himself fully acknowledged), Taylor writes: "there is little or no conformity. To date, no cultural synthesis, no picture of the life of any site or any group of sites, has come from his pen. Nor has he used his empirical data to analyze or discuss specifically and detail any cultural process, regularity, 'law,' or so-called non-material aspect. He has 'done' neither historiography nor cultural anthropology."[36] The indictment is well taken. Unfortunately, however, Taylor likewise suffered from an inability to operationalize his methodological ambitions. His own alternative, a synthesis of paleoecological and archaeological data called the "conjunctive approach," proved similarly ineffectual in practice.[37]

The frustrations of these early critics of traditional Mesoamerican archaeology demonstrate, among other things, the extreme difficulty with which the discipline was able to transcend its descriptive, particularistic habits. The elusive goal for Kidder, Kluckhohn, and Taylor was to write "culture history to the full extent of the data," to achieve reconstructions of prehistoric life on the order of the descriptions of existing cultures being collected by ethnographers. Relative to the study of pre-Columbian architecture, success in that agendum would have merged very near to the concept of an "architectural event" (presented in the following chapter and pursued for the rest of this project), providing insights into the interrelations between the built, the natural, and the socioeconomic environments; into the activities and performances that transpired in the buildings; and even into the religious and psychological dispositions of the human users. Yet, when, in the 1960s, the priorities of the traditional archaeology were finally superseded by the ballyhooed "new archaeology" — a genuine revolution in the methodological orientation of Mesoamerican studies — the bounty for such an "eventful" approach to pre-Hispanic architecture was actually quite lean.[38]

Contrary to the "pictures of culture life" to which Kluckhohn and Taylor aspired, the so-called new archaeology concerns itself with laws of cultural change and what are perceived as evolutionary relationships between measurable systems such as trade, population growth, social organizations, and the resources of particular environments. Welcomed progress aside, two aspects of the new archaeological orientation seriously restrict its contribution to the sort of study of pre-Columbian art and architecture that might content hermeneutically based historians of religions.

The first obstacle derives from the fact that, as a cure to their interpretive malaise, the new archaeologists imbibe heavily of materialist doctrines, particularly those of V. Gordon Childe on Near Eastern and European cultural beginnings.[39] Having fortified their theoretical orientation in this way, they invariably explain the dynamics of New World civilizations by focusing on what Julian Stewart calls the "cultural core": cultural-ecological adaptations, technological-economic-demographic systemic patterns and articulations.[40] In so doing, this strain of archaeology either relegates to a derivative, "secondary" status — or ignores entirely — the ideological, aesthetic, and religious dimensions of the ancient cultures they are investigating.[41] William Sanders and Barbara Price, for instance, two of the key players in this movement, are completely forthright regarding this materialistic arrangement of priorities: combining Leslie White's neo-evolutionary line with Childe's notion of cultural "revolutions," they hold that "the non-material aspects of culture [including art and religion] have evolved as adaptations to technological revolutions."[42] This "Marxist-materialist" approach to pre-Hispanic Mesoamerica (if prefiguring certain deconstructivist tendencies currently making their way into the field) is hardly congenial to studies that insist on seeing pre-Columbian art and architecture as primary, and largely autonomous, rather than derivative of socio-technical developments. Moreover, this materialist orientation is even less congenial toward approaches to pre-Columbian architecture (like the one advocated in this book) that demand center place for the nonmaterial aspects of ritual performance and users' preunderstandings.[43]

The second major deterrent to a hermeneutical, "eventful" approach to Mesoamerican architecture is the thoroughness with which the new archaeologists abandon the particular for the universal. Reacting against the extreme particularity of their positivistic predecessors (a complaint that traces back at least to Kidder), the new archaeological passion is for abstract theoretical models and the postulation of generalized cultural "laws" that can be tested in excavation. The description or plausible explanation of a sequence of historical events is of interest to systems theorists only insofar as it illustrates generalizable evolutionary processes.[44] As Willey and Phillips explain, anthropological archaeology (that is, the "new archaeology") necessarily concerns itself with unique events, but its ultimate purpose is actually the discovery of "regularities that are, in a sense, spaceless and timeless."[45]

In sum then, on the negative side, historians of religions (along with art historians) will complain that new archaeologists fail to respect the independence of art and architecture (and religion) from other sociocultural processes, and that they are preoccupied with universal processes and with a grand scale that fails to appreciate the uniqueness of specific works of pre-Columbian art and architecture.[46] On the positive side, however, by their willingness to generalize, new archaeologists do introduce a refreshingly more theoretical element into the study of Mesoamerican art and architecture. By their more wide-angled perspective, they provide unprecedented insights into the arrangement of space on a regional scale — for instance, areal settlement patterns, urban orientational schemes, and characteristic responses to ecological zones. Moreover, by their Marxist proclivities — and thus their tendency to shift the focus away from the grand public architecture of ceremonial centers onto the surrounding periphery, presumably where the "common people" lived — new archaeologists initiate an unprecedented appreciation of residential and "nonpedigreed," vernacular Mesoamerican architecture. (All these are, by the way, developments that will figure prominently in formulating new solutions to the Tula–Chichén Itzá problem.) And finally, to cite a more oblique contribution, by slanting the researches of the mainstream in this universalizing direction and deliberately neglecting "the small and the irregular" that had so fascinated their predecessors, the new archaeologists do, albeit unwittingly, open a niche for the second important strain of dissent against traditional Mesoamerican archaeology — namely, art history.[47]

Art History: Architecture as Art

> Anthropological conclusions about a culture do not automatically account for the art of that culture . . . because aesthetic activity lies in part outside culture, and because it is anterior to culture as a possible agent in the processes of change.
>
> *George Kubler, 1984*[48]

In addition to the criticism from within its own ranks, traditional Mesoamerican archaeology has been admonished by a more loosely affiliated lineage of art historians. The progenitor of this strain, Herbert Spinden, beginning in the teens and twenties, warned that the new, "scientific" emphasis on factual data in Mesoamerican archaeology was nurturing the seeds of its own undoing. He deplored increasing specialization for the way it emphasized the spectacular fringes and directed attention away from the "great central truths" of the subject.[49] A student of Roland Dixon and Alfred Tozzer, Spinden never abandoned the broadly archaeological goals of his Harvard training; yet, he was the first scholar of the Maya to devote himself particularly to the study of their art and architecture. A master of generalization and synthesis (and thus a major contributor with respect to the slash between universal and particular), he produced, amid a heap of daring though expendable grand theories, a core of insights about Maya art and architecture that continue to be exceedingly useful even now.

Spinden's *A Study of Maya Art* (1913), which combines his exceptional aesthetic sensibility with this generalizing spirit, is, then, typically (though not unanimously) considered the wellspring of the art historical strain.[50] Alternatively, George Kubler, inarguably the dominant figure in the field since the 1940s (and the most uncompromising critic of anthropological, "new archaeological" approaches to pre-Columbian art), traces the roots of his enterprise to nineteenth-century German art historian Franz Kugler.[51] While acknowledging Spinden's important contribution to the field, Kubler contends that "Spinden, however, was mainly an anthropologist, concerned with culture, and his work used Maya art to extract information about the civilization. . . . It remained for others, such as Pál Kelemen and José Pijoán [in the 1940s], to consider ancient art for its own sake rather than as a documentary file on cultural themes."[52] And, Cecelia Klein considers that pre-Columbian art history is not baptized as a discipline (at least in the United States) until Donald Robertson, a student of Kubler's at Yale, earns the first doctorate in the field in 1956.[53]

Its debatable origins aside, this art historical strain steadily gained momentum after the 1950s,[54] fashioning its embattled independence primarily on the basis of two sorts of remonstrations against archaeology and anthropology. First was a protest against presumably "reductive approaches" to pre-Columbian art and architecture (a plea for disciplinary autonomy parallel to that of historians of religions who claim that they alone are attending to an "irreducibly religious" dimension of the human experience that other disciplines neglect).[55] Art historians complain that the prevailing materialist orientation (epitomized by "new archaeologists") is simply the latest and most blatant expression of an untoward tendency to assess pre-Columbian artistic productions in terms of their "economic and political purposes," a reductively condescending approach that can be tracked clear back through the earliest, nontechnical remarks on indigenous art by sixteenth-century writers like

Sahagún, Landa, and Cieza de Leon.[56] By contrast, art historians define themselves as "humanists," who free ancient art (and architecture) from its status as a documentary file on socioeconomic and culture themes and thus appreciate art for its own sake.[57] Kelemen, for instance, explains that, where the archaeologist is preoccupied with unraveling the sequence of cultural development, "the art historian endeavors to evaluate the production of these cultures in the light of esthetics, setting it among the arts of the rest of the world."[58] Similarly, art historian Justino Fernández says, "the [pre-Columbian] objects we shall look at will be treated, arbitrarily if you wish, as works of art. We shall not be concerned in any strict sense with archaeology, or linguistics, or ethnography, or history."[59] And Kubler, the most strident of all in this regard, manifestoes that anthropological conclusions about a culture never fully account for its works of art "because aesthetic activity lies in part outside culture."[60]

Art historians of this ilk, then, celebrate the "uselessness" of art and architecture and deny emphatically that works of art are principally about facilitating cultural, or even religious, activities.[61] Thus, on the positive side (from the perspective of a hermeneutical history of religions), their perspicacity into the style and form of pre-Columbian architecture and into the subject matter and symbolism of iconographic art is unrivaled by any other strain of Americanists. Less positively, however, this antireductive stance, by its commitment to transcending the apparently prosaic historical and sociological dimensions of the art, contributes little to queries about the specific uses and functions of pre-Columbian works of art and buildings. Their laudable sensitivity to the content of the art comes, frequently, at the expense of due consideration to either the general sociopolitical context or the specific ritual performative context in which that art is involved (both of which are crucial to the "eventful" approach to architecture developed in the next chapters).[62] Too often, loosing pre-Columbian art and architecture from their sociocultural significance reifies some set of iconographic significances, thus disengaging the "symbolism" of buildings from any specific pre-Columbian actors or activities. When art historians interpret the iconography on a Maya temple's facade by telling us, for instance — and the standard literature is filled with claims of this sort — that the sculpted image of an arm across the chest signifies submission, a mat signifies royalty, or five circles signify Venus, we are left wondering: for which pre-Columbian social constituencies and in what ritual circumstances do these significances obtain?[63]

In any case, the second major set of protestations by art historians is aimed at the grand, neo-evolutionary schemes of the new archaeologists. Kubler, for instance, contends that such rigid schemes of cultural development place an inordinate emphasis on discontinuity and rupture in the history of Mesoamerican art and so neglect the important continuity in regional and local artistic traditions. Thus, where archaeologists tend to produce historical (re)constructions diagrammed into separate compartments (that is, art as "packages"), art historians usually produce descriptions of complex flow (that is, art as "tapes").[64] Art historians are, in other words, uniquely sensitive to, and adept at discovering, the historical relationships between specific works of art and architecture. It is, moreover, in this initiative to situate works of art with respect to their historically related precedents and progeny that art history makes its superlative contribution to a hermeneutical, "eventful" approach to pre-Columbian architecture: namely, an appreciation of *the decisive role of tradition* in both the production and subsequent human experience of works of art and architecture. Art historians' deciphering of historical sequences in art, evolutions in style, and deliberate "archaisms" or imitations of previous art styles outstrips by far the archaeo-anthropological contribution on that front. Determining the historical relatednesses between the artistic and architectural styles of, for instance, Tula and Chichén Itzá will prove crucial to the hermeneutical interpretation of those sites, and no other group of Mesoamericanists contributes so much to that project as do art historians.

Given their history of antagonism, then, it is ironic that the current vitality of pre-Columbian art history is largely the result of the ascendancy of the new archaeology.[65] The new archeologists' preoccupation with the ecological landscape, modes of production, habitation patterns, and the unelaborate artifacts of the peasantry — in short, the nonelite elements of Mesoamerican civilization — opened up a void with respect to serious consideration of the "fine" art masterpieces of the elite. Archaeology's shift in emphasis, in a sense, stigmatized the study of monumental art and architecture on which earlier generations of scholars had been fixated and, thus, in Klein's assessment, "study of the precious and symbolic aspects of Mesoamerican culture in particular were ripe for relocation in another, more congenial discipline . . . it seems fair to suggest that pre-Columbian art history came into being in this country in part specifically to carry on what archaeology had ceased to do."[66] Moreover, art historians, generally speaking, declined to accept the new archaeological resolution to the universal/particular problem. As Americanist archaeology concentrated on measurable, quantifiable, and predictable cultural laws on a grand scale, deliberately passing by individual particularities, it fell to the art historian, according to both Klein and Clemency Coggins, to retrieve the small and the irregular, "to re-educate archaeologists to the cultural significance of the unique, and the idiosyncratic, and the beautiful."[67]

Pre-Columbian art history, then, like all other approaches to the Mesoamerican materials, continues to define itself in relation to the archaeological mainstream. In a conciliatory spirit, Klein suggests that art historians may find future benefits in applying new archaeological methodologies to their own research (and there are signs that art historians are increasingly sensitive to matters of historical context).[68] By contrast, Kubler basks in what he calls the "outsider's position," neither anticipating nor aspiring to any reconciliation of the two approaches — for "only by preserving the independence of outside opinion can the art historian continue to ask the questions that are ignored in social science."[69] In either case, historians of religions (even further outside the Mesoamericanist mainstream) can benefit from the uneasy relations between archaeology and art history. If art historians are less than completely reliable in resolving matters of pre-Columbian history and social organization (and less attentive to the specific ritual uses of buildings than we might hope),[70] nevertheless, by their continuing discontent with the strictly archaeological analyses of pre-Columbian art and architecture (and thus their continuing interest in matters of aesthetics, symbolism, and meaning), art historians provide a uniquely evocative resource for the hermeneutical inquiry into Mesoamerican architecture. And, moreover, as Chapter 4 will demonstrate, nowhere have art historians' iconoclastic challenges to the old wisdoms of archaeology been more provocative than at Chichén Itzá.

Ethnohistory: Ethnographic Analogy

> In the New World, ethnohistory is the bridge to the past; without it one could not even glimpse prehistoric cosmology, interpret ancient public buildings, understand the contexts of ritual

paraphernalia, or analyze the iconography of long-dead Panamanians.

Joyce Marcus, 1978[71]

A third major chorus of discontent with traditional Mesoamerican archaeology has issued from the ranks of ethnohistory.[72] In 1940 the most articulate ethnohistorian of his era, J. Eric S. Thompson, like Spinden, an apostate from strict archaeology, initiated a career-long polemic against archaeology's overspecialization and tepidness toward the textual and ethnological evidence.[73] For Thompson, ethnohistory's enormous potential derived from the fact that the indigenous cultures of Mesoamerica, particularly the Maya, did *not* die with the Spanish conquest: "Maya culture, like, for instance, that of the Jews, is still very much alive."[74] Accordingly, Mesoamericanists should find two of their most rich resources in the substantial body of written materials produced either directly or indirectly by the Indians themselves in the post-contact era[75] and in the perseverance with which the Maya, especially, have clung to their language and culture. In Thompson's assessment, however, traditional archaeology — "the study of dead cultures" — neglected both:

> Maya culture . . . has a continuity from the first centuries of the Christian era to the present day; the correlation of all the data from colonial writings and observations of survivals among the present-day Maya with the information archaeology yields alone will give us a true picture of Maya life . . . we cannot permit archaeology, like some nineteenth century prima dona at a recital, to be the sole performer. This is, of course, the approach of the ethnohistorian.[76]

The inception of Mesoamerican "ethnohistory" is variously traced to Sahagún and the sixteenth-century compilers, to Leon y Gama (1792–1832), to Lewis Henry Morgan (1887), and to the influential historico-ethnological method of Eduard Seler (1880s–1920s).[77] All of the major archaeologists of the early twentieth century — Bodwitch, Tozzer, Morley, Spinden, Gates, and, preeminently, Ralph Roys — utilize, to a greater or lesser extent, the relevant documentary-pictorial corpus in consonance with the excavationary materials.[78] However, it is not until the 1950s that ethnohistory enters the literature as a recognizable and expanding subspecialization of anthropology; Howard Cline thinks that, possibly, the term is finally "sanctified" by its usage in the influential *Handbook of Middle American Indians* in 1972.[79] In any event, ethnohistory, as an approach concerned with the retrieval of pre-Columbian New World cultures from written (and, to an extent, ethnographic) sources is, by now, an established subspecialty and a major complement to strict, excavationary archaeology.

Residing in the hinterland between history and anthropology, the goals and methods of ethnohistory are continually disputed, primarily because the particularistic and diachronic tendencies of historians are never comfortably synthesized with the generalizing and synchronic motives of anthropologists (one more dimension of the universal/particular problem).[80] Yet, despite one lacking consensual methodology, ethnohistorians make singularly important contributions to the hermeneutical, "eventful" approach to Mesoamerican architecture in two areas. First, ethnohistorical approaches, more than any others, cast light on the use and function of pre-Hispanic buildings (which is particularly important to my project, because discerning the indigenous usages of buildings is both absolutely pivotal to "eventful" interpretations of architecture and despairingly difficult in the case of ruined sites such as Tula and Chichén Itzá). Second, in addition to recording particulars about indigenous ritual practices, ethnohistorians, by reading the transcribed myths and "histories" of Mesoamerican peoples and conversing directly with present-day Indians, enjoy the most explicit access to the mental dispositions or spiritual "preunderstandings" of the participants in those ritual-architectural occasions. Being attentive to the transmaterial, intellectual achievements of both pre- and post-Hispanic Indians, ethnohistorians team with iconographers to raise questions about the meanings and native perceptions of the monuments — another dimension that is critical to a hermeneutical understanding of those monuments but that largely eludes the methods of traditional archaeology.

Unfortunately, the utility of ethnohistoric researches in regard to either the ritual usage of pre-Hispanic buildings or the psychological and religious dispositions of the native users of those buildings is severely constrained by the exceedingly lopsided distribution of the extant textual sources. Where there is a relative abundance of sixteenth-century Central Mexican documentary sources, particularly with reference to the Aztecs, there is an almost complete void of written texts in all other eras (the Mixtec pictorial codices and Maya glyphs standing as two great exceptions). Attempts to redress this extreme unevenness in the textual record by analogizing, extrapolating, and generalizing the results of those Central Mexican colonial documents (still very fragmentary in themselves) have fueled a controversy of major proportions on the question: To what extent are the Aztecs on the eve of (or immediately after) the conquest representative of the more ancient and far-flung peoples of Mesoamerica? Moreover, this controversy regarding the viability of extrapolating from the Aztecs to other pre-Columbian cultures exposes the deep suspicions that many scholars have regarding the role of any sort of comparison and generalization in Mesoamericanist studies.

For the most part, since the mid-twentieth century, Americanists have employed two sorts of analogical approaches: "general comparative" and "specific historical."[81] So-termed general comparative analogy (which would include most history of religions morphological methods) allows inferences that are drawn from general life situations, without restriction as to time or space. Unfortunately (particularly for the present project), such nonhistorical comparative methods, for many Mesoamericanists, still evoke (however inappropriately) the specter of crackpot, overextravagant diffusionist theories, of imagination untempered by academic rigor. Thus, while nominally endorsed as a last resort by some Mesoamericanists (H. B. Nicholson for instance), in the main, reactions to cross-cultural comparison of any sort typically range from disinterest to disdain.[82] The notion, for instance (outlined momentarily), that the interpretation of the ruins of Tula and Chichén Itzá can be enriched in responsible ways via cross-cultural comparisons with the sacred architectures of India, Japan, Europe, and elsewhere is certain to offend the methodological sensibilities of most Mesoamericanists.

In any case, alternatively, specific historical analogy, or "ethnographic analogy," which permits inferences only within geographically and historically defined contexts, spawns a prodigious, if controversial, fund of interpretation in Mesoamerica. In other words, while rejecting nonhistorical, morphological comparative methods, nearly all Americanists do endorse the legitimacy of interpreting archaeological cultures with the aid of ethnographic or ethnohistoric accounts that relate Indian cultures that share a direct historical line of descent with one another.[83] Two such modes of specific historical analogy have been particularly prolific in Americanist studies: (1) "upstreaming" (a term more in vogue forty years ago), which involves the use of ethnographic data from a modern culture to criticize and reinterpret older accounts of its ancestor cultures,[84] and (2) the "direct historical approach" (like upstreaming, the direct legacy of Seler), which depends upon the logic of working from known or living cultures to unknown or archaeological cultures.[85] Likewise, virtually all Mesoamericanists applaud the use of ethnohistorical documents to unravel otherwise insoluble historical problems — two relevant and important instances being Roys's reliance on colonial-period texts to disentangle (at least to an extent) pre-Columbian Yucatán history, and Jiménez Moreno's ethnohistorically grounded "solution" to the Tollan-Tula problem.[86] And, with specific regard to the interpretation of Mesoamerican architecture, at least since Catherwood and Prescott (both of whom published major works in the 1840s), it has been standard practice to bolster archaeological descriptions of pre-Columbian buildings with Sahagún's and Landa's accounts of colonial-period native rituals; Tozzer's opus on Chichén Itzá is classic in that regard.[87]

More recently, Mesoamericanists' willingness to loosen the strictures of direct descent lines and immediate geographies, and thus widen the field for ethnographic analogy, has depended directly on confidence (or skepticism) about the basic continuity and overall cultural unity of the area.[88] Opinions on this matter settle into two camps (reflecting yet another controversy on the slash between universal/particular). On the one hand, those scholars who adhere to a fundamentally "unitary" view of Mesoamerican art and civilization (for instance, Bernal, Willey, Coe, Joralemon, Nicholson, Furst, and a host of other scholars) venture to utilize freely Central Mexican, contact-period ethnographic and ethnohistorical data to interpret antecedent cultures, most daringly, the Olmec, who lived a thousand years earlier in the Gulf Coast region.[89] Even these advocates for ethnographic analogy are, however, reticent to involve cross-cultural comparisons and analogies with any historical contexts *outside* Mesoamerica.

On the other hand, there is a significant though smaller contingent of scholars, evident as early as Hermann Beyer (1922), that expresses serious reservations about the presumed existence of a pan-Mesoamerican approach to life and art, and that thus is dubious about extrapolating from Aztec sources to any other Mesoamerican context, particularly to much earlier indigenous cultures like the Olmec or Teotihuacán.[90] Kubler, for instance, the most uncompromising spokesman for this latter opinion, completely rejects both the notion of a unitary Mesoamerican art world and, consequently, the viability of generalizing from one pre-Columbian culture to another.[91] He supports his wholesale rejection of ethnographic analogy by invoking Erwin Panofsky's "law of disjunction," a principle derived from the observation that medieval European art borrowed the *forms* of Classical Antiquity, but assigned to them entirely different *meanings* or *significances*.[92] Kubler explains:

> Disjunction, which is a mode of renovation, may be said to happen whenever the members of a successor civilization refashion their inheritance by gearing the predecessors' forms to new meanings, and by clothing in new forms those old meanings which remain acceptable. *Continuous form does not predicate continuous meaning, nor does continuity of form or of meaning necessarily imply continuity of culture.* . . . [Thus] we may not use Aztec ritual descriptions as compiled by Sahagún about 1550 to explain murals painted at Teotihuacán a thousand years earlier, for the same reason that we would not easily get agreement in interpreting the Hellenistic images of Palmyra by using Arabic texts on Islamic ritual. *The idea of disjunction . . . makes every ethnographic analogy questionable by insisting on discontinuity rather than its opposite whenever long durations are under discussion.*[93]

Kubler's flaying of ethnographic analogy — almost certainly overstated — does, nonetheless, focus a number of the basic issues regarding the use of ethnographic and ethnohistorical resources in the comparative hermeneutics of sacred architecture, both within and outside Mesoamerica. Kubler's terse remarks accentuate (as will my analysis) the fabulous complexity of the relations between artistic form, culture, and meaning, particularly when those relations are examined over long stretches of time.[94] Additionally, his cautionings become all the more piquant in relation to the present project because the famous similitude between the architectures of Tula and Chichén Itzá (while not an instance of "disjunction" in precisely Panofsky's and Kubler's sense) does involve an unmistakable commonality at the level of *artistic form,* which has, for generations, masked an equally significant contrariety between the respective *artistic meanings and intentions* of the two cities. Failure to appreciate the inevitable flux, or slippage (or perhaps "disjunction") between the art forms and what those forms come to mean at the two respective sites has, in fact, been the principal obstacle to satisfactorily resolving the Tula–Chichén problem.[95]

Moreover, Kubler's diatribe against ethnographic analogy is useful in accentuating the limitations of any interpretive approach that relies solely on the formal and constructional characteristics of Mesoamerican buildings without penetrating into the specific ceremonial usages of those buildings and into the specific conceptual worlds of the pre-Hispanic users. Nevertheless, to part company with Kubler, inferring on the basis of ethnographic and ethnohistorical researches has been, and remains, the most promising entrée into both those realms.[96] Ethnohistory enlivens the formal and technical descriptions of archaeology — in a sense, giving voice, movement, and intellect to, for instance, the faceless, innominate human forms that stand alongside the buildings in Tatiana Proskouriakoff's meticulous (re)construction drawings of Chichén Itzá and other Mesoamerican sites.[97] In so doing, ethnohistory lays the groundwork for hypotheses about the use and function of buildings and about the native perceptions of those buildings without which a hermeneutical, "eventful" approach to Mesoamerican architecture would be hopelessly frustrated.

To bring the first half of these methodological reflections to an abrupt conclusion: no major strain of Mesoamerican studies has consistently asked the sorts of hermeneutical questions or employed the sorts of comparative methods that would content most students of *Religionswissenschaft.* Together, however, traditional archaeology, new archaeology, art history, and ethnohistory — by their cooperation and their antagonism — provide an exciting bank of historical and theoretical resources for the hermeneutical interpretation of pre-Columbian sacred architecture. It remains for historians of religions (still new players in this game) to capitalize on those resources and to resolve the indomitable slashes between subjective/objective and universal/particular in their own characteristic ways — that is, in ways that eventuate in what is, from their perspective, a more "significant organization" of Mesoamerica's architectures (and, thus, in ways that provide a foundation for a fresh take on the old problem of Tula and Chichén Itzá). Yet, before embracing that task and presenting an alternative, hermeneutical principle of organization, this very general survey of the four strains of Mesoamerican studies can be complemented by a somewhat more specific and less-conventional survey of the seven alternative principles of organization by which Mesoamericanists have, so far, imposed order on the wild heterogeneity of pre-Columbian architecture.

Principles of Organization

> Rigid definitions and attempts to form classifications of art forms on the basis of precisely defined similarities may only impede the discovery of those distinctions which are significant in art development. . . . In exploring new approaches, standards of scholarship, precision and "objectivity" must take second place to the formulation of ideas which could enable us to describe a work of art and to relate it to other works, not as form, but as a vehicle of expression.
>
> *Tatiana Proskouriakoff, 1950*[98]

Organization by Form: An Appearance of Objectivity

> It is not, however, only from written records that our knowledge can be increased.
>
> *Alfred P. Maudslay, 1889*[99]

Organization and comparison that focus on the size and shape of buildings — the most obvious of classificatory criteria — have enjoyed a prolific, albeit checkered, career in Middle American studies. Preponderantly formal approaches to pre-Columbian art and architecture arise in three distinct streams: (1) the speculative diffusionist, (2) the traditional archaeological, and (3) the art historical.

First, and least auspicious, are those daring leaps from a coincidence in form to a (re)construction of historical events. A barrage of antiquarian (and modern) diffusionist phantasms depend, almost exclusively, on parallels between the architectural forms and artistic motifs of Mexico and the Old World. Among that host is Carlos de Sigüenza y Góngora (1645–1700), "beyond doubt the most erudite man of his time in Mexico," who considered the pandemic form of the cross as "proof" of the Mesoamerican travels of St. Thomas and who drafted the coincident contours of Mexican and Egyptian pyramids as "evidence" of the existence of an intervening continent, presumably Atlantis.[100] Count Jean Frederic Waldeck's (1830), and later G. Eliot Smith's (1924), risible claim that the long-nosed masks in the sculptures and wall decorations of Central Yucatán were elephants, and thus proof of pre-Hispanic contact with Asia and Africa, is likewise conjecture based on a coincidence in artistic form,[101] as is Charnay's posit of an Eastern origin for the American natives because, among other things, "their architecture is so like the Japanese as to seem identical."[102] More recently and less extravagantly, Gordon F. Ekholm and Robert Heine-Geldern exploit shared artistic patterns — most notably Hindu, Buddhist, and Maya lotus motifs — as evidence of two-way traffic between southeast Asia and America.[103] The list of examples of diffusionist theorizing on the basis of formal similitude in art and architecture is endless (and entertaining).[104]

Strange bedfellows, a second stream to focus almost exclusively on the formal characteristics of pre-Columbian architecture was early positivistic archaeology. Preceded by the evenhanded descriptions of John Lloyd Stephens and the precise drawings of Frederick Catherwood, the real harbingers of this organizational strategy were American William Henry Holmes's *Archaeological Studies of the Ancient Cities of Mexico* (1895–97) and Englishman Alfred P. Maudslay's *Archaeology* (1889–1902).[105] Radical in their avoidance of speculation and theorizing (and omitting Stephens's digressions on the women and food of Mexico), both Holmes and Maudslay reckon it irresponsible to conjecture about the age of the monuments, the dispositions of their inhabitants, or the possible function of the buildings. Yet, to describe the formal (and, to an extent, constructional) characteristics is to remain safely within the bounds of "scientific archaeology."[106] Holmes, after a whirlwind tour of the monuments of Yucatán, Chiapas, Oaxaca, and the Valley of Mexico, synthesizes the data with means that are scrupulously formal.[107] He builds innumerable sententious classifications of roof types, floor plans, and wall perforations (for instance, simple rectangular doorways versus compound doorways versus arched doorways);[108] he compares ideal-typical forms (for instance, a "generalized Palenque building" versus a "generalized Yucatán building" versus a "generalized Mitla building");[109] and he isolates representative formal types (for instance, the Castillo at Chichén Itzá is "the type of the Maya pyramid-temple," and the Temple of the Sun at Palenque is "the type of its class").[110]

Maudslay, while more particularistic than Holmes, likewise concentrates on the outward appearance of the monuments to the self-conscious exclusion of function and chronology.[111] The (seemingly) objective potentialities of mechanical drawing, plaster casts, and, most especially, newly discovered photography are uniquely suited to Maudslay's agenda of preserving the endangered "scientific truth" of the ruined architecture.[112] His opus, *Archaeology,* deliberately offers no conclusions, no syntheses, and no generalizations; yet, it is a landmark of empirical rigor and impeccable formal description, a thoroughly reliable source even today.

The singularity with which Holmes and Maudslay rely on the organization of pre-Columbian architecture by form passes quickly, particularly in the wake of a burgeoning preoccupation with chronology (that is, organization by time). Nevertheless, the early archaeological literature is overstocked with attempts to organize Mesoamerican architecture and architectural elements by preponderantly formal criteria that bear little relation to the age, location, cultural context, or function of the buildings.[113] Arch-systematizer Tozzer, for instance, is tireless in classifying pre-Columbian architecture in terms of "terraces, courts, pyramid mounds, cropped mounds, stairways, batters, door jams, columns" and then, employing his so-called comparative method, cataloging the incidence of those formal types at various sites and eras.[114] Pursuing substantially the same encyclopedic-comparative method, Mexican archaeologist Ignacio Marquina, the first to write a comprehensive work on Mesoamerican architecture — *Arquitectura Prehispánica* (1951) — makes a chart with formal architectural characteristics on one axis and then along the other axis checks them, *si o no?,* against the major sites of Central Mexico and Yucatán.[115] And H.E.D. Pollock, the Carnegie archaeologist who published the most on architecture, takes essentially the same conservative tack; his topical review, *Round Structures of Aboriginal Middle America* (1936), for instance, aside from noting some possible relation between circular buildings and Quetzalcoatl, is simply a descriptive, classificatory, and distributional catalog of round architectural forms.[116] The bibliography of parallel sorts of cautious archaeological cataloging efforts is, in short, enormous.

The third major stream in Mesoamerican studies to concentrate on the formal character of architecture is the art historical, within which there are two distinct pulses: archaeology-based art history and the more strictly art historical. The first is inaugurated by Spinden's seminal *A Study of Maya Art: Its Subject Matter and Historical Development* (1913).[117] Spinden distances himself from the diffusionists — "writers who, on the strength of this or that similarity, cheerfully leap the bounds of space, time and reason to derive the religious and artistic conceptions of the Maya from Egypt, India or China" — and, likewise, from the unembossed archaeological descriptions of Stephens, Holmes, Maudslay, and Maler, all of whose works are, from Spinden's ambitious perspective, "in reality hardly more than storehouses of selected materials."[118] Nevertheless, Spinden is the compeer to both the diffusionists

Alfred P. Maudslay, at work in the Chichén Itzá Nunnery in 1889. Seldom venturing speculations on the pre-Columbian origins or usages of specific ruins (at least in his academic writings), Maudslay produced a remarkable fund of meticulous descriptions, line drawings, and photographs of Maya architecture, which remain an invaluable resource for contemporary researchers. (Photo by H. M. Sweet.)

William Henry Holmes's panorama view of Chichén Itzá. Holmes, an artist, geologist, and head curator of the Field Columbian Exposition in Chicago, as well as an archaeological researcher, brought an unprecedented precision to his maps and drawings of pre-Columbian ruins. This rendition of Chichén Itzá, which was based on measurements Holmes made during an expedition in 1894, was labeled as follows: A, Nunnery or Palace with its annexed buildings, B and C; D, Akab-Dzib; E, Caracol or round tower; F, Chichanchob or Red House; G, ruined pyramid-temple [i.e., Deer House]; H, Ball-court or Gymnasium; I, El Castillo; J, two considerable temple-pyramids connected with an extensive system of ruins of which little is yet known [i.e., the Warriors Temple Complex]; K, Cenote Grande; and L, the Sacred Cenote. (William H. Holmes, *Archaeological Studies Among the Ancient Cities of Mexico*.)

and the positivists in his preoccupation with shapes and appearances of pre-Columbian art and architecture. Even so, the strictly formal, synchronic portion of his work is unique by virtue of its attentiveness, first, to the subject matter of Maya art (the human figures, gods, reptiles, birds, etc.) and, second, to the "processes of imaginative modification" that act upon that subject matter.[119]

Beyond mere description or distributional cataloging (but in advance of the chronological sequencing of works of art), Spinden undertakes the "stylistic comparison" of artistic elements and combinations of elements as they appear in Maya architectural decoration, the minor arts, and the codices.[120] He compares, for instance, various manifestations and permutations of "the face with the curled nose ornament," "the plant and fish motive," and "astronomical signs combined with birds and animal heads."[121] His assiduous treatment of the serpent motif — he isolates eighteen distinct parts that characteristically make up the serpent head in Maya art and then considers the range of "reptilian enrichment" relative to those elements — is the quintessence of his formal, comparative analysis.[122]

In the later portions of Spinden's own work, chronological priorities dominate, and the progeny of his strictly formal analysis are scarce. Tatiana Proskouriakoff, the most significant among them, provides a unique aperture into the formal characteristics of Maya buildings with her famous restoration drawings in *An Album of Maya Architecture* (1963), yet she laments that so few others have followed Spinden's lead in this regard.[123] Proskouriakoff is disenchanted with the conventional hybrid organization of pre-Columbian art styles according to geographical-ethnic categories (for instance, Olmec art, Totonac art, Huastec art, and Zapotec art), a scheme that, while satisfactory to no one, had

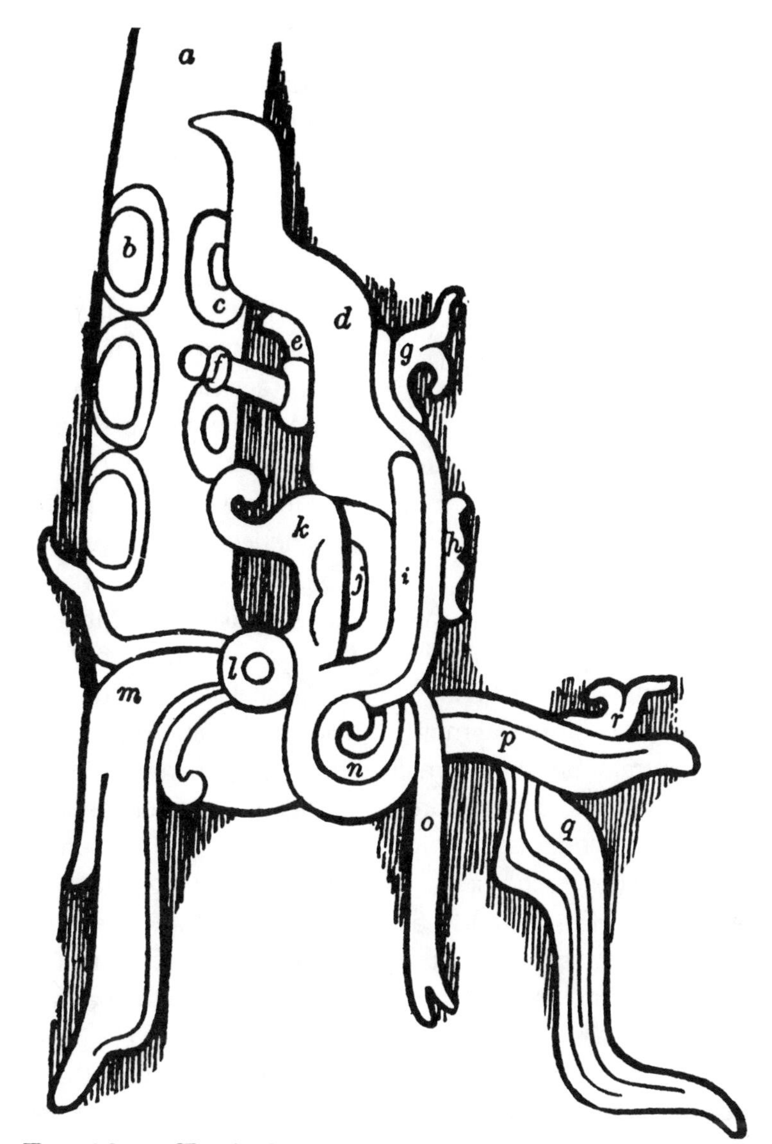

Fig. 30. — **Typical conventionalized serpent head:** *a*, **body;** *b*, **belly markings;** *c*, **back markings;** *d*, **nose;** *e*, **nose scroll;** *f*, **nose plug;** *g*, **incisor tooth;** *h*, **molar tooth;** *i*, **jaw;** *j*, **eye;** *k*, **supraorbital plate;** *l*, **ear plug;** *m*, **ear ornaments;** *n*, **curled fang;** *o*, **tongue;** *p*, **lower jaw;** *q*, **beard;** *r*, **incisor tooth.**

Herbert Spinden's drawing of a "Typical [Maya] Conventionalized Serpent Head," 1913. In the accompanying text, Spinden meticulously described variations and permutations on each of the eighteen elements. Concentrating (at this point) strictly on the formal appearance of this motif, Spinden's work was nonetheless comparative insofar as the drawing represented a generalized, imagined composite based on his survey of countless specific cases. (Herbert Spinden, *A Study of Maya Art*.)

become entrenched in the literature by the middle of this century. She argues instead for a strictly formal principle of organization, that is, a retrieval and more broad application of Spinden's approach.[124] Addressing the organizational problem head-on in the fifties, she writes:

> our first objective must be to find an efficient way to deal with the rich variety of designs that we find in Middle American collections . . . it seems to me that our only course is to study the general properties of form and to find among them significant features that can be compared in different designs. Only then can we proceed to define styles by the pattern of their formal properties.[125]

In any case, alongside this archaeo-art historical strain, the more strictly art historical corps — without harkening directly to Spinden's approach — employ three principal methods that likewise concentrate on the formal qualities of pre-Columbian art and architecture: (1) descriptive analysis, (2) connoisseurship, and (3) iconography.[126] Consider each briefly.

The earliest of all art historical methods, as old as Pliny the elder and Pausanias, is the exact description, recording, and cataloging of the visible forms of works of art.[127] There is a profusion of descriptive analyses of Mesoamerican art and architecture, which owes to the ironic dovetailing of this time-honored art historical approach and the descriptive propensities of the nineteenth-century positivistic archaeologists (for instance, Holmes and Maudslay).[128] Pál Kelemen's two-volume *Medieval American Art* (1943), for instance, is an early art historical work that epitomizes the near interchangeability of the two agenda.[129] Displeased with the chronological obsessions of the archaeology of his day, Kelemen endeavors to evaluate pre-Columbian art and architecture not as a barometer of cultural change but "in light of aesthetics."[130] Yet, rather than a fresh alternative, Kelemen's work — and his written descriptions of pre-Columbian art are still among the best available — is essentially a resurrection of Maudslay's style of presentation in *Archaeology,* namely, cautiously noninterpretive, descriptive commentary on photographs.[131] In other words, as Middle American archaeology, after the teens, abandoned strictly formal description in favor of "historical reconstruction" and temporal principles of organization, aestheticians like Kelemen and José Pijoán emerged to reassert the banner of ahistorical, formal analysis.[132]

In regard specifically to architecture, the aestheticians spewed countless site-by-site commentaries that make virtually no attempt at comparison or integration. (This is still the most common type of art historical treatment of Mesoamerica.) Kubler, however, exercising a more synthetic urge, parlayed this tradition of stodgy, particularistic description into an intriguing set of generalizations about pre-Columbian architecture while, at the same time, preserving intact the formal, nonhistorical approach. For example, he distinguished Mesoamerican architecture from its occidental counterpart on the basis of a number of strictly formal criteria: (1) in Mesoamerica vast masses are more important than enclosed spaces; (2) assemblages of masses and the spaces between them, not individual buildings, are the crucial units; and (3) American architecture engages in a hierarchic differentiation by height that is absent in Old World architecture.[133] Furthermore, he isolated ideal formal types — for instance, the pathway site, the pyramidal platform, the open-cornered versus the closed-cornered courtyard, and the patio building — and then collected cross-regional examples of each.[134] And finally, Kubler organized the whole of Mesoamerican spatial arrangement into three formal (and possibly, but only secondarily, chronological) categories: (1) fenced-in enclosures of geometric plan, (2) courtyards and plazas on several levels, and (3) chambered and roofed volumes.[135]

By contrast to the synthesizing vigor of Kubler's formal organizations, the second of the strictly art historical approaches, connoisseurship — *"la science des qualités"* — concentrated on the "artistic qualities" of single works of art, exercising a cultivated taste to determine the "best" among them.[136] Forever a customary practice among historians of Western art, qualitative assessments regarding the relative aesthetic merits of particular works of pre-Columbian art are, generally speaking, scrupulously avoided by modern Mesoamerican archaeologists and art historians alike, most likely in reaction to the obviously flawed, ethnocentric judgments of the antiquarian pre-Columbianists. Yet, of late, Esther Pasztory, among others, has retrieved connoisseurship and the selection of "masterpieces" in pre-Columbian art, "not as an idle pastime of forcing non-Western art into the categories developed in the study of Western art history, but [as] a way of determining the traditional limits imposed upon the artist, the latitude allowed for innovation, the visual sources available and the role of art in the larger social context."[137]

In any case, if the connoisseur's analysis is initially concentrated on the technique and form of a single work of art or architecture, it typically spreads "outward" to comparison with forms and techniques of related works and "downward" to consideration of the symbolic content of the work — blending at that point with the third mode of art historical formal analysis, iconography.[138] Iconography, the study of symbols and meanings in art, is, in Mesoamerica, the direct legacy of Seler (not of Spinden).[139] While iconographic analysis relies on a vigilant inspection of the formal characteristics of Mesoamerican art and architecture, as do the descriptive analysis and connoisseurship modes of art history (and, for that matter, as do the diffusionists, nineteenth-century archaeologists, and archaeo-art historians), iconography supersedes all of these by its attentiveness to both the historical context of the art and the mental disposition of the Indians. With these preferments, iconographers transcend the straightforward organization of Mesoamerican buildings according to their appearances and make an estimable contribution to the delineation of particular architectural "traditions." (Accordingly, discussion of iconography is deferred to the final section of the chapter, "Organization by Tradition.")

In sum then, the wide range of approaches that concentrate on the formal attributes of pre-Columbian buildings, by and large, simply takes for granted that analyzing, comparing, and arranging buildings according to their outward appearances are largely unobtrusive (if not wholly objective) procedures and that the resultant schemes are somehow significant. Visual appearances would seem the obviously appropriate starting point. Yet, as an end point, upon somewhat closer scrutiny, cataloging and assessing pre-Columbian buildings with respect to their shapes and sizes typically eventuate in comparative appraisements that are, from the perspective of the history of religions, either distorting or, at best, merely incidental. The untoward consequences of fixating on the formal parallels between Tula and Chichén Itzá are, of course, a paramount case in point.

Organization by Technique: Material Remains par Excellence

> Indeed, it would be impossible, with the best instruments of modern times, to cut stones more perfectly.
>
> *John Lloyd Stephens, 1841*[140]

Every generation of travelers to Mexico, from the Spanish conquistadors forward, marvels at the technical accomplishment of the pre-Hispanic monuments and wonders at the fine craftsmanship and enormous labor that must have been required. Prowess in building has, in fact, been invoked more regularly than any other element of indigenous civilization as indubitable evidence that the pre-Columbian peoples of America were, after all, "civilized." Moreover, building techniques and construction materials belong, even more than the formal appearance of buildings, to the "inorganic phases of civilization"; they are the "chemico-physical dimension" of ancient architecture, the material remains par excellence.[141] And because matters of construction are so available to direct empirical scrutiny, so seemingly noncontroversial, these issues enjoy a special legitimacy and incontestability that remain intact across innumerable shifts in the theoretical orientation of Middle American studies. That resilient prestige notwithstanding, sweeping classificatory schemes based exclusively on principles and materials of construction (for instance, wood construction versus stone versus brick) are surprisingly few in the history of the study of Mesoamerican architecture. More typically, as this quick survey shows, the criterion of building technology is incorporated into a mélange of other hybrid classificatory schemes.

Interest in pre-Columbian building strategies is as old as the study of ruins. Early nineteenth-century explorers of Maya ruins — Antonio del Río (1822), Guillermo Dupaix (1831), and Lorenzo de Zavala (1834) — are absolved of their other antiquarian excesses because they pay particular attention to building materials and methods of construction.[142] Désiré Charnay (1887) looses his theorizing proclivities on the constructional data and formulates, though to no particular advantage, a technical-evolutionary scheme for Mesoamerican building: he isolates "the cement epoch, the cement and cut stone [epoch], and the cut stone only [epoch]," and then searches out those supposedly successive eras in a variety of Yucatán sites, Chichén Itzá included.[143] And Edward Thompson, similarly attentive to the heterogeneity of building techniques within Chichén Itzá, dedicates an entire chapter of his autobiography to a digression on Maya construction principles and prowess.[144]

The documentation of Mesoamerican building techniques is even more perfectly suited to the more scientific archaeologists. Maudslay, and more so Holmes, bring their flatly descriptive agenda to the matters of masonry and construction.[145] Tozzer works his distributional sort of comparative method against a set of technical criteria (for instance, stoneworks, mortar quality, use of plaster, and use of paint).[146] In a similar vein, A. Ledyard Smith inventories the spread and distribution of the famed corbeled, or "Maya arch" across the entire New World, and Lawrence Roys, another of the Carnegie team, concentrates his efforts on "the engineering knowledge of the Maya."[147] Similarly, the early archaeo-art historians, Spinden (1913) and Thomas Joyce (1927), are exceedingly attentive (perhaps more than their methodological heirs) to the constructional attributes of Maya building and, specifically, the extent to which native art is confined by "technological limitations."[148]

The technical attributes of Mesoamerican buildings, already a preeminent concern of the early archaeologists, were afforded even greater respectability when, beginning in the 1920s, they were paired with chronological preoccupations. As suspicion with older methods of dating pre-Columbian buildings grew — Smith, for instance, exposed the fallibility of dating buildings by means of the inscriptions on presumably associated stelae, and Linton Satterthwaite, also a Carnegie researcher, demonstrated the unreliability of chronological architectural schemes based on formal characteristics[149] — modes and materials of

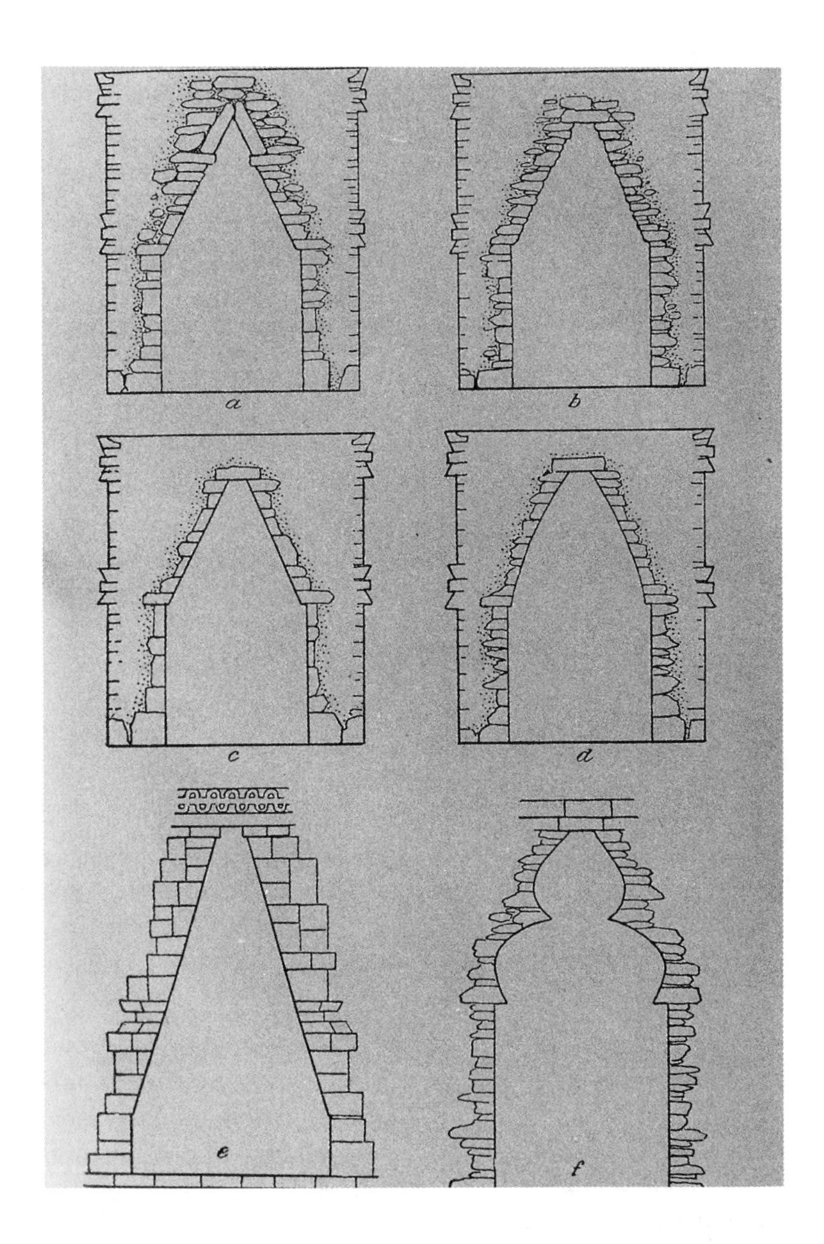

Holmes's categorization of "Types of Maya Arches" (1885), which were labeled as follows: *a*, section of cuneiform arch with acute apex, Chichén Itzá; *b*, section of ordinary arch with flat capstone; *c*, section of ordinary arch with dressed surfaces; *d*, section of ordinary arch with dressed surfaces and curved soffit slopes; *e*, portal arch with long slopes, showing masonry of exterior facing; and *f*, section of trefoil, portal arch of Palenque. If speculations on the pre-Columbian functions (and religious meanings) of ruined buildings fell outside the bounds of early scientific archaeology, cataloging the variety of Mesoamerican building techniques and materials has always been a thoroughly reputable (if sometimes dull) enterprise. (William H. Holmes, *Archaeological Studies Among the Ancient Cities of Mexico*.)

construction emerged unscathed as effective barometers of chronology. In 1940, Pollock, for instance, concluded that

> it has become increasingly clear that the technical aspects of masonry and construction are extraordinarily reliable and sensitive criteria of chronological and cultural change. Nearly all of the recent work has paid strict attention to these matters but the labors of [Earl] Morris and [Lawrence] Roys have been particularly valuable in describing, classifying and analyzing principles of construction.[150]

Later generations of archaeologists continue to acknowledge that charting the constructional attributes of pre-Columbian buildings does have the advantage of empirical verifiability, but they complain (as would historians of religions) that such presumably "neutral" classificatory principles shed little if any light on the realities of pre-Columbian indigenous life: W. W. Taylor, for instance, argues that while "hardness" (of pottery or building materials) remains an empirically valid criterion, Indians do not think of relative hardness in those terms, and it is, therefore, insignificant from any cultural point of view.[151]

The urge to simply catalog construction types flagged somewhat until the 1960s, when cultural materialism (via the "new archaeology") swept the field and technical building criteria received one more revival of prestige. The materialists (primarily followers of Gordon Childe, Leslie White, and Julian Stewart), confident that technology is the most basic and determining factor in cultural evolution, were drawn particularly toward the "technofacts" of tools, ceramics, and irrigation ditches and, thus, toward issues like the regional availability of building materials, increasing technical sophistication, and the constructional attributes of the ruins.[152] The innovation of their approach, however, lies in organizing the physical attributes of materials and techniques not simply into "objective," descriptive categories, but, furthermore (and more significantly), in seeing those attributes as culturally determinative components in an "ecological" model of Mesoamerican civilization.

In any event, whether as proofs of genuine "civilization" among the pre-Columbian peoples, as simply expedient criteria of classification, as barometers of time, or as determinants of culture, the diversity of constructional qualities in Mesoamerican building — the material remains par excellence — together with the formal appearance of those buildings, has been the starting point for every generation of architectural enthusiasts.

Organization by Time: The Enthronement of Chronology

> Chronology is admittedly an important factor in any archaeological research, and the earliest and surest method of establishing it is to be commended. But after a sequence of periods has been established, if then the very culture of those periods is unknown, we may justifiably ask "so what?"
>
> *Walter W. Taylor, 1948*[153]

How old are these ruins? Whether related ultimately to a human fascination with origins, or perhaps to a Western preoccupation with history, there is forever the assumption — not nearly so straightforward as it might appear — that in order to understand pre-Columbian buildings one must know how old they are. Not surprisingly, then, diachronic arrangements of Mesoamerican architecture — that is, taking the age of a building as the decisive criterion of organization — are vaunted, if differently, by both archaeology and art history. In each disciplinary stream, however, the motives and means of dating pass through several phases. In traditional Mesoamerican archaeology, where, for decades, time held an undisputed first place as *the* paramount principle of organization, dating efforts initially focused on the unique fund of epigraphic (presumably dated) inscriptions in the Maya zone, then on the chronologic capabilities of stratigraphic excavation, and then on the preoccupation with "historical reconstruction"; eventually, as priorities shifted and more technically sophisticated means of dating emerged, archaeologists' chronologic obsessions diminished considerably. Art historians, not quite so rabidly preoccupied with dating, pursued chronological organizations primarily in the interest of retrieving either "evolutionary sequences" in pre-Columbian art and architecture or in the interest of discerning artistic "traditions," that is, chains of historically related works of art.

In any case, this section, hardly a primer on the onerous issue of dating Mesoamerican architectures (a matter deserving of a volume of its own), briefly addresses in turn each of these variations on the organization of pre-Columbian art and architecture by time.

From their earliest "discovery," the cryptic inscriptions on the stelae and lintels of the Maya zone inspired optimism that these monuments could, eventually, be securely dated and sequentially arranged; and now, in the wake of recent epigraphic triumphs, Maya glyphs are once again the most prized chronological evidence.[154] Historically speaking, however, in an era when the glyphs remained largely enigmatic, the real breakthrough in the relative dating of monuments owed to the discovery of stratigraphic excavation. Where turn-of-the-century positivistic archaeologists had seized upon photography and plaster casts to preserve the "objective appearance" of monuments, their successors heralded stratigraphic excavation on the model of geology (that is, digging down through chronologically successive, layered deposits) as the means for transcending the formal-constructional description of artifacts and buildings without a loss of empirical rigor.[155] The influential Escuela Internacional de Arquelogía y Ethnología (founded in 1911 and directed successively by no less than Seler, Boas, Tozzer, Jorge Engerrand, and Manuel Gamio) pioneered this temporally predisposed "modern archaeology" in Mexico. For them, "modern" and "stratigraphic" were, in fact, essentially interchangeable terms.[156] Following their lead, interpretation in both the Mexican and Maya areas was funnelled into the single-minded quest after relative dates, and the merits of archaeological data were reduced almost wholly to their utility in that agenda. As Ignacio Bernal says, "the archaeologists of those days put all their energies into the search for a chronology."[157]

Through the teens and twenties, subsequent to the "stratigraphic revolution," unprecedented care was given to the sequential ordering of buildings. Where possible, stratigraphic principles were applied directly to the architecture (as, for instance, by Alfonso Caso in the Valley of Oaxaca).[158] In the main, however, attention was focused away from the monuments themselves onto potsherds and ceramic sequences. The countless sequential orderings of pre-Columbian architecture that issued from this generation were based *not* on the formal or constructional characteristics of the buildings themselves but on associated (presumably contemporaneous) ceramics types. Moreover, while this group was quite successful in assembling relative architectural chronologies, they had more trouble attaching absolute dates to specific buildings.

In any case, as the newfound capability for relative dating triumphed over every other priority, there was (appropriately enough) a protest against the presumption that the age of artifacts and buildings is the true measure of their significance. Kidder, for instance, the most influential in this regard, argued emphatically that the sequential ordering of material remains, albeit necessary, is only a point of departure; he aspired to "historical" rather than simply chronological principles of organization. Kidder maintained that beyond relative dating, the ultimate goal of archaeology (just as for the discipline of history) is no less than "recovering and interpreting the story of man's past . . . [that is] historical reconstruction."[159] Kidder's call to transcend chronology in favor of "culture history" signaled an important theoretical shift: Americanist archaeology from the 1930s and 1940s consistently positioned itself under the auspices of cultural anthropology, and explicated as its goal the "*reconstruction of history*."[160] George Vaillant (1930), for instance, typified the more expansive initiative when he noted that "archaeology has two chief aims, the reconstruction of the life of the people in the past and the arrangement of this life into an historical development."[161]

In this era there was, however (as noted earlier), a wide gap between theory and practice. Relative to the study of pre-Columbian architecture, the expanded archaeo-historical agenda, while still preoccupied with the temporal sequencing of buildings, aimed to retrieve as well the functions, cultural contexts, and artistic traditions of those buildings (all hermeneutically significant aspirations). Nevertheless, in practice, these ambitions continued largely to elude the ranks of traditional archaeology. As Taylor poignantly demonstrated, first in the 1940s and then again in the 1970s, Americanist archaeology (Kidder and Vaillant included), for all its high rhetoric, operated with an exceedingly limited notion of "history."[162] This era's supposed "historical reconstructions" of specific pre-Columbian sites (for instance, Acosta's conclusions about Tula and the Carnegie Institution's work at Chichén Itzá) were largely confined to improved stratigraphic ceramic sequences and chronological orderings of major events in the life of the Maya or Mexican elite — in Taylor's condemnatory phrase, "comparative chronicle."[163] Thus, the prodigious architectural reports of this era (exemplified by Pollock, A. L. Smith, Karl Ruppert, Tozzer, and Earl Morris, all of whom worked extensively at Chichén Itzá) augment Holmes's and Maudslay's meticulous formal-constructional description of the ruined buildings with an unprecedented reliability in dating, but the functions and cultural contexts of those buildings remain largely obscured. For decades, in fact, pre-Columbian architectural studies were bogged at this level, producing reports that are nothing more or less than thorough catalogs of the spatial and temporal distribution of formal-construction features (that is, organization by form, technique, and time).

Discontent with the chronological ordering of specific objects and events intensified with the emergence of the "new archaeology" in the 1960s. Diachronic proclivities persisted in relation to concerns for "cultural dynamics" and regularized process of change, but the dominant principles of organization for the new archaeology were "ecology" and "culture" rather than time. In reaction to the Carnegie Institution excavations, which were obsessed with retrieving chronology, new archaeologists no longer designed excavations to extract the maximum amount of chronological information.[164] They largely abandoned the "historical reconstruction" of unique cases in favor of pursuing generalized principles of cultural change, a reconfigured research agenda that was well served by the emergence of far more sophisticated means of dating and computer techniques, which facilitated quantitative analyses of systems of trade, population growth, the resources of particular environments, and so forth. With the advent of new dating technologies, archaeologists were freed from the constant concern with chronology and thus were allowed to concentrate on problems of context,

Repair of the Caracol at Chichén Itzá in the early 1930s. Academic and commercial interests have seldom been entirely compatible at Chichén Itzá. For instance, while the massive architectural (re)construction efforts of the Carnegie Institution of Washington and the Mexican government succeeded in fashioning the pre-Columbian city into a spectacular archaeological-tourist center, those projects likewise destroyed much of the more prosaic stratigraphic ceramic data on which an accurate chronology for the site might have been based. (Carnegie Institution of Washington photo, courtesy of the Peabody Museum, Harvard University.)

function, and process.[165] For them, arranging specific buildings along a time line was both easier and less satisfying than ever before. In this clime, the preoccupation with sequencing particular works of pre-Columbian art and architecture fell from archaeology to art history — where diachronic principles of organization had already had a distinguished run.[166]

Pre-Columbian art historians, very often, simply appropriate the chronological discoveries of archaeology (or epigraphy) and then proceed from there with their more aesthetically sensitive analyses. Assigning dates to specific works of Mesoamerican art and architecture, generally speaking, lies outside their province. There are, however, notable exceptions to that rule, wherein art historians have constructed chronological schemes from within the confines of their own discipline. Such efforts, while scarce, are particularly relevant and provocative for the comparative hermeneutics of sacred architecture, and no one is nearly so intriguing in this regard as Herbert Spinden.

Part II of Spinden's *A Study of Maya Art* (1913) convenes an art historical (or archaeo-art historical) tradition of organizing pre-Columbian art and architecture according to time that arises largely independently of the stratigraphic efforts of mainstream archaeology. In addition to his erudition of forms and styles in pre-Columbian art, Spinden has a passion for developmental, evolutionary schemes and, so, moves at every opportunity to impose a diachronic organization on his materials. Without being systematically separated, Spinden's chronologic agenda really has two phases, each with a respective goal and a respective foundational premise.[167]

In the first phase, the more properly art historical of the two, Spinden's goal is to formulate, on the basis of art styles alone, *relative chronological "sequences in art."* In contrast to sequencing on the basis of associated potsherds, he hazards to consider art and architecture themselves as historical documents. His basic premise here is that arrangements of art on the basis of form and technique necessarily engender arrangements of chronological significance.[168] In this project, which depends heavily on artistic intuition, Spinden is uncannily successful. Subtle variations in Maya art — for instance, fluctuations in foreshortening and perspective, shifts in body postures and poses, increasing complexity and flamboyance, and the development of round relief from flat relief — become, in his perspicacious view, not simply stylistic changes in Maya art but "criteria for chronological sequences."[169] Spinden's discussion of Maya architecture proper is likewise replete with developmental sequences based directly on variations in formal-constructional features. He divines, for instance, that: (1) the simple two-room ground plan evolves respectively into the sanctuary, portico, and palace; (2) the temples with the largest proportion of room space are the latest in construction; (3) roof constructions develop through stages from "cumbersome to airy"; and (4) irregular platform mounds are "decadent examples of the early artificial acropolis."[170] And, with the same eye to evolution over time in Maya architectural decoration, Spinden (re)constructs the origin of the mask panel, the development of geometric decoration, and the sequences of building for roof combs and crests.[171] All these evolutionary sequences are discerned strictly on the basis of the art or architecture itself!

The legacy of this amazing portion of Spinden's work is ironic. As other modes of dating, external to the actual art and architecture, continually bore out his efforts, even the most archaeologically minded scholars were awed by the accuracy of Spinden's form-derived sequences. Yet, in the wake of alternative dating techniques (especially epigraphy and stratigraphy), his method became, almost

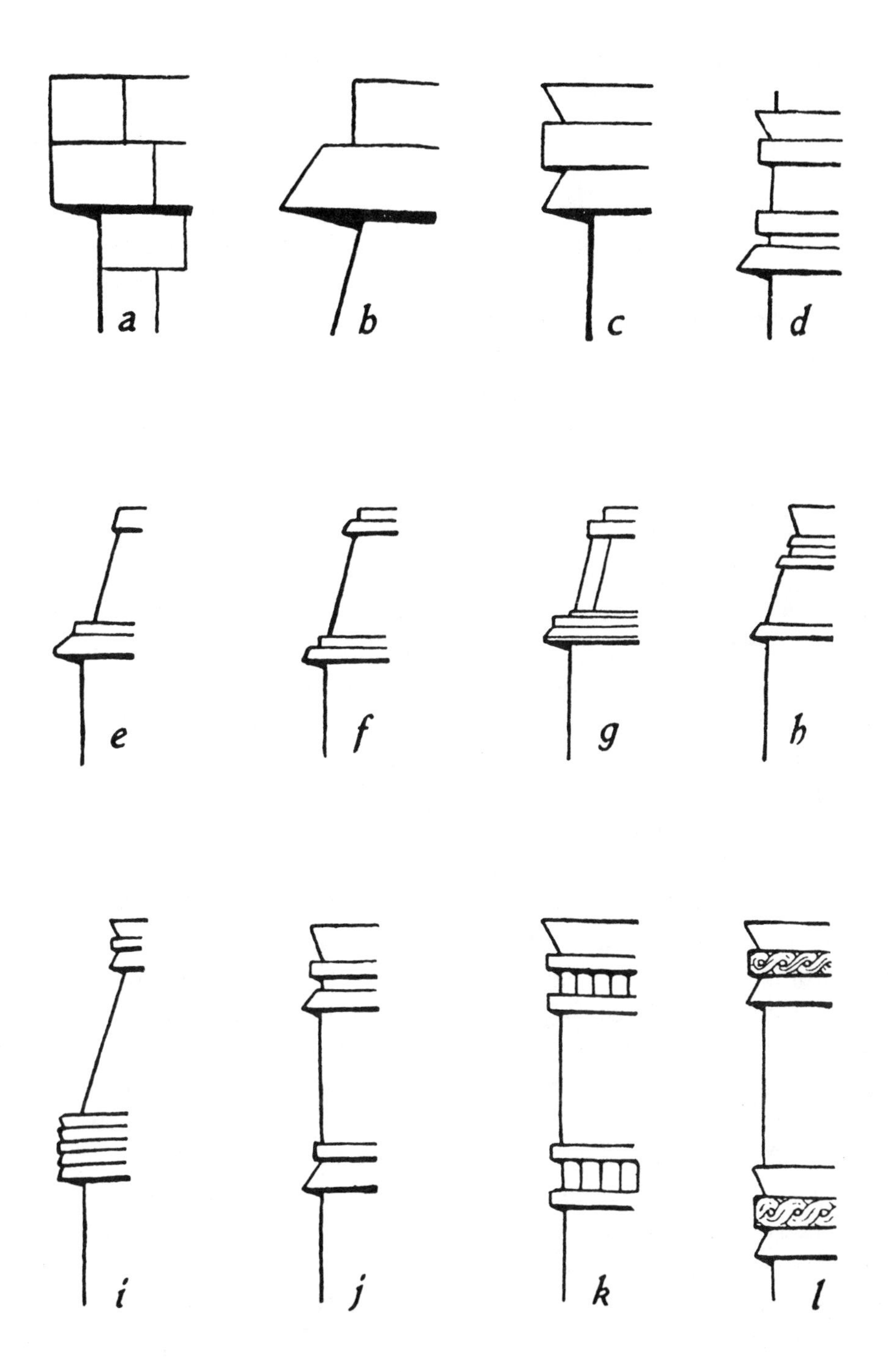

Spinden's categorization of pre-Columbian Maya cornice forms: *a*, southern area; *b*, Usumacinta area; *c*, northern area; *d*, *h*, *i*, and *j*, Chichén Itzá; *e*, *f*, and *g*, Palenque; *k*, Labná; and *l*, Chacmultún. At points, Spinden moved beyond the organization of Maya architecture in terms of strictly formal styles to render generalizations by geographical region and, even more daringly, to formulate "evolutionary sequences in Maya building" based directly on the art or architecture itself. (Spinden, *A Study of Maya Art*.)

immediately, a historical curiosity. Even Proskouriakoff, Spinden's most faithful follower, while similarly aspiring to retrieve a relative chronology of art forms (particularly of stelae in her case), considered that "it would be quite unreasonable to hope that we can date monuments precisely by an examination of their style."[172] Her *A Study of Classic Maya Sculpture* (1950) epitomizes the reversal of Spinden's strategy that typifies later archaeo-art historical studies. Proskouriakoff first arranges the monuments chronologically (in this case on the basis of Morley's epigraphic series from *The Inscriptions of Peten* [1937–1938]) and then undertakes "a systematic study of the manner in which their stylistic peculiarities develop."[173] In other words, she (and nearly everyone else) applies archaeologically derived chronologies to art; she does *not,* as Spinden had, claim to derive chronological series directly from the art itself.

George Kubler, despite taking his cue from Alfred L. Kroeber rather than Spinden, actually demonstrates a stronger fidelity to the premise that the organization of pre-Columbian art and architecture according to form will necessarily engender a significant chronological organization.[174] Kubler parlays Kroeber's method of sequencing pottery on the basis of form-time correlations into an ambitious theory of "transformations in art."[175] For Kubler, however, the simple chronological ordering of works of art, like the pigeonholing of works according to stylistic and formal commonalities, is wholly unrewarding and largely irrelevant.[176] Alternatively, Kubler holds that the history of art (in Mesoamerica and elsewhere) is punctuated by "prime objects," exceptional and unprecedented inventions in art, "things of great generating power" that spawn entire systems of replicas, reproductions, and derivatives.[177] Thus, where simply dating works of art is of little consequence, he considers it vitally important to retrieve, where possible, these "climactic entrances" and the linked sequences of replications that they spawn. Beyond just their chronological relationship, Kubler concentrates on the *historical* relationships between specific works of art and architecture, explaining their connections particularly via the processes of continuity and rupture, or "renascence" and "disjunction."[178] At this point, then, his more subtle initiative — the inadvertent bequest of the first phase of Spinden's chronologic program — transcends the notion of organization by time in favor of organization by "tradition" (and so will resurface at that portion of this chapter).

The second phase of Spinden's diachronic organization of Mesoamerican art and architecture espouses the more typically archaeological goal of "historical reconstruction"; he is, however, atypical (in fact, unique) in his optimism regarding the role of art in that agenda. For Spinden, art (including architecture) is, in fact, the quintessential diagnostic for the sequential ordering of Maya cultural events! His fundamental premise here is that the history of Maya art directly corresponds to (though is not derivative of) the wider politico-socio-economic history of the Maya. Thus, Spinden aims whenever possible to translate his creative "sequences in art" into more tangible and, in his view, more important statements about the evolution of Maya culture in general — for instance, the workings of their polities, their social organizations, and their migration and communication patterns. This portion of his work, considerably less successful, is likewise less enduring.[179]

Proskouriakoff, again typifying the moderation of the archaeo-art historical position, concurs with Spinden that there is a basic correspondence between developments in Maya art and developments in the sociopolitical realms of Maya culture, although, unlike Spinden, she is dubious that art can serve as a particularly reliable resource for retrieving those other dimensions of pre-Columbian life.[180] By contrast, Kubler and the more proper art historians have absolutely no sympathy with Spinden's use of art as an index of cultural development. Kubler follows Focillon in demanding the irreducibility and "special logic" of art; for them, art operates according to its own principles, independent of "history" on a grandeur scale.[181] Accordingly, their arrangements of art and architecture, while similarly employing time as a principle of organization, are explicitly antithetic to Spinden's insofar as they purport to be retrieving *artistic traditions* (that is, chains of *historically* related works of art) that, at least ostensibly, bear no direct relation to contemporaneous developments in Mesoamerican political hegemonies, economic processes, or patterns of migration. As pre-Columbian art history matures (parallel again the history of religions), many within its ranks feel that these claims of radical irreducibility and autonomy for art are, at this point, stifling and no longer appropriate;[182] the quest after the historical relations between specific indigenous works of art (for instance, at Tula and Chichén Itzá) remains, however, as urgent as ever.

In any case, generally speaking, the fervor for assigning dates to buildings has cooled considerably. The chronologic obsessions that, for decades, dominated Mesoamerican studies, including the study of pre-Columbian architecture, are permanently and unlamentably out of vogue, first, because many of the fundamental dating problems have been laid to rest or have fallen to the province of a highly sophisticated subspecialization of dating technologies, allowing Mesoamericanists to concentrate their efforts elsewhere, and, second, because no one in either archaeology or art history is any longer content to equate a pre-Hispanic building's significance with its date of construction.

Organization by Function: Temples, Palaces, or Whatever

> In Europe the building, the market, the courts of justice, the palaces and the houses are each directly recognizable as isolated and functionally definite entities. In Mesoamerican architecture such clear distinctions are often impossible . . . [it consists of] a system of poorly differentiated functional building types.
>
> *George Kubler, 1958*[183]

The pre-Columbian use and function of Mesoamerican monuments is never obvious.[184] Where the forms, construction techniques, and even ages of the ruins have proven retrievable, aside from a resigned consensus that what transpired in these pre-Columbian buildings was usually "ceremonial" and always "mysterious," their precise functions have remained disturbingly and perpetually elusive. Holmes's nineteenth-century frustration might well describe the current situation: "the question as to the function of the many buildings now found in various stages of demolition in the Maya province has been raised again and again and still remains somewhat imperfectly answered."[185]

Two fiascoes in the literature well instantiate the clumsiness with which functions have been assigned to pre-Columbian buildings. First, arising primarily as a reaction against Old World diffusionist theories, is the timeworn insistence that the pyramids of America, while formally resembling Egyptian pyramid-tombs, were in function not funerary monuments but simply giant substructures like the ziggurats of Babylonia. The tomb-versus-substructure formulation — repeated by Charnay, Joyce, Spinden, and a host of other commentators[186] — was virtual dogma until 1954, when Alberto Ruz Lhuiller excavated the fabulous pyramid-tomb of Lord Pacal in the Temple of the Inscriptions at Palenque.[187] Ruz, in other words, demonstrated indubitably that (at least some) Mesoamerican pyramids did serve a funerary function, and since his seminal excavations at Palenque it has become increasingly clear, contrary to the old conventions, that the architectural commemoration of the dead was certainly among the very highest and most widespread motivations for pre-Columbian building.[188]

Second, similarly untoward but even more tenacious, is the stock distinction between "temples" and "palaces" — ostensibly a bifurcation of pre-Columbian structures into "sacred" and "secular" functions. From the earliest colonial era, every structure that, however vaguely, connotes native spirituality (particularly pyramids) was declared a "temple," while the even more wildly inclusive category of "palace" (usually assigned to the multiroomed, rectangular structures that rest on relatively low substructures) became a catchall designation for any other impressive, though seemingly nonreligious building. Storage, administration, craft production, residence, and some ancillary ceremonial preparation are all routinely batted around as possible pre-Columbian functions for these so-called palaces.[189] In his *Views of Ancient Monuments* (1844), Frederick Catherwood, for instance, among countless examples, divides virtually all of Maya monumental architecture between "temples," where he feels certain that pre-Hispanic religious rituals were performed, and "palaces," which presumably housed more prosaic administrative or residential activities.[190] No one (including Catherwood) found this bathetic distinction satisfactory, but over the next hundred years, almost without addendum or alteration, the temple-palace bifurcation was entrenched in the archaeological (and art historical) literature.[191] In the 1960s, Maya "palaces" were redesignated by the more neutral (and more formal than functional) term "range structures," but their pre-Columbian function — and this problem is nowhere more trenchant than in the southern portion of Chichén Itzá (that is, "Old Chichén") — is still almost wholly a matter of conjecture.[192]

In short, none of the empirical certainty that applies to the formal, technical, and chronological status of pre-Columbian buildings obtains in discerning their original, indigenous functions. All strains of Mesoamericanist scholarship are forced to admit their unanimous frustration regarding just what sort of activities transpired inside (and on top of) these pre-Columbian buildings. Each strain, however, responds to the functional conundrum in its own characteristic way. The freewheeling antiquarians of last century, for instance, embraced the search after the uses of pre-Columbian architecture with characteristic abandon: Count Waldeck took flight from the arbitrary Spanish appellations of "Nunnery" and "Temple of the Dwarfs" at Uxmal (tellingly sophomoric in themselves) to re-create a detailed schedule of exotic monastic activities in those buildings;[193] and Le Plongeon is credited with the game surmise that the miniature temples of eastern Yucatán must have housed a devout race of pygmies.[194] Charnay, somewhat more reserved in his speculations on the use of pre-Hispanic structures, admitted that the ruins themselves shed little light on their original functions — "not that theories are wanting" — and, thus, based most of his own conjectures on analogies to the indigenous lifeways that are reported in the colonial texts.[195]

The successes of the archaeological mainstream in determining the functions of Mesoamerican buildings are more well tempered, but hardly greater. The positivistic Maudslay introduced a few implicit functional distinctions (for instance, stelae versus altars) but carefully qualified each such attempt so that he could not be accused of "speculating" on what was not immediately observable.[196] Traditional archaeologists, eminently curious about the usages of various buildings, have had

The so-termed Palace of the Governor at Uxmal, which is often described as the climax of the Maya "palace" or "range structure." The countless apocryphal names assigned to other structures in the same complex at Uxmal — for instance, the Pyramid of the Dwarf, the Quadrangle of the Nuns, the House of the Old Woman, the Cemetery Group, and the House of the Pigeons — testify to investigators' frustrations in discerning the pre-Columbian functions of these buildings. The same chaos in naming is evident at Chichén Itzá, where nearly every structure has been assigned innumerable eccentric misnomers. (Photo by Lawrence G. Desmond.)

somewhat more success in correlating distinctive formal types with their possible functions: Satterthwaite, for instance, located a number of similar buildings that seem assuredly to have been "sweat bathes";[197] since J. L. Stephens, Maya "ball courts" are rightly connected with their Aztec counterparts as described in the eyewitness accounts of the conquistadors; and Karl Ruppert surveyed a number of similarly odd Maya structures (the Caracol at Chichén Itzá included) before concluding with some confidence that they must have served as "astronomical observatories."[198]

For decades, these three — "sweat bathes," ball courts, and "observatories" — buildings of seemingly unmistakable usages were the only other functional types that could be respectably identified alongside the well-worn designations of "temples" and "palaces." A more ambitious functional organization came in what Sylvanus Morley described as his "Classification of Maya Buildings and Other Constructions According to Their Probable Uses" (1946).[199] Although Morley's categories are actually more formal than functional (they refer only vaguely to indigenous activities or events), he does chart the geographical distribution of twenty types of monuments, including pyramid-temples, small temples, palaces, astronomical observatories, ball courts, colonnades, arches or gateways, monumental stairways, reviewing stands, and causeways. Twenty years later, H.E.D. Pollock rejected Morley's scheme as misleading and speculative, but then, after surveying the more recent literature on the pre-Columbian uses of Maya buildings, presented an alternative scheme that, while ostensibly based on function, descends just as quickly to formal principles of organization; Pollock enumerates, for instance, temples, shrines, palaces, ball courts, sweat houses, ceremonial platforms, mortuary structures, oratories, towers, city walls, and causeways.[200] In short, the progress is minuscule.

Critics of traditional archaeology in the 1940s, predictably enough, denounced the timidity in hypothesizing about the functions of pre-Hispanic buildings and noted that any remark on the ceremonies attendant to these buildings had been "incidental and rather by-the-way."[201] These critics admitted that categorizing pre-Columbian cultural materials (buildings included) in terms of their generalized usages (and their techniques of manufacture) would be more inferential and speculative than formal organizations, but they considered the risks necessary if archaeologists were to have any success in "augmenting our knowledge of the cultural context."[202] Once again, the condemnatory diagnosis is apt, but these commentators were equally ineffectual in delivering a methodological remedy that shed any light on the indigenous functions of pre-Columbian buildings.

The more proper "new archaeologists" that follow express similar discontents, but they offer some redress by pushing the question of "function" away from the pre-Columbian rituals and activities in specific buildings toward a more generalized, Malinowskian version of structural-functional anthropology wherein the components of culture "function" to maintain the organic whole.[203] The reformulation of the problem by these more systems-oriented archaeologists, together with their wider concern for the nonelite sectors of indigenous society, does issue in some clarification regarding the pre-Columbian uses of residential architecture; and their interest in long-distance trade issues in the appreciation of some forms of vernacular architecture such as "warehouses" and "lighthouses."[204] Generally speaking, however, they too are largely ineffectual in fine-tuning the vaguely "ceremonial" usages of the more large-scaled, pre-Hispanic buildings.

A less direct but more productive archaeological strategy for discerning the functions of specific buildings involves the retrieval and identification of characteristic types of artifacts in those buildings — particularly so-called ritual indicators such as censers, caches, altars, and nondomestic pottery. R. E. Smith, for instance, attempted to distinguish ceremonial from domestic pottery as a means of ascertaining the functions of various Maya structures; and Proskouriakoff correlated types of architectural configurations with distinctive sorts of associated artifacts to hypothesize changes in ritual practice between the Classic and Postclassic eras.[205] More recently, Diane Chase, among others, has augmented this approach with a stronger dose of ethnohistorical research by systematically cross-checking documentary references to Maya ritual (particularly in Landa's *Relación*) against the archaeological evidence.[206]

In any case, where archaeologists are both desperately curious about the usages of pre-Hispanic buildings and deeply frustrated by their maladroitness in retrieving them, strict art historians, generally speaking, express a categorical disinterest in organizing art or architecture according to its function. Kubler,

TABLE VIII

CLASSIFICATION OF MAYA BUILDINGS AND OTHER CONSTRUCTIONS ACCORDING TO THEIR PROBABLE USES

Kind of Building, or Construction	Examples	
	Old Empire	New Empire
Pyramid-temples	Temples I, II, III, IV, V, Tikal; Temple 26, Copan	Castillo, Chichen Itza; House of the Magician, Uxmal
Small temples	Structures 20, 21, 33, 42, 44, Yaxchilan	Red House, Chichen Itza; House of the Old Woman, Uxmal
Palaces	Palace, Palenque; Palace (Structure A-V), Uaxactun	Monjas, Chichen Itza; Governor's Palace, Uxmal
Astronomical observatories	Structures E-I, E-II, E-III, E-VII, Uaxactun; Structures II, III, IV, VIII, Naachtun	Caracol, Chichen Itza; Round Tower, Mayapan
Ball courts	Structures 9 and 10, Copan; Structure 14, Yaxchilan	Ball court, Chichen Itza; Ball court, Uxmal
Colonnades	Structure J-2, Piedras Negras; Structure 74, Yaxchilan	Northwest Colonnade, Chichen Itza; Colonnade, Ake
Dance platforms	Structures 66, 78, 79, 80, 82, Tikal	Dance platform in front of Castillo, Chichen Itza; Structure 8, Tulum
Peristyle courts	Not yet found	Market-place and Structure 2-D-6, Chichen Itza
Vapor baths	Structure P-7, Piedras Negras	Structures 3-E-3 and 3-C-17, Chichen Itza
Arches, or gateways	Not yet found	Arch, Kabah; Portal, Labna
Shrines	Not yet found	Small structure at edge of Well of Sacrifice (Structure 1-D-1), Chichen Itza; Structure 7, Tulum
Skull platforms	Not yet found	Place of the Skulls, Chichen Itza; Platforms in Cemetery, Uxmal
Monumental stairways	Jaguar Stairway, Copan; Hieroglyphic Stairway (Structure 5), Yaxchilan	Not yet found
Reviewing stands	North side, West Court, Copan	Not yet found
Square stadiums for public spectacles	Great Plaza, Copan; Ceremonial Plaza, Quirigua	Not yet found
City walls	Becan*	Mayapan; Tulum
Causeways	Coba-Yaxuna; Coba-Kukicaan	Uxmal-Kabah; Izamal-Kantunil
Foundation platforms	Terrace of Group A, Tikal; Terrace of Group A, Uaxactun	North terrace, Chichen Itza; Terrace of the Governor's Palace, Uxmal
Bridges and aqueducts	Pusilha; Becan; Palenque	Not yet found

* A moat also has been found around this site, which may possibly be early New Empire rather than late Old Empire.

Sylvanus Morley's "Classification of Maya Buildings and Other Constructions According to Their Probable Uses," 1947. Morley's ambitious attempt to organize Maya architecture according to pre-Columbian functions actually reverts, in most cases, to simply formal criteria such as "peristyle courts" or "monumental stairways." It is noteworthy also that in the version of this chart that appears in the heavily revised third edition of Morley's *The Ancient Maya* (1956), George Brainerd replaces Morley's "historical" criteria (i.e., "Old Empire" and "New Empire") with presumably more neutral geographical criteria (i.e., "Central Area" and "Northern Area"). (Reprinted from *The Ancient Maya* by Sylvanus Griwold Morley with permission of the publishers, Stanford University Press. Copyright ©1946, 1947 by the Board of Trustees of the Leland Stanford Junior University.)

again polemical to archaeology, distinguishes between two classes of cultural artifacts — "objects of utility" and "useless objects," that is, objects of art — and then restricts his inquiry to the second of these. He writes: "The archaeologists and anthropologists classify things by their uses, having first separated material and mental culture, or things and ideas. The historians of art, who separate useful and aesthetic products, classify these latter by types, by schools, and by styles."[207]

Not surprisingly, art history (of this sort anyway) contributes even less than excavationary archaeology to the problem of the activities and uses of pre-Columbian buildings. In fact, to draw this discussion to an abrupt close, the only streams of scholarship to penetrate with any success into the particulars of pre-Columbian ritual occasions and ceremonial events are the ethnohistorical and the ethnographical. Where archaeology has made progress in this regard, it invariably has done so by looking to colonial-period texts and present-day native practices for plausible hypotheses that might be tested in excavation, that is, by relying on some form of ethnographic analogy. Negotiating the impasse regarding the indigenous usages of the "poorly differentiated functional building types" of Mesoamerica, especially the esoteric religious usages, depends directly upon the viability of ethnographic analogy or, perhaps even more promisingly (as this project does), on tapping the potential of creative and responsible cross-cultural comparison. In sum, while recovering the indigenous activities (or "ritual-architectural events") is an absolutely essential component of a hermeneutical approach to the ruins of, for instance, Tula and Chichén Itzá, virtually nowhere are the double-edged risks and rewards of comparison more keenly felt.

Organization by Geography: Expedience, Environment, Ecology

> For Kate firmly believed that part of the horror of the Mexican people came from the unsoothed dryness of the land and the untempered crudity of the flat-edged sunshine. If only there could be a softening of water in the air, and a haze above the trees, the unspoken and unspeakable malevolence would die out of the human hearts.
>
> *D. H. Lawrence, 1959*[208]

An interest in the natural environment of Mesoamerica forever accompanies the study of its monuments and civilization. The perpetuity of this concern for the bionomic as well as cultural landscape, and thus of geography as a principle for organizing and comparing Mesoamerican architecture, has been ensured by three successive academic motives: (1) encyclopedic expedience; (2) a concern for the natural environment as an essential component of pre-Columbian historical (re)constructions; and (3) more recently, a cultural-ecological school, which contends that the distinctive character of any pre-Columbian culture (including the peculiarities of its architecture) owes in large part to the natural ecological conditions to which it adapted. Because each of these variations on the geographical organization of pre-Columbian architecture presents its own problems and possibilities for interpreting pre-Columbian architecture, it is worth considering briefly the roughly chronological progression from, as it were, expedience to environment to ecology.

All of the more scientifically predisposed explorers of the nineteenth century were very much concerned with the natural environments as well as the cultural remains of Mesoamerica. For his second expedition to Yucatán (1841), John Lloyd Stephens, for instance, recruited naturalist Samuel Cabot Jr. to collect and identify the strange plants and animals he had noted on the previous journey;[209] and W. H. Holmes toured Mexico (1894) as the anthropological specialist on an interdisciplinary team that included a botanist, a geologist, and a natural historian.[210] Moreover, as they wrote up the results of their cartographic and archaeo-architectural surveys, both Stephens and Holmes adopted organizational arrangements that first outlined geographically distinct regions of Middle America (for instance, Eastern Yucatán, Middle Northern Yucatán, Chiapas, and Oaxaca) and then marched methodically through a site-by-site survey of the ruins in each area.[211] Their contemporaries, Catherwood and Maudslay, took precisely the same formulaic tack.[212] For these early writers, it could scarcely have been otherwise; the restraints of positivism censured speculation on the origins of the monuments, the chronology of the ruins was, as yet, impenetrable, and the uses of the buildings were absolutely obscure. Organization by geographical area (together with description of form and construction techniques) provided the obvious and expedient alternative, eminently appropriate for an "objective" presentation of the virginal data.

As Mesoamerican archaeology matured and garnered a more comprehensive knowledge of the pre-Columbian sites, the priority of expedient presentation dovetailed with that of encyclopedic comprehensiveness. By overlaying a grid on the map of Middle America, so the argument goes, no corner escapes methodological scrutiny. In that spirit of categorical efficiency, geographical organization was conventionalized by the archaeological (and art historical) community as a neutral common language — the perfect vehicle for their presumptions of impartiality, an organizing principle made safe precisely because of its *in*significance. In the early part of this century, the territory was variously reapportioned with respect to natural features (or, sometimes, modern political boundaries), but, typically, the purveyors of such geographic arrangements of pre-Columbian art and architecture claimed nothing more for their organizations than a convenient system of location, an orderly presentation of "what is," and where. The massive *Handbook of Middle American Indians,* for instance, includes the most comprehensive of countless surveys of American art and architecture that adopt geographical schemes in the interest of convenience and thoroughness: individual articles are dedicated to the respective architectures of large regions such as the Guatemalan Highlands, Maya Lowlands, Central Mexico, and then the architecture is arranged according to more specific geographical designations within those regions (for instance, the Río Bec, Chenes, Puuc, or Usumacinta River areas).[213] Most of the broadly framed art historical syntheses of pre-Columbian America during this era (and now) similarly espouse straightforward geographical organizations as a pragmatic necessity for completeness.[214]

While these encyclopedic surveys nearly always include perfunctory descriptions of natural features, their correlations of Mesoamerican architecture and the environment, generally speaking, amount to little more than refined versions of Holmes's survey of the regional availability of raw materials for building and the obvious constraints of terrain and climate.[215] By contrast, Alfred Kidder, again extending the boundaries of archaeology, exemplifies a tradition that demands a good deal more from its environmental studies. He wanted, in other words, more significant geographical organizations. Hypothesizing that the natural environment influenced pre-Columbian culture in direct and major ways, Kidder argued that thorough descriptions of specific environmental contexts constitute an essential component of the historical, ethnographic reconstructions to which he aspired — a backdrop for "full cultural pictures."[216] Because he considered the natural environment the logical point of departure for his interdisciplinary, pan-scientific approach to the major problems of Mesoamerican culture history, Kidder, beginning in the twenties, initiated unprecedentedly ambitious specialist studies into plant and animal biology, agronomy, hydrology, climatology, geology, and geography. Critically reviewing these early efforts (that is, looking back at the 1920s and 1930s from the 1950s), Kidder, as usual his own toughest critic, on the one hand judged this ambitious conception of an interdisciplinary approach that would situate reconstructions of pre-Columbian Maya culture history within its natural environmental settings to have been his most significant contribution to anthropology; yet, on the other hand, he felt compelled to admit that these specific researches had never been adequately synthesized.[217] Kidder, in other words, presaged but never attained a cultural-ecological, "holistic" conception of human populations and their environments as ecosystems.[218]

It remained for one branch of the "new archaeology" to employ geography and natural environment as significant, transdescriptive, "explanatory" principles of organization. Inspired particularly by the materialist theories of V. Gordon Childe, the 1960s witnessed a burgeoning interest in the articulations between ancient Mesoamerican cultures and their biological, climatological, and physical environments.[219] With this (re)emergence of both environmental determinism and cultural evolution, the specific processes of pre-Hispanic civilization were increasingly explained by focusing on subsistence, technology, and economics — all tied directly to the natural features of the landscape.[220] Julian Stewart, the principal figure in this environmental-evolutionary trend, held that different kinds of natural environments invariably spawn characteristic sorts of technological adaptations, which, in turn, would influence and condition other aspects of culture — including religion, art, and architecture.[221] William Sanders's conception of prehistoric Central Mexico as a "symbiotic region," Richard MacNeisch's search after the origins of New World agriculture, Karl Wittfogel's studies of hydrology and irrigation, and Gordon Willey's surveys of regional settlement patterns were (along with Stewart's work) taproots for a "cultural-ecological" school that elevated the natural environment to the status of a principal "causative agent" in Mesoamerican civilization. And in so doing, they espoused organization of pre-Columbian architecture that laced together geography with culture.[222]

The cultural-ecological school's most enduring principle of organization for art and architecture, borrowed from the study of modern ethnographic cultures, is that of the "culture area."[223] While the so-called culture areas (and subdivisions within those culture areas) that these new archaeologists delineate resemble the straightforward regional divisions of Holmes and Maudslay, they are more than convenient demarcations of the subject area. Culture areas are theoretical as well as descriptive categories; they endeavor to explain as well as locate pre-Columbian cultural remains, buildings included. The heuristic concept of a culture area is based on the notion of cultural adaptation to local environmental conditions, that is, the premise (à la Stewart) that the distinctive environmental features of a geographical province will necessarily spawn a set of cultural manifestations that are distinct from those of surrounding areas. Most famously, Paul Kirchhoff (1943) relied on the concept of a culture area to define and circumscribe the whole of "Mesoamerica" in terms of not only geographical boundaries but also a set of distinct cultural traits.[224] The same principle is particularized to distinguish ten significantly different cultural "sub-areas" of Mesoamerica, each presumably with its own characteristic art and architecture: the Maya Highlands, Maya Lowlands, Southern Periphery, Southern Veracruz-Tabasco, Oaxaca, Guerrero, Central Mexico, Central Veracruz, Huasteca, and West and Northern Frontier.[225] Moreover, the cultural subareas are further partitioned into innumerable "regions" (for instance, the Petén, the Usumacinta, the Montagua-Chamelecon, or the several divisions of Yucatán), within which are distinguished "localities" and, finally, individual "sites."[226] At each of these scales, the distinctiveness of the indigenous local culture (or building style) is, supposedly anyway, consequent of adaptation to the distinct local ecology.

With respect specifically to the hermeneutical interpretation of pre-Columbian art and architecture (and, more specifically still, the Tula–Chichén Itzá problem), the legacy of the cultural-ecological school and the concept of a culture area is mixed. The attempt to compare and explain differences between various pre-Columbian styles of art and architecture by reference to their respective environmental contexts is intriguing, to say the least. Eric Wolf, for instance, endorses the notion of ecologically derivative art when he maintains that the difference between Mexican and Maya art is a reflection of the climatic differences between high plains and rain forests: "The Mexican style is geometric, monumental. The Maya style, on the other hand, loves riotous movement, luxuriant form, flamboyance."[227] Yet, because the cultural-ecological school (in the universalizing spirit of the new archaeology) is concerned primarily to construct theoretical models of systems and processes — it rejects "particularism" in favor of laws and regularities[228] — these scholars (deliberately) dwell neither on the specific relations between environment, architecture, and ideology at single sites nor on the unique histories of those individual sites (as Kidder, for instance, had hoped to do). In their hands, local variations in architecture (or religion) typically are reduced to pawns in some theory of emergent civilizations or some model of ancient social structure, leaving the indigenous religious usages and meanings of those buildings largely unexplored. Even so, their project could be exceedingly interesting to historians of religions were it not for the disappointing disparity between methodological goals and realizations; they simply do not follow through with the interesting project of correlating distinctive natural environments (or, as Raffaele Pettazzoni, Mircea Eliade, or Ake Hultkranz might suggest, the *human experience* of distinctive natural environments) with characteristic types of architecture.[229]

Nevertheless, on the more positive side, despite the overbearing materialism of cultural ecology, both the study of space on a regional scale and the study of "nonpedigreed" Mesoamerican architecture in relation to the environmental context are treated with unprecedented sophistication. In reaction against the timeworn preoccupation with the elite and "fancy" architecture of Mesoamerican ceremonial centers (which is actually where our attention is focused with respect to the Tula–Chichén Itzá problem), the cultural-ecologists redirect their gaze toward house mounds and vernacular architecture. They concentrate especially on large-scaled, quantifiable issues such as regional land use, population density, resource management, subsistence patterns, and, particularly, intersite relations (including, for instance, relations between Central Mexico and Yucatán). Thus, if they do not contribute much to the study of individual buildings, or even individual sites, their efforts certainly do enrich and enlarge the scope of pre-Columbian architectural studies.[230]

In any case, these shifts and leaps in methodological sophistication eventually necessitate a serious reconsideration of the original concept of the so-called culture area. The old notion of mapping Mesoamerica in terms of distinctive ecologies that had bred distinctive cultures (and distinctive architectures) is challenged on several grounds: (1) because it distorts the shifts of cultural-geographical boundaries over time (most obviously, it becomes apparent that the borders of the culture area of "Mesoamerica" had fluctuated considerably over the centuries);[231] (2) because the culture area concept implies a linear model (that is, environment determines culture) rather than a more organic, systemic model (that is, human systems seen as parts of ecosystems);[232] and (3) because most archaeologists come to believe that sociocultural institutions (for instance, "information and commodity exchange networks") rather than the natural environment are responsible for the cultural geography of Mesoamerica.[233]

In short, as more data and more complex models of Mesoamerican civilization emerged through the 1960s, 1970s, and thereafter, correlating different sorts of natural environments with characteristic sorts of cultural adaptations became more, rather than less, difficult. There was, in fact, enough backpedaling and qualification of the correspondences between ecologies and cultures that the conventional culture areas and subareas descended to a status hardly more explanatory — or more significant — than their expedient, "objective" precedents. James Hester is probably correct when he says, "the greatest utility of the culture area concept [by the mid-1970s] is that it provides a framework well suited for the organization of data for teaching purposes."[234] Ecological explanation retreated to cartographic location and to pedagogy. The cycle of geographical principles for organizing Mesoamerican architecture, in a sense, came full circle, from expedience to environment to ecology and back to expedience. Or, from the perspective of a hermeneutical history of religions (or even archaeology), *significant* geographical organization lost its edge and ceded once again to insignificant, largely arbitrary classification.

Organization by Culture: Developmental Stages and Periods

> The evolution of the culture of mankind . . . is a fascinating story of adventure and progress, of a species lifting itself up by its bootstraps from the status of a mere animal to a radically new way of life.
>
> *Leslie White, 1949*[235]

During the French intervention in Mexico in the 1860s, Napoleon III initiated the Commission Scientifique du Mexique to study pre-Columbian antiquities, a commission that included, among others, Désiré Charnay and prominent architectural historian Eugene-Emmanuel Viollet-le-Duc (although the latter never actually visited Mexico).[236] The fruit of Viollet-le-Duc's participation in this venture, albeit preposterous in the extreme, was a "scientific analysis" to accompany an album of photographs by Charnay; together the pictures and text appear as *Cités et Ruines Américaines: Mitla, Palenque, Izamal, Chichén Itzá, Uxmal* (Paris, 1862–63).[237] Influenced both by the recent work of Compte Joseph-Arthur de Gobineau, *Sur l'Inéqualité des Races Humaines* (1853–55), and by the unrestrained diffusionist theories of the day, Viollet-le-Duc's bizarre essay undertakes to correlate various modes of architectural construction with the "instincts of particular races."[238] He is certain that the builders of the impressive pre-Columbian monuments could not have been indigenous Americans, but his supposed race-architectural correlations allow him to determine their original nationalities by reading the telltale racial signatures in the Mexican ruins: his fantastic reasoning holds, for instance, that because only

Aryans and Semites are capable of building in dry masonry, they must have influenced the ancient Americans; the ubiquity of mortar and plaster in the ruins is a sign of an infiltration of Turanian or Finnish blood; and the use of timber construction in some pre-Columbian monuments is more evidence of an infusion of Aryans into ancient Mexico.[239]

Although rightfully obscure, Viollet-le-Duc's race-architecture correlations earn him nominal membership in a prolific strain of Mesoamericanist scholarship that organizes the plentitude of architectural remains in terms of culture, or more properly, in terms of a hierarchy of cultural attainments — a strategy that is invariably tied to the currency of some sort of evolutionary theory of culture. There is typically (but not always) a chronological component to these sorts of developmental organizational schemes, but they are more ambitious (that is, more loaded and more evaluative) than strictly diachronic arrangements insofar as they presume to chronicle advances in cultural sophistication over time. For this group, it is the relative cultural attainments of the builders, not simply the age of a building, that is the decisive criterion of comparison and organization.

Arnold Toynbee's famous scheme for the historical development of civilizations and E. B. Tylor's notion of cultural evolution certainly provide more venerable pedigrees for this strain than does Viollet-le-Duc's racist-diffusionism, although the most substantial point of departure for this mode of operating is Lewis Henry Morgan's theory of unilinear evolution. Extending Darwin's revolutionary notion of biological evolution to the history of New World cultures, Morgan (another who believes that cultural traits are carried in the blood) dominates the fledgling field of Americanist studies in the United States from the mid-nineteenth century.[240] Foreshadowing the cultural materialism of the new archaeology, Morgan's influential *Ancient Society* (1877) presents an evolutionary scheme in which fixed developmental stages — specifically, savagery, barbarism, and civilization — correspond with certain types of subsistence and technology (including building types) as well as with characteristic types of sociocultural life. This infamous tripartite evolutionary scheme (along with subdivisions within each stage) should, according to Morgan, provide a means for significantly organizing and assessing the cultural productions of all peoples in all contexts, pre-Columbian Mesoamerica included. Thus, although Morgan's fieldwork was limited to contemporary North American tribal societies (particularly the Iroquois), he was able, with the faithful ethnohistorical assistance of Adolph Bandelier, to pry the contours of ancient Mexican culture history into his notorious three-stage sequence.[241]

Moreover, Morgan is particularly relevant to this project, not only because he embraces (one version of) the comparative method, but also because he applies this tripartite, unilinear organization explicitly to indigenous American architecture. His contribution is, however (particularly from the perspective of a hermeneutical history of religions), largely strangled by two conjoined factors. First is his thoroughly ethnocentric attitude that ancient (particularly non-Western) art is significant only as a demonstration of "the inferiority of savage man in the mental and moral scale, undeveloped, inexperienced, and held down by his low appetites and passions."[242] Second, and more specifically, is his equally untenable insistence that the Aztecs (whom he considered the "highest" of Mesoamerican peoples) were stunted in the "Middle Status" of barbarism: in Morgan's imagination (way offtrack at this point), Montezuma is reduced to a tribal chief, his palace to a communal dwelling, and the capital city of Tenochtitlán to a humble pueblo.[243] Accordingly, Morgan totally ignores the fabulous tradition of pre-Columbian public architecture — he considers that the great cities and monumental buildings of the Aztecs and the rest of Middle America existed only in the self-aggrandizing fables of the conquistadors — but he does impose his evolutionary organization on native American house architecture and the configuration of domestic groups.[244] In that context, he traces an ascending progress from "the hut of the savage, through the communal house of the barbarians, to the house of the single family of civilized nations."[245]

The undisputed reign of Morgan's unilinear evolution eventually passed. In fact, owing particularly to the enormous influence of Franz Boas who had absolutely no sympathy for these evolutionary theories, schemes of regularized cultural development were wholly expunged from the Americanist literature from 1900 until the 1940s, at which point, however, a "neo-evolutionism" reblossomed in the likes of Leslie White, Gordon Childe, and Julian Stewart.[246] About the same time, Wendell Bennett and Junius Bird produced an unassuming handbook, *Andean Culture History* (1949), which attempts to classify the artifacts of that region according to an evolutionary scheme.[247] They divide the early, middle, and late segments of Andean archaeological history into "culture-stages" on the basis of dominant modes of economic activity and political organization; each stage is labeled according to the "outstanding characteristics of the period as a whole" — namely, Cultist (1000–0 B.C.E.), Experimenter (0–600 C.E.), Master Craftsman (600–1000), Expansionist (1000–1200), City Builder (1200–1450), and Imperialist (after 1450).[248]

Mesoamericanists, impressed by the heuristic possibilities of this sort of classification by cultural stages, juxtaposed Bennett and Bird's South American scheme with an older tripartite cultural-chronological division of Central Mexican culture history (that is, "Archaic," "Toltec," and "Aztec"),[249] and then borrowed philological usage from Greek and Roman archaeology to whelp the indomitable trio — "Pre-Classic," "Classic," and "Post-Classic."[250] A new tripartite organization was born! Instead of Morgan's model of perpetual cultural ascent, however, the new hybridized Andean-Mexican-Greek system of classification adduced a bell curve model of pre-Columbian cultural history — an imaginal vision of American civilization rising, peaking, and declining, the influence of which can hardly be overestimated. In any case, it remained to assign the general categories to specific manifestations of pre-Columbian culture (and art and architecture). With respect to Central Mexico, "Classic" — presumably the best, greatest, and most sublime in Mesoamerican cultural development — was assigned to the florescence of Teotihuacán (still at this point termed "Toltec"), while Tula and Tenochtitlán, even in their respective primes, were designated "Postclassic," as though they were largely derivative of this Teotihuacán climax. In the Maya area, the same procedure obtained, with the lofty designation of "Classic" awarded, of course, to the cultures of the Southern Maya Lowlands, preeminently those sites and eras endowed with glyph-inscribed stelae. Earlier Maya occupations were considered Preclassic, implying that they were largely preparatory to the Petén climax, while the northern Maya sites, including Chichén Itzá, that were generally without initial series dates, were slotted into the degenerative Postclassic.

With the construction of this new tripartite scheme and its implementation in Mesoamerica, a lacuna in pedagogic classification was filled and a workable convention established; mere chronological classification would seem finally to have been transcended by a more significant organization in terms of the relative cultural attainments of various pre-Columbian societies. Almost immediately, however, there was ambiguity regarding the heuristic status of the Preclassic, Classic, and Postclassic categories, a bedevilment that would be reiterated with wearisome regularity: some scholars adopted both the logic and the terminology of the new system and thus employed the before, during-, and after-Classic units as "stages" of cultural development (that is, relative levels of achievement) while other, more conservative scholars adopted the new terms but employed them simply as neutral, chronological "periods." A third group, seemingly oblivious to the important difference, flip-flopped (sometimes even in the same article) between the conceptions of "Classic" as a "developmental stage" and as a "chronological period." Willey notes (though understates) the awkwardness of the resultant situation: "The ambiguity between strict chronology, on the one hand, and the characterization of social and cultural configurations and similarities through time, on the other, has given rise to confusion and misunderstanding. . . . Obviously we are dealing with two kinds of classification here."[251]

Confusingly enough, after the mid-twentieth century, virtually all Mesoamericanists were using some version of the Preclassic-Classic-Postclassic rubric, although they were actually operating with several quite different principles of organization. A number of influential classifications of Mesoamerican culture in the 1950s (for instance, by Armillas, Wauchope, Caso, Brainerd, and others) were explicitly developmental or "historical-developmental," although some, like that of Willey and Phillips (1958), denied being "evolutionary."[252] In either case, these developmental schemes relied particularly on technological, social, and political organization (and, to a lesser extent, religion and aesthetics) as criteria to isolate "cultural stages" (for instance, the Lithic, Archaic, Formative, Classic, and Post-Classic Stages) or "cultural types" (for instance, hunters and gatherers as opposed to agriculturalists or "irrigation civilizations" as opposed to "theocratic states"). These developmentalists could, at least ostensibly, correlate distinctive types of pre-Columbian architecture with respective levels of technological and sociopolitical organization; thus, they differentiated between, for instance, a characteristic "formative architecture," a characteristic "theocratic architecture," and so forth.[253] And, moreover, because their categories, theoretically anyway, were "free from the strict limits of time and space,"[254] these characteristic architectures should be identifiable in a variety of eras and locales across Mesoamerican culture history. Accordingly, their works are filled with formulations that correlate types of architecture with generalized stages of cultural development: Brainerd, for instance, considers that the distinguishing features of a pan-Mesoamerican "Classic Stage" include "the most formally planned religious centers . . . the most ornate architecture, and the most sophisticated and mature representational art in aboriginal America";[255] for Wauchope, the architecture of the "Village Formative" stage is, in every context, restricted to domestic dwellings, but the next stage in his scheme, the "Urban Formative," is signaled by the advent of public architecture in the form of pyramid platforms;[256] and for Willey and Phillips, the "Post Classic" stage in both Middle America and Peru is augured by "a decrease in the number, size, and elaboration of pyramid mounds and other types of religious structures [which] is one clue to the waning of religious authority."[257] (Via this logic, then, many of the similarities between Tula and Chichén Itzá could be explained by virtue of their parallel participations in a "Postclassic stage of development," even if there were absolutely no historical link between them.)

Examples of these sorts of historical-developmental arrangements are endless and their sweep ambitious. The organization of Mesoamerican architecture in terms of cultural stages is, however, limiting from the perspective of a hermeneutical history of religions for several reasons. First, the neo-evolutionists, like the cultural-ecologists, are, in the main, flagrant in their sociocultural reduction of art and architecture (not to mention religion). Second, their embracing correlations of culture and art are continually subverted by problematic regional differences in style; that is, they cannot adequately explain the diversity of artistic styles in regions of similar polities and social structures.[258] Third, and even more problematic, is their introduction of the notions of "progress" and "decline" (or "superiority" and "inferiority") into the arena of pre-Columbian aesthetics; most glaringly, in the Maya area, the adoption of a bell curve model of cultural history with the Petén Classic Maya as the apical standard of excellence in indigenous art and architecture consigns the contiguous artistic creations that precede the heralded stelae cult to a formative or Preclassic status (that is, not yet excellent), while those that follow — including, for instance, Chichén Itzá — are dismissed as decadent or Postclassic (that is, no longer excellent).[259] Moreover, when the "Classic" as a cultural developmental concept (based particularly on the high incidence of gylph-inscribed stelae in the Southern Lowlands) is exported to the Northern Maya Lowlands — the area that includes Chichén Itzá — it corresponds to virtually nothing in the indigenous Yucatecan culture.[260] As David Potter, writing specifically about architecture, notes, "this [Classic] period designation was established for the southern Maya lowlands and, when viewed as anything other than strictly a span of time, does not fit the situation in the northern Maya lowlands much better than it does in most non-Maya areas."[261]

In any case, despite the wide currency and the histrionic appeal of charting Mesoamerican cultural history in terms of grand sagas of the rise, peak, and collapse of various indigenous civilizations, many Mesoamericanists are dubious of such conspicuously loaded developmental terminology; they would prefer to stick with more strictly chronological arrangements. As early as 1959, Rene Millon, for instance, clamored for the substitution of a "neutral" (and strictly temporal) terminology based on Maya calendar dates (that is, "pre-Initial Series," "Initial Series," and "post-Initial Series").[262] And, as discontents mounted, in the 1970s there was a movement to adapt John Rowe's "master sequence" concept (another organization by time) from Peruvian to Mesoamerican archaeology and, with it, an alternative set of time-specific period names that would free such evaluative terms as Classic and Postclassic to designate only those stages that are explicitly developmental.[263] That changed nomenclature, however, never gained wide currency. Instead, a compromise solution prevails: most archaeologists (and art historians) opt to retain the conventional divisions of Preclassic, Classic, and Postclassic (presumed too deeply entrenched in the literature to eradicate) as *chronological* categories, but to drain that triad of any *cultural* significance. In other words, they feel compelled to retreat from organization by culture to organization by time. Kubler's assessment is typical: "Thus the content of the culture stages has been under constant correction and censorship, but their continuing use as 'empty' chronological containers seems to be of continuing value, by marking the pre-Columbian past into neutral periods called early, middle, and late which imply nothing either as to content or as to 'Zeitgeist.'"[264]

This compromise, though hardly satisfying, is widely accepted. Currently, then, the most common and safest way of organizing a survey of Mesoamerican art and architecture involves the use of Preclassic, Classic, and Postclassic in this resigned, culturally "empty" sense (with the Classic period running from 300 to 900 C.E., that is, the epoch circumscribed by the earliest and latest Initial Series dates on the stelae in the Southern Maya Lowlands)[265] and then, for completeness sake, overlaying that chronological scheme on a geographical survey of the area. Evolutionary assessments of culture are forced underground; relative positions in time and space once again are the only respectable comparative criteria. The connotation that there is some "significant" similitude between, for instance, Classic Maya architecture, Classic Teotihuacán architecture, and Classic Zapotecan architecture lingers — there is, in other words, an implicit presumption that each conforms to some shared standard of excellence — but the only explicit connection between the three is chronological contemporaneity.

In any case, epitomizing in one more way the awkwardness with which Mesoamericanists have been able to resolve the play of the slash between universal/particular, daring attempts at arranging specific works of pre-Columbian architecture with respect to the relative cultural attainments of their builders have been largely dismantled. In the same fashion that the venturesome, cultural-ecological correlation of specific environmental niches with characteristic architectures was forced back to more bland, geographical, locational principles of organization, the neo-evolutionists' ambitious coding of particular building types to particular stages of Mesoamerican cultural development was likewise forced to revert to a straightforward chronological ordering. Culturally significant organization ceded to insignificance. The daring, once again, retreated to the dependable.

Organization by Tradition: Historical Continuity and Transformation

> Everything made now is either a replica or a variant of something made a little time ago and so on back without break to the first morning of human time.
>
> *George Kubler, 1962*[266]

In the first decade of the nineteenth century, after examining the ruins of Mexico at the behest of Charles IV of Spain, professional soldier Guillermo Dupaix brought an atypical sympathy to his evaluation of pre-Columbian art.[267] Rather than blame the seemingly distorted proportions of carved human figures on the ineptitude of native artists, Dupaix attributed the peculiarities to political and religious conventions that in Mexico, as in Egypt, dictated a uniformity in style. This acknowledgment of the "tenacity of convention" or the "sway of style" is the ground for the last and, from the perspective of a hermeneutical history of religions, most promising mode of organizing Mesoamerican art and architecture — that is, organization according to tradition.

The barrage of technical definitions and casual usages of "tradition" spattered across the Mesoamerican literature are, in the main, queries into the issues of continuity and transformation among historically related cases. Organization by tradition here does *not* entail grouping works of art and architecture simply according to shared formal or technical criteria, *nor* eras of construction, *nor* functions or usages of buildings, *nor* geographic locations, *nor* in terms of the cultural attainments of the builders. Instead, organization by tradition depends upon reconstructing the connections between *historically related works* — in a sense, reuniting parent works with their siblings and offspring. Organization by tradition arises, in other words, from serious consideration of E. H. Gombrich's question, "Why should art have a history?"[268] Mesoamericanist archaeology, art history, and ethnohistory all venture responses to that query, and, as a segue into my own alternative means of organizing and comparing pre-Columbian architectures (in Chapter 3), this final section of Chapter 2 briefly surveys the respective efforts of each of those disciplinary strains.

An archaeologically defined "tradition," generally speaking, consists of the persistence of cultural forms through time. In Americanist archaeology, the concept of tradition was initially confined to the organization of pottery styles and individual technologies (for instance, the tradition of flat-bottomed vessels and the tradition of brick and mortar construction).[269] Eventually, however, the concept of discrete archaeological traditions was expanded in application to whole cultures (for instance, the American Southwest cultural tradition or the Mesoamerican cultural tradition).[270] By contrast to "culture areas," which are based on geographical distribution, or "cultural stages," which are based on generalized functional and developmental principles, the essential criterion for an archaeological "cultural tradition" is the identification of a particular, discrete history — "a long chronological persistence of the patterns concerned."[271]

This sensitivity to historical continuities does provide an alternative, more synthetic, more significant arrangement of various manifestations of indigenous culture; yet, from the perspective of a hermeneutical history of religions, archaeology's application of the concept of a cultural tradition to the transmaterial aspects of culture — particularly art and religion — is characteristically restrictive. According to Gordon Willey, for instance, each major cultural tradition "probably had a definite ideological pattern or world view," but, exemplifying his discipline's materialist leanings, the definitive touchstones for distinguishing one archaeological cultural tradition from another are subsistence patterns, technology, and ecological adaptations.[272] In other words, demonstrable continuities in architectural and artistic styles (and in religion for that matter) are, for the archaeological corps, significant primarily as reflections of continuities in these techno-economic spheres.

Not surprisingly, more subtle inquiries into historical continuities and transformations in Mesoamerican art and architecture issue from art history and ethnohistory. Two important themes particularly separate these efforts from their archaeological counterparts. First, where strict archaeologists consistently minimize any causative role for ideology (or religion) in the accomplishments of native cultures, art historians and ethnohistorians (much more in the spirit of the history of religions at this point) have been willing to place the mental workings or belief systems of indigenous peoples (to the extent that they can retrieve and characterize something like a native mindset) at the very center of their explanations of the continuous traditions in Mesoamerican art and architecture. And second, where archaeologists usually reduce art to a reflection of technologies and economic processes, art historians and ethnohistorians (again in a more hermeneutical vein) actively and sympathetically engage the subject matter of indigenous art. Iconographers in particular (as a subset within art history) concentrate on the matters of symbolism and aspire to penetrate beyond outward appearances to the "meanings" that are expressed in native art and architecture. Thus, for these academic strains, the organization of pre-Columbian art and architecture by tradition involves tracking continuities and transformations, not only of *form over time* but likewise of *meaning over time*. This is an exceedingly important advance.

Herbert Spinden was among the earliest to fashion an elaborate (if idiosyncratic) psycho-artistic theory of Mesoamerican art that manifests both these themes. Well in advance of the vogue for studying indigenous "world views" or "cosmovisions," Spinden argued that the accomplishments of traditional societies are animated by a kind of collective psychological predisposition, which he termed the "oversoul" or "psyche."[273] According to Spinden, the psyche, an embodiment of the beliefs and aspirations of the group, constitutes a mutual cooperation to advance the general good, a spiritual unitedness that makes almost any achievement possible. For him, then, pre-Columbian poetry, myth, art, and architecture are not expressions of individual whims or isolated genius; rather, they are testimony to the noblest dimensions of the group psyche. Furthermore, Spinden is very specific about how these indigenous mental processes involve themselves in the historical continuity and change of Maya art. He says that every artistic representation entails a conscious or unconscious manipulation of the realistic, "natural" subject matter: "to be exact, all art is conventional of necessity. In any representation there is always a compromise with truth and mental allowance for inadequacy."[274] He isolates four distinct modes of "compromise" or "processes of imaginative modification" in Maya art — simplification, elaboration, elimination, and substitution — and then amply illustrates how these processes have worked singly and in combination to produce identifiable, historically related series of representations, that is, artistic traditions.[275]

Thus, for Spinden, no work of Maya art or architecture is wholly unprecedented. Each can, at least ostensibly, be located with respect to its historically related precedents and its continually reworked derivative forms. Reconstructing chains of "imaginative modifications" — in his terms, "sequences in art" — is, however, more than chronological ordering; it is organization by tradition. And, while Spinden is most successful in sequencing representational Maya art (the conventionalization of carved serpent heads is his paramount example), he contends that architecture is likewise amenable to these processes of conventionalization.[276]

Spinden's concerns both for meticulous attention to the content of pre-Columbian art and for so-called conventionalized processes of modification (that is, changes in content over time) are perpetuated, albeit in a somewhat different guise, by those more recent pre-Columbian art historians who dedicate themselves particularly to iconography, the study of "the subject matter or meanings of works of art."[277] Once again deliberately distancing himself from the archaeo-art historical heritage, George Kubler, by his career-long preoccupation with the historical relations between individual works of art, is, nonetheless, the most prolific successor to this portion of Spinden's project.[278] Like Spinden, Kubler is adamant that no work of art (in Mesoamerica or elsewhere) is without precedent — "every important work of art can be regarded as a historical event . . . a replica or a variant of something made a little time ago."[279] In other words, because all art and architecture arises within the confines of tradition, he, like Spinden, considers that each single work is a participant in a "linked sequence of replications."[280] Thus, according to Kubler, the first task of the art historian (or the iconographer) is one of contextualization, of situating a work of art with respect to its historical antecedents and echoes.[281] But, iconographers — having claimed the interpretation of symbols as their special province — are never content with the chronological sequencing of works of art, nor even with the reconstruction of chains of historically related works. Iconographers, by and large, aspire somehow to go beyond outward appearances to retrieve the hidden significances and deeper meanings of pre-Columbian art and architecture. As H. B. Nicholson notes, "the essence of iconography . . . is a determined attempt to extract specific meanings from pre-Classic pictorial and sculptural representations, over and above purely esthetic-stylistic analyses."[282] Moreover, iconography, "among the most vigorous trends in Mesoamerican studies [in the 1970s],"[283] makes a unique contribution not only by transcending formal analyses but also by chronicling the fluctuations in those meanings over time. Kubler, for instance, holds that "the special insight conferred by iconographic studies arises from an examination of the changing relationships of form and meaning throughout very long durations."[284]

If iconographers accept this as their special charge, how best to attain this ambitious organization of form and meaning over time is, nonetheless, hotly debated. On the one hand, owing to the leaping sophistication of chronometric methods in the last decades, the arrangement of artistic forms into simple chronological order is, by now, a fairly straightforward procedure.[285] On the other hand, retrieval of the respective meanings of those forms is anything but straightforward (and this expectation of retrieving *the* meaning of a symbolic art form is a troublesome aspiration in its own right, as the next chapter will show). The tempest regarding appropriate strategies for penetrating to the indigenous meanings of pre-Columbian ruins blows students of Mesoamerican art into two camps or, more properly, into an established encampment that embraces ethnographic analogy as an *indirect* though viable procedure and a minority of dissidents who reject that inferential method and attempt to retrieve the meanings of ancient works of art *directly* on the basis of their intrinsic qualities.[286]

The strategy of the majority depends upon a collusion between art history (or iconography) and ethnohistory that dates back at least to Seler and the early 1910s and upon the working premise (discussed earlier) that because Mesoamerica is an essentially unified cultural area, similar art forms, regardless of their place and time within that area, probably carry generally similar meanings.[287] Emphasizing the continuities and persistences in Mesoamerican culture, these scholars claim the right of ethnographic analogy and the appropriateness of extrapolating from the unique wealth of sixteenth-century documents to retrieve the meanings of more remote works of art and architecture. Michael Coe, for instance, considers colonial-era Mexican monuments and texts very helpful in deciphering the symbolism of Olmec iconography that was carved centuries earlier and hundreds of miles away in the Gulf Coast region.[288] And a host of scholars — including Seler, Armillas, Caso, Jiménez Moreno, and Laurette Séjourné — rely heavily on this analogizing strategy to stretch the effusive Aztec materials across nearly a millennium to interpret the symbolism and supposedly retrieve the indigenous meanings of Teotihuacán's art and architecture.[289]

If suspiciously generalized, the fruits of this ethnohistorical–art historical alliance are, nonetheless, titanic (at least compared to the other alternatives). In fact, it is here that ethnohistory makes its strongest contribution to a hermeneutical study of pre-Columbian architecture[290] and here that historians of religions find the most satisfying syntheses of architectural forms with their probable uses and with the supposed perceptions of their pre-Columbian users. Where Spinden had simply applied a generalized theory of human psychology and art to Mesoamerica, a model he presumed equally applicable in any historical context, by contrast, ethnohistorical studies (pioneered by the likes of Angel M. Garibay and Miguel León-Portilla for the Nahua and by Ralph Roys and Eric Thompson for the Maya) begin to elucidate what is specific and unique to the conceptual world of Mesoamerica.[291] Studies into the oral, literary, and "philosophical" achievement of Mesoamerican peoples, both in colonial texts and ethnographic contexts, by providing the most direct access into native worldviews and "cosmovisions" — that is, conceptions of, for example, time, space, creation, and death — prove foundational for the retrieval of artistic and architectural meanings (and thus for the organization of works according to tradition). There is, however, an inherent methodological tension between the willingness to extrapolate from one Mesoamerican context to another (in a sense, working outside time and space to retrieve the meanings of specific works of art) and the initiative to chart changes in meaning over time. Ethnographic analogy is, as its detractors complain, invariably more attuned to pan-Mesoamerican continuities in iconography and architecture than to discontinuities.

Kubler, as the preeminent spokesman for the dissident minority, presents the most intriguing alternative. He shares the mainstream's concern for discerning continuities in both artistic forms and meanings over time — Kubler is, in fact, unsurpassed in recognizing instances of "renascence" (persistences or reassertions of conventionalized art forms) and "archaism" (self-conscious imitations of earlier art forms).[292] His more signal methodological contribution in this regard is, however, as a dissenting voice that accentuates transformations rather than continuities in Mesoamerican art and that proposes an ingenious alternative strategy for retrieving the meanings directly from remote works of pre-Columbian art and architecture themselves rather than indirectly via ethnographic analogy, a strategy that should be inestimably more sensitive to the uniquenesses of specific cases and, thus, for documenting changes in meaning over time.

As discussed earlier, Kubler stages a blitzkrieg against ethnographic analogy and the conventional presumption that the whole of Mesoamerica can be regarded as an *oikumene* of shared belief and symbolism.[293] More specifically, he invokes Erwin Panofsky's "principle of disjunction" to warn that, even among historically related works of art, there are disjunctive situations wherein form and meaning separate and recouple in different (re)combinations.[294] Thus, because, as Kubler says, "the idea of disjunction makes every ethnographic analogy questionable," he abstains entirely from using sixteenth-century sources as clues to the significance of earlier art and focuses instead on the structure and dynamics of discrete iconographic systems — that is, on the works of art themselves — as an entrée to their functions and meanings. This alternative strategy for retrieving meaning by direct analysis of ancient works of art and architecture (particularly works for which there are no coeval texts, like, for instance, Tula and Chichén Itzá) — a method Kubler terms "intrinsic configurational iconographic analysis" — relies on a linguistic model.[295] In this novel approach, each art form is examined for its "grammatical function" — whether noun, adjective, or verb — and then placed in a kind of "sentence" or context with respect to other forms with which it is typically associated. Thus, for instance, instead of the orthodox habit of explaining the art of Classic Teotihuacán by extrapolating back in time from sixteenth-century Aztec materials, Kubler resolves the entire Teotihuacán iconographic system into a few major "clusters," or sentence-like units of word-picture discourse (for instance, the rain god cluster, the butterfly complex, or the four-element group), each of which presumably articulates the "liturgical" priorities of a different Teotihuacán cult.[296]

Clemency Coggins considers Kubler's application of a linguistic model to the iconography of Teotihuacán and the Maya to be "perhaps the most important work in art historical theory" in recent decades, a method that is outstanding by virtue of its cultural specificity.[297] Where Spinden applied a universalistic psychological theory of art to his studies of Maya art, and the proponents of ethnographic analogy apply a generalized, nearly monolithic "Mesoamerican world view," Kubler endeavors to meet the subject matters of specific Mesoamerican works of art and architecture on their own unique terms. Only then, after engaging the particularities of individual cases, does he attempt to locate those works with respect to other historically related cases — that is, to organize indigenous works of art and architecture with respect to traditions.

From the perspective of a hermeneutics of pre-Columbian architecture, Kubler's intention is praiseworthy but the results disappointing. So-termed intrinsic configurational analysis is, as Kubler acknowledges, more viable for pictorial art than strictly architectonic forms, and his conclusions about associated liturgy and ritual are really too vague to be satisfying to most historians of religions. Moreover, the consensus of Mesoamericanists is that Kubler has overstated the case for discontinuity in indigenous art and religion; Nicholson, for instance, argues the more typical view that the most basic religio-ritual patterns were probably widely shared throughout Mesoamerica from Late Preclassic times onward.[298] Nevertheless, Kubler is exceedingly effective (more than anyone else) in dispelling the illusion that form and meaning have, as it were, strolled casually, hand-in-hand, across the history of Mesoamerican art and architecture (a realization that will prove crucial for our hermeneutical approach to the similitude between Tula and Chichén Itzá). Furthermore, Kubler provides fresh incentive for searching after historical connections between works of art by demonstrating that Mesoamerica has a plurality of retrievable iconographic lineages rather than a single domineering intentionality for all its art and architecture. Why, after all, if there is but one pan-Mesoamerican art tradition, has the organizational problem proved so vexing?

So far, neither the proponents of ethnographic analogy nor those few who favor intrinsic configurational analysis have been so precocious as to venture a thoroughgoing synthesis of Mesoamerican art and architectural history strictly in terms of chains of historically related works. Each strain does, however, make admirable strides toward locating individual instances of pre-Columbian art and architecture with respect to their historical precedents and derivatives. By reconstructing these artistic-architectural lineages — an initiative that is absolutely crucial to understanding the highly eclectic architecture of Chichén Itzá, wherein borrowings and imitations from all over the Mesoamerican world are patched into a cosmopolitan synthesis[299] — these various art historical methods are the strongest participants in what this section has loosely termed organization by tradition.

The preceding survey of inquiries into Mesoamerican art and architecture by four streams of scholarship (five, counting antiquarianism) recounts a dauntless, if rarely successful, struggle for satisfactory and significant generalization amid the tremendous diversity of pre-Columbian monuments. The quest after some acceptable resolution of the play of the slash between particular/universal is ceaseless. Scheme after ambitious scheme proves ineffectual or pedestrian to the shifting orientations of successive generations of specialists in Mesoamerica. And for comparativist historians of religions, the countless variations on the organization of pre-Columbian architecture according to formal appearance, construction technique, time, supposed use and function, geography, the culture of the builders, and even tradition are all stimulating — although none is thoroughly satisfying. In any case, I have carped enough about extant means of studying and comparing Mesoamerican architecture; the next chapter moves in a more constructive direction. Searching for a new point of departure into the old problem of Tula–Chichén Itzá similitude, and thus shifting, generally speaking, from a hermeneutic of suspicion to one of recovery (or retrieval), Chapter 3 outlines yet another alternative strategy for organizing and comparing the architectures of ancient Mesoamerica (and, ambitiously enough, anywhere else for that matter) — an alternative based on the notion of comparison via "ritual-architectural priorities."

Notes

1. Spinden, *Study of Maya Art,* 15.

2. Ibid.

3. The apparent lack of written texts has probably been the principal deterrent to students of *Religionswissenschaft* specializing in Mesoamerica. By far the most important exception of late is Davíd Carrasco. His energies in the past decade via the Mesoamerican Archive and Research Project of the University of Colorado at Boulder (and currently at Princeton University) have been unprecedentedly successful both in bringing the specific materials of Mesoamerica (particularly Aztec materials) to the attention of historians of religions and in bringing a history of religions approach to the attention of Mesoamericanists.

4. Readers concerned principally with the specifics of Tula and Chichén Itzá may find this entire chapter unnecessary; yet, because the viability of this larger project and its foundational concept — the organization of sacred architecture according to "ritual-architectural events" — hinges on its being a methodological alternative, it seems necessary and appropriate that I survey the more conventional approaches to Mesoamerican architecture.

5. Regarding this acknowledgment of the inevitable and productive interaction between the specific (or "historical") and the general (or "systematic"), see, for instance, Joachim Wach, *Introduction to the History of Religions,* ed. Joseph M. Kitagawa and Gregory D. Alles (New York: Macmillan Publishing Company, 1988), 53–79.

6. See, for instance, Gerardus van der Leeuw, *Religion in Essence and Manifestation,* trans. J. E. Turner (Gloucester, Mass.: Peter Smith, 1967), 2: 672.

7. Joseph Kitagawa, for instance, counseled his students that the first task in orienting oneself in an unfamiliar book should be to discern the author's "principle of organization." This advice has been of tremendous help in assessing and appreciating the "great books" on Mesoamerican art and architecture.

8. While there is an implied chronological succession — antiquarianism, traditional archaeology, new archaeology, art history, and ethnohistory — each persists as an active strain in the study of Mesoamerican architecture. Laying these five along one axis, and the seven principles of organization (such as form and technique) along a perpendicular axis, it is possible, at least in principle, to locate (or at least engage) the methodological orientation of any study of pre-Columbian architecture.

9. Mircea Eliade, *No Souvenirs: Journal 1957–1969,* trans. Fred H. Johnson Jr. (New York: Harper & Row, 1977), 245. Eliade's reflections on his encounter with Wiberto Jiménez Moreno (who is actually an ethnohistorian) in Mexico City in 1965 epitomize the continual frustration that historians of religions feel in dealing with the great bulk of Mesoamerican anthropological-archaeological literature.

10. Alfred V. Kidder, "The Development of Maya Research," *Proceedings of the Second General Assembly, Pan American Institute of Geography and History, 1935,* U.S. Department of State Conference Series, No. 28 (Washington: Government Printing Office, 1937), 218–25; reprinted in Richard B. Woodbury, *Alfred V. Kidder* (New York: Columbia University Press, 1973), 137.

11. George Kubler has repeatedly discussed the social scientific, anthropological domination in the study of New World art and architecture. See, for instance, George Kubler, "Science and Humanism Among Americanists," in Ignacio Bernal et al., *The Iconography of Middle American Sculpture* (New York: Metropolitan Museum of Art, 1973), 163–67. Clemency Coggins, "A Role for the Art Historian in an Era of New Archaeology," *Actes du XLII Congrès International des Américanistes, Paris, 1976,* 7 (1979): 315–19, discusses the same issue.

12. My remarks on the development of Middle American archaeology are informed especially by Bernal, *History of Mexican Archaeology;* Brunhouse, *In Search of the Maya;* idem, *Pursuit of the Ancient Maya;* Deuel, *Conquistadors Without Swords;* Keen, *The Aztec Image;* Walter W. Taylor, *A Study of Archaeology* (Carbondale: Southern Illinois University Press, 1964; first published in 1948 as No. 69 of the Titles in the Memoir Series of the American Anthropological Association); Robert Wauchope, *They Found the Buried Cities;* Gordon R. Willey and Jeremy A. Sabloff, *A History of American Archaeology,* 2d ed. (San Francisco: W. H. Freeman and Company, 1980); J. Ned Woodall, *An Introduction to Modern Archaeology* (Cambridge, Mass.: Schenkman Publishing Company, 1972); and Woodbury, *Alfred V. Kidder.*

13. In a very different context, Charles Long uses the phrase "play of the slash" with reference to J. Z. Smith's work, which concentrates on the slash between sacred and profane, and his own work, which concentrates on the slash between primitive and civilized. Charles H. Long, "The Study of Religion: Its Nature and Its Discourse," Inaugural Lecture of the Department of Religious Studies, University of Colorado, Boulder, October 7, 1980.

14. Bernal, *History of Mexican Archaeology,* 142–45, identifies 1800–1910 as the era of burgeoning positivism in Middle American archaeology and the earliest positivists as Eduard Seler, Alfred Maudslay, Ernst Forstemann, William H. Holmes, and Paso Troncosco. For the counterpart to this movement in American anthropology, Franz Boas and his followers are foundational.

15. Even Augustus Le Plongeon, perhaps the least inhibited and most speculative early student of Mesoamerican antiquities, was at least paying lip service to the ideal of "scientific" objectivity. In 1872 and repeatedly thereafter he disclaimed all reliance on "theory": "I have not advanced an opinion which is not founded on *facts* acknowledged by science, or events recorded in history." Le Plongeon quoted by Brunhouse, *In Search of the Maya,* 142–43. Lawrence Desmond, the most recent biographer of Le Plongeon, suggests that the eulogies of "the good doctor" to pure objectivity, which are obviously antithetical to the spirit of his own work, may actually be written in a sarcastic tone to mock the more staid establishment of Americanists from which he was always excluded. See Lawrence Gustave Desmond and Phyllis Mauch Messenger, *A Dream of Maya: Augustus and Alice Le Plongeon in Nineteenth-Century Yucatán* (Albuquerque: University of New Mexico Press, 1988).

16. Bernal, *History of Mexican Archaeology,* 144.

17. See Woodbury, *Alfred V. Kidder,* 59.

18. Gordon R. Willey, "Alfred Vincent Kidder," *Natural Academy of Sciences, Biographical Memoirs* 39 (1967): 302.

19. Alfred Kidder, "An Introduction to the Study of Southwestern Archaeology, With a Preliminary Account of the Excavation at Pecos," *Papers of the Southwestern Expedition,* no. 1 (New Haven: Yale University Press, 1924), 34; quoted by Woodbury, *Alfred V. Kidder,* 34. Woodbury thoroughly documents the consistency with which Kidder emphasized the importance of synthesizing the data, in contrast to mere "impressionistic" or descriptive reporting. Ibid., pt. 1.

20. See, for instance, Taylor, *A Study of Archaeology,* 37.

21. On the division of the history of religions into two main branches ("historical" and "systematic"), see Wach, *Introduction to the History of Religions,* 53–79.

22. To use Norman Hammond's words, in the first half of the twentieth century, the mainstream of Maya studies "created a massive data base devoid of explanatory models." Hammond, "Lords of the Jungle," 5.

23. A typical traditional archaeological report would include simply a description of the procedures followed, an account of the specimens found, and comparison of artifacts with similar tools of the same area. See, for instance, Woodall, *An Introduction to Modern Archaeology,* 8, 13.

24. Brunhouse, *In Search of the Maya,* 193, refers to Edward Thompson as "the last of the great amateurs" and gives a concise accounting of his activities at Chichén Itzá. Ibid., 171–76. Eric Thompson, in his introduction to Edward Thompson's *High Priest's Grave,* 10, considers that "Edward H. Thompson belonged to the old school that was content to consider archaeology as history," presumably, as opposed to archaeology as science.

25. Brunhouse, *In Search of the Maya,* 229–30, has a bibliography of Edward Thompson's writings.

26. Willard, *City of the Sacred Well,* 185. For other passages that explicitly celebrate the impenetrable mystery of Chichén Itzá, see ibid., 63, 68, 78. While Willard claims to know "this lovable, modest, blue-eyed six footer . . . perhaps, better than does any

other man" (ibid., vi), and Thompson himself endorsed the book, it can hardly be considered an accurate rendition of Thompson's exploits and ideas. Willard's work is a hodgepodge that laces Thompson's archaeological accomplishments with anecdotes, native legends, and reflections on the Spanish Conquest. Willard continually paraphrases (in quotation marks) remembrances of Thompson's, leading to perpetual confusion about whose notions are actually being presented. Ironically, here and elsewhere — for instance, T. A. Willard, *Lost Empires of the Itzáes and Mayas,* 14 — Willard claims that he is presenting "a record of the facts so far discovered . . . no theories." Moreover, Willard's book inadvertently causes its hero great difficulty by alluding to Thompson's shipping Maya artifacts out of the country, which led eventually to the Mexican government seizing Thompson's estate at Chichén Itzá. See Brunhouse, *In Search of the Maya,* 191.

27. Alfred M. Tozzer, "Architecture and Romance," *The Saturday Review of Literature,* 19 June 1926, 862.

28. Tozzer's lack of innovation in method is apparent in his keynote article, "Maya Research," in *Maya Research* 1:1 (July 1934): 3–19. Reflecting on the history of the study of the Maya and potentialities for the future, Tozzer trots out a few of Kidder's expansive theoretical dictums (a call to interdisciplinary research, to search after the "big questions," to transcend "mere description," and to compare across Mesoamerica), and some of Spinden's (for instance, to appreciate the "Archaic" level of Mexican culture), but Tozzer's real forte and concern is the collection of data and cataloging the "geographical distribution of traits."

29. Thompson, review of *Chichén and Cenote,* 119.

30. When, in 1929, Kidder took over directorship of the Carnegie Institution program from Morley, the goals were expanded considerably, but the actual results, much to Kidder's disappointment, continued essentially as they had previously. See Woodbury, *Alfred V. Kidder,* 54–87.

31. Willey and Phillips, *Method and Theory in American Archaeology* (Chicago: University of Chicago Press, 1958), 2.

32. Clyde Kluckhohn, "The Conceptual Structure in Middle American Studies," in *Maya and Their Neighbors,* ed. Hay et al., 41–51. Appropriately, this volume is a Festschrift to Alfred Tozzer.

33. Ibid., 51. Walter W. Taylor, "Clyde Kluckhohn and American Archaeology," in *Culture and Life: Essays in Memory of Clyde Kluckhohn* (Carbondale: Southern Illinois University, 1973), 18–23, discusses the impact and controversy surrounding Kluckhohn's famous essay.

34. Taylor's *A Study of Archaeology* was originally written as a doctoral dissertation under Kluckhohn at Harvard.

35. Kidder is actually a harsher critic of himself than is Taylor. Woodbury, *Alfred V. Kidder,* 74–85, especially paints Kidder as a sort of tragic hero, unnecessarily hard on himself in his retrospective assessment of his and the Carnegie Institution's accomplishments in Maya research.

36. Taylor, *A Study of Archaeology,* 45–46. For a more congenial and optimistic assessment of Kidder's work see Gordon Willey, "Alfred Vincent Kidder," 293–322.

37. Taylor, *A Study of Archaeology,* pt. II.

38. On the important differences between Taylor's position of 1948 and that of the "new archaeologists" of the 1960s, see Willey and Sabloff, *History of American Archaeology,* 187.

39. The influence of V. G. Childe is most apparent in the work of archaeologists Pedro Armillas and Williams Sanders and ethnologists Angel Palerm and Eric Wolf. See Willey and Sabloff, *History of American Archaeology,* 189. More recently, Eduardo Matos Moctezuma, principal excavator and interpreter of Tula, Hidalgo, and of the Templo Mayor in Mexico City, is a great champion of Childe's theories. It is ironic and telling of the Americanists' thirst for interpretive models that they should appeal to the grand theoretical systems of Childe, given that he himself virtually ignored all New World archaeological data and conceded in a letter to Robert Braidwood (1946), "as to my 'revolutions,' I have always been conscious that the Maya did not fit in . . . in the Old World urbanization was bound up with metal, the trade it required and the new transport facilities that it made indirectly possible." Sally Green, *Prehistorian: A Biography of V. Gordon Childe* (Bradford-on-Avon, Wiltshire: Moonraker Press, 1981), 86–87.

40. In other words, "the evolutionary position of most new archaeologists — although not always overtly formulated — assumes the technical-economic-realm of culture to be the primarily determinative one in change, with social and ideational realms changing in secondary relation to it." Willey and Sabloff, *History of American Archaeology,* 186.

41. This point is made by Henry B. Nicholson in his Introduction to *Origins of Religious Art: Art and*

Iconography in Preclassic Mesoamerica, ed. Henry B. Nicholson (Los Angeles: UCLA Latin American Center, 1976).

42. William T. Sanders and Barbara J. Price, *Mesoamerica: The Evolution of a Civilization* (New York: Random House, 1968), 9.

43. There are, however, encouraging signs that the extreme deprecation of the ideational sphere by mainstream archaeologists may be slackening. Nicholson, Introduction to *Origins of Religious Art,* ed. Nicholson, 4, for instance, expresses optimism in this regard, citing Gordon Willey and Geoffrey Bushnell as two leading materialistically oriented archaeologists who are urging more consideration of the "dimension of ideology."

44. This point is made by Coggins, "A Role for the Art Historian," 318. A good example of the neo-evolutionary approach to Mesoamerican architecture would be Kent V. Flannery and Joyce Marcus, "Evolution of the Public Building in Formative Oaxaca," in *Cultural Change and Continuity: Essay in Honour of James Bennett Griffin,* ed. Charles E. Cleland (New York: Academic Press, 1976), 205–21, wherein the authors attempt to document several evolutionary stages in the development of Zapotec religion on the basis of the evolutionary sequence of public buildings.

45. Willey and Phillips, *Method and Theory in American Archaeology,* 2. This tremendously influential book may be the single most important statement of the "new archaeology."

46. A telling example of the new archaeological tendency to look past the specific, artistic character of Mesoamerican architecture to more generalized sociocultural conclusions is Sidrys's computer-aided study of the weight and size of the massive serpent heads on the balustrades of the Castillo at Chichén Itzá to determine the "manpower requirements" for the transport of megalithic building materials. He abstains entirely on the religious or aesthetic significance of those snake heads. Raymond Sidrys, "Megalithic Architecture and Sculpture of the Ancient Maya," in *Papers on the Economy and Architecture of the Ancient Maya,* monograph 8, ed. Raymond Sidrys (Los Angeles: University of California Institute of Archaeology, 1978), 158, 161.

47. There is a very important difference between the study of Tula, Hidalgo, and that of Chichén Itzá. On the one hand, Tula was first investigated and excavated in the 1940s from the perspective of traditional archaeology (that is, by Jorge Acosta), then majorly reworked in the 1960s and 1970s from the perspective of the new archaeology (by Eduardo Matos Moctezuma and Richard Diehl, both of whom espouse precisely the goals outlined in this section; see Matos, *Proyecto Tula,* 7–16, and Diehl, *Tula,* 29–40, 97). Chichén Itzá, on the other hand, the focus of traditional archaeological efforts of the Carnegie Institution troupe, has *not* (primarily because of its importance as a tourist site) received the same thorough reworking from the new archaeological position. The implications of this difference become more apparent in the final chapters.

48. Kubler, *Art and Architecture of Ancient America,* 34.

49. Brunhouse, *Pursuit of the Ancient Maya,* 125.

50. Spinden, *Study of Maya Art.* Bernal's assessment of Spinden's work as the first really serious study of Maya (or any ancient Mesoamerican) art is typical: "despite its shortcomings, inevitable at the time, Spinden's work is a landmark." Bernal, *History of Mexican Archaeology,* 183.

51. Kubler, *Art and Architecture in Ancient America,* 37.

52. Ibid., 38. Kubler, whose remarks about Spinden are always a complex admixture of indebtedness and antagonism, attributes Spinden's anthropological leanings to the fact that he was "influenced by the 'technist' interpretations of primitive art from Semper to Haddon." Ibid. Kubler also cites the foundational art historical work of Salvador Toscano, Miguel Covarrubias, Paul Westheim, and Paul Gendrop. Ibid., 37.

53. Cecelia F. Klein, "The Relation of Mesoamerican Art History to Archaeology in the United States," in *Pre-Columbian Art History: Selected Readings,* ed. Alana Cordy-Collins (Palo Alto, Calif.: Peek Publications, 1982), 1.

54. Bernal, *History of Mexican Archaeology,* 183, considers that the pre-Columbian art history movement's main thrust came after 1950 but then discusses many earlier figures that paved the way. He also has interesting remarks about an unprecedented appreciation of ancient art in general around 1920, "for reasons that have little to do with archaeological research and more to do with changing aesthetic norms in Europe." Ibid.

55. Among his countless pleas for the irreducibility of religion, see, for instance, Mircea Eliade, "The History of Religions in Retrospect: 1912–1962," in *The Quest: History and Meaning in Religion* (Chicago: University of Chicago Press, 1969), 12–36.

56. See, for instance, Kubler, *Art and Architecture of Ancient America,* 33.

57. Kubler has argued strenuously for a nonreductive, autonomous Mesoamerican art history in several contexts, key among them: George Kubler, "Science and Humanism Among Americanists," in Ignacio Bernal et al., *The Iconography of Middle American Sculptures* (New York: Metropolitan Museum of Art, 1973), 163–67; idem, *The Shape of Time: Remarks on the History of Things* (New Haven: Yale University Press, 1962), vii–ix; idem, "Synopsis of the Meetings: Methodological Approaches," *Actes du XLII Congrès International des Américanistes, Paris, 1976,* 7 (1979): 283–89; and idem, Introduction, *Art and Architecture of Ancient America.* In addition to Kubler's discussions of the relations between Mesoamerican anthropology, archaeology, and art history, three other articles are particularly helpful in defining the discipline's autonomy: Klein, "Relation of Mesoamerican Art History to Archaeology"; Coggins, "A Role for the Art Historian"; and Donald Robertson, "Anthropology, Archaeology and the History of Art," in *Codex Wauchope: A Tribute Roll, Human Mosaic,* ed. Marco Giardino et al. (New Orleans: Tulane University, 1978), 73–80.

58. Kelemen, *Medieval American Art,* 8.

59. Justino Fernández, *A Guide to Mexican Art,* trans. Joshua C. Taylor (Chicago: University of Chicago Press, 1969), 7.

60. Kubler, *Art and Architecture of Ancient America,* 34.

61. On the "uselessness" of art, see Kubler, *The Shape of Time,* 14–16. The concept of "useless" or transutilitarian art is explored more fully in Chapter 3 in relation to "The Special Case of Architecture: Habitats and Worlds."

62. This criticism that an emphasis on the *content* (in this case, of works of art) comes at the expense of due consideration of *historical context* runs parallel to the criticism leveled at historians of religions who emphasize the "irreducibility" of religion and thus "non-reductionist" approaches to religion (like Eliade, for instance).

63. In other words, while art historians have been much concerned with the "symbolic" character of pre-Columbian art, they have tended to neglect what will be discussed in Chapter 3 as the "superabundance and autonomy of architecture."

64. Kubler, *Art and Architecture of Ancient America,* 32. Mesoamerican art history's and particularly Kubler's commitment to documenting the historical continuities and relatednesses between individual works of art is addressed later in this chapter in regard to "Organization by Tradition." This is also a crucial issue in Chapter 3 relative to "The Mechanism of Architecture: Tradition and Instigation."

65. Klein, "Relation of Art History to Archaeology"; and Coggins, "A Role for the Art Historian"; both argue cogently that pre-Columbian art history can and should fill a gap left by the shifting concerns of the new archaeology.

66. Klein, "Relation of Art History to Archaeology," 3–4.

67. Coggins, "A Role for the Art Historian," 318–19.

68. Klein, "Relation of Art History to Archaeology," 1.

69. Kubler, "Methodological Approaches," 289.

70. But then again, to the extent that epigraphy and deciphering of Maya glyphs are born of this strain of inquiry, art history is exceedingly productive in resolving matters of pre-Columbian history and social organization. (Recent advances in epigraphy have not been fully intergrated into this project.)

71. Joyce Marcus, "Archaeology and Religion: A Comparison of the Zapotec and Maya," in *Ancient Mesoamerica,* ed. Graham, 298.

72. Thompson, Introduction, *Maya History and Religion,* includes under the rubric of "ethnohistory" both reliance on documentary, written sources (the sine qua non of ethnohistory) and observations of modern-day Indians (typically the preserve of ethnology or anthropology). I follow his broad usage of "ethnohistory" in this section. As Hammond notes, the hallmark and most enduring portion of Thompson's great oeuvre arises from "a perceptive melding of archaeological, documentary, and ethnographic data." Hammond, "Lords of the Jungle," 23.

73. J. Eric S. Thompson, "Archaeological Problems of the Lowland Maya," in *Maya and Their Neighbors,* ed. Hay et al., 138.

74. Thompson, *Maya History and Religion,* Introduction.

75. See Howard F. Cline, "Introduction: Reflections on Ethnohistory," *Handbook of Middle American Indians: Guide to the Ethnohistorical Sources* (Austin: University of Texas Press, 1972), 12: 5.

76. Thompson, *Maya History and Religion,* xvi–xix. Two other strong examples of Mesoamericanists calling for the use of written records to solve archaeological problems are Ignacio Bernal,

"Archaeology and the Written Sources," *Actes du XXXIV Congrès International des Américanistes, Vienna, 1960* (1962): 219–25; and Henry B. Nicholson, "The Mesoamerican Pictorial Manuscripts: Research, Past and Present," *Actes du XXXIV Congrès International des Américanistes, Vienna, 1960* (1962): 199–215.

77. Cline, "Reflections on Ethnohistory," presents a very useful survey of the history of Mesoamerican ethnohistory tracing it back to Sahagún and the sixteenth-century compilers. Henry B. Nicholson, "Middle American Ethnohistory: An Overview," *Handbook of Middle American Indians: Guide to the Ethnohistorical Sources* (Austin: University of Texas Press, 1972), 15: 492, considers that Leon y Gama, "a talented Mexican astronomer," was the real founder of the modern Mexican ethnohistoric-archaeologic tradition. Karl H. Schwerin, "The Future of Ethnohistory," *Ethnohistory* 23 (Fall 1976): 323–41, argues that "ethnohistory goes back at least to the time of Lewis H. Morgan (1877) who drew on a wide variety of historical records in writing *Ancient Society.* Ibid., 323. And George Kubler, "Period, Style, and Meaning in Ancient American Art," in *Ancient Mesoamerica,* ed. Graham, 11–24, complains that "Seler's method of historico-ethnographical analogy still governs Mexican and Maya studies in all departments of archaeological and ethnographical research." Ibid., 21.

78. Nicholson, "Middle American Ethnohistory," 495. Alfred Tozzer and, even more, Ralph Roys deserve credit as tremendous ethnohistorians. Both concentrated their efforts on problems directly relevant to Chichén Itzá; their efforts ensured that the conventional wisdoms about Chichén Itzá really derive more from textual than archaeological sources. See Pierre Ventur, *Maya Ethnohistorian: The Ralph L. Roys Papers* (Nashville: Vanderbilt University Publications in Archaeology, 1978) for a bibliography of Roys's works and some fascinating correspondence between the pioneers of Maya ethnohistory. Likewise, the more anthropologically oriented Mesoamericanists of the first half of this century — for instance, Sapper, La Farge, Termer, Goubaud, Redfield (and Tozzer) — were sensitive (perhaps more sensitive than their heirs) to "survivals" of ancient Maya practices. See Thompson, *Maya History and Religion,* xvii.

79. Cline, "Reflections on Ethnohistory," 9. Volumes 12 and 13 of the *Handbook of Middle American Indians,* both edited by Cline, are dedicated specifically to the "ethnohistorical sources." Regarding the early development of ethnohistory, in 1972, H. B. Nicholson, "Middle American Ethnohistory," 504, wrote about the "cockcrowing and the morning star of this young field."

80. On ethnohistory as an incomplete synthesis of history and anthropology, see William C. Sturtevant, "Anthropology, History and Ethnohistory," *Ethnohistory* 13 (1966): 1–51. Cline, "Reflections on Ethnohistory," 9–11, follows and elaborates on Sturtevant's notion that anthropologists and historians have each pursued somewhat different conceptions of ethnohistory.

81. At this point I am following the analysis of Gordon Willey, "Mesoamerican Art and Iconography and the Integrity of the Mesoamerican Ideological System," in Bernal et al., *Iconography of Middle American Sculpture,* 153–62.

82. See H. B. Nicholson, "Preclassic Mesoamerican Iconography From the Perspective of the Postclassic Problems in Interpretational Analysis," in *Origins of Religious Art and Iconography,* ed. Nicholson, 173. Attempting to illumine Mesoamerican archaeological materials by nonhistorical, cross-cultural comparison (the very foundation of this project) is usually patronized as eccentric or "popular." John Carlson, "A Geomantic Model for the Interpretation of Mesoamerican Sites: An Essay in Cross-Cultural Comparison," in *Mesoamerican Sites and World-Views,* ed. Benson, 143–215, comparing Far Eastern "geomancy" with Mesoamerican site planning, is one of very few recent and serious attempts at nonhistorical, cross-cultural comparison in this area.

83. Willey, "Mesoamerican Art and Iconography," 155.

84. On "upstreaming" see William Fenton, "Collecting Materials for a Political History of the Six Nations," *Proceedings of the American Philosophical Society* 93 (1949): 233–38; and idem, "The Training of Historical Ethnologists in America," *American Anthropologist* 54 (1952): 329–39.

85. See Julian Stewart, "The Direct Historical Approach to Archaeology," *American Antiquity* 38 (1942): 195–99.

86. Both of these circumstances were described briefly in Chapter 1.

87. Catherwood, *Views of Ancient Monuments;* Prescott, *Conquest of Mexico,* Book I; and Tozzer, *Chichén and Cenote.* In the same vein, it is interesting to note that while John Stephens did not use

ethnohistorical sources in his first book, he makes strong use of them in the second, for example, to deduce the function of ruined Yucatec ball courts from Herrera's description of the Aztec ballgame. Stephens, *Incidents of Travel in Yucatán* 2: 304–8.

88. This paragraph owes greatly to Nicholson, "Preclassic Mesoamerican Iconography," 160. The problem of Mesoamerican unity was addressed with some thoroughness in Chapter 1.

89. For endorsements of a fundamentally "unitary" view of Mesoamerica, see Ignacio Bernal, *The Olmec World* (Berkeley: University of California Press, 1969), 7, 187–88; Willey, "Mesoamerican Art and Iconography"; Michael Coe, *America's First Civilization* (New York: American Heritage Publishing Co., 1968), 111–15; idem, "The Iconology of Olmec Art," in Bernal et al., *The Iconography of Middle American Sculpture,* 1–12; Peter David Joralemon, "The Olmec Dragon: A Study in Pre-Columbian Iconography," in *Origins of Religious Art and Iconography,* ed. Nicholson, 27–72; Nicholson, "Preclassic Mesoamerican Iconography," 160–73; and Peter Furst, "The Olmec Were-Jaguar Motif in Light of the Ethnographic Reality," in *Dumbarton Oaks Conference on the Olmec* (Washington: Dumbarton Oaks, 1968), 143–74.

90. On Hermann Beyer in this regard, see Manuel Gamio et al., *La Poblacíon del Valle de Teotihuacán,* vol. 1 (Mexico, 1922), 286.

91. See George Kubler, "The Iconography of the Art of Teotihuacán," in *Studies in Pre-Columbian Art and Archaeology,* no. 4 (Washington: Dumbarton Oaks, 1967), 11–12; idem, "Period, Style and Meaning," 140–44; and idem, "Science and Humanism Among Americanists."

92. The original exposition of the "law of disjunction" is in Erwin Panofsky, *Renaissance and Renascences in Western Art* (Stockholm: Almquist and Wiksells, 1960). The application of the principle to Mesoamerica is in Kubler, "Period, Style and Meaning," 21–22.

93. Ibid., 143–44, emphasis added. Nicholson, "Preclassic Mesoamerican Iconography," 160–61, quotes this portion of Kubler's stricture on ethnographic analogy and challenges the appropriateness of applying Panofsky's "disjunction principle" to Mesoamerica. Nicholson (and most Mesoamericanists would agree here) sees no sharp break in Mesoamerican culture history to parallel that between Classic paganism and Christianity in Western Europe. An important example in which ethnographic analogy has unquestionably gone awry (Alfonso Caso is the main culprit here) is in the application of Aztec models to the Mixtec codices. See Nancy Troike, "Fundamental Changes in the Interpretation of the Mixtec Codices," in *Ancient Mesoamerica,* ed. Graham, 277–96.

94. Kubler's skepticism about ethnographic analogy is matched, on somewhat different grounds, by Lewis Binford's position that "fitting archaeological remains into ethnographically known patterns of life adds nothing to our knowledge of the past." Binford, "Methodological Considerations of the Archaeological Use of Ethnographic Data," in *Man the Hunter,* ed. R. B. Lee and I. Devore (Chicago: University of Chicago Press, 1968), 13. On the appropriate correlation of archaeological and ethnohistorical sources, Malcolm Shuman strongly criticized Eric Thompson and Joseph Ball (that is, the two major figures responsible for the revised historical [re]construction of Chichén Itzá in the 1970s) for formulating their interpretations initially on the basis of the archaeological evidence and then scouring the documentary sources for supporting evidence. By contrast, Shuman maintained that ethnohistoric data are "weaker" than archaeological data and, therefore, should be utilized in the formulation of hypothesis that archaeology may then test — in no case is it admissible to test archaeologically derived hypotheses by ethnohistory. Malcolm K. Shuman, "Archaeology and Ethnohistory: The Case of the Lowland Maya," *Ethnohistory* 24 (Winter 1977): 1–18.

95. Chapter 4, "Deceptions in Form" will elaborate at length on this so-called disjunction between form and meaning at Tula and Chichén Itzá.

96. The relationship between my position and Kubler's with respect to "disjunctions" between artistic form and artistic meaning is important and subtle. While I wholeheartedly agree that apparent formal similarities (like those between Tula and Chichén Itzá) often mask more important differences — that, in fact, is the root of the Tula-Chichén Itzá problem — I will, however, be arguing (in Chapter 3) that the best way to respect that tendency for disjunction is *not* by forestalling comparison and ethnographic analogy (as Kubler implies) but rather by pitching the comparison above the consideration of formal parallels and contrasts to that of comparison according to "ritual-architectural events."

97. Tatiana Proskouriakoff, *An Album of Maya Architecture* (Norman: University of Oklahoma Press, 1963), contains drawings that hypothetically

reconstruct most of the major sites. These rightfully famous drawings have been endlessly reproduced in other publications.

98. Proskouriakoff, *Study of Classic Maya Sculpture*, 184.

99. Maudslay, *Archaeology*, 1: 3.

100. Bernal, *History of Mexican Archaeology*, 49–55, discusses the available sources by and on Carlos de Sigüenza y Góngora. His diffusionist ideas are also discussed, ibid., 24–26.

101. See Brunhouse, *In Search of the Maya*, 71; and Wauchope, *Lost Tribes and Sunken Continents*, 25.

102. Charnay, *Ancient Cities*, xiv.

103. Wauchope, *Lost Tribes and Sunken Continents*, 93–95. A refreshing alternative, in an era dominated by quick diffusionist leaps from similarities in art forms to historical connectedness, is Zelia Nuttall's expansive documentation of the swastika symbol in Old and New World art; she attempts to explain it, not by diffusion, but (more like Raffaele Pettazzoni) as the result of a shared experience of the heavens, that is, pole-star worship. See Zelia Nuttall, *The Fundamental Principles of Old and New World Civilizations* (Cambridge, Mass.: Peabody Museum, 1901).

104. Kubler, *Art and Architecture in Ancient America*, 474, n. 22, has a very helpful summary of current diffusionist statements.

105. Stephens, *Incidents of Travel in Central America, Chiapas and Yucatán;* and idem, *Incidents of Travel in Yucatán;* Catherwood, *Views of Ancient Monuments;* Holmes, *Ancient Cities of Mexico;* and Maudslay, *Archaeology*.

106. Taylor, *A Study of Archaeology*, 212–15, explains how, for these archaeologists, to proceed with positivistic rigor would require that one restrict inquiry to that which is directly observable, most obviously, the appearance of the ruins.

107. In Bernal's assessment, Holmes's *Ancient Cities of Mexico* consists of "long flat descriptions of ruins and objects; he makes no attempt either at historical perspective or at chronological sequences." Bernal, *History of Mexican Archaeology*, 102.

108. Holmes, *Ancient Cities of Mexico*, 39–42, 82.

109. Ibid., 160.

110. Ibid., 192. Although Holmes may be criticized for his staid presentation, in his defense, he is very accurate, his panorama drawings of whole ceremonial centers still have not been surpassed, and he has a far stronger generalizing spirit than the meticulous Maudslay. Holmes makes sweeping and viable comparisons of whole areas based on formal and constructional criteria, for instance: Maya versus Mexican stonework (and orientation), ibid., 26; Yucatán versus western Mexico ground plans, ibid., 69; Yucatán versus Palenque doorways and wall openings, ibid., 162; Yucatán mural sculpture versus Chiapas stucco modeling, ibid., 165; Yucatán versus Palenque stairways, ibid., 168; and Yucatán versus Oaxaca columns, ibid., 243.

111. Maudslay, *Archaeology*, 1: 3, explains the agenda of his classic work (that is, "sketch maps," plans, and photographs of the monuments of each site). He envisioned, though never carried out, a synthetic and comparative work to follow up this particularistic study. In his entire five-volume study there are only about a dozen clipped and tentative remarks on the functions of buildings; for instance, a wall at Copán is "possibly intended for defense" and underground chambers at Yaxché "possibly were for vapor bathes." For similar examples, see ibid., 1: 31, 32; 2: 23, 25, 27; 3: 34; 4: 11, 19, 29, 33.

112. The relationship between photography and "objectivity" is fascinating. Davis, *Désiré Charnay: Expeditionary Photographer*, Chapter 1, discusses the "golden era of expeditionary photography" (1850–1880) and the happy coincidence between "positivistic historians who accept science as their model" and the unique potentialities of photography, especially the early Daguerre process. In Middle America, Maudslay belonged to a class of pioneering photographers that included Stephens and Catherwood, Charnay, Le Plongeon, and Teobert Maler. Interestingly, Aldous Huxley lamented the extinction of the "artist-archaeologists" as exemplified by Catherwood (who is famous for his drawings rather than photographs), arguing that "when we pass from the precise reproduction of architectural details to the rendering of great monuments in their totality, as their creators meant them to be seen and as the mind's eye behind the spectator's eyes actually perceive them, the advantage is not always with the photographer." Aldous Huxley, Introduction to von Hagen, *Frederick Catherwood, Archt.*, xviii.

113. Strictly formal classifications have enjoyed an equally strong run in the nonarchitectural dimensions of Americanist archaeology. The organization of artifacts (for instance, arrow points, spearheads, and knives) according to "empirical types," designed to drain all subjective and speculative excess, is the target of some of W. W. Taylor's most searing criticism. Arguing that such categories correspond to nothing in the native culture or mentality, he writes,

"all this business of the objectivity of 'trait' lists, and the adding and percentaging of 'traits' is a fine instance of what Professor Sapir used to call 'spurious accuracy.'" Taylor, *A Study of Archaeology,* 137. Also see ibid., 70, 88, 122–27, 138.

114. See, for instance, Tozzer, *Chichén and Cenote,* 68–91. Tozzer's organizational schemes, while preponderantly formal, do intersperse constructional and functional criteria. Averse to speculation but thirsty for synthesis, Tozzer's notion of comparison is actually a survey of the geographical distribution of various architectural forms, for instance, "batters, or sloping walls on pyramid structures are absent in the buildings of the Yucatecan-Maya period but quite consistently present in both the early and late Mexican epochs at Chichén." Ibid., 69–70. Harry Pollock (the Carnegie archaeologist who did the most to perpetrate this approach to Maya architecture) praises Tozzer's systematization and influence: "Following the sound beginnings made by Holmes, Tozzer organized his material so adequately that the majority of subsequent site descriptions and architectural studies have followed his form of presentation." H.E.D. Pollock, "Sources and Methods in the Study of Maya Architecture," in *Maya and Neighbors,* ed. Hay et al., 191. This article has been a tremendous help in formulating this chapter.

115. Ignacio Marquina, *Arquitectura Prehispanica* (Mexico: Instituto Nacional Antropología et Historia, 1951). The chart is in a shorter article, idem, "Relaciónes entre los monumentos del norte de Yucatán y los del centro de Mexico," *Revista Mexicana de Estudios Antropológicos* 5 (1941): 147–48. Exemplifying the staid and particularistic attitude of the era, Pollock, "Study of Maya Architecture," 196, rebuffs Marquina's pioneering efforts at synthesis, saying, "it is questionable if our knowledge is sufficient at present to give validity to such a treatment."

116. H.E.D. Pollock, *Round Structures of Aboriginal Middle America,* Publication 471 (Washington: Carnegie Institution of Washington, 1936). Taylor, *A Study of Archaeology,* 49, 55, has critical remarks on Pollock's work. Pollock's thorough book on the Puuc architecture of Yucatán (very important for the second third of Chapter 4) is delivered from essentially the same methodological position. Idem, *The Puuc: An Architectural Survey of the Hill Country of Yucatán and Northern Campeche, Mexico* (Cambridge, Mass.: Peabody Museum of Archaeology and Ethnology, 1980).

117. Spinden, *Study of Maya Art,* 14, acknowledges G. B. Gordon, *The Serpent Motive in the Ancient Art of Central America and Mexico* (Philadelphia: Pennsylvania Department of Archaeology, 1905), as his only direct predecessor in this art historical mode; Gordon's work is very thin by comparison to Spinden's.

118. Spinden, *Study of Maya Art,* 1, 13–14. It is interesting to note that Spinden congratulates and embellishes virtually every one of the very few cases in which Maudslay goes beyond his purely descriptive mode to attempt stylistic comparison of artistic motifs, for instance: Spinden (ibid., 30) retrieves Maudslay's treatment of the serpent-bird motif (*Archaeology,* 1: 63), and Spinden (*Study of Maya Art,* 18) retrieves Maudslay's treatment of the two-headed dragon and the water-plant motifs (*Archaeology,* 4: 37–38).

119. Part I of *A Study of Maya Art,* "General Considerations of Maya Art," is the exclusively formal and nonhistorical portion of Spinden's work (and thus the part that champions form as the essential principle of organization). In this section he does discuss four "imaginative processes of modification" — simplification, elaboration, elimination, and substitution — that operate in the development and change of artistic motifs, so it is, in that sense, a diachronic study. Part I is not, however, about historical reconstruction or anything outside of the evolution of the subject matter of the art. Ibid., 38. In Eric Thompson's estimate, "this section, the most important in the book, is almost as pertinent now [1975] as when it was written." Eric Thompson, Introduction, in Spinden, *Study of Maya Art,* ix.

120. Spinden attempts, with less success, to bring the same sort of formal, stylistic comparison to bear on more strictly architectural features (such as substructures, ground plans, and roof structures). In these cases, he leaps almost immediately to developmental and sequential schemes that are addressed later with respect to "Organization by Time."

121. Spinden, *Study of Maya Art,* 17–18, 18–19, 20.

122. Ibid., 32–69. Spinden likes the serpent example enough to repeat it in his *Ancient Civilization of Mexico and Central America* (1928), 91.

123. Tatiana Proskouriakoff, "Studies on Middle American Art," *Middle American Anthropology,* Social Science Monograph V (Washington: Pan American Union, 1950), 29–38; reprinted in *Anthropology and Art: Readings in Cross-Cultural Aesthetics,* ed. Charlotte M. Otten (Austin: University of Texas

Press, 1971), 129–36. I will be citing page numbers from the reprinted version of this article.

124. Ibid., 129–36.

125. Ibid., 137. Proskouriakoff's elaborate framework for comparing the abstract formal properties of Maya art has four main categories: (1) principles of arrangement (including symmetry, rhythm of spacing, delineation of field); (2) principles of form definition (such as degree of isolation of elements and relation of field and form); (3) qualities of delineation (such as character of curvatures, typical devices of form distortion); and (4) qualities of elaboration (such as interior ornament, exterior ornament, and detail). Then, apparently in the spirit of Wach's concept of the "classical," she isolates and compares "ideal forms" that epitomize each of these formal properties. Ibid., 132–33. (See Joachim Wach, "The Concept of the 'Classical' in the Study of Religions," in *Types of Religious Experience: Christian and Non-Christian* [Chicago: University of Chicago Press, 1951], 48–57.) It is not entirely clear what Proskouriakoff intends by "ideal forms," but it is worth noting that Spinden likewise occasionally refers to "ideal-type forms" in Maya art, for instance, Spinden, *Study of Maya Art,* 121–22.

126. Kubler, "Methodological Approaches," 283–84, articulates five main approaches to pre-Columbian art history: (1) exact description, (2) connoisseurship, (3) visual morphology, (4) iconography, and (5) iconology. Klein, "Relation of Art History to Archaeology," 4, bifurcates pre-Columbian art history into descriptive, stylistic analysis and iconographic analysis. The tripartite division that I am using (connoisseurship, iconography, and formal, stylistic analysis) comes from Coggins, "A Role for Art Historians," 315.

127. Kubler, "Methodological Approaches," 283.

128. Klein, "Relation of Art History to Archaeology," 4, says that pre-Columbian art historians who do descriptive, stylistic analyses "continue the nineteenth-century tradition of describing objects, albeit with an eye now to 'aesthetic quality.'" I have relied upon her position.

129. Kubler, *Art and Architecture in Ancient America,* 38, lauds Pál Kelemen as among the first "to consider ancient American art for its own sake rather than as a documentary file on cultural themes"; but Kubler would probably not agree, as I contend, that Kelemen is primarily refilling a niche abandoned by archaeology.

130. Kelemen, *Medieval American Art,* 8.

131. Besides his fine descriptions, Kelemen does make some valuable generalizations within the now-antiquated framework of "Old Maya Empire" versus "New Maya Empire" versus the Mexican area.

132. José Pijoán y Soteras, *Arte Precolumbino: Mexicana y Maya* (Madrid: Espasa-Calpe, 1946).

133. George Kubler, "The Design of Space in Maya Architecture," *Miscellanea Paul Rivet, Octogenerio Dicata,* XXXI (Mexico, 1958), 527–30. This short article has proven tremendously provocative.

134. Ibid., 515–22.

135. Ibid., 526–27. These three categories are used below in Chapter 3 to organize the section on "sanctuary architecture."

136. Connoisseurship has been characterized by Henri Focillon, Kubler's mentor, as *"la science des qualités."* Kubler, "Methodological Approaches," 283.

137. Esther Pasztory, "Masterpieces in Pre-Columbian Art," *Actes du XLII Congrès International des Américanistes, Paris, 1976,* 7 (1979): 377–90. Marvin Cohodas is also involved in a retrieval of connoisseurship, but his special concern is studies on the pre-Columbian artist. See Marvin Cohodas, "The Identification of Workshops, Schools, and Hands at Yaxchilan, a Classic Maya Site in Mexico," *Actes du XLII Congrès International des Américanistes, Paris, 1976,* 7 (1979): 283–90.

138. See Coggins, "A Role for the Art Historian," 315.

139. Klein, "Relation of Art History to Archaeology," 4.

140. Stephens, *Incidents of Travel in Central America, Chiapas, and Yucatán,* 1: 151. He is writing in regard to the workmanship at Copán, Honduras.

141. Pollock, "Study of Maya Architecture," 197, stalwart of the traditional archaeological stream, sees the study of architecture as an "archaeological procedure," which should begin with scrutiny of the "inorganic phases of civilization [that deals with such questions as] ethnic groups and culture, geography and environment, chronology, construction, and design." In his opinion, any study of the aesthetic or religious significance of architecture depends upon these essential preliminaries.

142. Antonio del Río and Paul Felix Cabrera, *Descriptions of the Ruins of an Ancient City Discovered Near Palenque* (London, 1822); Guillermo Dupaix, *Antiquités Mexicaines* (Paris, 1834); and Lorenzo de Zavala, *Notice sur les Monuments Antiques d'Ushmal, dans la Province de Yucatán* (Paris, 1834). Pollock, "Study of Maya Architecture,"

183–84, excuses the unsophisticated theorizing in these works because of their meticulous attention to the construction techniques of the buildings, many of which were more ruined by the time modern archaeologists visited them. Of the three, Dupaix is the most interesting, particularly by virtue of his sympathetic appreciation of native art and by his recognition that the Maya zone (Palenque in particular) is distinct from the Valley of Mexico. See Brunhouse, *In Search of the Maya,* 17–30; and Bernal, *History of Mexican Archaeology,* 93, 96.

143. Charnay, *Ancient Cities,* 301, 327.

144. Thompson, *People of the Serpent,* 180–90.

145. Two good examples of Maudslay's concern for issues of Maya construction technology are a very detailed discussion of successive (re)building phases at the Monjas in Chichén Itzá (Maudslay, *Archaeology,* 3: 13–19) and his study of the nature and materials of roof construction for the various colonnades at Chichén Itzá (ibid., 3: 36–43).

146. Tozzer, *Chichén and Cenote,* 68–72.

147. A. Ledyard Smith, "The Corbeled Arch in the New World," in *Maya and Neighbors,* ed. Hay et al., 202–21 (which is succinctly summarized by A. L. Kroeber, "Conclusions: The Present Status of Americanistic Problems," in the same volume, p. 478); and Lawrence Roys, *The Engineering Knowledge of the Maya,* Publication 436 (Washington: Carnegie Institution of Washington, 1934), 27–105, which includes a "typology of Maya construction types."

148. Joyce, for instance, considered the greatness of Mesoamerican art to come from the Indians' transcending the confines of Stone Age technology. See Joyce, *Maya and Mexican Art,* 7, 9, 10, 12. Spinden, taking most of his constructional data from Holmes, began to work out an evolution of Maya construction types and argued (well in advance of the consensus on this issue in the 1930s) that classification of buildings by construction techniques was a "safer method" for determining their age than were formal criteria. In that spirit, he experimented with such hypotheses as "the temples with the largest proportion of room space are the latest in construction," and roof constructions develop from "cumbersome first attempts at Tikal to the airy superstructures at Palenque and in northern Yucatán." Spinden, *Study of Maya Art,* 107–8, 170, 186, 193.

149. On the inaccuracy of dating Maya buildings by associated stelae, see A. Ledyard Smith's remarks from the 1920s, cited in Pollock, "Study of Maya Architecture," 194–95. In the thirties, Satterthwaite noted the inaccuracy of dating buildings according to stylistic characteristics by documenting widely variant, although probably contemporaneous forms of architecture in adjacent regions, and variant styles even within the same region (see ibid., 195). As an alternative, Satterthwaite substituted two different means of eliciting chronology via construction techniques: one based on differences in masonry technique (for instance, at Yaxchilán) and a second (at Piedras Negras) that relied on a "wall-span index" and the dubious assumption "that there existed a continuing desire to widen rooms or reduce wall-thickness, or both, the desire limited by the technical ability to do so." Linton Satterthwaite, "Notes on the Work of the Fourth and Fifth University Museum Expeditions to Piedras Negras, Petén, Guatemala," *Maya Research* 3 (January 1936): 85–88.

150. Pollock, "Study of Maya Architecture," 195.

151. Taylor, *A Study of Archaeology,* 129.

152. See Woodall, *Introduction to Modern Archaeology,* 39–44. Margain, "Pre-Columbian Architecture of Central Mexico," 51, 75, working more in the mode of traditional archaeology than cultural materialism, has an excellent survey of regional Mesoamerican building materials and their physical properties. For similar sorts of remarks on available building materials in various regions, see Smith, "Architecture of the Guatemalan Highlands," 82; Pollock, "Architecture of the Maya Lowlands," 396; Andrews, "Archaeology and Prehistory in the Northern Maya Lowlands," 307; Thompson, *Rise and Fall of Maya Civilization,* 21–22, 26, 85–87; and Robertson, *Pre-Columbian Architecture,* 12.

153. Taylor, *A Study of Archaeology,* 60–61.

154. In the early decipherment of Maya inscriptions (and, consequently, chronological researches), no one was more important or ambitious than Morley. Brunhouse, *Sylvanus G. Morley,* 76–77, 87, 159, discusses Morley's obsessions with Maya dates and his influence in keeping chronologic issues at the fore of the Carnegie agenda. Interestingly, Morley's enthusiasm for hieroglyphic dates seems to have been matched by startling disinterest in ceramic, stratigraphic dating. On the history of the decipherment of Maya glyphs, see Michael D. Coe, *Breaking the Maya Code* (New York: Thames and Hudson, 1992). Coe's important and very relevant contribution appeared too late to be integrated into this book.

155. The beginnings of the stratigraphic method in Americanist archaeology (oddly, an innovation for which no one seems to claim credit) are discussed by Willey and Sabloff, *History of America Archaeology*, 84–93; and Bernal, *History of Mexican Archaeology*, 160–66.

156. Bernal, ibid., discusses the Escuela Internacional. Regarding its goals and shift in priorities, Engerrand wrote in 1913:

> the method adopted in archaeological studies is the modern, or stratigraphic one, which is fairly remote from what I propose to call the traditionalist. In the first, excavations are undertaken and accomplished by a careful scrutiny of whatever emerges from the successive layers, so that a fragment of sherd is accorded the same value as a fossil, as each is a fixed point in the chain of evidence and from its stylistic characteristics, one can proceed to allot at a relative position in time.

Engerrand quoted ibid., 161–62.

157. Ibid., 161. The work of Manuel Gamio, the first to conduct a stratigraphic excavation in Mexico, is a microcosm of the sweeping victory of stratigraphy and temporal principles of organization over the earlier formal, stylistic criteria. In 1909, prior to the Escuela Internacional, Gamio ordered his archaeological finds under the conventional formal categories of "heads," "spindle whorls," and the like; later, after realizing the hitherto unknown potential of stratigraphy, he reclassified the same artifacts in chronological order. Bernal discusses the significance of this shift in Gamio's (and all of Americanist) archaeology. Ibid., 194.

158. Bernal, *History of Mexican Archaeology*, 177, discusses Caso's work in Oaxaca; Bernal, ibid., 164–66, likewise discusses the chronologic preoccupations of Tozzer's work at this time.

159. In his unpublished Harvard Ph.D. thesis ("Southwestern Ceramics; Their Value in Reconstructing the History of the Ancient Cliff Dwellings and Pueblo Tribes: An Exposition from the Point of View of Type Distribution"), among other places, Kidder asserted that the first task of archaeological research is the use of stratigraphic evidence to establish a sequence of pottery types, which, in turn, makes possible chronological assignments to architectural data, burials, and other details. See Woodbury, *Alfred V. Kidder*, 32; and Willey, "Alfred Vincent Kidder," 297. Later, in his capacity as chairman of the Division of Historical Research for the Carnegie Institution, Kidder repeatedly proclaimed that archaeology, especially Maya archaeology, should aim at "reconstructing history." See, for instance, Kidder's contribution to the *Carnegie Institution of Washington Year Book 29* (1930): 91; cited by Woodbury, *Alfred V. Kidder*, 59.

160. W. W. Taylor has thoroughly and critically documented the endorsement of "historical reconstruction" as the principal goal of Americanist archaeology in this era; see, for instance, Taylor, *A Study of Archaeology*, 23–24.

161. George Vaillant, "Excavations at Zacatenco," *Anthropological Paper* 32:1 (1930): 9. Taylor, *A Study of Archaeology*, 24, quotes Vaillant — alongside very similar assertions by Julian Stewart (1944), J. B. Griffin (1943), and Alfred Kroeber (1937) — that the principal goal of archaeology is "historical reconstruction." In this regard, also see ibid., 93, 205, n. 36.

162. Taylor's original attack on the limitations of Americanist archaeology, *A Study of Archaeology*, first appeared in 1948. In his memorial review of Clyde Kluckhohn's impact (or lack thereof) on Americanist archaeology, Taylor lamented that "Middle American studies remain today [1973] much as they were before [Kluckhohn] wrote." Walter W. Taylor, "Clyde Kluckhohn and American Archaeology," in *Culture and Life: Essays in Memory of Clyde Kluckhohn*, ed. Walter W. Taylor et al. (Carbondale: Southern Illinois University Press, 1973), 14–27. Specifically with respect to the limited view of "history" espoused by archaeologists, Taylor focuses on Kidder: "to Kidder, history seems to be a series of episodic events and their dates of relative chronology. When he mentions a historical development he most often means a chronological development. . . . When he mentions a historical problem, he seems to mean a problem of chronology, or more specifically the chronology of large events." Taylor, *A Study of Archaeology*, 64–65.

163. Taylor, ibid., 59–65, defines and explains "comparative chronicle" as physical descriptions of architecture, ceramics, and cities placed in chronological order.

164. Coggins, "A Role for the Art Historian," 317–18, makes this point about the changed goals of archaeology. Note, however, that even if the Carnegie researchers were "obsessed with retrieving chronology," in the case of Chichén Itzá (where,

admittedly, they shared time with the Mexican government-sponsored archaeologists), the retrieval of chronological data, particularly ceramics, is woefully incomplete. The problems ensuing from the "public rather than academic" motives of these projects were discussed in Chapter 1 in regard to "Chichén Chronology: Empires and Overlaps."

165. See R. E. Taylor and Clement W. Meighan, eds., *Chronologies in New Archaeology* (New York: Academic Press, 1978), for a review of the stunning progress in dating technologies after 1950. Gordon Willey, "A Summary Scan," 516, in the same volume, comments on the new archaeology's freedom from the constant concern with chronology.

166. Coggins, "A Role for the Art Historian."

167. I am not aware of anyone else who has analyzed Spinden's method in these terms, but I consider his work important enough to deserve this involved scrutiny. Note that the two "phases" in Spinden's project that I am addressing do *not* correspond precisely to Spinden's own organization of his efforts; while Part III of *A Study of Maya Art* is entitled "Chronological Sequence," his attentiveness to matters of Maya art evolving over time actually begins in Part II, "Consideration of the Material Arts."

168. A lucid example of Spinden's dictum that arrangement by form leads to significant chronological arrangement is his organization of Maya stelae according to the proportions of the human figures carved on them: "it was found that this simple method threw them into a definite series in which other progressive variations were easily noted." Spinden, *Study of Maya Art,* 156.

169. For examples of Spinden exploiting each of these four sorts of variations in Maya art to retrieve chronological sequences, see respectively, ibid., 186, 191–92, 176–79, 184.

170. For discussions of each of the four "evolutions" in Maya architecture, see respectively, ibid., 99–100, 170, 186, 97.

171. For discussions of these three evolutions in Maya architectural decoration, see respectively, ibid., 121, 127–28, 111–12. Thomas Joyce, the other scholar to write a major synthesis of Mesoamerican art in this early era (1927), likewise shared the notion of a traceable "evolution" in Maya art; see, for instance, Joyce, *Maya and Mexican Art,* 42.

172. Proskouriakoff, *Study of Classic Maya Sculpture,* 8.

173. Ibid., 180. Spinden also occasionally developed chronological sequences in art and architecture on the basis of inscriptions on associated stelae. See, for instance, Spinden, *Study of Maya Art,* 185.

174. Kroeber, in 1927, published a statistical analysis of the Nazca pottery of southern coastal Peru based on the assumption that undated items belonging to the same "form-class" can be arranged in correct chronological order by shape-design correlations. Alfred L. Kroeber, "The Uhle Pottery Collection From Nasca," *University of California Publications in American Archaeology and Ethnology* 24 (1927).

175. The full exposition of Kubler's theory of transformations in art is in Kubler, *Shape of Time* (1962). He acknowledges his great debt to A. L. Kroeber on p. 2. George Kubler, "History — or Anthropology — of Art?" *Critical Inquiry* 1 (June 1975): 757–67, is an interesting retrospective discussion of *Shape of Time.*

176. In Kubler's own words, "establishing chronological order is not enough, for absolute chronology merely arranges the moments of time in their own sidereal succession." Kubler, *Shape of Time,* 79.

177. Kubler, ibid., 33–45, explicates this fundamental conception of art history as "formal sequences of prime objects and their replicas"; the same notion often reappears in his later writings.

178. See Kubler, "History or Anthropology of Art?," 759 et seq.

179. Spinden, *Study of Maya Art,* 155, says that his ultimate goal is "to reconstruct the ancient history of the Maya." His most ambitious projects in extrapolating his results outside the strict sphere of art into culture and history (ironically, the weakest portion of his work) include largely expendable theories of archaic American unity, of Maya primacy, and of a correlation of Maya and Christian calendars. Spinden himself considers this correlation of calendars (a project that would synthesize his relative sequences in art with an absolute chronology) to be his most important contribution; that correlation, now largely discredited, still enjoys periodic revivals. See, for instance, Arlen F. Chase, "Time Depth on Vacuum: The 11.3.0.0.0 Correlation and the Lowland Maya Postclassic," in *Late Lowland Maya Civilization,* ed. Sabloff and Andrews, 99–140.

180. While Proskouriakoff nominally accepts that her studies of Maya art are ultimately in the service of "historical reconstruction," she is much less inclined than Spinden to push her art studies into

the realms of politics, economics, and culture. She cautions, for instance, that "whatever [the stylistic appraisal of Maya sculpture] may suggest is tentative and must be correlated with other types of interpretation, before it can become part of a historic reconstruction." Proskouriakoff, *Study of Classic Maya Sculpture,* 180.

181. Kubler, "History — or Anthropology — of Art?," 757–58. This is directly related to some art historians' insistence on the "irreducibility" and autonomy of art, discussed earlier in relation to "Art History: Architecture as Art."

182. Cecelia Klein, for instance, the most articulate spokesperson for a more anthropological pre-Columbian art history, says, "there is no reason to go on insisting that art is 'explained' by religion or ideas and that the struggle for subsistence and advantage bears no relation to the images men make. Avoidance of the social and material basis of the concepts expressed by an artwork can seriously distort our understanding of the object's ultimate function, if not its meaning." Klein, "Relation of Art History to Archaeology," 5.

183. Kubler, "Design of Space in Maya Architecture," 528, 530.

184. With apologies to Radcliffe-Brown, Levi-Strauss, and Dumezil, "function" in this context refers to nothing more subtle than the activities that transpired in and around the architectural monuments of Mesoamerica.

185. Holmes, *Ancient Cities of Mexico,* 22.

186. Charnay, *Ancient Cities,* 132–33; Joyce, *Maya and Mexican Art,* 14; and Spinden, *Ancient Civilizations of Mexico,* 180, are among the legion who contrast Mesoamerican pyramids as substructures with Egyptian pyramids as tombs. To his credit, Holmes, *Ancient Cities of Mexico,* 206, recognized the Palenque pyramids as tombs some fifty years in advance of Ruz's definitive discovery.

187. Deuel, *Conquistadors Without Swords,* 357–62, explains the circumstances and significance of Ruz's discovery at Palenque.

188. See the section "Commemoration of the Dead: Ancestral Bones and Stones" in Chapter 3 for examples of the funerary function of Mesoamerican monuments.

189. See Pollock, "Architecture of the Maya Lowlands," 411; or Weaver, *Aztecs, Maya, and Their Predecessors,* 155, for some routine speculation about the function of Maya "palaces."

190. Catherwood, *Views of Ancient Monuments,* 126–29.

191. A smattering of those who resort to the temple/palace distinction includes: Charnay, *Ancient Cities,* 13; Thompson, *People of the Serpent,* 180; Spinden, *Ancient Civilizations of Mexico,* 78–79; Tozzer/Landa, 171, n. 895; Tozzer, *Chichén and Cenote,* 6–7, 72; Bernal, *Mexican Wall Painting* 12; Coe, *Maya,* 85; and art historians Kelemen, *Medieval American Art,* 1: 51, 62, and Robertson, *Pre-Columbian Architecture,* 15 et seq.

192. For instance, William A. Haviland, "A New Population Estimate for Tikal, Guatemala," *American Antiquity* 34 (1969): 429–31, comments on the redesignation of "palaces" as "range structures" and on how "a correct definition of Tikal now depends in part on clear-cut identification of the functions of these [range] structures." The second part of Chapter 4 directly addresses the controversy over the functions of the range structures in the southern portion of Chichén Itzá.

193. See Brunhouse, *In Search of the Maya,* 75.

194. Ibid., 155. See Desmond and Messenger, *A Dream of Maya,* for a more nuanced assessment of Le Plongeon's ideas.

195. Charnay, *Ancient Cities,* 108–9, 114–15, 125, 296–99, speculates on the functions of buildings.

196. For instance, Maudslay, *Archaeology,* 1: 33, 49; 2: 7.

197. Linton Satterthwaite, "An Unusual Type of Building in the Maya Old Empire," *Maya Research* 3 (January 1936): 62–73, discusses the incidence and character of Mesoamerican "sweat bathes." Becker, "Priests, Peasants and Ceremonial Centers," 8, reflects on Satterthwaite's "breakthrough in the evaluation of building functions."

198. Karl Ruppert, "A Special Assemblage of Maya Structures," in *Maya and Their Neighbors,* ed. Hay et al., 222–31, moves from the peculiar form and orientation of certain buildings to their probable astronomical function.

199. Morley, *Ancient Maya,* 1st ed., table 8, 355–56; Brainerd/Morley, *Ancient Maya,* table 8, 322–23.

200. Pollock, "Architecture of the Maya Lowlands," 409–12.

201. See Taylor, *A Study of Archaeology,* 71.

202. Ibid., 168.

203. See, for instance, Woodall, *Introduction to Modern Archaeology,* 33–34.

204. For instance, Jeremy Sabloff and David Freidel, "A Model of a Pre-Columbian Trading

Center," in *Ancient Civilization and Trade,* ed. Jeremy Sabloff and C. C. Lamberg-Karlovsky (Albuquerque: University of New Mexico Press, 1975), 375–76, 403, discusses Maya lighthouses; and idem, *Cozumel: Late Maya Settlement Patterns* (Orlando, Fla.: Academic Press, 1984), 188, discusses Maya warehouses. Fifty years earlier Frans Blom (1932) had suggested that there was a "lighthouse service" among seafaring Maya traders. See Tozzer/Landa, 5, n. 22.

205. See R. E. Smith, *The Pottery of Mayapán,* Papers of the Peabody Museum of Archaeology and Ethnology, no. 66 (Cambridge: Harvard University, 1971); and, more importantly, Tatiana Proskouriakoff, "Civic and Religious Structures of Mayapán," in *Mayapán, Yucatán, Mexico,* ed. Pollock et al.

206. Diane Z. Chase, "Ganned But Not Forgotten: Late Postclassic Archaeology and Ritual at Santa Rita Corozal, Belize," in *Lowland Maya Postclassic,* ed. Chase and Rice, 113–14, 117, 124, acknowledges Smith and, especially, Proskouriakoff as her predecessors.

207. Kubler, *Shape of Time,* 2–3.

208. D. H. Lawrence, *The Plumed Serpent (Quetzalcoatl)* (New York: Vintage Books, 1959), 443. Kate is the heroine of the novel and the one generally considered most nearly to share Lawrence's own attitudes.

209. Stephens, *Incidents of Travel in Yucatán.*

210. Holmes, *Ancient Cities of Mexico,* 9.

211. Note, for instance, the tables of contents in ibid. and Stephens, *Incidents of Travel in Yucatán.*

212. See Catherwood, *Views of Ancient Monuments,* and Maudslay, *Archaeology.*

213. In the *Handbook of Middle American Indians,* see, for instance, Smith, "Architecture of the Guatemalan Highlands"; Pollock, "Architecture of the Maya Lowlands"; and Margain, "Pre-Columbian Architecture of Central Mexico." Among the many archaeo-architectural surveys that use expedient regional categories, a straightforward example is G.H.S. Bushnell, *Ancient Arts of the Americas* (New York: Frederick A. Praeger, 1965). Even more common than strictly geographical organizations are hybrid geographical-ethnic classifications that name the regional art styles of Mesoamerica after the tribes living in the area at the time of the conquest (for instance, Totonac, Olmec, Zapotec, and Tarascan). For example, Hans-Dietrich Disselhoff and Sigvald Linné, *The Art of Ancient America* (New York: Greystone Press, 1966), employ such a scheme. Brainerd, *Maya Civilization,* 21, and Proskouriakoff, "Studies of Middle American Art," 133, both express dissatisfaction with these geographic-ethnic organizations, "a usage which is misleading but time-honored." Ibid.

214. See, for instance, Kelemen, *Medieval American Art,* and Kubler, *Art and Architecture of Ancient America.*

215. See n. 152 of this chapter for a brief sampling of works that correlate raw materials for building and regional architectural styles.

216. Woodbury, *Alfred V. Kidder,* 58, 63; and Brunhouse, *Pursuit of the Ancient Maya,* 69 review Kidder's initiative to study the natural environment.

217. Willey, "Alfred Vincent Kidder," 303–8.

218. Hammond, "Lords of the Jungle," 5, comments on the lack of methodological innovation among Mayanists during the Carnegie Institution–dominated years: "the field seemed to turn in on itself." Particularly relevant is the cool reception to the *Kulturkreise* school, which had such an impact on European archaeology and which, I suspect, could have contributed significantly to the discussion of relations between Middle American environment and culture.

219. Even before the advent of so-called cultural ecology, Arnold B. Toynbee's universal dictum that the environmental conditions under which a civilization will strive (and thrive) must be neither too soft nor too hard has been regularly invoked by Mesoamericanists for decades. Three Mesoamericanists particularly fond of citing Toynbee are Nigel Davies, Eric Thompson, and Ignacio Bernal. See particularly Ignacio Bernal, "Toynbee y Mesoamerica," *Estudios de Cultura Nahuatl* 2 (1960): 43–58. Waters, *Mexico Mystique,* 81–82, explicitly refutes the appropriateness of Toynbee's theory in Mesoamerica.

220. See Willey and Sabloff, *History of American Archaeology,* 150.

221. Ibid., 151.

222. William Sanders, *The Cultural Ecology of the Teotihuacán Valley* (University Park: Pennsylvania State University Press, 1965); Richard MacNeisch, "A Summary of the Subsistence," in *Prehistory of the Tehuacan Valley,* vol. 1, ed. D. S. Byers (Austin: University of Texas Press, 1967), 290–309; Karl Wittfogel, *Oriental Despotism* (New Haven: Yale University Press, 1957); and, of Willey's innumerable works on settlement patterns, see, for instance, Gordon Willey, ed., *Prehistoric Settlement Patterns in the New World* (New York: Viking Fund Publications in Anthropology, 1956). For a concise statement of the early cultural-ecology position, see Woodall, *Introduction to Modern Archaeology,* 44–47, 61–64.

223. Preceding its expropriation by the cultural-ecological school, Ralph Linton, in 1936, defined the "culture area" concept as follows:

> Various geographical areas present marked differences in climate and economic resources. Any society which settles in one of these environmental areas must develop cultural adaptations to the local conditions if it is to survive. In time these adaptations become increasingly complete and exact, so that its culture will diverge more and more from the cultures of tribes living in different geographic environments, even if these have the same remote basis.

Ralph Linton, *The Study of Man: An Introduction* (New York: Appleton-Century, 1936), 383–84; quoted by Freidel, "Culture Areas and Interaction Spheres," 36.

224. Paul Kirchhoff, "Mesoamerica: Its Geographic Limits, Ethnic Composition, and Cultural Character," trans. Norman McQuown, *Acta Americana* 1 (1943): 92–107; reprinted in *Ancient Mesoamerica,* ed. Graham, 1–10.

225. For the most influential use of these cultural "subareas," see Gordon Willey, *An Introduction to American Archaeology,* vol. 1, "North and Middle America" (Englewood Cliffs, N.J.: Prentice-Hall, 1966), 85–87.

226. For an explication of the classificatory scheme of culture area, subarea, region, locality, and individual site, see Willey and Phillips, *Method and Theory in American Archaeology,* 18–21.

227. Eric Wolf, *Sons of the Shaking Earth* (Chicago: University of Chicago Press, 1959), 90.

228. Klein, "Relation of Art History to Archaeology," 2–3, comments specifically on Julian Steward's attack on "particularism" in favor of laws and regularities; she also notes that "the regularities, moreover, were deemed explainable on the basis of environmental or, more properly, ecological factors." Ibid.

229. For poignant remarks on the viability of making morphological (rather than evolutionary or developmental) correlations between characteristic sorts of natural environments, forms of culture, and forms of religion, see Raffaele Pettazzoni, *The All-Knowing God,* trans. H. J. Rose (New York: Arno Press, 1978), 433–55. Regarding a "religio-ecological theory," see Ake Hultkranz, "Ecology of Religion: Its Scope and Methodology," *Review of Ethnology* 4 (1974): 1–12.

230. Hammond, "Lords of the Jungle," 22–26, has remarks on the developments and accomplishments of "regional archaeology" in the Maya area since 1970.

231. Gordon Willey, Gordon Ekholm, and Rene Millon, "The Patterns of Farming Life and Civilization," in *Handbook of Middle American Indians: Natural Environment and Early Cultures,* 1: 446–500 (Austin: University of Texas Press, 1964), discuss the time depth of "Mesoamerica" as a culture area and the fluctuation of its boundaries over time. More recently (1981), Willey, "Recent Researches and Perspectives in Mesoamerican Archeology," 4, discusses the continuing reassessment of the Mesoamerican concept, crediting Jaime Litvak King (1975) with the most signal advance. Litvak King examines the nature of the intercommunication network among various subareal and regional cultures within the Mesoamerican sphere and thus argues, as does Freidel, for replacing the culture area concept with that of the "interaction sphere."

232. See Willey and Sabloff, *History of American Archaeology,* 191–94.

233. Freidel, "Culture Areas and Interaction Spheres," 50–52, proposes the "interaction sphere paradigm" (he credits Joseph Caldwell, 1964, with the original development of the interaction sphere model), which attributes causality in the development of complex, elite social institutions to *regional* conditions via information and exchange networks rather than to *localized* conditions as the culture area paradigm implies. Freidel's review of the variations on the original culture area concept is particularly helpful. See ibid., 36–40.

234. James J. Hester, *Introduction to Archaeology* (New York: Holt, Rinehart and Winston, 1976), 90.

235. Leslie A. White, *The Science of Culture* (New York: Farrar, Straus and Giroux, 1949); excerpt reprinted in *High Points in Anthropology,* ed. with intro. by Paul Bohannan and Mark Glazer (New York: Alfred A. Knopf, 1973), 353.

236. See Keen, *Aztec Image,* 436–38; and Davis, *Désiré Charnay: Expeditionary Photographer,* 17. This would have been Charnay's first expedition to Mexico, when his efforts were largely restricted to photography.

237. The two-volume *Cités et Ruines Américaines* includes, along with Charnay's photographs, a popular travelogue essay by Charnay entitled "Le Mexique: 1858–1861: Souvenirs et impressions de

voyage" and the more technical (supposedly "scientific") essay by Viollet-le-Duc entitled "Antiquités Américaines." Charnay's preface to *Ancient Cities* demonstrates the racist influence of Viollet-le-Duc that Charnay seems to have muted but never entirely abandoned.

238. Jacques Barzun, *Race: A Study of Superstition* (New York: Harper & Row, 1965), 67, notes that an earlier work of Viollet-le-Duc, his dictionary of French architecture, published 1868, contains a "100 page essay that is pure Gobineau." Keen, *Aztec Image,* 438, describes Viollet-le-Duc's method as a "sociological-racist interpretation of architectural style," and notes, "that these erratic speculations could be published and taken seriously suggests how powerful was the influence of racism in Western thought in the nineteenth century."

239. Ibid., 438.

240. William Robertson, in his masterpiece, *History of America* (1777), anticipated the anthropology of Lewis Morgan at many points, including examining Aztec society within an evolutionary framework of three stages: savagery, barbarism, and civilization. See Keen, *Aztec Image,* 275–76.

241. Keen, ibid., Chapter 12, entitled "Montezuma's Dinner," is a fascinating and scandalous account of Morgan and Bandelier coercing the Aztec data into their evolutionary scheme. Green, *Prehistorian: V. Gordon Childe,* 94, 136, comments on how Childe was influenced by Morgan's savagery, barbarism, civilization scheme.

242. Lewis H. Morgan, *Ancient Society* (Cambridge, Mass.: Belknap Press of Harvard University Press, 1964); excerpt reprinted in *High Points in Anthropology,* ed. Bohannan and Glazer, 53–54.

243. Lewis H. Morgan, "The Seven Cities of Cibola," *North American Review* 58 (April 1869); discussed in Keen, *Aztec Image,* 385.

244. Lewis H. Morgan, *Houses and House-life of the American Aborigines,* Contributions to North American Ethnology, vol. 4 (Washington: Department of the Interior, 1881).

245. Morgan, *Ancient Society;* excerpt reprinted in *High Points in Anthropology,* ed. Bohannan and Glazer, 33.

246. Woodall, *Introduction to Modern Archaeology,* 27–28, discusses the "descriptive urge" of this anti-evolutionary period, dominated by Boas; these archaeologists were determined to organize the mass of stratigraphic, chronological data in "value-free taxonomies." The number and names of such "arbitrary segments" of time — including phases, foci, branches, complexes, and industries — is remarkable.

247. Kubler, "Period, Style and Meaning," 16–18, discusses the significance of Bennett and Bird's *Andean Culture History* for Mesoamerican studies.

248. Wendell C. Bennett and Junius B. Bird, *Andean Culture History* (New York: American Museum of Natural History, 1949), 113. (To add to the confusion somewhat, they refer to these culturally significant stages as "periods"; other authors [as noted momentarily] use "period" as a strictly temporal category in contradistinction to "stage," which is a cultural category.)

249. The "Archaic," "Toltec," "Aztec" scheme was standard usage in the Central Mexican archaeological reports of the teens and twenties by, for instance, Franz Boas, Manuel Gamio, and Alfred Tozzer. See Bernal, *History of Mexican Archaeology,* 162–70. The term "Toltec" was, at that time, applied to Teotihuacán culture, not to Tula, Hidalgo, as it is today.

250. The origins of the "Pre-Classic" (or "Formative"), "Classic," and "Postclassic" are complicated indeed. Early usages of the scheme include: Eric Thompson, "A Trial Survey of the Southern Maya Area," *American Antiquity* 9 (1943): 106–34; idem, "A Survey of the Northern Maya Area"; A. V. Kidder, J. D. Jennings, and E. M. Shook, *Excavations at Kaminaljuyú, Guatemala,* Publication 561 (Washington: Carnegie Institution of Washington, 1946); Robert Wauchope, "A Tentative Sequence of Pre-Classic Ceramics in Middle America," *Middle American Research Records,* Publication 15 (1950): 211–50; and Alberto Ruz Lhuiller, *La Civilización de los Antiguos Mayas* (Santiago de Cuba: n.p., 1957).

251. Willey, Ekholm, and Millon, "Patterns of Farming Life and Civilization," 477.

252. Explicitly developmental classifications in this era include: Pedro Armillas, "A Sequence of Cultural Development in Meso-America," in *A Reappraisal of Peruvian Archaeology,* ed. W. C. Bennett (Menasha, Wis.: Society for American Archaeology, 1948); Brainerd, *Maya Civilization;* Alfonso Caso, "New World Culture History: Middle America," in *Anthropology Today,* ed. A. L. Kroeber (Chicago: University of Chicago Press, 1953), 226–37; Wauchope, "A Tentative Sequence of Pre-Classic Ceramics in Middle America"; and, probably most influentially, Willey and Phillips, *Method and Theory in American Archaeology.* See ibid., 70–78, for their endorsement

of the "historical-developmental approach" but rejection of "cultural-evolutionary theory."

253. Richard E.W. Adams, *Prehistoric Mesoamerica* (Boston: Little, Brown and Co., 1977), 12–13, epitomized the developmental mode of organization when he surveyed the history of the whole of Mesoamerica as a "cultural concept" with reference to seven successive "stages of development" — Lithic, Incipient Agriculture, Preclassic, Protoclassic, Classic, Postclassic, and Protohistoric. He characterized each stage in terms of relative technology, settlement patterns, socioeconomic organization, as well as "philosophical and religious principles" and art and architecture.

254. Willey and Phillips, *Method and Theory in American Archaeology,* 64, espouse categories that are presumed to be free from time and space, that is, "levels of similar cultural attainment irrespective of their antiquity or geographical location." Others, like Adams, *Prehistoric Mesoamerica,* 12–13, assign specific dates to their developmental stages.

255. Brainerd, *Maya Civilization,* 21.

256. Wauchope, "A Tentative Sequence of Pre-Classic Ceramics in Middle America."

257. Willey and Phillips, *Method and Theory in American Archaeology,* 193.

258. Ibid., 187, addresses this problem of regional differences in style.

259. Tozzer, *Chichén and Cenote,* 254, n. 11, collects a very helpful set of the various terms that have been applied to this apical period in Maya history — for instance, "Classic," "Great Empire," "First Empire," "Old Empire," and "Initial Series Period."

260. By the same token, in Central Mexico, the misleading Preclassic, Classic, Postclassic terminology implies a single "cultural climax" at Teotihuacán, while later climaxes at Tula and Tenochtitlán are relegated to a presumably degenerate Postclassic. See *Weaver, Aztecs, Maya, and Their Predecessors,* 120.

261. David F. Potter, "Prehispanic Architecture and Sculpture in Central Yucatán," *American Antiquity* 41 (1976): 445. The most important and sustained objection to exporting the Preclassic, Classic, Postclassic scheme to the Northern Maya Lowlands came from Andrews IV, who proposed as an alternative: Formative, Early, Florescent, and Decadent periods. See E. Wyllys Andrews, "Archaeology and Prehistory in the Northern Maya Lowlands," 288–90, 330. For the transcript of a discussion between Sabloff, Proskouriakoff, M. Coe, A. Miller, and Kubler, all of whom agree that the "Classic"/"Postclassic" terminology distorts the situation in the Northern Maya Lowlands, see Elizabeth Benson, ed., *The Sea in the Pre-Columbian World* (Washington: Dumbarton Oaks, 1977), 91–93.

262. See Willey, Ekholm, and Millon, "Patterns of Farming Life and Civilization," 477–78.

263. John Rowe, "Stages and Periods in Archaeological Interpretation," *Southwestern Journal of Anthropology* 18 (1962): 40–54. Barbara Price, "A Chronological Framework for Cultural Development in Mesoamerica," in *The Valley of Mexico,* ed. Eric R. Wolf (Albuquerque: University of New Mexico Press, 1976), 13–27, argues for the application of Rowe's "master sequence" to Mesoamerica. Paul Tolstoy, "Western Mesoamerica before A.D. 900," in *Chronologies in New World Archaeology,* ed. Taylor and Meighan, 241–42, 248–49, 276, summarizes the movement for a "neutral" Mesoamerican chronological scheme. Diehl, *Tula,* 18–19, for instance, has a clear chart that lays side by side the old "Classic" scheme and the alternative, "neutral" scheme.

264. Kubler, "Period, Style and Meaning," 18.

265. Weaver, *Aztecs, Maya, and Their Predecessors,* 4, has a concise discussion of the way in which the term "Classic" is shifted from a "stage" (level of achievement regardless of time) to a "period" (an arbitrary block of time). She also discusses the priority of the 300–900 C.E. era in the Southern Maya Lowlands. Ibid., 93, 107, 117, 153.

266. Kubler, *Shape of Time,* 2.

267. Guillaume Dupaix, *Antiquités Mexicaines; Relation des Trois Expéditions du Capitaine Dupaix, Ordonnés en 1805, 1806, 1807 . . .* (Paris, 1834). On Dupaix, see Brunhouse, *In Search of the Maya,* 17–30; and Keen, *The Aztec Image,* 313–16.

268. E. H. Gombrich, *Art and Illusion: A Study in the Psychology of Pictorial Representation* (Princeton: Princeton University Press, 1969), Introduction.

269. See Willey and Phillips, *Method and Theory in American Archaeology,* 34, for a discussion of this original, restricted use of "tradition" and its eventually broadened application.

270. Willey, *Introduction to American Archaeology,* for instance, uses "major cultural traditions" of the Americans as its primary principle of organization; see particularly ibid., 4.

271. Ibid., 4, 24.

272. Ibid., 4.

273. Brunhouse, *Pursuit of the Ancient Maya,* 116–17, summarizes Spinden's theory of the "oversoul" or "psyche."

274. Spinden, *Study of Maya Art,* 39, operationalizes this portion of his theory of art.

275. Ibid., 38–49.

276. Ibid., 39–40.

277. Kubler, *Art and Architecture in Ancient America,* 39, 474, n. 31, adopts this definition of iconography from Erwin Panofsky and cites H. B. Nicholson as the authority on Mesoamerican iconography.

278. Kubler's iconoclastic and important position on the relationship between Tula and Chichén Itzá (he considers it to be a movement from Chichén to Tula rather than the other way) arose as a direct consequence of his career-long initiative to locate specific works of art with respect to their historical precedents and echoes. This is discussed more fully in Chapter 1 and Chapter 4. See Kubler, "Chichén Itzá y Tula."

279. Kubler, *Shape of Time,* 2, 33.

280. Kubler says, "historically only those situations related to one another by the bonds of tradition and influence are linked as a sequence." Ibid., 33.

281. In the same vein, H. B. Nicholson sees the first task of iconography as the arrangement of works of art into developmental series via what John Rowe has called "similiary seriation." Nicholson, "Preclassic Mesoamerican Iconography," 163, writes, for instance, "to establish valid iconographic continuities, I see no escape from the necessity of at least attempting to establish these developmental-sequential chains."

282. Ibid., 159. Nicholson explicitly acknowledges Panofsky for this notion of iconography.

283. Ibid.

284. Kubler, "Period, Style and Meaning," 21–22.

285. Taylor and Meighan, eds., *Chronologies in New World Archaeology* (quite outdated at this point) discusses some of the progress in dating techniques. An important exception to this general clarification in dating is Chichén Itzá, where the chronological succession of buildings and sculpture is anything but clear.

286. Nicholson, "Preclassic Mesoamerican Iconography," 169–70, states the problem of disjunctions between form and meaning over time this way: "granted, then, that various Mesoamerican iconographic continuities spanning relatively long time periods can be established, the much more difficult question remains: to what extent did their conceptual connotations hold constant during these long evolutionary sequences?"

287. This set of issues was addressed earlier in the chapter in "Ethnohistory: Ethnographic Analogy."

288. See Coe, "The Iconology of Olmec Art," 1–12.

289. Richard F. Townsend, *State and Cosmos in the Art of Tenochtitlán,* Studies in Pre-Columbian Art and Archaeology, no. 20 (Washington: Dumbarton Oaks, 1979), 11, collects these major examples of ethnographic analogy and then questions their wholesale reliance on Aztec materials to interpret the iconography of Teotihuacán.

290. The other major contribution of ethnohistory to the study of pre-Columbian architecture is, as previously discussed, the elucidation of the indigenous use and function of buildings.

291. Nicholson, Introduction, *Origins of Religious Art and Iconography in Preclassic Mesoamerica,* 4, considers the "broadly humanistic thrust" initiated primarily by Garibay and León-Portilla as a healthy antidote to the dominant materialist approach to the study of Mesoamerica. On Ralph Roys and Eric Thompson as the exceptions among the Carnegie Mayanists by their concern for "Maya mental processes," see Taylor, *A Study of Archaeology,* 54–55. Of course, at least as early as Daniel G. Brinton's *Essays of an Americanist* (1890) there had been interest in "the mental activity of the Maya"; see, for instance, ibid., 163.

292. On "renascence," a concept Kubler borrows from Erwin Panofsky, see, among other places, Kubler, "Period, Style and Meaning," 20–22, and idem, *Art and Architecture of Ancient America,* Introduction.

293. See Townsend, *State and Cosmos in the Art of Tenochtitlán,* 12, for additional remarks on Kubler's attack on ethnographic analogy.

294. Kubler, "Period, Style and Meaning," 143–44.

295. The seminal application of "intrinsic configurational iconographic analysis" comes from George Kubler, "The Iconography of the Art of Teotihuacán." The key application in the Maya area is by George Kubler, "Studies in Classic Maya Iconography," *Memoirs, Connecticut Academy of Arts and Sciences,* vol. 18, 1969. He does not really apply these efforts specifically to either Tula or Chichén Itzá.

296. Kubler, "Iconography of the Art of Teotihuacán," 5–11.

297. Coggins, "A Role for the Art Historian," 319.

298. H. B. Nicholson challenges Kubler's insistences on radical discontinuity and articulates a

more widely held position of moderation: "religious iconographic devices in all cultures undoubtedly undergo some shift in meaning over long time spans, but when the ideological systems whose concepts they graphically express do not undergo radical modification it seems likely that most of them retain their essential meanings more or less indefinitely." Nicholson, "Preclassic Mesoamerican Iconography," 172. Townsend, *State and Cosmos in the Art of Tenochtitlán*, 13–15, 71, similarly appreciates but moderates Kubler's position.

299. The remarkably eclectic character of the "Toltec" or northern portion of Chichén Itzá is discussed at length in Chapter 4's "The Ritual-Architectural Events of 'Toltec Chichén.'"

Atop the Nunnery in South Chichén Itzá in the early 1930s. Substituting henequen hook for obsidian blade, Yucatán Maya (re)enact one imagining of the sorts of ritual-architectural events choreographed by their pre-Columbian ancestors. (Photo by Luis Marden, courtesy of George Stuart.)

Chapter Three

Significant Alternatives: The Hermeneutical Interpretation and Comparison of Sacred Architecture

> If Yucatán were to gain a name and reputation from the multitude, the grandeur and the beauty of its buildings, as other regions of the Indies have obtained these by gold, silver and riches, its glory would have spread like that of Peru and New Spain. For it is true that in its buildings and the multitude of them it is the most remarkable of all the things which up to this day have been discovered in the Indies.
>
> *Bishop Diego de Landa, 1566*[1]

Agenda: Architecture as the Datum of Priority

The great dilemma of Maya religious studies lies in the perplexing disparity between a fabulous fund of ruined architectural monuments and (the abundant hieroglyphic inscriptions withstanding) a near-total void of contemporaneous written texts. Accordingly, virtually no area constitutes a more pregnant arena to explore the general problematics of retrieving the religious life of a people on the basis of nonliterary or, as they are sometimes called, "mute" architectural sources.[2] In the Maya zone — and for this reassessment of the Tula–Chichén Itzá problem, a problem that is after all based on an apparent similitude between the standing structures at the two sites — architecture becomes, by its handsomeness, and by default, the datum of priority.[3]

From the first view of the Spanish conquistadors, native architecture provided the most obvious gauge of the relative merits of indigenous American civilization. Yet, despite the glamour, abundance, and accessibility of pre-Columbian buildings, architecture has not always enjoyed uncontested preeminence among aficionados of the Maya. In fact, in the decades since the advent of serious Maya studies, there has been a kind of competition or rotational successorship among monumental architecture, ceramics, hieroglyphic inscriptions, and codices. Each has had its champions, each respectively has been lauded as "the key to the ancient Maya," and each enjoyed its era as the most prized sort of evidence.[4]

Given the Eurocentric bias for texts, it is not surprising, for instance, that even before the inception of a professional Americanist field, there was widespread optimism that "the truth" about the ancient Maya would emerge via their mysterious hieroglyphic writing system. In his official report on the first expedition to Palenque (1840), Patrick Walker, for example, writes, "Once a key is found to surmount the difficulty in deciphering [the hieroglyphs], as is the case with Egypt, the history, customs, manners and religious worship of Palenque may be correctly ascertained."[5] This enthusiasm for epigraphical problems as the most direct access into the calendrical, astronomical, and intellectual accomplishments of the Maya animates the earliest systematic studies in the field.[6] All of the pioneers of Maya epigraphy around the turn of the century — Ernst Förestemann, Charles Bodwitch, G. T. Goodman, Cyrus Thomas, Daniel Brinton, Eduard Seler, and Paul Schellhas — are confident that, in the phrasing of the last, "the decipherment of the enigmatic hieroglyphs presented . . . the first and most promising problem of this new branch of study."[7] And, with epigraphic leaps in the past two decades, which are recorded so engagingly by Michael Coe, the glyphs may once again stand in first place among the spectrum of evidences of the ancient Maya.[8]

Almost from the beginning, however, there was another voice in Maya studies that assessed the hieroglyphs (and the documentary evidence such as the *Popul Vuh* and the *Books of Chilam Balam*) as too arcane, too "symbolic," to be reliable in discerning the realities of pre-Columbian life. By the 1920s the initial preoccupation with epigraphical problems began to give way to the priorities of excavationary archaeology, and with the discovery of stratigraphic excavation and the unprecedented enthusiasm for chronology, pottery, while lacking the glamour of either big buildings or esoteric glyphs, was canonized as the most instructive realm of data.[9] Robert Wauchope, for instance, delivers the characteristic eulogy to the potsherd: "pottery is by far the most useful [of artifacts], since it underwent constant changes in fashion and style; and since it is found in such large quantities — either whole vessels or broken fragments — an archaeologist can usually obtain a large sample to analyze and interpret. Pottery was also traded widely and its style diffused over large areas."[10] Typical of an era that prized ceramic-rich garbage heaps over grandiloquent temples, Linton Satterthwaite similarly pined in the thirties that the "location of a large refuge-dump [at Piedras Negras] would be more important than a series of new temples."[11] And, while the passion for pots has not been unanimous — von Hagen, among many, complains that "Maya potsherds have been studied to delirium . . . the ancient Maya are not now [1960] more than animated pottery," and Kubler cautions that "pottery alone does not reveal much more than itself"[12] — even today, archaeologists shimmy at the possibility of a break in the ceramic record. David Freidel, for instance, admits that despite the current sophistication in Maya studies, "if [indigenous Mesoamerican] groups gave up pottery, they would be virtually invisible until other means of detecting them is [sic] devised. The prospect of a non-pottery using population in the lowlands is an epistemological nightmare."[13]

The champions of epigraphy and stratified potsherds notwithstanding, monumental architecture — ever the most pretentious evidence of ancient Maya civilization — emerges from such debates on the relative merits of different sorts of data more often as the spoiled brat than as the neglected child of Maya studies. Landa's ceaselessly quoted remarks about "the multitude, the grandeur and the beauty of [Yucatán's] buildings, . . . the most remarkable of all the things which up to this day have been discovered in the Indies . . ." are echoed in all of the early Spanish chronicles. The spectacle and availability of big beautiful pre-Columbian buildings likewise ensure architecture's unrivaled ascendancy among the earliest Mayanists. One of the first proponents for the preservation of the ruins, a priest named José Antonio de Alzate (1737–89), for instance, claimed that "a building lays bare the character and culture of a people";[14] Frederick Catherwood writes in 1844 that "monuments . . . are the most important aids we possess";[15] according to William Henry Holmes (1897), architecture "constitutes the best remaining index of the achievements of a race";[16] and Augustus Le Plongeon, working in a quite different mode but about the same time, similarly considered architecture an unerring standard of a people's degree of civilization, "as correct a test of race as is language, and more easily understood, not being subject to change."[17]

The irrepressible majesty of the big buildings of the Maya continued to hold the limelight for generations of scholars. Consequently, through the early part of this century, the study of the Maya was focused overwhelmingly on the huge and alluring ceremonial centers, and, thus, when the work of the Carnegie Institution came under fire in the late 1940s, criticism was based largely on its disproportionate attention to the monumental architecture. W. W. Taylor, for instance, chided this tendency to give public architecture preferential treatment (a favoritism that is quintessentially in evidence at the tourist-archaeological site of Chichén Itzá) by contending that "the Carnegie had sought and found the hierarchical, the grandiose. It neglected the everyday . . . [and had] a one-sided predilection for the grandiose and the 'fancy' in archaeology."[18] In keeping with their concern for the nonelite elements of pre-Hispanic society, the new archaeologists and their present-day heirs continue this harangue against the reduction of the ancient Maya to their high edifices and most spectacular elements. And yet, even if the insular study of the architectonic grandiloquence of the Maya is at this point pushed permanently (and appropriately) out of vogue, nevertheless, the massive pre-Hispanic constructions remain, as they have since Columbus's initial arrival, for dilettante, tourist, and scholar alike, the most incontrovertible testimony to the cultural accomplishment of the ancient Maya.

Unfortunately, however, for all the pother that Mesoamerican architecture has evoked, critical reflection on the unique potentiality and limitedness of architecture as a peculiar sort of window into the world of the ancient Maya has been distressingly scarce. Furthermore, although pre-Columbian architecture is invariably acknowledged as ostensibly "religious," Mesoamericanists have given little systematic consideration to the mechanism by which monumental architecture expresses and elicits meanings, religious or otherwise. And, while there have been ambitious attempts to cast specific Maya buildings against a broader Mesoamerican background, in the main, efforts at comparing pre-Columbian architectures either to other indigenous American contexts or, more cross-culturally and morphologically, to less proximate historical contexts have been, from the perspective of a hermeneutical history of religions, decidedly "insignificant."

This chapter, then, the most theoretical of the project, works to redress this insufficiency in critical scrutiny regarding the experience, the interpretation, and the comparison of pre-Columbian architectures.[19] In the spirit of theoretical alternatives that might be more satisfying to hermeneutically oriented historians of religions, the chapter presents two broadly framed sets of methodological recommendations. The first set, which evolves out of a reconsideration of the irrepressible subjective/objective problem, involves the exposition of an alternative means of constituting the interpretation of sacred architecture in terms of what I will call *the concept of a ritual-architectural event*. The second set of methodological proposals, which arises out of reflections on the equally inescapable tension between universal and particular, involves the presentation of an alternative, more hermeneutically and religiously significant principle for organizing and comparing specific sacred architectures, namely, *a framework of ritual-architectural priorities*. Together these paired theoretical proposals constitute an alternative point of departure into the problem of sister-city relatedness. They provide a preparatory pause or, as it were, a kind of hermeneutical calisthenics that will put us in shape for a fresh reconsideration of the similitude between the architectures of Tula and Chichén Itzá. Following this methodological prelude I will return to the historical specifics of those two sites in Chapter 4.

The Concept of a Ritual-Architectural Event

> A building standing empty is not a whole building. It is only a beginning. We cannot understand it until we fill it with people, if only in our imaginations.
>
> *Anita Abramovitz, 1979*[20]

> [Michelangelo's Sistine Chapel] is not an argument, a display of an iconographic program, or an illustration of verbal ideas, although all these things are present in the work. Rather, it is a Christian liturgical act and can be rightly understood only as it is apprehended in its performance.
>
> *John W. Dixon, Jr., 1987*[21]

Our five-step exposition of the "concept of a ritual-architectural event," quaintly enough, is arranged like the experience of a pyramid, with an ascent, a pinnacle in the middle, and then a descent. The first step is a brief historical review that traces the progressive scholarly recognition that hermeneutical reflection is a mode of human understanding that operates whenever strangeness or "otherness" is encountered. Second, sacred architecture is characterized as a "superabundant" or inexhaustible locus of possibilities from which "strangenesses" perpetually emerge, which thus reveals that the human experience of sacred architecture is itself an occasion of hermeneutical reflection. Third comes the apex of the argument: the experience of sacred architecture, which is itself an instance of hermeneutical reflection, is characterized as dialogical and game-like, that is, as a dynamic circumstance that cannot be interpreted adequately in terms of static, timeless buildings. Accordingly, the concept of a ritual-architectural event — a relational notion that subsumes the work of architecture, the human users, and the ceremonial occasion that brings the architecture and the people together into to-and-fro involvement — is proposed as the alternative principle of interpretation and comparison on which the entire rest of this project depends. The fourth and fifth steps in the argument are the descent or denouement that refines and qualifies this concept. The fourth step distinguishes architectural events from other occasions of hermeneutical reflection and reflects upon their unique potentialities and limitations as data for the history of religions. And the fifth explores the general twofold pattern and the specific mechanism by which ritual-architectural events transform and enlarge religious consciousnesses, playing particular attention to the decisive role of history and tradition in that process.

The Universality of Hermeneutical Reflection

> In the last analysis, Goethe's statement "Everything is a symbol" is the most comprehensive

> formulation of the hermeneutical idea. It means that everything points to another thing . . . the universality of the hermeneutical perspective is all-encompassing.
>
> *Hans-Georg Gadamer, 1964*[22]

> Hermeneutics must embrace the whole life of understanding and understanding is always already at play in every form of human life.
>
> *David Klemm, 1986*[23]

Hermeneutical reflection arises from the encounter with otherness.[24] By the grace of hermeneutics, distant meanings are brought close, strangeness becomes familiar, and bridges arise between the once and the now. When the sense of a text, action, or institution is immediately self-evident, understanding proceeds unimpeded; interpretation is noncontroversial, and no hermeneutical reflection is required. But the sense of symbols and of religio-historical phenomena is nearly always more elusive; pre-Columbian monuments, for instance, at once beckon us to understand and yet withhold the abundance of their meanings. This elusive doubleness of meaning — a conjoined familiarity and foreignness — gives rise to hermeneutical inquiry. A version of hermeneutics, in fact, manifests itself wherever the process of understanding meets resistance and then breaks through.

The acknowledgment of hermeneutical reflection as a widespread human mode of engaging the world — "[hu]man's true vital activity" — has sputtered ahead for generations.[25] The term "hermeneutics," common usage in the eighteenth century for an "understanding" sort of person, someone who knew how to relate to another human being and perceive what was only tacitly and inexplicitly expressed, virtually disappeared for a hundred years.[26] Then, in the early nineteenth century — as modern science and the application of critical historical methods to the Bible effectively dislodged the traditional self-evident quality of Scripture and made it "other" by exposing a text that is unsettlingly distant, ambiguous, and filled with seemingly preposterous supernatural eventualities — the concept of "hermeneutics" was retrieved.[27] Most importantly, Friedrich Schleiermacher embraced hermeneutics as an apt strategy to stem the attack of modernity and to translate the meanings and peculiarities of this suddenly alien Bible across the centuries to the world of modern Christians.[28] Moreover, if hermeneutics was revived first as an alternative mode of biblical exegesis, Schleiermacher quickly expanded the field of application for hermeneutical inquiry to include all written texts,[29] and then, dovetailing with the efforts of Wilhelm Dilthey, the other great founder of modern hermeneutics, the province of hermeneutics was stretched further still into a general method of understanding and interpretation that could apply to all human studies.[30] Hermeneutics, even at this point then, was broadly conceived as a disciplined method for coming to terms with the "strangenesses" of literature, of the past, or of peoples different from oneself.

This fledgling venture into the universalization of hermeneutical reflection took flight in Martin Heidegger's *Being and Time* (1927).[31] Heidegger challenged and extended Schleiermacher's and Dilthey's notions of hermeneutics in two ways that will have especial relevance for this project. For all their innovation, the hermeneutics of both Schleiermacher and Dilthey (in this regard, their theoretical orientation resembles that of the early positivistic Mesoamericanists) were characteristically "modern" insofar as they were *objectivist* (each granted a version of the Cartesian separation of a knowing subject and a known object), and *methodological* (each held as his mission to prescribe explicit rules for valid, self-conscious interpretation). By contrast, Heidegger marked the initiation of a "post-modern" stage in hermeneutics that is *relational* (rather than the conventional notion of an interpreter as "subject" who hopes for a prejudiceless understanding of the world as "object," Heidegger's notion of understanding depends upon the positive affirmation of the inescapable interrelatedness between interpreter and interpreted) and *ontological* (hermeneutical understanding is not one method of knowing alongside others but rather is the fundamental mode of human being).

Even without diverting ourselves too far into the philosophical nuances of Heidegger's project, we can note that each of these shifts is crucial not only for the broadened application of hermeneutics in general but also, more specifically, each has profound ramifications for how we might undertake a hermeneutics of pre-Columbian architecture. The first shift — the transition from objectivist to relational understanding — arises from Heidegger's insistence that the fundamental task of philosophy is to overcome the alienation of a human "subject" from a world that has been reduced to "objects" of experience and reflection. He disqualifies any theory of understanding — including those of Schleiermacher and Dilthey (or, for that matter, of the positivistic Mesoamerican archaeologists) — that relies on a subjective, disinterested human interpreter over against an object of the mind's attention. In other words, where the early professional Mesoamericanists like Seler, Maudslay, Holmes, and Boas legitimated their enterprise and distanced their efforts from those of their uninhibited antiquarian predecessors on precisely these grounds — by posturing themselves as thoroughly objective observers and collectors of unadulterated "raw data" — Heidegger would demand a wholesale reconsideration of the status of both the researcher and the researched. Rather than aspiring, as it were, to clean the slate of one's mind and adopt an attitude of presuppositionless objectivity, Heidegger argues that the prejudices of the interpreter (or the "preunderstandings" as Gadamer will call them) are precisely what makes understanding possible. Heidegger contends, in other words, that the quest after an objective discernment of "things as they are" (pre-Columbian artifacts and buildings, for instance) is neither a viable nor even compelling goal.

Heidegger's alternative — the notion of a relational rather than an objectivist understanding — was revolutionary. His radically contrastive solution to the subjective/objective problem challenged the very foundations of Western metaphysical thinking (not to mention the tacit presuppositions of traditional archaeology) by undercutting the concept of a transcendental ego (for Heidegger there is no free-floating interpreter independent of his or her relatedness to and immersion in the "event of being") and, likewise, by undercutting the traditional notion of being as substance (that is, there are no objectifiable, once-and-for-all neutral things or objects).[32] If he were to apply this notion of relational understanding to Meso-americanist studies, Heidegger would insist upon the inextricability of the knowing subject or researcher (for instance, the archaeologist) and the supposed object of that researcher's attention (for instance, the artifacts or buildings that the archaeologist unearths). Thus, where early (and not-so-early) Mesoamericanists conceived of their enterprise as, in Ignacio Bernal's terms, "the scientific study of things,"[33] Heidegger's view demands that the task of the researcher be drastically reconfigured. Instead of objectifying the phenomenon of one's attention (be it a manuscript, a building, a pottery shard, or an indigenous ritual), one would concentrate on "non-objectifying modes of disclosure." Instead of an objectivist understanding of the ancient Maya born of *self-conscious reflection on the world,* Heidegger would argue for a relational understanding that involves *direct engagement with the world.* In this view, neither the twentieth-century interpreter nor the ancient Mesoamerican phenomenon under consideration (for instance, the Maya glyph, pyramid, pot, or whatever) is a discrete, independent entity; rather, in every instance of hermeneutical reflection, the human interpreter and the interpreted phenomena are subsumed by the relation in which they are involved.[34]

The second Heideggerian shift beyond the positions of Schleiermacher and Dilthey — the transition from a methodological to an ontological hermeneutics — is even more explicitly universalizing, and, moreover, will have equally profound ramifications for this project. By subsuming the problem of hermeneutics under his general analysis of Being, Heidegger demonstrates that hermeneutical reflection (for instance, reflecting upon the possible meanings of a work of art or architecture) is not simply a mode of knowledge; rather, it is a mode of being — "the mode of that being who exists in comprehending Being."[35] Heidegger, in a sense, raises the stakes by moving beyond new canons of academic interpretation or new methodological proposals toward an explanation of what actually takes place in *every* event of human understanding.[36] He argues, in other words, that this sort of relational interactivity between interpreter and interpreted is not restricted solely to academicians' interactions with the phenomena of their scholarly attention (for instance, texts, art works, institutions, or historical circumstances). Rather, this sort of dynamically interactive engagement applies to *every* circumstance in which people are coming to terms with the strangenesses of their surroundings. For Heidegger, relational, interactive hermeneutical understanding is not simply an academic method; it is the ontological way of the world, an almost instinctual interpretive activity that informs our every interaction with the othernesses of our world. Thus, in *Being and Time,* the crucial question is not in what way being can be understood, but in what way understanding *is* being.[37] For Heidegger, understanding is the fundamental possibility for being human, and hermeneutics is the practical philosophy for realizing that possibility.[38]

If Heidegger is the progenitor of a fully universalistic hermeneutics, Hans-Georg Gadamer has been its guarantor. Gadamer's work, which will be foundational for my reassessment of the similitude between the architectures of Tula and Chichén Itzá, is, in fact, largely an attempt to explore the implications of the new starting point that Heidegger provides.[39] In the context of that exploration, Gadamer, among other things, advanced both Heideggarian shifts in hermeneutical theory in ways that will inform my interpretation of Mesoamerican architecture from here on. In the first case, Heidegger's notion of the relational character of hermeneutical interpretation is perpetuated and extended in Gadamer's elaborate exposition of understanding as an "ontological event" that subsumes the human interpreter and the interpreted phenomenon, a notion that will be crucial for my own concept of "a ritual-architectural event." And, in the second case, Gadamer echoes Heidegger's insistence that hermeneutics is an ontological rather than simply methodological process by emphasizing, at every turn, the unrestricted scope of the hermeneutical perspective. Gadamer is even more emphatic than Heidegger that hermeneutics operates not only in the scholarly interpretation of arcane texts but in *every* acquisition of practical wisdom. Again and again, Gadamer preaches on the inescapability, the endlessness, and the "universality" of hermeneutical reflection: "What I am describing is the mode of the whole experience of the world. I call this experience hermeneutical, for the process we are describing is repeated continually throughout our familiar experience."[40]

Each of these interpretive adjustments, as we will see momentarily, has profound ramifications for the interpretation of sacred architecture in Mesoamerica and elsewhere. Suffice it for now, however, to note with respect to the supposed universality of hermeneutical reflection that Heidegger's and Gadamer's positive affirmation of the interrelatedness between interpreter and interpreted — along with their contention that as human beings come to terms with the strangeness of the world they are, of necessity, caught up in some version of the "hermeneutical interpretation of ambiguity" — has, by this point, garnered a vast rainbow constituency of supporters. Enjoying the multilateral endorsement of philosophers, theologians, literary critics, art historians, anthropologists, and historians of religions, hermeneutics has outgrown its home as a problem of textual interpretation and has overstretched its bounds as an esoteric philosophical issue to become genuinely, in David Linge's phrase, "a new paradigm of reflection."[41] (Moreover, in our current postmodern clime, certainly scholars have been able to come to these same general methodological insights via routes other than Heidegger and Gadamer.)

The wide currency of hermeneutical theory notwithstanding, in Mesoamericanist studies (with rare exceptions[42]), this alternative interpretive paradigm has scarcely been tested. The cold reception has a number of plausible explanations. Heidegger and Gadamer provide an alternative resolution to the objective/subjective problem that affirms the subjectivity of the researcher, not as an obstacle to understanding but as the necessary basis of human understanding — including, for instance, an academic understanding of the pre-Columbian peoples of America. Yet, given the prolific success of more strictly positivistic approaches to the Mesoamerican materials, this notion of relational understanding is apparently perceived as a threat to the presumed objectivity that, by convention anyway, separates professional Americanists from their antiquarian predecessors. Invoking German philosophy seems to many Americanists a step backward rather than forward, an unhealthy compromise of the empirical rigor that legitimated their field in the first place. Continental philosophy, particularly of the hermeneutical sort, is judged by many Mesoamericanists as, at best, irrelevant, bringing excess Eurocentric baggage into the indigenous American context (as if more positivistic approaches did not) or, at worst, dangerously distorting and even irresponsibly romantic.

In short, we can (and should) anticipate considerable resistance to the notion that Heidegger and Gadamer might have something important to teach us about the realities of pre-Columbian Mesoamerican life, let alone about the resemblance between Tula and Chichén Itzá. Nevertheless, the next step in this experimental project is to explore how the notion of a "universalized hermeneutics" bears on sacred architecture, including pre-Columbian architecture, or, more precisely, the sense in which *the experience* of sacred architecture is itself an occasion of hermeneutical reflection.

The Autonomy and Superabundance of Architecture

> [Mesoamerican] architecture goes beyond metaphor; it *is* the space of power, sacred and secular; it *is* the meeting place of the real and the supernatural. Architecture becomes a deity, as a ruler becomes a god. Architecture transcends the manifest elements of which it is composed in a way that is awesome to the imagination.
>
> *Elizabeth P. Benson, 1985*[43]

> It is not an exaggeration to say that in some cases different groups visit "different" pilgrimage shrines located in the same building and at the same site.
>
> *Alan Morinis and N. Ross Crumrine, 1991*[44]

Architecture — particularly explicitly sacred architectures like temples, tombs, pyramids, palaces, mosques, and monasteries — constitute inexhaustible funds of otherness. Religious buildings arise as human creations, but they persist as transforming, life-altering environments; they are at once expressions and sources of religious experience. As created and creator, a religious building manifests human aspirations and intentions; the meaning of such buildings, however, "not occasionally, but always" surpasses its original intention.[45] Once erected, architects immediately lose control of the significance and meaning of their projects. What the builders have in mind is, invariably, but the first in an endless stream of ideas and sensations that their architectonic creations will evoke. Consequently, as *homo religiosos* live and worship in, reflect upon, and "play with" the built structures in their environment, they endlessly disrupt old meanings and awaken fresh ones.

Owing to this autonomy and superabundance of meanings, sacred architecture is a stellar instance of what Heidegger describes as the pandemic interwovenment of disclosure and hiddenness. Heidegger contends that "the conflict between revealment and concealment is not simply the truth of the work of art [though it is most in evidence there], but the truth of every being, for as unhiddenness, truth is always such an opposition of revealment and concealment. The two belong necessarily together."[46] Gadamer capitalizes on Heidegger's notion of the productive interplay of showing and concealing as the basis for his own discussion of "the ontological plenitude" or "excess of meaning," which is characteristic of all that is symbolic in life, most especially art.[47] Thus, the experience of art, in Mesoamerica and elsewhere, not only falls within the sweep of hermeneutical reflection, it wins a priority in Gadamer's exposition of understanding because the experience of art lays bare that which is less obvious in other realms of understanding. According to Gadamer, works of art (and architecture) are available to endless reinterpretation and revalorization because they hold within them inexhaustible reservoirs of "ontological possibility"; each work of art, as he says, "stands open for ever new integrations." Accordingly, Gadamer argues that "the creator of a work of art may intend the public of his own time, but the real being of his work is what it is able to say, and this being reaches fundamentally beyond any historical confinement. In this sense, the work of art occupies a timeless present."[48]

Moreover, Gadamer affirms that this open and "eventful" character of works of art not only has general validity when applied to the plastic arts, but, in a happy coincidence for this project, he says, "we shall find the most plastic of the arts, architecture, is especially instructive."[49] Because architecture is, on the one hand, a very accessible element of the practical sphere of utility and, on the other hand, a "genuine" work of art with an "excess of meaning," architecture is, for Gadamer, the paramount exemplar of revealment-concealment interplay that is characteristic of all hermeneutical reflection.[50]

This architectural interplay of concealment and revealment, of allurement and hiddenness, is, for instance, expressed with paradigmatic lucidity in the Greek labyrinth, which is, in the phrasing of Philippe Borgeaud, "the image of discourse conceived as architecture, strange and deceptive, but concealing something and at the same time leading to it."[51] Revealing itself differently (and incompletely) to each initiate, the superabundance of the Greek labyrinth is explicit and unmistakable. Yet, even so bluntly unelaborate architecture as the prehistoric menhirs of Britain and France, rudely honed monolithic stones merely lifted to an upright position, do not "simply stand there, mute and dumb";[52]

even these raw stones present a fabulous and evocative range of possibilities, a fund of potential meanings that have been (and will continue to be) imaginatively refigured by each generation of devotees and scholars that encounters them. Moreover, the combinations and recombinations of plausible meanings emerge from such monuments with an autonomy and unpredictability that would, most of all, surprise their original builders.[53] In the phrasing of architectural semiology, "certain 'symbolic' functions, especially in ancient architecture, survive the obliteration of their actual connotative and denotative functions."[54] The original intention of a building is, in short, but the first of countless re-creations.[55]

A particularly glamorous example of continually self-creating and superabundant architecture comes in the interminable career of the gigantic Pyramid of the Sun at Teotihuacán, the very frontispiece of Mesoamerican architecture. The origins of the great pyramid apparently reside in a modest Preclassic shrine, built to guard the entrance to a clover-shaped set of natural caves, presumably forming the backdrop for ritual reverence to this esteemed womb-like hierophany.[56] By the Classic period, Teotihuacános had, by increment, transformed the humble structure into a sculpturesque 250-foot pyramid-temple, the religio-civic focal point of Mesoamerica's largest urban complex and most splendorous state pageantry, only to have the great pyramid eventually ravaged by a cataclysmic fire and then abandoned for centuries, save for the eccentric devotions of a handful of squatters. Some 500 years after its destruction, in the so-termed Postclassic era, the Aztecs, thoroughly uninformed about the empirical history of the ancient Teotihuacán, revered the monumental ruined pyramid as the work of the gods and the site of the original cosmogony; for them, regular rituals at the old pyramid provided a source of cosmic legitimation for their new imperial ambitions. Following the Spanish Conquest, the Pyramid of the Sun was variously reappropriated into a whole series of creative ideological schemes, none of which, of course, remotely resembled the initial expectations of the pre-Hispanic architects: for those who imagine various Catholic saints as the supposed builders, the scale and splendor of the pyramid confirmed their Christian faith; for diffusionist antiquarians, the enormous pyramid was concrete "evidence" of transoceanic contacts with Phoenicians and Egyptians; and then, with more substantial excavations through the nineteenth and twentieth centuries, the Pyramid of the Sun became the provocative grist for ceaseless (re)constructive theorizing, treated by scholars as a kind of arcane text on ancient Mexico. In the meantime, the irrepressible pyramid was likewise exploited by governmental officials as a monumental pawn in countless political intrigues and symbolic declarations of Mexican nationalism; the great pyramid was, in those cases, revalorized primarily as an emblem of ethnic-civic pride. And today, in its latest manifestation, the pyramid is packaged as the focus of a fully equipped tourist attraction, which hundreds of visitors ascend daily and which anchors an imaginative, if garish, sound and light show in the evenings, another eventuality that could scarcely have occurred to the original builders.

This motley array of activities at Teotihuacán — "architectural events," if you will — all derive their impetus from the structure of the great Pyramid of the Sun; but, in terms of meanings, religious or otherwise, these circumstances share very little. Emerging variously as a pilgrimage shrine, a civic center, an archaeohistorical document, a national treasure, or a tourist attraction, the Pyramid of the Sun is more than a static structure; it is a cultural resource. This gargantuan pyramidal mound, continually reinvested with novel meanings, in a sense, created anew in each fresh circumstance, is magnificent testimony to the autonomy, inexhaustibility, and superabundance of possibility that reside in every instance of sacred architecture.[57]

The principal pyramid of Chichén Itzá, the so-called Castillo, has endured a similarly eccentric succession of usages, serving in the wake of the city's collapse as a home to squatters, an occasional pilgrim destination, a cannon turret for the Spaniards, a picnic ground, an archaeological textbook on the ancient Maya, and, in the mythical imagination of the nearby natives of Chan Kom, as the most tangible evidence of the miraculous efforts of the long-vanished race of the Itzá, or Chac Uincob — "the Red People," who supposedly constructed the grand edifices of Chichén Itzá and who are expected to return someday.[58] Thomas Gann, for instance, made the same point about the transient functions of intransigent buildings when he reflected in the 1920s on the "solid ugly old church" of Santa Cruz de Bravo, "still standing square and uncompromising," which had endured stints first as a Spanish Catholic sanctuary, then as the headquarters for the brutal cult of the Santa Cruz (which took its name from this monument), and finally, in revolutionary times, as a prison.[59] Even today, visitors to the area continually encounter either stately pre-Columbian monuments that have, over time, been reduced to totally prosaic functions like that of cattle pens or grain storehouses, or, at the other extreme, ancient ruins that are daily revalorized as pilgrimage sites or propitiatory contexts by present-day Indians and travelers.[60]

There is, however, much more at stake in the autonomy and superabundance of architecture than the shifting usages of old buildings. In addition to these fairly obvious permutations in meaning and function over time, Johanna Broda's detailed discussion of the Aztecs' Templo Mayor as "ritual space," for instance, recounts an amazingly variegated schedule of ceremonies that would have transpired at this monument in the span of a single year. In addition to hosting the infamous public rituals of the Aztec state cult — extravagant coronations, human sacrificial devotions to their patron deity Huitzilopochtli, and celebrations of warfare and militarism — the Templo Mayor played an ancillary role as host to a quite different, apparently more ancient set of traditions and an elaborate schedule of rites concerning nature, rain, and fertility.[61] Besides serving the Aztec elite's endeavors in religio-political statecrafting, the superabundant Templo Mayor likewise figured large in the more generalized ritual pursuit of agricultural fecundity, and, as Broda eloquently demonstrates, any full interpretation of the pyramid temple must acknowledge this highly diversified range of ceremonial usages. Methodologically speaking, to lay hold of a single immutable meaning, or even a set of meanings for the Templo Mayor (or for the Pyramid of the Sun or the Castillo), is impossible. Each of these monuments is, in an important sense, revalorized, embellished, and resculpted in each ritual occasion.[62]

Moreover, beyond the flux in meanings and functions between the different ceremonial occasions at a single monument, deciphering sacred architecture is complicated more still because, invariably, the built environment simultaneously evokes a range of disparate meanings from the heterogeneous constituency that is experiencing it. Like actors in an intricately choreographed pageant, individuals and factions play different roles and bring different preparednesses to their respective experiences of the architectonic world; not surprisingly, their sentiments and perceptions of that world are equally variegated. Anthony Blunt, for instance, explains how the common people of seventeenth-century Spain, equipped only with a familiarity with the legends of Catholic saints and their miracles, were terrifically excited by the popular Baroque churches of Andalusia but were, in a sense, blind to the sophisticated theological allusions in the paintings of El Greco, paintings that inspired intense religious feeling among the more intellectually astute.[63] In ancient Mesoamerica, Robert Carmack reflects upon the Quiché Maya lords of Utatlán in the Guatemalan Highlands, who perceived their towns as sacred by virtue of their fidelity to the archetypal urban model of Tollan and deemed the rustic hamlets as profane; yet, for their Quiché vassals, the situation was reversed: for them, the rural mountains and plains, as elements of the Earth Mother, were the most sacred, and the city was, at best, a particularly powerful manifestation of that deity.[64] Or, more obviously still, in the context of a single Aztec human sacrifice, we can be certain that the architectural presence of the Templo Mayor would have engendered drastically different sensations (and different meanings) from the presiding king, the executing priest, the sacrificial victim, the victim's family, and the audience at large.

Each of these circumstances demonstrates the essential problem: namely, that *the autonomy and superabundance of sacred architecture both threatens and enlivens its interpretation.* The malleability, openness, and character of possibility within religious buildings (a set of potentialities that is particularly evident in long-enduring edifices like those at Tula and Chichén Itzá) ensured a wealth of meanings that will never be given over in their description as static constructional forms — even the most coarsely honed menhirs do not just stand there mute and available for their once-and-for-all analysis as objects. No work of architecture is confined to a single meaning, or even set of meanings. In and of themselves, works of architecture do not "mean" anything. Wrenched from its relatedness to human beings and to some particular function or ceremonial occasion, a religious building loses its meaning or, more likely, its many meanings are set adrift without context or perspective. Because objectivist descriptions of architecture — and this includes the vast majority of the literature on architectural history in Mesoamerica and elsewhere — err in presuming a lock or constancy between buildings and their meanings, historians of religions must pursue an alternative interpretive course, that is, one that appreciates the "universality of hermeneutical reflection" and that respects the endless flux between buildings and their meanings. Announcing *the* meaning of an architectural configuration, a building, or an iconographic motif (as so often happens) is never sufficient.

This alternative methodological stance depends upon a recognition that — and this is the crucial point — the mechanism of hermeneutical reflection is manifesting itself on two levels here: in the *experience* of superabundant sacred architecture itself (for instance, in the experience of the Castillo by tenth-century Yucatán natives), and in the *interpretation* of the experience of sacred architecture (for instance, in the academic interpretation of the history and significance of the Castillo by twentieth-century historians of religions). At the first level, historical cases of revalorized architectural forms, transfigured meanings, fluidity in function, and a multiplicity of expectations and apprehensions among the users of any given work of architecture (like the examples just discussed) testify indubitably that hermeneutics is operating in the *experience* of sacred architecture. Following Gadamer, even the most untutored experience of an architectural monument, like the little boy's dialogical encounter with the stone angel, is (potentially anyway) an occasion of hermeneutical reflection. Moreover, at the second level, the scholarly interpretation of those historical cases is equally an occasion for hermeneutics. Thus, to say it again, the interpretation of sacred architecture is an exercise in hermeneutical reflection upon a circumstance that is itself an exercise in hermeneutical reflection.

Acknowledging this layering of hermeneutical situations gives my project an atypical slant. Even among the Gadamerian faithful who acknowledge the supposed universality of hermeneutics, the field of application for hermeneutical theory is typically restricted to excogitations on the plausibility of a scholar overriding or mediating the otherness of the religious, historical, or literary context that one hopes to interpret. Fascinating as the merger of "horizons" between researcher and researched is, my project points elsewhere. As a theoretical contribution, this project, together with its foundational concept — "the ritual-architectural event" — aims less at the hermeneutical relation between the world of the scholar and the "other world" of pre-Columbian Americans than at the relations to otherness that the pre-Columbians would have encountered in their own world. My reassessment of the Tula–Chichén Itzá problem focuses first of all on the ways in which indigenous Mesoamerican populations might have experienced and mediated the "othernesses" of the pre-Columbian monuments of those two sites and then, secondarily, on mediating the otherness between ourselves and those indigenous Mesoamericans (though certainly those two levels constantly interact). In other words, this project concerns itself preeminently with the interrelatedness between human beings and the architectural monuments of their worlds — a circumstance that can be epigrammatically framed as an encounter between a native Mesoamerican pilgrim and a pre-Columbian pyramid — and claims that the plenipotent language and theoretics of hermeneutical understanding are also applicable to this hypothetical confrontation. By regularly invoking this poignantly simply image of an indigenous pilgrim's encounter with a pyramid, I hope to provide a constant methodological reminder that, from the perspective of a hermeneutical history of religions, the study of pre-Columbian architecture must be constituted not in terms of buildings per se but in terms of people's *experience* of buildings — that is, as the next section explains, in terms of "ritual-architectural events."

The Eventfulness of Architecture: Conversation and Play

> In every condition of humanity, it is precisely play, and play alone that makes man complete; man plays only when he is in the full sense of the word a man, and he is wholly Man only when he is playing.
>
> *Friedrich Schiller*[65]

> Whatever is brought into play or comes into play no longer depends on itself but is dominated by the relation we call the game.
>
> *Hans-Georg Gadamer, 1962*[66]

To reiterate for a running start, the concept of a ritual-architectural event arises as an alternative to conventional interpretations of art and architecture, in Mesoamerica and elsewhere, that would presume to have retrieved *the* meaning of this ancient sanctuary, or *the* intention of that monumental sculpture, or *the* significance of some particular pyramidal temple. Embracing Heidegger's and Gadamer's resolution of the objective/subjective problem, this alternative approach rejects the viability of a researcher wiping away all preconceptions (or by *epoché* holding them in abeyance) in order to guarantee what Husserl termed a "pure seeing" or a "certitude of vision" that would lay bare the timeless significance of the work of art or architecture and afford an untainted grasp of "the meaning of the absolutely given."[67] Instead of constituting buildings as objects and then aspiring to disclose the meanings of those buildings in a process of self-conscious reflection (as most approaches to pre-Columbian architecture have), Heidegger and Gadamer refute the claim that the interpreters can ever thoroughly disconnect themselves from their life-worlds and, likewise, that the world can ever be adequately conceived as the realm of neutral things or objects. They claim, instead, that "truth is always an opposition of revealment and concealment" and, thus, that interpreters are naive in believing that they ever really "see" the total disclosure of any phenomenon. Because, from their perspective, phenomena — preeminently works of art and architecture — continually "withhold themselves," the act of human understanding is less a Cartesian, conquistadorial unveiling than a movement of history in which neither the interpreter nor the work of art can be thought of as autonomous parts.[68]

This notion of a dynamic, mutually interactive experience of the world (and particularly the experience of art and architecture) bears so little resemblance to "looking at pictures" that the standard metaphor of sight, while not wholly inappropriate, does not do justice to this alternative conception of the way in which people experience and understand the "other-nesses" (including the buildings) that surround them. Accordingly, Gadamer replaces the Husserlian notion of understanding as "pure seeing" with the more dynamic and dialogical metaphors of *conversation* and *play:* for Gadamer, the experience of a work of art or architecture, itself an exercise in hermeneutical reflection, is like a "dialogue between persons" or, even more graphically, like the "buoyance of a game in which the players are absorbed."[69] From this perspective, the interpreter does not stand over, above, or apart from the phenomenon that is under consideration; rather, the two are engaged as partners in a hermeneutical conversation, or players in a hermeneutical game. Moreover, owing to the encompassment of hermeneutical reflection, this status as interactive players in a game applies not simply to academicians and the phenomena they study but also, more poignantly, to all persons who are seriously involved in understanding the phenomena of their worlds. We must appreciate, for instance, that the indigenous pre-Columbian visitors to Tula Grande and "Toltec Chichén," beyond simply "looking at" the imposing pyramids and platforms, were, in an important sense, "playing with" (or engaging in conversation with) the monuments of those two sites. Play (or conversation) is, thus, the most adequate metaphor for the interactive relationship between the pilgrim and the pyramid.

With this as background, my project espouses the concept of a "ritual-architectural event" as an alternative that shifts the emphasis away from the interpretation of objectified built forms and toward the interpretation of *the human experience of architecture.* Instead of buildings per se, my reassessment of the architectural similitude between Tula Grande and "Toltec Chichén" is constituted in terms of events or circumstances in which people are interacting with buildings. The experience of sacred architecture is, in other words, located fully within the realm of hermeneutical reflection and, thus, is conceived not as "looking at buildings" but as participation in conversation-like, or game-like, ceremonial occasions. In that spirit, the concept of a ritual-architectural event demands, above all, that buildings not be reified as timeless objects but, instead, be contextualized in relation to the human users who bring with them their characteristic preunderstandings and in relation to the particular ceremonies that transpire there. In short, a ritual-architectural event encompasses the situation that includes the building, the people, and the activity. Interpretation is constituted in terms of ritual circumstances rather than buildings, and each of these constituent elements of the circumstance is essential: (1) the stone, wood, and iron of the buildings themselves as one player; (2) human beings — heavily burdened with expectations, traditions, and religious opinions — as another player; and (3) the ceremonial occasion as the activity or game that brings buildings and people into a to-and-fro involvement with one another.

Because the concept of a ritual-architectural event defines a situation, a happening, it likewise concerns itself with all that bears on that situation; it widens the field of interpretation rather than narrowing it. The history of sacred architecture, for instance, abounds with orientational schemes that draw celestial bodies, mountains, and weather phenomena into the province of the ritual-architectural event. The famous rock-cut temples of Malinalco, Mexico, and the mountain citadel of Machu Picchu, Peru, wedged in among boulders and spectacular overhangs, are only the most obvious proofs that the natural landscape also belongs within the concept of a ritual-architectural event. Smells and sounds assuredly assert themselves in the synesthetic experience of sacred architecture; and furniture, ritual paraphernalia, and costumes, by impinging upon the architectural circumstance, become germane as well. At Banaras, light is exploited as the most persistent image of Kashi; at Chichén Itzá's great Castillo pyramid, Quetzalcoatl is manifest in a shadow that creeps along the steps; and, the manipulation of light is the virtual signature of the Gothic — so certainly luminosity and shadow are elements of the concept of a ritual-architectural event. In sum, the concept of a ritual-architectural event wants inclusion. It defines not a built form but the circumstances that arise in relation to that form and, thus, hopes to encompass all the forces that act upon that circumstance.

This inclusive and situational conception of ritual-architectural events heeds Gadamer's warning that to interpret the experience of architecture either in terms of the subjective attitude of the human observer or in terms of the physical attributes of the building condemns one to miss that which is most important — namely, the "buoyancy" or the movement of "play" between the two.[70] Insisting on the interactive relation between superabundant architecture and its users, the buildings of, for instance, Tula and Chichén Itzá emerge not as static objects of reflection but, more appropriately, as dynamic partners in conversation or, in the case of the game analogy, as active, lissome players who both respond to and provoke responses from those who experience them. Both the pilgrim (as well as the academic interpreter) and pyramid are "players" in a game, an interactive exchange — or an architectural event — that transcends and subsumes the players. In Gadamer's phrasing, "the back and forth movement of the game has a peculiar freedom and buoyance that determines the consciousness of the players. It goes on automatically — a condition of weightless balance . . . whatever is brought into play or comes into play no longer depends on itself but is dominated by the relation that we call the game."[71] Accordingly, the intrinsically dialogical nature of the experience of art and architecture makes it less appropriate to imagine a pre-Columbian pilgrim craning his neck for a better view of the Castillo — as though it were simply an inert, inanimate, mute structure — than to conceive of the pilgrim and pyramid as mutual partners in lively repartee or, better still, as withy players in a brisk game that will, before its end, transform them both.

Moreover, besides insisting on the interdependent relatedness between monument and human, the metaphors of conversation and play call attention to three other qualities that are intrinsic to the situational concept of ritual-architectural events. Such occasions are, invariably: (1) active, (2) serious, and (3) productive or transformative.

In the first case, the athleticism of the play analogy points toward an active, performative element that is intrinsic to the experience of all arts, and especially to architecture. Gadamer insists that the presentation or performance of a work of art, while more obvious in the cases of drama and music, is, in every type of art, something essential not incidental — "for in this is merely completed what works of art already are: the being of what is presented in them."[72] Works of art and their meanings are dependent and inseparable from the ceremonial occasions in which the art plays an active part. Navajo sandpainting, for instance, provides radical exemplification of this indissolubility between works of art and their performative contexts. In Gary Witherspoon's phrasing, "to the Navajo the artistic or aesthetic value of the sandpainting is found in its creation, not in its presentation. Its ritual value is in its symbolic or representational power, and not in its use as a vehicle of conception. Once it has served that purpose it no longer has any ritual value."[73] And so, at the conclusion of the Navajo ceremonial, the sandpainting is regretlessly obliterated. To salvage a sandpainting from a hogan floor, consolidate it, and mount it in a suburban den — a venture that bewilders and amuses the Navajo — in a sense makes that painting a player without a game (or at least casts it into a very different league, with radically different rules). The meaning of a religious building, like that of the Navajo sandpainting, is inextricable from the human traditions and active performance in which it participates. Chichén's Castillo, for instance, "means" (in fact, *is*, according to Gadamer's radical ontological argument) something very different in the event of a Maya coronation, than in the event of human sacrifice, than in the event of propitiation for rain (not to mention the profoundly different ontology of the Castillo in relation to its interactions with twentieth-century scholars and tourists).

Second, for all the jovial connotations of the allusions to play, Gadamer hardly intends that the game-like experience of architecture is something trivial. To the contrary, he says, "play and seriousness, the exuberance and superabundance of life, on the one hand, and the tense power of vital energy, on the other, are profoundly interwoven. They interact with one another, and those who have looked deeply into human nature have recognized that our capacity for play is an expression of the highest seriousness."[74] Owing to the fundamentality of the issues with which ritual and art "play," there are profound existential risks at stake in many ritual-architectural events. When, for instance, in ancient Mesoamerica, pilgrims entered the closed world of the manipulative religio-civic "pyramid events" at Chichén Itzá or Tenochtitlán, they committed themselves to abiding by the rules of those ritual-architectural games; they were compelled to surrender cautious disinterest and expose themselves to the as-yet-unknown consequences. One who skirts the rules and declines to take them seriously remains an outsider, in Gadamer's terms, a "spoilsport" rather than a player.[75] Commitment, and thus risk, are essential to every ritual-architectural event: "the game is underway when the individual player participates in full earnest, that is, when he no longer holds himself back as one who is merely playing, for whom it is not serious."[76]

This willingness to accept the rules of the game, to loosen the intransigent confidence that one has in a particular view of the world, and to give serious and sympathetic consideration to the alternatives that the art and architecture present, leads to the third essential quality of ritual-architectural events: they are transformative or, in an important sense, generative. For Gadamer, the experience of art, like that of human understanding in general, is genuinely productive; it entails, in his terminology, an "increase of being," as things and ideas that were not, come to be. Similarly, in the gamelike exchange between buildings and persons, both experience productive transformations: the significance of monuments grows and changes as unprecedented combinations of superabundant meanings emerge, and the human spectators are transformed and awakened as they replace their preunderstandings and foreconceptions with previously unimagined alternatives. Thus, rather than relaxation or idyllic repose, ritual-architectural events are, very often, forums of jolting surprise, experimentation, and vicarious participation in frighteningly unfamiliar ways of knowing and being. In the productive experience of art and architecture, complacences are interrupted, aspirations and awarenesses are heightened or, at the very least, reorganized.

Gadamer describes the bittersweet appeal of being reworked in these situations, saying, "all playing is a being-played. The attraction of a game, the fascination it exerts consists precisely in the fact that the game tends to master the players."[77] Elsewhere he reiterates the same theme of the play's transformative power with explicit reference to the experience of art and architecture: "The work of art is not an object which stands over against a subject for itself. Instead a work of art has its true being in the fact that it becomes an experience changing the person who is experiencing it."[78] The conjoined seriousness and transformative power of ritual-architectural events is unmistakable, for instance, in the young initiates' experience of ceremonial death and then rebirth by their entry and exit of the Greek labyrinth, "a symbolic milieu that represented both a grave and a womb."[79] The productive realignment of one's world is equally explicit in the eventful experience of Mount Meru: in I. W. Mabbett's words, "to approach Meru is to change one's spiritual state; to arrive at the top is to transcend particularities of state altogether."[80] Richard Townsend's discussion of the elaborate Aztec coronation as a "royal rite of passage" in which the Templo Mayor "formed the central stage and touchstone" likewise showcases a ritual-architectural event that is explicitly and preeminently transformative: the ruler-elect enters the Templo Mayor coronation event as a mere human of contestable authority but passes out the other side as the legitimate, invulnerable, and divinely sanctioned *huey tlatoani,* or chief speaker.[81] And Allan Grapard's exposition of the "mandalization" of the landscape and temples of Japan — and the sense in which pilgrimage either across the country or through a single building constitutes the experience of a consciousness-altering mandala — provides a whole set of ritual-architectural events that are explicitly and, by design, transformative in a most serious fashion.[82]

To summarize then, hermeneutical reflection operates on two levels in, respectively, the *experience* and the *interpretation* of sacred architecture. The metaphors of conversation and play are relevant in both situations. On the first level, researchers must posture themselves not as omniscient observers but as questioning, listening partners in conversation; accepting a relational (rather than objectivist) resolution of the objective/subjective problem, they must willingly accept for themselves the status of players rather than referees. And on the second, even more important level, researchers must acknowledge that their "opposition," the other player, is actually itself a game — for instance, the game between the pilgrim and the pyramid — a ritual-architectural game in which human beings and buildings are interacting in ways that are active, serious, and transformative. By constituting the interpretation of sacred architecture, in Mesoamerica and elsewhere, in terms of "playful" or dialogical ritual-architectural events rather than as the more customary (and more objectivist) "meanings of buildings," we can respect both the wide applicability of hermeneutics and the superabundance of religious architecture. Moreover, by insisting on the "eventfulness" of the monumental architectures of Tula, Chichén Itzá, and elsewhere, we can provide an alternative, more "religiously significant" principle of comparison and organization than any of those reviewed in Chapter 2.

The Special Case of Architecture: Habitats and Worlds

> Thinking, feeling, and even the will have to be involved in the perception of the work of art. This is most evident in the work of architecture, where an ever-so astute analysis of the ground-plan cannot replace the feeling one receives from the light and shade pervading the spaces and the actual muscular communion with the whole that is experienced through walking around and into a building.
>
> *Konrad Oberhuber, 1985*[83]

> Architecture, it has often been said, is the Mother of the Arts.
>
> *Adrian Stokes, 1951*[84]

The final two steps in my exposition of the concept of a ritual-architectural event constitute the denouement, that is, a set of refinements and qualifications to the preceding discussion. Having argued that the experience of architecture is a particularly representative instance of the massively inclusive process of hermeneutical reflection and, as such, has the character of play (or conversation), we need to counter that exercise in inclusion by exploring the *uniqueness* of religious architecture and the sense in which the experience of sacred architecture is distinct from other occasions of hermeneutical understanding. In that spirit, this section explores the basis for architecture's special prestige among the arts and, thus, architecture's potentialities and limitations as a unique sort of data for the history of religions in general or, more specifically, as evidence for the resolution of a problem like that of the relationship between Tula and Chichén Itzá. Following that, the final step in this argument explores the specific mechanism by which ritual-architectural events engage and transform human consciousness, emphasizing particularly the decisive role of tradition and history in mediating those transformations. In short, this section reflects upon what sacred architecture is, the next, upon how it works.

The hermeneutical experience of architecture is, so it would seem, a specifically human phenomenon. Impressive as the building achievements of various animal species may be — the engineering feats of weaverbirds, beavers, bees, and termites are especially favored examples[85] — Gadamer, for instance, claims that humans have a thoroughly nonzoological way of relating to their environment, whether built or natural. His differentiation between the "habitats" (*Unwelt*) of animals and the "worlds" (*Welt*) of humans is as follows:

> It is thus clear that man, unlike all other living creatures has a "world" insofar as these creatures do not have a relationship to the world, but are, as it were, placed within their habitat. . . . It is also the case that, unlike all other living creatures, man's relationship to the world is characterized by freedom from habitat. Animals can leave their habitat and move over the whole earth without severing their environmental dependence. . . . For man, however, to rise above the habitat means to rise to "world" itself, to true environment.[86]

Gadamer insists, in other words, that there is a characteristically human tendency to strive self-consciously to expand one's "horizon of meaning," a tendency that depends upon linguistic and transcendental capacities that animals lack. Thus, as Alan Olson concludes, "It is the essence of 'habitat' to remain the same as fixed physical space, whereas the notion of 'world' expands and contracts relative to one's horizon of meaning."[87]

Animal researchers may disagree that the capacity to alter and enhance one's environment belongs uniquely to humans, but from Gadamer's perspective, architecture zooms to the fore in this process of world transformation and expansion because it is, in the first place, a very basic participant in the quotidian experience of the environment and, in the second place, an artful reminder of the more sublime aspects of life. Regarding what he terms "the greatest and most distinguished" of the arts, Gadamer reminds us that, in its most elemental and practical role, namely shelter, architecture is an indispensable, unavoidable, and unremitting presence in human life; building is a vital activity scarcely less ubiquitous than sleeping and eating. Invariably, however, the ordinary sheltering functions of architecture are laced with very extraordinary significances.[88] According to Gadamer, "we can call a successful building a 'happy solution,' and mean by this both that it perfectly fulfils its purpose and that its construction has added something new to the spatial dimensions of town or landscape. Through this dual ordering the building presents a true increase of being: it is a work of art."[89]

Gadamer is, however, only one of countless theorists to trace the uniqueness of architecture and its special status among the arts to this complementary participation in the "functional" realm of mundane utility and in an aesthetic realm that transcends the merely practical. Moreover, this dual fraternity is the ground of any number of more subtle mediations that distinguish architecture, and particularly the large-scale sacred architecture with which this project is primarily concerned. Architecture is, on the one hand, the biggest and most imposing art. Van der Leeuw, for instance, comments on the potential of expressing "the Holy" through massive and monumental architecture; Ruskin considers masses of "mere size" the most direct expression of sublimity; and novelist Elizabeth Bowen considers that "substantiality is itself a beauty."[90] Yet, on the other hand, architecture is the most familiar and most intimate of the arts, "for man apprehends it not as a remote object but as a close accomplice in his own reality."[91] Because it is most often built to facilitate a function, to generate a profit, or to further some practical mission beyond its own existence, architecture has been called "the most mercenary of the arts."[92] Yet, by its immediacy and ubiquity architecture is the sole "fine art" that everyone experiences almost continually.

Architecture has the character of a tool — pragmatic, expedient, and serviceable — yet, architecture, most especially sacred architecture, never exhausts itself in its role as an obedient servant to utility. "Great" architecture is, by nature, an insurgent against banality and a champion of transutility and nonexpedience.[93] Herbert Spinden and W. H. Holmes, for instance, both marveled at the recrementitious dimensions and "unnecessary complexity" in Maya building;[94] the monstrous pillars of Karnak in Egypt are, from a practical point of view, "placed all too near to each other"; and, the massive effort and expense outlaid for the pyramids and obelisks of the same context have been judged "an infinite waste of material."[95] Sir Herbert Read applauds sacred architecture's rebellion against the mundane, exemplified in the "superhumanity" of the Gothic, which aims at "the liberation of human faculties from the oppression of our personal, limited vision"; and

Gio Ponti waxes that "architecture lasts because it is art and surpasses its use."[96] Similarly, George Kubler's definition of "monumentality" in art and architecture depends not on bigness but on precisely this transutilitarian "uselessness." He says, "the main point is that [monumental] works of art are not tools. . . . In short, a work of art is as useless as a tool is useful."[97] Ironically, according to Kubler, uselessness connotes a superiority over mere usefulness because it presents world-stretching possibilities: "useful inventions alter mankind only indirectly by altering his environment; aesthetic inventions enlarge human awareness directly with new ways of experiencing the universe, rather than with new objective interpretations."[98]

Accordingly, then, "big and fancy buildings" like those in the plazas of Tula Grande and "Toltec" Chichén Itzá, being simultaneously tools and works of art, become not simply collaborators in the perpetuation of conventionalized routines but, moreover, arenas for the presentation of new possibilities. Yet, as an instrument for cultural innovation, monumental architecture is stuck in an ambiguous position. It has the privilege of immediacy and ineludibility, but the range of themes with which it can deal is seriously curtailed by the practical difficulties involved in major construction projects. Substantive messages communicated by architecture are significantly and qualitatively different from those enumerated by the minor and literary arts. Where pottery is easily transportable, brittlely evanescent, and exceedingly receptive to change — all the characteristics that make ceramics the preeminent indicator of chronology and migration — a major architectural construction never moves, always outlives its builders, and demands a commitment that cannot afford the levity of cultural fashion. Where sculpture and painting hold open to individualistic expression, large-scale building is patently without spontaneity and radically nonindividualistic, requiring tedious forethought and extraordinary expenditures of collaborative effort.[99]

Public, monumental architecture like that of Tula Grande and "Toltec Chichén" thus presents both special strengths and liabilities as a datum for the historian of religions. On the positive side, because large-scale architecture requires a degree of commitment and social cooperation not characteristic of the minor arts, it generally excludes that which is fickle, capricious, or eccentric in a people's spirituality, expressing instead deep, pan-generational (if highly conventionalized) insights and anxieties. In Mesoamerica, for instance, the architectural tradition demonstrates a measure of continuity that far exceeds that of pottery, the minor arts, or even mythology. Like a strong deep watercourse, its headwaters at the Olmec sites of the first millennium B.C.E., the characteristic arrangement of pyramidal volumes grouped around courts and plazas persists across Mesoamerican time and space until the Spanish Conquest.[100] There are meanders, forks, and tributaries to be sure, but wild innovation and unprecedented aberrations among the major projects in the history of pre-Columbian sacred architecture are very few. In that spirit, Carlos Margain argues, somewhat atypically, that art, and most especially architecture, is, even more than written texts, a direct access to that which is most important and ostensibly "religious" in the Mesoamerican experience. He writes,

> man creates art to project tangibly the spiritual aspects of his experience that are precious to him. With his artistic creations man creates for himself a significative and valuable world quite beyond the necessities for survival. Art . . . is the manifestation of values and aspirations which are difficult to express any other way. . . . The architecture produced in the course of many centuries presents eloquently and impressively the elements related to the

> aesthetic factor. There is both sincerity of expression and perfect identification between the philosophy of life and the formal expression of it.[101]

Balancing this important but none-too-tangible potential for passing directly through architecture to the most essential elements of a historical culture are a number of very serious limitations for architecture as data for the historian of religions. The most standard and well-publicized shortcoming, the perpetual complaint of Marxist new archaeologists, is that large-scale architecture expresses nothing other than the pretentious and self-glorifying image of an elite minority and, accordingly, reveals almost nothing of the character and aspirations of the more popular strata of society. Gallenkamp's assessment of the limitedness of "official" Maya art and architecture, for instance, is aimed particularly at sumptuous plazas like that of Chichén Itzá:

> [It is] intended primarily for the glory of the gods and the aggrandizement of the elite classes. Only rarely does it abandon its obsession with deities, rituals, mythology, or exalted rulers and priests to offer glimpses into the lives of ordinary people. Conspicuously absent are images of the common man, the peasant farmer, the laborers who worked tirelessly to erect and maintain the cities.[102]

A second major limitation of architecture as data relates to the interminable struggle in Mesoamerican studies to synthesize the literary evidence, particularly Spanish chronicles, with the material evidence revealed by archaeologists.[103] In the Yucatán area, Chichén Itzá included, the problem is exacerbated because the most thoroughgoing written source on indigenous Maya ritual, Bishop Landa's *Relación de las Cosas de Yucatán* (about 1566), describes ceremonies that are, for the most part, divorced from any really permanent architectural contexts. Tozzer summarizes the disappointing, and often overlooked, incongruity between the textual and architectural evidences: "in several places Landa speaks of altars and in these cases they seem to have been temporary affairs, erected at the time of the rite. This is still another indication that few if any of the rituals, witnessed and described by Landa took place in any of the stone buildings known to archaeology."[104]

A third severe limitation to the heuristic power of public architecture stems from the presence of cultures which, though well-endowed and thoroughly capable, simply decline to express their "deep anxieties and high aspirations" in monumental architecture. This problem is especially poignant for the study of Chichén Itzá by virtue of the belated recognition of a powerful merchant-warrior society that dominated the Gulf Coast and Yucatán Peninsula in the Terminal Classic and Postclassic periods and which apparently was, in large part, responsible for Chichén Itzá's florescence as a powerful capital city. The historical controversies surrounding these commercial geniuses — the Putun Maya — are discussed at other points in this book, but the persistent characterization, by now widely accepted, is that the Putun were "pragmatic," "materialistic" if not "secularistic," and highly mobile; they were, so the tentative consensus says, thoroughly preoccupied with trade and expansion and largely uninterested in exerting themselves to erect the elaborate ceremonial architecture generally presumed of Mesoamerican "empires."[105] This notable disparity between their modest architectural output and the vastness of the Putun's supposed accomplishments in other realms, if historically uncertain, does, nonetheless, serve as a sure methodological warning against any facile equation of excellence in monumental architecture with cultural or religious sublimity.

A fourth and probably the greatest obstacle to architecture as data for something like resolving the problematic connection between Tula and Chichén Itzá involves a shortcoming on the part of researchers rather than buildings. Our interpretive descriptions of remote historical architectural events and their participants are limited and distorting more by consequence of the narrowness of our understandings of sacred architecture than by anything inherent in the nature of architecture. Looking ahead to the next sections, because we are so much a part of the interpretive conclusions at which we arrive, we can best improve our scholarly determinations by widening the range of questions that we bring to those dialogical interpretive situations — that is, by enriching and improving ourselves as hermeneuts. In the end, we and our limited understandings of architecture are the most serious obstacles to architecture as data for the study of religion and for the resolution of problems like that of the sister-city resemblance. We need, in other words, to make ourselves stronger, wiser, and more interesting partners in conversation with architecture and with ritual-architectural events. And, as subsequent sections will argue, nothing will enhance our ritual-architectural interpretive skills more efficiently than comparison — cross-cultural, interdisciplinary, wide-searching comparison.

To summarize, large-scale public architecture is, precisely as the materialist archaeologists have charged, undemocratic, elitist, and narrowly orthodox; and, as the case of the Putun Maya well demonstrates, splendid building is hardly a perfect barometer of cultural strength and achievement. The monumental architectures of Tula and Chichén Itzá are, admittedly, spokesmen for the ideals of the hierarchy and the conventions of pre-Columbian society. The superabundance and longevity of architecture, however, ensure that the meanings of buildings far outrun the original prescribed messages of the religio-civic authorities. As Kubler's conception of "monumentality" implies, the messages of monumental architecture are never stodgy or stagnant. "Great architecture" — and a major portion of the twin cities' oeuvre is "great" in this sense — never simply expresses that which everybody already knew. By definition, "great architecture," like "great music," does not content itself with the mere reiteration of conventionalized wisdoms; it drives forward and presents new possibilities — startling, transforming, disorienting, and reorienting those who experience it.[106] With that in mind, the final step in this explication of the concept of a ritual-architectural event now turns to the mechanism by which sacred architecture works in this world-expanding role.

The Mechanism of Architecture: Tradition and Instigation

> On the contrary, it is exactly that blend of *the traditional* and *the inventive* which makes the work of art both understandable and interesting.
>
> *Terence Grieder, 1982*[107]

> Every work of art is the child of its time; often it is the mother of our emotions.
>
> *Wassily Kandinsky, 1947*[108]

Having appraised the mixed merits of architecture as a special sort of data for historians of religions, a final set of refinements to the concept of a ritual-architectural event entails an exploration of what might be termed *the mechanism of architecture,* that is, the twofold pattern of conventionality and innovation (or allurement and transformation) that typically characterizes the human experience of sacred architecture. Two qualifications are essential to understanding that pattern, both of which will prove crucial in my alternative assessment of the similitude between Tula and Chichén Itzá. First, the ebullience with which sacred architecture has been commended for its superabundance and inexhaustible possibility could foster an image of religious monuments that continually bubble and errupt, spraying out meanings harum-scarum to whoever is within eyeshot; thus, in order to moderate that volcano-like image of randomly dispensed architectural meanings, the following discussion accentuates the decisive role that history and tradition play in disciplining the superabundance of sacred architecture. And second, despite Gadamer's rejoinders about the seriousness of play, my appeal to that metaphor could, nonetheless, connote that the experience of art and architecture is typically a kind of carefree romp, that is, essentially a voluntary, self-motivated sort of process — another misconception in need of redress. Accordingly, this section emphasizes (much more than Gadamer himself does) that participation in ritual-architectural events is *not,* generally speaking, a matter of free choice or even self-conscious decision; more often, sacred architecture, particularly in ancient Mesoamerica, works a seduction of sorts that can compel even the most reluctant spectators into participatory and transformative involvement.

The pattern of ritual-architectural events, together with these two conjoined themes — the decisive role of tradition and the coercive instigation of architectural events — finds an unlikely analogue in the story of a young traveler who, after several months of exhilarating and good-fortuned touring, returns home to the disconcerting discovery of his beloved mother in the arms of a repulsive stranger. Deeply attached to his mother and pleased for her newfound happiness, he, nonetheless, finds her mysterious partner abhorrent in every way. His mother's new lover is ugly, rude in the extreme, and he smells bad, leaving the returning son wholly bewildered as to why his mother would have so enthusiastically invited this stranger into their life and home. Ignoring the situation, however, unpleasant though it may be, is not an option. The faithful son is compelled, even coerced, to enter into, in Gadamerian language, a kind of hermeneutical projection and revision, a maneuvering to make sense of the strange circumstance and to adapt. Albeit a less than obvious a parallel, the following discussion should demonstrate that the human experience of sacred architecture and the characteristic twofold pattern of ritual-architectural events is, in fact, more like this perplexing homecoming than, say, a stroll through a museum of art.[109]

Gadamer's contention that architecture is singularly adept at transforming and enlarging one's "world" depends upon what he terms (somewhat misleadingly) the "concept of decoration." He explains that

> architecture gives shape to space. Space is what surrounds everything that exists in space. That is why architecture embraces all the other forms of representation: all works of plastic art, all ornament. Moreover, to the representational arts of poetry, music, acting and dancing it gives their place. By embracing all the arts, it everywhere asserts its own perspective. That perspective is: decoration.[110]

Gadamer's so-termed concept of decoration, in other words, points to the architectural creation of appropriate and efficacious contexts — the architectural choreography of the sort of felicitous spatial arrangements that afford people meaningful and productive experiences of other art forms, for instance, painting, sculpture, or drama. But the perspective of decoration makes architecture more than a stage. In elaborating the nature of architectural decoration, Gadamer rejects the usual Kantian distinction between "a proper work of art" and "mere decoration" and presents in its stead something more like Paul Wheatley's notion of the "centripetal" and "centrifugal" functions of ceremonial centers and traditional cities.[111] According to Gadamer, the nature of decoration in architecture consists in performing a twofold mediation, "namely to draw the attention of the viewer, to satisfy his taste [a centripetal sort of function], and then to redirect it away from itself to the greater whole of the context of life which it accompanies [a centrifugal sort of function]."[112]

With respect to the epigrammatic pilgrim and pyramid, this twofold mediation implies that the pilgrim first experiences the allurement of the pyramid and is drawn, even sucked, into its proximity; and then, following what Gadamer terms a significant "transformation of his being," the pilgrim is redirected away. In the most extreme hypothetical scenario, the pilgrim, originally repulsed by the notion of ritual killing, is yanked from his complacent domestic home into the resplendently grizzly event of pre-Columbian human sacrifice. Once engaged with the pyramid, the pilgrim is "played" hard, in a sense, issued an irrefusable offer to see the world in a new light, and so experiences a radical revision of his projections of the world, perhaps even coming to endorse the urgent agendum of massive human sacrifice.

Albeit an ultraistic circumstance, the transformative mechanism that operates in this hypothetical event of human sacrifice on the pyramid epitomizes the pattern and mechanism that operates in all effective ritual-architectural events. In each case, the potency of the ritual-architectural event depends upon the interplay of a conservative, reassuring component of order — that is, in Gadamer's terms, a "continuity of tradition" — and a disconcerting component of variation, or, as befits an occasion of hermeneutical reflection, a component of "strangeness" or "otherness." In other words, the generalized pattern of ritual-architectural events is twofold: first, there must be a requisite element of familiarity that allures and instigates the human involvement (for instance, the traveler's mother) and, second, there must be an element of strangeness, or the evocative presentation of unfamiliar alternatives (for instance, her repulsive lover).

Architectural theorist Christian Norberg-Schultz addresses this twofold structure of ritual-architectural events in his exposition of the productive tension between order and variation in architecture.[113] Norberg-Schultz, like E. H. Gombrich and a host of other psychologists of art, sides with Heidegger against "objectifying reflection" by insisting that the perception of one's environment is neither objective nor passive.[114] Following Wittgenstein, Norberg-Schultz contends that "to perceive is to interpret" and that the "active character of perception" relies on socially derived "schema," or typical, stereotyped reactions to a situation, that is, habits of perception.[115] The importance of so-called schema is so great, according to Norberg-Schultz, that "we may almost put a sign of equality between schema and perception. . . . We cling to schemata and are afraid of the insecurity which would result if the world should lose its schema-bound stability."[116] Through schematization one attains a satisfactory, livable perception of order and, moreover, develops the perspectives that breed enthrallment toward some architectures and indifference toward others.

Norberg-Schultz invokes Leonard B. Meyer's conception of "style" in music to elucidate further this conservative component in one's perception of the built and natural environment. For Meyer, musical styles are culturally established probability systems out of which arise the conventions and expectations upon which musical theory is built;[117] and, just as every historical context generates characteristic musical styles, so each context brings forth characteristic schematizations of space.

Whether in a musical or architectural situation, there are many possibilities for the choice of our perception, some more acceptable than others, based on an acquired "system of expectations," that is, a style. Thus, according to Norberg-Schultz, the enthusiasm with which a person is drawn to specific buildings is highly subjective, and the nature of that subjectivity is culturally determined. Gadamer, of course, would deplore the subjectivist formulation of the problem, yet, even so, Norberg-Schultz is describing something generally compatible with Gadamerian "pre-understanding" or "fore-knowledge" as the basis for one's initial allurement into the worlds of some works of architecture and complete indifference to other works.

Countless theorists have acknowledged similarly that any transaction of meaning in the experience of art (architecture or written texts included) depends upon the initial fulfillment of conventionalized expectations that allow people to find something familiar, reassuring, and orienting in the work of art.[118] Notable among scholars of Mesoamerica, Herbert Spinden developed an elaborate psycho-evolutionary theory of art that required art, first, to comport with the group "psyche," that is, to reinforce the shared value system and then from there to effect "progress" and the advancement of civilization.[119] George Kubler similarly concedes this decisive role of conventionalized tastes and preunderstandings by employing Erwin Panofsky's concept of the "mental habits" of different historical contexts.[120] In Gadamer's intricate language, the initial experience must be simultaneously one of self-forgetfulness and reconciliation with self: "Precisely that in which he loses himself as spectator requires his own continuity. It is the truth of his own world, the religious and moral world in which he lives, which presents itself to him and in which he recognizes himself . . . so the absolute moment in which the spectator stands is, at once, self-forgetfulness and reconciliation with self."[121]

The importance of this conservative, familiar element that sets in motion the ritual-architectural game cannot be overemphasized for the historian of religions because, in so many historical contexts — and Tula and Chichén Itzá are quintessential examples in this regard — architectures take their characteristic forms precisely in the interest of instigating the participatory involvement of reluctant spectators. In all sacred architectures, but particularly in the public monuments like those of Tula Grande and "Toltec Chichén," the greatest energy is expended on strategies to get people involved, to convince people that the architecture is relevant to them, that the messages within it are *their* messages. Where the instigatory strategies succeed, pilgrims are lured from their statuses as disinterested spoilsports and swept into the buoyance of the game; where the instigatory strategies fail, those same pilgrims can simply pass by with causal disinterest — there are no ritual-architectural games, and no transaction of meaning.

Moving to the second half of the twofold pattern (that is, moving from what might be termed the "front half" to the "back half" of the pattern), for a ritual-architectural event to be productive and transformative, this requisite component of conservatism and familiarity must be counterpoised to an element of disorientation and deviation from predictability. Once the dialogue between pilgrim and pyramid is instigated, it must be dialogue about something — pilgrims to the pyramid must learn something they had not known before; they must experience something strange, something other. As in the case of music, the conservative or stylistic component must be complemented by a creative deviation from style. A melody that conforms perfectly to the style and is, thus, completely consonant with expectations is neither meaningful nor meaningless; it is, according to Meyer, neutral with respect to meaning: "Musical meaning arises when our expectant habit responses are delayed or blocked — when the normal course of stylistic mental events is disturbed by some form of deviation."[122]

Thus, for Meyer, making meaningful (and "great") music depends upon a kind of intentional disorientation that he calls "planned uncertainty." A very similar sort of deliberate cultivation of unpredictability informs the juxtaposition of repetition and variation that David McAllester finds in Navajo music, where "such modes of variation as interruption, alternation, return, pairing, progression, transaction, and ambiguity . . . may be seen as contrapuntal to the theme of repetition."[123] Planned uncertainty finds direct architectural analogues in Bernard Rudofsky's concept of "intended irregularity" and in Chinese *feng-shui* planning, which militates against perfect regularity and axiality by holding that any straight lines of flow — whether in watercourses, mountain ranges, valleys, or streets — are dangerous because they carry "noxious influences."[124] In the same vein, each of the "processes of imaginative modification" that Spinden finds working in Maya art and architecture — that is, simplification, elaboration, elimination, and substitution — is a necessary and productive counterpoint to perfect predictability.[125] Likewise, Norberg-Schultz aptly describes the fruitful consequences of stifled expectations and disorientation in the experience of architecture using Whiteheadean terms:

> [An architectural system] should be characterized as a system of probabilities . . . it warrants order as well as variation. . . . Order and variation belong together, as a "variation" which does not refer to an order is an arbitrary and meaningless fancy which tends to destroy the existing architectural system. An order which does not allow for variation, on the other hand, leads to known banal cliches.[126]

In other words, then, if the experience of the pyramid is to be a genuinely productive and meaningful ritual-architectural event, the expectations that the pilgrims bring will *not* be affirmed. Instead, where the transformative mechanism of architecture really works, pilgrims will be confronted by unanticipated, disturbing, or perhaps exhilarating realizations that significantly alter their conceptions of themselves, the pyramid, and the world.[127]

As the preceding range of cross-disciplinary illustrations amply testifies, the productive interaction of conventionality and innovation, of order and variation in art and architecture, has not been neglected. Nearly all scholars would agree, for instance, that Proskouriakoff's assessment that "the [pre-Columbian Maya] artist . . . had to rely in his work on the affective qualities of novelty, and to achieve a proper balance between the traditional and the new to win the appreciation of his work" is likewise applicable to virtually any historical context.[128] The more subtle implications of this productive interplay between "the traditional" and "the new" for the experience of sacred architecture (and for the concept of a ritual-architectural event) have not, however, been so unanimously appreciated. In short, the crucial point is the decisive role of history and tradition. As variation must be embedded in order, so too, ritual-architectural events are necessarily embedded in historical traditions. The absolute necessity of a conservative, stabilizing component of tradition with which the spectator finds some identity reins in the superabundance of sacred architecture. The transactions of meaning within architectural events are, in a sense, legislated by the strictures of history and tradition; not all possibilities are available to all persons in all circumstances.[129] Without a continuity of tradition, that is, without the centripetal function that characterizes the "concept of decoration," architecture's power is disenfranchised. If the pilgrims see nothing of themselves in the pyramid event, nothing that convinces them that what is going on is relevant to them, the ritual-architectural game never gets under way.

Owing to the decisive role of tradition, every ritual-architectural event has a limited constituency. Unless they find in the monument and the circumstance that requisite, stabilizing, orienting component, spectators are willing to remain precisely that; for them, the monument has no magnetism. If an architecture is perceived as thoroughly strange, without any moorings of convention, spectators can persist with respect to it as casual "spoilsports" rather than serious, committed players. An aborted project in the 1930s to reproduce the great Castillo of Chichén Itzá on the Tulane campus in New Orleans provides an extreme, if somewhat eccentric, illustration.[130] Where the original Yucatán pyramid-temple had presumably been host to an abundance of solemn and transformative ritual events — truly life-altering ceremonies — its Louisianan counterpart, wrenched from its historical context and totally disconnected from its mythological and cosmological traditions, would, in all likelihood, have been more bewildering than alluring. Even if the physical form had been exactly replicated, the essential component of familiarity and allurement that instigates ritual-architectural events would have been absent. The appeal of the great pyramid is culturally specific not intrinsic; thus, instead of engendering awe and respect as its pre-Columbian counterpart had, the duplicate Castillo could easily have been dismissed by most North Americans as a curious anomaly bearing no relation to their lives or existential concerns, which perhaps explains why the plan was never realized.[131]

The Aztecs' ritual-architectural choreography at the Templo Mayor in Tenochtitlán provides a less-affected example of the continuity of tradition, or sense of self-identification, that is required to spark a meaningful experience of architecture. The Aztec empire, typically assessed as poorly integrated, loosely knit, and perpetually on the verge of collapse,[132] struggled to bring this quality of allurement to the Templo Mayor by incorporating a remarkable abundance of building materials and offerings both from the geographical periphery of the Aztec empire and from the temporal periphery, that is, from the esteemed Toltec, Teotihuacán, and Olmec eras. Quite reasonably, this symbolic integration of the periphery into the central pyramid has been interpreted as an attempt by the Aztec elite to rectify the fragmentary political situation;[133] but, moreover, and more relevantly, this synthesizing initiative might also be understood as an attempt to fabricate the continuity of tradition that would empower and instigate the ritual-architectural events at the Templo Mayor. Presumably (to the extent that this ritual-architectural ploy worked), when the peripheral populations visited the capital city and were confronted by this eclectic monument, they were confronted by some portion of themselves — the conservative, familiar component was present — and, thus, they were drawn into serious dialogue with the alternatives, that is, the substantive content that the Templo Mayor had to speak. Abstaining and standing aloof from participation in the Aztec agenda was no longer an option.

In the end, the experience of Mesoamerican pilgrims as they approached the pyramids of Tenochtitlán, Tula, or Chichén Itzá was like that of the traveling youth who returns home to his mother and her ugly lover. Upon his homecoming, the son would sooner ignore entirely the repugnant stranger and the disturbing disorientation that comes with finding that things are not as he had presumed, but his connectedness to his mother, as to one's tradition, is unconditional and tight. Like it or not, the returning son (and the pilgrim who finds both something strange and some self-identification in the ritual-architectural proceedings of a pre-Columbian city) is cast into a kind of hermeneutical reflection that will spawn a new order of things, an alternative orientation, a transformed sense of himself, of his mother, and of his home-world. Moreover, this twofold mechanism of allurement and transformation, besides denoting a generalized pattern for ritual-architectural events in all sorts of historical contexts, will emerge with especial piquancy for the sister-city problem as I argue (in Chapter 4) that the highly eclectic architecture of "Toltec" Chichén Itzá, even more than the Templo Mayor or any other city in Mesoamerican history, was a strenuous and ingenious effort to establish, by whatever means possible, a continuity of tradition that would bring its very heterogeneous audience into play with its monuments. In sum, the transformative mechanism of ritual-architectural events depends upon the consideration of the challenging and novel possibilities that superabundant architecture offers, but that process can commence only where the unfamiliar variations are juxtaposed with a component of familiarity, tradition, or allurement.

A Framework of Ritual-Architectural Priorities

> The endless variety of phenomena which the history, psychology, and sociology of religion provides us must be organized. Typological categories are designed to do that.
>
> *Joachim Wach, 1955*[134]

> A particular problem of organizational theory is that of avoiding "reification" of the organization, the notion that it has, so [to] speak, organic life and a will, while at the same time keeping in mind that an organization is something more than the mere sum of its constituent parts.
>
> *Staale Sinding-Larsen, 1984*[135]

The latter half of this methodological prelude to my reassessment of the Tula–Chichén Itzá problem casts the concept of a ritual-architecture event into the realm of comparison. Having outlined in some detail an alternative conception of the experience and mechanism of sacred architecture — a conception that ultimately derives from an alternative, more relational than positivistic resolution of the objective/subjective problem — the remainder of this chapter goes back to work on the other ineludible problem in Mesoamerican studies, namely, the play of the slash between universal and particular. Having expressed my discontent with the arrangement and comparison of Mesoamerican architecture according to commonalities in building form, structural technique, era of construction, geographical location, or the ethnicity of the builders, and then having insisted that the interpretation of architecture must, of necessity, be constituted in terms of dynamic ritual events rather than static constructional forms, I return to the estimable problems of significantly organizing and comparing various architectures. Alternatively, then, in the interest of more hermeneutically and "religiously significant" approaches both to the comparison of architectures in general and to the specific problem of the similitude between Tula and Chichén Itzá, I will propose *a framework of ritual-architectural priorities*.

Styled after intrepid, jungle-slashing expeditionaires like Stephens, Teobert Maler, and Frans Blom rather than their more meticulously descriptive Mayanist heirs like Maudslay and Holmes, this comparative section is more suggestive and exploratory than definitive and precise. It both acts on the complaint that the most serious limitation to architecture as data for historians of religions is our own limited appreciation of the nature and mechanism of architecture and then embraces the proposed solution that wide-searching, cross-cultural comparison provides the most apt redress. Even a cursory comparative survey of relevant cross-cultural materials quickly demonstrates that, while ritual-architectural events in virtually all historical contexts may conform to a characteristic twofold pattern of conventionality and innovation, there is most certainly a stupendous diversity in terms of the strategies of allurement, the informational content, and the modes of presentation that characterize the endless spectrum of particular ritual-architectural circumstances. Yet, on the other hand, cross-cultural foraging likewise demonstrates that specific architectural events are never absolutely unique; there are always significant parallels. In short, every ritual-architectural circumstance — including those of Tula and Chichén Itzá — can be illumined by critical comparison.

To that end, the concluding half of this methodological rehearsal harkens (with some trepidation) to the notion of typology as the most dexterous mediator between specific cases and general patterns as the most constructive means of resolving the ineludible particular/universal problem.[136] Accordingly, the typology of ritual-architectural events — or, more properly, *the framework of types of ritual-architectural priorities* — that this section outlines consists of eleven general categories that describe the range of alternative priorities that give individual ritual-architectural events their distinctive character. The interpretive framework, in other words, presents eleven alternative ways of describing various relationships between monuments and ritual, eleven prospective paths for hermeneutical reflection upon individual ritual-architectural events, or, to invoke the dialogical metaphor for the experience and interpretation of architecture, eleven general topics of conversation with which to engage the specific ritual-architectural events of Tula and Chichén Itzá.

I. Architecture as Orientation:
The Instigation of Ritual-Architectural Events
- A. Homology: Architecture that presents a miniaturized replica of the universe
- B. Convention: Architecture that conforms to abstract principles or standardized rules
- C. Astronomy: Architecture that is aligned to celestial bodies or phenomena

II. Architecture as Commemoration:
The Content of Ritual-Architectural Events
- A. Divinity: Architecture that commemorates or houses a deity or divine presence
- B. Sacred History: Architecture that commemorates an important mythical or miraculous episode
- C. Politics: Architecture that commemorates or legitimates a political or social system
- D. The Dead: Architecture that commemorates revered ancestors

III. Architecture as Ritual Context:
The Presentation of Ritual-Architectural Events
- A. Theatre: Architecture that provides a stage or backdrop for ritual performance
- B. Contemplation: Architecture that serves as an object of meditation or devotion
- C. Propitiation: Architecture that intends to please, appease, or petition the sacred
- D. Sanctuary: Architecture that provides a refuge of perfection or purity

Fig. 1. A Framework of Types of Ritual-Architectural Priorities

The logic and structure of this somewhat cumbersome typological framework (outlined in Fig. 1) should become apparent once the respective entries are explicated and illustrated with specific examples. I must from the outset, however, emphasize in the strongest terms that, while the general categories do audaciously claim a measure of relevance to the ritual-architectural events of any and all historical contexts, this framework is *not* a universalistic system of classification. Rather, it is *a heuristic tool* designed to evoke productive, hermeneutical conversations between interpreters and specific ritual-architectural circumstances; it is a methodological stimulant rather than a system of cataloging. The eleven so-called types, then, must be appreciated, *not* as Linnean classificatory pigeonholes but, instead, as *alternative ritual-architectural priorities,* or as competing parameters of design. Together the eleven categories denote a heuristic vocabulary designed to keep the interpretive dialogue with the monuments of Tula and Chichén Itzá (or elsewhere) at the level of ritual-architectural events rather than descending to that of reflections on once-and-for-all meanings of buildings.

Accordingly, two interrelated clarifications regarding the status and utility of the categories in the framework are particularly important. The first involves the nonmutual exclusivity or overlapping of the respective entries. Because every ritual-architectural occasion arises from a complex play (or competition) between highly variegated priorities — including, for instance, sociopolitical interests, economic forces, technological capabilities, environmental conditions, artistic conventions, not to mention specifically "religious" aspirations — any single ceremonial occasion will participate simultaneously, to one degree or another, in many of the eleven ritual-architectural priorities: an elaborate religio-political ritual like a ninth-century New Fire Ceremony at Chichén Itzá, for instance, would span nearly the entire spectrum of typological priorities. Nevertheless, even in the most multifaceted ritual-architectural event, two or three types of priorities invariably assert themselves as the dominant priorities, while others become significant primarily by their *un*importance or, sometimes, deliberate avoidance. We could argue, for instance, that in that New Fire Ceremony, the synchronization of calendrical time and architectural space (homology, priority I-A) was exceedingly important, while the ritual-architectural commemoration of the dead (II-D) was relatively unimportant.[137] Typology-aided hermeneutical reflection on any particular circumstance, then, is never exhausted by ramming the case into some dovecoat-like designation. Instead, the interpretive procedure entails determining relative emphases by reflecting on how and to what extent each of the types of ritual-architectural priorities is pertinent. It is, in fact, the combination and recombination, the alliance, dance, and divorce of types (and, in fact, countless subtypes) that is, in the end, the most provocative.

The second major clarification concerns the nonparallel, wildly heterogeneous character of the priorities themselves. The first of three sets of priority types — (I) *architecture as orientation: the instigation of ritual-architectural events* — concentrates on three alternative strategies for alluring participants into the ceremonial occasion, three ways of recruiting willing and/or unwilling players into the architectural game (that is, the conservative, or "front" half in the general twofold pattern of ritual-architectural events). The second set — (II) *architecture as commemoration: the content of ritual-architectural events* — considers four major sorts of information that are communicated once the players have shed their "spoilsport" statuses, in a sense, exploring the range of conversation topics that sacred architectural events address (that is, the innovative, or "back" half in the general twofold pattern of ritual-architectural events). And the third set, the most motley collection — (III) *architecture as ritual context: the presentation of ritual-architectural events* — considers four other priorities that play against one another to determine the tone and choreographic staging of particular ritual-architectural performances, that is, the ambience in which the entire ritual-architectural event transpires. Arranged in this tripartite fashion — (I) *mode of instigation,* (II) *nature of the content,* and (III) *means of presentation* — it may appear as though the proposed method of interpreting architectural events were tantamount to ordering a Mexican *comida corrida* (literally a row or file of food) wherein one selects a soup, entrée, and dessert from each of three respective menu lists. In practice, however, nothing so slick is either possible or advisable. Rather, the typological framework of priorities and its highly variegated quality stem from the attempt to respect rather than reduce the bizarrely disparate sorts of forces that determine the unique design and character of any specific ceremonial-architectural circumstance. Ritual-architectural choreography is, for instance, forced somehow to reconcile rarified theological doctrines with prosaic concerns about the strength and availability of construction materials; fidelity to the canons of tradition must compete against the constraints of climatic conditions; and propagandistic sociopolitical interests are pitched against the choreographic potentialities of color, light, and sound. The framework, by working to organize ritual-architectural events according to the priorities that win out in these complex frays of rival forces, is, of necessity, as peculiarly variegated as those heterogeneous forces themselves.

Ambiguities notwithstanding, interpretation according to these types of ritual-architectural priorities makes heuristic strides in several directions, three of which can particularly enhance our reconsideration of the problem of sister-city similitude. First, as a method for *synchronic comparison,* the typological approach, on the one hand, exposes the perils of presuming that formally similar architectures are likewise parallel at the level of religious meaning and intention and, on the other hand, brings together specific cases that ostensibly have little in common. For instance, despite "Toltec" Chichén Itzá's obvious formal similarity to Tula, upon reconsideration with respect to ritual-architectural priorities, Xochicalco (another Central Mexican site, which does not "look" a great deal like Chichén Itzá) will, surprisingly enough, actually emerge as a more "religiously significant" match to the Yucatán capital.[138] Second, as an aid to *diachronic comparison,* the framework provides a means of charting not only remodelings or changes in the appearance of buildings over time but, more importantly (or more "religiously significantly"), a means of assessing the ways in which those formal changes reflect shifts and rearrangements of ritual-architectural priorities. We could, for instance, employ these categories to write something like a "ritual-architectural reception history" of Chichén's Castillo, which would respect the pyramid's superabundance by chronicling the succession of revalorizations and radical transformations in the ceremonial usage and perceptions of this long-enduring monument.[139] And third, the alternative categories of the typological framework provide us with a fresh means for significantly organizing, assessing, and orienting ourselves with respect to timeworn academic debates regarding specific Mesoamerican architectural phenomena, most poignantly, the old party lines about Tula and Chichén Itzá.[140]

Because it provides a strategy for holding the discussion up to the level of ritual-architectural priorities and events (instead of, for instance, the age or appearance of buildings), I am optimistic that the benefits of such a typological comparative approach outweigh the liabilities. The remainder of this chapter proceeds, therefore, by presenting, for each of the eleven categories, a brief exposition of the generic type of ritual-architectural priority with respect to specific cross-cultural examples, followed by an assessment of the relevance and problematics of the type with respect to Mesoamerica generally, and then, where possible, some intimation as to the specific applicability of that respective priority to the Tula–Chichén Itzá problem. Convinced, in other words, of the futility of standing mute before the remains of Tula and Chichén Itzá, waiting for "the facts to speak," I am adopting a more aggressive, more interrogational, and more comparative hermeneutic. Instead of silently objectively observing, I aspire to approach the ancient ruins as a provocative and worthy conversation partner, overbrimming with questions and supposals, types, patterns, and cross-cultural analogies of all sorts — but, as befits a good conversationalist, prepared to listen and not unduly certain of anything.[141]

Architecture as Orientation: The Instigation of Ritual-Architectural Events

> Ancient Mexico is a world of order, in which everything and everybody has a place. . . . Everything has its perfect place, there is a formula for everything. . . . One discovers things that appear to be disorder according to our judgment, but afterwards one discovers a much more fantastic order . . . the orderly structure can be seen in every-thing.
>
> *Paul Kirchhoff*[142]

> It all depends on the place a man occupies on the earth. The fortune and misfortune of men can be explained if we remember what connection they have to the land.
>
> *Canek: Maya Hero*[143]

The complex and exciting interrelatedness of orientation, architecture, and ritual has spawned a substantial body of interpretive literature. Some historians of religions have argued that there is, in fact, an important sense in which orientation *equals* religion. Charles Long says, "For my purposes, religion will mean orientation — orientation in the ultimate sense, that is, how one comes to terms with the ultimate significance of one's place in the world";[144] and Jonathan Smith affords a similar preeminence to orientation in space when he writes that "the question of the character of the place on which one stands is the fundamental symbolic and social question. Once an individual or culture has expressed its vision of its place, a whole language of symbols and social structure will follow."[145] Architectural theorists like Norberg-Schultz stress particularly the crucial role of building in this quest after meaningful orientation and the necessity of "supplementing the physical milieu with a symbolic milieu — that is, an environment of meaningful forms. . . . Human life can not take place anywhere; it presupposes a space which is really a cosmos, a system of meaningful spaces."[146] And countless historians of architecture — while noting exceptions like that of Michelangelo and the Mannerists, who validate an atmosphere of doubt, conflict, and tragedy — have, by and large, tended to equate "excellence" in architecture with building programs that exude harmony, regularity, balance, and symmetry, that is, architectures that seem to foster a sense of stability and orientation.[147]

The ritual-architectural events of archaic contexts, where presumably the "religious experience is a total one,"[148] have been particularly vaunted for their comprehensive orderliness, and in Mesoamerica specifically, studies of orientation continue to enjoy a flourishing vogue. David Carrasco's inquiry into Mesoamerican urbanism, for instance, is based on the premise that the quest for orientation was a causative agent of first importance — "the story of ancient Mexico is the story of places and symbols of places."[149] Kubler accentuates the extraordinary "monumentality" of Mesoamerican architecture, by which he means not bigness but dexterousness in overriding disorientation and "inscribing some meaning upon the inhuman and hostile wastes of nature."[150] And Octavio Paz has creatively interpreted the Spanish Conquest as an occasion of catastrophic "disorientation" and the post-Conquest embrace of Catholicism by Meso-american Indians as a desperate attempt to retrieve "a sense of their place on earth."[151] In a similar vein, Mesoamericanists are pursuing the possibility of a tradition of Mesoamerican "geomancy," that is, the systematic divination of one's place in relation to the play of cosmic and natural forces, which parallels the practices of Chinese *feng-shui*.[152] Other scholars have pounced on the radically inflexible grid layout of Teotihuacán as incontestable witness to an "orientation motive" in Mesoamerican architecture.[153] And now, in the wake of an explosion in archaeoastronomical research, even the Maya centers that had long been disparaged as "haphazard . . . without careful orientation"[154] are being lauded for their purposive, sophisticated, and precise orientational systems.[155] Equally important has been the increasingly sensitive and "eventful" acknowledgment by Mesoamericanists, preeminently Johanna Broda, that the orientational schemes and correspondences between calendrics, myth, society, and ancient Mexican building forms were transformed from static abstractions into relevant and lived realities in the ritual usages of those buildings.[156]

This burgeoning appreciation of the subtle connections between orientation, architecture, and ritual is promising indeed. Yet, in a more critical vein, we must insist that almost no ritual-architectural event, in ancient Mesoamerica or elsewhere, is exhausted in the simple presentation of generalized world order. More typically, an architecture's initial presentation of unity, harmony, and order functions as the strategy that *allures* ritual participants from their "spoil-sport" status into the religio-architectural game. The demonstrations of fidelity to cosmic or conventionalized aesthetic standards that help to orient spectators with respect to a particular architectural situation typically function *not* as the sum of the ritual-architectural event but as that requisite conservative component that invites (or, in cases, demands) serious consideration of the more substantive content that the situation has to offer. Architectural presentations of symmetry, harmony, and orderliness typically constitute introductions or strategies of allurement; they are the starters or catalysts that open the way to participation in the "back half" of a ritual-architectural event, the more explicit articulation of the very specific privileges and responsibilities that are concomitant with one's particular "place" in that world order.

We can, then, make a soft correlation between orientation and the so-called front half or the conservative, instigatory component in the characteristic twofold pattern of ritual-architectural events. Fine-tuning and pursuing that correlation, the following section explicates three types of orientation, or three alternative catalytic instigatory strategies, or, perhaps most accurately (because it admits to the inevitable interpenetrability of the three types), three sorts of orientational priorities that can be termed for expedience sake: homology (priority I-A), convention (priority I-B), and astronomy (priority I-C). Each of these typological alternatives is a variation on the presentation of a prerequisite foundation that orients and impresses the spectator and, thus, that certifies the ensuing architectural event as the harbinger of real, viable alternatives and not simply an occasion for promoting idiosyncratic or expendable frivolities. As we will see, any attempt to differentiate absolutely between these typological alternatives is ultimately in vain — the three variations overlap constantly — but the hermeneutical exercise does, nonetheless, pave the way for reassessing the Tula–Chichén Itzá problem.

Homology: Literal Images of the Universe

> The creation of the world is the exemplar for all constructions. Every new town, every new house that is built imitates afresh, and in a sense repeats, the creation of the world. . . . Just as the town is always an *imago mundi*, the house is always a microcosm.
>
> *Mircea Eliade, 1949*[157]

Among historians of religions, Mircea Eliade's model of sacred space has proven the dominant and most enduring paradigm for interpreting and comparing various religious architectures.[158] Eliade's renowned formulations regarding the symbolism of the center, humanly constructed imitations of celestial archetypes, and religious buildings that are conceived as microcosmic replicas of the cosmos at large have, in fact, been invoked (sometimes with disturbing ease) as a kind of interpretive panacea for making sense of the religious architecture of virtually every historical context. Nevertheless, the tendency for overgeneralization notwithstanding, with respect to the present typological framework, Eliade's rightfully preeminent theory of sacred space, and particularly his conception of temples as *imago mundis* or miniaturized reproductions of the universe, provides an apt point of departure for exposition of this first category of homologized architecture (priority I-A). (For all its heuristic potency, I should likewise note at the outset, however, that the other ten categories in this framework might be considered alternatives to the interpretive hegemony that Eliade's model has enjoyed.)

The principle of homology, whether drawn from Eliade's work or elsewhere, depends upon a "cosmological conviction,"[159] that is, a confidence in an encompassing world order and a commitment to attune all dimensions of life to that order.[160] By virtue of this sort of confidence in a deep structural unity that embraces all of the seemingly disparate realms of existence, the respective parts of a building can be variously correlated with (or homologized with, or identified with) particular celestial bodies, biological species, colors, body parts, systems of polity, or mythico-historical events. Via ritual-architectural homology, a built structure can, in an important sense, become a kind of microcosmic summation of the entire structure of the macrocosm. The South American Barasana, for instance, imagine that their longhouse or *maloca,* a humble structure some 80 feet long and 40 feet wide with a tent-like gable-roof, quite literally *is* the universe itself: the roof *is* the sky, the house posts *are* mountains that support the sky, and the floor space *is* the earth.[161]

The global illustration of this sort of cosmogrammatic architecture by Eliade and like-minded collaborators has been so thoroughgoing that even a brush with the hulking literature on homologized architecture reveals a spectacular range of exemplary cases. Borobudur, Ankor Thom, Banaras, Mount Meru, Tibetan monasteries, and the three-tiered *yaka calai* room where the *yakam* or South Indian fire sacrifice is performed have all been interpreted as architectural cosmograms.[162] Likewise demonstrating the manifestation of the homology priority at every conceivable scale, in Japan, houses, temples, and even the whole of the country have been elucidated as literal images of the universe.[163] Moreover, to cite but a few salient examples, the humble though symbolically munificent house of the Atoni of Indonesian Timor,[164] Sudanese Dogon longhouses and the vernacular architecture of West Africa,[165] Shoshone and Ute sun dance lodges,[166] the Salteaux Indian villages of Manitoba,[167] and the *ceque* system of the Incas (which embraces the entire region surrounding the pre-Columbian capital city of Cuzco)[168] have similarly been interpreted (though not always with critical rigor) as human constructions designed to mirror the cosmic order. In short, despite a tendency for scholars to appeal too often to this familiar interpretive solution, the range of viable cross-cultural instantiations of the homology priority (I-A) is, nonetheless, immense.

Mesoamerica is hardly an exception in this regard. To the contrary, owing especially to the recent preoccupation with Middle American "cosmovisions,"[169] there is a superfluity of evidence that the homology priority (I-A) has been exceedingly important in virtually all eras, areas, and scales of Mesoamerican art and building, from textiles to monumental architecture.[170] Regarding, for instance, the symbolism of the center, omnipresent conventionalized crosses in Mesoamerican art, and particularly the famous Maya "tree of life" or "world tree," have been appreciated as (what Eliade would term) "*axis mundis*" for decades.[171] In the thirties Robert Redfield wrote, "the shape of the cross, as a symbol of power and protection, pervades the thinking of the people [of Yucatán] so that they see crosses everywhere. . . . Indeed a home is a lacework of crosses."[172] More recently, Gary Gossen, in his discussion of present-day Tzotzil Maya cosmology, concluded that "most basic to Chamula [that is, Tzotzil Maya] spatial organization is the belief that they live at the center . . . 'the navel of the earth.'"[173] In the same vein, Evon Vogt comments on the "sacralization of natural features" and the networks of cross shrines that serve as "doorways" or channels of communication to some deity in the cosmological system of the present-day Zinacantecos of highland Chiapas.[174] Also with respect to the symbolism of the center, Clemency Coggins first documented the notion of a central cosmic axis that governed the orientational and iconographic program among the Classic Maya[175] and then, in her more recent work, with respect to the Preclassic Izapa of Chiapas, where preoccupations with the zenith and center seem to have been the root cause for the original creation of the 260-day ritual calendar at that site.[176]

Furthermore, the vigorous exercise of the homology priority (I-A) is evident in a wide array of Mesoamerican strategies for uniting space and time or, more specifically, architecture and calendars. Perhaps the most unmistakable space-time coupling comes in the Classic Maya's erection of dated monolithic pillars or stelae, which explicitly commemorate in stone the passage of certain epoches. But Mesoamericans interknit the built environment with each natural, sacred, and historical time in a series of more subtle ways. The Pyramid of the Niches at El Tajín, for instance, with its 365 recessed compartments, each presumably correlated to a day in the solar calendar, is a stunning instance of homologized pre-Columbian architecture.[177] And the meticulous "right timing" of important ceremonies constitutes another vivid (and alluring) exercise of the homology priority (I-A). Diego Durán's *Book of the Gods and Rites* and *The Ancient Calendar,* for instance, document thoroughly how the Aztecs (like other Mesoamerican groups) unified architectural space, calendrical time, and the processes of nature via a carefully scheduled annual cycle of ritual-architectural events that celebrated each phase in the agricultural cycle of planting and harvesting.[178] And also, along with the rhythms of nature, the "historical" record of past events, together with the timing of coronations, battles, and truces, was likewise ingeniously manipulated by the ancient Mesoamericans to yield a set of ritual-architectural events that announced the homologous unity of space, time, religio-political authority, and ethnic or national destiny.[179]

Besides encompassing natural, sacred, sociopolitical, and historical dimensions, the homology priority (I-A) manifests itself on every scale in Mesoamerica, from regional layouts to

The Pyramid of the Niches at El Tajín, Vera Cruz. With 365 recessed compartments, each presumably correlated to a day of the solar year, this structure provides clear instantiation of the homologized unification of space and time. Though seldom quite this obvious, the deliberate correlation of architectural forms with cyclical calendars is a recurrent theme across Mesoamerica. (Photo by the author.)

incense burners. Joyce Marcus, for instance, hypothesizes a huge, regionally homologized scheme (not unlike the Inca *ceque* system) in which Tikal was the grand ceremonial center or "capital" that had dynastic links with four regional capitals that were geometrically positioned to correspond with *bacabs*, the divine brothers of Maya mythology who bore the sky in the north, east, south, and west.[180] At the scale of individual sites, there is not only very substantial evidence of cosmogrammatic, four-quartered pre-Columbian cities,[181] but likewise, ample documentation that Maya villages, both before and after the arrival of Europeans, were routinely arranged with four principal entrances, each guarded, at least figuratively, by a *balam* or jaguar.[182] Individual pre-Columbian buildings that mirror the cosmos are likewise abundant. David Freidel, for instance, interprets single buildings at Cerros, Uaxactún, and Tikal as "miniature models of the world";[183] the Templo Mayor is an arresting example of cosmogrammatic construction;[184] and the great Castillo pyramid of Chichén Itzá (as discussed in the next chapter) is perhaps the most self-consciously and elaborately homologized monument in Mesoamerica.[185] Moreover, even the constituent elements of buildings — for example, the tripartite columns at Chichén Itzá that are correlated with heaven, earth, and underworld[186] — are, in many cases, homologized constructions. And finally, at an even smaller scale, the ritual accoutrements in Mesoamerican architecture — for instance, offertory boxes[187] and *incensario* lids[188] — are often homologized cosmograms.

In short, the documentation of the principle of homology (priority I-A) in Mesoamerican building has been thoroughgoing and indisputable. Therefore it becomes less important to announce once more the plenipotence of homologization in ancient Mexico — a task already embraced with rigor and success — than to guard against being lulled to believe that Eliade's famous categories of *axis mundi* and *imago mundi* explain more than they actually do. We must insist, in other words Mesoamerican builders' undoubted dedication to cosmological unification notwithstanding — that the homology priority (I-A) had major competitors in the design of this region's ritual-architectural events. Thus, the ensuing enumeration of the other ten categories in this framework aspires to counteract any interpretive lethargy or overconfidence that Eliade's potent model may afford by charting the less-well-documented priorities of sacred-architectural design that operate alongside the ubiquitous cosmological conviction.

As but one among many ritual-architectural priorities, the articulation of cosmic harmoniousness, nonetheless, retains a distinctive prestige; it is less an alternative beside the other priorities than a substratum underneath. Homologized architectures like the Barasana longhouse, the *ceque* system, or Chichén's Castillo do articulate a generalized unity and cosmic wholeness, but, invariably, that is the *beginning* of the architectural event's significance rather than its end. The display of fidelity to cosmic dictates in Mesoamerican and other architecture, generally speaking, serves as that essential conservative component that initiates or sets in motion the ritual-architectural event. By demonstrating its integral involvement in the cosmological fabric, a cosmogrammatic monument (like the Castillo) is perceived as (or, at least, the architects hoped that it is perceived as) reliable, legitimate, and worthy of a hearing. Again and again in ancient Mesoamerica the presentation of an aura of cosmological correspondence serves as the strategy that allures participants and spectators away from their status as spoilsports and into the ritual game, opening them to the kind of suspension of disbelief or receptive vulnerability that is requisite to the transaction of meaning and the transformative experience of architecture. Moreover, appreciating that homologization typically serves in this evocative, instigatory role (and not as the full initiative of any ritual-architectural program) is, as we will see, crucial for our reassessment of the similitude between Tula and Chichén Itzá.

Convention: Codified Prescriptions of Order

> The thickness of the frame in front is to be equal to one twelfth the height of the door, and is to diminish towards the top a fourteenth part of its width.
>
> *Vitruvius*[189]

Otto von Simson argues that the symbolism of the Gothic cathedral has been misunderstood.[190] In his attempt to remedy that error he articulates (albeit inadvertently) what amounts to a distinction between architecture as a literal image of the universe (homology, priority I-A) and architectural adherence to codified prescriptions of order that were discovered by earlier generations and canonized by tradition (convention, priority I-B). Von Simson repeatedly describes the Gothic cathedral, which attains its classic expression at Chartres, as a "symbol of heaven," a "model of the universe," and an "image of the Celestial City" — all metaphors for homologized architecture (priority I-A).[191] Yet, he argues with great rigor that the nature of the relations between symbolic cathedral and cosmos is *not*, as H. Sedlmayr has contended, "representation," and even less is it "optical illusion."[192] Rather, von Simson contends that the cathedral and cosmos are linked by "the tie of analogy"; there is, in other words, a particular set of abstract laws of measure and proportion, which are deemed "universal" by the Western Christian tradition, that are considered to inform both the whole cosmos and the humanly constructed cathedral. According to von Simson, the Gothic architectural form is not conceived so much as a reflection of the cosmos (as in the case of the homology priority, I-A) as it is the reflection of a commitment to replicate the traditionally validated standards of "Augustinian aesthetics of number and proportion."[193]

The distinction between homologized architecture (priority I-A) and building programs that take conformity to the standards of convention as their first priority (priority I-B), and even more the *experience* of these two modes of ritual-architectural orientation, is by no means absolute. More likely, this pair represents two points on a single continuum. Both these types of priorities involve the instigation of ritual-architectural events by alluring presentations of reliability, stability, and incontestably legitimate order. In both cases, the ideals of world harmony, correspondence between various realms of existence, and parallelism between microcosm and macrocosm are paramount. Still, the contrariety is significant. Instead of demonstrating conformity to and participation in the cosmic order by actually constructing a microcosmic duplicate of the universe (as, for instance, in the case of the Barasana longhouse, exemplum of the homology priority, I-A), participants in this second sort of orientational strategy demonstrate harmony and orientational legitimacy by conforming to abstract principles that carry the prestige of history and tradition. In the case of the convention priority (I-B), meticulous systemizations of space and proportion that may have arisen originally from the direct observation of nature, geometry, music, or human anatomy (or, in other instances, from some divine revelation) actually owe their lasting prestige to processes of historical amplification and canonization. Conventionalized orientation (I-B), thus, typically has less to do with literally replicating the cosmos than with the imitation of historical precedents and respect for tradition or, in some situations, with rote conformity to standardized codes and rules of ritual-architectural design.[194]

There is, in any event, considerable debate regarding the earliest Western manifestations of this sort of conventionalized sacred architecture. Many scholars, notably Rudolf Wittkower, associate the notion of architecturally reproducing the secret rhythms of the universe primarily with the Renaissance and the "Age of Humanism."[195] Von Simson, however, sees this sort of conventionalized abstraction already in Gothic architecture; Whitney Stoddard, drawing attention to a medieval tradition of "magic numbers," finds strong evidence for this sort of compliance to codified prescriptions earlier still in Romanesque architecture;[196] and Vincent Scully moves the origin of the notion back even further by connecting the advent of architectural adherence to standardized principles with the growth of philosophical speculation in Postclassic Greece.[197] Doubtless there are still earlier Western manifestations of rigorously conventionalized building (and, in fact, probably no architectural design proceeds without some sort of reference to the precedents of tradition). Nevertheless, it is in Renaissance Italy and particularly in relation to the proliferation of manuals of proportional building standards, quintessentially represented by Leon Battista Alberti's *De re Aedificatoria*

(1485), that the convention priority (I-B) finds perhaps its most lucid illustration.

Alberti, the paradigm of the Renaissance architectural tradition, made his greatest contribution not with the design of a particular building but with his famous handbook for the working architect, a virtual recipe for integrating abstract principles and the practical construction process.[198] His perspective epitomizes the Renaissance confidence in scientific Copernican cosmology and in a universe that is systematically and rationally ordered according to abstract, general rules, that is, "the first principles of Nature," immutable laws that can be discovered in the harmonic tones of music and the measurements of the human body and then replicated in perfectly proportioned architecture.[199] Thus, architecture, for Alberti, as for Vitruvius,[200] became a science of partitioning space according to the harmonic patterns of nature, a science in which the supreme priority was proportion — the correct relationship of parts to the whole — which he outlined thoroughly in his treatise.[201] The influence of Alberti's manual of design, along with those of his successors Serlio, Vignola, and Palladio,[202] was enormous, as conformity to the practical prescriptions of proportion and style outlined in these treatises (whether in a rote fashion or more selectively) overpoured both ecclesiastical architecture and Italy. For our purposes, this abundant (and continuing) legacy represents, among other things, a giant reservoir of buildings — particularly institutional buildings — whose plea for legitimacy (or "strategy of ritual-architectural allurement") is based on precisely this fidelity to historically canonized standards of architectural design (that is, convention, priority I-B).

The Renaissance conception of space as a homogeneous substance that can be endlessly dissected, arranged, and rearranged lends itself particularly to a codification of architectural principles. Any number of other traditions, however, likewise embrace the agendum of abstract systematization or, in some cases, a kind of "architectural legalism." In India, for instance, the fabulously intricate Hindu "science" of *vastu sastra* is codified in *Silpa Sastra* building manuals that detail both appropriate temple proportions and fastidious procedures for ritual construction;[203] and handbooks of axiomatic architectural stipulations are similarly replete in the Chinese practice of *feng-shui,* the most complete being the *Lo-ching chieh.*[204] Parallel if exceedingly diverse examples are likewise abundant at different points within the Abrahamic traditions: the Jewish halakic ("religious-legal") literature, for instance, addresses numerous issues related to appropriate spatial layouts;[205] the synthesis of mathematics, rhythm, and spirituality likewise figures large in the geometrical design of Islamic architecture;[206] and, speaking to the resilience of this ritual-architectural priority (I-B), faithful adherence to the prescriptive canons of proportion recorded in the *"Painter's Manual" of Dionysius of Fourna,* apparently written sometime during the Turkish occupation of Greece, continues to inform the design of Orthodox iconography and churches in both Eastern Europe and even the United States.[207]

Where the priority of homologized architecture (priority I-A) leaps from the Mesoamerican data, evidence for the convention priority (I-B), at least in the form of this sort of adherence to codified prescriptions, is considerably more elusive. Intensely geometrical and repetitive pre-Columbian facades, for instance at Mitla in Oaxaca and the Puuc sites of Central Yucatán, suggest that some kind of rarified principles of composition may have been at work,[208] and there are tentative intimations among art historians that the monumental sculpture of the area was designed according to canons of harmonious proportion.[209] John Carlson's scouring of the Mesoamerican materials for "sacred ratios" and measuring schemes that are parallel to those of Oriental geomancy is, however, largely in vain: he concludes that "the presence of these factors in Mesoamerica is, at best, speculative,"[210] although, leaving the possibility open, Carlson does anticipate that, "since the Classic Maya had a penchant for numerical complexity coupled with arithmetic exactitude, we may yet discover complex geometrical and mathematical relationships in their site plans and architecture."[211] One major advance in this regard is Aveni's and Hartung's hypothesis that the "seemingly haphazard" layouts of several Maya sites (including Chichén Itzá) may actually be arranged according to arcane and precise systems of "radians" and "multiple orthogonal axes" and of "conceptual lines" that intersect in right angles, form isosceles triangles, and converge on noteworthy points.[212] They conclude, for instance, that the four-structure Nunnery Complex at Uxmal, previously deemed a paragon of asymmetry because of its deviation from right angularity, is actually a rigorously executed forum for the expression of a whole series of abstract geometrical interbuilding relationships.[213]

With respect more specifically to the problem of the similitude between Tula and Chichén Itzá, among the most exciting (if highly uncertain) intimations of Mesoamerican codified standards of architectural design involves cryptic allusions to the *u tzibal Tulán,* or chart-maps of the Toltecs of Central Mexico. Sahagún says that, as they journeyed toward "the East" (presumably Yucatán), the Toltec priests took with them "all their paintings in which they had all the things of ancient times and of the arts and crafts."[214] The *Popol Vuh* recounts how the Lord Nacxit (the Guatemalan appellation for Quetzalcoatl) gave to the Quiché Maya princes, among other things, "the paintings of Tulan *(u tzibal Tulán),* the paintings as those were called in which they put their chronicles."[215] And in Yucatán, Bishop Landa saw and described "Itzá books," which likewise may have been connected with this famed Toltec literature.[216] At this point, it would be conjectural in the extreme to venture that these paintings (if they ever existed) contained specific prescriptions for building or that they ever made their way to Chichén Itzá.[217] Even so, there is the intriguing possibility that the organization of the "Toltec" portion of Chichén Itzá derived, at least in part, from conformity to a set of architectural standards and proportions that were originally codified in Central Mexico and then were transported in some literary form to the Yucatec context.

Be that as it may, a more certain set of manifestations of ritual-architectural conventionalization (that is, priority I-B) comes with the exceedingly widespread pre-Columbian practice of deliberately imitating the prestigious art and building styles either from other contemporaneous Mesoamerican sites or from the renowned architectures of the past.[218] This sort of architectural mimicry and borrowing (a more straightforward variation on the convention priority, I-B), in fact, appears to have been among the most pervasive (and perhaps persuasive) of indigenous strategies for enhancing the prestige and legitimacy of one's ritual-architectural program. Particularly intriguing instantiations of this mode of allurement are those circumstances in which architectural alignments that originated as empirical, functional astronomical references (that is, astronomy, priority I-C) were subsequently imitated, sometimes centuries later, in contexts where those traditionally revered systems were totally irrelevant to empirical celestial phenomena (thus, in that case, evincing instead the convention priority, I-B). An orientational pattern uniquely relevant to the skies of Copán, for instance, was duplicated at several other Maya sites where the

The Nunnery Quadrangle at Uxmal, adjacent to the Adivino pyramid. Because of the quadrangle's obvious deviations from right angularity, the layout of the Nunnery Complex was long described as haphazard and imprecise. Recently, however, Anthony Aveni and Horst Hartung have hypothesized that the seemingly irregular courtyard configuration actually conforms to an exceedingly precise system of "conceptional lines" that intersect in right angles, form isosceles triangles, and converge on noteworthy points. In that case, instead of lax orientation, the Nunnery may provide an instance of highly rarified and rigorously conventionalized architectural design. (Photo by William M. Ferguson, courtesy of the University of Texas, Austin.)

same celestial views are *not* possible.[219] Even more famously, the 17 degrees east of north orientation of Teotihuacán, probably originating in response to the movements of the Pleiades with respect to the mountains of that site, was mimicked as a nonoperative alignment by a whole family of sites, including several built hundreds of miles away in the mountainless Yucatán, nearly a millennium after the collapse of Teotihuacán.[220]

More typically, however, these Mesoamerican exercises in ritual-architectural appropriation were much less subtle. Often this mode of ritual-architectural allurement (convention, priority I-B) involved simply copying one or several distinguished building styles or esteemed sculpture techniques, or perhaps synthesizing well-known pictographic elements from several important sites into a single eclectic iconographic program, and, thereby (presumably anyway) partaking in the prestige associated with those sites. Moreover, because there is reason to believe that the notorious formal similarities between Tula and Chichén Itzá owe in large part to precisely this sort of mission in allurement via eclecticism, it is this more blunt version of the convention priority (I-B) that will, in the end, prove most important in my reassessment of the problem of the sister cities.

Astronomy: The Power of Prediction

> The universality of sky symbolism in the history of religions would seem to suggest that the sky has expressed more fully than any other symbol at least a part of the religious experience of life.
>
> *Peter C. Chemery, 1987*[221]

Students of the comparative history of religions from Charles Francois Dupuis to the "Panbabylonianists," to Max Muller, Raffael Pettazzoni, and Mircea Eliade have been unanimously impressed by the seemingly ubiquitous human fascination with the sky.[222] In Mesoamerica specifically, the acknowledgment of astronomical alignments in the architecture is virtually as old as the study of those constructions. Already in the early eighteenth century Guillermo Dupaix was convinced of pre-Columbian astronomical knowledge.[223] John Lloyd Stephens (1841) guessed that Copán was host to a congress of priest-astronomers settling discrepancies in their calendar.[224] Alfred Maudslay (1882–1902) found astro-architectural alignments especially clear at Tikal.[225] Eduard Seler (1901), a vehement "Astralist," was overpowering in his advocacy for astronomical-religious-calendrical-architectural connections.[226] Herbert Spinden (1913) argued that astronomy was of "first importance" in Maya art and architecture.[227] Thomas Joyce (1927) concluded that "[pre-Hispanic] religion was intimately connected with astronomy, and that the 'temples' were used to a great extent as observatories."[228] Robert Willson (1924), John E. Teeple (1931), and C. A. Guthe (1932) all lauded Maya astronomical prowess;[229] and Carnegie archaeologists Tozzer, Morley, and especially Karl Ruppert, with "A Special Assemblage of Maya Structures" (1940), ushered the study of astro-architectural orientation into the comparative realm.[230] And now, in the wake of much Stonehenge balderdash and an "explosion of new interest in the astronomical knowledge of ancient and contemporary non-Western cultures since the 1970s,"[231] Anthony Aveni and Horst Hartung have ensured Mesoamerica's continued prominence in the related fields of archaeoastronomy, ethnoastronomy, and astroarchaeology.[232]

The turbulent debate about Stonehenge that was so important in reviving enthusiasm about these issues typically counterpoised Stonehenge as an astronomical observatory (Lockyer, Thom, and Hawkins) against Stonehenge as a center for ritual (Atkinson and Daniel),[233] an antithesis that largely reflects argumentation about the intellectual capabilities of "primitive" peoples — that is, could they possibly have been intelligent enough to think of such things? — and a presumed incompatibility between the "scientific" and "religious" purposes of megalithic structures.[234] However, as the Mesoamerican cases well demonstrate, in ancient astronomy the quest after empirical data was virtually always subservient to the wider orientational agenda of homologized unification of space, time, society, and polity (as well as to matters of sociocultural convention).[235] The Maya's willful distortion of observed celestial cycles and freewheeling synchronization of recorded history, termed "chronological coercion" by Morley and "mass compulsion neurosis" by Tozzer, have been a continued source of consternation to scholars for decades.[236] Ancient Mesoamerican astronomy was, as Schele says in reference to Palenque, "a

William H. Holmes's section drawing of the Caracol at Chichén Itzá, with hypothetical profile, 1895. Even the earliest investigators suspected that there were significant celestial alignments in many pre-Columbian buildings. Holmes, who described this famous round tower as "the most unique and extraordinary structure in Yucatán," was among a very few writers, before or after, who declined to speculate on the usage of the Caracol as an astronomical observatory. (William H. Holmes, *Archaeological Studies Among the Ancient Cities of Mexico*.)

different type of astronomy, in which the goal was to interlock cosmic cycles and visual phenomena with the functions and definitions of Palenque rulership."[237] Therefore, rather than try to wrestle apart the "scientific" from the "religious," we must, in Broda's phrasing, "put the emphasis on the particular mental and social processes by which astronomical observations became immersed in myth and ritual, thus leaving behind the terrain of 'objective' scientific knowledge."[238]

Acutely aware, then, that the significance of astro-architectural events is virtually never confined to the disinterested, empirical observation of natural processes, celestially oriented building in Mesoamerica and elsewhere emerges as an excitingly multifaceted phenomenon that intrudes into a variety of the categories of the present typological framework. British megaliths, for instance, according to Aubrey Burl's interpretation, were astronomically referenced primarily in the interest of incorporating the sun and moon into rituals concerned with dead ancestors and fertility (that is, commemoration of the dead, priority II-D).[239] In Rome, while the suburban areas were oriented cardinally, the urban core was rotated some 36 degrees to conform to solar equinoxes and, thus, to distinguish itself as an especially sacred realm (that is, sanctuary, priority III-D).[240] Or, among North American Indians, constructions were directed toward personified celestial phenomena that were conceived as the protagonists of mythical narratives (that is, commemoration of sacred history, priority II-B).[241]

However, as the Mesoamerican data show perhaps better than any other, the special potentiality of astronomically aligned architecture (and thus its viability as a distinct category in this framework of ritual-architectural priorities) rests, most of all, on the power of prognostication and the seeming ability to predict the future that those configurations provide. Where homologized and conventionalized orientations (priorities I-A and I-B) initiate architectural events with announcements of perfect harmony, astronomically referenced architecture (priority I-C) can instigate participation by seizing upon predictable celestial phenomena to confirm the right and propitious timing of ritual events. By demonstrating a seemingly remarkable foreknowledge of sky phenomena — that is, anticipating celestial occurrences before they actually happen — astro-architectural allurement can drive beyond orientation with respect to the conventions of the past, or the homologous correspondences of the present, to give ritual participants a sense of place with respect to a presaged and, to an extent, predictable future.

Particularly in ancient Mesoamerica — where there would seem to have been a near-pathological obsession with omens, oracles, prophecy, divination, and sortilege[242] — the orchestration of ritual-architectural events that could provide some sense of prognostic foreknowledge of the ever-uncertain future had especial appeal. Innumerable structures were designed explicitly as observatories for collecting predictive astronomical data. The Caracol at Chichén Itzá is perhaps the most renowned of many such buildings,[243] but Aveni has likewise shown how, for instance at Copán and Palenque, whole cities acted as superlunary registers of celestial data.[244] Moreover, beyond their perspicuous function as astronomical instruments, Mesoamerican "observatories" also capacitated ritual-architectural events that integrated those observational data into a system of cosmic orientation. Coggins, for instance, considers that the famous Structure E-VII sub at Uaxactún, the earliest known Maya pyramid, was constructed not only to observe celestial cycles but, likewise, to symbolize the completion of those cycles and, furthermore, to serve as the backdrop for a specific predictive ritual "associated with the casting of seed in divination and with auguries of the named Katun."[245]

Paralleling the catalytic presentation of perfect harmony that issues from the exercise of homology and convention sorts of ritual-architectural priorities (that is, I-A and I-B), it is important to appreciate that the alluring celestial-architectural synchronization of sky, building, and ritual (that is, the astronomy priority, I-C) is typically the initiatory spark to a ceremonial program rather than its summation. Mesoamerican ritual planners, in other words, seized on celestial occurrences and particularly startling meteorological coincidences as irrefusable offers to acknowledge the seriousness and legitimacy of their ritual programs. This strategy of celestial opportunism, moreover, required that ritual-architectural choreographers capitalize on the unique topographical and astronomical configurations that each respective site had to offer: at Palenque, for instance, westward-looking phenomena, particularly sunsets, were favored;[246] at La Venta, in consonance with their feline obsessions, the Olmec apparently oriented their buildings toward a constellation of stars that seemed to form a cat's mouth;[247] at Teotihuacán, the melodrama of violent seasonal thunderstorms seems to have been integrated into the agricultural rites of Tlaloc and the solar year;[248] and at Chichén Itzá, the zenith sunset, the setting of the Pleiades, and the first appearance of Venus as the evening star at the beginning of the rainy season may have been the most compelling and carefully monitored celestial phenomena.[249]

Moreover, synchronization with a predictable coincidence of more than one celestial phenomenon would constitute an even more emphatic announcement that the orientations and obligations prescribed in the subsequent ritual event carried the weight of a cosmic imperative. The puzzling 17 degrees east of north alignment of Teotihuacán, for instance, has been interpreted as a possible reference to the biannual celestial coincidence of the heliacal rising of the Pleiades and the zenith passage of the sun (that is, twice a year these two celestial bodies come up on the horizon at the same place, and that place nearly corresponds to the east-west baseline of the city).[250] Recent research into a Maya hieroglyph termed the "shell-star event" reveals a scenario in which the Classic Maya seized upon a rare celestial coincidence — the simultaneous inferior conjunction of Venus and a solar zenith passage — as the day for an extravagant heir-designation ceremony that involved a ritual battle and the final celebration of the victors.[251] To cite a similar (and similarly hypothetical) pre-Columbian attempt at astro-architectural allurement, at Copán, the ingenious configuration of built forms and the strategic scheduling of an elaborate kingship rite seem to have been designed to exploit the periodic coincidence of the sun setting along a baseline demarcated by two outlying stelae and the reappearance of Venus on the horizon as viewed through a slit-like window in Temple 22.[252] The simultaneous (and contrived) observance of these two celestial phenomena, with the sun appearing to disappear into the earth and Venus reappearing in its place as the evening star (presumably an astronomic metaphor for the sowing and sprouting of maize), served as the catalytic, instigatory, or "front half" of a royal ritual-architectural event that would entice the assembled spectators into serious consideration of the specific politico-religious agenda of the lords of Copán (that is, the component of variation, new information, or the "back half" of the event). To the extent that this strategy of allurement worked, even reluctant visitors could not refuse such a spectacular celestial invitation; in a fabulous ritual stroke of astro-architectural choreography, the king of Copán was (hypothetically anyway) able to weave himself into the very cosmological fabric of the universe and thus legitimate his royal initiative.

To conclude, then, the already impressive fund of evidence for many and diverse sorts of celestial alignments in the architectures of ancient Mesoamerica continues to grow, perhaps faster than ever. While there is certainly much stronger evidence of the astronomy priority at Chichén Itzá than at Tula, in either case, these celestial referencings are important to our hermeneutical reassessment of the two sites, particularly in their role as alternative or, more often, complementary or supplemental strategies of allurement that helped to coax people into involvement with the subsequent ritual-architectural proceedings. Instead of demonstrating the literal homologization of disparate realms of existence (as priority I-A does), or conformity to historically entrenched prescriptions of convention (as priority I-B does), allurement via astronomy (priority I-C) relies on seductive synchronicity with the dramas of the sky. Moreover, to borrow a distinction from G. van der Leeuw between "passive harmony" and "active control," the predictive component of this sort of astro-architectural seduction may allow ritual participants to push beyond the sense of acquiescence to the world that comes with being "caught up and ruled by a rhythm" in favor of a greater confidence that comes with "subjugating the world by mastering a rhythm," a more audacious orientational option than either the homology or convention strategies can offer.[253] Yet, in actual historical practice, these three orientational modes — homology, convention, and astronomy — are typically complimentary rather than antagonistic. These three types of priorities, as we will see in relation to Tula and Chichén Itzá, invariably blend and dissolve into one another as they collaborate in their crucial role as the instigatory component or "front half" of a ritual-architectural event that set ceremonial occasions in motion. Keeping the three neatly separated is neither advisable nor even possible.

The next sections of this chapter, with equal futility, work to systematize the "back half" of the characteristic pattern of ritual-architectural events, that is, the range of substantive issues with which those events might deal, by considering a series of four similarly overlapping types of commemorative or informational priorities.

Architecture as Commemoration: The Content of Ritual-Architectural Events

> A traditional monument, as the origin of the word indicates, is an object which is supposed to remind us of something important. That is to say, it exists to put people in mind of some obligation they have incurred: a great public figure, a great public event, a great public declaration which the group pledged itself to honor.
>
> *J. B. Jackson, 1980*[254]

Ritual-architectural events, by definition, are never content to leave things and thoughts as they are. Each architectural event transforms and enlarges human consciousness (or "being") by the presentation of new information, the retrieval of forgotten meanings, and participation in otherwise inaccessible realms. Ritual-architectural events play havoc with the neat succession of time and the boundedness of physical space by commemorating circumstances from the past, present, and future. In the experience of sacred architecture, mythical realms are visited, dead ancestors revived, deities engaged in conversation, and impending epochs lived and tested. These space-time flights are not simply occasions for generalized adoration and wonderment; they, moreover, lay before the ritual participants and spectators very specific information about ancestral history, programs for social action, systems of politico-economy, apportionments of power, and allocations of responsibility.

Thus, where the previous section aimed at various strategies for drawing people into these magically transformative events, this section explores the manifold diversity of the substantive content — the messages — of ritual-architectural events, that is, the component of variation and information, or the "back half" of the twofold pattern. This section asks, what, once the pilgrim and the pyramid were engaged in dialogue, was the topic of conversation? The range of potential topics that might be annunciated and assayed in such hermeneutical, human-monument conversations is then organized by discussing successively four types of ritual-architectural commemorative priorities, four sorts of thematic issues that ritual-architectural events are inclined to explore: commemoration (A) of divinity, (B) of sacred history, (C) of politics, and (D) of the dead.

Often, the messages of architecture are presented with blunt, didactic clarity. In Mesoamerica, for instance, the explicitly informative potential of architecture blossoms in a fabulous tradition of murals,[255] in the iconographic inscriptions that grace so many pre-Columbian buildings, and in the abundant Maya stelae, which, cloaked with epigraphy, refer in a very direct, text-like fashion to specific deities, cosmologies, historical events, and places.[256] Yet, even beyond these unmistakably communicative cases, the prevailing tendency in Mesoamerica architecture to eschew interior sheltering spaces for "monumental," exterior-sculptured volumes[257] witnesses to a building tradition that is intentionally, unabashedly, and aggressively loaded with commemorative information.[258] Mesoamerica's rich tradition of "sculptural-architecture" is epitomized, for instance, by the expressive facade of alternating feathered serpent and Tlaloc masks on the Pyramid of Quetzalcoatl at Teotihuacán or, in the Maya area, by the molded form of Pyramid E-VII sub at Uaxactun, "the most sculptural of all Maya structures."[259] And the same tendency is likewise manifest in a multitude of Mesoamerican constructions that, scaled impossibly beyond human use, are more commemorative sculptures than "functional" buildings; for instance, the "simulated" or "fake temples" of the Río Bec area, with their deity mask facades, insurmountable stairways, and false doorways, are notable in this regard,[260] as is the Great Ball Court at Chichén Itzá, whose gigantic scale suggests that it was built to host divine rather than human contests.[261]

Moreover, in addition to this sort of expression of rarified mythological and ostensibly "religious" themes, architecture (in Mesoamerica or elsewhere) can be even more categorically informational when constructed in the service of a specific ideology or political initiative.[262] In Postclassic Quintana Roo, for instance, the "ruthless modifications of the Classic buildings and deliberate covering of any decorative facades" appear to have been the unsubtle architectural expression of "a shift in ideological orientation" or the announcement of "a new world view" by adherents of a radical Maya "revitalization movement."[263] Examples of this sort of carefully contrived self-presentation via architecture are abundant in all eras of Mesoamerican history.[264]

Furthermore, particularly in ancient Mesoamerica, where the demonstration of a distinguished cultural pedigree is an ever-present concern (and a preeminent strategy of religio-political legitimation), architectural programs were very often (including, for instance, at Tula and especially at Chichén Itzá) dedicated to the commemoration, replication, or imitation of previous building styles. The motivations for historical allusions and retrogressive references in pre-Columbian architecture were, however, by no means constant.[265] Sometimes there is a concerted effort to revive intact the entire form-meaning, ritual-architectural package. For instance, Postclassic Maya "revitalization movements" seem to have gone to great pains to refurbish and re-erect monuments of previous eras as a means of retrieving those older, "more pure" religious practices.[266] In other cases, architectural styles were repeated more casually. Spinden, for instance, long ago coined the term *archaistic* to address those reversions to earlier Maya artistic forms and techniques that seem to have been motivated more by pragmatic ease than anything else.[267] Other cases show architectural imitation as a willful political manipulation, and others still as a coercion from the outside. Innumerable Mesoamerican cities, for instance, deliberately patterned themselves after Teotihuacán as a self-initiated strategy of legitimation, but, in some cities, most notably Kaminaljuyú in Guatemala, the replication of Teotihuacán seems to have been forcibly imposed from the outside.[268] Finally, in other cases, ironically enough, retrogressive imitation proceeded with an almost complete ignorance of the original intention of those architectural forms, as, for instance, in those cases in the Río Bec area where the considerable reverence for antique hieroglyphic stelae was so uninformed that the old monuments were re-erected upside down and in ridiculous combinations.[269]

In short, architecture, including Mesoamerican architecture, can act as the well-laden bearer of a fabulously diverse range of information and, accordingly, the human experience of architecture is often a world-altering occasion of transformation and learning. In many cases, the messages are self-consciously crafted, direct, and unambiguous. Yet, nearly always, owing to the autonomy and superabundance of architecture, beneath (and alongside) the deliberate and explicit ritual-architectural messages are countless additional, more subtle, and often unintended meanings — meanings and issues that do *not* fit neatly into our categories of divinity (II-A), sacred history (II-B), politics (II-C), and the dead (II-D). Tinkering in the next four subsections with these alternative types of ritual-architectural priorities will, nonetheless, provide us with a set of provocative questions (and a heuristic vocabulary) with which to assess the substantive content of the respective architectural events at Tula and Chichén Itzá and, moreover, to lift the synchronic comparison of those sites beyond the analysis of shared architectural forms to a more religiously significant and "eventful" level.

Divinity: Bodies, Abodes, and Abstractions

> The [Hindu] temple is at once the notion of God, the dwelling of God, the body of God, and the holy act of man utilizing tangible substance to realize all these abstract ideas.
>
> *Nelson I. Wu, 1963*[270]

Vincent Scully maintains that "all Greek sacred architecture explores the character of a god or group of gods."[271] He considers that the chronological development of Greek sacred architecture is constituted of a series of expressions and explorations of the relationships between nature, humanity, and divinity, that is, relationships between the natural environment, the built environment, and divinity — between "the earth, the temple, and the gods." Accordingly (at least in Scully's highly "eventful" reading of the evidence), the Hellenic tradition presents not one but a whole evolutionarily linked set of variations on the ritual-architectural commemoration of divinity (priority II-A).[272] For our purposes, three aspects of that complex evolution are particularly intriguing: architecture that *is* the deity, architecture that *houses* the deity, and architecture that *expresses* in some abstract fashion the character of a deity.[273]

Scully's history of the evolution of Greek architecture begins with the great Cretan palaces, the paradigm of which is at Knossos. In this earliest phase (the phase that will find the most direct counterpart in ancient Mesoamerican building), the palace architecture embodies and celebrates the central tenent of Minoan religion — namely, an unquestioning reverence for a great nurturing goddess of the earth. Consequently, the siting, orientation, and design of the Minoan palace all conspire to erect a form that is literally, even magically, identified with the actual body of the earth goddess; the architecture *is* the goddess.[274] Later, according to Scully, the Mycenaean culture witnessed a transition toward a more "human centered view of experience" and, thus, a movement away from the conception of a magical unity between the goddess and the architecture that had dominated Minoan planning.[275] By Homeric times nature was perceived more as hostile than venerable, and the conception of divinity was characterized by a plurality of gods who, aside from immortality and fantastic power, were not too different from humans.[276] These Homeric, pre-Classic conceptions are reflected in the archaic Greek temple which, rather than itself "being" a deity, *houses* the image of a deity. The Pre-classic temple represents the presence of a god rather than the literal image of the god, although, by its sculptural qualities, the temple makes visible the otherwise hidden character of the god.[277]

The development from body, to abode, to abstraction culminated in the Classic Greek temple, in Scully's assessment, "the ultimate refinement of the Stone and Bronze Age tradition." The Classic Greek temple, like much of Mesoamerican architecture, eschews the function of "elaborated shelter"[278] and the facilitation of activities in favor of the commemorative presentations of a conception of divinity.[279] The Classic temples of Hera, Demeter, Artemis, and Aphrodite are not designed spatially, nor as backdrops to ritual performance; rather, according to Scully, they are "articulated sculptural bodies" and, as such, personifications and commemorations of a deity's attributes.[280] Employing a purely abstract, transhuman scale (a strategy very similar to that employed by the pre-Columbian Maya in the Río Bec-Chenes area of Yucatán), the Classic Greek temple at once denies human entry and delivers a theological statement about the nature of divinity and of humanity's and nature's relatedness to divinity.

Each stage in the continuum from literal to abstract architectural commemoration of divinity (priority II-A), so clearly exemplified in the evolution of Greek sacred architecture, finds many counterparts in other world architectures as well.[281] Hindu temples, which actually participate in the full spectrum of options,[282] provide among the most vivid instantiation of the actual equation of architecture with the body of a god. Soundara Rajan, for instance, describes how the erection of temples in India was considered "the emergence of the corporeal body and vesture of God, replete with flesh, bones, tendons, and nerves, and breathing with life. The temple itself was looked upon as God transcreated."[283] The conception of architecture as the "house of God," or a place for the incarnation of a divine presence in a structure, is even more widespread.[284] And, though somewhat more difficult to document, there are innumerable cross-cultural parallels at the more rarified end of the spectrum of variations on the ritual-architectural commemoration of deity. Consider, for instance, those Catholic churches that celebrate the Christian conception of divinity, the Trinity. The Austrian Baroque Church of the Trinity at Stadl-Paura (1714–25), among countless such examples, is triangular in plan; each of three identical facades is framed by three towers, and each of three portals and three altars is dedicated to a member of the Trinity.[285]

The search for parallel instances of the ritual-architectural commemoration of divinity in Mesoamerica is seriously complicated (as it should be) by the profound difficulties in ascertaining indigenous American conceptions of the sacred, a problem that has been debated at some length. Beginning with sixteenth-century friar-chroniclers, there was for centuries a largely uncritical presumption that native American peoples (supposedly like "pagan idolaters" in general) operated with a "pantheon" of anthropomorphic "gods" not unlike that of the

Classic Greeks. More recently, however, Mesoamericanists have rejected these heavy-handed ethnocentric supposals with such rancor that at least some scholars would favor a wholesale excision of the terms "pantheon," "deity," and "god" from the academic literature on Mesoamerica in favor of more culturally specific, indigenous terminologies (for instance, the Mixtec term *nuhu,* the Zapotec term *pè,* or the Maya terms *ku* and *ik*), which connote something more like "vital forces" (that is, wind, breath, or spirit) that make all things move, rather than "gods" with distinct "spheres of control."[286] The understandable antipathy toward Hellenic analogies notwithstanding, Scully's work on Greek sacred architecture, and even more on the Cretan context, does present a provocative set of parallels to Mesoamerica's architectural commemoration of divinity (priority II-A) and a line of hermeneutical inquiry that has not been well explored.

There are, most certainly, countless fairly straightforward examples of pre-Columbian architectures that "house" deities (or spiritual entities of some sort). Perhaps the most prominent such instance is the specially designed sanctuary of the Aztecs, where the "gods" of conquered peoples were installed as slaves in cells, niches, or, in some cases, wooden cages.[287] The far more vigorous and sublime exercises in theomorphizing Mesoamerican architecture are, however, the serpent-mouth temples of the Río Bec, Chenes, and Puuc regions of Central Yucatán, close neighbors to Chichén Itzá in both space and time.[288] Paul Gendrop describes the lurid elegance of the wall-sized masks and zoomorphic portals of these Central Yucatán temples as "mythical surrealism."[289] And Eric Thompson (among the strongest scholarly voices for a Maya "pantheon of gods") explained these zoomorphic facades by a kind of triple identification between Itzamná (that is, "Iguana House, the greatest god of the Yucatec Maya"), the Maya conception of the universe as a house, and the temple construction itself.[290] Thompson says, "Supporting evidence for this belief [in a triple identification] is supplied by those Maya temples with facades sculptured to represent the faces of celestial monsters, the doorway, often set with teeth, representing the creature's mouth."[291] Now, however, in the wake of considerable skepticism about the viability of a Maya "pantheon of deities," and particularly about the pivotal role that Thompson ascribes to Itzamná,[292] the dragon-throated temples of Central Yucatán seem more likely to have been representations of the earth itself, or perhaps of an earth monster, than representations of a supereminent creator god (as Thompson had argued). These famous zoomorphic temples may, in other words, actually represent a variation on the ritual-architectural commemoration of divinity (priority II-A) quite like the equation of the Cretan palace with the body of the Minoan earth goddess. Elizabeth Benson's hypothetical (re)creation of the serpent-mouth temple event as an experience of death and cosmogonic rebirth, for instance, depends upon just such a symbolic identity of architecture, god, and earth: "One goes into the cosmologically defined world when one enters the doorway; coming out through the god mouth one re-enacts the ancient emergence from the primordial cave, from the earth."[293]

There are many similar mask facades and zoomorphic doorways throughout the Maya zone, notably, Temples 11 and 22 at Copán, and, even more relevantly, several buildings in South Chichén Itzá have this sort of configuration.[294] Moreover, the seemingly literal equation of architectural forms with conceptions of divinity, most particularly with earth monsters, likewise animates a host of other very different-looking Mesoamerican constructions. The great zoomorphic sculpted boulders that so

Structure II at Chicanná, in the Río Bec-Chenes area of south central Yucatán. This structure, with its wall-sized mask facade — complete with eyes, nose, and teeth over the doorway-mouth — provides one of the best extant examples of the "serpent mouth" or "dragon-throated" temples. Such temples, which may have represented an earth monster deity or perhaps the earth itself, are common throughout the Maya zone, including at Chichén Itzá. The ritual entry of these zoomorphic temples may have facilitated a symbolic death (or a return to the womb) and then, upon exiting, a sensation of rebirth. (Photo by Lawrence G. Desmond.)

impressed John Lloyd Stephens at Copán and Quirigua, for instance, were interpreted by Spinden as Maya gods and culture heroes in the form of grotesque reptile, bird, and mammal composites[295] and, more recently, by Michael Coe, as representations of "crouching earth monsters or sky deities with humans seated among their snake like coils."[296] This general motif of a carved humanoid figure seated inside the body of an earth monster is likewise elaborated in a variety of different, cave-like architectural forms spread all across Mesoamerica that appear to "house" or "clothe" either another deity or a deceased ruler or ancestor.[297] In addition to particularly noteworthy examples of these sheltering zoomorphs at La Venta, Tres Zapotes, and Izapa, a different sort of variation on the cave-niche monster-mouth theme appears at the late Postclassic Central Mexican site of Malinalco, where the motif was synthesized with the pyramid form and with symbols of the Aztec eagle and jaguar military orders.[298] Moreover, likewise speaking to the breadth and pervasiveness of this pre-Columbian tendency to build architectonic images of deities (priority II-A), Broda considers that, "on the mythological level the Templo Mayor, the sacred mountain, was the earth itself, the earth as a voracious monster devouring human victims and blood";[299] and finally, on a somewhat larger scale, the entire layout of the Olmec ceremonial center of La Venta seems to have depicted a gigantic jaguar mask and thus identified itself with the feline deity.[300]

With respect to the ritual-architectural commemoration of divinity (priority II-A), when confronted by the strange and marvelous monuments of Mesoamerica, the single most common question of Spanish friars, antiquarian explorers, and modern tourists alike has been the methodologically naive inquiry: "To which god is this temple dedicated?" Even more scholarly Mesoamericanists, while increasingly sensitive to the inadequacy of simply extrapolating stereotypical notions of paganism into the Native American context, remain, nonetheless, very tentative in their understandings of the indigenous conception(s) of divinity. Whether because of some actual peculiarity in indigenous pre-Columbian American notions of the supernatural or because of the limitedness and unevenness of the academic literature (which is more likely), at this point anyway, the literal end of the continuum of the architectural commemoration of divinity (as epitomized by Minoan earth goddess temples) stands out in far higher relief in Mesoamerica than does the sort of rarified architectural abstraction that informs the Classic Greek temple. In all probability, however, if we allow the more thorough documentation regarding plausible strategies for the ritual-architectural commemoration of divinity from, for instance, Greece and India to inform the hermeneutical questions that we bring to the Mesoamerican materials, evidence for these higher levels of abstraction will be forthcoming.[301]

Sacred History: Myths and Miracles

> For mythical thinking the relation between what a thing "is" and the place in which it is situated is never purely external and accidental; the place is itself part of the thing's being, and the place confers very specific inner ties on the thing.
>
> *Ernst Cassirer, 1955*[302]

In traditional contexts, the cosmogony, the fabulous adventures of ancestors and culture heroes, and the miraculous (and not-so-miraculous) happenings of the post-primordial time meld together into an unbroken course of "sacred history."[303] In these contexts, the memory of one's sacred history is the foremost of spiritual responsibilities and, as John Ruskin pontificated a century and a half ago, architecture has a rare appetency in this mnemonic charge. He writes, "there are but two strong conquerors of the forgetfulness of men — Poetry and Architecture."[304] Architecture is, therefore, and should be, according to Ruskin, an embodiment of history, characterized by a "richness of record."[305]

This prolific collusion between remembering and architecture has sired an unwieldy and diverse collection of ritual-architectural events whose priority lies in the commemoration and preservation of myths, miracles, and religious history (that is, sacred history, priority II-B). The most obvious expressions of this priority involve that vast set of architecturally created "stages" whereupon the narrative dramas of myth and history are re-enacted, and thus re-experienced anew by the progeny of those traditions. In Mesoamerica, for instance, the most pellucid examples are those low square stages or tribunes (typically termed "dance platforms"), which are common both throughout Central Mexico and at "Toltec Chichén," where Bishop Landa surmised that they had served as the stages on which "farces were represented, and comedies for the pleasure of the public."[306]

Beyond this ancillary stage-setting function, however, the ritual-architectural commemoration of sacred history — and, particularly, of cosmogonies or creation myths — likewise manifests itself in a number of much more direct and ingenious constructional embodiments of religious narrative. The architectural arrangement of the moat-encircled Angkor Vat in Cambodia, for instance, is a very literal manifestation of a Southeast Asian cosmogony: the balustrades of the causeway over the moat to the city gates are formed by rows of giant stone figures who are holding an enormous nine-headed serpent, which, in Buddhist myth, was used to churn the world into existence. By virtue of the architectonic presence of these mythical protagonists, according to R. Heine-Geldern, "the whole city became a representation of the churning of the primeval milk ocean by gods and demons, when they used the serpent king Vasuke as a rope and Mount Meru as a churning stick."[307] Likewise, Egyptian pyramids have been interpreted as architectural embodiments of cosmogony that depict the first mound to rise out of the watery abyss, a symbol of the body of Atun, the omnipotent Egyptian god;[308] and the Incas, using a different strategy of architectural commemoration of cosmogony, fashioned a cult temple out of live rock at Pacaritombo ("Origin Lodge") to designate the emergence cave from which hero-founder Manco Capac (or Manqo Qhapaq) and his followers began their journey to found the future imperial capital of Cuzco.[309] Moreover, the same incentive to concretize the cosmogony is well represented in ancient Mesoamerica. The alternating serpent and Tlaloc masks on the sculpted facade on the Temple of Quetzalcoatl at Teotihuacán, for instance, have been interpreted as deity heads projecting up out of a primordial sea, thus depicting "the initial creation of the universe from a watery void through a series of dual oppositions."[310] The famed Aztec Calendar Stone, at least since Spinden, has typically been assessed as "a record of the cosmogonic myth of the Aztecs and the creations and destructions of the world."[311] And the cave paintings of Olmec creation scenes at Juxtlahuaca and Oxtitlán in Guerrero, some of the oldest known in the New World, likewise evince the Mesoamerican propensity for enlivening and sustaining their cosmogonic traditions through architecture.[312]

Besides the specific commemoration of creation myths, ritual-architectural events in many cases memorialize significant episodes in the careers of deities and culture heroes. To choose from a plethora of diverse cross-cultural examples: Fred Clothey terms a whole set of South Asian ceremonials and attendant architectural contexts "theofests" (festivals designed explicitly to commemorate some aspect of a god's activity) to distinguish them from "ecofests," which commemorate some important agricultural or astronomical event;[313] the rock-cut temples of Ajanta, India, sheathe magnificent frescoes, which both preserve episodes in the mystic and historical life of the Buddha and grant a foretaste of the paradise where the Buddhas and bodhisattvas reign;[314] Navajo sandpainting rituals rejuvenate the *Diyin Dine 'e* and other deities by depicting and recounting their most significant mythical adventures;[315] and the explicit intention of the bulk of Bernini's theatrical sculpture-architecture was to freeze the climactic moment of some mythic or saintly story that it might be available for re-experience and participation.[316] In Mesoamerica, the interpretation of Aztec human sacrifice on the Templo Mayor as the reenactment of the myth of Huitzilopochtli's birth and ferocious slaying of his 400 brothers and his sister, Coyolxauhqui, on the mythical

Temple of Quetzalcoatl at Teotihuacán. With respect to the ritual-architectural commemoration of cosmogonic myth, Michael Coe suggests that the alternating feather-collared serpents and goggle-eyed Tlaloc masks on this facade may depict "the initial creation of the universe from a watery void through a series of dual oppositions." Davíd Carrasco suggests that this feathered serpent imagery at Teotihuacán is connected to a paradigmatic myth of urbanism that would inform a whole series of subsequent ceremonial centers or "other Tollans," including Tula and Chichén Itzá. (Photo by William M. Ferguson, courtesy of the University of Texas, Austin.)

mountain of Coatepec is likewise lurid testimony to the very literal ritual-architectural dramatization of sacred history.[317] And, despite the lack of specific corroborating myths for Tula and Chichén Itzá, we can imagine parallel ritual-architectural strategies there as well.

An even larger set of architectural events is less concerned to facilitate an actual reenactment of episodes from sacred history, than simply to mark the site or to display the material evidence of a mythical or miraculous event, thus, almost invariably, creating a destination for pilgrims. One of the most famous pilgrimage temples of Indochina, the Shwe Dagon Pagoda at Rangoon, for example, was built specifically to enshrine eight hairs supposedly given by Gautama himself to two Buddhist merchants.[318] The Dome of the Rock, the mosque at Jerusalem, preserves a footprint of Muhammad and marks the spot where Moslems believe he ascended with the archangel Gabriel on his eagle-winged horse to visit the seven heavens of Islam.[319] And the reliquary geography of late medieval Europe, particularly in the wake of the post-Tridentine enthusiasm for miracles and relics, was overladen with monuments that commemorate the heroes of Catholic sacred history and, thus, denote destinations for Christian pilgrims.[320] Tepoztlán, the Central Mexican pueblo renowned across indigenous Mesoamerica as the site of the legendary discovery of the intoxicating drink *pulque,* and, thus, invariably linked to debauchery and orgy, was the goal of a more rambunctious style of commemorative pilgrimage but one that, nonetheless, preserved a mythological event by connecting it inextricably to a particular parcel of sacred geography.[321] And here again, despite lacking the specific corroborating mythic or ritual evidence, the renown of Chichén's Sacred Cenote as both a pre-Hispanic and colonial-era pilgrimage site suggests that this could be a very live line of hermeneutical inquiry.[322]

Perhaps the most intriguing issue in relation to Mesoamerican manifestations of this particular ritual-architectural priority (and the issue that has the most direct ramifications for my hermeneutical reassessment of the similitude between Tula and Chichén Itzá) involves major regional and ethnic discrepancies in the pre-Columbian enthusiasm for the artistic commemoration of narrative sacred history (priority II-B). John Graham, for instance, recognizes a great enthusiasm for recounting narratives in Izapan art (a style named for the huge Pre-classic site of Izapa on the Pacific coastal plain near the Chiapas-Guatemalan border) but a patent disinterest in storytelling among the arts of the Olmec and Maya.[323] In his assessment, Olmec art is preoccupied with monumentality and with full, swelling masses, while Maya art favors elite portraiture. In contrast to these nonnarrative approaches, for Izapan art of the Chiapas region, "the chief purpose seems to have been the depiction of narrative scenes often depending to a great extent on movement and dramatic action for their clarity and effect."[324]

This notion that particularly the Classic Maya were more reticent to depict narrative themes in their monumental art than other Mesoamerican peoples (including, for instance, Tula Toltecs) has been widely accepted. To be sure, there has long been a willingness to acknowledge that Classic Maya architecture and sculpture is replete with storiological mythic and historic allusions. Spinden, for instance, appropriately recognized the unnaturally combined Maya zoomorphic sculptures (for instance, quetzal birds and jaguars) as "characters that appear in the mythology and religion";[325] carved lintels such as those at Yaxchilán are generally considered to chronicle actual scenes of conquest and ceremonial life with associated dates and glyphs;[326] and the hieroglyphic stelae of the Maya have proven to be highly specific historical documents. Likewise, to be sure, there is a very full exposition of the sacred stories of the Classic Maya in other, less strictly architectural genres of art, for instance, vase painting, murals, and codices where the genealogies, marriages, conquests, and episodes in the lives of both notable historical and mythical personages were recorded in great detail.[327] Nevertheless, the range of subject matter treated in Classic Maya architecture and sculpture has typically been assessed as narrow, static, and nonnarrative. The prevailing opinion remains, as Proskouriakoff wrote in 1950, that in "the Classic [Maya] monumental style . . . action is seldom depicted and always restrained in character."[328] Accordingly, scholars have often relied on the presence (or absence) of a narrative, documentary component as a diagnostic (albeit an uncertain one) for determining whether an extant archaeological building or sculpture was constructed by "pure Maya" or other native peoples (an academic procedure that, among other things, helps to sustain the old image of the Maya as an isolated special case).

Moreover, feeding the supposed polarization of Maya and Central Mexican peoples, if Classic Maya architectural decoration is typically judged as decidedly nonnarrative, by contrast, the Tula Toltecs are regularly lauded for their exceedingly documentary, "historical" approach to art and architecture — a stock contradistinction that is nowhere more apparent than at Chichén Itzá. Conventional interpretations of Chichén Itzá have, in fact, routinely described the "Toltec" intrusion into Yucatán as the intrusion of a more explicitly informational and so-called secular style of art and architecture (that is, the intrusion of a more vigorous enthusiasm for the artistic commemoration of narrative sacred history, priority II-B). George Brainerd, for instance, was typical of his era when he concluded that two different approaches to narrative art at Chichén Itzá denote two different eras of occupation and two different ethnic groups: "the art of the Toltec period [at Chichén Itzá] is more naturalistic and narrative than that of the northern Maya . . . [and] shows many specific identities with that of Tula. . . . The greatest quantity of such representational material is the several hundred figures of warriors and various functionaries shown singly on the faces of the square columns in the colonnades."[329]

Besides the storiological "Toltec" bas-reliefs and murals at Chichén Itzá, gold disks found in the Sacred Cenote are also deemed "non-Maya" by Brainerd and others largely because their repoussé designs have a "narrational character and show scenes of warfare in which the Maya are unquestionably on the losing side."[330]

This simple bifurcation of Maya and non-Maya artistic elements at Chichén Itzá is (as noted in Chapter 1) hardly acceptable. Thus, lest the characterization of Maya art and architecture as static and nonnarrative be too categorical, a final example from Palenque provides a healthy antidote. According to Linda Schele's analysis, the first three Late Classic rulers of Palenque — Pacal the Great, Chan-Bahlum, and Kan-Xul — were not simply all-powerful sovereigns; they were the protagonists of a "mythology of kingship" that established the patterns to which all later rulers were obliged to adhere.[331] The major constructions of these primogenitorial rulers — the Temple of the Inscriptions, the Group of the Cross, and the north buildings of the Palace — functioned, according to Schele, as "texts" to articulate the paradigmatic mechanisms for the exercise and transference of royal power. In her phrasing, "the orientation of the buildings housing the monuments of the three rulers is designed to repeat the mythological pictures of the ascension and death events."[332] Moreover, as performative architectural events, the kingship rituals at these buildings well conform to that pattern wherein astronomical occurrences (in this case, solstice sunset phenomena) are seized upon to instigate the ritual-architectural game and to promote a sympathetic hearing for a very practical program of information. Schele summarizes the pragmatic effect of these carefully timed royal rites this way:

> [both the Temple of the Cross and the Temple of the Inscriptions are situated] so that large numbers of people could and can view the [solstice] hierophanies. The generality of the events, the accessibility to them, their dramatic characterization and their grandiose scale and publicness argue for a direct linkage between the perceptions of the real events in the heavens and the mythology that explained the relationship of man to the cosmos and the function and identity of rulers.[333]

In short, celestial phenomena acted as the conservative, instigatory component of these Palenque kingship ritual-architectural events (astronomy, priority I-C), and the radical component of new information (that is, the "back half" of these events) explained the relations between cosmos, kings, and citizenry. The political expediency of this synchronization of mythology, astronomy, and building at Palenque, besides memorializing the king-heroes of its sacred history (priority II-B), moreover, demonstrates the very frequent merger of this narrational priority with the design incentive that is next up for review — the ritual-architectural commemoration of temporal, or political, authority (politics, priority II-C).

Politics: Legitimation of Authority

> Although ritual was (and is) a cultural resource employed in the creation and maintenance of symbolic worlds of meaning, it was (and is) also used as a political tool in the competition for and the control of the seat of power.
>
> *Gary Ebersole, 1989*[334]

Abbot Suger, often termed the "founder" of Gothic architecture, undertook his massive rebuilding of the Abbey of St. Denis largely to promote his grand political design for France and the Capetian monarchy.[335] The Fifty New Churches built in London and the suburbs in the early eighteenth century, besides their otherworldly significances, were, according to Kerry Downes, monuments to the Tory government and to Queen Anne, as well as to the High Church party of the Church of England.[336] And Louis XIV, apparently inspired by the Assyrian conqueror Sargon's glorific palace at Khorsabab (built in the eighth century B.C.E.), proclaimed his own immodest hegemony by laying his bed at the center of the palace of Versailles upon which roads from Paris and a host of other places converge.[337] So too, the *ceque* system of Cuzco, Peru, orchestrated by Inca sovereign Pachacuti, was, among other things, a grand scheme for the political integration of the empire, as were the mandala organizations that characterized the "galactic polities" of Southeast Asia.[338] Likewise, in India, according to Soundara Rajan, "architecture served [the rulers] as their most spectacular and accredited publicity agents and promoters."[339] And, in an even more extreme linkage of architecture and polity, Heine-Geldern explains how, in the Hinayana Buddhist empires of Burma, Siam, and Cambodia, the power of kingship resided not in an individual but in the palace itself.[340]

Each of these cases, and countless others in Mesoamerica and elsewhere, testify to the munificent collusion of politics and buildings and to an enormous set of ritual-architectural events that have as their priority the manipulation of public sentiments, the validation of socioeconomic systems, the glorification of sovereigns, and the legitimation of oligarchies — in sum, the commemoration of temporal authority (that is, politics, priority II-C).

Very often, the ritual-architectural articulation of legitimate political hegemony is initiated via the imitation of other well-known and respected art forms, a conventionalizing strategy of allurement (priority I-B) that serves to demonstrate — or, just as often, to fabricate — some sort of genealogical claim to power. Particularly in ancient Mesoamerica, boldly expropriating and imitating prestigious building styles in the interest of announcing one's authoritative, if contrived, pedigree was a frequent ploy. The Aztecs, for instance, were only one of several groups that, though lacking any actual hereditary connection to the esteemed Toltecs, duplicated their architecture and, thereby, participated in the Toltec mystique.[341] A whole family of Mexican cities — including Tenayuca, Tepozteco, and Tula, together with portions of the Yucatán centers of Dzibilchaltún and Chichén Itzá — copied the prestigious, though by then nonfunctional, astronomical orientation of their famed forebear, Teotihuacán, apparently as a strategy of self-legitimation.[342] Likewise related to the construction of fictive pedigrees, Eric Thompson's durable explanation of the "Toltec" style at Chichén Itzá holds that the Putun Maya, militarily and materially well endowed but wholly without cultural standing, ushered Topiltzin Quetzalcoatl and his Toltecs (then on the lam from Tula) into their city to provide the prestige and legitimation that the Putun so craved.[343]

In addition to this quest after pedigree through architecture (one sort of manifestation of the politics priority, II-C), the endemically violent atmosphere of conquest, occupation, and intimidation in pre-Columbian Mesoamerica ensured a flamboyant politicization of nearly all public architecture and ritual, particularly in the urban ceremonial centers.[344] Effecting a kind of symbolic exportation of the center, the Quiché, for instance, rulers of the most powerful Highland Maya state, marked the extent of their imperial penetration into peripheral territories with garrisons that were scaled-down copies of the civic buildings of their capital, Utatlán.[345] Likewise evincing a kind of politicized ritual-architectural homology (that is, merging priorities I-A and II-C), the Cocom ruler of Mayapán seems to have held his subsidiary lords hostage in the thirteen colonnaded halls of the civic core that were, in turn, correlated to the dependent provinces.[346] Even the Aztecs, notorious for their disinterest in refashioning the spirituality of conquered peoples, on occasion resorted to architectural announcements of authority, as at the rock-cut site of Malinalco, where they overlaid the symbols of their eagle and jaguar military orders on earlier structures.[347] Or, to note a far less subtle manifestation of this theme of intimidation by architecture (another variant of the politics priority, II-C), consider the daunting Maya bas-reliefs of bound figures, for instance at Tikal and Naranjo, which Spinden compares to ancient Far Eastern conquest monuments that picture the foot of the king on the neck of a captive.[348]

Equally blunt, the intimidating ritual-architectural spectacle of human sacrifice, whether in the civic plazas of Tula, Chichén Itzá, or Tenochtitlán, likewise was, at least in part, as a number of scholars have concluded, "a public demonstration of power."[349] Richard Townsend's sensitive analysis of Aztec coronation at the Templo Mayor provides an even better illustration of the pattern in which conventional, noncontroversial symbols were used to instigate an architectural event that detailed a program of political authority. Townsend believes that the rulers of Tenochtitlán were deeply concerned with the incorporation of ancient forms as well as the invention of new ones; consequently, the Templo Mayor and its royal rites presented the masterful integration of "an architectural vocabulary that was traditional" with an original, innovative expression that was specific to the time and needs of the Aztec imperial context.[350] Embedding the particulars of the political agenda within the incontestable canons of convention assured that the demands of the *huey-tlatoni* (or Aztec chief speaker) were not perceived as aberrant, opportunistic, or exploitative. Instead, according to Townsend, "This allowed the events of a present, unfolding history to be perceived as an inevitable, preordained outcome of a cosmic process that had been established since the time of origins, since the beginning of things."[351]

Even, however, where Mesoamerican architecture is not tied explicitly to the coercive administration of authority, there is often a very thoroughgoing symbolic correlation between the built environment and the sociopolitical hierarchy. Sidrys, for instance, argues that monuments of the ancient Maya functioned as highly visible symbols of national prestige, labor organization, and political power and, as such, were the megalithic pawns in a shrewd tournament of "competitive building" between the rival chiefdoms of the

Aztec human sacrifice at the Templo Mayor. Besides reenacting the mythical scenario of the birth of the patron deity Huitzilopochtli, ritual human sacrifice at the Templo Mayor provided a threateningly blunt announcement of political supremacy and the dire consequences of resisting Aztec hegemony. Where the Toltec rituals of Tula Grande have nearly always been imagined as spectacles of intimidation, scholars were much slower to acknowledge the similarly politicized nature of Classic Maya ritual. (From *Book of the Gods and Rites and the Ancient Calendar,* by Fray Diego Durán. Translated and edited by Fernando Horcasitas asn Doris Heyden. Copyright ©1971 by the University of Oklahoma Press.)

Early Classic Northern Lowlands.[352] Similarly, Robertson describes how an attempt by the impertinent Tlatelolcan builders to outsize the Templo Mayor with their own local pyramid was considered so gross an affront that the Aztecs were compelled to respond militarily.[353] Antonio de Herrera and Landa each recognized a concentric socio-spatial hierarchy in Mayapán, Yucatán, wherein, moving out from the temples at the center of the city, in the latter's words, were "the houses of the lords and priests, and then those of the most important people . . . [then] came the houses of the richest and of those who were held in highest estimation nearest to them, and at the outskirts of town were the houses of the lower class."[354] Likewise speaking to this socio-spatial theme, Dzibilchaltún, also in northern Yucatán, was a focal point in an extensive system of raised causeways that, in the opinion of Andrews V, were constructed less as pragmatic communication routes than as symbolic statements of a superlocal integration of society and politics.[355] And Carmack describes a virtual equation of the social and architectural organizations in the Quiché capital of Utatlán, where "buildings occupied by the lineages became as important symbolically as the lineages themselves — hence the name *nim ja* ('big house') as the general term for lineage."[356]

Among the most subtle studies of the interrelatedness of Mesoamerican building and polity is George Cowgill's "cross-cultural ethnoarchaeology of public architecture."[357] Aiming specifically at the Ciudadela, the extensive complex generally believed to have been the governmental seat of Teotihuacán, Cowgill implies what amounts to three general variations on the ritual-architectural commemoration of temporal authority: (1) architecture that glorifies a particular ruler, (2) architecture that facilitates the day-to-day operation of a government, and (3) architecture that functions as a symbol of the stability of the state.[358] Working the second of these two variations against the third, he concludes that while the Ciudadela was probably the center of everyday administration and political management at an early point in Teotihuacán's evolution, the structure's more essential role as the physical embodiment of the stability and intransigence of the Teotihuacán state precluded its being modified and expanded enough to keep pace with the increasingly complex bureaucratic routines of a growing city, which were, consequently, moved to other quarters.[359] Cowgill, moreover, concludes that the other alternative, architecture that glorifies specific individual rulers (epitomized, for instance, at Chan Chan, the Chimu capital on the north coast of Peru where each new ruler constructed a new residential complex that was forever identified with his individual persona),[360] is apparently less relevant to Teotihuacán's Ciudadela than to the royal palaces of Montezuma and his Aztec predecessors at Tenochtitlán.[361]

In the Maya zone, we note that it is precisely the viability of this mode of individuated ritual-architectural commemoration (one variation on the politics priority, II-C) that has sustained perhaps the most famous debate regarding the significance of Maya monuments and hieroglyphs. At one end of the spectrum, old-guard Mayanists (Morley, Spinden, and Eric Thompson), holding that the inscriptions on Maya monuments are cosmological and "religious" rather than political, are emphatic that these "are in *no* sense records of personal glorification and self-laudation like the inscriptions of Egypt, Assyria, or Babylonia";[362] the middle ground (Covarrubias, Bernal, and Bushnell) claims that Maya art and architecture commemorate royal offices but not individuals;[363] and the present consensus (following Proskouriakoff and the Tikal Project) holds that, assuredly, "[Maya] authority focused powerfully upon personal rule and that political motives affected the art and architecture at least as strongly as did religious and aesthetic sensibilities."[364]

This infamous controversy regarding the political nature of Maya art and architecture has a special legacy for the interpretation of Chichén Itzá. Tozzer, having fully espoused the image of the peaceful, apolitical Maya, and having formulated his ideas about Maya iconography and epigraphy before Proskouriakoff's revolutionary recognition of individuality and historicity in the inscriptions, based his fabulously influential interpretation of Chichén Itzá on three now-antiquated presuppositions: (1) that the abundant human figures in southern Classic Maya art, whether on stelae, altars, or walls, refer neither to specific individuals nor to any sort of worldly, "nonreligious" issues or events;[365] (2) that the Puuc Maya of the Northern Lowlands (including the original Yucatecan inhabitants of Chichén Itzá, who supposedly built "Old Maya Chichén") entirely avoided anthropomorphic representations of any kind, most of all people engaged in domestic or civic activities;[366] and (3) that, in diametric opposition, the Toltecs (the supposed builders of "New Toltec Chichén") were obsessed with propagandistic depictions of the events and personages of "secular" political history. The baseline of Tozzer's whole interpretation of Chichén Itzá is, in other words, a contradistinction between an "indigenous Maya" component, which shunned entirely the architectural commemoration of politics and worldly affairs (that is, priority II-C), and the "foreign Toltecs," who vigorously depicted specific individuals and events, particularly those relating to their conquest of the city. Thus, according to Tozzer's dubious position, the Toltecs were presumably responsible for all of the art at Chichén that displays "actual historical pictures . . . showing phases of the capture of a native people by an invading host," a theme that would hold little interest for the more spiritually predisposed Maya artists.[367]

The overwrought stereotypes of the apolitical, otherworldly Maya and the "secular" Toltec invaders may, by now, have been exposed. Certainly, the Maya, if pursuing somewhat different religio-civic strategies than the Tula Toltecs, were likewise very energetic participants in a whole range of variations on the ritual-architectural commemoration of temporal authority (politics, priority II-C). Accordingly, in any reassessment of the phenomenon of "Toltec" Chichén Itzá, we must resist the lingering tendency of Tozzer and Eric Thompson to equate the politicization of art and ritual with cultural degradation[368] and, instead, appreciate the exciting diversity of ways in which Mesoamerican politics, ritual, and building coalesce. In short, no serious study of the sacred architecture of Tula and Chichén Itzá (or anywhere else for that matter) can afford to neglect the omnipresent infiltration of socioeconomic forces and political interests into the spheres of religion and art.

The Dead: Ancestral Bones and Stones

> The habitation of the living may be poor, even wretched, but the tomb on the contrary has to be vast and attract attention. . . . The eternal abode has to stand out for its solidity and fine appearance. . . . The tomb is visible wealth, and some ruin themselves in building it.
>
> *Raymond Decary, 1962*[369]

We can, for heuristic and expedience sake, partition the abundance of religio-architectural manifestations of the fascination, fear, and awe of death (the commemoration of the dead, priority II-D), into two overlapping categories. The first entails the literal transmutation of ancestors into stone, the second, the accommodation and strategic location of the physical remains of the deceased — in other words, architecture that in some sense *is* the dead and architecture that *houses* the dead.

Perhaps the best instantiation of the first option is megaliths. Aubrey Burl, for instance, in a refreshingly "eventful" study of European megaliths, while acknowledging a whole range of possible religio-ritual usages and significances, concludes that these monuments were first and foremost accoutrements of necromancy, stone constructions that facilitated continued communication between the living and the deceased but, nevertheless, very active "undead."[370] Burl contends that even the irrefutable astronomical alignments of monuments like Stonehenge were primarily mechanisms for communicating with the dead,[371] an assessment that finds some support in Sullivan's insistence that megalithic religion is *not* about prescientific stargazing. "Rather," Sullivan writes, "the meaning of the religious perception of the heavens is involved with the megalithic religious experience of the dead, of stone, of space ordered permanently in stone, of the Earth, and of fertility; for these are the realities brought together in megalithic material sites."[372]

Likewise, Heine-Geldern and Eliade both interpret the megalithic constructions of western and northern Europe as manifestations of a pervasive Neolithic cult of ancestors. For Heine-Geldern, megaliths are architectural manifestations of people's hope that their names will be remembered through the agency of stone, a memory "fixed" in the rock.[373] And Eliade invokes his work on lithic symbolism to explain that, whereas the houses of Neolithic peasants were modest and ephemeral, the dwellings for the dead were built of stone. For Eliade, slabs of stone reveal duration without end, modalities existing independently of temporal being and thereby constituting an inexhaustible reservoir of vitality and power.[374] According to this interpretive line, megaliths in Europe (and perhaps in Mesoamerica) were, in other words, not simply sites for the worship of esteemed forebears but, moreover, in a seemingly more magical sense, stones animated with life that worked to transcend or conquer death and to keep the ancestors present. Somewhat surprisingly, then, from this vantage, monoliths find among their closest analogues those rock-cut Hindu shrines that are, according to Mabbett, conceived quite literally as the "live bodies" of dead ancestors: "often [a Hindu shrine's] life is an embodiment of the soul of a real human being, a deceased chieftain, ruler, dignitary, or human sacrifice, for whom his new home is regarded as a lodging in exactly the same way as was his body during his life."[375]

If megaliths and rock-cut temples epitomize one major variation on the ritual-architectural commemoration of the dead (the transmutation of ancestors into stone), a somewhat more obvious set of manifestations involves the assiduous treatment and strategic location of the physical remains of the dead. Chinese *feng-shui* geomancy, for instance, provides a rarified version of this sort in which human bones, whether living or dead, are understood to give off a powerful sort of energy termed *chii* (that is, vital forces of nature or "local currents of cosmic breath"). Accordingly, the task of the Chinese geomancer, and the first priority in *feng-shui* spatial planning (whether at the scale of cities, villages, or — especially — individual domiciles), is to decipher the convoluted relations among *chii,* bones, and the living and then to exploit those relations in a fashion that preserves the interactive, "umbilical" connections between living descendants and dead ancestors.[376] Moreover, the Far Eastern ancestral rites associated with *feng-shui* building likewise provide one of countless more straightforward sorts of examples wherein the ritual-architectural context is conceived as a kind of residence that houses either the physical remains or at least the spiritual presence of the honored deceased, thus facilitating their ongoing and very active otherworldly existences. In fact, cross-cultural examples of ritual-architectural events that are dedicated primarily to placating and propitiating highly esteemed and influential "undead" ancestors with food, drink, money, and the other practical necessities for their activities in the netherworld are too numerous to require much comment (though, of course, culturally specific conceptions of the status of the dead vary tremendously).

Looking to Mesoamerica, the pervasiveness of death in pre-Columbian art has never been in doubt. In 1913, Spinden, for instance, was writing that "symbols of death are found everywhere in the codices and sculpture."[377] But contributors from all sectors of Mesoamerican studies have lately pushed that nascent recognition of the artistic commemoration of the dead (priority II-D) — and particularly the pivotal role of pre-Columbian ancestor worship — from the wings to center stage.[378] In fact, Mesoamerican mythology, ethnohistory, ethnography, and archaeology all bear splendid testimony to a commingling of both major forms just discussed — the transmutation of ancestors into stone and the reverential treatment of ancestral bones.[379]

The veneration of stones in general, and particularly as a means of maintaining access to forebears, is, in fact, a featured theme in mythico-historical traditions all across Mesoamerica.[380] The Yucatán cosmogonic account in *The Chilam Balam of Chumayel,* for instance, says that "God" was hidden in a stone when there was neither earth nor day and that later he left that stone, fell into a second stone, and there declared his divinity *(Kuil).*[381] With direct relevance to the "Toltecization" of the Mayaland, the Quiché Maya documents repeatedly allude to the stone that Nacxit (or Quetzalcoatl) gave as a gift to those tribes when they departed Tulán-Civán (that is, Tollan). This stone, "which the kings and the people worshipped [and which] they used in their incantations," was enshrined in the Great Edifice of Tohil and guarded as the paramount symbol of authority and sovereignty because it was the tangible, pertinacious link with their revered and authenticating "Toltec" ancestry — as the *Popol Vuh* says, the "reminder of their fathers."[382] Moreover, the preeminence of sacred, ancestral stones in Mesoamerican myth is matched by the equal prominence of ancestral bones. In Aztec stories, Quetzalcoatl creates the current people of Mesoamerica by "bleeding his member" on the precious bones of a previous human race,[383] and in the *Popol Vuh,* the decapitated head of Quiché Maya cultural hero Hun Hunahpú becomes the anthropomorphic fruit of a tree, which then spits on and impregnates a maiden who eventually gives birth to the ancestors of future generations.[384] Furthermore, the *Popol Vuh* emphasizes that among the essential attributes of a great Quiché lord is respect for his ancestors — "recognition of their having been created" — and, in that spirit, the text traces back the genealogy of the Quiché kings to the very beginning of time.[385]

Besides the mythic record, the colonial documentary sources likewise strengthen the case for a very vital Mesoamerican ancestor worship. Landa, for instance, describes a Yucatec practice of cremating the bodies but preserving the skulls of important people (a practice that Eric Thompson confirmed archaeologically and interpreted as evidence of an ancestor cult among the aristocracy of Yucatán and, possibly, Guatemala).[386] Las Casas says that the cadavers of famous Quiché lords were burned and their bodies joined together with gold thread and precious stones to form "mummies," which were entombed and held in great veneration by people who burned incense and made sacrifices to them during important temple ceremonies.[387] And Herrera and Sahagún both refer to circumstances in which Central Mexican chieftains were "mummified" and interred in caves. Moreover, research into Maya hieroglyphic writing and iconography, especially at Palenque, has verified that these people were "deeply obsessed with the cult of the honored dead."[388] It is plausible, for instance, that both the strategic placement of the "bone element" in the iconography of the sarcophagus lid of Lord Pacal's tomb in the Temple of the Inscriptions at

Temple of Inscriptions at Palenque. The remarkable sarcophagus of Lord Pacal beneath this pyramid, complete with a "psychoduct" or stone tube that runs from the subterranean crypt to the temple floor, perhaps designed to maintain contact with the deceased king, was not (re)discovered until 1952. That find sparked a new appreciation of the pre-Columbian Maya concern for ancestor worship and for the ritual-architectural commemoration of the dead. (Photo by the author.)

Palenque, and the "psychoduct" (a stone tube that runs from Pacal's subterranean crypt up to the temple floor) are contrivances to send posthumous guidance, or more likely, in the manner of the *chii* forces of *feng shui*, to channel the "life, breath, and soul" of Pacal to the living.[389] Equally significant has been the discovery by modern ethnographers that, of all Maya divinities, it is the ancestral gods who are most active, relevant, approachable, and interested in the daily lives of contemporary Maya people.[390]

Reassessing the archaeological data in light of the mounting ethnohistorical, epigraphical, and ethnographic evidence suggests that, from the earliest European assessments, the centrality of ancestor worship in Mesoamerican, and particularly Maya, religion (and, thus, the prolific pre-Columbian ritual-architectural commemoration of the dead, priority II-D) has been seriously underestimated. The Spanish friars' vituperative cries of Mesoamerican "idolatry," for instance, were based largely on the dubious presumption that the stone images that they found in so many of the indigenous temples were (after the fashion of Greek pagan statuary) "idols" to "gods." It now appears, however — at least in the Zapotec-Mixtec region of Oaxaca, where the stupendous tombs of Monte Albán and Mitla make this a paradigm of Mesoamerican funerary architecture — that virtually all of these sacred images represent deceased rulers, megalithic ancestors, as it were, whose actual physical remains were housed in elaborately decorated masonry vaults that formed the foundations for the same temples.[391] Likewise, that widely distributed motif of a figure seated inside an earth-monster arch now appears more likely to represent a "stone ancestor" than a deity.[392] The belated discovery of the spectacular tomb of the Lord Pacal in the Temple of the Inscriptions, Mesoamerica's most famous "funerary temple," undermined the old notion that Maya pyramids were simply substructures rather than crypts for the actual royal remains.[393] And the controversy over Classic Maya stelae also rears its head once more in this context, as the figures on the carved megaliths of the Petén area, contemporaneous with the Zapotec ancestral stone effigies, are, one by one, identified as late, great historic rulers.[394]

Nevertheless, as the revisionist assessment of Maya ancestor worship continues to be honed, the legacy of an earlier paradigm stubbornly lingers at Chichén Itzá.[395] In the era of the Carnegie Institution's work, the assessment of the artistic commemoration of death was (like so many other things) swept into the larger project of polarizing "Toltec" over against "Maya." The conventional stereotypes of that day clustered the depiction and worship of the dead with "militarism" and "secularism" as the distasteful hallmarks of Central Mexico and the Toltecs. The indigenous Maya, by contrast, were applauded for their disinterest in representing death and for an art that was "religious," "peaceful," and "alive." Of Chichén Itzá specifically, Tozzer announced summarily that "most of the figures of death seem to be Toltec."[396] Accordingly, in his so-termed Chichén I stage (presumably the era of indigenous Yucatán Maya occupation), "death and the ideas surrounding it are not especially prominent"; later, however, in the Chichén II and III stages, the "Toltecs" supposedly introduce the characteristically Mexican morbidity, and "the death god . . . is especially in evidence."[397] Subsequently, according to the (re)constructions of Tozzer and Eric Thompson, there was a reassertion of Maya values at Chichén Itzá that was characterized by a healthy restraint from representations of death;[398] but then, this short-lived Maya renaissance, to continue with the Carnegie party line, was followed by a final era of Toltec-instigated decadence and militarism — in Thompson's phrasing, "the rise of secular forces at the expense of sacerdotal control, [and] a vulgarization of the spiritual aspect of religion."[399] In the context of this decadent anticlimax, the traditional religion of the Maya elite supposedly waned as Chichén Itzá, and even more Mayapán, experienced "a growth of cults, of which ancestor worship was conspicuous and the transference of much of ceremonialism to the private dwelling."[400]

This late and little assessment of ancestor worship at Chichén Itzá, together with the pejorative entanglement of ancestor worship in a complex of militarism and secularism, is, at this point, simply bogus. Chichén Itzá is now available for fresh consideration as a major participant in a resplendent tradition of indigenous Maya ritual-architectural commemoration of death (priority II-D). Perhaps this round, instead of using death in art and architecture as a stiff criterion for polarizing the Maya and the "Toltec" elements of Chichén Itzá, can be used to explore the meaning of, and the extent to which, two very basic expressions — ancestor worship (typically associated with the Classic Maya), and devotion to genealogical paradigms (typically associated with the Central Mexicans and specifically with the endurance of the Quetzalcoatl-Tollan paradigm) — are alternative responses to a single religious motivation, namely, connectedness to one's forebears.

Architecture as Ritual Context: The Presentation of Ritual-Architectural Events

> It was for the performance of liturgy that any church was ever built.
>
> *Staale Sinding-Larsen, 1984*[401]

The mendicant orders emerge from Wolfgang Braunfels's survey of European monastic architecture as something of a special case. Committed to peregrination rather than building, neither St. Francis nor St. Dominic reflected particularly upon the layouts of their houses of worship, nor did the question possess any great importance in the eyes of their immediate successors. Thus, as Braunfels explains, "The fruit of this casualness toward what they considered superficial was the adoption [by Franciscans and Dominicans] of the traditional Benedictine scheme for all their establishments."[402]

The significance of this case notwithstanding, nonchalance about the built environment in which one practices the religious life is certainly an exception rather than the rule, even among monastic communities. In general, the ritual ambience is scrutinized with the same rigor that applies to the ceremonial scheduling, the sanctity of the ritual paraphernalia, and the preparedness of the actors. The concept of ritual-architectural events, in fact, demands that the buildings and architectural decorations themselves be understood as active participants in the ritual proceedings. By way of organizing and comparing the plethora of strategies whereby architecture concocts an efficacious context for ritual, the following section isolates four basic types of presentational priorities: (A) theatre, stagecrafting for dramatic ritual performance; (B) contemplation, presentation of architectural features as foci for meditative devotion; (C) propitiation, circumstances in which construction itself becomes ritual; and (D) sanctuary, the fabrication of refuges of pristine sacrality.

Considerably more varied than the set of three orientational priorities or the four commemorative priorities, the tetrad of presentational priorities — theatre (III-A), contemplation (III-B), propitiation (III-C), and sanctuary (III-D) — besides throwing into the ring that many more contenders for what may have been happening at Tula and Chichén Itzá, is particularly useful in explaining the contrast, competition, and play among the ritual-architectural priorities of specific ceremonial contexts. In concert, these four categories provide a vocabulary for the significant comparison of, for instance, the sumptuously choreographed liturgical events of Cluny versus the secluded worship of Cistercian monasteries versus the architecturally aided contemplation of Gothic cathedrals; or, for distinguishing the shifting ritual-architectural priorities between the Classic Greek temple and its progeny, the Roman temple; or, in Mesoamerica, for charting the fluctuating ritual priorities of Early Classic, Late Classic, and Postclassic Maya architectural events. In other words, these four types of presentational priorities belong together not because they are parallel but because they play off one another so productively in the hermeneutical discussion about alternative strategies for choreographing the allurement and content of ritual-architectural events.

Theatre: Pomp, Procession, and Pageant

> In all the long catalogue of superstitious rites that darken the pages of man's history, I cannot imagine a picture more horribly exciting than that of the Indian priest, with his white dress and long hair glotted with gore, performing his murderous sacrifices at this lofty height, in full

view of the people throughout the whole extent of the city.

López de Cogolludo, 1688[403]

Perhaps *the* fundamental problem in the study of Mesoamerican architecture has been the disengagement of monuments from ritual, of edifices from events. Confronted, however, by the magnificent processional ways and "pageant-spaces" of ancient Mexico, even the most staid reporters have been swept into imaginative re-creations of the pre-Columbian ritual-architectural events. From the brink of Monte Albán's ruined yet sumptuous Great Plaza, a typically impassive William H. Holmes pines,

> How striking must have been the effects when these pyramids were all crowned with imposing temples, when the great, level plaza about them, six hundred by one thousand feet in extent, was brilliant with barbaric displays, and the enclosing ranges of terraces and pyramids were occupied by gathered throngs. Civilization has rarely conceived anything in the way of amphitheatric display more extensive and imposing than this.[404]

A hundred years later, the same vista moved George Kubler to an uncharacteristic flourish on "the stirring fusion of stone and ritual . . . the sumptuous life of religious pageantry" in which "processions in costumes were probably the living sculpture which moved over the platforms and stairways of Monte Albán . . . the most grandiose of all American temple centers."[405]

The evocative Zapotec-Mixtec center of Monte Albán is located picturesquely atop a steep hill in the valley of Oaxaca, yet, rather than accentuate the pregnant vistas, its most important feature is, in Jorge Hardoy's words, "its negation of topography and natural environment."[406] Monte Albán's Great Plaza takes control of the space and, despite an appearance of perfect regularity, shuns absolute geometric proportions to achieve its choreographic ideal, the creation of an amphitheatre that encloses large gatherings of people and rivets their attention on the performative drama of Zapotecan ritual.

This choreographic contrivance to seduce and to shock is the hallmark of the theatric ritual-architectural priority (III-A), a priority that is both exceedingly prominent and exceedingly well documented in ancient Mesoamerica. At best high drama, at worst garish pretension, where the theatric priority dominates, ritual-architectural events typically begin by taking one's breath. Such spectatorial events are inclusive in the extreme; they compel participation by ostentation, spectacle, and amazement and then proceed, via religious showmanship, to convey their messages. A simply expedient division between ceremonial movement along processional ways (as epitomized in the lush liturgical marches at Cluny) and stationary pageant events (like those contrived by Bernini's elaborately sculpted Baroque architecture) organizes a set of illustrations that, while wildly disparate in content, are decidedly similar by their theatric presentational strategy (priority III-A).

Virtually all sacred architecture is informed by ritual proprieties, and, not infrequently, the demands of liturgical stagecrafting overpower all other parameters of design. The competition and interaction between circular and longitudinal European church plans, for instance, and particularly the controversy over (and eventually rejection of) Bramanti's sixteenth-century proposal of a round plan for the rebuilding of St. Peter's in Rome, illustrates both a play of typological priorities and the victory of the theatric mode (priority III-A).[407] On the one hand, Bramanti's round design was well suited to expressing the Renaissance conception of God's perfection and harmony (that is, the commemoration of divinity, priority II-A);[408] yet, on the other hand, the circular plan was severely criticized as inadequate to the needs of ecclesiastical ceremony: it had no adequate sacristy, few chapels for the worship of individual saints, and, most condemnatory of all, no nave — a feature essential to house a large congregation and to provide a suitable setting for liturgical processions. The traditional cross-shaped basilica, by contrast, had endured hundreds of years of transformation and refinement to bring it into accord with the demands of Christian liturgy, an evolution that culminated in the monumental third abbey church of Cluny (1088–1130), where, as Braunfels explains, "building was to one end only: the life of the monks was almost exclusively devoted to the celebration of liturgy."[409] At Cluny, gigantic scale, munificent lavishness, and sublime symbolism were coordinated into a longitudinal basilica that aspired, above all, to provide the backdrop for theatrical ceremony and, particularly, for elaborate liturgical processions.[410]

In colonial Mexico the merger between this mode of Christian processionary choreography and a similarly enthusiastic indigenous preoccupation with ritual ambulation eventuated in ubiquitous religious parading so grand that, at least according to the comparative assessment of globe-trotting Englishman William Bullock, "in order and regularity, in the grandeur of the vestments, and in the silver and gold . . . the processions of Rome, or any other city in Europe suffer much in comparison."[411] This vibrant Mesoamerican tradition of ceremonial walking, still prominent today,[412] was solidly established at least by 300 C.E., a rough date for the famous Miccaotli, or "Street of the Dead," at Teotihuacán.[413] Leading nowhere, this consummate processional seam bisects the Pyramid of the Moon and imposes an intense longitudinal order on a ceremonial center whose artistic oeuvre, most explicitly, its mural iconography, is distinguished above all by its "strongly marked liturgical character."[414]

The fascination with munificently staged parades at Teotihuacán was, if the representational art is any indication, paramount in the other great sites of Central Mexico as well. At Tula, for instance, the procession represented in the "frieze of the caciques" on a bench in the colonnade of the main temple is but one of several rows of warriors, priests, and animals inscribed on the city's lintels, altars, walls, and benches.[415] And at Tenochtitlán, innumerable surfaces are similarly decorated — most famously, the Stone of Tizoc, showing fifteen pairs of processing figures.[416] Likewise, at Chichén Itzá (particularly in the northern portion of the city), there are more than a dozen major relief carvings and murals of elaborately clad persons in file. Yet, because these processional scenes at Chichén Itzá (the largest of which shows some 114 figures arranged in seven lines in the Lower Temple of the Jaguars) are invariably associated with undulating serpents and what are conventionally identified as "Toltec warriors," they are one more feature that is typically (although dubiously) considered "non-Maya" and thus fundamental corroboration of the old story of a Tula-Toltec invasion of Yucatán.[417]

Be that as it may, the Maya zone is not without its own indigenous tradition of sumptuous processional ways. In the "island," or "archipelago cities" of the central Petén region, the elaborate causeways and ramps that traverse swampy ravines to connect the various raised platforms and buildings acted, in some cases (Tikal, for instance), as dams on transport routes; yet, in virtually all cases, these causeways are well oversized for their simply utilitarian functions.[418] Moreover, speaking to the pervasiveness of Maya ritual marching, J. Antonio Villacourt and Recinos both described great celebrative processions of, in the southern region, conquering warriors and lords into and along the *beyawoc,* or "main street" of

Utatlán.[419] And in the north, the area around Cobá and Chichén Itzá is crosshatched by a remarkable system of wide, stone causeways or *sacbe* ("white roads"). Thomas Gann, among the earliest to explore the *sacbe* network, while mistaken in his geography (the network does *not* aim directly for the Sacred Cenote at Chichén Itzá, as he thought), was probably closer in his brusque assessment of its function: "It was completely useless . . . the only explanation was a purely ceremonial road or *via sacre*."[420] The grand avenue that does connect the Sacred Cenote with the Castillo pyramid some 300 meters away — given the prominence of processional reliefs at Chichén Itzá, the nature of the spatial remodeling of the city in the era of the Castillo's erection, and the double endowment of the Maya and Central Mexican ritual ambulatory traditions — seems to have been stage to longitudinal ceremonial events of dazzling glitz and gore, with human sacrifices at the pyramid on one end and then again at the Cenote on the other.[421]

Shifting now from the ambulatory manifestations of the theatric priority (III-A) to its more stationary manifestations — from processional ways to pageant spaces — the latter mode of ritual-architectural presentation finds classical exemplification in the emotive stagecrafting of Baroque architecture, and especially in the work of its most renowned artisan, Gian Lorenzo Bernini. A sculptor by trade, Bernini's preoccupation in his later years became architecture and the creation of whole environments that embodied his sculptural ideal: the production of art that invites the spectator to be moved, the creation of ambiences that provide occasions for enlightenment and inspiration, not through liturgy, but via direct participation in the reality to which the art refers. As Wittkower says, "In Bernini's churches . . . the architecture is no more and no less than the setting for a stirring mystery revealed to the faithful by sculptural decoration."[422] Bernini typically achieved this ideal by freezing in art the "crucial moment" in the life of a saint or biblical figure; captured in art, climactic religious circumstances thereby become accessible to the spectator and their full significance is, in fact, forced to recognition. The mystical experience of Teresa of Avila, for instance, is concretized in his fabulous sculpture, the *Ecstasy of St. Teresa* (1645–52).[423] And the passion and resurrection of Christ are ossified, and thus re-actualized, in the architectural space of the Crossing at St. Peter's. In Lavin's words, "the Christ figure charges the physical space of the Crossing with the meaning of a dramatic action: we are actually at Jerusalem and salvation is being achieved before our eyes."[424] The informational content of Bernini's work, whether in sculpture or more explicitly architecture, deals, in other words, primarily with the commemoration of the circumstances and individuals of Catholic sacred history (priority II-B), but his manner of presentation relies upon histrionic devices, emotional pleas, and the arousal of astonishment (theatre, priority III-A).[425]

Such highly theatric architecture, Bernini's included and Cluny even more so, not infrequently draws charges of vulgarity, superficiality, and degeneracy. In Mesoamerica, for instance, the so-called Toltec style (whether at Tula or Chichén Itzá), owing to its obviously dramatic character (and its relative technical inferiority), has been singularly dispraised on exactly those grounds. Particularly the Toltec architecture of Tula is generally dismissed as bold, ambitious, even flashy, but shoddily executed, lacking in detail and realism — in Covarrubias's oft-cited words, "meant to impress but not to last."[426] And the "Toltec" style at Chichén Itzá, notable for its "spaciousness of planning"[427] and commitment to "maximum spectator participation, pomp and ceremony,"[428] has (by contrast to indigenous Maya architecture) likewise received

Great Plaza of Monte Albán, Oaxaca. Somewhat surprisingly, this mountaintop plaza, regarded by George Kubler as "the most grandiose of all American temple centers," is arranged so that the pregnant vistas are blocked rather than exploited. Instead of fostering outside views, the amphitheatric space seems to have been designed to focus all the attentions of large audiences inward, that is, onto the performative drama of Zapotecan ritual. (Photo by William M. Ferguson, courtesy of the University of Texas, Austin.)

almost unanimously condescending reviews. Bernal's assessment is typical: "Toltec-Maya art produces a very spectacular architecture and sculpture, colorful but at the same time more superficial and emptier than those of the Classic period; it is a nouveau-riche art suitable to the taste of warriors who have lately achieved power."[429]

If despised by most modern critics, this supposedly transient and degenerate Toltec style was, nonetheless, the most deeply revered and widely copied in all of pre-Columbian Mesoamerica. The Aztecs, like a number of groups, wholly enamored of all that was "Toltec" — religion and architecture particularly — not only perpetuated the theatrical Toltec mode of ritual architecture but, in the proceedings of the state cult at the Templo Mayor, gave it hyperbolic expression. The *teopantli* (or serpent-walled) precinct around the Templo Mayor, not unlike that at Tula Grande, was the wide-open, public stage for a carefully scripted drama of Aztec sacred history and political imperialism.[430] William Prescott (1845), for example, seized upon the gory showmanship of "the dismal rites of the sacrifice [that] were all visible from the remotest corners of the capital" as the ideal foreshadowing to his Victorian account of the confrontation between the "quixotic" Spanish conquistadors and their "barbarian" adversaries.[431] Prescott's romantic excesses notwithstanding, recent excavations and interpretations of the Templo Mayor have done nothing to dispel his vision of the lush theatrics of the Aztec state cult's public rituals. Carrasco, for instance, accentuating the political dimension of Aztec human sacrifice (priority II-C), describes the choreography of motion, color, sound, and gesture in the Templo Mayor event as a "drama of intimidation" and thus concludes that "the ritual extravaganza was carried out with maximum theatrical tension, paraphernalia and terror in order to amaze and intimidate the visiting dignitaries who returned to their kingdoms trembling with fear and convinced that co-operation and not rebellion was the best response to Aztec imperialism."[432]

Once again evincing the polarization of pre-Columbian Indians, there has been one strain of interpreters that hoped (not wholly inappropriately) to exclude the Maya from the gaudy ostentations of the Central Mexicans. Joyce, for instance, argued that, in contrast to the horridly visceral Aztec statue of the beheaded Coatlicue, "on the whole, Maya sculptural art is not emotional; [instead], for the most part, it is characterized by a calm and almost superhuman serenity, a kind of lurking strength";[433] and Brainerd noted that Classic Maya architecture, being smaller, "more subtle and esoteric" than Mexican, "suggests an emphasis on quality rather than quantity, on enlightenment rather than power in the code of Maya values."[434] Scholars both before and after these Maya aficionados, however (if often rationalizing it as a foreign, Mexican intrusion), generally have acknowledged the steamy histrionics of Maya public ceremony. Cogolludo is perhaps the most graphic, reflecting upon the "horribly exciting" spectacle of Yucatán human sacrifice;[435] but Landa also emphasizes the "great show and company of people" at Yucatán rituals.[436] Similarly, Catherwood imagined "great exhibitions of pomp and splendor";[437] Stephens, "the theatre of great events and imposing religious ceremonies";[438] and Francisco de Fuentes (circa 1700), "the great circus of Copán."[439] More recently, Spinden and Kubler re-echoed these assessments of the theatrical character of Copán,[440] and Kelemen went directly for the parallel to Bernini's work to describe the Copán plaza as "an ideal arena. . . . Baroque it is — in feeling, in its complication of design and ebullience of detail, in the dramatic dynamics of its whole conception, in the untrammeled freedom of its execution . . . a ceremony witnessed here must have been immensely awe-inspiring."[441]

In sum then, examples of the scholarly appreciation of the theatrical character of Mesoamerican architecture (including that of the indigenous Maya), both in its processionary and stationary modes, could be multiplied almost endlessly. Nevertheless, as the telling label "Maya Baroque" suggests (a comparative appellation that, while at times illuminating, has been overextended to describe all that is complex, ornate, or exuberant in Maya art),[442] there has been (and is) a tendency to dismiss the unmistakably theatrical character of pre-Columbian art and architecture as a mere pandering of emotions — a "meretriciousness; a constant striving after the grandiose and impressive."[443] Moreover, there has been a tendency to assess all pre-Columbian ritual-architectural choreography as preeminently theatrical. Thus, for our purposes the irrefutable glamour and posh in Mesoamerican ritual architecture notwithstanding, it becomes perhaps more important to explore other, "nontheatrical" explanations for this commitment to ostentation. The contemplation and propitiation priorities (III-B and III-C) are offered as two major alternatives. Also, we must attend to those many cases in which the theatric priority (III-A) is notable most of all by its deliberate avoidance, as Mesoamericans opt instead for exclusivistic, private ritual space, which is the hallmark of the sanctuary priority. (III-D).[444]

Contemplation: Props for Devotion

> *We* may no longer have much leisure to contemplate the images before us, but people once did; and they turned contemplation into something useful, therapeutic, elevating, and terrifying. They did so in order to attain a state of empathy . . .
>
> *David Freedberg, 1989*[445]

In most cases, sacred architecture contributes to the experience of ritual *in*directly by creating an efficacious ambience. Theatric architecture (priority III-A), for instance, crafts constructional elements into a stage for participatory dramatics, and sanctuary architecture (priority III-D) facilitates ritual by providing an environment of distractionless purity. This section, however, addresses a mode of ritual-architectural presentation in which the link between building elements and ritual participants is direct, immediate, and unmitigated. Moreover, while theatric architecture typically either seduces or coerces participation, where the so-termed contemplation mode (priority III-B) prevails, architectural events typically begin at the voluntary, even enthusiastic, behest of the worshipper. Ritual-architectural contemplation (priority III-C), as defined here, involves, in other words, architectural forms that serve willing participants as props for devotion or foci for meditation that, by their direct apprehension, lift those devotees to new spiritual awarenesses. The viability of this as a distinct type of priority is embodied in the East by the rich tradition of mandala architecture and in the West by Gothic architecture and the resilient career of "the theory of anagogical illumination."

In Guiseppe Tucci's Jungian language, mandalas are "psycho-cosmogrammata that lead the neophyte by revealing to him the secret play of the forces that operate in the universe and in us, on the way to reintegration of consciousness."[446] Where Tucci's work is based primarily, the mandala paintings of Tibet, the same principle materializes on a monumental scale in the cosmogrammatic architecture of Angkor Vat in Indochina and Borobudur in Java. These multivalent mandala temples are certainly, as Tucci says, concretizations of mental states and homologized maps of the universe (homology, priority I-A); likewise, they are filled with representations and allusions to Buddhist mythology (sacred history, priority II-B); moreover, Borobudur as a whole can be considered an elaborate *stupa* and, as such, an architectural "substitute" for the Buddha (commemoration of divinity or perhaps the dead, priorities II-A and II-D).[447] Yet, as monumental vehicles for devotion, "means of integration," these stupendous mandala architectures are even more instructive as illustrations of the contemplation mode of ritual-architectural presentation (priority III-B).

Where "reading" a two-dimensional Tibetan painted mandala requires a sort of mental journey as one concentrates on successive elements of the printing's pattern until eventually reaching its center, the pilgrim's experience of Borobudur is a microcosm of the spiritual life that requires literally walking the circuitous paths of the ninth-century shrine. Ascending through a long series of gateways and dim lower galleries that encircle the monument, many decorated with relief panels based upon the life and enlightenment of Gautama, the pilgrim eventually emerges from this confining space and is granted an open view of the great crowning *stupa,* encircled by seventy-two smaller *stupas,* each containing an image of the Buddha.[448] Presumably a metaphor for the path to enlightenment (or, as Tucci would say, "reintegration of consciousness"), the experience of physically climbing Borobudur is, like all successful ritual-architectural events, profoundly transformative. Moreover, as is characteristic of the contemplation mode (priority III-B), the architecture is in this case more than a backdrop; the built form plays an essential, direct, and pivotal role in that liberating transformation.

The mandala-induced transition facilitated by Borobudur, which Grapard terms "from manifestation to source . . . from form to essence,"[449] finds Western counterparts in Thomas Aquinas's dictum that "men apprehend intelligibles through sensibles" or, somewhat earlier, in Dionysius the Pseudo-Areopagite's "theory of anagogical illumination," which explains the mechanism whereby people can be transported by the "material to the immaterial."[450] Architecturally speaking, it is precisely this confidence that physical forms can expedite spiritual transformations that provides the informing notion behind Abbot Suger's innovative building program for the abbey church at St. Denis, France, "the first Gothic cathedral." In Suger's treatise on the building of St. Denis (in which he makes explicit both his intention to adapt fully the metaphysical system of the Pseudo-Areopagite to the realm of architecture and his obvious self-satisfaction in having succeeded), he relates how contemplation of the architectural elements of St. Denis, in this case the precious stones and altar ornaments, lifts him from his quotidian boundedness to "some strange region" of ethereal bliss:

> When — out of my delight in the beauty of the house of God — the loveliness of the many-colored stones has called me away from external cares, and worthy meditation has induced me to reflect, transferring that which is material to that which is immaterial, on the diversity of the sacred virtues: then it seems to me that I see myself dwelling, as it were, in some strange region of the universe which neither exists entirely in the slime of the earth nor entirely in the purity of Heaven; and that by the grace of God, I can be transported from this inferior to that higher world in an anagogical manner.[451]

Suger thus contrived at St. Denis, in every way possible, to construct an atmosphere of sumptuousness and ostentation. Borobudur, with its massive gilded surfaces, nearly two miles of narrative reliefs, and more than 500 Buddha statues, was no less flamboyant.[452] Yet, the experience of the Gothic or of Borobudur is *not* primarily of the affective, theatric sort (priority III-A); *nor* is it, in essence, like the sensations that are obliquely evoked by indefectible sanctuary spaces (priority III-D). Rather, at both Borobudur and St. Denis, the relation between the human and the architectural forms is more direct. The artistic forms are, to use Levi-Strauss's term, "effective symbols"[453] insofar as they evoke a transformative experience, an experience that Suger considered not psychological but "religious." Meditating on the shiny surfaces of the Gothic cathedral and, even more, on the light filters through the stained glass induces a trance-like state, described by Panofsky as a "spiritual illumination."[454] The constructed elements that issue from the contemplation priority are, in von Simson's phrasing, "objects of mystical contemplation . . . gateways leading the mind to ineffable truths"[455] or, in Suger's own words, "anagogical windows [that] urge us onward from the material to the immaterial."[456] Art and architecture, in this case, are not only a helpful guide to transcendence, they are indispensable — for Suger the only route to God is through material things.[457]

As yet, Mesoamericanists have done very little to explore the relevance of this sort of contemplative ritual-architectural priority (III-B) with respect to pre-Columbian building and decoration. Among notable exceptions: at the fringes, Laurette Séjourné, Irene Nicholson, and Frank Waters each employ a Jungian perspective to interpret Mesoamerican motifs, particularly Quetzalcoatl and the quincunx pattern at Teotihuacán, as mandala symbols that function as props for psychic unity and reinterpretation;[458] much earlier, Eduard Seler had interpreted the Codex Borgia, a set of hieroglyphic Mixtec paintings, after the fashion of a mandala;[459] and Eric Thompson, on occasion, described the intentionally circuitous route and manipulation of open and closed spaces in Maya planning in a manner that recalls the pilgrim's path at Borobudur.[460] The far louder strain of interpretation, however, beginning with the turn-of-the-century pioneers, has seized upon the fabulous superfluity of decoration, particularly in Maya architecture, not as possible objects of contemplation but as evidence of a *horri vacui*, or fear of space, which was generally explained by analogy to the European Baroque (an analogy that implies, among other things, that Mesoamerican decoration is primarily an expression of the theatric priority, III-A). Catherwood, for instance, experienced tremendous frustration in reproducing the ebullition of people, reptiles, flowers, and bird plumes that "oozed like voluptuous ectoplasm" out of the principal designs of Copán stelae;[461] Holmes, confronted by the convoluted mask-covered walls and flying facades at Uxmal and then by the geometric intricacies of Mitla, wondered at a "love of display" so pronounced that "at least nine-tenths of the labor expended on a building is represented in show alone";[462] and Joyce, deeply enamored of the arrangement, spacing, and perspective of Maya composition, considered that "the sole criticism which could be leveled at Maya relief art would be that the main design is often obscured by a superabundance of detail, and that the sculpture was obsessed by the *horri vacui*."[463]

While such luxuriant ornamentation assuredly does testify to an architecture of flash and drama (theatre, priority III-A), the conventional tag "Maya baroque"[464] obscures two other modes of ritual-architectural presentation that may be equally relevant. First is the propitiatory priority (III-C) and the notion that the act of elaborate construction was itself a ritual display of devotion and adoration; second is the present contemplative priority (III-B), the possibility that the exuberant decoration of Mesoamerican architecture functioned as a prop for meditation. The pursuit of this latter possibility raises this discussion to a new height of tentativeness, yet, several areas of Mesoamerica provide especially fertile grist for hermeneutical hypothesizing.

First, consider the interminable (and typologically convoluted) Maya stelae controversy. By typically counterpoising the old notion that stelae were the cosmological monuments of the time-worshipping Maya (thus foregrounding homology and astronomy, priorities I-A and I-C) versus the newer consensus that stelae are, after all, very specific political-historical documents (thus foregrounding the commemoration of sacred history and politics, priorities II-B and II-C), scholars have been slow to affirm what may have been the most important ritual function of Maya stelae — namely, their possible role as objects of contemplation and devotion (priority III-B). At Copán, for instance, where the convoluted designs on the stelae and their collateral altars so perplexed Catherwood, the simple record of dates and events (whether cosmic or historic) is so radically and systematically embellished that a direct, meditative, "mandala-like" engagement between the worshipper and monument seems more than plausible.

Furthermore, in the more strictly architectural realm, the stunningly complex facade decorations in the Zapotec-Mixtec region of Oaxaca, the Río Bec-Chenes region of Central Yucatán, and the Puuc region (which bears so directly on the southern section of Chichén Itzá, that is, "Old Chichén") provide especially pregnant candidates for meditative, contemplative ritual-architectural events. At Mitla in Oaxaca, for instance, the Mixtecs discarded the grand amphitheatric "pageant-spaces" of their distinguished neighbor and precedent, Monte Albán, but seized upon and honed the Classic Zapotec tradition of ornament into a magnificent system of geometric, fretted wall decoration; two primary elements, the key fret and the spiral fret, are combined into a "vocabulary" of eight typical forms that are ingeniously arranged and rearranged in some 150 extant panels of mosaic decoration, which cover friezes or, in some cases, whole walls.[465] Analogously, at the Puuc site of Uxmal (like the southern portion of Chichén Itzá), geometrically arranged squares of cut stone coat the buildings, and (as if the wall surfaces themselves were not space enough) flying facades that extend well above the buildings proper are likewise decked with veritable explosions of mosaic ornament.[466] Here too, a small number of "typographical elements," each carved with a geometric shape, are variously combined like puzzle pieces to compose multitiered, conventionalized faces and designs or, in some cases, giant wall-sized masks with doorways for mouths.[467] And, in the neighboring Río Bec-Chenes area, the compulsion for abstract ornamentation intensifies still more as geometric and mask facades of even greater elaboration are superimposed on "sham temples" that, though fitted with pseudo-doorways, are wholly without interior space and are accessible (or actually inaccessible) only by impossibly steep stairways.[468]

The extremity of Río Bec decoration has generally drawn dispraise. Coe, for instance, dismisses it as "fakery . . . an aberrant architectural style [in which] showiness rather than function is what was apparently sought."[469] But even the more flattering scholarly assessments of the abundant ornamentations at Mitla and Uxmal reveal almost nothing about the ritual-architectural events in which those decorations participated. Kubler, among the few who even venture an "eventful" interpretation of these elaborate facades, gamely, but with due tentativeness, submits that the various decorative motifs at Mitla may refer to different Mixtec towns or principalities and, thus, in combination, become a kind of nationalistic symbol of confederated unity (commemoration of politics, priority II-C),[470] and that the rhythmic ordering of ornament at Uxmal may somehow correspond to the complexities of Maya time computation (that is, a variation on the homology priority, I-A).[471] Kubler is, however, neither convinced nor convincing, and the possibility that these amazing facades could — by playing on the hypnotic patterns of repetition, order, and variation — lead one through a series of meditations seems at least as plausible.[472]

Providing neither sanctuaries nor theatres, this genre of effusively ornamented pre-Columbian architecture declines almost entirely to define interior space; moreover, its dedication to abstract geometric shapes suggests a patent disinterest in communicating any explicit information, whether mythic, historical, or political. This leaves contemplation (and propitiation) as the most viable ritual use(s) of this decorative exuberance, which is perhaps what Spinden intended when he wrote of this Maya decoration, "pure geometric art reacts directly upon our senses and does not appeal at all to our intelligence."[473] Thus, while it may be premature to hypothesize a strain of Mesoamerican mystical contemplation on the basis of this

East Facade of the West Building of the Nunnery Complex at Uxmal. The beauty and technical workmanship displayed by these intricate Puuc-style facades, which have strong parallels in South Chichén Itzá, have never been in doubt. The role of these lush wall carvings in pre-Columbian ritual, however, remains elusive. That they could have served as mandala-like props for contemplation or guides to meditation is a possibility that deserves more consideration. (Photo by William M. Ferguson, courtesy of the University of Texas, Austin.)

diffident argument by subtraction, it would be more rash to ignore the intriguing possibility of a neglected set of pre-Columbian contemplative ritual-architectural events (priority III-B) that began primarily at the worshipper's own instigation and that were buoyed along by deliberate concentration on architectural props for devotion. Furthermore, this line of conjecture becomes all the more significant for my reassessment of the sister-city resemblance when one notes that the southern portion of Chichén Itzá, a tangential participant of the Río Bec-Chenes-Puuc tradition of lavishly decorated architecture, has an extensive sampling of this sort of elaborate and geometric ornament[474] while, by contrast, both Tula and the northern portion of Chichén Itzá (that is, "New" or "Toltec Chichén") are almost totally without such intimations of ritual-architectural contemplation. This disparity suggests, at the very least, one more path for hermeneutical reflection worth exploring in the next chapter.

Propitiation: Building as Offering and Adoration

> Nay, I do not want marble churches at all for their own sake, but for the sake of the spirit that would build them. . . . It is not the church we want, but the sacrifice; not the emotion of admiration, but the art of adoration: not the gift, but the giving.
>
> *John Ruskin, 1848*[475]

Edward Thompson, "the Schliemann of Yucatán" and longtime owner of the hacienda that included the ruins of Chichén Itzá, provides an engaging, if largely fanciful, (re)construction of a ritual-architectural event at Chichén's Sacred Cenote that casts it almost exclusively as a desperate petition to a belligerent "No Hock Yum Chac," the Maya god of rain:

> The priestly procession, with living victims and rich offerings [passed] between the Snake-Head columns down the steps of the temple of Chichén Itzá. . . . As they approached the Sacred Well, the droning beat of the *tunkul* and the shrill notes of the whistles would have ceased, while the High Priest, from the platform of the stone shrine on the brink of the well, made an invocation to the Rain God. In slow-spoken words he would have sought to appease the offered deity, that the needed rain be once more allowed to quench the thirst of a sun-parched earth and let the green things grow that give life to the suffering people.[476]

Thompson's rendition of the Cenote ceremony, albeit enhanced by his chimerical freewheeling, is faithful to the oldest and most standard explanation of Mesoamerican ritual-architectural events: the ceremonials in the ancient "adoratorios"[477] were, so it seemed to nearly every generation of Euro-American observers, all essentially occasions for the Indians to ask for rain and to give thanks for corn.[478] To avoid accepting too easily this quasi-panacean explanation, this section reviews somewhat more critically the relationship between propitiation and sacred architecture.

As a general heuristic category, propitiatory ritual-architectural events (priority III-C) have as their priority to please and appease the sacred, whether the divine is conceived in terms of deities, apotheosized ancestors, or simply as a cosmic equilibrium. Propitiatory events, the most broadly encompassing category in the entire framework, are typically instigated by a sense of responsibility, adoration, anxiety, or, in Redfield's phrase, "just in case."[479] Stirring a whole complex of issues — offering, petition, sacrifice, fertility, worship, and atonement — the unwieldy mass of relevant data and themes is organized by a heuristic division between *the propitiatory ritual use of architecture,* a gigantic and well-respected set of events, and the somewhat more neglected sense in which *architectural construction itself is a propitiatory ritual.*

Johanna Broda, analyzing the more than eighty offertory caches from the Templo Mayor, concludes that two significantly different aspects of Aztec religion are represented.[480] The first involves the flamboyant public rituals of the state cult that were primarily concerned with the specific legitimation of Aztec authority (and, thus, stalwart exemplars of the political and theatric priorities, II-C and III-A). The second, less-glamorous aspect of Aztec religion, evidenced in the basic form of the twin pyramid and all the offerings buried inside, derives from an older, more popular pan-Mesoamerican cult of mountains, caves, and water and has as its basic cultic motivation, according to Broda, the "control of the contradictory manifestations of natural phenomena" — that is, an explicitly propitiatory priority (III-C).[481] Moreover, Broda believes that the sacralization of mountains, caves, and water, together with the related cult of maize and fertility, constitutes the "nucleus of Indian peasant religion" that remains basically intact from the Preclassic to the present,[482] a ubiquity that, among other things, ensures a nearly pan-Mesoamerican relevance for the propitiatory priority.

The endurance of this sturdy strain of "ancient nature worship" is evidenced architecturally both in the ritual burial of offertory caches that, as at the Templo Mayor, apparently accompanied virtually every major pre-Columbian construction in Central Mexico and the Mayaland,[483] as well as in countless native propitiatory rituals that required more temporary constructed ambiences. Consider, among innumerable examples, the *cha chac,* the ceremony conducted by both ancient and contemporary Maya to rouse the *chacs* who control the rain and all meteorological phenomena after their dormancy in the winter dry season. The four-day series of purifications, animal sacrifices, oblations, and offerings to the *chacs* is sometimes conducted in a cave (as, for instance, at Balankanche, an extensive system of underground caverns just 4 miles from Chichén Itzá);[484] more often, however, huts or, in some cases, simply four-sided altars, are erected expressly for the *cha chac* event and then are completely destroyed at the end of the ceremony.[485]

Mesoamerican propitiatory rituals such as the *cha chac* have usually been interpreted as occasions for human devotees to enter into conversation and negotiation with their deities. Eric Thompson, for example, long argued that, "essentially, Maya religion is a matter of a contract between man and his gods";[486] Redfield contended that Yucatec folk religion was based on a detailed "keeping of accounts" with gods, saints, and *yuntzilb* (the protectors of the fields and woods), and a "preservation of balance expressed in offering and ritual performance";[487] and, more recently, T. Lee, E. Vogt, and G. Foster each describe a "bargaining process" between Highland Maya and the supernatural.[488] All of these mercantile metaphors imply that ritual-architectural events in which propitiatory priorities dominate are occasions for religious bartering, for the buying and selling of divine favor, and thus that splendorous monuments might somehow increase one's market share of the sacred. Alternatively, however, it may be that the indigenous logic of propitiation depended, not unlike Melanesian cargo cults or Kwakiutl potlatch redistribution, on a cosmic system of mutual relatedness and equilibrium.[489] In that case, then, Mesoamericans would have been conceiving of themselves not as merchants of the sacred but as integral elements in something like a "cosmological system of circulation," who thus felt both an obligation to participate by offering and exchanging and a confidence that their actions in the human realm would "provoke a corresponding response in all associated realms."[490]

Leaving aside that important and subtle debate (together with an equally significant debate about whether Mesoamerican ritual petitions are generally aimed at deities, ancestors, or animated forces of nature),[491] the propitiation priority (III-C) has a second quite different (and less well-acknowledged) set of manifestations that involve the sense in which the *act of construction itself is an offertory ritual.* Where the seemingly obvious objective in most modern construction is to raise buildings as quickly, inexpensively, and expediently as possible,[492] the erection of sacred architecture as a propitiatory ritual espouses precisely the opposite priority — nonexpedience or, better, "transexpedience." This phenomenon of transexpedient ritual construction, never the simple means to an end, takes two principal forms: building for periodic renewal and building as a demonstration of devotion.

The first option, a favorite theme for Eliade, has been amply documented in countless contexts. In India, for instance, the elaborate ritual prescriptions applied to building materials, craftsmen, and techniques are all couched in explicit metaphors of founding a new world, and, once erected, even if structurally sound, the very brick, mortar, and timber members are subject to periodic ritual renewal.[493] The construction of the Barasana longhouse and the Oglala *hocoka* or camp circle,[494] or the "breaking to pieces" and rebuilding of a South African Tongo village following the death of a headman, among dozens of examples, have also been explicitly recognized as exercises in ritual regeneration through building.[495] In Mesoamerica the concept of periodic, transexpedient building as a regenerative process (one sort of manifestation of the propitiatory priority, III-C) has likewise been famously well documented. At the domestic level, Landa, for example, was struck by the Yucatecans' seemingly inordinate changes in residence and, moreover, by their annual compulsion for sweeping and destroying household utensils only to replace them with near-duplicates at the first of the new year.[496] On a more public scale, Tozzer wondered at the pan-Maya evidence of "an almost feverish restlessness to demolish and rebuild or to cover up a smaller by a larger construction."[497] In the Quiché region, Tovilla (1635), describing the passing of the lord of Utatlán, says that "when the king died, they rewhitened all the streets and palaces inside and out, and painted new histories."[498] In Central Mexico as well, perpetual rebuildings of perfectly serviceable structures proceeded either: (1) in conjunction with calendrical regularity — the pyramid of Tenayuca, where each of six successive campaigns of enlargement and remodeling may correspond to the conclusion of fifty-two-year calendar cycles, has been the classic example;[499] (2) with changes in leadership — the Templo Mayor, for instance, was substantially refurbished by each of seven successive Aztec rulers;[500] or (3) in some cases, on a schedule imposed by the availability of resources — the humble Otomi, for example, sedentary peasants of the high plains of Mexico, took down and replaced their temple only as often as they could afford.[501]

All these and endless other cases in Mesoamerica are testament to Eliade's theme of regeneration through ritual wreckage and rebuilding,[502] an especial compulsion given a pan-Mesoamerican cosmogonic tradition that gives the destruction of the cosmos equal time with its creation.[503] Furthermore, in addition to the ritual-architectural reenactment of cosmogony (and thus foregrounding the homology and sacred history priorities, I-A and II-B, along with propitiation, III-C), each of the preceding cases likewise demonstrates the more explicitly propitiatory character of building itself as an act of devotion. In other words, besides a participatory exercise in creation, ritual building can be a tangible expression of commitment to supernatural authority, a sign of pure adoration, or an admission of createdness. Thus, ironically, the ostentatious, the intricate, and the high in sacred architecture may actually be signs of humility and of acknowledging one's subservience in the face of the divine. In this sense, all those overscaled and elaborately ornamented architectures cited earlier as contenders for the theatric and contemplation priorities (III-A and III-B) — the Gothic cathedrals that were hundreds of years in the making, the Baroque spaces of unbelievable complexity, or the spectacular Río Bec and Puuc facades — may be, likewise, monuments to the extreme inconvenience the faithful will endure to express modesty and abasement before the sacred (that is, yet another sort of manifestation of the propitiatory priority, III-C).

There is a fabulous fund of cross-cultural evidence for such an architecture of adoration in which expedience is a totally foreign priority. Herod's essay to rebuild Zerubhabel's temple, for instance, was complicated immensely by the Jewish decision to forestall completion rather than compromise tradition by expediting the process with iron tools.[504] Inaccessibly sited Jain temples in South India apparently were built less for congregational use than as exercises in social virtue and meritous action.[505] In Navajo sandpainting, the end product is wholly valueless outside of the ritual process of its construction, and thus regretlessly destroyed.[506] And southwestern kiva wall paintings are similarly painted over at the completion of their ceremonial composition.[507] Also, there has been an enduring if tacit consensus that ancient Mesoamericans, ever nervous of their human ephemerality, built to express devotion and abasement before the gods and, more pragmatically, to demonstrate worthiness and to cultivate divine favor. Vaillant, for instance, characterized Mesoamerica as "a civilization that glorified not themselves but the gods who permitted them to exist . . . Maya and Mexican ceremonial structures were true monuments to the glory of the gods."[508] Margain, who describes their large pyramids as "devotional monuments," believed that Mesoamericans "built colossal architectural assemblages in propitiation for [gods'] favors."[509] Eric Thompson astutely considered that the act of building offered the most available opportunity to move beyond passive acquiescence to active participation in Maya religion.[510] And, more generally, the growing appreciation of Mesoamerican self-sacrifice and emasculation, particularly among the Maya, suggests that abasement before the divine was a very important component of Mesoamerican religion.[511]

The stronger evidence of Mesoamerican construction as a devotional act is, however, in the art and architecture itself. Particularly in Central Mexico, a number of structures, for instance, the gargantuan Pyramid of the Sun at Teotihuacán and the even larger pyramid at Cholula, engender respect not for their beauty or craftsmanship but for the tremendous outlay of labor that was involved.[512] At Mitla, Holmes puzzled at the fabulous intricacy of the geometric facades — "the amount of work involved was great, but these strange people were evidently not adverse to work" — and, more perplexing still, was the fact that a great deal of that artful exertion was hidden in sealed tombs.[513] There is, then, amid the justifiable charges of ostentation and panache, as Holmes was recognizing, a pervasive strain of Mesoamerican art and architecture that secretes away its best for the exclusive perusal of the divine patrons or, as at Mitla, the ancestors. That strain reverses the priority of theatric display (III-A), committing itself instead to recondite shows of devotion such as the elaborately carved downsides of sculptures that, once positioned, are forever hidden from human view (still another sort of manifestation of the propitiatory theme, priority III-C). A similar logic animates Maya murals that were stowed deep in caves, in Ian Graham's words, "like Ghirlandajo's frescoes . . . painted for the eyes of gods, not men."[514] Likewise, magnificent Olmec masks, never meant to be displayed, were buried almost immediately upon being made;[515] and, in fact, all the sumptuous artistic creations retrieved from dedicatory caches were, from a Western point of view, distressingly exempted from public view.

This strain of offertory "art for the Other" finds its most radical expression in the vigorous Mesoamerican tradition of ritual destruction.[516] Sometimes a necessary prerequisite to regenerative rebuilding (homology, priority I-A), and in other cases a brutal sign of military conquest (politics, priority II-C), the ceremonial ruination of art and architecture has a third possible motive in the desire to give human creations over to the superhuman (that is propitiation,

Pyramid of the Sun at Teotihuacán. A number of monumental pre-Columbian structures are most impressive, not because of their beauty or intricate craftsmanship but simply by virtue of their enormous size and the outlay of human labor that must have been involved. Such massive constructions may, ironically, have served as propitiatory admissions of humility before the divine. (Photo by Lawrence G. Desmond.)

priority III-C). Frequently, fine Mesoamerican ceramics and metal objects were ritually "killed," first by deliberate mutilation and then again, by being cached in offerings or burials. The vast majority of precious goods dredged from Chichén Itzá's Sacred Cenote, for instance, had endured this fate, as had much of the pottery retrieved from Maya lake sacrifices.[517] Architectural elements and, in some cases, whole buildings were similarly ritually defaced: a number of Classic Maya stelae were deliberately smashed and then buried; huge Olmec stone carvings were likewise mutilated and buried;[518] and, at Chichén Itzá, whether for military or offertory motives, several buildings were subjected to what Tozzer terms "a pre-Columbian desire to mutilate."[519] And, while it is generally conceded that the architectural carnage at Tula and Mayapán was militarily wrought, the more enigmatic destructions and abandonments of Teotihuacán and the Classic Petén Maya centers could be interpreted, albeit very tentatively, as giant-scale propitiation events.[520]

In sum then, the widely inclusive category of propitiation (priority III-C) gathers together a suspiciously disparate collection of ritual-architectural events; dedicatory caches, rain ceremonies, regenerative building programs, constructional displays of commitment and humility, and ritual destructions of art and architecture are all roped together by a shared priority of appeasement and adoration of the sacred. General enough to be relevant to virtually every religious architectural event, the propitiatory priority on occasion holds the spotlight, as in the *cha chac,* or, in other cases, is deeply submerged, as in the Aztec state cult. The concern for propitiation is sometimes allied with the commemoration of deity (priority II-A), as in those very specific calls to gods of rain and of maize. Sometimes, as with Zapotecan funerary architecture, propitiation joins with the commemoration of dead ancestors (priority II-D). At other times, propitiation works in concert with the homologized passage of time (homology, priority I-A), as in the case of regularly scheduled New Fire Ceremonies. As the final chapter shows, each of these alternative pairings arises in the history of Chichén Itzá, and, by that lurking presence and shifting pattern of alliances, the propitiatory priority (III-C) more than earns its heuristic keep in the interpretive framework.

Sanctuary: Refuges of Sacrality

> He will mark off a portion of this field by means of walls, which set up an enclosed, finite space over against amorphous, unlimited space. . . . This lesser, rebellious field, which secedes from the limitless one, and keeps to itself, is a space *sui generis* of the most novel kind, in which man frees himself from the community of the plant and the animal, leaves them outside, and creates an enclosure apart which is purely human, a civil space.
>
> *Jose Ortega y Gasset, 1951*[521]

In the traditional foundation legend of Rome, Romulus plows a circular ditch, the *sulcus primigenius,* which designates the configuration of the city walls. When his twin, Remus, flippantly jumps over the furrow, Romulus immediately slays him and premonishes, "thus perish any who leaps over my walls." The furrow was deserving of reverence because it marked an inviolate boundary that circumscribed a sacred precinct within the profane landscape.[522] Analogously, the camp circle of the Oglala Indians, the *hocoka,* demarcated a space inside which everything was irrefutably Oglala, safe, knowable, and auspicious; outside the *hocoka* were the enemies, the inconsistencies of everyday life, the evil spirits, and later, Europeans.[523] The stone circles of the British Isles have been interpreted similarly, not only as demarcations of sacred from profane space but also as spiritual barriers that prevent the ghosts of those buried within the circle from leaving their graves.[524] In this sense, Rome, the *hocoka,* and Stonehenge each epitomize the final entry to the typological framework: an architecture that encloses space, carving from the generalized pedestrian environment a hermetic refuge of sacrality, a retreat from the mundane — that is, sanctuary, priority III-D.

The creation of sanctuary spaces, which is relatively inconsequential for outward-looking designs, becomes the first priority in building agenda of containment, control, and exclusion. For instance, the Hellenistic architecture, which Scully applauds for its reciprocal and collaborative relationship with nature (its "outward-looking design"), stands in radical contrast to Roman building that, in general, aimed for complete disconnectedness from the landscape. In Scully's words, "Roman theatres, like those at Orange in southern France and Aspendos in Asia Minor, were intended, like most Roman buildings, to provide an enclosed experience totally shut away from the outside world."[525] In a military empire like that of Rome, the objectives of security and dominion ascend to priority so that, unlike the Classic Greek temple's analogy to the attributes of a deity (commemoration of divinity, priority II-A), the Roman temple is rigidly symmetrical, logical, self-sufficient, and bastioned (thus epitomizing the sanctuary priority, III-D).[526] Scully explains that the fabric of the Roman structure is no longer itself holy; nor do the Roman architectural forms serve worshippers directly as props for contemplation (priority III-B), as in the case of the Gothic cathedral. Instead, as is characteristic of the sanctuary priority, the Roman temple works *in*directly to create ritual ambience — it simply encloses space. The temple at Lykosoura, for instance, "is in no way intended to be a solemn physical embodiment of its god but is purely a shell enclosing space . . . the volume of space to be created . . . is the determinant of the design."[527]

Deliberately rejecting the exhortatory Gothic machinations of his contemporary, Abbot Suger, in favor of privacy and seclusion, the building agenda of Saint Bernard of Clairvaux and his Cistercians was likewise dominated by the sanctuary priority (III-D).[528] For Saint Bernard, the church was not, in essence, "the house of God"; rather, the church was an oratorium, the place of the soul's communion with God, and the monastery was a pristine, autonomous refuge wherein all energies were enlisted in perfect conformity to the Rule of St. Benedict.[529] The simplicity and geometrical clarity of Bernard's plan for Clairvaux (which was repeated in some 742 Cistercian monasteries, virtually all of which were located at remote rural sites) were intended to facilitate a perfectly disciplined life exempted from the corruption and distractions of the worldly mainstream.[530] Life in the Cistercian cloister was ideally an image and foretaste of paradise, an ideal that Bernard termed *"paradisus claustralis."*[531] Bernard thus vehemently spurned both the spectactorial inclusiveness of Cluniac decoration, sculpture, stained glass, and towers (ritual-architectural ideals consonant with the theatric priority, III-A) and Suger's anagogical logic that material art forms are the essential vehicles to spiritual illumination (contemplation, priority III-B). By contrast, Bernard extolled the more exclusivistic ideals of poverty, retreat from the world, and a renewed spirit of Benedictine regulation (goals that reflect the preeminence of the sanctuary priority, III-D).[532]

The priorities of detachment and isolation are manifest even more radically in the medieval French Charterhouses, where Carthusian hermits literally pass their entire solitary existences in architectural cells or envelopes.[533] And, among countless cross-cultural examples, the Cretan palace at Knossos, patterned after Minos' labyrinth and, thus, so complex in plan that neither the Minotaur nor his victims could find their way out, is another gem of hermetic architecture.[534] An even more intriguing variation on the sanctuary theme comes, however, in the architecturization of the Japanese concept of *ma*. *Ma* refers to the "interval" between two (or more) spatial or temporal things or events; thus, it carries meanings such as gap, opening, space between, or — like the related term, *kekkai* — areas of "pregnant nothing."[535] According to Richard Pilgrim, Japanese architecture prizes the intervals and gaps between buildings because, by their openness and purity, these are the spaces most receptive to *ki*, or the spiritual power of *kami:* "Although these spaces may be located within shrine buildings or, for example, caves, their paradigmatic model is the cleared out, white rock-covered spaces surrounding shrines or even predating shrines — spaces variously referred to as *shiki, yuniwa, iwakura, tamajari,* and *kekki.*"[536] Especially in ancient Shinto, these spaces often framed a single tree, rock, or pillar, which acted as a magnet or target for the sacred power of *kami*. In the words of Matsuoka Seigow, "rather than not know at all where *kami* might make its temporary appearance, our ancestors took to demarcating an 'area of *kami*' by enclosing a particular space with twisted rope thus sanctifying it in preparation for the visit of *kami*. This area was called *kekkai*."[537] In *ma*-inspired architecture, then, all obstacles are cleared away, all distractions silenced; space is opened up, cleared out, and purified in anticipation of the coming and going of *kami;* a gap or crevice is created in the mundane, a "negative space," a sacred *ma,* a vacuum into which rushes the formless energy *(ki)* of *kami*.[538]

The characteristically sculptural architecture of Mesoamerica, exceptional by its concentration on monumental, exterior volumes and the relative scarcity of interior spaces, might at first appear the very antithesis of exclusivistic, hermetic sacred architecture, as though pre-Columbian architects were largely uninterested in the sanctuary priority (III-D). With even a little probing, however, Mesoamerica, beginning with a remarkable and enduring strain of ritual-architectural events that exploit naturally formed sanctuaries — especially caves, which are tremendously important in pre-Columbian religion[539] — displays an exceedingly diversified oeuvre of architectural refuges of sacrality, with counterparts for virtually every manifestation of the priority just discussed. For heuristic sake, a sampling of the wealth of Mesoamerican sanctuary spaces can be surveyed according to: (1) fenced-in enclosures, defined mainly by thin-walled construction, (2) courtyards or plazas bounded by impressive masses such as pyramids and platforms, and (3) chambered buildings and roofed volumes such as colonnades.[540]

The first set of options — open-air, fenced-in enclosures — is instantiated at every scale, from the walling of whole pre-Columbian cities downward. The function of Mesoamerica's abundant city walls and huge triumphant arches — are they defensive or "symbolic"? — has been endlessly debated;[541] yet, accounts such as that of the long and rigorous ritual purification process demanded of the Quiché militia before they could reenter the gates of their own city of Utatlán attest that, generally speaking, the defensive character of the walls was exceeded by a more explicitly religious function similar to that on which Romulus had insisted at Rome.[542] At an intermediate scale, the great sunken plaza of the ancient Olmec site of La Venta in Vera Cruz, roughly 60 by 75 meters, is delimited literally and definitively by an intimidating row of close-set, hexagonal basalt columns.[543] And the *coatepantli,* or serpent wall, surrounding the ceremonial precinct at both Tula and Tenochtitlán, provides an equally straightforward, unambiguous cordoning of sacred space from the wider city.[544] Somewhat more prosaically, Lacandon Indians in Chiapas, even now, in a daily display of reverence, routinely clean their feet before crossing an unseen but very real boundary and embarking to work in the sacred enclave of the milpa field.[545] And, at the most modest level, the *emku,* for instance, the Yucatán coming-of-age ceremony described minutely by Landa, could proceed only in a temporarily "walled" space delimited, like the Japanese *kekkai,* by four *chac* priests holding a rope.[546]

Along the same lines, although relying on more subtle strategies than actual fencing, the builders of some Mesoamerican cities, especially in the lush tropical regions, announced an inviolate boundedness from the wider surroundings by means of "artificially" rigid straight lines, constructions of stark plain stone, and red-colored platforms and pyramids, all of which established sharp contrasts with the curved and leafy green natural setting. "In this way," according to Broda, "ancient Mesoamerican architecture created an artificial order in contraposition to nature; it imposed a new structure, a 'human order' upon the 'natural order'"[547] — a ritual-architectural strategy of clearly distinguishing

Arch at Labná, in the Puuc region of west central Yucatán. Elaborate archways and remnants of walls at several of the Puuc Maya sites seem less likely to have served as defensive fortifications than as symbolic boundaries, which clearly separated a sacred precinct from the wider, more prosaic surrounding areas. (Photo by the author.)

between culture and nature that may find a European parallel in the Parisian revetments, which, in Frampton's unsubtle description, protected "the 'civilization' of the city from the 'idiocy' of the countryside."[548]

The second set of options — open precincts formed by the arrangement of surrounding buildings or platforms — served not only to differentiate the city from the wilds in general but, moreover, to articulate complex religio-spatial hierarchies within individual pre-Columbian sites. The Nunnery Complex at Uxmal, for instance where four inward-looking range structures enclose a quadrangular courtyard, and the Great Plaza of Monte Albán, similarly surrounded by inward-oriented buildings that completely close off the potentially spectacular outward vistas, constitute especially tightly controlled ceremonial precincts within the already sacred totality of their respective ceremonial centers.[549] Whether these sorts of uncluttered spaces engendered between and among pre-Columbian buildings are, in any significant sense, parallel to the "pregnant nothings" of *ma*-inspired Japanese architecture, or whether those open-air courtyards were conceived as anything like "targets" for a Mesoamerican counterpart to *ki*-like spiritual energy, remains intriguing (and as-yet untested) topics for hermeneutical reflection.

As Kubler emphasizes, this initiative to delineate religio-spatial hierarchies within a single city by juxtaposing bulky volumes and open spaces is reflected in the vertical as well as the horizontal layout of sites in both the Mexican and Maya regions, particularly in the Early Classic period.[550] Differentiation by height — "a cardinal objective of the American Indian architect in all periods and all regions"[551] — was achieved occasionally by genuine superimposition of stories (for instance, in the Palace at Palenque) or, more typically, by augmenting natural contours with extensive earth sculpting and platform constructions. At Xochicalco, for example, the entire mountain site was refashioned into a magnificent escalating series of courtyards, each screened from the other, as if to define a veritable hierarchy of sacred, more sacred, and most sacred spaces.[552]

Though pre-Columbian architecture, generally speaking, has very limited interior spaces, a third, somewhat more obvious set of manifestations of the sanctuary priority (III-D) includes roofed volumes such as colonnades together with actual rooms or cave-like chambers.[553] In the central Maya area (and in the southern portion of Chichén Itzá), whether constrained by engineering or convention, the construction of interior rooms never advanced beyond the heavy-walled, exceedingly small, cell-like cloisters of Palenque.[554] The incongruity of dark little temple spaces atop megatherian platforms has led, reasonably enough, to conjectures that the attendant ritual events were of the most exclusive and esoteric sort. Eric Thompson, for instance, opined that "much of the [Classic Maya] ritual, there is reason to believe, took place inside the temple where there was room for only a handful of priests or chiefs; congregational participation must have been almost nil."[555] This same pattern of rigid socio-religious exclusion and hierarchy (characteristic of the sanctuary priority, III-D) is even more clear in the two-room plan of the Zapotec *yohepèe,* literally the "house of *pè*" (that is, wind, breath, or spirit). Reminiscent of the Temple of Herod, in which the prepotent Inner Court was reserved exclusively for Jews and separated by a balustrade from the lesser Court of Gentiles,[556] the outer room of the *yohepèe* was open to people who wished to make an offering, but the actual sacrifice was performed on an altar called *pecogo* or *pe-quie* (stone of *pè*) in a second, "more sacred" room to which no layman was ever admitted but which the priests rarely left.[557]

Likewise, this sort of fully enclosed ritual-architectural expression of the sanctuary priority (III-D) is evident in a whole series of more transient, special-use constructions: the Yucatán Maya, for instance, deem it necessary to construct annually a thatched hut in the forest that is used exclusively as a controlled environment in which to carve and store idols;[558] and in Guatemala, the Quiché Maya would specially construct a *raxaja,* or "green house" (so named because this temporary hut was kept ever-new and pure with fresh leaves that were continually replaced as they dried out), where a solitary priest would do penance for up to a year, bleeding himself and offering gifts to the deities.[559] In a similar set of variations on the theme of sanctification via architecture, the continence and fasting that are prerequisite to all Maya ceremonies were (and are) facilitated by quartering the participants in isolation beforehand: Las Cass, for instance, reports that the Maya in Guatemala were "accustomed to separate from their wives and take up residence in special men's houses near the temples for 60, 80, or even 100 days before some great festival"; and Landa says that before major ceremonies in Yucatán, "all had to sleep, not in their homes, but in houses that for the time of the penance were near the temples."[560] As is evident in Cogolludo's mocking remarks about the seventeenth-century Maya, even the simplest domestic dwellings must be ritually segregated from their profane surroundings: "whenever they made new houses, that is every ten or twelve years, they won't enter or live in them until an old sorcerer comes from a distance of one, two, or three leagues to bless them with silly charms."[561]

In sum, the sanctuary priority (III-D) constitutes the final entry to this heuristic framework, the last lap in our preparatory hermeneutical calisthenics. As with each previous category, the sanctuary priority displays itself in countless permutations. Natural cave sanctuaries, targets for spiritual energy, juxtaposed volumes and voids, city walls, regenerative seclusions, eremitical refuges, spatializations of exclusion and hierarchy, and fabricated foretastes of heaven are all looped together as manifestations of a shared priority to isolate the sacred from the mundane.

By this delineation of variations within thematic priorities, subpriorities within priorities, the framework of ritual-architectural priorities has exposed, not eleven, but dozens of alternative means for exploiting the superabundant potentialities of sacred architecture and dozens of conceptions of the relatednesses between architecture and ritual. If at times tedious, this practice in cross-cultural foraging and in morphological comparison according to ritual-architectural priorities improves our chances for delivering fresh interpretations of the old problem of Tula–Chichén Itzá similitude. With this broadly comparative background, we return to that more specific comparative problem and those two sites as more able hermeneutical conversation partners, better equipped with heuristic questions and more well prepared to appreciate the answers that the monuments speak.

Notes

1. Landa, *Relación,* 170–71.

2. Davíd Carrasco, *Religions of Mesoamerica: Cosmovision and Ceremonial Centers* (San Francisco: Harper & Row, 1990), 30, for instance, advisedly uses the term "mute texts" to refer to "stones, sacred stones, ceremonial architecture, pottery, and even human bones."

3. Circumscribing this project by concentrating on one sort of evidence — namely, architecture — conforms to a timeworn, albeit untoward, tradition in Maya studies. Even the most prolific Mayanists have, in the main, focused their efforts on a single dimension of the pre-Columbian resources. Brunhouse, *Sylvanus G. Morley,* 85, for instance, describes how when Sylvanus Morley and Herbert Spinden traveled shoulder-to-shoulder through Yucatán, the former scoped in on hieroglyphic inscriptions while the latter fixed his gaze on the art and architecture. Eric Thompson, in his introduction to Spinden's *Study of Maya Art,* Dover ed., viii, remarks on Spinden's ineptness with archaeological materials other than art and architecture. Similarly, in Spinden's review of Morley, *The Ancient Maya,* in *American Historical Review* 53 (1947): 92, he holds that Morley was, for all his breadth of interest, "first and last a student of inscriptions and calculations in the famous calendar"; and Brainerd's review of the same work, *American Antiquity* 14 (1948): 135, criticizes Morley for the "disproportionate weight" he attributed to epigraphic data and for his neglect of ceramic data, particularly as the basis for chronology. Woodbury, *Alfred V. Kidder,* 73, appropriately cites Eric Thompson as the great and rare example of a Mayanist who was able to conquer several realms of data.

4. David Freidel's comments on the idiosyncratic capabilities and limitations of various sorts of data for retrieving the ancient Maya and the necessity of "cross-correlation of artifact categories" are very relevant to this notion of "data of priority." Freidel writes, "each major artifact category [for instance, pottery, axes, monumental art, and architecture] can thus provide a different cultural geography when mapped out across the lowlands"; see Freidel, "New Light on a Dark Age," 308–9. Similarly, with respect to the issue of Toltec and Puuc "overlap" in the Northern Lowlands, Andrews and Sabloff, "Classic to Postclassic," 449–50, discuss complications implied by the fact that "different classes of material

culture [particularly architecture and art versus ceramics] may not be telling us the same things and that the association between them cannot be assumed."

5. Walker quoted in *Palenque: The Walker-Caddy Expedition*, ed. Pendergast, 176.

6. Bernal, *History of Mexican Archaeology*, 176, following Kidder's assessment, maintains that the purely epigraphic study, especially of Morley, is what sparked all the other types of work in Maya studies. Klein, "Relation of Art History to Archaeology," 2; and Hammond, "Lords of the Jungle," 14, 18, also comment on the significance of epigraphy in early Maya studies.

7. Paul Schellhas, "Fifty Years of Maya Research: 1885–1936," *Maya Research* 3 (April 1936): 129–39. Schellhas's work is actually restricted to hieroglyphs in manuscripts and excludes stelae glyphs.

8. See Coe, *Breaking the Maya Code*.

9. I have discussed the significance of the discovery of stratigraphy more fully in Chapter 2 in the section on "Organization by Time: The Enthronement of Chronology."

10. Wauchope, *They Found Buried Cities*, 12. Other succinct eulogies to pottery as the data of priority include: Brainerd, *Maya Civilization*, 13; Morley, *Ancient Maya*, 2d ed., 367; Woodall, *Introduction to Modern Archaeology*, 26–27, 49; and Anna O. Shepard, *Ceramics for the Archaeologist*, Publication 609 (Carnegie Institution of Washington: 1968.

11. Satterthwaite, "Notes on Museum Expedition to Piedras Negras," 86.

12. Von Hagen, *World of the Maya*, 78; and Kubler, "Period, Style and Meaning," 14–15.

13. Freidel, "New Light on a Dark Age," 293. Unfortunately, the paucity of stratigraphic trash mounds in the Maya area, particularly in northern Yucatán, where the limestone has only a thin soil covering (and even more at Chichén Itzá, where that slim record was neglected in the original excavation), has been a chronic problem. For instance, Tozzer, "Maya Research," complains in the thirties of the disparity between the Maya zone and the Valley of Mexico in this regard; Taylor, *A Study of Archaeology*, 52–56, laments "the scarcity of stratigraphic excavation in the Maya area as a whole . . . [and] the readiness with which stratigraphic excavation was abandoned for a mound"; and Benson, *Maya World*, 90–91, remarks that the scarcity of Maya middens has made caches and burials the richest finds for Maya archaeologists.

14. José Antonio de Alzate, quoted by Bernal, *History of Mexican Archaeology*, 77.

15. Catherwood, *Views of Ancient Monuments*, 119.

16. Holmes, *Ancient Cities of Mexico*, 21.

17. Le Plongeon, quoted by Tompkins, *Mysteries of the Mexican Pyramids*, xvii.

18. Taylor, A *Study of Archaeology*, 55–57, 64, notes particularly Alfred Kidder's awareness of the Carnegie program's unbalance and his frustrated attempts as director to change directions. Thompson, "Archaeological Problems of the Lowland Maya," 132, 135; Deuel, *Conquistadors Without Swords*, 319–20; and Bernal, *History of Mexican Archaeology*, 175–76; all comment on the Carnegie's inordinate concentration on monumental architecture, particularly at Chichén Itzá.

19. Chapter 3 of this project is a highly abbreviated version of Lindsay Jones, *The Hermeneutics of Sacred Architecture: Experience, Interpretation, and Comparison*, unpublished working manuscript, which accentuates the pre-Columbian Mesoamerican evidence.

20. Anita Abramovitz, *People and Spaces* (New York: Viking Press, 1979), 5.

21. John W. Dixon Jr., "The Christology of Michelangelo: The Sistine Chapel," *Journal of the American Academy of Religion* 55 (Fall 1987): 503.

22. Hans-Georg Gadamer, "Aesthetics and Hermeneutics," reprinted in *Philosophical Hermeneutics*, trans. and ed. David E. Linge (Berkeley: University of California Press, 1976), 103. Gadamer's work, as will soon become evident, is the primary inspiration for the first portion of this chapter.

23. David E. Klemm, *Hermeneutical Inquiry* (Atlanta: Scholars Press, 1986), 2: 2.

24. The flipside of hermeneutics involves appreciating the strangeness of the familiar, for instance, the ways in which the study of pre-Columbian Mesoamerica awakens us not only to insights about *them* (as "the other") but, moreover, to the "othernesses" of ourselves as well.

25. Gerardus van der Leeuw, in his famous "Epilegomena" to *Religion in Essence and Manifestation*, trans. J. E. Turner (Gloucester, Mass.: Peter Smith, 1967), 675–76, argues, on the basis of his reading of Edmund Husserl, that "phenomenology . . . is not a method that has been reflectively elaborated, but is man's true vital activity." However, on the negative side, van der Leeuw has been criticized for "hovering above objects like a god," which is precisely

antithetical to the sort of hermeneutics being espoused in this section; see Charles Long, *Significations: Signs, Symbols, and Images in the Interpretation of Religion* (Philadelphia: Fortress Press, 1986), 41.

26. See Hans-Georg Gadamer, "Aesthetic and Religious Experience," reprinted in *The Relevance of the Beautiful and Other Essays,* trans. Nicholas Walker, ed. with an intro. by Robert Bernasconi (Cambridge: Cambridge University Press, 1986), 141.

27. Hans-Georg Gadamer, "On the Problem of Self-Understanding," reprinted in *Philosophical Hermeneutics,* ed. Linge, 46.

28. See Friederich Schleiermacher, "The Christian Faith" (1830); reprinted in Klemm, *Hermeneutical Inquiry,* 1: 13–24. On Schleiermacher's pioneering role for modern hermeneutics, see Klemm, *Hermeneutical Inquiry,* 1: 1–60; 2: 1–13. Klemm's reflections, together with the major works on hermeneutics, which he collects in this book, have been very important in the formulation of this section.

29. Klemm, ibid., 2: 2, locates the real turning point for the "universalization of the hermeneutical problem" in Heidegger's *Being and Time* (1927); but he argues that, having now come to the notion of a "hermeneutics of existence," it is possible to read it back also into the earlier tradition of modern hermeneutics, that is, Schleiermacher and Dilthey. On the universalizing dimension of Schleiermacher's hermeneutics, also see Gadamer, "Aesthetic and Religious Experience," 141; idem, "On the Scope and Function of Hermeneutical Reflection," reprinted in *Philosophical Hermeneutics,* ed. Linge, 23; and Paul Ricouer, "Existence and Hermeneutics," reprinted in Klemm, *Hermeneutical Inquiry,* 2: 186.

30. According to Dilthey, "inner reality" *(Erlebnis),* or the immediate experience of a self relating to the world, is intrinsically meaningful by virtue of a primordial thinking process or capacity for understanding, and this process "extends over the whole of life and relates to any kind of speech or writing." Wilhelm Dilthey, "The Development of Hermeneutics" (1900); reprinted in Klemm, *Hermeneutical Inquiry,* 1: 93–105. See Klemm, ibid., 1: 89–92, on Dilthey's attempt to universalize Schleiermacher.

31. See the excerpt from Heidegger's *Being and Time* together with Klemm's commentary in *Hermeneutical Inquiry,* 2: 83–112, and Gadamer's extensive remarks on Heidegger, particularly in *Philosophical Hermeneutics,* pt. 2. David E. Linge's Introduction to *Philosophical Hermeneutics* is also very useful in deciphering Heidegger's complex philosophy.

32. See Linge, Introduction to *Philosophical Hermeneutics,* xi.

33. See Bernal, *History of Mexican Archaeology,* 144. This was discussed in Chapter 2 in relation to "Traditional Archaeology: Beyond Antiquarianism."

34. Gadamer, "On the Problem of Self-Understanding"; reprinted in *Philosophical Hermeneutics,* ed. Linge, 50, explores this dimension of Heidegger's philosophy more fully.

35. Charles Long, *Significations,* 44, summarizes Heidegger's universalizing agenda this way but implies that Heidegger has not taken history seriously enough.

36. See Linge, Introduction to *Philosophical Hermeneutics,* xxxvi.

37. Gadamer, "On the Problem of Self-Understanding," 49, uses this formulation to describe Heidegger. Klemm, *Hermeneutical Inquiry,* 2: 83, discusses the sense in which Heidegger's conception of hermeneutics as "fundamental ontological thinking" is more than a methodology.

38. Klemm's discussion of hermeneutics as "practical philosophy" and as "speculative ontology" (ibid., 1: 37–44) is exceedingly relevant to and supportive of this concept of a universalized hermeneutics. By contrast, Paul Ricouer is unwilling to push hermeneutics into the realm of practical philosophy and speculative ontology and thus develops a complex critique of Heidegger's universalizing notion of hermeneutics. See Ricouer, "Existence and Hermeneutics"; reprinted in Klemm, *Hermeneutical Inquiry,* 2: 185–202.

39. On Gadamer's debt to Heidegger, see, for instance, Linge, Introduction to *Philosophical Hermeneutics,* xlix-l. Linge holds that "Gadamer's principle contribution to hermeneutics is to be found in his concerted effort to shift the focus of discussion away from techniques and methods of interpretation, all of which assume understanding to be the deliberate product of self-conscious reflection, to the clarification of understanding as an event that in its very nature is *episodic* and *trans-subjective.*" Ibid., xxviii.

40. Hans-Georg Gadamer, "The Universality of the Hermeneutical Problem"; reprinted in *Philosophical Hermeneutics,* ed. Linge, 15.

41. Klemm, *Hermeneutical Inquiry,* 1: xii, lauds hermeneutics as "a new paradigm of reflection."

42. Some exceptions that do attempt to combine hermeneutical approaches with Mesoamerican

materials include: Charlotte Zimmerman, "The Hermeneutics of the Maya Cult of the Cross," *Numen* 12 (April 1965): 139–59; Willard Gingerich, "Heidegger and the Aztecs: The Poetics of Knowing in Pre-Hispanic Nahuatl Poetry," in *Recovering the Word: Essays on Native American Literature,* ed. Brian Swann and Arnold Krupat (Berkeley: University of California Press, 1987), 85–112; and Harald Johnsen and Bjornar Olsen, "Hermeneutics and Archaeology: Philosophy and Contextual Archaeology," *American Antiquity* 57 (1992): 419–36.

43. Elizabeth P. Benson, "Architecture as Metaphor," 188.

44. Alan Morinis and N. Ross Crumrine, "La Peregrinación: The Latin American Pilgrimage," in *Pilgrimage in Latin America,* ed. Alan Morinis and N. Ross Crumrine (New York: Greenwood Press, 1991), 7.

45. I borrow this phrase from Hans-Georg Gadamer, *Truth and Method,* trans. W. Glen-Doepel (London: Sheed and Ward, 1975), 280, where he is speaking of the inexhaustibility of texts.

46. Heidegger, *Holzwege;* quoted by Linge, Introduction to *Philosophical Hermeneutics,* liii.

47. Hans-Georg Gadamer, "The Relevance of the Beautiful," reprinted in *The Relevance of the Beautiful,* ed. Bernasconi, 31–34, explains "symbolic" as half-revealed and half-concealed.

48. Gadamer, "Aesthetics and Hermeneutics," 96.

49. See Gadamer, *Truth and Method,* 119, 138–42, for explicit remarks on architecture that are brief and difficult.

50. This dual participation of architecture in utility and in art is explored more fully in this chapter in "The Special Case of Architecture."

51. Philippe Borgeaud, "The Open Entrance to the Closed Palace of the King: The Greek Labyrinth in Context," *History of Religions* 14 (August 1974): 26. Borgeaud discussed the experience of the Greek labyrinth as an initiation, a circumstance that could aptly be considered a "ritual-architectural event."

52. I steal this line from Heidegger's polemic against the existence of timeless "objects."

53. George Baird, "'La Dimension Amoureuse' in Architecture," in *Meaning in Architecture,* ed. Charles Jencks and George Baird (New York: George Braziller, 1970), 79–100, addresses the problem of the autonomy and superabundance of architecture from a different angle when he castigates Walter Gropius's notion of a "total architecture" that would presume to control and predetermine totally the experience of an environment as an exercise in both arrogance and futility. Alan Colquhoun, "Typology and Design Method," also in *Meaning in Architecture,* ed. Jencks and Baird, 267–68, 274–76, discusses a number of other modern architects who espouse "objective," "determinist," or "functionalist" design methods.

54. Gillo Dorflores, "Structuralism and Semiology in Architecture," in *Meaning in Architecture,* ed. Jencks and Baird, 44.

55. In Paris, for instance, the Pontes of St. Denis and St. Martin have long lost their intended meanings as gateways to the city, but have since become landmarks related to the festive atmosphere of their districts; and the Parc Monceau rotunda, once a port of entry for taxing imported goods, has ceded its economic significance and become the gate to a park for recreation and leisure. Francoise Choay, "Urbanism and Semiology," in *Meaning in Architecture,* ed. Jencks and Baird, 31.

56. See Heyden, "Caves, Gods, and Myths"; and Doris Heyden, "An Interpretation of the Cave Underneath the Pyramid of the Sun in Teotihuacán, Mexico," *American Antiquity* 40 (April 1975): 131–47, on the cave discovered beneath the Pyramid of the Sun.

57. Erwin Panofsky's influential study of the medieval reclamation of the art forms of classical antiquity (discussed last chapter in reference to ethnohistory and the dangers of ethnographic analogy) also illustrates that the hinge between architectural form and meaning is never locked tight. See Kubler, "Period, Style and Meaning," 22, for a concise summary of Panofsky's "principle of disjunction" as it applies to Mesoamerica.

58. There are passing remarks about the attitudes of Chan Kom villagers toward Chichén Itzá and the American archaeologists who worked there (and who are, in some cases, identified with the Itzá, Chac Uincob, or Red People) in Robert Redfield, *Folk Culture in Yucatán* (Chicago: University of Chicago Press, 1941), 14, 45, 158, 308, 311; and Robert Redfield and Alfonso Villa Rojas, *Chan Kom: A Maya Village* (Chicago: University of Chicago Press, 1934), 6, 12, 30, 206. A fuller but still brief account appears in Robert Redfield, *A Village That Chose Progress: Chan Kom Revisited* (Chicago: University of Chicago Press, 1950), 13–19.

59. Gann, *In an Unknown Land,* 32–34. In the same vein, Gann, ibid., 137, for instance, discusses the use of ruined temples at Cozumel as "drying

houses for their tobacco"; and Stephens, *Incidents of Travel in Yucatán,* 1: 196–98, corroborates Cogolludo's sixteenth-century allusions to Indians burning incense and making offerings at ruins of Uxmal with his own observations there 200 years later.

60. Evidence of such practices continues to be common at the remote sections of Chichén Itzá, and even more so at Maya ruins all through Guatemala.

61. Johanna Broda, "Templo Mayor as Ritual Space."

62. Gadamer, "Composition and Interpretation"; reprinted in *Relevance of the Beautiful,* ed. Bernasconi, 69, for instance, notes that "we have only to interpret that which has a multiplicity of meanings."

63. Anthony Blunt, "The Iberian Peninsula and the New World," in *Baroque and Rococo: Architecture and Decoration,* ed. Anthony Blunt (New York: Harper & Row, 1978), 311–12.

64. Carmack, *Quiché Maya,* 182–83.

65. J. C. Friedrick von Schiller, *On the Aesthetic Education of Man,* trans. with intro. by Reginald Snell, (New York: F. Unger, 1965), 79.

66. Gadamer, "On the Problem of Self-Understanding," 53.

67. Husserl, *Idea of Phenomenology;* quoted in Walter L. Brenneman, Stanley O. Yarin, in association with Alan M. Olson, *The Seeing Eye: Hermeneutical Phenomenology in the Study of Religion* (University Park: Pennsylvania State University Press, 1982), 80.

68. Gadamer invokes Heidegger's distinction between "objectifying reflection" (the Cartesian position) and "non-objectifying awareness" (Heidegger's alternative) in his own exposition of the experience of a work of art as an exercise in hermeneutical reflection. See *Truth and Method,* 91 et seq.; also see Linge, Introduction to *Philosophical Hermeneutics,* li.

69. Linge foregrounds the metaphors of conversation and play in Gadamer's work. Ibid., xix–xx. Gadamer follows Schleiermacher in taking "significant conversation" as the model of understanding. For Schleiermacher, "hermeneutics is a theory of understanding that takes the communication existing between friends as a standard for more sophisticated reflections on human texts"; see Klemm, *Hermeneutical Inquiry,* 1: 57–58. Gadamer, *Truth and Method,* 97–105, 462–65, is his definitive discussion of "play" or "game" as the most appropriate metaphor for the process of understanding, but he summarizes those thoughts repeatedly; "On the Problem of Self-Understanding," 53–54; and "Man and Language," 66 — both reprinted in *Philosophical Hermeneutics* — are two succinct cases.

70. Gadamer, *Truth and Method,* 104.

71. Gadamer, "On the Problem of Self-Understanding," 53.

72. Gadamer, *Truth and Method,* 118; also see Hans-Georg Gadamer, "The Festival Character of Theatre"; reprinted in *Relevance of the Beautiful,* ed. Bernasconi, 58–59.

73. Gary Witherspoon, "Beautifying the World Through Art (Navajo)," in *Native North American Art History,* ed. Z. P. Mathews and A. Jonaitis (Palo Alto, Calif.: Peek Publications, 1982), 208.

74. Hans-Georg Gadamer, "The Play of Art"; reprinted in *Relevance of the Beautiful,* ed. Bernasconi, 130.

75. Gadamer, *Truth and Method,* 92.

76. Gadamer, "Man and Language," 66.

77. Gadamer, *Truth and Method,* 95.

78. Ibid., 92.

79. Borgeaud, "The Greek Labyrinth in Context," 5.

80. I. W. Mabbett, "The Symbolism of Mount Meru," *History of Religions* 23 (August 1983): 68.

81. Richard Townsend, "Coronation at Tenochtitlán."

82. In Grapard's words, the Buddhist experience of pilgrimage along a sacred network of roads or through a mandala-temple involved processes that were "complex and had to become the basis for a complete change in the pilgrim's consciousness and perspective on the universe. The pilgrimage was an exercise in rebirth and magical transformation"; Allan Grapard, "Flying Mountains and Walkers of Emptiness: Toward a Definition of Sacred Space in Japanese Religions," *History of Religions* 20 (February 1982): 206. Note that Heidegger and Gadamer conceive of the experience of art and architecture not as transformative of "consciousness and perspective" but of "ontological being."

83. Konrad Oberhuber's Preface to Gottfried Richter, *Art and Human Consciousness,* trans. Burley Channer and Margaret Frohlich (Spring Valley, N.Y.: Anthroposophic Press, 1985), xi.

84. Adrian Stokes, *Smooth and Rough* (London: Faber and Faber Limited, 1951), 55. Also see idem, *The Invitation in Art* (London: Tavistock Publications, 1965), 45, where Stokes holds that "building is the most extensive and unavoidable of man-made things. Hence, architecture once again is seen as the mother of the arts."

85. See, for instance, Bernard Rudofsky, *The Prodigious Builders: Notes Toward a Natural History of Architecture With Special Regards to Those Species That Are Traditionally Neglected or Downright Ignored* (New York: Harcourt Brace Jovanovich, 1977), 62; and Yi-Fu Tuan's praise of termites, *Space and Place: The Perspective of Experience* (Minneapolis: University of Minnesota Press, 1977), 101–2.

86. Gadamer, *Truth and Method,* 402–3.

87. Alan Olson, "Unfolding the Enfolding: Hermeneutics and Mysticism," in Brenneman, Yarin, and Olson, *The Seeing Eye* (University Park: Pennsylvania State University Press, 1982), 45. This highly subjective, "world-expanding" perception of space and of one's environment (a formulation of which Gadamer would not approve) has been discussed endlessly, particularly by psychologists of perception. For a smattering of good ideas on this theme, see E. H. Gombrich, *Art and Illusion: A Study in the Psychology of Pictorial Representation,* 2d ed. (Princeton: Princeton University Press, 1972), intro. and Chapter 9; Rudolf Arnheim, *The Power of the Center: A Study of Composition in the Visual Arts* (Berkeley: University of California Press, 1982), 4, 42; Irving Hallowell, *Culture and Experience* (Philadelphia: University of Pennsylvania Press, 1955), 187; Kent C. Bloomer and Charles W. Moore, *Body, Memory, and Architecture* (New Haven: Yale University Press, 1977), 31–32.

88. See, for instance, Gadamer, *Truth and Method,* 137–38.

89. Ibid., 138.

90. Gerardus van der Leeuw, *Sacred and Profane Beauty: The Holy in Art,* trans. David E. Green (New York: Holt, Rinehart and Winston, 1963), 206–7; John Ruskin, *The Seven Lamps of Architecture,* 3d printing (New York: The Noonday Press, 1971), 72; and Elizabeth Bowen comments on the "substantiality" of the Aurelian Wall in *A Time in Rome;* quoted in Stanley Abercrombie, *Architecture as Art: An Esthetic Analysis* (New York: Van Nostrand Reinhold Co., 1984), 17.

91. Abercrombie, *Architecture as Art,* 169.

92. Ibid., 7.

93. I take my notion of "great" architecture, by analogy, from Leonard B. Meyer's remarks on "great" music as that which disturbs our complacence and makes us aware of "ultimate uncertainties — and at the same time ultimate realities"; Leonard B. Meyer, "Some Remarks on Value and Greatness in Music," *Journal of Aesthetics and Art Criticism* 17:4 (June, 1959): 486–500. Meyer considers that the experience of great music "gives rise to a profound wonderment — tender, yet awful — at the mystery of existence. And in the very act of sensing this mystery, we attain a new level of consciousness, of individualization. The nature of uncertainty too has changed. It becomes a means to an end rather than an end to be suffered." Ibid., 498. Christian Norberg-Schultz, *Intentions in Architecture* (Cambridge: M.I.T. Press, 1965), 70–71, 157, 176, 197, recognizes the value of Meyer's work on music for the interpretation of architecture. Similarly, Dominick La Capra discusses "great texts," or what Gadamer calls "eminent or significant texts," as those that both challenge and reinforce existence (see Klemm, *Hermeneutical Inquiry,* 2: 5–6); and Robert Bernasconi, in his Introduction to Gadamer's *The Relevance of the Beautiful,* xiii, explains that where Heidegger's account is explicitly confined to "great art," Gadamer attempts to transform those concepts so that they become generally applicable to the broader range of art.

94. Spinden, *Study of Maya Art,* 172, comments on the "unnecessary complexity" of Maya art; and Holmes, *Ancient Cities of Mexico,* 52, comments on the fabulous outlay of Maya labor imposed by "the demands of symbolism and aestheticism."

95. Van der Leeuw, *Sacred and Profane Beauty,* 206, alludes to these Egyptian cases.

96. Herbert Read, *Icon and Idea,* quoted by Abercrombie, *Architecture as Art,* 28; and Gio Ponti, *In Praise of Architecture,* quoted in the same volume, 99.

97. Kubler, "Design of Space in Maya Architecture," 515. John Graham, "Antecedents of Olmec Sculpture at Abaj Takalik," in *Pre-Columbian Art History,* ed. Cordy-Collins, 9, disassociates monumentality and bigness in a somewhat different way: "characterized by a preoccupation with volume, that is, a feeling for full swelling masses, which together with consistent application of a highly refined system of proportion accounts for the overall impression of grand, inherent monumentality that distinguishes even the smallest of fine Olmec objects."

98. Kubler, *Shape of Time,* 14–16. In the same vein, John Ruskin went to the antifunctionalist extreme by maintaining that "the most beautiful things in the world are the most useless, peacocks and lilies, for instance." Ruskin quoted in Abercrombie, *Architecture as Art,* 103.

99. Kubler has written on the general implications of architecture's unique "immobility" and "indestructibility"; see, for instance, ibid., 41, 52; and idem, "Period, Style, and Meaning," 12. And Abercrombie, *Architecture as Art,* 8–9, 30, has expansive remarks on the social cooperation and commitment required to construct large works of architecture.

100. Weaver, *Aztecs, Maya, and Their Predecessors,* 89–91, 232–34, discusses the emergence and continuity of the "Mesoamerican pattern," a concept that is not restricted to architecture. Tozzer, among others, documents the "very striking similarity" among the pyramid mounds of various eras in Guatemala, Yucatán, and the Valley of Mexico; see *Chichén and Cenote,* 69. In the same vein, Spinden, *Ancient Civilizations of Mexico,* 61, argues that the difficulties of working in stone rather than clay make "stone art less subject to caprice than ceramic art."

101. Margain, "Pre-Columbian Architecture of Central Mexico," 72. Margain draws on the rangy remarks of Lewis Mumford to further his argument on this issue. George Cowgill, "Rulership and the Ciudadela: Political Inferences From Teotihuacán Architecture," in *Civilization in the Ancient Americas,* ed. Leventhal and Kolala, 313, 329, engaging in what he calls the "ethnoarchaeology of public architecture," is another who argues strenuously that architecture, particularly in contexts devoid of textual information (like Teotihuacán), and particularly when considered in a comparative light, can tell a great deal more about the nonmaterial aspects of Mesoamerica than has generally been presumed.

102. Charles Gallenkamp, *Maya: The Riddle and Rediscovery of a Lost Civilization,* 2d rev. ed. (New York: Penguin Books, 1981), 102. He takes the term "official" art from artist-scholar Miguel Covarrubias, *Indian Art of Mexico and Central America* (New York: Alfred A. Knopf, 1957). Similarly, Carrasco, *Quetzalcoatl and the Irony of Empire,* 7, cites Robert McC. Adams, *The Evolution of Urban Society* (Chicago: Aldine, 1967), 21–34, on the general limits and possibilities of archaeological evidence.

103. Discussed in Chapter 2 in relation to "Ethnohistory: Ethnographic Analogy," the history of the integration of texts and material evidence in Mesoamerica is an exceedingly interesting and complex issue. John L. Stephens, in a sense the founder of Mesoamerican archaeology, complained in 1839 that the pre-Hispanic past was being reconstructed almost entirely on the basis of the written record and that "the monuments and architectural remains of the aborigines have heretofore formed but little groundwork for these speculations"; *Incidents of Travel in Central America, Chiapas and Yucatán,* 1: 97. Bernal, *History of Mexican Archaeology,* has a number of helpful comments on progress and opinions about correlating written and archaeological evidence in the past 150 years; see particularly 7–8, 108, 115–17, and 181. Another interesting debate in this regard involved the outcry by "new archaeologists" in the 1950s against Franz Boas's claim that "nothing pertaining to the intangible aspects of life can be rescued with the help of the spade"; they argued instead that even the simplest archaeological data are "culturally significant"; see Taylor, *A Study of Archaeology,* 154–56, 171, 219.

104. Tozzer/Landa, p. 163, n. 854.

105. This conception of the pragmatic Putun merchant-warriors is dangerously hung up with Eric Thompson's older notion of a "decadent," "secular" Postclassic. David Freidel and Jeremy Sabloff, *Cozumel: Late Maya Settlement Patterns* (Orlando, Fla.: Academic Press, Inc., 1984), 181, 192–93, among other places, argue that Putun were "materialistic" but not "secular."

106. Note the remarks earlier in this section on "great" architecture and "great" music in n. 93.

107. Terence Grieder, *Origins of Pre-Columbian Art* (Austin: University of Texas Press, 1982), 11.

108. Wassily Kandinsky, *Concerning the Spiritual in Art and Painting in Particular* (New York: Wittenborn, Shultz, 1947), 23.

109. Another, even less-likely analogue for the pattern of ritual-architectural events comes in that restaurant situation in which one is unthinkingly chewing a fine cut of meat until, to one's consternation and surprise, one is interrupted by something hard and gritty between the teeth. Here, too, ignoring the circumstance — unpleasant though it may be — is not an option. As one conjectures as to what has made its way into one's mouth, one is forced into what might be loosely termed an occasion of hermeneutical reflection, a maneuvering to make sense of the disconcertingly strange circumstance and to adapt.

110. Gadamer, *Truth and Method,* 139.

111. Ibid., 141; and Paul Wheatley, *The Pivot of the Four Quarters* (Chicago: Aldine, 1971), 257–67. Gadamer and Wheatley make no reference to one another.

112. Gadamer, *Truth and Method,* 140.

113. Christian Norberg-Schultz, *Intentions in Architecture,* relies heavily on sociological concepts and terminology drawn from Talcott Parsons and on the language philosophy of Wittgenstein and Piaget; thus, he tends to see architecture as both derivative and supportive of socialization. Nevertheless, his concern for socialization is not altogether unlike Gadamer's concern for tradition; moreover, there is an even stronger parallel between Gadamer's notion of the interplay of projection and revision and Norberg-Schultz on expectation and (un)fulfillment in the experience of architecture. Accordingly, Norberg-Schultz's attempt to provide a "satisfactory theory of architecture that is capable of covering all possible historical contexts" is highly relevant.

114. See E. H. Gombrich, *Art and Illusion.* His notion of "making and matching," or "schema and revision" is directly relevant to the interplay of order and variation.

115. Wittgenstein paraphrased in Norberg-Schultz, *Intentions in Architecture,* 34.

116. Norberg-Schultz, *Intentions in Architecture,* 41.

117. Leonard B. Meyer's full exposition of "style" in music comes in his *Emotion and Meaning in Music* (Chicago: University of Chicago Press, 1956); he addresses the issue more concisely in Leonard B. Meyer, "Meaning in Music and Information Theory," *Journal of Aesthetics and Art Criticism* 15:4 (June 1957): 414–15.

118. With respect to the transformative experience of literature, Giles Gunn's exposition of "hypothetical otherness" in Giles Gunn, *The Interpretation of Otherness: Literature, Religion and the American Imagination* (New York: Oxford University Press, 1979), 52–91, argues for precisely this pattern; as does Hans Robert Jauss's exposition of an "aesthetics of reception and impact," in "Literary Theory as a Challenge to Literary Theory," *New Literary History* 2 (Autumn 1970): 7–37. Both are directly indebted to Gadamer.

119. Brunhouse, *Pursuit of the Ancient Maya,* 116–18, discusses this portion of Spinden's theory of art in a brief but helpful way.

120. Kubler, *Shape of Time,* 28. Erwin Panofsky discusses his concept of "mental habit" in, among other places, *Gothic Architecture and Scholasticism* (New York: World Publishing, 1957).

121. Gadamer, *Truth and Method,* 113.

122. Meyer, "Meaning in Music and Information Theory," 414–15.

123. David McAllester, "The First Snake Song," unpublished manuscript; quoted in Witherspoon, "Beautifying the World Through Art," 210. In the same article Witherspoon seconds McAllester by commenting on the "compulsive power" of Navajo music: "the repetitive nature of many Navajo songs is adorned with and enlivened by various modes of variation." Ibid.

124. See Rudofsky, *Prodigious Builders,* 104, and Jeffery F. Meyer, "*Feng-shui* of the Chinese City," *History of Religions* 18 (November 1978): 142. Carlson, "A Geomantic Model for Mesoamerica," 176–77, also has interesting remarks on *feng-shui* planning, "symmetrophobia," and "the conscious avoidance of perfection"; he concludes that "the intentional asymmetrical placement of structures and residences to acquire benefit and good fortune, and to avoid evil, is implicit in geomantic thinking." Ibid., 177.

125. Spinden, *Study of Maya Art,* 38–43.

126. Norberg-Schultz, *Intentions in Architecture,* 187.

127. Geographer Yi-Fu Tuan's remarks on the perilous yet productive experience of an alien environment are appropriate here. He writes, "experience is the overcoming of perils. The word 'experience' shares a common root (per) with 'experiment,' 'expert,' and 'perilous.' To experience in the active sense requires one to venture forth into the unfamiliar and experiment with the elusive and the uncertain. To become an expert one must dare to confront the perils of the new." Tuan, *Space and Place,* 9.

128. Proskouriakoff, *Classic Maya Sculpture,* 3. Kubler, *Shape of Time,* 80–82, considers Adolf Göller, an architect and psychologist of artistic form in Stuttgart (1880s), to be the first to consider systematically the productive interplay of order and variation and to observe that "familiarity breeds contempt." Certainly the discussion, if "nonsystematic," is much older.

129. This is an exceedingly complex issue. Where some theorists locate the origin of the orderly, conservative component in the "socialization process" and others imply that it arises from "psychological habits," artistic conventions, or possibly individual idiosyncrasies, Gadamer argues for the more appealing alternative that one's preunderstandings and expectations are grounded in what he calls "tradition."

130. Brunhouse, *Frans Blom: Maya Explorer,* 119, 138, 262, n. 6, discusses Blom's connection with plans to reproduce Maya buildings in the United States.

131. The radically different contexts notwithstanding, owing to the autonomy and superabundance of architecture, we can imagine that a replica of Chichén's Castillo in New Orleans would engender a host of meaningful (though probably eccentric) ritual-architectural events; any connection between these events, however, and those of the pre-Columbian Maya would be slim at best.

132. For instance, see, Robert McC. Adams, *The Evolution of Urban Society,* quoted by Carrasco, *Quetzalcoatl and the Irony of Empire,* 2; or Friedrich Katz, *The Ancient American Civilizations,* trans. K. M. Lois Simpson (New York: Praeger Publishers, 1972), 314–17.

133. Carrasco, "Templo Mayor: Aztec Vision of Place," 278, 288–91.

134. Joachim Wach, *The Comparative Study of Religions,* ed. with an intro. by Joseph M. Kitagawa (New York: Columbia University Press, 1958), 25–26. Joseph M. Kitagawa, "Verstehen and Erlosung: Some Remarks on Joachim Wach's Work," *History of Religions* 13 (February 1974): 40, provides an apt clarification of Wach's typological project: "To be sure, Wach is not advocating the sheer amassing of historical data; what is important to him is discovering the principle that structures historical facts and events without which it would be impossible to find meaning in the configurations of the vast amount of data that are available to us."

135. Staale Sinding-Larsen, *Iconography and Ritual: A Study of Analytic Perspectives* (Oslo: Universitetsforlaget AS, 1984), 129.

136. Joachim Wach, *Sociology of Religion* (Chicago: University of Chicago Press, 1944), Chapter 1, for instance, argues that "types" are the best strategy for mediating between universal and particular.

137. On the possibility of New Fire Ceremonies at Chichén Itzá, see the section in Chapter 4 on "New Fire Integration: Toward a Summation."

138. On the parallel between "Toltec Chichén" and Xochicalco, see the section in Chapter 4 on "Quetzalcoatl's Role: Serpent Column Synthesis." Moreover, in the realm of synchronic comparison, by relying on this framework of ritual-architectural priorities, regional characterizations and contrasts, typically developed along formal and stylistic lines, may be reassessed more significantly as differences in ritual priorities: accordingly, one might, for example, move beyond the typical remarks about each respective Mesoamerican region's facade decorations and vaulting techniques to generalize that Central Mexico shows a strong predisposition for inclusive, theatric ritual architecture (theatre, priority III-A), the Puuc area of central Yucatán for building that fosters meditation and introspection (contemplation, priority III-B), and the Classic Petén Maya area for esoteric, exclusivistic ritual events (sanctuary, priority III-D).

139. Moreover, in a diachronic vein (though, admittedly, this is not a particularly strong method for resolving specific historical questions), typological analysis of ritual-architectural priorities can expose facile diffusionist claims based on formal parallels and thus contributes significantly to the evaluation of specific historical problems such as migratory patterns and intrasite relations, issues that are poignantly relevant to the Tula–Chichén Itzá problem.

140. One could, for instance, rely on this framework to organize (in a more religiously significant fashion) the issues in the interminable controversy over the significance and ritual use of Maya inscriptions on stelae and buildings by noting that this controversy has typically counterpoised the old-guard Mayanists, who insisted that indigenous epigraphy was exclusively cosmological and calendrical (homology, priority I-A), over against the more recently dominant view that Maya inscriptions contain genealogical and historical records of specific Maya rulers (sacred history, priority II-B, and politics, priority II-C). Amid the long-winded controversy, however, scholars have likewise imaginatively re-created the Maya stelae events as occasions for the commemoration of the dead (priority II-D), or of deities (priority II-A), or as contexts for propitiation (priority III-C), or for contemplation (priority III-B), and even as sessions for astronomical observation (priority I-C). For concise summaries of the history of this debate see, among innumerable options, Deuel, *Conquistadors Without Swords,* 383–87; Benson, *Maya World,* 75–79; Weaver, *Aztecs, Maya, and Their Predecessors,* 113–15; Adamson, *Ruins of Time,* 210, 226–31; Jones, Coe, and Haviland, "Tikal," 302–3; Peter Mathews and David M. Pendergast, "The Altun Ha Jade Plaque: Deciphering the Inscription," in *Ancient Mesoamerica,* ed. Graham, 239–42; Grieder, *Origins of Pre-Columbia Art,* 73–76; and Hammond, "Lords of the Jungle," 23–25.

141. To invoke the other favored metaphor for the experience and interpretation of sacred architecture — that of play — this typological discussion serves not as a classificatory scheme for stating my conclusions but as a kind of preparatory hermeneutical calisthenics that will ready me for the challenging interpretive games at Tula and Chichén Itzá.

142. Johanna Broda, "Astronomy, *Cosmovision*, and Ideology," 103, quotes Paul Kirchhoff's unpublished notebooks.

143. Abreu Gomez, *Canek: History and Legend of a Maya Hero,* 37.

144. Long, *Significations,* 7.

145. Jonathan Z. Smith, "The Influence of Symbols Upon Social Change: A Place on Which to Stand," *Worship* 44 (October 1970): 472. For an explicit application of Smith's position to Mesoamerica, see Carrasco, *Quetzalcoatl and the Irony of Empire,* 104.

146. Norberg-Schultz, "Meaning in Architecture," in *Meaning in Architecture,* ed. Jencks and Baird, 225–26.

147. Norberg-Schultz, *Meaning in Western Architecture,* 130, has emphasized the atypicality of Michelangelo and the Mannerists' rejection of harmony. There are, of course, any number of other cases in which conflict, doubt, and incongruity supersede harmony and all-encompassing order as design parameters for sacred architecture. An eccentric smattering of examples follow. Whitney S. Stoddard, *Art and Architecture in Medieval France: Medieval Architecture, Sculpture, Stained Glass, Manuscripts, the Art of the Church Treasuries* (New York: Harper & Row, 1966), 279–326, describes French Flamboyant and Rayonnant architecture that, while looking like Baroque, does not stem from confidence (as did the Baroque) but rather from disillusionment, nominalism, and skepticism. Alfonso Ortiz, *The Tewa World: Time, Space, Being and Becoming in a Pueblo Society* (Chicago: University of Chicago Press, 1969), 134–37, demonstrates that there are intentional asymmetries in Tewa Indian ritual and architecture but that those asymmetries are resolved over longer spans of time. And Irving Goldman, *The Mouth of Heaven: An Introduction to Kwakiutl Religious Thought* (Huntington, N.Y.: Robert E. Krieger Publishing Company, 1975), Chapter 9, shows that in Kwakiutl cosmology, and thus architecture, interdependence between realms is more important than perfect parallelism between those realms.

148. I lift this general characterization of archaic contexts from Sullivan, "Astral Myths Rise Again," 17.

149. Carrasco, *Quetzalcoatl and the Irony of Empire,* 1.

150. Kubler, "Design of Space in Maya Architecture," 516.

151. Octavio Paz, *The Labyrinth of Solitude: Life and Thought in Mexico* (New York: Grove Press, Inc., 1961), 89–90.

152. Carlson, "A Geomantic Model," 143–216. Carlson cites as his only precedents in the study of Mesoamerican "geomancy" Ricketson, Kubler, and Millon. Ibid., 187–88.

153. For instance, Anthony F. Aveni, *Skywatchers of Ancient Mexico* (Austin: University of Texas Press, 1980), 218–21.

154. Spinden, *Study of Maya Art,* 97–98. Eric Thompson, in an ironic underestimation of his beloved Maya, makes perhaps the most famous denial of careful and precise orientation at Maya centers. See Aveni and Hartung, "Precision in the Layout of Maya Architecture," 63–70, for a summary and critique of Thompson's remarks. Among the most recent authoritative sources to perpetuate the traditional characterization of the "amorphous nature of Maya settlement" is Coe, *Maya,* 83, 84, 88.

155. Aveni and Hartung have been the most thoroughgoing in documenting purposive and precise, albeit obscure, systems of orientation in Maya sites that had earlier been judged as random and haphazard; "Precision in the Layout of Maya Architecture" is but one of their many relevant articles.

156. Johanna Broda, "Astronomy, *Cosmovision,* and Ideology"; and idem, "Templo Mayor as Ritual Space."

157. Mircea Eliade, *Patterns in Comparative Religion,* trans. Rosemary Sheed (New York: Meridian Books, 1967), 379 (originally published as *Traite d'Historia des Religions* [Paris: Payot, 1949]).

158. Mircea Eliade, *The Myth of the Eternal Return: Cosmos and History,* trans. Willard R. Trask (Princeton: Princeton University Press, 1954), Chapter 1, provides among the clearest expositions of the principal elements of Eliade's famous theory of sacred space.

159. Cornelius Loew's concept of "cosmological conviction" has been concisely summarized by Jonathan Z. Smith, *Map Is Not Territory: Studies in the History of Religions* (Leiden, Netherlands: E. J. Brill, 1978), 151–53.

160. The origin and explanation of the organizing principles that are replicated in a wide variety of otherwise seemingly unrelated contexts — most especially the homologous relations between cosmology and society — have, of course, been the subject of debate among social scientists for decades. Eliade maintains that the homologization of diverse levels of reality is possible because of the nature of symbols and that the ultimate model is embedded in the cosmogony. Dumezil attributes the presence of homology among Indo-Europeans to an all-pervasive "ethnic mystique" or "tripartite ideology." Levi-Strauss traces the phenomenon of homologized realms to the structures of the mind. And Durkheim explains homology as the fruit of social facts yielding supernatural facts.

161. See Stephen Hugh-Jones, *The Palm and the Pleiades: Initiation and Cosmology in Northwest Amazonia* (Cambridge: Cambridge University Press, 1979), 150.

162. Mabbett, "Symbolism of Mount Meru," 76, discusses architectural homologization with respect to Mount Meru and summarizes the landmark work of Paul Mus on Borobudur as a cosmogram. And Hiram W. Woodward, "Borobudur and the Mirrorlike Mind," *Archaeology* (November-December 1981): 40–47, has a concise interpretation of Borobudur and a bibliography of other recent works on this monument. Wheatley, *Pivot of the Four Quarters,* 437–38, discusses Ankor Thom and the traditional Chinese city with direct reference to Eliade's model of sacred space. Diana Eck, *Banaras: City of Light* (Princeton: Princeton University Press, 1982), 146, 256, 283–84, 322, discusses the city of Banaras as a mandala and representation of the universe. In the same vein, see Romi Khosla, "Architecture and Symbolism in Tibetan Monasteries," in *Shelter, Sign and Symbol,* ed. Paul Oliver (Woodstock, N.Y.: Overlook Press, 1975), 71–83. Fred Clothey, *Rhythm and Intent: Ritual Studies From South India* (Madras: Blackie and Son Publishers, 1983), 149–51, discusses the tantric principle known as *vastu-purusa mandala* that underwrites a homology between the portions of a ritual room, the limbs of a human body, and the regions of the cosmos; he also explains how the *yaka calai* is constructed as a literal image of Vedic and Puranic cosmologies (in some traditions the *yaka calai* has five rather than three tiers; see ibid., 148). Clothey also provides a splendid example in which the dedication of the Hindu temple is explicitly homologized to the founding of a cosmos, see ibid., 190.

163. Keith Critchlow, "*Niike*: Siting of a Japanese Rural House," in *Shelter, Sign and Symbol,* ed. Oliver, 219–226, develops the interesting angle of an architecture that not only homologizes time and space but also acupuncture and the health of an individual at various times of the day. On homologization in Japanese temples, see Bruno Taut and Shiro Hiral, *Fundamentals of Japanese Architecture* (Tokyo: Kokusai Bunka Shinkokai, 1936); cited in *Shelter, Sign and Symbol,* ed. Oliver, 31. Richard B. Pilgrim, "Intervals (*Ma*) in Space and Time: Foundations for a Religio-Aesthetic Paradigm in Japan," *History of Religions* 25 (February 1986): 255–77, also adeptly explores the homologization of space and time in Japanese architecture. Grapard, "Flying Mountains and Walkers of Emptiness," 214–18, discusses the progressive expansion of the concept of mandala until the entire country of Japan came to be viewed as sacred space on *shinkoku* (that is, "divine nation").

164. See Clark E. Cunningham, "Order in the Atoni House," in *Right and Left: Essays on Dual Symbolic Classifications* (Chicago: University of Chicago Press, 1973), 204–38.

165. Alexander-Phaedow Lagopoulos, "Semiological Urbanism: An Analysis of the Traditional Western Sudanese Settlement," in *Shelter, Sign and Symbol,* ed. Oliver, 206–18, stresses particularly the Dogon conception of the longhouse as a "cosmic egg" in which the "plan of the house is converted into a sort of summary of its three-dimensional spatial reality." With respect to West African vernacular architecture, David Dalby explains that in Hausa, the principal language in the eastern half of the West African Savannah, *garii,* the basic term for individual settlement, that is, a village or town, can be used on a flexible scale to refer to any category of human settlement or territorial unit up to the whole world itself; see David Dalby, "The Concert of Settlement in the West African Savannah," in *Shelter, Sign and Symbol,* ed. Oliver, 197–205, and especially p. 203.

166. Joseph G. Jorgensen, *The Sun Dance Religion: Power for the Powerless* (Chicago: University of Chicago Press, 1972), 177–205, discusses the cosmic design of Ute and Shoshone sun dance lodges.

167. On Salteaux village arrangement, see Irving Hallowell, *Culture and Experience* (Philadelphia: University of Pennsylvania Press, 1955), 187–201.

168. See R. T. Zuidema, *The Ceque System of Cuzco: The Social Organization of the Capital of the Inca* (Leiden, Netherlands: Brill, 1964).

169. Broda, "Astronomy, *Cosmovision*, and Ideology," 81–85, for instance, strikes very close to the issue of homology when she describes "cosmovision" as "the structured view in which the ancient Mesoamericans combined their notions of cosmology into a systematic whole."

170. Aldous Huxley noted the parallels between native Mexican weavings and the geometric patterns on the walls of the temples at Mitla, Oaxaca, and thus described them as "petrified weaving"; see Victor von Hagen, *The Aztecs: Man and Tribe* (New York: New American Library, 1961), 151. Spinden notes the parallels between textile arts and architecture among the Maya in *Ancient Civilizations of Mexico*, 88; and Robertson makes a similar sort of observation relative to "suggestive similarities between [Peruvian] textiles and the patterns and plans of Chanchan buildings," *Pre-Columbian Architecture*, 120. More recently, Cecelia Klein has discussed the homology between weaving and the other realms of Mesoamerican existence in "Woven Heaven, Tangled Earth: A Weaver's Paradigm of the Mesoamerican Cosmos," in *Ethnoastronomy and Archaeoastronomy in the American Tropics*, ed. Aveni and Urton, 1–36.

171. Although there is effusive evidence for the symbolism of the center in Mesoamerica, the evidence regarding orientation with respect to the four cardinal directions (another pillar of Eliade's model of sacred space) is much more ambiguous. B. L. Gordon, "Sacred Directions, Orientation, and the Top of the Map," *History of Religion* 10 (February 1971): 211–27, for instance, pleads a near universality for cardinal orientation, but its wholesale applicability to Mesoamerica may have come too incautiously. At least as early as Holmes, *Ancient Cities of Mexico* (1895–97), 24, 102, 154, 215, 226, 231, 290, it was generally agreed that cardinal axiality was considerably more revered by the peoples of Oaxaca and the Valley of Mexico than by the Maya of either Chiapas or Yucatán. Among the most notable recent discussions of this long-standing Maya-Mexican dichotomy is one by Clemency Coggins, who argues that, while Teotihuacános were always obsessed with quadripartition, the Maya were originally more interested in organization by threes than by fours and that the appearance of a four-part axiality in the Maya zone is largely a Mexican imposition. Coggins, "A New Order and the Role of the Calendar: Some Characteristics of the Middle Classic Period at Tikal," in *Maya Archaeology and Ethnohistory*, ed. Hammond and Willey, 44; and idem, "The Shape of Time: Some Political Implications of a Four-Part Figure," *American Antiquity* 45 (October 1980): 727–30, 736. Likewise noteworthy is Franz Tichy's claim that the four cardinal directions are largely irrelevant to all of Mesoamerica and that solar solstitial directions are actually responsible for Central Mexican axiality. Tichy, "Order and Relationship of Space and Time in Mesoamerica: Myth or Reality?" in *Mesoamerican Sites and World-Views*, ed. Benson, 218, 221.

172. Redfield and Villa Rojas, *Chan Kom*, 111. Tozzer, *Chichén and Cenote*, 109, has collected a number of early references to trees as *axis mundis* in the Maya tradition. More recently, Pearce, *View from the Temple*, 40, has summarized the significance of the Maya sacred tree as an *axis mundi*, particularly with respect to its most lucid exemplification at Palenque.

173. Coggins, "Zenith, Mountain, Center and Sea," 111. Ibid., 116, she summarizes Gossen's work on Chamula spatial organization.

174. Evon Z. Vogt, *Tortillas for the Gods: A Symbolic Analysis of Zinacanteco Ritual* (Cambridge: Harvard University Press, 1976), particularly chapters 1 and 3. Gordon Brotherson and Dawn Ades, "Mesoamerican Description of Space I," *Ibero-Amerikanisches Archiv*, NS 1:4 (1975): 279–305 (cited by Coggins, "Zenith, Mountain, Center and Sea," 111), come to similar conclusions about the role of centers in the cosmology and orientation principles of the sixteenth-century Yucatecan Maya.

175. See Coggins, "Zenith, Mountain, Center and Sea," 111.

176. Ibid.

177. See, for instance, Kubler, *Art and Architecture of Ancient America*, 137–41.

178. On the annual cycle of rituals associated with the Aztec *xihuitl* (the natural or solar calendar), see Fray Diego Durán, *Book of the Gods and Rites* and *The Ancient Calendar*, trans. and ed. Fernando Horcasitas and Doris Heyden (Norman: University of Oklahoma Press, 1971). Also on the coordination of space and time in Aztec monthly ceremonies, see, for instance, Broda, "Astronomy, *Cosmovision*, and Ideology," 81–84, 93, 99.

179. Coggins, "A New Order and the Role of the Calendar"; and Thompson, *Maya History and Religion*, 24–25, discuss the Maya manipulation

of historical chronologies and records to fit cosmological schemes. Tozzer/Landa, 21, comments on Morley's idea of a "chronologic coercion" or a compulsive neurosis urging the Itzá to do things when "the times were ripe for change." Broda, "Astronomy, *Cosmovision*, and Ideology," 102, relying on Paul Kirchhoff as her authority, discusses the same sort of homologization of history by the Aztecs. Also, in what seems to be a parallel to the Inca *ceque* system, Phillip C. Thompson (cited by Andrews V, "Dzibilchaltún," 327) has documented a pattern among the Yucatecan Maya of rotational movements from one political office to another that is correlated to Maya calendrical cycles.

180. Joyce Marcus, "Territorial Organization of the Lowland Classic Maya," *Science* 180 (1973): 911–16. Linda Schele, "Sacred Site and World-View at Palenque," 108, 110, 115, extends Marcus's notion of a pan-regional cosmological orientation in Maya site planning, emphasizing particularly Palenque's role in that scheme as "the western portal to the Underworld . . . the place where the sun and the moon died," and Copán's conception as "the eastern portal out of the Underworld, or into it, whichever way you want it." William R. Bullard, Jr., "Maya Settlement Patterns in Northeastern Petén, Guatemala," *American Antiquity* 25 (1960), had earlier explored the possibility of regional planned Maya territories. Thompson, *Rise and Fall of Maya Civilization*, 89, also has some remarks on Mesoamerican regional planning and cosmological planning, as do Tozzer/Landa, 26, n. 136; and Leslie Byrd Simpson, *Many Mexicos* (Berkeley: University of California Press, 1969), 80. Robert Carmack sees evidence of regionally homologized space among the Quiché Maya of the Guatemala highlands: "[the Quiché] may have come to see these towns as mirroring the spatial universe, with Kúmarcaaj [the city of Utatlán] in the center, Pismachi on the south, Pilocab on the north, and Panpacay and Panqúib on the east and west." Carmack, *Quiché Maya*, 184–85. Despite these examples, Carlson, "A Geomantic Model," 202, concludes his review of the research into the large-scale spatial organization of sites and long-distance alignments in Mesoamerica with a lament that much more study is needed.

181. See Wheatley, *Pivot of the Four Quarters*, 234.

182. Thompson, *Maya History and Religion*, 215, 291; and Redfield and Villa Rojas, *Chan Kom*, 114, discuss quadripartite Maya village organization. Landa discusses the spatial organization of Mayapán, wherein the closer one lives to the center the greater one's social prestige. See Brainerd/Morley, *Ancient Maya*, 95, 158, 261.

183. Freidel (1981: 217), cited by Benson, "Architecture as Metaphor," 184, discusses the late pre-Classic Structure 5C–2nd at Cerros as a miniature model of the world; Freidel also addresses the cases of Uaxactún and Tikal; see "Cultural Areas and Interaction Spheres."

184. Rudolph van Zantwijk, "The Great Temple of Tenochtitlán: Model of Aztec Cosmovision," in *Mesoamerican Sites and World-Views*, ed. Benson, 71–86, is among many who discuss the cosmogramic quality of the Templo Mayor.

185. On the homologous character of the Castillo, see especially the section on "The Ritual-Architectural Events of 'Toltec Chichén'" in Chapter 4.

186. Tozzer, *Chichén and Cenote*, 119, interprets the columns at Chichén Itzá in this way.

187. Benson, "Architecture as Metaphor," 188, describes offertory boxes as cosmological models, using Offering 31 from the Templo Mayor as a specific example.

188. Janet Catherine Berlo describes how Manuel Gamio in 1922 astutely observed that incensario lids from Teotihuacán seemed to be miniature temples; Berlo advances the argument, describing the architecture itself as a miniature of the natural order. Berlo, "Artistic Specialization at Teotihuacán: The Ceramic Incense Burner," in *Pre-Columbian Art History*, ed. Cordy-Collins, 90–99.

189. Vitruvius, *The Ten Books of Architecture*, trans. Morris Hicky Morgan (New York: Dover Publications, 1960).

190. See Otto von Simson, *The Gothic Cathedral: Origins of Gothic Architecture and the Medieval Concept of Order* (New York: Harper & Row, 1956).

191. Ibid., 37.

192. Ibid., xvii.

193. See ibid., Chapter 2, "Measure and Light."

194. It is plausible that this trio — homologized architecture, rationalized compliance with abstract principles, and rote conformity to codified prescriptions — constitutes a historical evolution, but thus far I am not comfortable positing it as such.

195. Wittkower's work is tremendously useful in distinguishing between Gothic and Renaissance architectures, but it is decidedly "uneventful," that is, he has very little to say about the use of buildings or the spectator's point of view; rather, he is

concerned to understand the intentions of the architect, and that he does very effectively. Rudolf Wittkower, *Architectural Principles in the Age of Humanism* (New York: W. W. Norton and Company, 1971), pt. 4.

196. Stoddard, *Art and Architecture in Medieval France,* 58, connects the architectural adherence to universalistic principles to Medieval European magic numbers and finds many examples in the Romanesque.

197. Vincent Scully, *The Earth, the Temple, and the Gods: Greek Sacred Architecture,* rev. ed. (New Haven: Yale University Press, 1979), 198–201, 210, has connected the advent of architectural adherence to universalistic principles to the growth of philosophical speculation in Postclassic Greece. Where the Classic temple is "a particularly active embodiment of a specific kind of power" (that is, particularly participating in the commemoration of divinity priority, II-A, as discussed later), the Postclassic Greek temple was conceived as "a correct, generalized abstraction" (that is, convention, priority I-B). Scully's discussion of the "purely geometrical control of space developed by Hippodamian city planning" is also directly relevant to this type of rationalized architecture. Ibid., 187.

198. Alberti's *De re Aedificatoria* (1485) appears in English as Leone Battista Alberti, *The Ten Books of Architecture,* trans. James Leoni, ed. Joseph Rykwert (London: Alec Tiranti Ltd., 1955).

199. The ascendancy of rarified proportionality and architectural rule books in the Italian Renaissance was, of course, abetted by a congenial and all-encompassing theoretical orientation. Joan Godal, *Leon Battista Alberti: Universal Man of the Early Renaissance* (Chicago: University of Chicago Press, 1969), for instance, explains that the God of the Renaissance was the "Great Artificer of Nature," himself an architect who had fashioned the cosmos according to immutable metric laws.

200. While Vitruvius' *Ten Books of Architecture* contains no real theory of proportion, it is a crucial concern for him; see, for instance, 109 and 130.

201. See Wittkower, *Architectural Principles,* pt. 4.

202. A reworking of Vitruvius' famous architectural treatise, Alberti's *De re Aedificatoria* (1485), is the most prestigious in a distinguished line of Italian rulebooks that includes the influential manuals of Sebastiano Serlio, *Tutte l'Opere de Architecttura* (1531–51); Giacomo Barozzi da Vignola, *Regola Delli Cinque Ordini d'Architettura* (1562); and Andrea Palladio, *I Quattre Libri Dell'Architettura* (1570). Wittkower, *Architectural Principles,* 18, characterizes Serlio's treatise as "pedestrian and pragmatic, consisting of a collection of models rather than expressions of principle . . . we can not expect to find here any of Alberti's philosophical concepts." Also on Serlio's treatise, see Peter Murray, *The Architecture of the Italian Renaissance* (New York: Schocken Books, 1963), 196–200. For a concise discussion of Vignola and his treatise, see ibid., 200–208. Palladio's treatise, available in English as *The Four Books of Architecture* (New York: Dover Publications, 1965), is concerned almost entirely with practical issues, though it is arranged very rationally and precisely. Wittkower, *Architectural Principles,* 21 et seq., stresses Palladio's continuity with Alberti. James Ackerman, *Palladio* (New York: Penguin Books, 1966), 25–29, claims that Serlio was Palladio's most influential model.

203. Clothey, *Rhythm and Intent,* 183–84, for instance, discusses the *Silpa Sastras.* For a particularly vivid example of conventionalized design, see Soundara Rajan, *Invitation to Indian Architecture,* 19–20, 32, where he recounts the fastidious textual requirements for correctly proportioned *Vimana* (the pyramidal storied shrines that proliferate in southern India).

204. See, for instance, Jeffery Meyer's discussion of *feng-shui* handbooks, "*Feng-Shui* of the Chinese City," *History of Religions* 18 (November 1978): 139–50; or Else Glahn, "Unfolding the Chinese Building Standards: Research on the *Yingzao fashi,*" in *Chinese Traditional Architecture,* Nancy Shatzman Steinhardt et al. (New York: China House Gallery, 1984), 47–58. Regarding the continuing enthusiasm for these building practices in contemporary China, see Raymond Lo, Feng-shui *and Destiny* (Lutterworth, Leicestershire, England: Tyron Press, 1992). All these cases demonstrate in Chinese architecture (as in Hindu) a major juxtaposition of adherence to supposedly universal principles and a hierophonic, heterogeneous conception of space that is profoundly different from that of the Italian Renaissance conception of homogeneous space.

205. See, for instance, Yossi Katz, "The Jewish Religion and Spatial and Communal Organization: The Implementation of Jewish Law in the Building of Urban Neighborhoods and Jewish Agricultural Settlements in Palestine at the Close of the Nineteenth Century," in *Sacred and Profane Places,* ed. Jamie

Scott and Paul Simpson-Housley (New York: Greenwood Press, 1991), 3–19.

206. See, for instance, Titus Burckhardt, *Art of Islam: Language and Meaning* (World of Islam Festival Publishing Company, 1976), especially Chapter 4 on "The Sphere and the Cube."

207. See Paul Hetherington, *The "Painter's Manual" of Dionysius of Fourna* (London: Sagittarius Press, 1974). An article from the *Chicago Tribune,* 25 December 1985, sec. 5, p. 1, for instance, describes the ongoing construction of a Ukrainian Catholic church on the northwest side of Chicago that is proceeding with meticulous conformity to this manual. Or, to draw on a radically different sort of example, Le Corbusier's famous "Modular" proportioning system, based on the "miracle of numbers" and the so-termed golden rectangle and golden section, provides yet more vivid instantiation of the convention priority (I-B). Abercrombie, *Architecture as Art,* 79, 82, for instance, has a brief discussion of Le Corbusier's "Modular."

208. For another way of understanding the significance of the geometrical and repetitive designs on Mesoamerican facades (most prominent at Mitla in Oaxaca and at the Puuc sites of Central Yucatán), see the discussion later in this chapter of the contemplation priority (III-B).

209. For instance, Justino Fernández, *Coatlicue, Esthético del Arte Indígena Antiguo,* stresses the importance of proportional analysis; and Beatriz de la Fuente, "La proporción armónica en la escultura monumental Olmeca," *Actes du XLII Congrès International des Américanistes, Paris, 1976,* 7 (1979): 337–56, argues that the famed colossal heads of the Olmecs have harmonious proportions that reflect a conception of perfection. George Kubler, "Synopsis of the Meetings," 287, alludes to both these works in a summary of a discussion on the study of proportions in Mesoamerican art; however, the real crux of his discussion is that this is an avenue of research that has been sorely neglected.

210. Carlson, "A Geomantic Model," 202.

211. Ibid.

212. See particularly Aveni and Hartung, "Precision in the Layout of Maya Architecture"; and on "conceptual lines," see Hartung, "Alignments in Architecture and Sculpture of Maya Centers: Notes on Piedras Negras, Copán, and Chichén Itzá." With specific reference to Chichén Itzá, Hartung, ibid., 234–37, argues that the Caracol served as the point of departure for the entire northern or "Toltec" portion of the city.

213. It is somewhat ironic that Aveni and Hartung, pathfinders in discerning astronomical orientations in Mesoamerican buildings (astronomy, priority I-C), have, in the case of the Nunnery Complex at Uxmal, provided a stellar example that, while not entirely without celestial references, is preeminently an inward-looking exercise in orientation with respect to abstract principles of geometry (convention, priority I-B). See Hartung, "Precision in the Layout of Maya Architecture," 71–77. Kubler, *Art and Architecture in Ancient America,* 241; and Gualberto Zapata Alonzo, *Guide to Puuc Region: Uxmal, Kabah, Sayil, Xlapac, Labná* (Mexico: Dante, published after 1983), 41–43, both present the typical position that the skew of the Nunnery buildings at Uxmal is motivated by "aesthetics" or "a deliberate aim at perspective correction."

214. Sahagún, *Florentine Codex;* quoted by Recinos, *Popol Vuh,* 77–78, n. 2.

215. Recinos, *Popol Vuh,* 78, n. 2, refers to this line of the *Popol Vuh.* (He says that the line is in Chapter 5 of Part 4, but actually it is in Chapter 6 of Part 4; see p. 209 of the same work.) Recinos, ibid., 209, n. 6, describes how the Oidor Zorita found paintings in Utatlán, Guatemala, the ancient capital of the Quiché, that were, in 1550, considered to be "of more than eight hundred years" and then concludes that they "could well have been the paintings brought from Tulán [that is, the *u tzibal Tulán*]." Unfortunately, these paintings have not survived.

216. Landa, *Relación,* 28, 169.

217. Wolfgang von Hagen, *World of the Maya* (New York: The New American Library, 1960), 202–4, though without any real substantiation, has been willing to speculate that the Toltecs brought these "books" (the *u tzibal Tulán*) with them to Yucatán and used them as patterns for the refashioning of Chichén Itzá.

218. In this respect, an appreciation of the convention priority (I-B) is very closely related to my discussion in Chapter 2 regarding "Organization by Tradition" and the initiative to locate specific works of art and architecture with respect to their historical precedents and antecedents.

219. Aveni, *Skywatchers of Ancient Mexico,* 240–41.

220. For instance, Andrews, "Dzibilchaltún," 330–31, discusses the imitation of the 17 degrees east of

north, Teotihuacán alignment at Dzibilchaltún in northern Yucatán.

221. Peter C. Chemery, "Sky: Myths and Symbols," *Encyclopedia of Religion*, ed. Mircea Eliade, 13: 346.

222. Sullivan, "Astral Myths Rise Again," 12–13, treats the significance of Charles Francois Dupuis, *De l'origine de Tous les Cultes* (originally 1798), and the Pan-Babylonianists in the history of the study of the relationship between astronomy and religion.

223. See Brunhouse, *In Search of the Maya*, 20.

224. Stephens, *Incidents of Travel in Central America, Chiapas, and Yucatán*, 1: 159–60. Deuel, *Conquistadors Without Swords*, 243, reflects on the significance of Stephens's Copán theory.

225. Maudslay, *Archaeology*, 2: 48, says, "no other temples in Central America offer such support to the theory that the position and form of the buildings were due to astronomical considerations as those at Tikal."

226. Peter van der Loo, "Thematic Units in Mesoamerican Religion: Why Deerhunting and Adultery Are a Dangerous Combination," in *The Imagination of Matter*, ed. Carrasco, 31–50, takes Seler to task for his overbearing "Astralism," a style of interpretation that tried to explain all gods in any religion as ultimately representing, or deriving from, celestial phenomena. Seler's commentary on the Codex Borgia is particularly replete with astronomical alignment interpretations.

227. Spinden, *Study of Maya Art*, 12.

228. Joyce, *Maya and Mexican Art*, 14–15.

229. Robert Willson, "Astronomical Notes on the Maya Codices," *Papers of the Peabody Museum of American Archaeology and Ethnography* 6:3 (Cambridge: Harvard University Press, 1924).

230. For instance, Tozzer, *Chichén and Cenote*, 83, notes work on astro-architectural orientations at Copán, Uaxactún, and the Caracol structure at Chichén Itzá but then in a skeptical fashion says, "the data on these observations has not been entirely verified." Morley, *Ancient Maya*, 2d ed., 227–60; and Karl Ruppert, "A Special Assemblage of Maya Structure," in *Maya and Their Neighbors*, ed. Hay et al., 222–31, both comment on the expression of astronomical knowledge in Maya buildings. Ruppert was also the primary excavator of the indubitably astronomical Caracol structure at Chichén Itzá.

231. Sullivan, "Astral Myths Rise Again," 13.

232. "Archaeoastronomy," now the most vogue and encompassing of the terms, is the interdisciplinary study of ancient peoples' view of the cosmos as gleaned from both the written and unwritten record; "ethnoastronomy" studies the astronomic understandings of contemporary peoples; and "astroarchaeology," a term already apparently on its way out, is actually the most directly relevant to this project; Aveni, *Skywatchers of Ancient Maya*, 4, defines it as "the study of the astronomical principles employed in ancient works of architecture and the elaboration of a methodology for the retrieval and quantitative analysis of astronomical alignment data."

233. Peter Lancaster Brown, *Megaliths, Myths and Men: An Introduction to Astro-Archaeology* (New York: Taplinger Publishing Company, 1976), 1–161, devotes seven chapters to reconstructing the Stonehenge debate in great detail.

234. Sullivan, "Astral Myths Rise Again," 14–15, discusses the inappropriateness of the typical dichotomy between megaliths as "astronomical observatories" (that is, "scientific," practical, systematic, and generative of precise knowledge) and as "ceremonial centers" (that is, "religious," impractical, imprecise, and unproductive of increments in precise data). He notes that false dichotomy, while nearly ubiquitous in the literature on megalithic Europe, is largely absent in the archaeoastronomic investigations of North America, Mesoamerica, the Andes, and Southeast Asia. However, statements such as Karl Ruppert's on Maya observatories — "[their function] in the original instances may have been astronomical but provincially and decadently became ritualistic" (Ruppert, 1937; quoted by Kubler, "Design of Space in Maya Architecture," 519) — demonstrate that Mesoamerica has not been wholly immune to this problem.

235. Anthony Aveni, "Introduction: Whither Archaeoastronomy?," in *World Archaeoastronomy*, ed. Anthony F. Aveni (Cambridge: Cambridge University Press, 1989), 10, for instance, notes, "After all, ancient astronomy was what it was and it may have meant something entirely different to its practitioners than either scientist or social scientist can conceive."

236. Tozzer, *Chichén and Cenote*, 36, 256, recounts Morley's explanation of the "curious coincidence" by which the katun date of 8 Ahau in the Maya calendar is repeatedly the recorded date for important events in Yucatán history. Tozzer himself contributes

several more examples of Toltecs, Itzá, and Aztecs engaging in the same sort of willful distortion. The general issue of correction, adjustment, and manipulation of the Maya calendar has been discussed endlessly. See, for instance, Spinden, *Study of Maya Art,* 111, 140, 143; Thompson, *Rise and Fall of Maya Civilization,* 177–178; Adamson, *Ruins of Time,* 40, 212; and Coe, *Maya,* 158–59. More recently (and more interestingly) Aveni in *Skywatchers of Ancient Mexico,* 187, 190, among other places, has discussed the willful distortion of empirical astronomical data by the ancient Mesoamericans.

237. Schele, "Sacred Site and World-View at Palenque," 104.

238. Broda, "Astronomy, *Cosmovision,* and Ideology," 100.

239. Aubrey Burl, *Rites of the Gods* (London: J. M. Dent and Sons, Ltd., 1981), accepts the existence of astronomical alignments in the megaliths of Western Europe, but, in his estimate, neither cosmic harmony (homology, priority I-A) nor astronomical prediction (astronomy, priority I-C) is nearly so important as veneration of revered ancestors (the dead, priority II-D).

240. Kenneth Frampton, "Labor, Work and Architecture," 156. I suspect that Frampton got this example from Joseph Rykwert, *The Idea of a Town: The Anthropology of Urban Form in Rome, Italy and the Ancient World* (Princeton: Princeton University Press, 1976).

241. Spinden, *Ancient Civilizations of Mexico,* 144, for instance, implied a distinction in Mesoamerican astronomy between the personification of celestial bodies and the consideration of abstract celestial rhythms and cycles.

242. One very often encounters this fatalistic and predictive obsession in the Mesoamerican materials; suffice it here to note Weaver's assessment that, "whether one is considering the Maya Indians of the Petén region of Guatemala, the Zapotecs of Oaxaca, the Mixtecs of Puebla, the Nahua of the basin of Mexico, or the Tarascans of Michoacán, the predominating reason for such an exact record of passing time and the attendant writing systems seems to have been intimately related to astrology and prognostication of the future." Weaver, *Aztecs, Maya, and Their Predecessors,* 93.

243. See Anthony Aveni, Horst Hartung, and Sharon Gibbs, "The Caracol Tower at Chichén Itzá: Ancient Observatory," *Science* 18 (June 1975): 977–85.

244. Aveni, *Skywatchers of Ancient Mexico,* 165.

245. Coggins's discussion of Structure E-VII sub at Uaxactún is particularly apt because she makes her case by contrasting E-VII sub as a "calendrical ritual" (homology, priority I-A) and E-VII sub as a "locus of ancestor veneration ritual" (commemoration of dead, priority II-D) with what she considers to be its primary significance as astro-architecture with a divinatory intention (astronomy, priority I-C). Coggins, "Shape of Time," 731–32.

246. Schele, "Sacred Site and World-View at Palenque," 105.

247. Marion Hatch, "An Hypothesis on Olmec Astronomy With Special Reference to the La Venta Site," *Papers on Olmec and Maya Astronomy, Contributions of the University of California Archaeological Research Facility* 13, Berkeley, Calif., 1971.

248. Coggins, "Shape of Time," 735, reflects on the ritual integration of rainy skies, Tlaloc, and the solar year at Teotihuacán.

249. Susan Milbrath, "Astronomical Images and Orientations in the Architecture of Chichén Itzá," in *New Directions in American Archaeoastronomy,* ed. Anthony F. Aveni (Oxford, England: B.A.R. International Series 454, 1988), 57, suggests that "the most important orientations" at Chichén Itzá seem to be toward these phenomena.

250. Anthony Aveni, "Concepts of Positional Astronomy Employed in Ancient Mesoamerican Architecture," *Symposium on Native American Astronomy in Ancient America,* Colgate University, Hamilton, N.Y., 1975; cited by John Carlson, "The Case for Geomagnetic Alignments of Precolumbian Mesoamerican Sites — The Maya," *Katunob: A Newsletter-Bulletin on Mesoamerican Anthropology* 10 (June 1977): 78–79.

251. Carlson, "Ancient Skies," 27–28, describes the collaboration between Mary Miller and Floyd Lounsbury that led to this interpretation of the so-called shell-star event. In the same vein, Coe, *Maya,* 174, suggests that, in general, the Maya connected Venus dates with martial action, capture, and conquest; by contrast, Jupiter was connected with the ascension of rulers.

252. This possible scenario at Copán involving Temple 22, the sun, Venus, and the rites of kingship (while still highly tentative) provides a particularly fortuitous example because the same circumstance has been subject to sophisticated archaeoastronomical scrutiny by Anthony Aveni, "The Real Venus-Kukulcán in the Maya Inscriptions and Alignments,"

rev. version of unpublished paper presented at the Sixth Mesa Redonda de Palenque, June 1986; and ethnohistorical, ritual interpretation by Mary Miller, "The Meaning and Function of the Main Acropolis, Copán," in *The Southeast Classic Maya Zone, A Symposium at Dumbarton Oaks,* 6–7 October 1984, eds. Gordon R. Willey and Elizabeth Hill Boone (Washington, D.C.: Dumbarton Oaks Research Library and Collection, 1988) 149–89.

253. I am using van der Leeuw's distinction between "passive harmony" and "active control" in a quite different context than he does; he raises the issue in connection with two types of sacred dance. See van der Leeuw, *Sacred and Profane Beauty,* 24–25.

254. J. B. Jackson, *The Necessity of Ruins and Other Topics* (Amherst: University of Massachusetts Press, 1980), 91.

255. The interpretation of the fabulous Mesoamerican mural tradition, while not specifically architectural, could be, to some benefit, reworked in terms of commemorative architectural events. Robertson, *Pre-Columbian Architecture,* 33–35, among many, gives a concise summary of extant ancient mural paintings in Mesoamerica.

256. Robertson, ibid., 11, says of Maya stelae: "so directly do they adhere to their architectural role that they were, in the strict sense of the phrase, sculptural architecture rather than mere sculptural monuments."

257. Kubler stresses particularly the priority of exterior volumes over interior spaces in Mesoamerican architecture; it is, in his phrasing, not "elaborate shelter" but "monumental form . . . [that] commemorates a valuable experience by distinguishing one space from others in an ample and durable edifice." Kubler, "Design of Space in Maya Architecture," 515.

258. Robertson, Kubler's student, similarly stresses the interdependency of sculpture and architecture in Mesoamerica. He collects the finest examples of sculptural architecture in Central Mexico and then for the Maya zone. Robertson, *Pre-Columbian Architecture,* 29–31, 31–32.

259. Robertson considers the Pyramid of Quetzalcoatl at Teotihuacán the finest example of sculptural architecture in Central Mexico, ibid., 19; and Pyramid E-VII sub at Uaxactún the best in the Maya zone, ibid., 22, 29. It is significant that sculptural architecture in Mesoamerica does *not* arise as a decadent elaboration in later times but is evident from the beginning of pre-Columbian building.

260. Pollock, "Architecture of the Maya Lowlands," 427–28, discusses the "simulated temples" of the Río Bec and Chenes areas of Yucatán.

261. Kubler, *Art and Architecture in Ancient America,* 295, makes this unconventional suggestion about the Great Ball Court at Chichén Itzá.

262. Commemorative pre-Columbian architecture, while particularly concerned with the communication of rarified mythological themes and specific political ideologies, moreover, gives voice to an immense range of more prosaic concerns. For instance, the Curi-chanca, or "Golden Enclosure" in the heart of urban Cuzco, Peru — described by sixteenth-century chronicler Pedro de Cieza de Leon as a kind of artificial garden paradise where the stems of leaves, corn cobs, llamas, and even clods of earth were reproduced in fine gold — seems to be a kind of architectural acknowledgment of their agricultural, peasant foundations; see Pedro de Cieza de Leon, *The Travels of Pedro de Cieza de Leon,* trans. Harriet de Onis, ed. Victor von Hagen (Norman: University of Oklahoma Press, 1959). The murals of Tlaloc's paradise at Tepantitla, near Teotihuacán, is a possible parallel to this architectural commemoration of the pristine (see, for instance, Kubler, *Art and Architecture of Ancient America,* 54, 66–67); and the much discussed representation of modest Maya houses in the super-elaborate stone friezes at Uxmal, Labná, and Kabah (see, for instance, Kelemen, *Medieval American Art,* 75–76), may similarly have been an architectural ode to the simple, pre-urban life.

263. See Robert Fry, "Revitalization Movements Among the Postclassic Lowland Maya," in *Lowland Maya Postclassic,* ed. Chase and Rice, 127–32.

264. To cite a different sort of example, earlier this century, when the Yucatecan villagers of Chan Kom (Robert Redfield's "village that chose progress") made their petition to the Mexican governnment to be upgraded to the status of "pueblo" (and thus receive the concomitant financial assistance) by revamping their town according to the European architectural forms of plaza, rectilinear street, and masonry house, they were participating in an ancient Mesoamerican pattern of self-definition by architectural mimicry. See Redfield and Villa Rojas, *Chan Kom,* 25, 31, 45. Note also that they quote seventeenth-century historian López de Cogolludo to the effect that ever since the arrival of

the Spaniards in America the plaza, rectilinear street, and masonry house had been the primary symbols of Europe and of "civilization." Ibid., 31.

265. Kubler, "Period, Style and Meaning," admonishes against facile presumptions of continuity in meaning just because forms are replicated, which is exceedingly relevant here.

266. Fry, "Revitalization Movements," 129.

267. Spinden, *Study of Maya Art*, 175, uses a distinction between "archaistic" and "the truly archaic" in Maya art.

268. Davies, *Ancient Kingdoms*, 87–89, discusses the extent to which other centers, particularly Kaminaljuyú, were influenced by Teotihuacán.

269. Thompson, *Maya Archaeologist*, 260, describes the uninformed retrieval of stelae at Río Bec. Satterthwaite, "Expeditions to Piedras Negras," 84, describes even greater decadence in the retrieval of previous buildings at Piedras Negras wherein old carved stones were salvaged, broken up, and reused as mere building stone. This phenomenon, common all over Mesoamerica, could perhaps be termed "inadvertent architectural commemoration."

270. Nelson Wu, *Chinese and Indian Architecture: The City of Man, the Mountain of Gods, and the Realm of the Immortals* (New York: George Braziller, 1963), 21.

271. Scully, *Earth, Temple and Gods*, 1.

272. Scully's work is particularly appealing for this project by virtue of his highly "eventful" approach, which takes into account the religious disposition that spawns a particular architectural form, the ceremonial occasion of its use, and, particularly, the integration of the built form with the surrounding landscape. Together these constitute the appropriate unit of study or, what he calls, "one ritual whole." Ibid. 56.

273. Scully himself does *not* explicitly differentiate between these three modes of ritual-architectural commemoration of divinity (though it is implied in his discussion).

274. Ibid., Chapter 2.

275. Ibid., 35.

276. Ibid., 42–43.

277. Ibid., 46.

278. Kubler, "Design of Space in Maya Architecture," 515, argues that Maya architecture is not "elaborated shelter."

279. Scully, *Earth, Temple and Gods*, 62, states explicitly that the Classic Greek temple is totally unique, *not* a "solid mass like an Egyptian or Maya pyramid" (though it seems to me that, as sculptural commemorative architectures, the Mesoamerican and Classic Greek cases actually have much in common).

280. Ibid., 55.

281. While Scully's work is useful in denoting a range of variations on the ritual-architectural commemoration of divinity (priority II-A), I certainly would not want to imply that there is a universal, fixed-stage evolution from the literal to abstract variations.

282. On the interpenetrability of the three variations of the commemoration of divinity in the Hindu temple, see, for instance, Wu, *Chinese and Indian Architecture*, 21.

283. Soundara Rajan, *Invitation to Indian Architecture*, 15. Regarding the conception of architecture itself as the body of a deity, see Mabbett, "Symbolism of Mount Meru," 75, who explains the sense in which the Indian *stupa* serves as "the shrine or cult object at which the otherwise inaccessible divinity was worshipped turned into the divinity in person." (It is intriguing that Mabbett seems to describe an evolution in the architectural commemoration of divinity from abstract to more literal, the opposite of that which Scully documents with respect to Greek sacred architecture.)

284. Regarding architecture as "the house of God," for instance, Clothey, *Rhythm and Intent*, 186–200, recounts the performance of the *pratistha*, a Hindu ceremonial process by which icons can be embodied with the fullness of the divine, wherein the deity Venkatesvara was literally transported from India to his new home in the Penn Hills Temple at Pittsburgh. And an equally fantastic genre of deity-inspired architecture stems from the Hindu notion that temples are the temporal abodes of the divinities where they are to be duly pampered as we do a child — thus Siva, who is *abhiseka-priya* (fond of ritual bath), is indulged by an *anda-deul* (sunk-shrine) type temple, as at Tiruanaikka near Tiruchirapalli in Tamil Nadu, where the sanctum floor is laid below the level of the water table so that it is nightly flooded and then manually baled out before worship each morning; Soundara Rajan, *Invitation to Indian Architecture*, 22–23, gives examples of several *unda-deul*, sunk-shrine type temples.

285. See Laing, "Central and Eastern Europe," 217. Irving Lavin, *Bernini and the Crossing of St. Peter's* (New York: New York University Press,

1968), 17, likewise discusses the representation of the Trinity at St. Peter's, the Latern, and the church of Santa Maria dei Monti at Rome.

286. Marcus, "Religion and Archaeology," 299–305, for instance, reviews and convincingly challenges the stock notion, advanced most forcefully by J.E.S. Thompson, that the Classic Maya had a vast "pantheon" of "gods." She attributes the origin of this misconception to the Classical educations of the early Spanish chroniclers, "including knowledge of the ancient Greco-Roman pantheon that served as their model for an 'idolatrous' religion"; moreover, she argues that the so-called idols of "gods" that the Spanish found in so many Zapotec temples were more probably sacred images of deceased rulers. Nancy Troike, "Fundamental Changes in the Interpretation of the Mixtec Codices," in *Ancient Mesoamerica,* ed. Graham, 282–83, reviews the 1976 meeting in Paris of the International Congress of Americanists in which the consensus was that the nature of the Mixtec supernatural was distorted by the standard terms "god" and "deity" and concludes that those terms "should probably be eliminated pending the determination of appropriate categories." Alternatively, the ancient Mesoamerican conception of the supernatural is now being described more in terms of "vital forces" that make all things move, rather than as "gods" with distinct "spheres of control." Troike, ibid., for instance, discusses the Mixtec term *nuhu* and compares it to *mana*. Marcus, "Religion and Archaeology," 299, 305, considers the Zapotec term *pè* — variously translated as "wind," "breath," or "spirit" — and the Maya terms *ku* ("sacred" or "divine") and *ik,* which also meant "wind," "breath," and "life."

287. For instance, see Brundage, *Two Earths, Two Heavens,* 80. Mesoamerica is, of course, also replete with instances in which not the building itself but the architectural ornament is dedicated to the commemoration of deity: the long-nosed masks of Chaac, the Maya god of rain, prevalent in central Yucatán architecture (see Gendrop, "Dragon-Mouth Entrances," 146–50), and the alternating images of Tlaloc and Quetzalcoatl on the Citadel pyramid at Teotihuacán are obvious examples. Other clear instances of Mesoamerican theomorphic architectural decoration include: the stone carvings of Ah Muzencahs, that is, the bee or "diving" gods placed above doorways at Tulum and Cobá, among other Maya sites (see Henderson, *World of the Maya,* 223); the doorways, joints, and facades of all the major temples at Copán that are ornamented with stone friezes of the rain god, young maize god, and other deities (see Coe, *Maya,* 88); and the stucco reliefs of the nine lords of darkness, which decorate the walls of the tomb of Pacal in the Temple of the Inscriptions at Palenque (see Adamson, *Ruins of Time,* 239).

288. Gendrop, "Dragon-Mouth Entrances," describes the stylistic variation and geographical distribution of dragon-mouth entrances. He is in general accord with Eric Thompson that the facades of Central Yucatán temples represent Itzamná, "the multifaced creator god"; and he likewise accepts the traditional assessment that the long-nosed masks typically associated with these facades are representations of Chaac, the Maya god of rain.

289. Gendrop, ibid.

290. Thompson, *Maya History and Religion,* Chapter 7, has a famous discussion of "the major gods of the Maya pantheon," with special attention to Itzamná. The phrase "triple identification" is my term for Thompson's equation of Itzamná, the Maya universe, and the serpent-mouth temples. It is also noteworthy that the Maya conception of the universe as a house is very like that of the Barasana, discussed earlier in this chapter in reference to homologized architecture (priority I-A).

291. Thompson, *Maya History and Religion,* 215.

292. On the status of the Maya "deity" question and especially for a challenge to Thompson's understanding of the significance of Itzamná, see Daniel Schavelzon, "Temples, Caves or Monsters? Notes on Zoomorphic Facades in Pre-Hispanic Architecture," in *Third Palenque Round Table,* 1978, pt. 2, ed. Merle Greene Robertson (Austin: University of Texas Press, 1980); also see Benson, "Architecture as Metaphor," 185, 188.

293. Benson, "Architecture as Metaphor," 185. Benson apparently sees her interpretation as complimentary rather than antithetical to Eric Thompson's earlier interpretation.

294. Copán Temple 22 was addressed earlier in this chapter in the section on "Astronomy: The Power of Prediction" Gendrop, "Dragon-Mouth Entrances," 148, has a picture of Temple 11 (fig. 11).

295. Spinden, *Study of Maya Art,* 15–16.

296. Coe, *Maya,* 90.

297. Benson, "Architecture as Metaphor," 183–84, has collected a whole series of examples of this "figure within a monster deity" theme from both Central Mexico and the Maya area. Scholars have related

this recurrent motif of a humanoid figure seated inside the architectonic body of a zoomorphic god (for instance, at La Venta, Tres Zapotes, and Izapa) to: (1) origin myths in which the deity-ancestors are returned to the place of emergence, (2) earlier beliefs that gods and spirits of nature were "housed" in specific natural phenomena, (3) natural cycles, and (4) the relationship between kingship and deity. See ibid.

298. Richard Townsend, "Pyramid and Sacred Mountain," in *Ethnoastronomy and Archaeoastronomy in the American Tropics,* ed. Aveni and Urton, 37–62.

299. Broda, "Templo Mayor as Ritual Space," 64, bases her assessment of the Templo Mayor as a voracious earth monster particularly on the iconography of Cihuacoatl-Coatlique-Coyokauhqui and on the Tlaltecuhtli representations on relief stones.

300. See Weaver, *Aztecs, Maya, and Their Predecessors,* 54.

301. One interpretation that does recognize the rarified architectural commemoration of divinity in Mesoamerica is Justino Fernández's assessment that the famous Aztec statue of Coatlicue (the goddess, Serpent Skirt) does not represent a being but an idea, "the embodiment of the cosmic-dynamic power which bestows life and which thrives on death in the struggle of opposites." Fernández, *A Guide to Mexican Art,* 42–45.

302. Ernst Cassirer, *The Philosophy of Symbolic Forms,* vol. 2, in *Mythical Thought* (New Haven: Yale University Press, 1955), Chapter 2; quoted by Klimkeit, "Spatial Organization in Mythical Thinking as Exemplified in Ancient Egypt," *History of Religions* 14 (May 1975): 277.

303. Mircea Eliade, *The Quest: History and Meaning in Religion* (Chicago: University of Chicago Press, 1969), 85, defines "sacred history" as "the fabulous epoch [between the creation of the world and historical time] when the ancestors were roaming about the land." I have expanded the term in both directions to include the cosmogony proper and the mythico-historical events of the post-primordial era.

304. Ruskin, *Seven Lamps of Architecture,* 169.

305. Ibid., 170.

306. Landa, *Relación,* 179; cited in Tozzer, *Chichén and Cenote,* 81.

307. Robert Heine-Geldern, *Conceptions of State and Kingship in Southeast Asia,* Data Paper no. 18, Southeast Asia Program, Cornell University, 1956, 19. Mabbett, "Symbolism of Mount Meru," 71, 82, has also commented on the cosmogonic significance of the Angkor Vat balustrade.

308. William Mullen, "A Reading of the Pyramid Texts," *Pensée;* cited by Frank Waters, *Mexico Mystique,* 162.

309. Brundage, *Two Earths, Two Heavens,* 3–4, 38; or Gary Urton, *The History of a Myth: Pacariqtambo and the Origin of the Inkas* (Austin: University of Texas Press, 1990).

310. Michael Coe, "Religion and the Rise of Mesoamerican States," in *The Transition to Statehood in the New World,* ed. Grant D. Jones and Robert R. Kautz (Cambridge: Cambridge University Press), 168; cited by Benson in "Architecture as Metaphor," 184.

311. Spinden, *Ancient Civilizations of Mexico,* 217.

312. Weaver, *Aztecs, Maya, and Their Predecessors,* 63.

313. Clothey, *Rhythm and Intent,* 78.

314. Short, *History of Religious Architecture,* 89–90, 95. These frescoes date from the first century B.C.E. to the seventh century C.E.

315. Gary Witherspoon, "Beautifying the World Through Art," in *Native North American Art History,* ed. Mathews and Jonaitas, 219; or Witherspoon, *Language and Art in the Navajo Universe* (Ann Arbor: University of Michigan Press, 1977), 167 et seq.

316. Howard Hibbard, *Bernini* (Baltimore: Penguin Books, 1965). Bernini's work is discussed more fully in the section on theatric sacred architecture.

317. Carrasco, "Templo Mayor," 284–85; and Broda, "Templo Mayor as Ritual Space," 45, among others, interpret Aztec human sacrifice in terms of Huitzilopochtli's birth.

318. Short, *History of Religious Architecture,* 98.

319. Von Hagen, *Frederick Catherwood, Archt.,* 34, recounts how this renowned illustrator of Yucatec antiquities was, in 1833, the first to sketch the interior of the Dome of the Rock.

320. Anthony Blunt, Introduction to *Baroque and Rococo,* ed. Blunt, 10; and Laing, "Central and Eastern Europe," 221, discuss the strong affirmation of saints and relics in the Council of Trent and the consequent developments in architecture. In the same vein, note also that the Cappella della S. S. Sindome, among dozens of such commemorative examples, was built specifically to safeguard and display the Holy Shroud of Turin, in spite of its authenticity having been officially denied by the Church in the later Middle Ages; see Blunt, Introduction, 10. And, the pilgrimage church of the Wies (1746–54), the final

masterpiece of Dominikus Zimmermann and the seat of one of the most enduring pilgrimages in Bavaria, was built specifically to house a crude image of the Scourged Christ at the Column after that image was seen to have shed tears; see Laing, "Central and Eastern Europe," 269. Laing's discussion of Vierzehnheiligen, a German church built over the spot where, in 1445, a shepherd had had a vision of the Christ child surrounded by fourteen other children, later interpreted as the Fourteen Saints in Time of Need, is an equally good example of this sort of architectural commemoration of sacred history (priority II-B).

321. Oscar Lewis, *Tepoztlán: Village in Mexico* (New York: Holt, Rinehart and Winston, 1960), 17. An even more visceral expression of the desire to actually lay hands (or feet) on the real estate of one's sacred history is evidenced in contemporary pilgrimages to the small New Mexican village of Chimayo, where pilgrims journey to obtain dirt, eat it (geophagy), and use it with saliva to make the sign of the cross on children's foreheads; in this regard, Ronald Grimes, *Symbol and Conquest: Public Ritual and Drama in Sante Fe, New Mexico* (Ithaca, N.Y.: Cornell University Press, 1976), 71, explains: "space becomes objectified as land . . . *tierra del Santo* [sacred soil] . . . and insofar as space becomes objectified as land one can 'carry space' back with him in the form of a jar of dirt."

322. On the Sacred Cenote as a pilgrimage destination, see, for instance, *Chilam Balam of Chumayel*, ed. Roys, 65, n. 4; 133, n. 7; and 176.

323. Graham, "Antecedents of Olmec Sculpture at Abaj Takalik," 9–10.

324. Ibid.

325. Spinden, *Study of Maya Art*, 34.

326. Coe, *Maya*, 93.

327. Regarding Maya vase painting, for instance, Michael Coe has argued that the majority of it relates to a lost epic literature of which the *Popol Vuh* is a surviving fragment, and Richard Adams has argued for specific historical depictions on particular vases; see Hammond, "Lords of the Jungle," 31. Similarly, regarding Maya mural paintings, Benson, *Maya World*, 83, for instance, argues that, "whereas Maya sculpture had a narrow range of subject matter, mural painting was apparently much freer and more telling."

328. Proskouriakoff, *Study of Classic Maya Sculpture*, 4–5.

329. Brainerd, *Maya Civilization*, 82–83.

330. Ibid., 93.

331. Schele, "Sacred Site and World-View at Palenque," 96.

332. Ibid., 99.

333. Ibid., 104.

334. Gary Ebersole, *Ritual Poetry and the Politics of Death in Early Japan* (Princeton: Princeton University Press, 1989), 266.

335. Abbot Suger believed that the king of France was a "vicar of God" and that the authority and unity of France were symbolized and vested in the Abbey of St. Denis. See Abbot Suger, *On the Abbey Church of St. Denis*, ed., trans., and annotated by Erwin Panofsky (Princeton: Princeton University Press, 1979), 2. Von Simson, *Gothic Cathedral*, 89, shows that Suger's two principal strategies for implementing his master plan in the sphere of politics were the manipulation of the Carolingian "histories" and the prodigious rebuilding of St. Denis.

336. Kerry Downes, "England," in *Baroque and Rococo*, ed. Blunt, 159.

337. Short, *History of Religious Architecture*, 23–24, suggests this connection between Sargon and Louis XIV. Blunt discusses the Place Vendôme and the earlier Place des Victoires, which were royal squares "designed first and foremost to glorify the king [Louis XIV] whose statues they framed" and, moreover, Louis XIV's conception of monarchy as reflected in explicitly ecclesiastical buildings. Anthony Blunt, "Baroque and Rococo," in *Baroque and Rococo*, ed. Blunt, 130, 133. Kent Bloomer and Robert Moore, *Body, Memory, and Architecture* (New Haven: Yale University Press, 1977), 12, comment on the placement of Louis XIV's bed at Versailles and allude to a sense in which the gardens there symbolize an integration of nature and imperial authority.

338. Stanley Tambiah, *World Conqueror and World Renouncer: A Study of Buddhism and Polity in Thailand Against a Historical Background* (Cambridge: Cambridge University Press, 1977), Chapter 7.

339. Soundara Rajan, *Invitation to Indian Architecture*, 51.

340. Heine-Geldern, *Conceptions of State and Kingship in Southeast Asia*, 24. Mabbett, "Symbolism of Mount Meru," 79–81, explains that, "in much of Southeast Asia, royal legitimacy was sanctified in great measure by the construction of an impressive shrine rather than a secular palace, as a symbolic Mt. Meru and ritual center of the kingdom."

341. Carrasco, *Quetzalcoatl and the Irony of Empire,* explains the Toltec/Aztec relationship in resplendent detail.

342. Aveni, *Skywatchers of Ancient Mexico,* 237. The revered alignments of Copán were similarly adopted in a number of Maya centers despite their astronomical ineffectualness. See ibid., 233, 270–80. Likewise demonstrating the twofold pattern wherein astronomy and homology (priorities I-C and I-A) are used to instigate an architectural event that communicates a specific political agenda (priority II-C), Coggins, "Zenith, Mountain, Center, Sea," 115, reviews the ingenious correlation of the revered imagery of zenith and center, the movement of the sun, and the experience of the volcano of Tacana (cosmology, astronomy, and geography) with the specific privileges and demands of rulership in the kingship rituals of Izapa, Chiapas.

343. Thompson, *Maya History and Religion,* Chapter 1.

344. The strength of the materialist position in Mesoamerican studies has ensured that this political character of architecture and ritual has been very well documented; Kubler, *Art and Architecture in Ancient America,* 41, cites Cecelia Klein and Johanna Broda (somewhat unfairly I think) as exemplars of the "hard materialist" approach that has class struggle as a dominant theme and in which "the place of art is reduced . . . to propaganda for the state."

345. Henderson, *World of the Ancient Maya,* 232.

346. Ibid., 221.

347. Kelemen, *Medieval American Art,* 1: 38, 48, contrasts the Aztec remodeling of Malinalco with their more typically disinterested occupation of Mitla, where "they seem to have left little impression on the place."

348. Teobert Maler considered the bas-reliefs of bound figures at Tikal and Naranjo as evidence of Maya human sacrifice, but Spinden, *Study of Maya Art,* 21–22, 178, considers that these and others like them symbolize success in war. These pre-Hispanic Maya bas-reliefs of bound figures find an even stronger parallel in the grim post-Hispanic image of two mailed knights standing on the heads of conquered Mayas on the doorway of Montejo's colonial palace in Mérida, Yucatán. And similar to Montejo's palace, but more drastic still, is that architectural event in which the Incas led captives in triumph through Cuzco, forced them to lie prone in front of the Sun Temple, and then trod on their necks to symbolize victory; see, for instance, von Hagen, *Realm of the Incas,* 200.

349. John Pohl, "The Significance of Human Sacrifice in the Codex Zouche-Nuttal," Paper read at the 1977 meeting of the Society for American Archaeology, New Orleans; cited by Troike, "Interpretations of Mixtec Codices," 281. Broda, "Templo Mayor as Ritual Space," 41, similarly discusses how, at the main temple of the Aztecs, "it was political power transformed into supernatural power by means of sacrifice."

350. Townsend, "Coronation at Tenochtitlán."

351. Ibid., 406. Demonstrating a similar sort of pre-Columbian reliance on familiar old imagery to legitimate a novel new political agenda, Carolyn Tate, "The Maya Cauac Monster's Formal Development and Dynastic Contexts," in *Pre-Columbian Art History,* ed. Alana Cordy-Collins (Palo Alto, Calif.: Peck Publications, 1982), describes how a jaguarian-anthropomorphic motif known as the Cauac Monster, originally an apolitical and universalistic depiction of the devouring and regenerative earth (and, as such, perfectly suited to initiating a ritual-architectural event), was later enlisted as a stylized pedestal by specific Maya leaders and thus became an emblem of the legitimacy of their rulership; see especially ibid., 33, 52.

352. Raymond Sidrys, "Megalithic Architecture and Sculpture of the Ancient Maya," in *Papers on the Economy and Architecture of the Ancient Maya,* monograph 8, ed. Raymond Sidrys (Los Angeles: Institute of Archaeology, UCLA, 1978), 155–57.

353. Robertson, *Pre-Columbian Architecture,* 20–21.

354. Landa, *Relación,* 62; quoted in Tozzer, *Chichén and Cenote,* 73. For Herrera's remarks on the concentric spatial-social organization of Mayapán, see ibid., 83. Recent settlement pattern studies have challenged the archaeological validity of Landa's idea of Mayapán planning, and particularly its overgeneralization to other Maya sites; see, for instance, Chase, "Ganned But Not Forgotten: Late Postclassic Archaeology and Ritual at Santa Rita Corozal, Belize."

355. Andrews, "Dzibilchaltún," 329, 332.

356. Carmack, *Quiché Maya,* 159–64.

357. George Cowgill, "Rulership and the Ciudadela: Political Inferences From Teotihuacán Architecture," in *Civilizations in the Ancient Americas: Essays in Honor of Gordon R. Willey,* ed. Richard

M. Leventhal and Alan L. Kolata (Albuquerque: University of New Mexico Press, 1983), 313–43.

358. Ibid., 329–32.

359. Cowgill admits that his interpretation of the Ciudadela as one of the central symbols of the state, apart from any specific ruler and apart from the day-to-day operation of government, directly follows from the interpretation of Rene Millon. Ibid., 331.

360. Ibid., 330. It is interesting typologically that, while the Inca is alive in his palace, it is an operative bureaucratic center (that is, primarily an instance of the commemoration of politics, priority II-C), but once he dies, the same building is, by prearrangement, transformed into a tomb-shrine or *huaca* (primarily commemoration of the dead, priority II-D).

361. There may actually have been a major diachronic shift with respect to the artistic commemoration of specific individuals. Weaver, *Aztecs, Maya, and Their Predecessors,* 136, basing her opinion on work by Kubler, Millon, and Sanders, says that after 500 C.E. at Teotihuacán there was "a trend away from purely religious symbolism toward individual glorification and warfare." Also, the great stone heads of the Olmec, among the oldest major monuments, are so highly realistic and individualistic that it seems likely that they represent specific historical leaders.

362. Morley quoted by Deuel, *Conquistadors Without Swords,* 383. Likewise, Joyce, *Maya and Mexican Art,* 41, argues that Maya human representation was conventionalized and impersonal; "portraiture, as we understood it, did not exist"; and Spinden, *Study of Maya Art,* 23, says, "it is exceedingly doubtful whether any [Maya] sculptures were seriously intended as portraits of individual chiefs or priests." Deuel, *Conquistadors Without Swords,* 383–87, has a brief historiographical account of the controversy.

363. Bernal, *Mexican Wall Paintings,* 16, cites Miguel Covarrubias as his authority for concluding that the regalia, ornaments, and accessories of office are far more important than human figures in Maya murals; similarly, with respect to Maya sculpture, Bushnell concludes that "most examples give the impression that the office mattered more than the man." Bushnell, *Ancient Arts of the America,* 106.

364. Jones, Coe, and Haviland, "Tikal," 303. Stephens, *Incidents of Travel in Central America, Chiapas, and Yucatán,* 1: 139, 153–58, deserves credit for anticipating this position in the mid-nineteenth century.

365. Tozzer, *Chichén and Cenote,* 151, claims, in consonance with the old standard position, that "in the Maya Great period the only example of any personal identification by sign or by glyph is on the limbs of some prisoners such as those on Lintels 8 and 12 at Yaxchilán and Lintel 12 at Piedras Negras." To his credit, Tozzer does identify a number of depictions of Classic Maya personages on stelae, lintels, pottery, and architectural foundations, which appear to commemorate temporal circumstances — particularly gestures of military defeat and submission, and scenes of captive prisoners — but these he considers exceptions. Ibid., 178.

366. Ibid., 167.

367. Ibid., 176. Tozzer, ibid., 151, 155, also emphasizes that, at both Tula and Chichén Itzá, individual warriors are identified by tribe, town, and name.

368. See especially Thompson, *Rise and Fall of Maya Civilization.*

369. Raymond Decary, *La Mort et les Costumes Funéraires à Madagascar* (Maisonneuvre, 1962); quoted by Michel Ragon, *The Space of Death: A Study of Funerary Architecture, Decoration, and Urbanism* (Charlottesville: University Press of Virginia, 1981), 35–36.

370. Burl, *Rites of the Gods.* The variegated interpretations in Aubrey Burl's provocative study of European megaliths and their ritual usages cut a wide swath across the framework of ritual-architectural priorities: besides their indubitable astronomical alignments (astronomy, priority I-C), the stone circles of the British Isles encapsulated a sacred space within the prosaic landscape (sanctuary, priority III-D); the chambered tombs in the same area served as stage-like backdrops for cult practice in their forecourts (theatre, priority III-A); the megalithic temple-tombs were the loci of prayerful petitions of news and favors (propitiation, priority III-C); and, it has even been claimed (see ibid., 85), albeit unconvincingly, that some megaliths are formalized representations of deities (divinity, priority II-A). It is also noteworthy that English architect Indigo Jones, after careful measurements, mistook Stonehenge for the ruins of a proportional Roman temple and thus a participant in the adherence to universal principles (convention, priority I-B). See Wittkower, *Architectural Principles,* 143. Nevertheless, the priority most poignantly illustrated by Burl's work on megaliths is the architectural commemoration of the dead (II-D).

371. Burl's contention that European megaliths are primarily mechanisms for communicating with the dead finds support in Gordon Childe's dour acknowledgment of the primacy of ancestor worship in French megalithic culture — "superstition absorbed all their energies; the cult of the dead overshadowed all other activities." Gordon Childe, *The Dawn of European Civilization* (London: Kegan Paul, Trench, Trubner and Co., 1925), 284–85.

372. Sullivan, "Astral Myths Rise Again," 15, is in perfect accord with Eliade on this point.

373. See Eliade, *History of Religious Ideas,* 1: 123.

374. Ibid., 115.

375. Mabbett, "Symbolism of Mount Meru," 74. On the same theme, also see Soundara Rajan, *Invitation to Indian Architecture,* 26–27. Though somewhat less dramatic, Cistercians similarly champion strict, unadorned stone construction for its unadulterated purity and for precisely this temporal intransigence; see Braunfels, *Monasteries of Western Europe,* 74.

376. The complex and dynamic interplay between *chii,* bones, and the living has been summarized this way: "Every living body is a concentration of energy [or *chii*]. The energy condenses and forms bones. When a man dies, only the bones remain. Therefore it is a principle that a buried corpse can influence latently its descendants by returning the energy from the bones." The *Tsang-shu* of Kuo P'u; quoted by Carlson, "A Geomatic Model," 170. Also see Joseph Needham, *Science and Civilization in China* (Cambridge: Cambridge University Press, 1962), 4, pt. 1.

377. Spinden, *Study of Maya Art,* 85. There was, at one time, a stereotype that exempted the Classic Maya from the typical Mesoamerican preoccupation with death; for instance, Tozzer, *Chichén and Cenote,* 111–12, says, "it has often been said that death and the ideas surrounding it are not especially prominent in Maya art in Classic times."

378. Marcus, "Archaeology and Religion," 297–99, 311, for instance, has strong remarks on the misunderstanding and underestimation of royal ancestor worship in Mesoamerica generally and among the Zapotecs and Maya particularly.

379. I am indebted to Carlson, "A Geomantic Model," for the general organization of evidence for Mesoamerican ancestor worship in terms of mythology, ethnohistory, ethnography, and archaeology; I have supplemented his excellent examples with others of my own.

380. Heyden, "Caves, Gods and Myths," 10, for instance, gives examples and says that "stone was worshipped in many parts of Mesoamerica, especially flint and obsidian, and some groups believed themselves to be the descendants of great rocks, the way others saw their primeval forebearers as trees." Heyden's interpretation owes explicitly to Eliade's work on stones.

381. Recinos, *Popol Vuh,* 190, n. 13. In regard to the general significance of stones for Mesoamericans, Recinos, ibid., also notes that the mythico-history in *The Annals of the Cakchiquels,* from the Southern Highlands area, speaks of the obsidian stone, or Chay Abah, to which the nation rendered homage; also see ibid., 209, n. 3; 225, n. 2. Recinos considers the crucial theme to be "the constant association of the divinity with stone" (ibid., 190), but recent research demonstrates that in Mesoamerica the commemoration of ancestors is actually more relevant than the commemoration of deities (that is, the dead, priority II-D, rather than divinity, priority II-A).

382. Recinos, *Popol Vuh,* 190, 205–6, 225, (re)constructs this account of Nacxit's (Quetzalcoatl's) gift of stone to the Quiché from references in both the *Popol Vuh* and the *Título de los Señores de Totonicapán.*

383. See, for instance, Miguel León-Portilla, *Aztec Thought and Culture: A Study of the Ancient Nahuatl Mind,* trans. Jack Emory Davis (Norman: University of Oklahoma Press, 1963), 99.

384. Recinos, *Popol Vuh,* 118. Carlson, "A Geomantic Model," 190–93, cites both this example and the previous one related to Quetzalcoatl reviving the bones of a former race to demonstrate the devotion to ancestral bones in Mesoamerican myth.

385. Ibid., 226, 228–30. This genealogy, of which Quetzalcoatl is an integral member, demonstrates that the commemoration and worship of ancestors, together with the fascination for pedigrees and distinguished lines of descent — directly relevant to the resilient career of the Quetzalcoatl-Tollan paradigm and thus to the Tula–Chichén Itzá problem — need to be considered as part of one giant complex of issues.

386. Landa, *Relación,* describes the postmortem preservation of the heads of Mayapán Cocom lords at p. 131, human heads used as trophies at pp. 120 and 123, and the cremation of "nobles and persons of very high rank" and the placement of their ashes in urns and wooden statues at pp. 18–19. Carlson,

"A Geomantic Model," 193; Tozzer, *Chichén and Cenote,* 218–19; and Coe, *Maya,* 131, all make use of these references.

387. Bartolomé de Las Casas, *Apologetica Historia de las Indias* (Madrid: Nueva Biblioteca de Autores Expanoles, 1909), 630; quoted by Carmack, *Quiché Maya,* 194.

388. Coe, *Maya,* 8–9.

389. Carlson, "A Geomantic Model," 195–99, explores this intriguing if speculative hypothesis.

390. According to Ruth Bunzel, *Chichicastenango* (Seattle: University of Washington Press, 1959), "the Ancestors" dominate Chichicastenango religion and provide the great moral standard against which all ethical behavior is judged; the Ancestors constitute the highest tribunal, meting out punishment, sickness, and even death. Accordingly, in Chichicastenango, altars are set up in most of the private homes where, after the fashion of the Chinese household cults, family prayers are offered to them. In the churches, specific areas are designated — the high altar being the domain of the First People — where the Ancestors receive prayers from the public. Also see Pearce, *View From the Temple,* 154–58, who bases his remarks about modern Maya ancestor worship particularly on ethnography by Bunzel, E. Vogt, T. Lee, and C. Guiteras-Holmes.

391. Marcus, "Architecture as Metaphor," 298–301, argues that the Spaniards never understood Zapotec royal ancestor worship and that their distortions have persisted until today. Kelemen, *Medieval American Art,* 1: 47, emphasizes the character of the Zapotec tombs as literal houses for the "undead"; they remind him of the Etruscan graves of Tuscany and Umbria.

392. Ibid., 183–84. This motif was discussed more fully earlier in this chapter in relation to the architectural commemoration of divinity (priority II-A). Furthermore, with direct relevance to the Tula–Chichén Itzá problem, even Kukulcán/Quetzalcoatl and his Toltecs, who together with the Itzás traditionally have been castigated for bringing "idolatry" to Yucatán, may eventually prove instead to have been devotees of royal ancestor worship. Tozzer repeatedly documents the traditional assessment that idolatry was not present among the Maya until it, together with human sacrifice, was introduced by Kukulcán (or Kukulcán II); see, for instance, Tozzer, *Chichén and Cenote,* 38, 208. So far as I know, no one has discussed the "idolatry" of Kukulcán as a manifestation of royal ancestor worship.

393. Suggesting multiple sorts of manifestations of the ritual-architectural commemoration of the dead (priority II-D) in a single monument, Coe, *Maya,* 103, considers that the most appropriate term for the Palenque's Temple of the Inscriptions is "funerary temple" because it captures the dual sense in which the Maya used their pyramid structures as "burial grounds," often intruding innumerable graves into an older substructure while continuing to carry on ceremonies in the superstructure. In the same vein, Benson, "Architecture as Metaphor," 185, interprets the sarcophagus of Pacal, equipped with all the royal accoutrements and retainers due an active king, as "a small cosmic house inside a large cosmic model."

394. Marcus, "Archaeology and Religion," 311, notes the contemporaneity of the Zapotec commemoration of royal ancestors in tombs, murals, and sculpture with the Maya commemoration of royal ancestors in the carved stelae.

395. The Castillo at Chichén Itzá (along with the Temple of the Inscriptions at Palenque) is Carlson's arch example of a *feng-shui* geomantic-like monument in Mesoamerica; but, aside from noting the Castillo's orientation toward the two cenotes that "gave entrance to the Underworld," his interpretation is actually better support for the Castillo as homologized architecture (priority I-A) than commemoration of the dead (priority II-D). Ibid., 179–87.

396. Tozzer, *Chichén and Cenote,* 163.

397. Ibid., 111–12.

398. Thompson, *Rise and Fall of Maya Civilization.*

399. Ibid., 144, 268; and idem, *Maya History and Religion,* 187–88, 199.

400. Pollock et al., *Mayapán, Yucatán, Mexico,* 16.

401. Staale Sinding-Larsen, *Iconography and Ritual: A Study of Analytical Perspectives* (Oslo: Universitetsforlaget AS, 1984), 9.

402. Braunfels, *Monasteries of Western Europe,* 132. Franciscans and Dominicans are, of course, not wholly ambivalent about their religious structures; nowhere is this more clear than in colonial New Spain, where church building was a giant priority and a major pillar of the spiritual conquest of Mexico. Tozzer/Landa, 74–75, n. 335, 177, has several telling references to Franciscan friars making the Indians work on "the very sumptuous monasteries which they have built without ceasing to build." Leslie Byrd Simpson, *Many Mexicos,* 4th rev. ed. (Berkeley: University of California Press, 1969), 75,

86–87, has some astute remarks on "the architectural conquest" of Mexico by the mendicant orders and on the transplantation of "the Renaissance tradition of magnificence; the more beautiful the church the greater the glory to God, and the greater credit to themselves."

403. López de Cogolludo, *Historia de Yucatán*, 1688, in regard to human sacrifice at the Adivivo Pyramid in Uxmal, Yucatán; quoted by Stephens, *Incidents of Travel in Yucatán*, 1: 192–93.

404. Holmes, *Ancient Cities of Mexico*, 221. Holmes, dedicated to "objective description," has very few such forays into imaginative (re)construction.

405. Kubler, *Art and Architecture of Ancient America*, 163.

406. Hardoy, *Pre-Columbian Cities*, 106–13. As an enclosure that shuns exterior views, Monte Albán's Great Plaza likewise participates in the sanctuary priority, III-D; see the final section of this chapter.

407. After several attempts at compromise, Bramanti's circular design was eventually jettisoned in favor of the Latin cross plan that exists at St. Peter's today. A number of authors discuss the history and controversy of the sixteenth-century rebuilding of St. Peter's. Besides Wittkower, *Architectural Principles*, pt. 1; and Murray, *Architecture of the Italian Renaissance*, 124–25; see Blunt, Introduction, 25–26.

408. Wittkower, *Architectural Principles*, 20–30, argues that the shift from the basilical cross form to centralized church plans is the architectural expression of a fundamentally changed conception of the godhead that separated the Middle Ages from the Renaissance.

409. Braunfels, *Monasteries of Western Europe*, 51. On the evolution of the basilica form, also see Stoddard, *Art and Architecture in Medieval France*, 53.

410. Norberg-Schultz, *Meaning in Western Architecture*, 75–91, interprets procession through the longitudinal Romanesque form as a metaphor for the teleological salvation route of Christianity.

411. William Bullock, *Six Months Residence and Travels in Mexico* (London: John Murray, Albemarle-Street, 1824), 146, 152–53. Stephens, *Incidents of Travel in Central America, Chiapas, and Yucatán*, 1: 153–54, 210–20, 215–17, likewise comments on the prevalence and elaboration of processions in nineteenth-century Mexico.

412. Besides the elaborate parades that accompany nearly all political and ecclesiastical events in modern Mexico, the streets of small Mexican towns are regularly graced with impromptu processions for weddings, graduations, saints' days, and — especially in the days before Christmas — for nightly "posadas," in which small groups sing on their way to one another's houses.

413. Kubler, *Art and Architecture of Ancient America*, 51–54.

414. George Kubler, "The Iconography of the Art of Teotihuacán," in *Studies in Pre-Columbian Art and Archaeology*, no. 4 (Washington: Dumbarton Oaks, 1967), 12. Margain, "Pre-Columbian Architecture of Central Mexico," 73–74; and Weaver, *Aztecs, Maya, and Their Predecessors*, 117, 134, both benefit from and extend Kubler's assessment of the "liturgical character" of Teotihuacán art.

415. Tozzer, *Chichén and Cenote*, 164.

416. Ibid., 163–64.

417. Ibid.

418. Kubler, *Art and Architecture of Ancient America*, 207.

419. Carmack, *Quiché Maya*, cites both Villacourt and Recinos as ethnohistorical sources in this regard at 197; and he summarizes the archaeological data on the "Main Street" of Utatlán at 299–302.

420. Thomas Gann, *Mystery Cities* (London: Gerald Duckworth and Co., 1925), 103–27; quoted by Deuel, *Conquistadors Without Swords*, 305.

421. The probable character of the ritual-architectural events at Chichén Itzá's Sacred Cenote and Castillo will be addressed more fully in the final chapter.

422. Wittkower, *Art and Architecture in Italy*, 199; quoted by Hibbard, *Bernini*, 151.

423. Bernini's *Ecstacy of St. Teresa* has also been described as a prop for contemplation (for instance, by Hibbard, *Bernini*, 138) and thus as a participant in the contemplation priority (III-B) as well as the theatric priority (III-A).

424. Irving Lavin, *Bernini and the Crossing of St. Peter's*, 18 et seq.

425. Curves, movement, color, and light — a fusion of painting, sculpture, and architecture all collaborate in Bernini's architectural thespianism as demonstrated in his small church of Sant'Andrea al Quininale in Rome (begun 1658); see Hibbard, *Bernini*, 144–48. And, on a much larger scale, Bernini's design for the piazza in front of St. Peter's (only a portion of which was actually built) is flanked by two free-standing colonnades, likened by Bernini to the outstretched arms of the Church welcoming the faithful — a ploy that epitomizes the inclusiveness and exhortative suasion typical of manifestations of

the theatric ritual-architectural priority (III-D). See ibid., 155.

426. Miguel Covarrubias, *Indian Art of Mexico and Central America* (New York: Alfred A. Knopf, 1957). For other typical negative assessments of Tula's architecture see, for instance, Margain, "Pre-Columbian Architecture of Central Mexico," 76; Fernández, *Guide to Mexican Art*, 27–28; Weaver, *Aztecs, Maya, and Their Predecessors*, 202; and Hester, *Introduction to Archaeology*, 408.

427. Pollock, "Architecture of the Maya Lowlands," 434–35, has characterized "Toltec Maya" architecture in this fashion, particularly as contrasted to the Classic Maya and Puuc Maya styles.

428. Weaver, *Aztecs, Maya, and Their Predecessors*, 225–27, summarizes the conventional characterization of the "Toltec Maya" style at Chichén Itzá. Thompson (for instance *Rise and Fall of Maya Civilization*, 126–30) has been very influential in propagating this negative assessment of the "Toltec" style at Chichén Itzá.

429. Bernal, *Mexican Wall Paintings*, 21.

430. Regarding the theatrical character of Aztec ritual-architectural choreography, Brundage, *Two Earths, Two Heavens*, 33, contrasts the inclusive, public *teopantli* of Tenochtitlán with the Huacaypata, the great square of Cuzco that was a familial and exclusive space. Von Hagen, *World of the Maya*, 119–20, makes the explicit parallel between the European Baroque city and the Highland Maya city (which has close Toltec affiliations). He claims that both demonstrate that "absolutism and enormous plazas belong together." Thus, while the content of the Aztec state-sponsored human sacrifice was largely dedicated to the commemoration of sacred history (particularly the mythic birth of Huitzilopochtli) and of political authority (priorities II-B and II-C), the manner of presentation was pure theatrics (priority III-A).

431. Prescott, *The Conquest of Mexico*, 45, imagines the rites of the Aztecs this way: "From the construction of their temples, all religious services were public. The long processions ascending their massive sides, as they rose higher and higher toward the summit, and the dismal rites of the sacrifice which were performed there, were all visible from the remotest corners of the capital, impressing on the spectator's mind a superstitious veneration for the mysteries of his religion, and for the dread ministers by whom they were interpreted." Quoted in Catherwood, *Views of Ancient Monuments*, 126.

432. Carrasco, "Aztec Vision of Place," 292; or idem, *Quetzalcoatl and the Irony of Empire*, 186. In the same vein, Broda, "Templo Mayor as Ritual Space," 40–41, explains how each successive ruler enlarged the Templo Mayor, particularly in a fashion that produced an increasingly spectacular frontal view, and then invited the lords of allies and enemies alike to witness extravagant inaugurations that began with displays of the architectural embellishments and tributes of luxury goods from the conquered provinces and climaxed in massive human sacrifices of captives from resisting populations.

433. Joyce, *Maya and Mexican Art*, 41.

434. Brainerd, *Maya Civilization*, 26. Brainerd does, however, suspect that the elaborate costumes of the Maya priests were designed to evoke "religious awe" from the commoners. Ibid., 66.

435. López de Cogolludo, *Historia de Yucatán*, 1688; quoted by Stephens, *Incidents of Travel in Yucatán*, 1: 192–93.

436. Landa, *Relación*, 119.

437. Catherwood, *Views of Ancient Monuments*, 126–29, seems to have simply extrapolated Prescott's notion of Aztec ritual into the Maya context.

438. Stephens, *Incidents of Travel in Central America, Chiapas and Yucatán*, 1: 143, seems to have used Cogolludo as his main inspiration for Maya ritual; also see idem, *Incidents of Travel in Yucatán*, 1: 192–93.

439. Francisco Antonio de Fuentes y Guzmán, writing of Guatemala in about 1700; cited by Stephens, *Incidents of Travel in Central America, Chiapas and Yucatán*, 1: 131.

440. Spinden, *Study of Maya Art*, 96, considers that "the plaza [of Copán] is surrounded by a stepped wall as if it were a sort of theatre." Kubler, *Art and Architecture of Ancient America*, 217, seconds that "a primary platform, rightly called the acropolis . . . provides a theatrical setting for the [Copán] ball court."

441. Kelemen, *Medieval American Art*, 1: 57–61.

442. Von Hagen, *World of the Maya*, 113–14, 159, for instance, described virtually all Maya art as "baroque" because of its elaboration.

443. Gann, *In an Unknown Land*, 62, actually made this sarcastic charge in reference to the little plaza in San Miguel, the capital of Cozumel, and what he terms "the neo-Mexican culture — the keynote of which is meretriciousness — a constant striving after the grandiose and impressive in architecture, institutions, and culture, a

lamentable falling short, and attainment only of the ridiculous."

444. Regarding the deliberate avoidance of the theatric priority (III-A), for instance, where the Maya architecture of the Preclassic and Early Classic periods generally has a theatrical openness, Robert E. Fry, "Revitalization Movements Among Postclassic Lowland Maya," in *Lowland Maya Postclassic*, ed. Chase and Rice, 134, sees in the Late Classic a kind of "deep structure change" that is reflected both ritually and architecturally: "rituals were increasingly isolated from large scale public viewing; plazas which were previously quite open became cut off from the populace; and rites in the temples were conducted in small rooms out of sight of the viewers." Following this important interlude of elitist and esoteric ritual architecture (demonstrative especially of the sanctuary theme, priority III-D), in the Postclassic, the participatory theatric priority (III-A) was reasserted: "the emphasis was on broad open areas on top of pyramid substructures, unless impermanent temple structures were used. Both imply a more open access and greater possibility for visual participation in rituals, harking back to an early Preclassic and possibly Early Classic period." Ibid.

445. David Freedberg, *The Power of Images: Studies in the History and Theory of Response* (Chicago: University of Chicago Press, 1989), 161.

446. Guiseppe Tucci, *Theory and Practice of the Mandala*, vii.

447. Woodward Jr., "Borobudur," provides a very helpful interpretation of the experience of Borobudur.

448. Drawing his analogy from the two complementary mandalas of Japanese Shingon Buddhism, Hiram Woodward, ibid., 43–46, believes that the dim lower galleries of Borobudur correspond to the "womb mandala," the real world, the trial, and that the upper open terraces and apical *stupas* correspond to the "diamond mandala," the ideal world as known by the Bodhisattvas, the reward for lessons learned in the dark galleries.

449. Alan Grapard, "Flying Mountains and Walkers of Emptiness: Toward a Definition of Sacred space in Japanese Religion," *History of Religions* 20 (February 1982): 209.

450. Turner and Turner, *Image and Pilgrimage in Christian Culture*, 234–35, invokes this dictum of Thomas Aquinas to explain what is happening in Marian pilgrimage and, in so doing, articulates the sense in which Catholic pilgrimage churches participate in the contemplation priority (III-B).

451. Abbot Suger, *The Abbey Church of St. Denis*, 21; quoted by E. Panofsky in his Introduction to that treatise. On the uniqueness of Abbot Suger's treatise, besides Panofsky's thorough introduction to Suger's treatise, see von Simson, *Gothic Cathedral*, 102.

452. Woodward, "Borobudur," 47, hypothesizes that Borobudur may have had more gilded "mirror-like" surfaces than is typically acknowledged and that these surfaces symbolized elements of existence that were "reflected" and without "real" existence.

453. Claude Levi-Strauss, "The Effectiveness of Symbols," in *Structural Anthropology*, trans. Chris Jacobson and Brooke Grundfest Schoepf (New York: Basic Books, Inc., 1963), 186–205.

454. Panofsky's Introduction to Abbot Suger, *The Abbey Church of St. Denis*, 21. Whereas, in archaic contexts architectural forms presumably "correspond" by literal homology to the structure of the cosmos (priority I-A), and in the Italian Renaissance architectural forms "correspond" to abstract laws of proportion (convention, priority I-B), the architectural elements of Borobudur and St. Denis "correspond," and thus provide the otherwise unavailable access, to immaterial reality. Similarly Charles Long, *Alpha*, 27–30, has emphasized that symbolic art is a necessary dimension of religion because in art forms the relationship of humans to their world is objectified, made concrete, and therefore accessible for participation and communion.

455. Von Simson, *Gothic Cathedral*, 38–39, 109.

456. Abbot Suger quoted in Panofsky's Commentary on Suger's *The Abbey Church of St. Denis*, 203.

457. Adding another twist to the play of priorities, quite often the dominance of the theatric priority (III-A) and that of the contemplation priority (III-B) succeed one another in the experience of a single building. For instance, Santa Maria Tonantzintla and San Francisco Acatepec, two nineteenth-century churches near Cholula in Central Mexico, both of which feature literally hundreds of small cherubic faces scattered through a riot of Churrigueresque decoration, initially stun the human observer by their ultraistic histrionics (theatre, priority III-A), but then they sustain interest as the patron's attention fastens on one or on a series of the exuberant elements as an object of contemplation (priority III-B). Significant also are accidental or inadvertent architectural props for devotion; a water-stained wall or a crack in the floor may become the habitual focus of

some worshipper's attention and, as such, ironically, surpass the altar in transformative power.

458. Laurette Séjourné, *Burning Water: Thought and Religion in Ancient Mexico* (Berkeley, Calif.: Shambhala, 1976), 89–96; Irene Nicholson, *Mexican and Central American Mythology* (London: Paul Hamyln, 1976); and Frank Waters, *Mexico Mystique: The Coming Sixth World of Consciousness* (Chicago: Swallow Press Inc., 1975), 141–42, 180–81, who speaks about pre-Columbian "mandala symbols" that "evoke a psychic effect from all [their] imparted meanings."

459. Waters, ibid., 140–42, discusses Seler's allusions to mandala-like symbolism in his commentary on the Codex Borgia.

460. For instance, Thompson, *Rise and Fall of Maya Civilization*, 74–75.

461. Von Hagen, *Maya Explorer*, 115, uses this dramatic language to describe Catherwood's problems in reproducing the Copán decoration.

462. Holmes, *Ancient Cities of Mexico*, 38, 89, 248–49.

463. Joyce, *Maya and Mexican Art*, 39–41.

464. Tozzer, *Chichén and Cenote*, 14, is another who uses the term "Maya baroque."

465. Kubler, *Art and Architecture of Ancient America*, presents his ideas on the historical and stylistic relationship between Monte Albán and Mitla at 169–70. The notion of a Mixtec "vocabulary" of eight typical forms is also Kubler's; he explicates and graphically reproduces these, ibid., 174–75.

466. Spinden, *Study of Maya Art*, 110–12, comments on the Maya's seemingly compulsive need to garner even greater surfaces for decoration by extending the walls above the roof; his five-stage developmental sequence for the Maya roof-comb seems to be a parallel to the Gothic attempt to push the cathedral higher and higher.

467. See Kubler, *Art and Architecture of Ancient America*, 269–70, for a discussion of the recombination and, in some cases, salvage and re-use of constituent, "typographical" elements at Uxmal. Kubler, ibid., 169, 173, 236, also notes that besides their mutual use of geometrical mosaic panels, Mitla and Uxmal share the otherwise very rare formal characteristics of outward-leaning, "negative batters" and open-cornered courtyards formed by four unconnected buildings. Holmes, *Ancient Cities of Mexico*, 88–89, 248–49, was perhaps the earliest to comment on the repetition and rearrangement of a limited number of elements both at Uxmal and at Mitla.

468. The mask panel phenomenon is typologically complex in the extreme. Earlier in this chapter, I discussed the sense in which these Río Bec and Chenes temples could participate in the commemoration of divinity, priority II-A; and there is likewise a strong possibility that mask buildings are connected with mummy burials and, thus, the commemoration of the dead, priority II-D. See Coe, *Maya*, 58.

469. Ibid., 104.

470. Kubler, *Art and Architecture of Ancient America*, 175.

471. Ibid., 243. Rosemary Sharp, "Architecture as Inter-elite Communication in Preconquest Oaxaca, Veracruz, and Yucatán," in *Middle Classic Mesoamerica*, ed. Pasztory, 169, has also made the suggestion that Mesoamerican geometric architectural decoration may represent a coding of calendrical data, that is homology, priority I-A.

472. The issue of repetition and variation from repetition in architecture is complex. Walter Gropius, *The New Architecture and the Bauhaus*, trans. P. Morton Shand with an intro. by Frank Pick (Cambridge, Mass.: The M.I.T. Press, 1965), 37, 85, for instance, discusses the concept of "a manifold simplicity arrived at by deliberate restriction to certain basic forms used repetitively . . . for it is commonplace that repetition of the same things for the same purposes exercises a settling and civilizing influence on men's minds." Abercrombie, *Architecture as Art*, 31–32, discusses the sense in which repetition is among the architect's most basic tools for inspiring awe.

473. Spinden, *Study of Maya Art*, 48.

474. In the southern sections of Chichén Itzá, for instance, the Monjas, Iglesia, Casa Colorado, House of the Deer, and especially the Temple of Three Lintels all have Puuc-like decoration.

475. Ruskin, *Seven Lamps of Architecture* (originally published 1848), 25, makes this remark in reference to architecture and "the lamp of sacrifice."

476. Thompson, *People of the Serpent*, 58.

477. Stephens, *Incidents of Travel in Yucatán*, 1: 52, notes that the name given by the Spaniards to the large structures of America was "adoratorio," implying that they were essentially places for petitioning favor from the deities.

478. Landa mentions the Sacred Cenote of Chichén Itzá six times, and in each instance he stresses that the exotic ritual machinations there,

particularly throwing live persons into the sink-hole, were primarily in the interest of propitiating rain. See Tozzer, *Chichén and Cenote,* 212.

479. Redfield, *Folk Culture in Yucatán,* 230.

480. Broda, "Templo Mayor as Ritual Space," 38, 43, 51, is quite original in connecting the Great Temple of the Aztecs with this more basic substratum of Mesoamerican religion.

481. Of course, this substratum of ancient pan-Mesoamerican religion is scarcely exhausted in the propitiation priority (III-C); the other especially relevant categories are the commemoration of the dead (priority II-D), commemoration of divinity (priority II-A), and homology (priority I-A).

482. Ibid., 59. Broda, perhaps inadvisedly, uses the terms "philosophy of nature" and "natural philosophy" in reference to the enduring cosmological concepts of the ancient Mesoamericans. Ibid., 46, 65.

483. Thompson, *Maya Archaeologist,* 163, generalizes that "an offering was placed in every Maya structure when it was dedicated or enlarged." Also see Thompson, *Maya History and Religion,* 178–79. Benson, *Maya World,* 91, has a generalized discussion of typical locations and contents of Maya caches; and Tozzer, *Chichén and Cenote,* describes the offertory caches at Chichén Itzá, ibid., 209–10, and at other Maya sites, ibid., 85.

484. Heyden, "Caves, Gods, and Myths," 27, describes and gives examples of the strong continuity between ancient and modern Mesoamerican cave ritual and symbolism. More specifically, E. Wyllys Andrews IV, "Balankanche — Throne of the Tiger Priest," *Explorers Journal* 49:4 (1971), describes how Balankanche, "an archaeological treasure trove," had been lost even to the local Maya until it was rediscovered in 1959, at which time Maya *h-men* explained the rumored existence of such a lost adoratorio dedicated to the rain god and insisted on performing the *cha chac* immediately and in toto to placate the disturbed deity. Gallenkamp, *Maya: The Riddle and Rediscovery of a Lost Civilization,* 207–14, has a summary of the rediscovery of Balankanche.

485. Gann, *In an Unknown Land,* 55, witnessed a *cha chac* ceremony "from beginning to end" in which the Maya constructed and, upon completion, burned "two rude huts." Following Irwin Press, *Tradition and Adaptation: Life in a Modern Maya Village* (New York: Greenwood Press, 1975), Pearce, *View From the Temple,* 48–49, describes a four-sided *cha chac* altar; Pearce also notes the interesting case in which the tiny village of Telchaquillo, near the ruins of Mayapán, holds the *cha chac* inside the ancient city's walls. Ibid., 49.

486. Thompson, *Maya History and Religion,* 170.

487. Redfield, *Folk Culture in Yucatán,* 115, 128.

488. T. Lee, *Jmetic Lubton: Some Mexican and Pre-Hispanic Ceremonial Customs in the Highlands of Chiapas, Mexico,* New World Archaeological Foundation 28 (Provo, Utah: Brigham Young University, 1970); Evon Vogt, *The Zinacantecos of Mexico* (New York: Holt, Rinehart and Winston, 1970); and George Foster, *Tzintzuntzan* (Boston: Little, Brown, and Company, 1967), which, while it is a study of Michoacán, is considered generally applicable to the Maya Highlands. Pearce, *View From the Temple,* 155, 174, 247, uses these three sources as evidence of the "logic of bargain or contract" among the Maya. Marcus, "Archaeology and Religion," 299, similarly argues that, among Zapotecs, "all relationships — whether with ancestors, animals, other Zapotecs, or supernaturals — were considered reciprocal, with something offered in return for every concession."

489. Regarding the possibility that Mesoamerican propitiatory ritual-architectural events were probably more often occasions to shock the cosmic system equilibrium into responding than occasions to beg or buy divine favor, see, for instance, Smith, *Map Is Not Territory,* 304–8, who discusses Melanesian cargo cult logic; and Irving Goldman, *The Mouth of Heaven: An Introduction to Kwakiutl Religious Thought* (Huntington, N.Y.: Robert E. Krieger Publishing Company, 1975), 122–43, who provides a fresh interpretation of Kwakiutl potlatch redistribution.

490. See Goldman, ibid., 85, 123–24. Where the older view of Mesoamerican propitiatory ritual as conversation with their gods ties the propitiatory priority (III-C) particularly to the commemoration of divinity (priority II-A), Goldman's notion of cosmic equilibrium and interdependence implies a special linkage to the homology priority (I-A).

491. Evon Vogt, "Some Aspects of the Sacred Geography of Highland Chiapas," in *Mesoamerican Sites and World-Views,* ed. Benson, 120–25, for instance, provides strong evidence that in most cases, the Highland Maya, at least, were propitiating ancestors rather than deities.

492. Walter Gropius, *New Architecture and the Bauhaus,* 43, for instance, as the voice of the "New Architecture" of the Bauhaus, campaigned

incessantly for simplicity and economy in building, a "rationalized construction" that could raise buildings quickly and expediently.

493. Clothey, *Rhythm and Intent,* 183, describes building the Hindu temple as "founding a world" and notes the extensive religious as well as technical training required of Hindu craftsmen. Soundara Rajan, *Invitation to Indian Architecture,* 25, recounts the celebrated and ancient practice of renewing the building materials of Hindu temples; his specific example is the Jagannath temple at Puri (Orissa), where rites of renewal coincide with the twelve-year sidereal period of Jupiter.

494. On the Barasana case, see Hugh-Jones, *Palm and the Pleiades,* 28. On the *hocoka,* see Powers, *Oglala Religion,* 41–42.

495. Regarding the Tongo of South Africa, Oliver, Introduction to *Shelter, Sign and Symbol,* 7–8, recounts how, when a headman dies, or a village is struck by lightning, or the land has been exhausted, a ritual specialist invokes astragalomancy (the use of divining bones) to select a fresh site, then consummates the choice by sexual intercourse, and embarks upon a lengthy process wherein the old village is "broken to pieces" and the new village erected and sacralized, thus allowing the Tongo to experience "a phoenix-like opportunity for rebirth of the community with the rebirth of the village." Oliver's principal source is Henri A. Junod, *The Life of a South African Tribe* (London: Macmillan and Co., 1927).

496. See Landa, *Relación,* 18, for his mention of the many changes of residence; and ibid., 206, for the oft-cited account of the ritual destruction and replacement of household utensils.

497. Tozzer, *Chichén and Cenote,* 35; similar is idem, "Maya Research," 11–12.

498. M. A. Tovilla, *Relación Histórica Descriptiva de las Provincias de la Verapaz y de la del Manche* (1635); quoted by Carmack, *Quiché Maya,* 194–95. Carmack considers the archaeological evidence for this "rewhitening" agenda, Ibid., 295.

499. Vaillant, *Aztecs of Mexico,* 92, originally contended that the pyramid at Tenayuca was rebuilt according to fifty-two-year cycles, but that has since been challenged; Kubler, *Art and Architecture of Ancient America,* 89, holds tentatively to Vaillant's position.

500. Broda, "Templo Mayor as Ritual Space," 42.

501. Jacques Soustelle, *The Four Suns: Recollections and Reflections of an Ethnologist in Mexico,* trans. E. Ross (New York: Grossman Publishers, 1971), 115–19.

502. It is quite possible that the same logic that informs the chronic destruction and rebuilding is operating in the Mesoamerican notions of ritual filthiness and cleansing (see Thompson, *Maya History and Religion,* 174; and Landa, *Relación,* 161) and ritual feasting followed by purgation and ritual vomiting (see Tozzer, *Chichén and Cenote,* 207–8).

503. Heyden, "Caves, Gods, and Myths," 12, makes explicit use of Eliade to explain how, in Mesoamerica, building and the settling of new territories "reiterated the cosmogony."

504. See, for instance, Short, *History of Religious Architecture,* 47.

505. Ibid., 91. Though not speaking specifically of architecture, John Strong, "The Transformative Gift: An Analysis of Devotional Acts of Offering in Buddhist Avada-na Literature," *History of Religions* 18 (February 1979): 221–37, provides a relevant discussion of the sense in which meritous acts in Buddhism (that is, *bhakti* and *karma)* are, like architectural events, profoundly transformative.

506. Witherspoon, *Language and Art in the Navajo Universe,* 167–70.

507. Bushnell, *Ancient Arts of the Americans,* 127; and Marvin Cohodas, "Style and Symbolism in the Awotobi Kiva Murals," in *Native North American Art History,* ed. Mathews and Jonaitis, 167, both make reference to kiva wall paintings that were immediately painted over.

508. Vaillant, *Artists and Craftsmen in Ancient Central America,* 21–23.

509. Margain, "Pre-Columbian Architecture of Central America," 90.

510. Thompson, *Rise and Fall of Maya Civilization,* 303.

511. Coe, *Maya,* 172, for instance, describes how Classic Maya stelae, once thought to have been concerned with water and fertility, are now understood to portray blood dripping from mutilated members; Pearce, *View From the Temple,* 11, collects several references to a penis mutilation cult in Yucatán; and Schele and Miller's Introduction to *The Blood of Kings* places bloodletting at the very center of Maya religion.

512. Ruskin, *Seven Lamps of Architecture,* 27, contributes the very relevant general rule that "we should consider an increase of apparent labor as an increase of beauty in the building." Sidrys, "Megalithic Architecture and the Sculpture of the Ancient

Maya," among others, attempts to calculate the prodigious labor to build the Mesoamerican, particularly Maya, buildings.

513. Holmes, *Ancient Cities of Mexico,* 250–52.

514. Ian Graham, in conversation with Adamson; quoted in Adamson, *Ruins of Time,* 258; Ghirlandajo (1449–94) was one of the finest Florentine painters of frescoes and a master of Michelangelo.

515. Bushnell, *Ancient Arts of the Americas,* 135.

516. Fry, "Revitalization Movements," 129–35, discusses the pervasiveness of the Maya tradition of ritual destruction of art and architecture and especially its possible relationship to revitalization movements.

517. Tozzer, *Chichén and Cenote,* 197, recounts the "killing" of offerings at Chichén Itzá and elsewhere; Deuel, *Conquistadors Without Swords,* 378–80, discusses the phenomenon of "ceremonially smashed" pottery and underwater archaeology; Thompson, *Maya History and Religion,* 180, comments on the pervasiveness and resilience of Maya offerings to lakes; and Bushnell, *Ancient Arts of the Americas,* 135, laments the fact that most of the bowls retrieved from New Mexican burials had been ritually "killed."

518. Weaver, *Aztecs, Maya, and Their Predecessors,* discusses the deliberate destruction and burial of Maya stelae at Tikal, ibid., 160; and at Kaminaljuyú, ibid., 83; and of Olmec stone carvings in the Gulf Coast area, ibid., 51–45.

519. Tozzer, *Chichén and Cenote,* 259, n. 16. The most obvious examples of deliberately defaced buildings at Chichén Itzá are the Caracol, the Temple of the Little Heads, the Temple of the Warriors, and the Atlantean figures. Ibid., 45.

520. Weaver, *Aztecs, Maya, and Their Predecessors,* 207, discusses the deliberate destruction of Tula; and Henderson, *World of the Ancient Maya,* 222, discusses the military destruction of Mayapán. Weaver, *Aztecs, Maya, and Their Predecessors,* 139, following Rene Millon, discusses the sudden, catastrophic, and total destruction of Teotihuacán, seemingly from within; and Munro Edmonson, "Some Postclassic Questions About the Classic Maya," in *Ancient Mesoamerica,* ed. Graham, 225, suggests that the "destruction" of Classic Maya cities may have been largely ritual and symbolic and that the "abandonment" was probably an evacuation by the ruling dynasty rather than the total population.

521. José Ortega y Gassa, 1951, on the transition from village to city; quoted in George Andrews, *Maya Cities: Placemaking and Urbanization* (Norman: University of Oklahoma Press, 1975), 7.

522. *Encyclopaedia Britannica,* 1965 ed., vol. 19, 151–52. Mircea Eliade, *Occultism, Witchcraft and Cultural Fashions: Essays in Comparative Religions* (Chicago: University of Chicago Press, 1976), 22–23, emphasizes that the foundation of Rome and Romulus' plowing of the circular ditch is tantamount to a cosmogony.

523. Powers, *Oglala Religion,* 41.

524. Burl, *Rites of the Gods,* 164.

525. Scully, *Earth, Temple and Gods,* 194.

526. Ibid., 211–12.

527. Ibid., 202–3. So too, the Romanesque Christian basilica, directly indebted to this Roman tradition, perpetuates the stratagem of designing from the inside out and of space-enclosing volumes; see L'Orange, *Art Forms and Civic Life in the Late Roman Empire,* for an elaboration on this point.

528. The distinction between the respective building agenda of Saint Bernard and Abbot Suger is a central issue in Panofsky's Introduction to Abbot Suger's treatise, *The Abbey Church of St. Denis.*

529. Braunfels, *Monasteries of Western Europe,* Chapter 5.

530. This imitation and standardization among Cistercian monasteries represents something of a shift away from the sanctuary priority (III-D) toward that of conventionalized architecture (priority I-B).

531. Von Simson, *Gothic Cathedral,* 44. Braunfels, *Monasteries of Western Europe,* 37–46, discusses the astonishing plan for "an ideal Carolingian monastery" that was found in the library of St. Gall; this is an excellent example of an attempt at a construction that would provide a foretaste of paradise.

532. Modern proponents of "functionalism" and "nonbourgeois architecture" (for instance, the Bauhaus architects) adopted white, beige, gray, and black as their colors, and championed a stark simplicity of form that harkened to that of the Cistercians; the formal coincidence is particularly intriguing and ironic given the radically different intentions of the two groups. See Wolfe, *From Bauhaus to Our House,* 24–27, for a satirical discussion of the "functionalist" ideal.

533. Braunfels, *Monasteries of Western Europe,* Chapter 6.

534. See, for instance, Borgeaud, "The Greek Labyrinth in Context." And, on a totally different plane, Simpson, *Many Mexicos,* 147, among many such examples, recounts a number of instances in which

fugitives from the law sought refuge in the colonial Catholic churches of Mexico and, thus, spawned fascinating debates between the civil and ecclesiastical notions of sanctuary.

535. Richard B. Pilgrim, "Intervals *(Ma)* in Space and Time: Foundations for a Religio-Aesthetic Paradigm in Japan," *History of Religions* 25 (February 1986): 255–77, is my main source for the discussion of *ma*. By collapsing the distinction between time and space, *ma*-inspired architecture also participates in the homology priority (I-A); see particularly ibid., 255–56. Günter Nitschke, "'Ma': The Japanese Sense of 'Place' in Old and New Architecture and Planning," *Architectural Design* 36:3 (March 1966), which Pilgrim uses, connects *ma* explicitly with architecture.

536. Pilgrim, "Intervals in Space and Time," 263.

537. Matsuoka Seigow, "Aspects of *Kami*," in *MA: Space-Time in Japan* (New York: Cooper-Hewitt Museum, n.d.); quoted by Pilgrim, "Intervals in Space and Time," 262. The strategy of demarcating a sacred space with ropes finds a direct parallel in Maya initiation ceremonies that take place inside just such a tethered precinct. See Landa, *Relación*, 103–4, 153.

538. Pilgrim, "Intervals in Space and Time," 266, says, "such experimental 'places' evoke, by their very nature, a sense of reality characterized by a dynamic, active, changing, poetic immediacy." Thus, where the Romans built sanctuaries to protect and facilitate activities, and the Cistercians to experience a foretaste of paradise, these Japanese cases employ sanctuary architecture (priority III-D), in a role more typically usurped by the orientation priorities, namely, the instigation of a ritual-architectural event. Pilgrim, ibid., 263, explains that the term *kekkai* persists in Buddhism to describe the special room in a temple set aside for a priest's spiritual renewal, a ritual event reminiscent of the Shinto practice of regenerative seclusion, especially in caves, tombs, and *tama-bako* ("soul-boxes") that — though containing nothing — are filled with sacred power to be imparted to those who have entered them.

539. Mesoamerican cave sanctuaries, as Doris Heyden's work "Caves, Gods and Myths" proves, deserve an entire study unto themselves. As is the case in a number of Buddhist monasteries, innumerable Mesoamerican buildings are built over cave shrines; and the Hindu homologization of cave, womb, and temple (see Kramrish, *The Hindu Temple*, 1: 162–63) similarly has countless parallels in ancient Mexico. At Chichén Itzá, aside from the many caves within the site proper, immediately adjacent there is an extensive warren of caves called the Balankanche that are typically interpreted as shrines to the Mexican gods, the Tlalocs, and Xipe Totec. See Andrews, "Balankanche."

540. This three-part organization owes directly to Kubler, "Design of Space in Maya Architecture," 526–27. This article (in which Kubler presents this scheme as a presumably evolutionary sequence) is remarkably provocative, but it is very short, quite old, and hardly representative of his subtle thinking on the diachronic development of Mesoamerican architecture. I have expanded his three categories (and abstained on the diachronic implications) in ways that he probably never intended.

541. On the old problem of the defensive versus the symbolic function of Mesoamerican city walls and archways, Stephens, *Incidents of Travel in Central America, Chiapas and Yucatán*, 1: 142, puzzles over the seeming contradiction between Copán's apparently defensive walls and the virtual absence of war-related iconography. Holmes, *Ancient Cities of Mexico*, 94, resolved his puzzlement over the apparent defensive ineffectuality of the elaborate archways at Labná, Kabah, Mayapán, Uxmal, and Chichén Itzá by concluding that the Yucatecans must have intended to build walls between them but had never finished. Thompson, *Maya Archaeologist*, 70, mentions excavating the foundations of an arch at Chichén Itzá that Holmes apparently did not see. And Spinden, *Study of Maya Art*, 109, also discusses these triumphant arches. More recently, Miller, "The Maya and the Sea," 132, summarizes the debate over the defensive versus the symbolic character of the walls at Tulum, Quintana Roo.

542. Recinos's account of the Quiché warriors reentering Utatlán is cited by Carmack, *Quiché Maya*, 183.

543. Kubler contends that La Venta's stone-encircled courtyard represents a survival or vestige of a primitive mode of monumental enclosure, far older than his second class of American architecture, that is, precincts formed of pyramids and platforms. Ibid., 527.

544. There is some evidence (discussed next chapter) that a wall similar to Tula's and Tenochtitlán's *coatepantli* may have enclosed "Toltec" Chichén Itzá.

545. Brunhouse, *Frans Blom*, 173.

546. Landa, *Relación*, 103–4, 153.

547. Broda, "Astronomy, *Cosmovision*, and Ideology," 101, argues that Mesoamerican architecture has within it two opposing tendencies: the tendency to achieve harmony with nature by creating an architectural replica (this recalls Scully's discussion of Greek architecture that integrates and dialogues with nature, but is actually most relevant to the homology priority, I-A) and the tendency to differentiate architecture from the natural surroundings (which is more like Roman architecture and especially relevant to the sanctuary priority, III-D).

548. Kenneth Frampton, "Labour, Work and Architecture," in *Meaning in Architecture*, ed. Jencks and Baird, 155, suggests that inside the walls of the city (Paris in this case) is "culture" and outside is "nature"; the quote from José Ortega y Gassa, used as an epigraph to this section on the sanctuary priority (III-D), is likewise relevant here.

549. See Horst Hartung, "Monte Albán in the Valley of Oaxaca," in *Mesoamerican Sites and World-Views*, ed. Benson, 55–59. Monte Albán's Great Plaza was also discussed earlier in this chapter as a major example of an amphitheatric space (theatre, priority III-A), and the so-termed Nunnery Complex at Uxmal was discussed in relation to the convention priority, I-B.

550. Kubler, "Design of Space in Maya Architecture," 523–24.

551. Ibid., 528. Spinden, *Study of Maya Art*, 96–97, describes the "artificial" acropolises, which characterize the central Maya area, for instance, Copán, Quirigua, and Tikal.

552. Kubler, "Design of Space in Maya Architecture," 528–29, uses Tikal, Copán, Piedras Negras, Yaxchilán, and Palenque to illustrate the concept of "the ascending ranks of courts rising in hierarchic order"; he does not mention Xochicalco in this context, though I think that it is the best example of all. Carrasco, *Quetzalcoatl and Irony of Empire*, 126–33, presents a very helpful "walk-through" of Xochicalco.

553. Kubler, "Design of Space in Maya Architecture," 526, hypothesizes that in Late Classic times there was a profound shift away from this manipulation of sculptural masses and open plazas (the second option that I have discussed) toward this third option — chambered buildings and "organized interior volumes of increasing spatial complexity."

554. Spinden, *Study of Maya Art*, 100, records the ground plans of the dark, cell-like sanctuaries at Palenque, Copán, Tikal, and Chichén Itzá. The great exception to the characteristic Mesoamerican pattern of cramped quarters and airless rooms appears at Tula and, likewise, in the "Toltec" architecture of Chichén Itzá, where hollow interior volumes and large-roofed colonnades enjoy an unprecedented success. These impressive interior spaces — the Mercado colonnade at Chichén Itzá is 165 by 150 meters — while assuredly enclosing space in a unique fashion, are tentatively considered to have been markets rather than explicitly religious buildings. Both Tula and Chichén Itzá are amply endowed with other ostensibly ritual structures that do conform to the more typical Mesoamerican pattern. Tozzer, *Chichén and Cenote*, 80, discusses the many cell-like sanctuary spaces at Chichén Itzá, particularly the inner rooms of the Castillo and the High Priest's Grave.

555. Thompson, *Maya History and Religion*, 163, admits that he is really speculating here; the quote continues, "[but] for all we know to the contrary, attendance may have been obligatory."

556. The Inner Court of the Temple of Herod was furthermore segmented into the Court of the Women, the Court of Israel, and the Court of the Priests; the Temple of Solomon was apparently likewise partitioned according to various classes of sacrality. See Short, *History of Religious Architecture*, 48.

557. Marcus, "Archaeology and Religion," 299, 311, explains that this arrangement of a "highly sacred inner room" and a "less sacred outer room" is characteristic of the Maya as well as the Zapotecs. There are several such floor plans in the southern portion of Chichén Itzá.

558. Landa, *Relación*, 160. On the same page, Tozzer's nn. 825, 828, and 831 give parallel examples among other Mesoamerican peoples. Morley/Brainerd, *Ancient Maya*, 219; and Thompson, *Rise and Fall of Maya Civilization*, 289, use this same example.

559. Las Casas's description of this Guatemalan refuge is summarized in Carmack, *Quiché Maya*, 198. Alfredo López Austin, *Hombre-Dios, Religion y Politica en el Mundo Nahuatl* (Mexico City: Universidad Nacional Autonoma de Mexico, 1972), 106; and Davies, *Toltecs Until the Fall of Tula*, 292–93, also use this same example.

560. Thompson, *Maya History and Religion*, 172–75, describes preparation for Maya ceremonies, citing not only Las Casas and Landa but a number of

strong ethnographic references; Tozzer, *Chichén and Cenote,* 76, gives more sources on the same issue.

561. López de Cogolludo, *Historia de Yucatán* (1688); quoted by Thompson, *Maya Archaeologist,* 132. Thompson also describes taking part in an all-night vigil for the consecration of the hut in which he was living; ibid., 132.

From left, Efraín Tamayo Matu, Gregorio Moo Camal, and Esteban Moo Camal, Maya residents of Chan Kom alongside the author's truck in 1988. Chan Kom, which is some 15 kilometers southeast of Chichén Itzá, was immortalized in the anthropological literature by Robert Redfield and Alfonso Villa Rojas as "a village that chose progress." (Photo by the author.)

Chapter Four

Deceptions in Form: The Ritual-Architectural Events of Tula and Chichén Itzá Reconsidered

The shortest line by land between the two sites [that is, Tula and Chichén Itzá] is not less that 800 miles . . . to the peoples of Middle America in the tenth century the distance was immense. . . . Yet there are the closest resemblances in the sculptural art, the architecture, the planning of religious symbolism, and even the details of costume, ornaments, and weapons of the two cities. The extraordinary fact is that nowhere between central Mexico and Yucatán have buildings in this distinctive style been found.

Eric Thompson, 1966[1]

Continuous form does not predicate continuous meaning.

George Kubler, 1970[2]

Agenda: Interrogation and Interpretation

Having digressed from the specifics of Tula, Hidalgo, and Chichén Itzá, Yucatán, for two long chapters to explore a more general set of problems related to the experience, interpretation, and comparison of sacred architectures, the discussion returns to the particular problem of the sister cities, presumably stronger and better equipped, and assuredly more determined than ever, to assess the relevant monuments *not* simply in terms of their formal and technical attributes, *nor* their ages, *nor* the cultural attainments of their builders, but rather as dynamic and superabundant participants in pre-Hispanic ritual-architectural events. Returning, then, to these two particular sites, the discussion becomes much more tightly focused. A couple of final methodological clarifications are, however, in order.

First, it is important to make explicit that mine is a decidedly nonhistorical comparative method. Thus, acutely aware of the wadded uncertainty of even state-of-the-art knowledge of the historical peoples and circumstances that link Tula and Chichén Itzá (and frustrated that as the old historical paradigms of Tozzer, Morley, and Thompson have toppled, no equally thoroughgoing replacements have emerged), the following analysis espouses only a minimal (and not particularly original) set of propositions about Tula–Chichén Itzá *historical* relatedness as a working hypothesis.[3] Rather than attempt to solve the historical problem (an initiative to which my comparative hermeneutical method is *not* particularly well suited), I endeavor, instead, to compare the famous pair *non*historically, morphologically, synchronically, and typologically — that is, in terms of a set of "religiously significant" questions. Where answers to the vexing chronological dimensions of the Tula–Chichén Itzá problem will most likely issue, at some point, from archaeological (or perhaps epigraphical) efforts, my project, by contrast, is dedicated to elucidating and comparing in a more synchronic fashion the play, interaction, and competition of ritual-architectural priorities that gave a distinctive quality to the buildings and ceremonial occasions of the two sites.

Second, I should be equally explicit about the generalizing nature of this hermeneutical reassessment. While the concept of a ritual-architectural event requires that I pay at least as much attention to the human actors and actions as to the buildings of Tula and Chichén Itzá, my hermeneutical approach simply does not provide the means for retrieving specific ritual movements and individual attitudes that may have informed any particular pre-Columbian ceremonial occasion. Instead, I am working at a somewhat higher level of generalization. While it may *not* be possible to retrieve the specific utterances, movements, and personalities of ancient Tula and Chichén ritual events, it is entirely plausible to retrieve at least the most pervasive and characteristic types of ritual-architectural priorities. Furthermore, our best hope for succeeding in that initiative comes via cross-cultural, morphological comparison, that is, by reference to the workings and meanings of sacred architectures in other, more accessible historical contexts like those discussed in the previous chapter.

In a sense then, after fashioning the hammer in the preceding chapters, this one delivers the blow. If disconcerting by its violence (and more so by the violence it implies toward the indigenous Mesoamerican context), the mallet metaphor intends, in Adolph Jensen's phrase, "to call a spade a spade,"[4] that is, to accept — enthusiastically even — that all hermeneutical reflection proceeds by a projection and revision, by a dialogical questioning and being answered.[5] Thus, hardly the reporting of a disinterested, "objective" bystander, this hermeneutic does not hover above, observing silently and unseen. My approach has no confidence in waiting passively, "letting the facts speak." Instead, it is unabashedly an interrogational hermeneutic, a third degree that, like the small boy in the Cuernavaca cathedral, puts its hands all over the monuments of Tula and Chichén Itzá, questioning, badgering, prodding the architectures and the architectural events of those sites and then watching and listening for their responses.[6] Moreover, it is a hermeneutic that revels in (rather than reduces) the superabundance and inexhaustibility of those sacred architectures, never landing on one meaning as *the* meaning nor trusting that the originally intended meanings of the pre-Columbian designers had any great endurance.

In that interpretive spirit, then, the ensuing discussion, moving in three large sections, relies heavily on the eleven types (and innumerable subtypes) of ritual-architectural priorities outlined in Chapter 3 as lines of inquiry, or points of departure, that initiate successive hermeneutical dialogues with the architectural events of: (1) Tula, Hidalgo; (2) South Chichén, that is, the portion of the city that is considered, according to convention, the older, indigenously Maya, "pre-Toltec" portion of the city; and (3) "Toltec Chichén," or North Chichén, the great and presumably somewhat newer plaza of the Castillo pyramid wherein Charnay was first awestruck by the uncanny similitude to Tula.

In each of these three cases, I will address (not always in quite so formulaic an order) five sorts of themes. The beginning two themes are preliminary and stage-setting. First is a very brief reiterative summary of the study of the particular site by antiquarians, archaeologists, ethnohistorians, and art historians. Second is a similarly brief background statement describing the historical ambience of the site, its specific dilemmas and special resources — the nature of the historical circumstances that gave rise to its specific ritual-architectural events. The final three subsections of each third of the chapter, which rely more explicitly on the comparative method outlined in the previous chapter, discuss the respective character and priorities of the ritual-architectural events of Tula, South Chichén, and "Toltec Chichén" in terms of: *the strategy of allurement,* or the "front half" of the respective architectural events, which typically involves a play of instigative or orientational priorities (homology, convention, and astronomy, priorities I-A, I-B, and I-C); *the manner of presentation,* that is, the choreographic strategy of the respective events or the nature of the ritual context that arises (usually at least) in the tension between the priorities of theatre (III-A), contemplation (III-B), propitiation (III-C), and sanctuary (III-D); and *the content or fundamental message* of the respective ritual-architectural events — the main idea or the substantive issues those events explore, which typically (though not always) arise from the play of commemorative priorities (divinity, II-A; sacred history, II-B; politics, II-C; and the dead, II-D).

Comparing the ritual-architectural events of Tula, South Chichén, and "Toltec Chichén" in terms of these five themes — scholarly inquiry, historical background, instigation, presentation, and content — elicits a complexly compartmentalized, cross-hatching interpretive framework, the discussion of which may tend both toward tedium and a false sense of analogical rigor. Churning through this long-winded interrogation of Tula's and Chichén Itzá's architectures is, however, not intended to render a definitive verdict nor, even less, to ram the pre-Hispanic perpetrators into dovecote-like explanatory cells. Rather, this pattern of formulaic questioning intends to stimulate productive hermeneutical dialogue with the old monuments and *to organize significantly* their fascinating and ever-paradoxical responses. These heuristic hermeneut-monument interviews reveal that Tula Toltec, South Chichén Puuc, and "Toltec Chichén" are not only three distinct architectural styles but as it were, three unique personalities and participants in three very different sorts of ritual-architectural agenda. Most relevantly of all, these hermeneutical conversations reveal that scholars, from Désiré Charnay forward, have typically been deceived by the striking formal resemblance between the ceremonial plazas of Tula Grande and "Toltec Chichén." The analysis demonstrates, in short, that the famed similitude in architectural forms masks a more important, more "religiously significant" *dis*similitude in ritual-architectural priorities.

At the risk of deflating all suspense, the basic hypotheses with respect to each of the three major sections follow. First, Tula was the first major Central Mexican center to rise out of the chaos following Teotihuacán's collapse. Tula made a ferociously gallant attempt to restore order, and its religio-civic architectural events were expressly dedicated to synthesizing the city's internal ethnic diversity so as to stand against unflagging external competition and, more specifically, to promote the Toltecs' daringly new concept of authority (then largely unprecedented in Mesoamerica) that hegemony rightfully belongs to those with military supremacy. Second, South Chichén, a case unto itself, participated (at least tangentially) in the very different problems and aspirations of the Puuc "Great Cities" of west central Yucatán and bears no special relation to Tula, either in the form of its architecture or the morphology of its ritual-architectural events. And third, North or "Toltec Chichén," to shorten a very long, complex story (and to leave aside, for now, the problem of its historical relatedness to Tula), was presumably founded from a position of far greater material wealth and stability than Tula ever enjoyed. The architects of "Toltec Chichén," faced with a dilemma that had more to do with winning the respect of their gathered audiences than with intimidating them, came forward with a design solution that not only looked different than the southern portion of the city but, moreover, expressed a considerably different set of ritual-architectural priorities than those that prevailed at either Tula or South Chichén.

With respect, then, to the direct morphological comparison between the ceremonial-architectural events of Tula Grande and those of "Toltec Chichén" — ostensibly, the root question from which this entire project grows — I will be arguing that both urban plazas engage, in similar strategies of allurement and both relied on similarly extravagant, theatrical, inclusive modes of presentation (although, with Chichén's vastly greater resources, it elevates those shared tactics to a substantially higher subtlety). It was, however, in regard to their respective messages or substantive contents (their "back halves") that the architectural events of Tula and "Toltec Chichén" differed most sharply. Despite conventional wisdom about the rampant "secularization" and militancy of the invading Toltecs (and notwithstanding the explicit Tula-like images of warriors, human sacrifice, and battle that are so abundant in "Toltec Chichén"), my hermeneutical interpretation suggests that the ritual-architectural events of the Yucatán capital did *not* announce the martial intimidations, the ultimatums of acquiescence or death that issued from Tula. Instead, quite to the contrary, to pose an unconventional hypothesis, these "Toltec Chichén" religio-civic events deliver a declaration (or at least a hope) of unity, reconciliation, and integration by promoting the idea that the remarkably diverse peoples that had come under the sway of "Toltec" Chichén Itzá — among the most cosmopolitan constituencies in the history of ancient Mesoamerica — shared a common cosmogonic tradition, a common history, a common conception of divinity, and, essentially, a common human condition.

This triune of specific hypotheses about Tula, South Chichén, and "Toltec Chichén," both iconoclastic and very involved (together with the more general methodological argument about the inadvisability of presuming a tight lock between architectural forms and religio-architectural meanings), should become, if not convincing, at least considerably more clear in the discussion that follows.

The Ritual-Architectural Events of Tula

> The house of Quetzalcoatl at Tollan was built with consummate care, majestically designed; it was the place of worship of their priest, whose name was Quetzalcoatl; it was quite marvelous. It consisted of four abodes. One was facing east; this was the house of gold. For this reason it was called the house of gold; that which served as stucco was gold plate applied, joined to it. One was facing west, toward the setting sun; this was the house of green stone, the house of fine turquoise. For this reason it was called the house of green stones, of fine turquoise. One was facing south, toward the irrigated lands; this was the house of shells or of silver. That which served as stucco, the interior walls, seemed as if made of these shells inlaid. One was facing north, toward the plains, toward the spear house *tlacochcalcopa,* this was the red house, red because red shells were inlaid in the

interior walls, or those stones which were precious stones, were red.

Fray Bernardino de Sahagún, 1569[7]

Tula: Embattled in History and Scholarship

Tula rose to prominence in a time of unprecedented confusion in the Valley of Mexico. The collapse of Teotihuacán had left a chaotic decentralization of power and Tula, for all its adolescent imperfections, deserves great credit as the first successful attempt to reconstruct order after the Classic collapse.[8] Described as a "halfway house between Teotihuacán and Tenochtitlán," Tula constituted a kind of experiment, a "more or less starting from scratch," in a sense, an invention of the type of military aggression and coercive, centralized authority that the Aztecs would later perfect.[9]

Yet, as the victor in the post-Teotihuacán scramble for control, Tula's was forever an embattled success. Where Teotihuacán had enjoyed a relatively confident and undisputed hegemony and was the dominant partner in a pan-Mesoamerican trading network, Tula, far smaller and more tenuous, perched itself on a defensible site surrounded on three sides by cliffs. The Tula Toltecs, even at their apex, were "perennial frontiersmen,"[10] ever facing potentially hostile competition from El Tajín to the east, Cholula to the southeast, Xochicalco to the southwest, the Tarascans to the west, and, above all, because it was located at the northern limit of "civilized" Mesoamerica — the encroachment of "barbarian" elements from the hinterland.[11] The Aztec empire, typically chided for instability and poor integration, was as much as ten times larger and in every way more well synthesized than the antecedent Tula Toltec empire.[12] In short, if Tula was the most potent force of its age, its hegemony over Central Mexico was, nevertheless, always precarious and strictly military: it never gained commercial dominance; it faced continual rebellion; its borders shifted radically and rapidly; and, in the end, its demise was as violently abrupt as its ascent.[13]

If Tula's pre-Hispanic historical career was at every turn wrought with difficulty, pressure, rebellion, inconfidence, and disrespect, modern scholars have scarcely been more tender with the city in their retrospective assessments of its art and architecture. By way of setting the stage for a reassessment of Tula's ritual-architectural events, the next two sections summarize quickly the various approaches to Tula and, particularly, the virtually unanimous dispraise of its artistic production.

The Study of Tula: Five Voices

To recapitulate briefly from the first two chapters, the investigatory history of Tula, Hidalgo, constitutes a perfect microcosm of the wider history of Mesoamerican studies. Each major stream of scholarship sweeps past the Hidalgo site with its characteristic style of questioning, and each makes discoveries commensurate with its interests. Representing the prescientific, antiquarian contingent, Désiré Charnay sashayed into Tula in the late nineteenth century and conducted rambunctious excavations on portions of two houses and the Adoratorio, a small platform that sits at the very center of the plaza of Tula Grande, the main ceremonial precinct.[14] On the basis of these limited diggings and his perusal of the other ruined and heavily looted structures at Tula, Charnay divined that this was, just as he had suspected, the paradisiacal Tollan of the documentary sources. From there, he was able to expound his glamorous vision of Tula as the original Toltec capital from which this superpeople launched their pan-American conquests. Even as Tula was increasingly appreciated through the twentieth century, Charnay's gushingly generous assessment of the site has never been equalled.

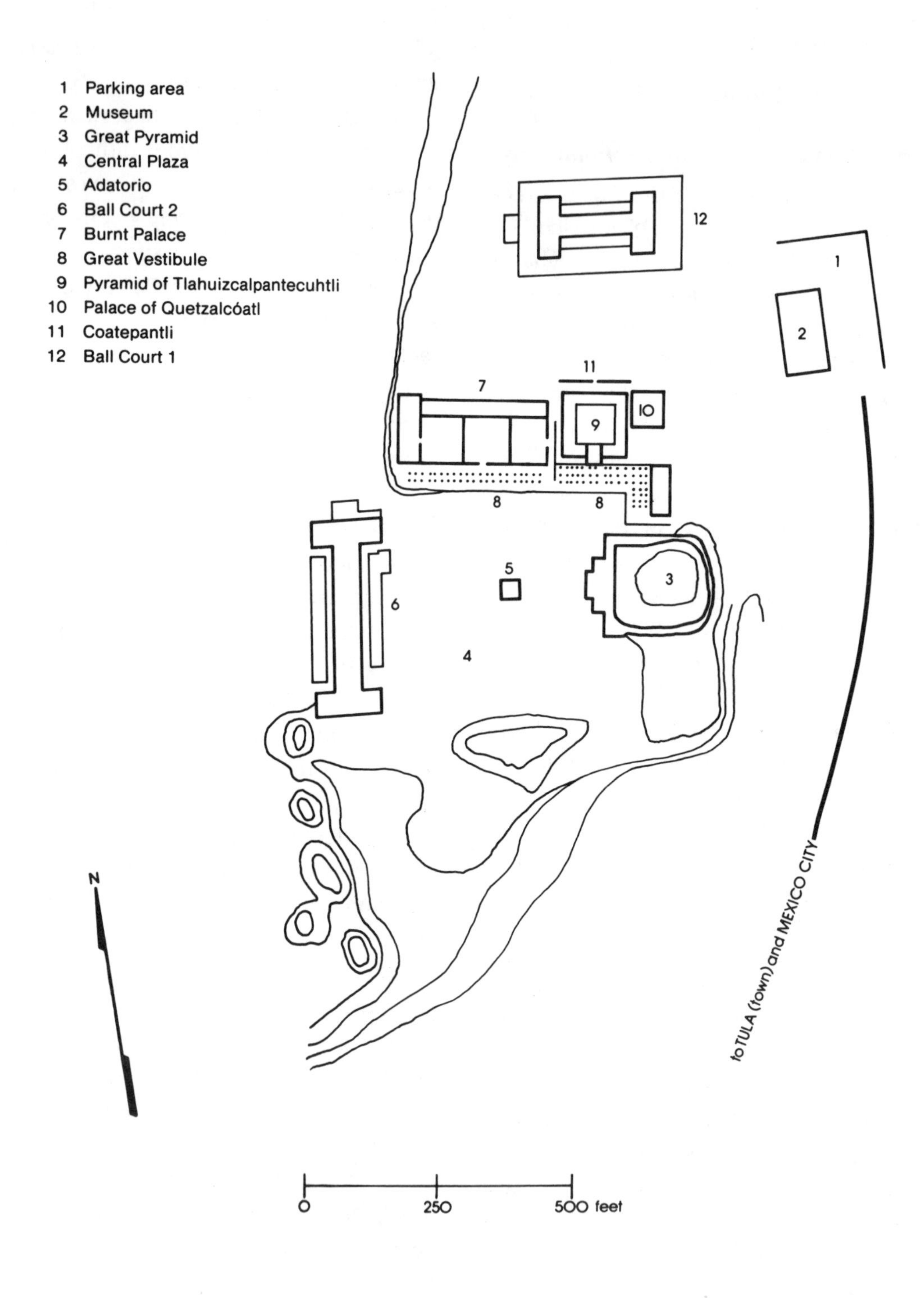

Tula. (From *The Complete Visitor's Guide to Mesoamerican Ruins*, by Joyce Kelly. Copyright ©1982 by the University of Oklahoma Press.)

The second strain of scholarship to look closely at Tula (of which Charnay is a tangential participant) was the ethnohistorical. While there are absolutely no extant written texts contemporaneous with Tula's florescence, the colonial-period documents are filled with Aztec reflections and reminiscences of the fabulous "Toltec" city of Tollan, some of which include explicitly architectural references, for instance, to a "frog temple" constructed for the water goddess and to a royal house known as the Quillaztli.[15] Even more thorough are Fray Sahagún's elaborate praises of the Toltec "spearhouse," the four "houses of feathers," and — the most highly praised of all the structures in the quasihistorical city of Tollan — the "houses of Quetzalcoatl" (Sahagún's description of which was quoted at the beginning of this section on Tula).[16] Any one-to-one correlation of these colorful Aztec odes to the urban perfection of Tollan with the earthly remains of either Tula, Hidalgo, or Teotihuacán has, however, proven unconvincing.[17] These poetic descriptions of Tollan, at first sight a boon to our understanding of Tula, are, in fact, of disappointingly little direct help in (re)constructing the historical ritual-architectural events of the Toltec capital.

Nevertheless, more generally, these ethnohistoric texts are the basis of Wigberto Jiménez Moreno's famous historical (re)construction of the rise and fall of the Toltecs — and, thus, of his equation of the mythical Tollan with the site of Tula, Hidalgo — which won majority support in the early 1940s and which remains today the orthodox position.[18] Paul Kirchhoff, the other pioneering ethnohistorian to address these problems, seconded the basic identification of Tula as the geographic analogue to the mythical city of Tollan, but proposed a different historical scenario, particularly for the fall of Tula.[19] And Nigel Davies, more often in accord with Kirchhoff than Jiménez Moreno, has more recently carved out a third and daringly more detailed (re)construction of Tula's rise and fall primarily on the basis of the documentary evidence. Davies's work is particularly notable for his exploration of the ethnic diversity of ancient Tula (discussed momentarily).[20]

The third strain of scholarship to attack the problem of Tula is that of traditional archaeology. While there had been a certain amount of archaeological knowledge about the presumed "Toltec" culture from early twentieth-century excavations at Teotihuacán (by Gamio) and at Chichén Itzá (by Morley), the first modern archaeological investigations of Tula, sponsored by the Instituto Nacional de Antropología e Historia (INAH) and directed by Jorge Acosta, did not begin until 1940. This initial round of excavations then ran a full two decades as the results far exceeded expectations. Acosta was able to establish a site chronology based on changes in pottery over time (which is still fairly reliable) but, characteristically, he focused his energies on the excavation and (re)construction of the most ostentatious civic structures in that portion of the city known as "Tula Grande." Thus, Acosta is not only responsible for the names, common wisdoms, and physical (re)construction of virtually all that the tourist now sees at Tula, he also provides the solid archaeological basis for the nearly unanimous identification of Tula, Hidalgo, with the Tollan of the documentary sources and for the archaeological-historical framework generally accepted today.[21]

The dust settled on Acosta's excavations at precisely that moment when Americanist archaeology was undergoing its radical reorientation, and as the "new archaeologists" took the field. Thus, when INAH began again at Tula in the late 1960s, this time under the directorship of Eduardo Matos Moctezuma and in cooperation with the University of Missouri–Columbia (UMC) Tula Archaeology Project headed by Rich-

Lower portion of one of the so-called Atlantean figures at Tula, from Désiré Charnay's *Ancient Cities of the New World*. Consistent with his extravagant assessment of Tula and the Toltecs, Charnay composed this wood engraving so that the pre-Columbian sculpture appears at least twice its actual size.

ard Diehl, the priorities were significantly rearranged. Both projects intentionally distanced themselves from the agenda of reconstructing large civic structures (though Matos did reconstruct the second major ball court in Tula Grande) and espoused instead an orientation that was patently "new archaeological" and cultural materialist.[22] Diehl stated his basic aim as the documentation of social, economic, and political processes, together with the "daily life of the ordinary people living in the city";[23] and Matos, even more enthusiastic about the gospel of Gordon Childe and anthropological archaeology, seized every occasion (even tourist guides) to shift the emphasis from the elite structures of Tula Grande to nonelite activities and cultural processes.[24] Their more sophisticated investigations of the ceramic stratigraphy, settlement patterns, and residential complexes of both the "micro" and "macro areas" of Tula (a style of archaeological initiative that, unfortunately, has no substantial counterpart at Chichén Itzá) were exceedingly thorough.[25] However, because of their mode of digging and refilling (as contrasted to the reconstructive agenda of Acosta), the efforts of this strain of archaeology are now virtually imperceptible to the casual visitor to Tula.

Finally, art history, a fifth perspective on Tula, chimes in with its characteristic antimaterialist, productively iconoclastic contribution. The still-lingering debate of the 1960s between George Kubler (who continues to hold his "reverse migration" hypothesis wherein Tula is reduced to "a frontier garrison at the extreme edge of the civilized world" that imitates rather than models for "Toltec" Chichén Itzá) and Alberto Ruz (who upheld the more conventional west-to-east model of Tula–Chichén connectedness) is a controversy sustained especially by creative interpretations of the art and iconography of the two sites.[26] Aside from that old (though still important) debate, providing a kind of converse to the archaeological situation, art historical work at Tula in recent decades has, with few exceptions, stagnated. Thus, while at Chichén Itzá the most exciting revisionist developments are issuing from art history, the deeply entrenched tendency simply to dismiss Tula art and architecture as brutal and superficial is seldom challenged. Aside from Mayapán (supposedly another "Toltec" creation in Yucatán), Tula has no competition for the bottom rung in conventional rankings of Mesoamerican art, an assessment that continues to be generally taken for granted. Before launching into my own hermeneutical reassessment of Tula's artistic works (that is, perhaps offering a sixth academic take on Tula), I will consider briefly the pervasiveness of this pejorative evaluation.

Tula Art and Architecture: Unanimous Dispraise

Charnay, again the odd man out, was enthralled equally with the women and the ruins that he encountered in Tula during the last century and, consequently, filled his work with superlatives for the vision and technical expertise of this, the supposed fountainhead of Middle American culture.[27] His literal reading of Tula as the Tollan of the documentary sources was probably more responsible for this excessive eulogy than anything he observed at the site, yet virtually no one since Charnay has shared his exuberant assessment of Tula's artistic accomplishment. In fact, where Aztec art is so often disdained for its brutal conception and sanguinary subject matter, it is likewise generally redeemed by its exquisite execution. Toltec art and architecture, by contrast, are dispraised doubly for their overbearingly martial content and, even more unanimously, for their shoddy craftsmanship. The style of Tula is conventionally dismissed as the bad art of a difficult time, a shallow and unappealing conception paired with a lackadaisical execution.

Tula Grande plaza with the Adoratorio platform in the foreground and Pyramid B, also known as the Pyramid of Quetzalcoatl (or of Tlahuizcalpantecuhtli), in the background. (Photo by Lawrence G. Desmond.)

Tula, the whipping boy of pre-Columbian art, draws disapprobation from virtually all fronts. Séjourné, for instance, deems the identification of Tula with the fabulous Tollan of the sources ludicrous, and calls Tula "a second-rate civic center which, except for a few remarkable sculptures, contains only crude copies and imported motifs, and thus cannot possibly have been the cradle of a glorious culture."[28] Weaver disparages Tula artisans for what she terms "a characteristic stiffness and monotony . . . a far cry from the imaginative elegance achieved by their Preclassic and Classic ancestors. Indeed, the remains at the site of Tula itself give the impression of having been put together in haste, skilled and unskilled alike having had a hand in the carving and modeling."[29] Similarly disenchanted with the site, Bushnell laments the usurpation of the lively little figures and floridity of Teotihuacán painting in favor of a total preoccupation with war at Tula;[30] Fernández deems the sculptural execution of Tula "very rigid and dry";[31] and Coe reproaches the nearly exclusive representation of war-related themes and the "singular secular cast of Tula . . . a state of affairs usually interpreted as the result of the encroachment of the military over the spiritual."[32]

Reflecting the wider paradigm of Maya-Mexican polarity, Tula Toltec art has suffered particularly in its juxtaposition with Maya art. Waters, for instance, considers that Tula as a whole "lacks homogeneity" and is "the direct antithesis of Maya art" but then excuses this lack of focus because of Tula's difficult position: "it stood at a crossroads of space and time, between two peoples and at a decisive moment when the fulcrum was tipped to the militaristic future."[33] Eric Thompson is far less forgiving in his Toltec-versus-Maya comparison: he considers "Toltec" architecture, both at Tula and Chichén Itzá, to be symptomatic of a "morally weaker culture" with "lower standards" than the Maya, a "showy but unstable architecture," characterized by "incredible stiffness" and "depressed monotony."[34]

Even those commentators who are more matter-of-fact in their evaluation of the spirit of Toltec art (and even those who are bucking for an equation of Tula with the marvelous Tollan of tradition) are, nonetheless, unimpressed by its technical execution. Something of an apologist for the Toltecs, Jorge Acosta, for instance, considers that Tula architecture is of "majestic conception but mediocre execution."[35] Diehl seconds that opinion, pointing specifically to crude carvings, mass-produced frieze elements that were rapidly assembled with frequent mismatches of adjacent pieces, and to basic construction standards in Tula architecture and crafts products that were definitely inferior to either earlier Teotihuacán or later Aztec standards.[36] Davies, deeply enamored of the Toltecs' reassertion of order in the chaotic wake of Teotihuacán's fall, likewise admits the Toltec tendency toward "quick and even shoddy finish."[37] And, in perhaps the most widely cited of all evaluations of Tula Toltec architecture, Miguel Covarrubias concludes that "the construction technique was rather poor . . . these buildings were meant to impress, but not to last."[38]

The sole quality for which Tula art and architecture is grudgingly commended is originality.[39] Robertson, for instance, emphasizes that the general conception of Tula's central plaza (Tula Grande) with its low, four-sided platform at the center (the Adoratorio) is an enclosed space "producing a self-contained effect" that is quite different from the linear, axial, open-ended plan of Teotihuacán.[40] And besides the unprecedented preoccupation with motifs of war and human sacrifice, the first appearance of many specific architectural elements is typically attributed to Tula: for instance, the *coatepantli* (or serpent wall), the *chacmool,* the serpent column, friezes of marching jaguars and eagles, square pillars decorated with warrior reliefs, skull racks, I-shaped ball courts with stone rings, and rectangular colonnaded halls with large interior rooms and benches, as well as new styles of stone carvings and ceramic production.[41] It is, as some critics may point out, possible to find precedents in ancient Mesoamerican art history for virtually every one of these elements (and they are all indubitably present in "Toltec" Chichén Itzá as well as at Tula). Yet, because the unanimously dispraised artisans of Tula probably were the first to elaborate all of these design elements in consonance, art historians are forced, if unobligingly, to grant them at least a tacit measure of prestige and respect.

Tula Divided: Three Sorts of Tension

The wide dispraise for Tula notwithstanding, the efforts of these various streams of scholarship, particularly this latest round of archaeology, make it possible now to rise above the conventional bashing of Toltec art and architecture and to consider alternative interpretations. We can, at this point, for instance, present a series of somewhat more subtle hypotheses about the religio-artistic priorities that characterized Tula's ritual-architectural events and, particularly, about how those events might compare with their counterparts at Chichén Itzá.

For decades, one of the most manageable aspects of the Tula–Chichén Itzá problem has

Désiré Charnay's wood engraving of young girls at Tula in 1880. Charnay was equally enthusiastic about the women and the ruins of Tula. Subsequent scholars, however, have been inclined to see Tula as the worst rather than best of Mesoamerican art and architecture. (Désiré Charnay, *Ancient Cities of the New World*.)

been the relative consistency and unity of the phenomenon of Tula. Where Chichén Itzá's so-called Sacred Cenote was site to perhaps Mesoamerica's most convoluted series of occupations, abandonments, reoccupations, conquests, and ethnic admixtures, Tula was conceived much more simply as an urban phenomenon with a beginning, a middle, and an end — "all one piece" — "a primarily Postclassic phenomenon with rather slender roots reaching down to epiclassic levels."[42] Where Chichén Itzá holds an incredibly complex oeuvre of different architectural styles, even Acosta conceded the impossibility of recognizing any real evolution of style in the art of Tula; and Davies, for all his convoluted (re)constructions of the Toltecs' historical triumphs and tribulations, similarly concludes that Tula architecture is "more or less all of one pattern."[43]

However, as the later INAH and UMC archaeologists expanded the field of inquiry spatially away from the Main Ceremonial Precinct (that is, Tula Grande), and temporally both before and after the "Golden Century of Tollan" (that is, 1000–1100 C.E.), and as Davies widened the ethnohistorical base to include more than the strictly Aztec sources, the conventionalized monolithic image of Tula began to crack.[44] Three particularly important sorts of tensions have emerged: (1) a tension in time between Tula Chico, the original center of the city, and Tula Grande, the later and more famous civic plaza; (2) a tension in the ethnic composition of Tula between the Nonoalca and the Tolteca-Chichimeca; and (3) a tension in religious ritual between Tula's public, civic cult and its less-glamorous domestic worship.

Two Times: Tula Chico and Tula Grande

The most dramatic challenge to the "one Tula" model came in Eduardo Matos's excavation of "Tula Chico," a group of medium-sized mounds located just 1 kilometer north (literally within sight) of the Main Ceremonial Precinct or "Tula Grande," the famous plaza where all earlier archaeological efforts had been concentrated. Despite its proximity to the area of Acosta's major (re)construction efforts, this second major concentration of mounds had, heretofore, been virtually ignored. Test pitting and then refilling Tula Chico (it appears virtually indistinguishable from the surrounding desert at this point), Matos discovered that this complex had constituted the original locus of Tula, had been constructed and then abandoned well in advance of the city's "Tollan phase" florescence at Tula Grande and, moreover, well in advance of all of the traditional, ethnohistorically derived dates for the founding of Tula.[45] Matos, in other words, revised the orthodox Tula chronology not by rearranging it but by adding a major, earlier phase onto the front end of the time line. Whereas Acosta and most Mesoamericanists had accepted Jiménez Moreno's date of 856 C.E. (or something around 900 C.E.) for the origin of Tula, Matos associated the Tula Chico structures with the considerably earlier Metepec ceramic phase of 650–750 C.E., already known at Teotihuacán.[46]

The implications are several. First, where Tula had generally been considered entirely posterior to Teotihuacán, Matos's "new Tula chronology" implied a kind of Central Mexican "overlap theory" by holding that, if not Tula itself, at least "the Tula area" had been under Teotihuacán control.[47] Moreover, and even more importantly, it became apparent that Tula's growth had been marked by *two* distinct immigration and population increases. The first major occupation of the Tula ridge (800–900 C.E.), which had largely eluded Acosta, probably entailed some 19,000–27,000 people and had Tula Chico as its major civic-religious zone.[48] The second period (950–1100 C.E.), previously considered the sum total of Tula's development, has an uncertain population estimate of 30,000–40,000, as the city achieved its maximum size and importance.[49] In other words, in this second phase, the Tula Chico complex was abandoned and the adjacent Tula Grande became the civic-religious center of the city.

This fairly radical revision in the historical (re)construction picture of Tula is, however, less revolutionary with respect to the characterization of Tula Toltec civic architectural events. In fact, there is virtually no evidence to suggest a qualitative shift in the ritual-architectural priorities between the earlier and later Tula plazas. Everything in Matos's reports implies that Tula Chico, so named for its close similarity to the main plaza at Tula, formally (and typologically) resembled its later and larger counterpart. Matos notes at every turn the parallels between the orientation and distribution of buildings in the two plazas: Tula Chico has mounds corresponding to the preeminent Pyramids B and C in Tula Grande (that is, the Pyramid of Tlahuizcalpantecuhtli and the Great Pyramid); there is a similarly located colonnaded hall; and there are two Tula Chico ball courts in positions analogous to those of Tula Grande.[50] In short, all the evidence, incomplete as it is, suggests a continuity between the types of ritual-architectural events at Tula Chico and at Tula Grande.[51]

More problematic than any qualitative discrepancy between the two civic plazas is the uncertain possibility that Tula Grande contains, beneath the now-visible buildings, a set of earlier constructions, contemporaneous with those of Tula Chico (at this point, however, no one seems particularly optimistic that early Tula actually had two coterminous and adjacent ceremonial plazas).[52] Even more elusive are the forces that led to the eventual abandonment of Tula Chico and the elaboration of Tula Grande next door (though Matos and Diehl have both speculated that the shift from Tula Chico to Tula Grande may have represented the ascendancy of one ethnic or religious faction over another).[53] And the greatest mystery is that, following its abandonment, the site of Tula Chico was surrounded by dense residential settlement, yet, the area of old plaza itself remained an empty, open space, totally devoid of later structures or even rubbish.[54]

To summarize with respect to the tension between Tula Chico and its more famous heir, Tula Grande, while the typical laments of scant data are in order, the repercussions for this study are less earth-shattering than they might first have appeared. There is no reason to presume any radical disjunction between the respective ritual-architectural priorities of the two successive plazas.[55] In fact, as the next sections demonstrate, both the ethnic tensions between Nonoalca and Tolteca-Chichimeca and the religious tensions between civic ritual and domestic ritual constitute considerably more significant challenges to the conventional notion of "one Tula" than does this belated discovery of two distinct eras at the Toltec capital.

Two Peoples: Tolteca-Chichimeca and Nonoalca

The debates regarding the ethnic composition of Tula (a problem explored more fully by ethnohistorian Nigel Davies than anyone else) are exceedingly complex.[56] It is, however, fairly certain that Tula's big growth spurts in both cases were the result of immigration rather than internal accretion, that the immigrants came from several directions with various dispositions and orientations that were never thoroughly integrated, and that, upon Tula's decline, these immigrants variously departed, again in several directions. Thus, ironically, where claims to "Toltec" heritage would eventually become the consummate sign of national purity and pedigreed authority across Mesoamerica, the historical Toltecs of Tula were, from beginning to end, an exceedingly heterogeneous ethnic conglomeration.

Davies has general support in identifying two major sets of immigrants: the Tolteca-Chichimeca and the Nonoalca. The times, origins, and precise circumstances of their respective migrations are, however, highly debatable.[57] The Tolteca-Chichimeca, somewhat easier to pin down archaeologically, were mainly Nahuatl speakers of modest cultural attainments from the margins of Mesoamerica north of Tula. Their name, originally a negative appellation for "less civilized," came later (that is, among the Aztecs) to signify a measure of rugged manliness or hardiness, and implies that they themselves were a conglomeration of disparate elements of varying cultural attainments and ethnic allegiances.[58] In any event, the Tolteca-Chichimeca seem to have constituted the majority in Tula and to have contributed, in addition to a distinctive style of pottery, the colonnaded hall, which becomes a hallmark of Toltec architecture, as well as most of the death motifs in the religion, and perhaps the Tezcatlipoca cult.[59]

The Nonoalca, on the other hand, are mentioned more prominently in the documentary sources than the Tolteca-Chichimeca but are more elusive archaeologically. Their homeland is generally thought to have been the lowlands of southern Veracruz and Tabasco (that is, the same interjacent area from which the Itzá or

Putun Maya presumably embarked, in the other direction, to Chichén Itzá). Jiménez Moreno and Piña Chan, however, consider that the Nonoalca originally came from Teotihuacán,[60] and Davies suggests that they included middle- and upper-class peoples dislocated from Teotihuacán, Monte Albán, Xochicalco, El Tajín, and other centers, who were wandering in search of new lives because of problems on their respective home fronts.[61] Thus, even more than the Tolteca-Chichimeca, the Nonoalca element appears to have been ethnically and linguistically diverse. But, in sharp contrast to the Tolteca-Chichimecas, the Nonoalca were renowned as a kind of craft and intellectual elite. In Davies's words: "[the Nonoalca] stand out as par excellence the *Kulturvolk,* the bearers of the most prized arts and skills of Mesoamerica and the guardians of the ancient lore. . . . It was largely through the practice of their skills and the manifestation of their genius that the words 'Tollan' and 'Toltec' eventually became synonymous with refinement and splendor."[62] Likewise, where the Tolteca-Chichimeca are credited with the cult of Tezcatlipoca, Davies argues (against some resistance) that the Nonoalca were originally responsible for the Quetzalcoatl cult at Tula.[63] In any case, more certain than the geographic origin or specific contribution of the Nonoalca is that, although they were a minority, they maintained a certain cultural and political ascendancy in Tula and remained forever a group apart, never fully integrated into the wider population.[64]

Remembering the traditional mythico-historical account of Tollan's dramatic rise and fall, it is tempting simply to correlate the wise Nonoalca with the deity Quetzalcoatl and the priest-king Topiltzin and the sturdy Tolteca-Chichimeca with the darker figures of Tezcatlipoca and Huemac. Jiménez Moreno, Kirchhoff, and Davies, however, provide detailed (though different) explanations for why so neat a correlation scenario is unacceptable, why exactly the opposite is equally plausible, and why, in short, there can be no strict ethnic-religious-political bifurcation of Tula.[65] Furthermore, while it is clear that disparate ethnic groups departed the declining Tula at different times and in different directions, there is no warrant for arguing that any particular group (the Nonoalca would be the most likely candidates) emigrated directly from Central Mexico to Yucatán or Chichén Itzá.[66]

While the specifics are uncertain, it is most probable that the great "Tula Toltecs," hardly a monolithic superrace, were, instead, an exceedingly heterogeneous, mutually exploitative union of immigrant peoples, all of whom were already highly fragmented themselves even before their respective arrivals at Tula. In fact, the entire restive history of Tula — from rise, climax, to collapse — was, in all likelihood, dominated by these two factors: a perpetual ethnic diversity and an unceasing flow of immigrants. Tula, in other words, seemingly owed its beginning to a migratory convergence of complementarily endowed elements, a "natural partnership" so to speak, "a new amalgamation of peoples";[67] its vigorous ascent and estimable successes likewise depended on the creative tension between the respective talents and orientations of this motley congregation; but, by the same token, the violent fall of Tula seems to have derived largely from the hostilities that arose between the imperfectly synthesized factions in the face of a burgeoning tide of unwanted foreigners from the northern frontier.[68] Ethnic diversity would, in short, appear to have been both the decisive strength and weakness of the Toltec capital.

Moreover, to anticipate briefly the forthcoming discussion of Tula's civic ceremony, the public architecture, first at Tula Chico and then at Tula Grande, was perhaps the most enduring manifestation of this perpetual struggle at Tula to create from its factional elements a viable, unified whole that could stand against the endemic threat of hostile outsiders. Tula's appearance was fierce, unsubtle, and showy. It was the architecture of a tenuously admixed population in constant defense of its territory. The civic ceremonial precincts of the Toltecs at once failed to exude the calm assurance shown by their predecessors at Teotihuacán and presaged the ostentatious paranoia of Aztec public ceremony. Even in its ruined condition, the shrill ritual-architectural announcement of a right to exist, and to dominate, continues to resonate from Tula Grande.

Two Religions: Civic and Domestic Rituals

The third major challenge or qualification to the old concept of a monolithic Tula is the existence — alongside the public, civic ritual of the great plazas — of a more modest domestic and neighborhood religion. The "new archaeologists," having worked to switch the emphasis from sacred to profane and from elite to proletarian dimensions of pre-Columbian society, almost inadvertently uncovered a substantial fund of evidence for an "old religion" of ancestors and fertility. This other aspect of Toltec religion, evidenced particularly in the domestic and vernacular architecture of the site (not unlike the more popular devotional stratum that Broda recognizes among the Aztecs) presumably preceded, paralleled, and then postdated the more flamboyant ceremonials of Tula Chico and Tula Grande.[69]

Though all of the earlier archaeological efforts at Tula had concentrated on the ceremonial plazas, the "Toltec house" already in the nineteenth century enjoyed a certain dubious prestige by virtue of Charnay's audacious claim that the modest residences of Tula prefigured the more public architecture of site, which, in turn, had served as the prototype for all of Mesoamerican architecture.[70] The UMC project of the 1970s was, however, the first to undertake a systematic study of the nonpedigreed architecture of Tula by excavating a number of houses and two small temples in the more outlying sections of the city and, consequently, was the first to provide substantial materials for theorizing about ritual-architectural priorities outside of Tula Grande.[71]

With respect to the excavation of principally residential structures, the discovery of a pattern wherein several houses were typically arranged around a central courtyard — which, in each case, featured a small rectangular altar or shrine faced with "Toltec Small Stone Construction" — suggests some sort of neighborhood clan organization or possibly extended family rituals.[72] Though heavily looted (both pre- and post-Hispanically), the evidence of well-stocked burials in every one of these platform shrines, together with the discovery of burials in virtually every domestic subfloor, suggests, as Healan and Diehl hypothesize, that this residential worship was linked to the veneration of familial ancestors (that is, the ritual-architectural commemoration of the dead, priority II-D).[73] Moreover, while the Tula houses were generally without exterior ornamentation, recovered fragments suggest that some were decorated with symbols of the rain god Tlaloc and others with stone carvings of human skulls — more evidence of a concern for fertility and the propitiation of natural phenomena (priority III-C).[74] Furthermore, the household debris contained an abundance of figurines (particularly of women, but also of the deities Tlaloc and Xochiquetzal), and the fact that nearly all of these molded figures had been ritually "killed" has led to the reasonable conjecture that, as elements of healing rituals, they were broken "to insure destruction of the cause of illness."[75]

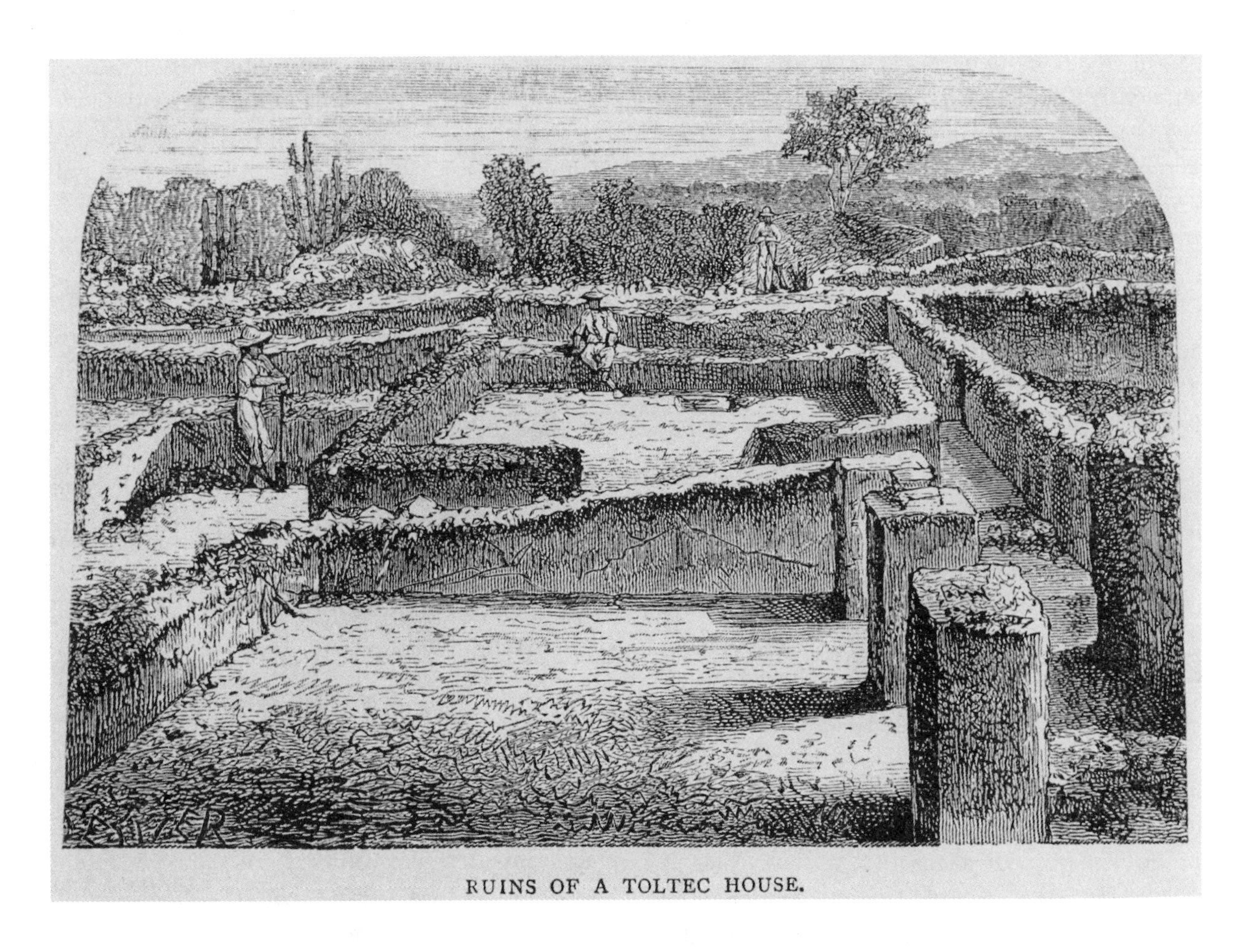
RUINS OF A TOLTEC HOUSE.

Désiré Charnay's wood engraving of ruins of a Toltec house at Tula. (Désiré Charnay, *Ancient Cities of the New World.*)

The two small, outlying temples excavated by the UMC project likewise seem to correspond to something like neighborhood socioreligious units.[76] The smaller of the two, the "Canal Locality Temple," a rectangular structure only a few meters on a side, built on a 1-meter-high platform and surrounded by rooms and courtyards, had at least four building phases, all contemporary with the Tollan phase of Tula Grande.[77] Also heavily looted, this structure too is notable for associations with human bones and with Tlaloc (that is, incensario fragments bearing Tlaloc's image, Pacific coast shells, and rosette stones with *Chalchihuitl* symbols)[78] and for the characteristic two-room plan of its tiny superstructure — presumably a little antechamber and a smaller inner sanctuary.[79] The other apparently nonresidence in Tula's residential zone, the "Corral Locality Structure," which was somewhat less thoroughly excavated by the UMC project, is larger and more elaborate than the Canal Locality Temple.[80] Likewise contemporary with the Tollan phase florescence of Tula Grande, and also located well away from the main plaza, it also contained a rectangular altar faced with Toltec Small Stone Construction over a burial and offerings, along with significant Pacific coast debris and a large quantity of scattered bone fragments. In the end, however, this structure actually raises more questions than it answers.[81]

All these evidences of explicitly religious activity in the nonelite structures of Tula, albeit fragmentary and generic, point to that stratum of popular or "old" religion, which Broda contends was held more or less universally at the family and community levels across Mesoamerica.[82] This ancient pan-Mesoamerican tradition of cosmological thought, doubtless a crucial force in binding together the disparate ethnicities of Tula, according to Broda, was devoted, first of all, to the observation, petition, and control of natural phenomena, particularly rain and fertility as epitomized in the abundant symbols of Tlaloc and the sea coasts, and, secondly, to the veneration of ancestors as demonstrated by the ample burials and effigy figurines.

In sum then, as a set of ritual-architectural events, the specifics of Tula's domestic and neighborhood ceremonials remain, as yet, equally irretrievable as those of the more public ritual. The play of typological priorities in this more popular devotion is, nevertheless, reasonably clear. There is some evidence of homologized and conventionalized orientational priorities (I-A and I-B) in the grid layout of suburban Tula but little reason to conclude that the nonelite structures were aligned to any specific celestial phenomena (astronomy, priority I-C). The ritual-architectural commemoration of deities (priority II-A), particularly of Tlaloc, may have been a motive in Tula's nonpedigreed facade decoration, and more so in the effigy figurines, but specific references to sacred history (priority II-B) and politics (priority II-C) are notably absent. The residential courtyard arrangement suggests a ritual theatre context of modest proportions (priority III-A) but, more probably, denotes an attempt to seal off a ritual space from the city at large (sanctuary, III-D), a priority that is certainly at stake in the two-room plan of the Canal Locality neighborhood temple. And, to continue this typological inventory, the Toltec Small Stone Construction, a decidedly nonexpedient technique for veneering the domestic altars and the frequently repeated expansion of the Canal Locality Temple, may be signs of ritualized building (that is, one sort of manifestation of the propitiation priority, III-C) and/or a variation on the contemplation priority (III-B).[83]

The tangential manifestation of all these concerns notwithstanding, two types of priorities, as is typical in the nonelite ritual-architectural events of Mesoamerica, tower above the rest: (1) the commemoration of the dead (priority II-D) as demonstrated in the ubiquitous burials and effigy figurines and (2) a wide range of propitiation interests (priority III-C), from bodily healing to the petition of rain and general well-being. Important as this belated documentation of a resilient strain of Mesoamerican popular religion that persists independently and alongside the state ceremony of Tula Grande may be, even more interesting is the considerable and significant overlap between the elite and nonelite architectures of Tula. Of most specific interest is the way in which Tula Grande feeds on the domestic ritual-architectural practices or, in other words, the sense in which the vocabulary of Tula popular religion constitutes a fund of conservative or "instigatory" elements for Tula's civic architectural events. With this little foreshadowing, the discussion now moves to that more public Toltec forum.

The Main Event: Tula Civic Ceremony

Having acknowledged that the grand pageantry of Tula Grande was preceded, probably in kind, by Tula Chico, that the audience to Tula ceremony was anything but a monolithic block of purebreds, and that the bulk of the people's personal "religious" needs were probably addressed outside this large-scale public forum, the discussion at last moves to the interpretation of those more haughty politico-ritual-architectural events at Tula Grande. We can reflect in turn upon the types of ritual-architectural priorities that seem to have characterized: (1) the conservative or instigatory elements of Tula's civic ceremonies, (2) their manner of presentation, and (3) the substantive content or informational aspects of those events.

Instigation: Coercion by Eclecticism

If the internal diversity and external pressure that dogged Tula posed an unusually perilous situation, its civic ceremonies were nowise exempt from the usual necessity of all ritual-architectural events to interweave order and variation, to juxtapose the conservative and the radical, the reliable and the revelatory, the alluring and the transformative. The architects of Tula public ceremony, like ritual choreographers everywhere, had to fashion the sort of ritual-architectural invitation that would incite their constituencies to real, committed participation before the hermeneutical game could begin. Without familiar, alluring elements in which the citizenry saw something of themselves and their own — "reconciliation with self" in Gadamer's terms[84] — there would be no possibility of ever convincingly communicating the specific agenda of Tula polity. Moreover, playing to an especially diverse, eclectic audience, the designers of Tula civic events, of necessity, had recourse to an instigatory strategy that would have had an equally broad-based appeal. The Toltec solution to this problem of heterogeneity was to invoke a similarly eclectic strategy of allurement that incorporated conservative, time-honored elements drawn, not simply from one pillar of tradition but, rather, from the roots of each dimension of its variegated constituency (a ritual-architectural ploy that would blossom in epic proportions in the ceremonial staging at "Toltec" Chichén Itzá).[85] The instigation of Tula civic ceremony relied primarily on orientation via an appeal to ritual-architectural convention (priority I-B) — or, more properly, appealed to a sweepingly eclectic range of conventions.[86]

Backtracking Mesoamerican art styles and motifs, and discerning historical paths of inheritance and borrowing (organization according to tradition), is always a difficult task.[87] It is fairly certain, however, that Teotihuacán, even in collapse, remained in the Postclassic era, Central Mexico's primary reservoir for images of urban legitimacy, familiarity, and dependability. Not surprisingly, then, Tula is replete with allusions to its insuperable predecessor. The characteristic talud-tablero pyramidal substructure of Tula Grande's principal temples and platforms, the respect for grids and right-angularity, the 17 degrees east of north orientation (astronomically irrelevant in Tula's context),[88] the articulation of great processional ways, the renowned feathered serpent imagery, and perhaps the entire man-bird-serpent concept all owe directly to Teotihuacán.[89] Yet, rather than slavish imitation, each of these Classical elements is transfigured at Tula by juxtaposition either with those of another tradition or with an original Toltec innovation. For instance, at Tula, the familiar pyramid substructures carry temples with wooden roofs and warrior column supports, neither of which are known at Teotihuacán. Likewise, the axiality and devotion to procession from Teotihuacán are respected, but rather than linear, open-ended avenues, Tula Grande seals off the ends to effect a closed, four-sided arena (more like the Great Plaza of Monte Albán) and then concentrates all its most important structures in one corner of that plaza.[90] And, speaking to the same sort of innovative imitation, the famous carved serpent heads of Teotihuacán's Ciudadela are also reiterated, although in the Tula serpent columns, the snake faces are attached to erect, full bodies and tails as if descending from the sky.

Reconstruction drawing of Tula Grande. (Courtesy of the Mexican National Museum of Anthropology.)

Besides these general Teotihuacánoid allusions, each immigrating ethnicity respectively contributed more idiosyncratic components to the synthesis of Tula Grande. Of constantly debated provenance, the colonnaded hall, which became a stamp of Toltec architecture, seems to be the contribution of the Tolteca-Chichimeca,[91] while the Nonoalca contingent, probably the carriers of most of the Teotihuacán elements (including the variations and elaborations on the Quetzalcoatl theme) seems to have been the conduit that brought to Tula glyphic designs similar to those of the Mixteca and Zapoteca regions of Oaxaca[92] and relief patterns from Central Veracruz.[93]

Along with these endeavors in deliberate artistic and architectural archaism, the integration of the ball game into Tula's civic plazas (there are three ball courts in both Tula Grande and Tula Chico) may likewise have been a ploy at allurement. The first of the major ball courts at Tula Grande (excavated in the 1940s by Acosta) seems to owe its formal inspiration to Xochicalco and Monte Albán,[94] while the other major Tula Grande ball court (excavated by Matos in 1968–70) — which is the biggest in all Mesoamerica except for its even bigger, near twin, the Great Ball Court at Chichén Itzá — has reliefs that are indebted to El Tajín.[95] More important in the present discussion of instigatory strategies than the search for specific historical precedents to the various Tula ball courts is the general observation that, while ball courts are *not* a crucial element in

A broken *chacmool* is positioned at the south end of the ball court that lies on the west side of Tula Grande. This ball court, which Jorge Acosta excavated in the 1940s, most resembles those at Xochicalco and Monte Albán. (Photo by the author.)

Teotihuacán's organization,[96] Tula looked elsewhere to seize upon the pan-Mesoamerican tradition of the ball game that, by virtue of both its far-reaching roots and its intrinsic spectatorial appeal, served as an especially adept mechanism for alluring the heterogeneous citizenry of Tula into its civic ceremonial events. The Tula ball games — and this may be true of Mesoamerican ball games generally — were ultimately less important as ritual events unto themselves than as the conservative elements that drew people into participatory involvement in the more encompassing "game" of Tula public ritual.

The final, and perhaps most irresistible, fount of conservative, instigatory elements for Tula civic ritual-architectural events came from the vocabulary of its more modest, popular, or domestic religion. The overlap between Tula's domestic and civic religions is, as noted earlier, considerable and significant. The low, square Adoratorio platform, for instance, which sits at the very center of Tula Grande's open plaza, seems not to have supported a building but rather to have been simply a more elaborate (and contemporaneous) version of the courtyard altars found in the residential areas of Tula, complete with a high-status burial and intimations of ancestor worship.[97] The conventional two-room plan of the neighborhood temple seems to have been transported virtually without change, except for the addition of the massively elaborated pyramidal bases, to the most preeminent temples of Tula Grande.[98] And the abundance of Pacific coastal and marine fragments in the residential caches finds a direct counterpart in the shell decorations of Tula Grande's civic temple substructures.[99]

Moreover, similarly drafting elements from Mesoamerican popular religion into the role of instigatory devices for the civic proceedings — fashioning, in Gadamer's terms, "continuities in tradition" — the *coatepantli,* or serpent wall, that extends along the northern side of Tula Grande's monumental Temple of Tlahuizcalpantecuhtli provides perhaps the most highly condensed juxtaposition of symbols from the shared "old religion" with the specific innovations of the urban Toltecs. This elaborately carved stone wall, some 10 feet high and 130 feet long, is composed of five long rows of repetitive ornament. The middle row is decorated with the gruesome scene of a serpent that has swallowed a dead person, except for the skull that protrudes from the snake's jaws.[100] This gory configuration of undulating serpents and human skulls and bones, the notorious leitmotif of Tula, is repeated along this middle row for the full length of the wall. This original Toltec motif (that is, the particularistic content of Tula civic architecture) is, however, sandwiched between two lines of a simple ascending and descending stepped design that is, almost certainly, a reference to the ancient cult of the mountains; above that, the full length of the crest of the *coatepantli* carries an equally simple repetition of scroll-like designs and conventionalized shells that are generally associated with water.[101] The *coatepantli,* in marvelously concentrated form, pleads for the interrelatedness of the irreproachable devotion to mountains and water (the conservative component or, in a sense, "the mother") with the ferocious new Toltec agenda of supereminence in arms and combat (the radical component or, as I termed it last chapter, the ugly lover).[102]

Thus, as caricatured in the *coatepantli,* the impressive range of syncretic historical allusions in Tula Grande from Teotihuacán, from the immigrants' respective homelands, and from the shared domestic religion cannot be dismissed either as sentimental respect for forebears nor as unoriginality. Instead, these familiar elements are part of an eclectic strategy of instigation — pale and rudimentary by contrast to that which "Toltec" Chichén Itzá will undertake but, nonetheless, a shrewd campaign to announce roots, to project reliability, and to remind the respective constituencies of their connectedness and responsibility to participate in the imperial mission of Tula.

Presentation: Glitz and Gore

The means of presenting these instigatory elements in Tula civic ceremony were equally shrewd. The cloistered temple plan, the *coatepantli* barrier, and the completely enclosed arena arrangement of Tula Chico (and later Tula Grande) all bespeak a concerted effort to differentiate the ceremonial precinct from the wider city or to delimit sacred from profane space (an expression of the sanctuary priority, III-D). Clearly, however, the even more important choreographic priority at Tula was the crafting of a stage for emotionally overpowering ritual-architectural drama (theatre, priority III-A). The stock recriminations against Tula architecture — that it is showy but shoddy, glamorous but unstable, standardized and monotonous rather than individuated — evince that Toltec building was less an exercise in transexpedient devotion or meditative consideration of detail (that is to say, the propitiation and contemplation priorities, III-B and III-C, were *not* particularly important) than the expedient creation of a histrionic forum, a backdrop for pomp, panache, and propaganda. For

The *coatepantli* or serpent wall, which runs along the north side of Pyramid B. By positioning familiar symbols associated with the ancient cults of mountains and water above and below the more radical images of undulating serpents, skulls, and human bones, the *coatepantli* provides a microcosm of the productive play of conventionality and innovation that informs the entire ritual-architectural program of Tula Grande. (Photo by Lawrence G. Desmond.)

example, while it is conceivable that the six rapidly successive remodelings of the Pyramid of Tlahuizcalpantecuhtli were motivated by the passing of cosmic calendrical cycles (and, thus, principally manifestations of the homology and propitiation priorities, I-A and III-C),[103] more probably, as Acosta believes, the frequent rebuildings at Tula Grande were necessitated by perpetually failing structural techniques and, most of all, by the pragmatic desire to show always a seamless face of invulnerability — particularly when the city actually was in danger of coming apart at the seams.[104]

In other words, Tula civic ceremony was characterized less by a play of presentational priorities than by the wholesale domination of the single priority of affective, theatrical stagecrafting (priority III-A), unmistakable in each of its mobile and stationary manifestations. While the specific ceremonial movements remain a matter of conjecture, the ubiquitous portrayal on Tula's benches, friezes, and wall paintings of elaborately adorned warriors, jaguars, and eagles — all in file — leaves little doubt about the Toltec fascination with ritual ambulation, with ceremonial procession and

Pyramid B, with remains of colonnaded hall in the foreground. This structure, also known as the Pyramid of Quetzalcoatl (or Tlahuizcalpantecuhtli), was apparently remodeled six times in quite rapid succession. (Photo by Lawrence G. Desmond.)

parade. Diehl, for instance, imagines that the colonnade halls were "council halls" from which these courtly promenades emanated: "The procession [depicted in the frieze of the Burnt Palace colonnade in Tula Grande] seems to march toward the front exits and out into the vestibule between the building and the plaza, perhaps portraying actual processions which began in the building and made their way over to Pyramid B [that is, the Pyramid of Tlahuizcalpantecuhtli]."[105] Moreover, demonstrative of the theatrical priority in its more stationary mode, the "self-contained effect" or the "centralized composition" of the Tula Grande Acropolis[106] leaves little doubt that Toltec civic ritual, in manner of presentation, was the direct precedent to the inclusive, spectator-oriented, and intimidating stagecraft of the Aztecs, a historical context for which we have the eyewitness accounts that are totally lacking in the case of Tula.

By this combination of eclectic instigative elements and theatric presentation, Tula civic ceremony becomes the epitome of that sort of ritual-architectural event that does not simply solicit interest but, instead, demands and coerces the participation even of reluctant onlookers. Tula Grande delivers an ungentle ritual-architectural invitation that cannot be easily refused. In contrast to elitist sanctuary events

The so-termed atlantean figures, which stand in file atop Pyramid B, continue to serve as a kind of emblem for the capital of the Toltecs. (Photo by William M. Ferguson, courtesy of the University of Texas, Austin.)

or self-motivated exercises in architectural contemplation (expressions of priorities III-D and III-B), civic Tula exemplifies inclusiveness, extending its withy embrace just as far as it can and so, presumably, apprising all of Central Mexico of the unslakable destiny of Tula and the Toltecs.

Content: A New Concept of Authority

As the fiercest in the fierce ambience of Early Postclassic Central Mexico — a chaotic age beset by new rules and a new martial orientation — Tula was the frontline propagandist for the redirected values. Where Teotihuacán's slow, laborious ascent to imperial dominance and prestige had been paved by combined superiority in crafts, commerce, and war, Tula's innovation in effrontery, not nearly so balanced, was to launch a bid for supremacy by sheer force of arms. The notion of a centralized state based wholly (or, at least, preponderantly) on supereminence in war was apparently quite novel in this era of Mesoamerican culture history. Consequently, Tula's civic architectural events were saddled with a heavy informational burden — namely, rallying the diverse elements of the city's population to their common purpose, recruiting them, like it or not, as participants in a callow, largely unprecedented concept of sovereignty that was based upon an ultimatum of acquiescence or obliteration. The grim message of Tula civic ceremony was first about internal unity or codependency, the transformation of gathered separate interests into one citizenry — "we are one." Even more emphatically, however, it was a message to their neighbors that the Toltecs were strongest and, thus, the rightful sovereigns of Central Mexico (that is, a specific variation on the ritual-architectural commemoration of temporal authority, priority II-C, which far supersedes that of any other informational priority).

There are any number of theories regarding the ways in which the Toltecs refashioned and elaborated Quetzalcoatl, already a potent presence at Teotihuacán and throughout Central Mexico, into the sort of god (or god-man) that would serve their unprecedentedly martial agenda.[107] For instance, many scholars identify the prominent figure in the carvings on Pyramid B as Tlahuizcalpantecuhtli, a form of Quetzalcoatl as the Morning Star that is apparently manifest for the very first time at the Toltec capital.[108] In the main, however, Tula iconography hardly seems to represent a tour de force in theological innovation and abstraction, and the deities (or culture heroes) that do appear in Tula art are portrayed in static poses rather than in the context of mythic or narrative scenes as in the lively murals of Tlaloc's paradise at Teotihuacán.[109] That is to say, there is little in the extant architectural data to suggest that Tula civic ritual was greatly concerned to explore the subtleties of divinity (priority II-A); nor does the recitation of mythic, sacred history (priority II-B) seem to have been an especially important priority (though that is certainly a more likely possibility).

Political sacred history (another dimension of priority II-B) is, perhaps somewhat surprisingly, likewise largely absent from Tula's pictorial art. For instance, while both the ball game and Tula's endemic campaigns in war constituted pregnant contexts for participants to display their skills and, thus, win individual distinction, the ubiquitous warrior figures in Tula's art are virtually all standing at attention or in file; none are shown in the context of specific battles as they are in the murals of "Toltec" Chichén Itzá, and none are identified as specific heroic individuals as in the hieroglyphs of South or "Old Chichén."[110] And the commemoration of ancestors and the dead (priority II-D) is similarly quite limited: Tula Grande is, for instance, overburdened with images of human

Relief carvings on the *coatepantli* depicting feathered serpents devouring partially skeletalized human figures. The panel on the right is a reproduction. At Tula Grande, the abundance of images of human carnage, decapitation, and half-eaten bodies would seem to deliver a blunt ritual-architectural ultimatum of acquiescence to Toltec hegemony or death. (Photo by the author.)

carnage, decapitation, and half-eaten bodies, but, aside from the presumed burials in the Adoratorio, there are no elaborate tombs of ancestral rulers like those of the Oaxaca and Maya areas and no obvious preoccupation with prestigious lineages like that evinced by the Aztecs and virtually every other pseudo-heir to the Toltec legacy.[111]

Arguing by subtraction, and according to the more general historical background, the message of Tula civic ritual-architecture is not only overbearingly political (an expression of priority II-C), it is political propaganda of a very specific, one-dimensional sort. It presumes neither to legitimate one particular royal family or one ethnic constituency nor to document its own specific mythico-historical climb to paramountcy. Instead, the ritual-architectural agenda of Tula Grande would seem to concentrate on selling a new concept of hegemony — namely, the viability of a centralized authority underwritten solely (or, at least preeminently) by military force. Neither coy nor devious in the least, civic Tula announces, snarls, and panders over and again both its military peerlessness and the dire consequences of resistance. Once visitors and citizens were lured into Tula Grande's ritual-architectural game by the dramatic stagecrafting of allusions to old Teotihuacán, to their diverse nationalistic roots, and to the ubiquitous popular religion — once they had been beckoned to committed involvement by assurances of motherly familiarity and respectability — indifference became impossible. And then, opened and vulnerable, the spectator-participants were confronted with equal drama by the ugly lover, the terrifying, albeit irrefutable, injunction of acquiescence to the grisly military-imperial destiny of Tula.

The physical forms of Tula Grande would subsequently be borrowed, copied, and revalorized in the context of other more subtle and intricate ceremonial contexts, preeminently at Tenochtitlán and "Toltec" Chichén Itzá. But, if I am correct in my hermeneutical reassessment (this portion of which does not actually deviate too radically from conventional assessments of Tula), nowhere again would Mesoamericans see ritual-architectural events that were more blatantly extreme in their coercive instigation, their theatrical presentation, or their single-mindedly politicized content.

Tula Revalorized: Tenochtitlán and Chichén Itzá

By every criterion (except possibly that of originality), Tula's art and architecture pale beside that of Tenochtitlán. Yet, ironically, to the Aztecs themselves, Toltec works were the very epitome of the "all good, all perfect, all wonderful, all marvelous."[112] Moreover, rather than simply admire from afar, the Aztecs launched a massive effort of rape and rescue at Tula, 50 miles to the north of their capital, which entailed ravaging every building in the decaying city, public and residential, heisting every sculpture, and prying loose every facade decoration they could.[113] Owing to this vandalizing expression of esteem, every bit of the exterior ornamentation of Pyramid C, the largest structure of Tula Grande, was expropriated. The famous frieze panels of marching warriors, eagles, and jaguars on Pyramid B, the other principal structure in Tula Grande, remained intact only because they were, by the era of the Aztecs, buried beneath a later elaboration of the adjacent Palacio de Quetzalcoatl. All the rest of the decoration was wrenched loose and, in a visceral demonstration of revalorization, the very physical architectural elements of Tula Grande were carried to Tenochtitlán, where they were perhaps rehung in the context of the Aztecs' own civic architectural events.[114]

The vigorous Aztec borrowing of Toltec styles and stones presents an intriguing (though little-discussed) parallel to the situation of the more famous similitude between Tula and Chichén Itzá.[115] Given the Aztecs' aspirations to position themselves as the "new Toltecs," it is not surprising that the respective plazas of the Templo Mayor and Tula Grande share a number of strikingly resemblant architectural elements: besides the generally similar layouts of pyramids and plazas, carved panels of characteristically Toltec armed warriors, the regalia of the eagle and jaguar orders, human sacrifice–related *chacmool* statuary, and artistic referencings to Quetzalcoatl are abundant and unmistakable at Tenochtitlán. And the possibility that, in cases, the very same carved stones were literally transferred from one site to the other provides the very quintessence of formal similitude. The indubitable correspondence in "Toltec" forms is, however (as in the case of Tula–Chichén Itzá similitude), dangerously deceptive. Generally speaking, the presentation of Aztec religio-civic ceremony may have been as theatrical as that of Tula Grande, the beckoning to participation equally coercive and non-negotiable, the ritual choreography equally gory, and the substantive agenda equally propagandistic; it would appear that the same general sorts of ritual-architectural priorities prevailed in both cases. Even so, the respective roles of these particular shared Toltec elements were significantly different. Where, at Tula, those carved warriors and heart-devouring eagles had articulated the radical new "might makes right" agenda of Toltec polity, by the reign of the Aztecs some 300 years later, the same gory iconography, no longer shockingly innovative, was revalorized as part of the Aztec claim to conservatism and legitimacy, to roots and respectability.

Despite the irrefutable formal resemblances between the ceremonial centers of Tula and Tenochtitlán, the contrast between the respective public ritual-architectural events of the Toltecs and Aztecs is significant (and, moreover, highly instructive with respect to a reassessment of Tula–Chichén similitude). Where, in the context of the eleventh- and twelfth-century civic events of Tula Grande, the images of carnage and war had carried the new and disturbing message of centralized authority legitimated by martial superiority (those images had served, in other words, as the radical and substantive component of the Toltec ritual-architectural events), by the fourteenth and fifteenth centuries, when the Aztecs took center stage, that brutal conception of rulership had become a familiar Central Mexican reality. Consequently, for the Aztecs, those very same militaristic Toltec images were exploited (or revalorized) in Tenochtitlán, not for their revolutionary content but, to the contrary, as emblems of venerable tradition, as signs of the Aztecs' continuity with the prestigious Toltec heritage. The once-novel images of carnage and war, which had functioned as the informational, "back half" of Tula's civic architectural events, were, somewhat ironically, recast in Tenochtitlán as conservative components in a complex strategy of ritual-architectural allurement and thus were repositioned in the "front half" of those events, where the Toltec elements could serve to coax tradition-conscious audiences into the theatrically staged public ceremonies of the Aztecs. In a sense, the ugly lover of Tula became the mother of Tenochtitlán.

Granted, the reassigned role of Toltec art forms in Tenochtitlán may not have been quite so absolute as this neat formulation implies. Nevertheless, this passing glimpse at the deceptiveness of the formal resemblance between Tula and Tenochtitlán provides an important clue for my more detailed hermeneutical reconsideration of the famous similitude between Tula and Chichén Itzá. To anticipate my forthcoming argument, "Toltec Chichén," which presumably hosted ritual-architectural events that were more substantially different from those of Tula than were the Aztec events, constitutes a similar, though even more acute instance of this sort of "disjunctive revalorization."[116] In this later case, according to the hypothesis that I will elaborate momentarily, the juvenescent Yucatán capital, roughly contemporaneous with Tula (and thus looking across the countryside at the embattled success of the Toltec capital rather than back in time as the Aztecs had), likewise found in Tula perhaps the richest of available resources for its own construction of a convincing strategy of ritual-architectural allurement. The designers of "Toltec Chichén" (as the Aztecs would subsequently do) thus widened the already eclectic ritual-architectural oeuvre of their city to include a very strong representation of decorative and formal elements from Tula. Yet, even more than in the case of Tenochtitlán, at Chichén Itzá, those familiar Toltec elements were reconfigured and recast in decidedly different ritual-architectural roles.

Anticipating a bit more of my subsequent hypothesis, the fierce images of Tula were retrieved and transferred to Yucatán *not* to articulate the specific nature and program of Chichén's own polity; because the lords of Chichén Itzá were not involved in the sort of

Frieze panels on Pyramid B featuring jaguars and eagles holding human hearts in their beaks. The Aztecs, who were enamored of all that was Toltec, apparently pried loose virtually all the exterior ornamentation on the buildings of Tula. These famous panels remained intact only because they were buried beneath later elaborations of the adjacent structure. (Photo by the author.)

endemic struggle for their existence that plagued the Toltecs, they did not require that sort of threatening ultimatum. Instead, those Central Mexican elements were utilized as components in the highly cosmopolitan, "event-starting" program of "Toltec" Chichén Itzá. Thus, when the graphically martial images of Tula reappeared at Chichén Itzá (not unlike what would eventually happen at Tenochtitlán), those images had, in a sense, descended from their status as radical, specific, and programmatic messages to become one (albeit very important) of many instigatory contrivances or lures that the Maya architects of "Toltec Chichén" used to draw a multinational audience into their ritual-architectural events. With respect to the twofold pattern of ritual-architectural events, the notoriously similar forms that had originally constituted the "back," or radical, component of the events in Tula Grande were eventually replicated and repositioned in the "front," or conservative, component of the events at "Toltec Chichén." To that extent, the respective revalorizations of Tula art and architecture at Tenochtitlán and Chichén Itzá constitute parallel cases.

However, to accentuate the most important difference between these respective revalorizations, *unlike* the general continuity between the priorities of Toltec and Aztec public ceremony, at Chichén Itzá, there was a decidedly more pronounced rearrangement of types of ritual-architectural priorities. In the case of Tenochtitlán, the formally resemblant Toltec images were shifted to a different relative position in a set of Aztec architectural events that, nonetheless, demonstrated essentially the same arrangement of general ritual-architectural priorities as those that had prevailed at Tula. By contrast, in the case of "Toltec Chichén" (which actually preceded Tenochtitlán by several hundred years), not only were the Toltec forms repositioned in the "front" rather than "back half" of Chichén events, but, moreover, these Yucatecan events demonstrated a significantly different arrangement of ritual-architectural priorities than would have been witnessed at Tula. In sum, those architectural forms that are so famously shared by Tula and Chichén Itzá not only filled significantly divergent roles in their respective events but, moreover, found themselves participating in qualitatively different sorts of ritual-architectural events at each capital.

The Ritual-Architectural Events of South Chichén

> The architecture [of Chichén Itzá] shows two distinct styles: (1) a Maya period, the buildings of which date from the sixth to tenth centuries, pure Maya in style; and (2) a Maya-Mexican period, the buildings of which date from the eleventh to fourteenth centuries and show many architectural features imported from central Mexico.
>
> *Sylvanus Morley, 1946*[117]

> In short, Chichén Itzá is best interpreted as an integrated whole community. The settlement pattern and architecture provide no evidence of ethnic heterogeneity at the site. Rather the picture is one of a highly stratified and internally political society that was *probably* ethnically uniform and Maya.
>
> *Charles Lincoln, 1986*[118]

Two Chichén Itzás: The Roadway Runs Through It

From the earliest colonial era until the 1980s, when it was finally redirected, the main thoroughfare from the east coast of Yucatán to the capital city of Mérida passed directly through the ruins of Chichén Itzá. Besides holding the ancient capital in the public view — these ruins were never lost in the jungle — a prophetic coincidence in routing inexactly bifurcated the city along a northeast-southwest axis between

Aerial photo of Chichén Itzá, showing the old highway that roughly separates "Old Maya Chichén Itzá" and "New Toltec Chichén Itzá." That road was rerouted around the ruins in the 1980s. (Photo by William M. Ferguson, courtesy of the University of Texas, Austin.)

what Edward H. Thompson would eventually term, in the late nineteenth century, "Old Chichén" and "New Chichén."[119] Far more than adjacent neighborhoods, these two respective sides of the roadway became (and remain) the spatial and temporal loci, the essential terms of debate, for every (re)construction of Chichén Itzá's long and convoluted past.

Alfred Tozzer, again exercising his enormous influence, was particularly responsible for elaborating and systematizing this serendipitous division between the northern and southern portions of the ruins. Where Thompson had distinguished the two halves simply according to their presumed ages, Tozzer, in the context of his overpowering effort to counterpoise absolutely all that was "foreign" or "Mexican Toltec" in Chichén Itzá over against all that was "indigenous Maya," correlated the two districts not only with space and time (that is, South/North and Old/New) but with ethnicities — thus, the respective labels "Old Maya Chichén" and "New Toltec Chichén," which continue to appear regularly on maps and signs around the site.[120]

The vexing terminological situation is complicated even more by the fact that every building and section of Chichén Itzá has, over the past centuries, been assigned a crazily mixed variety of Maya, Spanish, and English names, none of which are remotely reliable designations of the actual pre-Hispanic uses of these structures. Nevertheless, in Tozzer's scheme, the northern portion of the site, designated as "Toltec Chichén," includes the Sacred Cenote and the five major structures located on the giant platform or La Gran Nivelación: the Castillo; the Great Ball Court Complex, including the Temple of the Jaguars and the adjacent *Tzompantli* (or skull rack); the Temple of the Warriors; the Court of a Thousand Columns Colonnade; and the Mercado. The smaller Platform of the Eagles and Jaguars, together with the Platform of Venus, both located within the great plaza of the Castillo pyramid, also belong to this well-integrated assemblage of "Toltec Chichén" structures. According to Tozzer, this fairly tight cluster of buildings was the locus of activity in "post-Mexicanization" phases that he terms Chichén II, III, and IV.

The other major "half" of the site — so-termed South Chichén — presumed by Tozzer to be the older and more purely Maya component of the city, consists essentially of everything else outside La Gran Nivelación. This far more scattered collection of buildings includes, most prominently, the loosely related group of large structures some 500 meters to the south of the Castillo: the Caracol, the House of the Deer, the Casa Colorado, the Iglesia, the giant Monjas (or Nunnery) and its annexes, and the Akab-Dzib or Temple of the Obscure Writing. Additionally, four smaller clusters of structures scattered farther to the south in Thompson's "Old Chichén" (an area that on some maps is called "Old Old Chichén") are also typically lumped into this catchall designation of South or Old Chichén. These far-spaced clusters are variously termed: (1) the Initial Series Group or the Date Group, also sometimes called the Group of the Phalli; (2) the Southwest Group, including what is popularly known as the Castillo of Old Chichén and the Jaguar Temple of Old Chichén; (3) the group including the Temple of the Lintel, the Temple of the Three Lintels, and the Temple of the Four Lintels; and (4) the Group of the Hieroglyphic Jambs. Actually linked only by their nonparticipation in the "Toltec Chichén" plaza to the north, a number of these supposedly indigenous Maya structures, particularly in the outlying clusters, do, in fact (as Tozzer fully acknowledged), show many "Toltec" features. Moreover, the blanket assessment of their anteriority to the "Toltec Chichén" plaza has always been contested. Nevertheless, Tozzer designated this conglomeration of largely unrelated buildings, some twenty five major structures in all, as the spatial correlate to his "Chichén I" stage, that is, in his estimate, the "pre-Toltec" or "pure Yucatán Maya" era at Chichén Itzá.[121]

Problematic as it may be, Tozzer's notion that the modern roadway (rerouted around the ruins in the 1980s) conveniently separates Old Maya South Chichén and New Toltec North Chichén has proved exceedingly resilient.[122] This polarized, bilateral vision of two Chichén Itzás was canonized by the early 1950s with the Carnegie Institution's map of the site, which continues to serve as the pattern for virtually all schematic representations of Chichén Itzá. On the Carnegie map (and thus nearly all other diagrams of the site), the Sacred Cenote, presumably the original pivot of the city, is situated at the very top of the page so that absolutely no structure north of the Sacred Well is depicted. The Castillo and the "Toltec" plaza lie slightly below (that is, south of) the Cenote, while the supposedly earlier, "non-Toltec," "indigenous Maya" structures are strewn over the lower (or southern) two-thirds of the frame.[123] Not inconsequentially, the fenced-in precinct of the current archaeological-tourist zone likewise conforms to these general boundaries.

In South Chichén, serpent head on the stairway of the Caracol. Though most of the Tula-like iconographic and architectural elements are concentrated in the northern portion of the ruins, there are many characteristically "Toltec" features in the southern portions of the site as well. (Carnegie Institution of Washington photo, courtesy of the Peabody Museum, Harvard University.)

Variations of this oft-reproduced Carnegie map, which are nearly always cropped so that the Sacred Cenote appears at the topmost edge, and which invariably label the alternate sides of the old roadway as Old and New Chichén Itzá, are all too often simply accepted uncritically as an objective rendering of the pre-Columbian reality. The old map continues to have a disturbingly powerful impact on the way in which both scholars and tourists visualize Chichén Itzá. Charles Lincoln, however, emphasizing that the consistently flat terrain presents no ecological factors that would have militated against even settlement on all sides of the Sacred Cenote (except for the Xtoloc Cenote, which is south of the Castillo and typically considered to have served more utilitarian purposes), considers that the seemingly matter-of-fact site plan is misleading in the extreme and that the conventional notion of Old and New Chichén on respective sides of the roadway is simply wrong. He argues, instead, that, in all likelihood, the Sacred Cenote lay near the center of Chichén's wider area of pre-Hispanic habitation rather than at the far northern extension (as both the Carnegie map and the layout of the present archaeological zone connote) and, moreover, that entire site was a single integrated whole.[124] Yet, even in Lincoln's iconoclastic hypothesis of "total overlap" — his argument for a complete contemporaneity and ethnic unity for all parts of Chichén Itzá — his fundamental distinction between respective "public" and "private" sectors of the city runs generally along the traditional roadway axis.[125]

Thus, ironically enough, 400 years of antiquarian and academic reflections on the site have not provided a more workable division of Chichén Itzá than that marked by the unreflective routing of the old road. Tozzer's contradistinction between two Chichén Itzás, completely satisfactory to no one, endures as the basic framework for virtually every critical and casual discussion of Chichén Itzá. Even his harshest detractors are forced to take as their starting point an unmistakable incongruity between the ruined architecture of the central plaza of the Castillo and that of the rest of the site; no acceptable alternative has emerged. Thus, while the current academic literature on Chichén Itzá culture history works to jettison the old stereotypes of the pacific Maya and brutal Toltecs, the legacy of the paradigm of Maya-Mexican polarity and of the fabled "Toltec Conquest" of Yucatán remains very much alive. With various amendments, in the broad strokes, South Chichén continues to be regularly depicted as the "non-Toltec" (or "pre-Toltec"), native, and

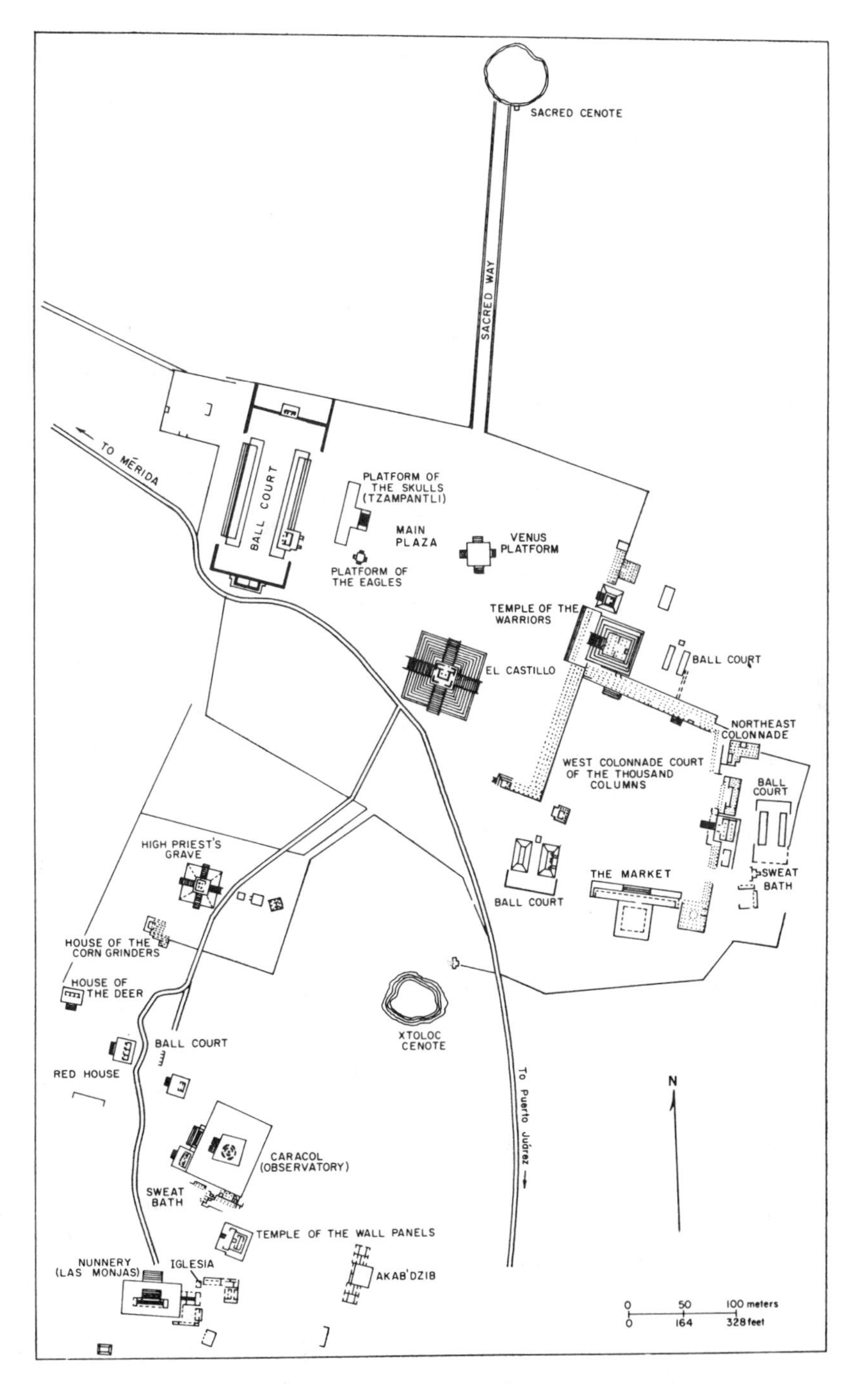

Chichén Itzá
(after Morley and Brainerd)

Chichén Itzá. Variations on the Carnegie Institution of Washington map of the site have been reproduced in countless academic and popular publications. (Reprinted from *The Ancient Maya* by Sylvanus Griswold Morley with the permission of the publishers, Stanford University Press. Copyright ©1946, 1947 by the Board of Trustees of the Leland Stanford Junior University.)

purely Maya portion of the city that existed before the decadent cloud of Tula Toltec idolatry and militarism darkened northern Yucatán and settled down in North Chichén Itzá.

Furthermore — and this is what has made the ruins of Chichén Itzá uniquely provocative to both dilettantes and critical scholars — where the aged stereotypes of the benign and intellectual Maya and the ferocious Central Mexicans have usually pitched Classic Maya sites in the Guatemalan jungle against Mexican sites hundreds of miles away on the high plateau, the dichotomy between South Chichén and North Chichén encapsulates the paradigm of Maya-Mexican polarity in the space of a few hundred meters. Accordingly — to restate once more the principal factor that has sustained the enthusiasm and "enigma" of Chichén Itzá — from the top of either the Monjas in the southern portion of the city or the Castillo in the northern sector, a visitor to Chichén Itzá can collect, even now, in one potent eyeshot, the radical poles of Mesoamerican architectural history. A visitor atop either of these buildings can see at once specimens that represent, according to the old script, the sublime style of the Puuc Maya victims and the gaudy artistic production of their Toltec conquerors — by common decree, the very best and the worst in pre-Columbian aesthetics.

If preserving, then (despite serious reservations), the traditional north/south spatial division of Chichén Itzá, we can, nonetheless, provide more nuanced and "religiously significant" reassessments of each respective portion. In that spirit, the final two-thirds of this chapter proceed with hermeneutical interpretations, first of the ritual-architectural events of the southern, ostensibly Maya sector of the city, and then of the more tightly circumscribed plaza of "Toltec" Chichén Itzá and the Sacred Cenote to the north.

The Study of South Chichén: Tangential Interest

Southern and outlying Chichén Itzá has generally been defined by negation as that portion of the site that lies outside the obviously integrated plaza of "Toltec" Chichén Itzá. South Chichén is the seemingly less-anomalous sector of the city, whose architecture resembles that of the Puuc Maya sites to the west and that, unlike North Chichén, shows no special affinity with the styles of Central Mexico. Although it has been typically designated as the unremarkable or "the other" part of Chichén, that has not usually been a pejorative label. To the contrary, each of the early nineteenth-century pioneers (Stephens, Charnay, Holmes, and Maudslay) commented favorably and at length on the buildings of South Chichén, particularly the Monjas, the largest structure by volume anywhere in Chichén Itzá.[126] While noting that the architecture of this southern portion of the site is different and rather "more beautiful" than that to the north, none of these early explorers, however, assessed this area as temporally earlier or ethnically distinct from the rest of the city. The claim of anteriority and the title "Old Chichén" both seem to originate around the turn of the century with Edward Thompson (though Thompson, like his antiquarian predecessors but unlike Tozzer, declined to assign any distinct ethnic status to the builders of these southern structures).[127]

By the time the major Chichén Itzá projects of the Carnegie Institution and the Mexican government began (in the 1920s), the northern "Toltec" plaza had become the primary focus of interest. Accordingly, the emphasis of this generation's massive efforts, both in traditional archaeology and in rebuilding the pre-Columbian monuments so as to attract tourists, was on that northern precinct.[128] However, if South Chichén was marginalized at this point, it was not entirely ignored. In the thirties, Russell

Smith and John Bolles, both of the Carnegie Institution, did undertake a major architectural study of the famously elaborate Iglesia structure and of the Monjas together with its adjacent annexes; Bolles's work remains the most thorough description of these "Old Chichén" buildings.[129] And, in the same era, Paul Martin, also of the Carnegie, did the only thorough archaeological (re)construction of a southern building at the Temple of the Three Lintels. This impressive structure, which provides the most thoroughly Puuc-style architecture anywhere within Chichén, because of its outlying location, is today seen only by more adventuresome visitors.[130]

At Tula the ambitious efforts of this era of traditional archaeology (in that case the work of Jorge Acosta) was followed by a second round of "new archaeological" research, but Chichén Itzá has been host to no similarly thorough reworking. The more embracing archaeological surveys of outlying settlement patterns and nonelite structures, for instance, and the more sophisticated chronological studies that would be of inestimable help in understanding the scattered constructions lumped under the title "South Chichén," have, unfortunately, scarcely begun at Chichén Itzá. Likewise, art historians from the Carnegie era forward have been enthusiastic about the fabulous Puuc Maya architecture of west-central Yucatán and, thus, very interested in the variations on that style that appear in "Old Chichén," but, where there has been a lot of provocative new art historical work on North Chichén, recent works concentrating on the art and iconography in the southern portion of the city are depressingly rare.[131] So too, the ethnohistorical record of Chichén Itzá aims primarily at the northern portion of the city: *The Books of Chilam Balam,* for instance, address particularly events related to the Sacred Cenote; Landa's eyewitness account of Chichén Itzá focuses on the Castillo and its plaza as though there were no other major constructions;[132] the reconnaissance of Chichén Itzá by the Spanish conquistadors is confined to the staging of armaments on the Castillo with no mention of the outlying constructions; and colonial-era accounts of resurgent native religion around Chichén Itzá — for instance, the aborted pilgrimage of the Xui in 1536 — are likewise generally confined to the area of the Sacred Cenote and the Castillo.[133]

By contrast to this near dearth of literary (or "book") evidence, the buildings of South Chichén are graced with abundant hieroglyphic inscriptions, a resource that is almost totally lacking in North Chichén. Advances in deciphering these ample glyphs, currently the most promising line of evidence, have fostered a genuine revolution in the thinking about "non-Toltec" Chichén. David Kelley, Michel Davoust, and Jeff Kowalski, for instance (though not in total agreement), each provide readings of these epigraphic texts that illumine specific names and dates for Chichén Itzá "kings" and thus for the substantive content of South Chichén ritual-architectural events, specifics that, in Tozzer's era, would have been entirely inconceivable.[134] With these (and future) epigraphic revelations, certainly the most exciting point of entry into South Chichén at the moment, this portion of the city may finally win more than the tangential attention for which "the other part of Chichén" has always settled.[135]

Style and Context: Tangential Puuc

The buildings of South Chichén do not belong to the mainstream of any major Mesoamerican formal style of architecture, an independence that led Eric Thompson to the understated musing: "one would like very much to know what were the circumstances that gave rise to this aberration."[136] Yet, of the various stylistic affinities represented in South Chichén, all run distant seconds to the majestic Puuc style of the

In South Chichén, facade of the east end of the Monjas Annex with the upper levels of the Monjas in the background. Encrusted with elaborate decoration, the buildings in this portion of the ruins have been considered by nearly all modern observers as far more beautiful than the monuments in the northern, supposedly "Toltec" portion of the site. (Photo by Lawrence G. Desmond.)

"Great Cities" of west central Yucatán — Sayil, Labná, Kabah, and, preeminently, Uxmal.[137]

Unmistakable for building facades absolutely coated with incredibly elaborate mosaics of geometric designs and stylized masks, Puuc architecture is, by age-old consensus, the very apex of pre-Columbian building, the most beautiful and "the best," the direct antithesis of the vulgar aesthetic of Tula Toltec architecture. In 1588, Fray Antonio de Ciudad Real, for instance, while visiting the "very renowned edifices of Uxmal," praised the "great delicacy" of the Puuc facades whereupon "there are many figures of serpents, idols and shields, many screens or latticework and many other carvings that are beautiful and fine, especially if one looks at them at a distance like a painting of Flanders."[138] Similarly impressed in 1843, John Stephens, like virtually all subsequent critics, echoed these extravagant praises of the Puuc style when he waxed that "tried by the severest rules of art [the Puuc facade decoration of Kabah] would embellish the architecture of any known era . . . it stands as an offering by American builders worthy of the acceptance of a polished people."[139]

Thus, where Tula Toltec architecture (and to a lesser extent that of "Toltec" Chichén Itzá) is typically berated as the epitome of bad taste and poor execution (Mayapán building being its only serious competitor in infamy),[140] the Puuc style has been, and continues to be, almost universally drenched by rave superlatives.[141] Moreover, perhaps not surprisingly, the Yucatecan Terminal Classic context (roughly 600–900 C.E.) that gave rise to the "Great Cities" of the Puuc is typically characterized as peaceful and stable, the very antithesis of the violent chaos in which Tula arose. Once having conquered Yucatán's limitations of scarce water with a system of *chultunes* or underground cisterns, the hilly Puuc region some 80 miles west of Chichén Itzá ("Puuc" means hill or low ridge) became the peninsula's most prosperous and populous region, the locus of what Morley had termed the "New Maya Empire."[142] Where the brashly innovative style of Tula's architecture issued from the desperate and daring spasm of a single city struggling to fashion order out of chaos, the mature Puuc style, peaking at Uxmal, was apparently the climax of a slow, relatively calm, internal evolution involving dozens of healthy communities over a span of some 300 years. None of the Puuc cities seem to have endured the rampant migration, the ethnic competition, nor the military opportunism that racked Tula and shaped its design.[143]

South Chichén is, however, only a tangential participant in this renowned tradition of Yucatecan architecture. Of the numerous buildings in the southern portion of the city, only the Temple of the Three Lintels is absolutely and purely Puuc.[144] Yet, because nearly all the other structures in this portion of the site have strong Puuc associations, an analysis of this fabulous tradition provides the most obvious entrée into retrieving the play of priorities in Chichén's "non-Toltec" ritual-architectural events. Inconveniently, though, the assessment of Puuc architecture itself is, at present (like so many other dimensions of the Tula–Chichén problem), undergoing considerable revision. The older, conventional interpretation of Puuc architecture (promulgated especially by Morley and Tozzer), which is actually more faithful to the paradigm of Maya-Mexican polarity than to the empirical historical realities of pre-Columbian Yucatán, accentuates two essential attributes: first, Puuc architecture is applauded for its nonmilitant, apolitical, abstract, and seemingly "metaphysical" character; and, second, the Puuc is likewise praised for its purity as an indigenous Maya accomplishment, free from either Toltec or any other outside influences.[145]

Throughout the Tozzer era, this twofold, laudatory assessment of the Puuc was typically extrapolated wholesale to South Chichén Itzá, so that the ritual-architectural agenda of this portion of the city (particularly in contrast to North Chichén) was deemed apolitical and uncontaminatedly Maya. There is now, however, important controverting evidence on both counts. First (signaled especially by Kowalski's discovery of specific rulers and royal families in the inscriptions of Uxmal), it has become increasingly difficult to accept that Puuc ritual-architectural events were wholly otherworldly, "metaphysical," and calendrical in character. To the contrary, pre-Hispanic Puuc events now seem, as do most public Maya rituals, to have been designed at least in part to promulgate very specific and highly politicized agenda.[146] As part of the broader reassessment of the "darker" and more worldly Maya, the older view that the rituals associated with the Puuc style would have been wholly abstract and exclusively "religious" (as though homology, I-A; astronomy, I-B; and the commemoration of divinity, II-A, were the sole ritual-architectural priorities) is giving way to a new appreciation of the very pragmatic and highly political nature of these Puuc rites (and thus, the importance of the ritual-architectural commemoration of temporal authority, priority II-C). Kelley's and Davoust's parallel work on the inscriptions in South Chichén is similarly forcing scholars to acknowledge that the legitimation of specific rulers and dynasties was at least as important in the architectural events of this portion of the city as was devotion to stars or to time (as the older view would have implied).

Second, although somewhat more difficult to assess, are challenges to the old contention that Puuc architecture was a strictly indigenous, thoroughly "uncontaminated" Yucatecan Maya accomplishment. As part of the wider revisionist appreciation of the mobility and interactivity of ancient Mesoamericans in general, there has been a growing acknowledgment of the significantly eclectic character of Puuc architecture. As early as 1950, Proskouriakoff, for instance, recognized obviously "foreign" (specifically Central Mexican) iconographic elements in the Puuc sites.[147] Andrews IV, a decade later, remarked on the occurrence of "Mexican-looking" glyphs and architecture in the Puuc region, specifically a *tzompantli* in the Terminal Classic context of Dzibilchaltún.[148] And in the 1970s, Ball, concerned especially with the chronological implications of these earlier-than-expected Mexican influences in Yucatán, articulated the current consensus that the florescence in Puuc Maya architecture was actually the amalgam of three distinct components: (1) indigenous developments in the Puuc hill region, (2) influences from the more strictly Maya style of the Río Bec-Chenes area to the south, and (3) "foreign" influences from the Gulf Coast and Central Mexican Highlands.[149]

If "pure" Puuc itself is significantly eclectic, then South Chichén architecture, as a tangential participant in the Puuc, is even more so. Indebted most of all to its impressive neighbors to the west, South Chichén integrates Puuc design with an older block masonry construction, with a significant number of southern Petén Maya elements, and with an ample share of both Río Bec-Chenes Maya and Central Mexican components.[150] The consequences of this considerable eclecticism in what had, by convention, been deemed the strictly Yucatán Maya portion of Chichén Itzá are complex. Perhaps the most important implication for our understanding of the Tula–Chichén problem has to do with the way in which the builders of North, "Toltec" Chichén would find a precedent in South Chichén for their own, even more ambitious efforts in synthesizing diverse styles. Yet, with more direct relevance to South Chichén itself, despite the increasing appreciation of the significantly eclectic character of the architecture in this portion of the city, there is nothing to suggest the measure of multi-ethnicity that plagued (and energized) Tula. Where ethnic diversity and international mixing were both Tula's greatest strength and its fatal liability, the multinationalism of South Chichén attained no such drastic proportions. In short, South Chichén faced lesser pressures and very different problems than those that beset either Tula, Hidalgo, or "Toltec" Chichén Itzá; accordingly, it responded with very different types of public ritual-architectural events, events to which I now turn my attention.

"Many-Minded" Ritual-Architectural Events

I accept as a working hypothesis the partial (but not total) chronological overlap of South Chichén and "Toltec" Chichén. On that basis, it would appear that the former portion of the city (while neither so isolated nor so idyllic as the old stereotypes connote) arose in a historical context more like that of the contemporaneous, steadily prosperous "Great Cities" of the Puuc hill region than of the pressurized and unprecedented circumstances that challenged the builders of Tula and "Toltec Chichén." Accordingly, regarding allurement, South Chichén ritual-architectural events had no need, like those of Tula or "Toltec Chichén,"

East end of the Monjas Annex. Though indebted most to the Puuc Maya style of west central Yucatán, the eclectic architecture of South Chichén also integrates elements from the Petén, Río Bec, and Chenes Maya regions as well as from Central Mexico. (Photo by Lawrence G. Desmond.)

to beg, cajole, or coerce the participation of a strange or fragmentary audience; instead, these events could be instigated much more easily and on an entirely different basis. Moreover, because this ritual-architectural program did not issue at one of those precarious turning points in Mesoamerican history (as those of Tula and "Toltec Chichén" would), the designers of South Chichén architecture and ceremony were not saddled with the burden of communicating one unmistakable and novel message, political or otherwise; instead, much less pressured than their Toltec counterparts, the architects of South Chichén were allowed to explore a more sweeping range of issues about divinity, sacred history, and royal ancestry. As the following sections will elaborate, where Toltec and Puuc architectures typically land at the opposite extremes in standard formal-aesthetic comparisons, jacking the comparison up to the level of ritual-architectural events, if on somewhat different grounds, scarcely mitigates the sharp contrast between South Chichén and either Tula or "Toltec Chichén."

Instigation: Invitation Not Coercion

For all the adulations heaped on Puuc architecture, scholars were for a long time hard-pressed to discern any sort of coherent orientational strategy for the layout of these beautiful sites. Most general characterizations of Puuc city planning have, in fact, agreed with Spinden's assessment of 1913 that the area's sites "lack careful orientation" and that, particularly in contrast to either the grid layouts of Central Mexico or the compact, integrated arrangement of connecting courts and plazas of many southern Maya centers, Puuc structures are scattered, "seemingly haphazard," except for certain courtyard configurations.[151] Pollock's more recent, wide survey of the Puuc area (definitely the most thorough descriptive source on this region) nudges that stock assessment of orientational indifference by finding an approximate north-south axis, sometimes accentuated by causeways and avenues, in six of the major Puuc sites (Sayil, Kabah, Labná, Uxmal, Oxkintok, and X'kukican) and by showing that the vast majority of Puuc public structures are oriented, to varying degrees, somewhat east of north.[152] The same could be argued for South Chichén, where many buildings have an east of north orientation and are, with the exception of the Hieroglyphic Jambs Group, clustered along a generally north-south roadway (Sacbe no. 7). There is, however, nothing in South Chichén (or any Puuc site for that matter) remotely like the four-quartered spatial scheme of Tenochtitlán or a Teotihuacán-style axial grid, which is to say that the homology priority (I-A) is not particularly well expressed.[153]

Especially given the location of the famous Caracol "observatory" in this southern portion of the city, the case for celestial references in "Old Chichén" (astronomy, priority I-C) is somewhat more promising. The Caracol is, however, a very special case, with a complicated history of several major rebuildings and realignments, and, while there is considerable uncertainty in this regard, most scholars credit "Mexican Toltecs" (rather than indigenous Maya) with the later remodelings that gave the Caracol its characteristic circular shape and very elaborate set of astronomical references.[154] At least one archaeoastronomer is dubious of the entire long-standing assumption that the Caracol, even in its final circular manifestation, was ever really an astronomical observatory.[155] Anyway, perhaps more important for our purposes than the eccentricities of the Caracol would be the discovery in other portions of South Chichén of the sorts of sophisticated celestial alignments that Aveni and his colleagues are currently (if belatedly) documenting for other Puuc sites, specifically Uxmal, whose orientations had long been dismissed as largely purposeless and "haphazard."[156] Most of that work, however, remains to be done for the outlying sections of Chichén Itzá.[157]

Intimations of axial and astronomical alignments notwithstanding (that is, evidence for the homology and astronomy priorities, I-A and I-C), it would appear that the instigation of ritual-architectural events in South Chichén, just as in the Puuc area generally, depended far more heavily on the presentation of familiar, highly standardized forms, techniques, and decorative elements, each juxtaposed with somewhat atypical modifications (a variation on allurement via convention, priority I-B). Most Puuc buildings seem to have been designed with respect to traditionally prescribed patterns and rules and were arranged primarily with respect to one another rather than to the sky or some vision of the cosmos.[158] Thus, not only does conventionality appear to have been the preeminent orientational priority in Puuc building, it was conventionality of a quite specific sort.

Instead of relying on the syncretistic display of eclectic historical allusions that would be so important at Tula Grande and even more so at "Toltec Chichén" (and which represents one sort of manifestation of orientation and allurement by an appeal to artistic convention, priority I-B), the instigation of Puuc architectural events relied on a more rarified, abstract variation on the notion of allurement

Aerial photo of principal structures in South Chichén, with the Nunnery in the foreground. The loosely clustered structures of South Chichén, with the exception of the astronomically aligned Caracol (the round tower in the photo), would seem to be primarily oriented with respect to one another rather than according to any axial or celestial referencing. (Photo by William M. Ferguson, courtesy of the University of Texas, Austin.)

via conventionalization.[159] The favored strategy for legitimating and instigating Puuc ritual-architectural events involved beginning with a set of standardized, artificial if you will, constituent elements — such as masks, geometric motifs, and prototypical floor plans — as the starting point for deviation from those conventions (a somewhat more subtle variation on priority I-B). Accordingly, nowhere is the interplay between order and variation, the typical and the atypical, the conventional and the novel — which is the characteristic pattern of ritual-architectural events — more clear than in the experience of Puuc (and, to a great extent, South Chichén) architecture. It is almost as though Puuc designers began their projects with a kind of generic, prototypical building form — a long, low rectangular structure, perforated along the front by a series of rectangular doorways, each of which leads to a small, windowless, corbel-vaulted room — and then adapted that standard form to each individuated circumstance. This basic "palace" or "range structure" form operated as the conservative element in Puuc architectural design, as a thoroughly respectable, noncontroversial anchoring point of departure from which the "restless energy of Puuc builders"[160] launched endless elaborations in: (1) the ground plans of individual structures, (2) the arrangement of groups of structures, (3) construction techniques, and, (4) perhaps most vividly, the lush architectural decorations of the Puuc. Consider briefly these four arenas for the interplay of order and variation in Puuc building generally and more specifically their possible applicability to South Chichén.

First, the shuffling and reshuffling of the windowless little rooms in Puuc ground plans is a particularly obvious demonstration of variation within the tightly ordered parameters of convention.[161] Close to the prototypical plan, the Adjacent Palace at Chunhuhub and the Serpent Head Palace at Itzimté, for instance, have three simple doorways to three rooms in a line, all facing one direction;[162] South Chichén's Casa Colorado and Deer House similarly share this simple arrangement; and the Akab-Dzib, also in "Old Chichén," may likewise originally have had this very basic floor plan.[163] Other Puuc buildings, like Structure 1A5 at Kabah, retain the simple ground plan but employ more elaborate columnar entrances to vary the rhythm of the openings.[164] Even more Puuc structures — like the main building at Xlapak, which has a bank of nine rooms with doors on both sides and both ends — enhance the familiar layout by employing more complicated plans and entrance configurations.[165] For example, the Akab-Dzib in its final form had some eighteen chambered rooms, and South Chichén's Monjas, constantly rebuilt, eventually had several tiers of rooms facing in all directions, though both structures always remained faithful to the basic prototypical pattern.[166]

Second, this basic prototypical form was, moreover, used in groups as the primary element for composing courtyards and plazas. The magnificent Nunnery Complex at Uxmal, a roughly rectangular configuration formed by laying elaborated range structures along each side, is the quintessential example. Deceptively simple in design and seemingly relaxed in its imperfectly squared layout, the Nunnery is actually constructed of an amazingly intricate, assuredly premeditated system of angles and sight lines and, as such, constitutes the most sophisticated exercise in the sort of abstract, conventionalized orientation that characterizes the Puuc generally.[167] There are several other similar range-lined quadrangular courtyard configurations at Uxmal and innumerable more modest examples throughout the Puuc hills. In South Chichén specifically, virtually all the range structures participate in this sort of interbuilding arrangement, thus creating clustered wholes that are greater than the sum of the individual parts.

Third, similarly manifesting the pattern of order and variation, Puuc construction techniques, while consistently maintaining the same basic design, were variously modified and reworked in a number of ingenious ways. For instance, while most Puuc buildings (including those in South Chichén) rest on relatively low platforms or terraces, in some cases, like the "Miradors" (inappropriately termed "lookouts") at Sayil, Labná, and elsewhere, the basic range structure is situated atop a high, steep, pyramidal base. The Adivino (or Temple of the Magician) at Uxmal similarly lifts a modest range form high into the sky on a huge pyramid, and South Chichén's Red House and Deer House are likewise simple range structures raised up on large platforms, in these cases rounded rectangular substructures instead of pyramids. Where the builders of many sites in the Puuc hills were able to exploit naturally rising terrain to achieve a multistoried effect, in South Chichén, which is generally flat, a similar effect was achieved (for instance at the Monjas) by filling in older rooms and then building on top of them.[168] Puuc ceiling and vaulting techniques, as Pollock's survey demonstrates, provided one more constructional arena for the endless manipulation of a simple, conventional prototype. Pollock, in fact, concludes that "almost every aspect of the design of the 'normal' [Puuc] vault was at one time or another omitted, modified or substantially changed."[169]

Fourth, the interplay of convention and novelty crystalized in the insuperable facade decorations to which Puuc architecture owes its greatest renown. Usually concentrating the decoration in the upper zone of the building face, or on "flying facades" that extend well above the building proper, many Puuc buildings actually appear to be little more than hangars for their exterior embellishment.[170] The ample decoration, which graces virtually every Puuc structure, is most typically composed of a repetitive array or parquetry of *"chac"* (or *"chaac"*) masks and geometric designs. As Kubler says, "mosaic decorations of small units easily re-used in new combinations are the rule."[171] The *chac* mask motif — the most characteristic of all Puuc decorative elements — a highly stylized face with eyes, mouth, and a long, hooked nose, is (like the basic rectangular range building form) both invariably respected and endlessly manipulated so that there is remarkable diversity not only between different sites but even between the masks on any one building. At its most basic, a single face is inlaid on a flat wall surface (though even in these cases there are individuated features), and countless other masks are bent around the corners of buildings, as though peering out in two directions at once. At South Chichén, for instance, the Temple of the Three Lintels and the Monjas and its associated buildings all have both the flat and corner sorts of masks.

Other Puuc buildings use the *chac* masks in combination, sometimes stacking them two high, as in Chichén's Monjas Annex; sometimes they are three or even five high, as in several instances at Uxmal. Uxmal's Palace of the Governor, the climax of the range form, arranges *chac* masks in a snake-like, ascending and descending pattern. In other cases, such as the principal building at Xlapak, the bodiless heads are squashed together so that the teeth or beard of the upper one appears as the eyebrows of the lower face. On the Codz-Pop of Kabah, the ultimate Puuc mask facade with more than 300 masks rowed together, there is likewise incessant tinkering with the basic prototype: some of the stone faces have two ears others share an ear with their neighbor and others, placed inside the antechambers, have their noses molded into a step used to enter the inner room.

So too, the geometric ornament that accompanies the *chac* masks is a virtuoso exercise in the juxtaposition of convention and novelty, the arrangement and rearrangement of small interchangeable units. Zigzag dentate, frets, circles, diamonds, balls, chevrons, crosses, and stars,[172] all relatively simple in themselves, are, nonetheless, easily combined into almost endless complex and fresh designs. Exemplified in the brocaded facade of the Adivino at Uxmal, the "typographical" units, possibly even salvaged from some older edifice, are arrayed to create, after the fashion of Chenes serpent-facades, full, wall-sized masks of stunning complexity. In Kubler's words, "it is like typographical design: from a number of small units, each carved with a geometric shape, large pictures are formed . . . in Puuc design [the serpent-mask facades] are like typewriter pictures, composed with key and ribbon from a small number of conventional signs available in quantities as needed."[173] Exemplifying this approach in South Chichén, the flying facade of the Casa Colorado and the facades of the Monjas Annex and the Iglesia, which provide the premier extant Puuc decoration at the site, appear at first glance impenetrably intricate — an effect assuredly redoubled when they were brightly painted. Yet, upon more careful examination, the relatively simple, none-too-perfect constituent blocks emerge, and it becomes evident that the stunning general effect is only the result of a meticulous accumulation of very humble parts.

Although South Chichén may lie somewhat aside from the Puuc mainstream, the same basic instigatory strategies would seem to apply. As in the Puuc generally, the ritual-architectural events of South Chichén apparently allured their constituents from "spoilsport" status into committed participation by presenting familiar architectural conventions that had been manipulated and elaborated in appealingly novel ways (a quite different variation on the convention priority, I-B, than the eclectic accumulation of allusions to other Mesoamerican architectures that was intended to initiate the events of Tula Grande and "Toltec Chichén"). Caricaturing the twofold pattern of ritual-architectural events, South Chichén participates with a vigor equal to Tula's in juxtaposing familiar and unfamiliar, the secure and the unknown. To stretch the analogy of mother's ugly lover, if Tula civic events resembled the jarring experience of finding one's parent (the conservative and familiar component) embracing a repulsive stranger (the radical and unfamiliar component), the invitation into the events of South Chichén would have been considerably less rattling, more liable to inspire wonderment and puzzlement (instead of horror) as the mother one knew so well revealed for the first time a very different and largely unanticipated side of herself. This Puuc architecture, in other words, by transcending the bland and the predictable, engendered a sense of awe and surprise but hardly the irrefusable demand to reorientation provoked by the events of Tula Grande (or, for that matter, "Toltec Chichén"). South Chichén, so it would seem, presented a welcoming invitation to explore and to experiment with new possibilities and permutations, an option rather than an imperative to participate.

Presentation: Nontheatrical Choreography

Scholars of every generation have been struck not only by how different South Chichén looks from the area around the Castillo and the Sacred Cenote but also by the profoundly different "feel" or "attitude" of its architecture. Eric Thompson, for instance, reflects in his journal that, unlike North Chichén, "there is a Puritan stolidity about those thick-walled Maya buildings of Classic [that is, South] Chichén."[174] Moreover, he considered that, because the builders of Puuc-style architecture had elsewhere proven themselves fully capable of constructing good-sized windows, that the dark heavy effect of these South Chichén buildings was intentional (and, furthermore, proof that these were "religious" rather than residential structures). Thompson writes: "I think this lack of light was not regarded as a drawback, but as a desideratum for the secret rites of the old Maya priesthood, who seem to have wished to break contact with the outer world when performing their mysteries, for they were much given to worshipping in the recesses of dark caves."[175] Arguing emphatically, then, that "there can be no doubt that these stone buildings were never permanently inhabited," Thompson proposes that the tight, copal-stained spaces of South Chichén had served as cells for preparatory fasting and purification prior to more public ceremonials that were carried out elsewhere in the city, presumably in North Chichén.[176]

More recently, Charles Lincoln, though explicitly rejecting the assessment that these could not have been primarily residential structures, nonetheless, echoes Thompson's sense

Decorative panels from the upper level of the Monjas. The lush facade ornamentation on several of the structures of South Chichén, particularly the Monjas, clearly instantiates the characteristic Puuc strategy of building up seemingly complex designs via the creative rearrangement of relatively simple and highly conventionalized geometric elements. (Photos by Lawrence G. Desmond.)

that there is something profoundly different about the mood of South Chichén. Thus, despite arguing that the two very different-looking portions of the city do not represent two successive epochs in time nor the respective efforts of Toltec and Maya ethnicities as Tozzer and Thompson had claimed, Lincoln emphasizes that, in contrast to the large and "not-very-subtle" iconographic adornments of North Chichén (for instance, images of warriors, skulls, and feathered serpents), the architecture of South Chichén is characterized by a "limitation of access." He also argues that the intricate hieroglyphic inscriptions that are so plentiful in South Chichén (but largely absent in North Chichén) would have been decipherable only by the literate middle and upper strata of Chichén society and, moreover, were positioned largely out of view of any large spectatorial congregation.[177] On the basis of these marked differences, Lincoln then concludes that the two sectors of the city constitute "two contrasting [but completely contemporaneous] types of architectural context . . . one [that is, North Chichén] appears to be public, the other [that is, South Chichén] private."[178]

Lincoln's conclusion that the range structures of South Chichén had a "private function, probably, but not always necessarily residential,"[179] does not seem warranted. Thompson's older opinion that these buildings had housed largely esoteric rites (if qualified somewhat) is actually more compelling. In either case, their general agreement that the activities that transpired in these buildings, whether ritual or residential, must have involved only a highly restricted set of participants does mesh, albeit inadvertently, with my own more "eventful" interpretation of the mode of ritual-architectural presentation that characterized South Chichén, a mode that is quite unlike that of either Tula or "Toltec Chichén."

As I argued in the previous chapter, Puuc building (probably together with that of the Mixtecas of the Oaxaca region) participated in a strain of Mesoamerican ritual-architectural choreography that largely eschewed extravagant ceremonial spectacles that would play to large assembled audiences — the sort of inclusive theatrical ritual events that were Tula's (and "Toltec Chichén's") first preoccupation — in favor of more exclusive and voluntarily instigated ritual-architectural events, events that are typically characterized more by introspection and devotion than by the promulgation of a programmatic sociopolitical agenda. Accordingly, the affective power of the lavish Puuc facade decoration notwithstanding, I argued that the stock designation of the Puuc as "Maya Baroque," which implies a histrionic ritual-architectural staging after the fashion of Bernini (thus placing the theatre priority, III-A, in first place), is actually quite misleading. Alternatively, I hypothesized that Puuc events were, more likely, dominated by the contemplation priority (III-B) and that worshippers apprehended the intricate forms of the Puuc in a direct and meditative fashion (as opposed to the indirect apprehension of architecture facilitated by theatric, stage-setting ritual-architectural presentation). Thus, in that case, Puuc events actually find much stronger analogues in the experience of, for instance, either Gothic architecture (wherein, according to Abbot Suger, stained glass and lush cathedrals serve "to transport one [via anagogical illumination] from the material to the immaterial") or Borobudur mandala architecture (wherein the physical forms lead one, both literally and figuratively, through an ascent to something like spiritual illumination).[180] Moreover, the section on the propitiatory ritual-architectural priority (III-C) suggested that the very construction of these same elaborate Puuc facades, anything but prosaically streamlined, was quite probably

In South Chichén, east end of Monjas Annex. Though this facade has evoked (and continues to evoke) countless ingenious philosophical and mythological interpretations, few investigators have seriously considered the possibility that it might have served as a mandala-like prop for contemplation or a guide to introspective meditation. (Photo by Lawrence G. Desmond.)

itself an act of devotion, thanksgiving, or petition to the primary Puuc protagonist, Chac, the rain god. The unequaled care, precision, and finesse of Puuc construction would seem, in fact, to represent the quintessence of nonexpedient building typically associated with the propitiation priority.[181]

Having already made a case that Puuc architecture demonstrates an ascendancy of contemplation and propitiation priorities (III-B and III-C) over those of a theatric sort (III-A), the present discussion can focus particularly on Puuc strategies for delimiting refuges of sacrality (the sanctuary priority, III-D). Such refuges seem to have been much more important in South Chichén than the characteristic "Toltec" preoccupation with staging large-scaled spectatorial events. The preeminence of the sanctuary priority (III-D) over that of theatre (III-A) is suggested, for instance, by the fact that the open-air acropolises or spectator arenas of the sort that one finds at Monte Albán, Tula, Tenochtitlán, or in the southern Maya ruins are rare in Puuc sites.[182] Instead, the vast majority of Puuc buildings are arranged so as to form closed-off courtyards — fully enclosed, flat, paved rectangular enclaves that are accessible only through narrow tunnels in the surrounding buildings. At Uxmal alone, for instance, there are some dozen of these somewhat exclusive quadrangular arrangements extant, many with the narrow portal passageways still intact.[183]

Often these tightly circumscribed Puuc courtyards feature a small, centrally located platform that resembles, at least formally, the low, flat Adoratorio platform at the center of Tula Grande or the famous tribunes that lie between the Castillo and the Sacred Cenote in "Toltec" Chichén Itzá.[184] Despite the formal resemblance to the Toltec tribunes, however, these Puuc daises seem to have functioned very differently. Instead of serving as "dance platforms" or as stages for what Landa termed "farces" for the entertainment and edification of a large assembled audience, the Puuc platforms typically served as substructures for monolithic altars or, in a few cases, carved stelae. The Puuc platforms were, in other words, not stages on which ritual actors played out their roles but architectonic objects of devotional attention (thus, instantiating the contemplation priority, III-B, rather than that of theatre, III-A). Moreover, rather than maximizing spectatorial viewing, physical access and sight lines into these Puuc courtyard spaces were highly restricted by the small openings through the flanking buildings, suggesting that only the participation of a relatively elite few was allowed (again more characteristic of the exclusive sanctuary mode, III-D, than the more inclusive theatre mode, III-A).[185]

In sum, the manner of presentation in South Chichén ritual-architectural events is almost diametrically opposed to the inclusively vocative, theatrical choreography of either Tula or North Chichén. In fact, in South Chichén the theatre priority (III-A) is the least important of the four generalized modes of ritual-architectural presentation. The lavish facade decorations of South Chichén did, in all likelihood, perform as mandala-like props for meditative devotion (thus expressing the contemplation priority, III-B). The willingness to decorate even the unseen, inaccessible portions of these structures and to use exceedingly precise and nonexpedient means of construction suggest that the very process of building South Chichén was itself a worshipful ritual of adoration (thus instantiating the propitiation priority, III-C).[186] And the characteristically Puuc delineation of a complex network of restrictive, exclusive precincts speaks strongly of a deep concern for the sanctuary priority (III-D). In virtually no South Chichén case, however, is the appeal to large spectatorial audiences, which is characteristic of the theatre mode (III-A), allowed to usurp these other modes of ritual-architectural presentation.

Content: Deities, Concepts, and Kings

Although the manner of presentation of South Chichén ritual-architectural events may be somewhat illumined by retrieving Thompson's notion of "the secret hide-away attitude of Maya priests in the Classic period,"[187] his intimations that they sat in the dark pondering the wholly otherworldly mysteries of cosmic time and an "almost-monotheism" are by now completely unacceptable. The informational content, that is, the message of Puuc-style architecture, long enjoyed a reputation as ethereal, "metaphysical," and apolitical, especially at South Chichén, where that style is laid right beside a "Toltec" art that would seem to be screaming with explicit images of war, conquest, and coercive authority. This timeworn appraisal that South Chichén was home to the "religious Maya" prior to the arrival of the "secularizing Toltecs," an obvious expression of the wider paradigm of Maya-Mexican polarity, has been challenged indirectly by any number of generalized reassessments of the politicized nature of the pre-Columbian Maya.[188] The most direct and irrefutable challenge, however, comes with the recent epigraphic studies of South Chichén and Uxmal inscriptions. These new researches into the glyphs confirm, contrary to the old

In South Chichén, the Iglesia *left,* and Monjas Annex. Whether these heavy walled, tight-spaced structures could have served as residences has long been a subject of debate. Typically arranged in closed-off courtyards, which contrast sharply with wide-open ritual-architectural spaces of North Chichén, these structures more probably hosted exclusive, esoteric rites of some sort. (Photo by Lawrence G. Desmond.)

stereotypes, that Puuc-style architecture was not, after all, abstract and "religious" in lieu of worldly, practical concerns but rather in the interest of such concerns. These epigraphic studies force us, among other things, to reconsider seriously the play of thematic ritual-architectural priorities in South Chichén.

Particularly before the highly politicized inscriptions of South Chichén had been deciphered, nearly all scholars assumed that the veneration of Maya rain deities was by far the most important substantive concern of Puuc-style architecture (suggesting, in other words, that the commemoration of divinity, II-A, and perhaps propitiation, III-C, were the first priorities of Puuc designers).[189] According to most interpretations, the omnipresent architectonic masks were the visage of Chac, the famous rain god, who would sneer, as it were, at his pre-Columbian patrons for several rainless months at a time, while the level of the *chultun* cisterns progressively receded, until finally in the spring he let loose with his seasonal torrents. Certainly, precipitation extremes in the Yucatán Peninsula have consequences that are positively dire, and, thus, the ubiquity of this same general image of the rain god, albeit with endless permutations, would seem to express, reasonably enough, the principal obsession of an agrarian culture in an environmental context where water is the scarcest and most essential resource. The situation is mediated somewhat at South Chichén by the proximity of two cenotes (a feature not generally present in the Puuc hills), but the precipitation paranoia remains, nonetheless, severe in the extreme.

The Puuc-style facades of South Chichén, perhaps most vividly on the east facade of the Monjas, not only showcase the typical Puuc *chac* masks, they also integrate that motif with the more characteristically Río Bec-Chenes serpent mouth portals, wherein the entire exterior wall becomes a huge stone face with the doorway as its mouth.[190] Formally, this famous Monjas facade closely resembles those at the Chenes site of Chicanná (to the south in Campeche), and, more importantly, its configuration suggests a set of ritual events at South Chichén similar to those performed at Copán's Temple 22, at the Aztec Templo Mayor, and perhaps even at Minoan earth monster temples (each of which was a featured example in last chapter's discussion of the divinity priority, II-A).[191] In all these cases, as noted earlier, the architecture seems to have facilitated a pattern of ritual (re)entry into the earth-cave-womb-temple, and thus the experience of a symbolic death followed by a presumably cathartic rebirth upon exiting. These situations exemplify, in other words, a somewhat more subtle manifestation of the ritual-architectural commemoration of divinity than the supposed ceremonial negotiations with Chac in the interest of rain.

The synthesis of this basic earth imagery with that of rain and the sky testifies to South Chichén's solid participation in the sort of generic agricultural and fertility rites that flourish all across Mesoamerica (thus holding in the foreground the divinity and propitiation priorities, II-A and III-C). Important as these themes are, unfortunately, scholars' fascination with the spectacularly abstract facial and geometrical iconographic elements has often led them to neglect the richly diversified, and particularly the more historically specific, content that is likewise present in the architectural decoration of South Chichén. Tozzer, for instance, concluded that, in comparison with either "Toltec Chichén" or the southern Maya sites, there is a real lack of specificity and "realism" in South Chichén art. He was able to identify almost no depictions of individual personages, few pictorial bas-reliefs, and little fresco painting — in general, virtually no references to the particulars of sacred or political history (priorities II-B and II-C).[192] Pollock's somewhat more recent and more thorough survey of Puuc decorative themes challenged the old notion that the Puuc were dedicated solely to mystical abstraction by cataloging a wealth of naturalistic carved serpents, birds, turtles, houses, jaguars, and, more importantly, a healthy sampling of very realistic human figures, particularly marching in procession and seated on thrones.[193] Though Pollock noted that many of these veristic figures are accompanied by substantial hieroglyphic texts, he did not really consider the interpretive implications.

With the breakthroughs in deciphering the glyphic inscriptions at Uxmal and South Chichén, scholars are, however, forced into an unprecedented appreciation of the specificity of the messages of Puuc architecture. In the late 1960s, David Kelley, for instance, demonstrated that the South Chichén inscriptions that Morley and his generation had considered strictly calendrical and astronomical (as if homology, I-A; astronomy, I-C; and perhaps divinity, II-A, were the sole priorities) actually contain an abundance of very specific historical information (thus signaling as well a concern for the ritual-architectural commemoration of sacred history, politics, and the dead — priorities II-B, II-C, and II-D).[194] Kelley argued that a certain series of

In South Chichén, the west or front facade of the Iglesia. This compact structure is the best extant example at Chichén Itzá of the earth monster or dragon-throated temples, which are prevalent throughout the Maya zone. Besides rows of stylized *chac* masks and stacks of long-snouted masks at the corners, the entire facade of the Iglesia appears as a huge face with large eyes, a hooked nose, and the doorway serving as a mouth. Ritualized entry and exit of this sort of temple may have provided an experience of symbolic death and rebirth. (Photo by Lawrence G. Desmond.)

glyphs, which he located fourteen times on the lintels of South Chichén buildings, can be read phonetically as Kakupacal,[195] the name of a prominent Itzá captain who had long been known from references in *The Books of Chilam Balam* and other colonial-period documents.[196] Moreover, this glyphic series is often followed by two other glyphs that Kelley now thinks mean something like "ruler of lords" or "king of kings."[197] Michel Davoust advances this case for the historical particularity of the South Chichén inscriptions even further by discerning in the glyphs the names of ten specific "kings" of Chichén Itzá, a list that Kelley accepts with only one exception.[198]

The discovery of these abundant, highly specific inscriptions in South Chichén (something that Morley, Tozzer, and Thompson had never anticipated) almost certainly confirms that the ritual-architectural commemoration of temporal authority (politics, priority II-C) was at least as important as the more otherworldly concerns that scholars had so long associated with these monuments. Furthermore, and perhaps even more importantly, these politicized glyphs suggest a means of ritual-architecturally legitimating authority that is qualitatively different either from the Classic Maya cities of the Southern Lowlands or from Tula and "Toltec Chichén." Where the southern Classic Maya inscriptions typically refer to the successive episodes in an individual ruler's life (such as birth, ascension to kingship, and death), the inscriptions of South Chichén, rather than commemorate living or even recently deceased Chichén kings, seem to be parallel statements made by one king — Kakupacal — about a number of his ancestors.[199] Kelley's interpretation of the tightly clustered Chichén inscription dates suggests that most of the major South Chichén buildings were constructed in an eighteen-year period between 866 and 884 C.E., presumably Kakupacal's reign, and that they were formally dedicated in a series of rituals honoring Kakupacal's ancestors — ritual-architectural events that, while legitimating temporal authority (politics, priority II-C), are quintessentially about the commemoration of royal forebears (the dead, priority II-D).[200] To follow the conclusions of Kowalski, who is leading parallel work on the inscriptions at Uxmal, where both south and north Maya cities legitimated political authority by presenting dynastic histories in the context of their ritual-architectural events, the southern sites typically emphasized the personal biography of rulers, while the northern cities — specifically, Uxmal and South Chichén — emphasized the ritual commemoration of ancestors.[201]

The difference between the political content of the architectural events of South Chichén and those of Tula (or of "Toltec Chichén") is less subtle. Where Tula was saddled with the imposing task of articulating a radically new conception of sovereignty, specifically a kind of "might makes right" ultimatum in which specific leaders and individuals were relatively incidental, in South Chichén, the informational burden was neither so great nor so revolutionary. If less biographical than the Classic southern Maya sites, South Chichén, nonetheless, still works a time-honored pattern of legitimating authority on the basis of a highly particularistic family history, a royal lineage that reaches back to Palenque and the older southern centers. Thus, in contrast to the brash Tula announcement that because they are the strongest they are entitled to rule, Kakupacal's entitlement to authority is based on a genetic right, a heredity claim. (A third option, which is exercised in "Toltec Chichén," will be discussed toward the end of this chapter.)

In any case, I can summarize my general hermeneutical interpretation of the ritual-architectural events of South Chichén, the supposedly indigenous Yucatán Maya, "pre-Toltec" portion of the Yucatecan capital, in terms of four principal issues, each of which emerges as somewhat counter to the academic common wisdom about "Maya Chichén" and counter to the pre-Columbian architectural events of either Tula or "Toltec Chichén." First, the architecture of South Chichén, which integrated elements from the Petén South, the Río Bec-Chenes area, and Central Mexico with an approach to design that was preponderantly Puuc, was *not* (contrary to older assessments) a myopically local development; rather, South Chichén building was significantly eclectic, though not so much as Tula architecture, and not nearly so much as the adjacent plaza of "Toltec Chichén."

Second, South Chichén ritual-architectural events, while significantly cosmopolitan (somewhat more cosmopolitan than the more mainline Puuc sites), apparently did *not* rely upon a strategy of coercive instigation by pandering these eclectic elements as Tula did (one variation on allurement via convention, priority I-B), nor did they seduce participation primarily by displaying a conformity to homologized world order or to astronomical rhythms (that is,

In South Chichén, hieroglyphic lintel at Temple of the Inscription, bearing what is generally considered the oldest date at the site. Prior to the 1960s, the only hieroglyphs at Chichén Itzá that had been deciphered were dates. Since then, scholars have been increasingly successful in identifying glyphic allusions to specific historical individuals, a development that changes drastically our conception of the pre-Columbian rituals that may have taken place in this portion of the city. (Carnegie Institution of Washington photo, courtesy of the Peabody Museum, Harvard University.)

homology and astronomy, priorities I-A and I-C, both of which are crucial to the instigatory strategy of "Toltec Chichén"). Rather more calmly, after the fashion of the Puuc, South Chichén invited (instead of forcing) involvement in its ceremonial occasions by presenting intriguing variations on conventionalized architectural forms, techniques, and decorations (a somewhat more rarified version of allurement via convention, priority I-B).

Third, regarding the mode of ritual-architectural presentation, South Chichén, unlike Tula Grande and the Gran Nivelación, with their inclusive, amphitheatric spaces, scarcely bespeaks a concern for reaching large assembled audiences. Instead, South Chichén events, generally speaking, provided a set of cloistered contexts for meditative and petitionary reflection, thus suggesting that sanctuary, contemplation, and propitiation (III-D, III-B, and III-C) were all more important priorities than theatre (III-A).

Fourth, the substantive content of South Chichén architectural events actually embraced an impressive range of worldly and otherworldly themes far wider than Tozzer or Thompson would have imagined and, more significantly, far wider than at either Tula or "Toltec Chichén." In the "many-minded" architecture of South Chichén (as opposed to the largely single-minded architecture of Tula), the characteristic Puuc *chac* masks and Río Bec-Chenes earth monster doorways were espoused and ingeniously elaborated in ways that, as scholars have long noted, well instantiate a concern for commemorating and expressing conceptions of divinity and mythological sacred history (priorities II-A and II-B). Moreover, the detailed records of dynastic history in the inscriptions (a dimension of South Chichén's architecture that earlier generations of scholars failed to appreciate) signal not only a concerted effort to legitimate temporal authority (politics, priority II-C), they likewise demonstrate a very pronounced concern for the commemoration of ancestors (the dead, priority II-D), a filial initiative that was unsurpassed in Tula, North Chichén, or perhaps even the Maya cities of the Southern Lowlands.

In all these respects, then, South Chichén bears no special relationship, either historically or morphologically, to Tula, Hidalgo, and, whether antecedent or coterminous with the city's more glamorous "Toltec" half, South Chichén does present a very different religio-architectural world.

The Ritual-Architectural Events of "Toltec Chichén"

> This building [the Castillo of Chichén Itzá] has four staircases, which face the four points of the compass. Each of them is thirty-three feet wide and has ninety-one steps, so that it is extremely trying to climb them. . . . At the time when I saw it, there was at the foot of each balustrade a fierce mouth of a serpent, all of one piece and very (carefully) carved. . . . This building had around it, and still has today, many other well built and large buildings and the ground between it and them covered with cement, so that there are even traces of the cemented places, so hard is the mortar of which they made them there. At some distance in front of the staircase on the north, there were two small stages of hewn stone, with four staircases, paved on top, where they say that farces were represented, and comedies for the pleasure of the public. From the court in front of these stages a wide and handsome causeway runs, as far as a well [the Sacred Cenote] which is about two stones' throw off.
>
> *Bishop Diego de Landa, 1566*[202]

The Study of "Toltec Chichén": History and Architecture

On the northern side of the old roadway, and ever in the mainstream of Mesoamerican studies, lies the Sacred Cenote and the giant plaza of the Castillo that constitutes so-called Toltec Chichén Itzá. When Landa, for instance, chose but three ruined sites to describe in detail, the plaza of the Castillo was, not surprisingly, one of them.[203] North Chichén is likewise a primary locus of activity in the native accounts of *The Book of Chilam Balam of Chumayel, of Tizimin,* and *of Mani.*[204] While virtually ignoring South Chichén, the colonial-period histories of Gaspar Antonio Chi (1582), Tomas López Medel (1612), Bernardo de Lizana (1633), and Diego López de Cogolludo (1688) all include elaborate renditions (however imaginal) regarding what may have happened at "Toltec Chichén" and around the Sacred Cenote.[205] So too, every eighteenth- and nineteenth-century antiquarian Mesoamericanist, none more vigorously than Augustus and Alice Le Plongeon, awarded North Chichén's Castillo and Sacred Well a central place in their historical phantasms.[206] In short, for most visitors to Yucatán, the plaza of "Toltec Chichén" has been (and remains) the "real" Chichén Itzá — and even *the* exemplary Mesoamerican ruin — the postcard image that impresses most and endures longest.

The great plaza of North Chichén, shown here with the old roadway still intact, constitutes a far more well-integrated architectural unit than the scatter of buildings in South Chichén. (Photo by William M. Ferguson, courtesy of the University of Texas, Austin.)

A vastly more well-integrated unit than the mélange of South Chichén buildings, the major constructions of "Toltec Chichén" are all situated on a single massive platform or leveled terrace, "La Gran Nivelación," which lies midway between the Sacred Cenote and the main south group. The principal structures of "Toltec Chichén" — the giant Castillo pyramid, the Great Ball Court Complex (which includes by far the largest "playing field" in Mesoamerica, the Upper and Lower Temples of the Jaguars, and the adjacent *Tzompantli* skull rack), the Temple of Warriors, the Court of a Thousand Columns, the similarly colonnaded Mercado, and the smaller tribunes known respectively as the Venus Platform and the Platform of the Eagles and Jaguars — each find stunningly direct formal counterparts in the buildings of Tula, Hidalgo. Moreover, if the building forms speak an unmistakable correspondence between Tula Grande and "Toltec Chichén," the shared sculptural program of reclining *chacmool* figures, atlantean statues with their upraised arms, feathered serpent columns and iconography, and the vivid reliefs of warriors, jaguars, and eagles shout even more loudly for some sort of preternatural relationship between these two grand ceremonial plazas. As Charnay declared more than a century ago, there is "a striking analogy" between the ruins of "Toltec Chichén" and Tula Grande, a curious affinity that no one can deny.[207]

Though providing a somewhat less neat microcosm of Mesoamericanist studies than does the investigatory history of Tula, each strain of Middle American scholarship does bring its characteristic set of questions to bear on "Toltec" Chichén Itzá. Each generation, in an important sense, (re)discovers and (re)invents its own plaza of the Castillo. Following Charnay's seminal recognition of the special Tula-"Toltec Chichén" similitude, the turn of the century, for instance, juxtaposed the earliest positivistic archaeologists — best represented by Alfred Maudslay and his exact descriptions and tersely tempered remarks about the somehow "foreign" character of "Toltec Chichén"[208] and "the last of the great amateurs," Edward Thompson, who held forth with his freewheeling historical (re)constructions and spectacular accounts of his dredging and diving operations at the Sacred Cenote.[209] This early clash of styles between the reticent Maudslay and the reckless Thompson is instructive, moreover, because it foreshadowed the tension between the scientific and the sensational, the academic and the popular, archaeology and tourism that would be "Toltec Chichén's" mixed blessing from then on.

This composite pattern of popular, political, and pedagogical motives and incentives, nascent even in Charnay's era, intensified in the 1920s as Sylvanus Morley, at once an epigrapher, archaeologist, and publicist for the Maya, maneuvered the mammoth backing of the Carnegie Institution of Washington and initiated the massive program of studies that would hold Chichén Itzá in the limelight for the next several decades. This huge Carnegie initiative, ever sensitive to American public opinion, first seized upon (re)construction of the Temple of the Warriors (the mirroring counterpart of Tula's so-called Temple of Tlahuizcalpantecuhtli) as the best vehicle to showcase both its own and the Maya's accomplishments.[210] At the same time, the Mexican INAH, similarly blending the causes of scholarship and tourism, let loose great resources and its leading archaeologists on the "Toltec Chichén" plaza; their principal initiatives at this point were the (re)construction of the Great Ball Court, the Temple of the Jaguars, the various platform stages, and, most ambitiously, the enormous Castillo pyramid.[211] The joint efforts of these Carnegie and Mexican powerhouses eventuated in not only a dazzling tourist attraction but, moreover, a library of data on Chichén Itzá — almost (but not quite) enough to absolve them of their inattentiveness to the prosaic ceramic data that might have provided the sure chronology that, ironically, is still so sorely lacking for this most worked of all sites. The visual aspect of "Toltec Chichén" has remained largely unchanged since this initial flurry of (re)construction, save for the eventual rerouting of the old highway and the installation of innumerable banks of electric lights to illumine nighttime extravaganzas, which rely on music and dramatic narrations to provide one more colorful rendition of "Toltec Chichén's" pre-Columbian past. Also, just adjacent to the plaza they have opened a major new museum-visitor complex.

Besides bringing world attention to the site, it was this generation of Carnegie and INAH labors (both archaeological and ethnohistorical) that set in place nearly all of the assumptions and paradigms about the "history" of "Toltec Chichén" that persist today as the "old" or "traditional view." In that era the images of antipodean Maya and Mexican peoples, and the story of the violent "Toltec Conquest" of Yucatán, which had been lurking in the ethnohistoric record for centuries, found their most articulate narrative exposition. The now timeworn view that emerged at this point, commensurate (at least in the broad strokes) with

Between 1906 and the early 1930s, the Mexican government restored the stone facings and stairways on the north and west sides of the great Castillo pyramid, giving it essentially the appearance it has today. The Carnegie Institution sponsored reconstruction of the adjacent complex of the Warriors Temple and its associated colonnades, which was, according to Morley, "nothing but a mound, covered with stones and overgrown with trees" when work commenced in 1925. (Photo by William M. Ferguson, courtesy of the University of Texas, Austin.)

Tozzer's position, holds that "Old" (or "Yucatán Maya") South Chichén had been an undistinguished Classic Maya center until it was overwhelmed in the Postclassic period by a gang of militant Mexicans (or Mexican-related groups), at least some of which originated from Tula, Hidalgo. Just to the north of the old Maya settlement, these foreign interlopers, so the story goes, built (or at least designed) the "New," "Mexican" or "Toltec" Chichén Itzá — in Morley's term, "the greatest post-Classic metropolis."[212] And then, according to this familiar version (the version that would come to be known as the "linear succession" or "no overlap" model), Chichén Itzá embarked upon some two centuries of prosperity and dominance as the one and only important political and commercial center in the Postclassic Northern Lowlands.[213]

We should note, however, that, despite all the Carnegie's and Mexican government's digging and (re)building at the actual site of "Toltec Chichén" during this era, this traditional (re)construction of the "Toltec Conquest" scenario actually depends much more heavily on the colonial-era ethnohistorical traditions of the

Carnegie-sponsored repair of the Caracol in the 1930s. During this era especially, strictly archaeological motives were sometimes at odds with the initiative to fashion the ruins into a compelling and picturesque tourist attraction. (Carnegie Institution of Washington photo, courtesy of the Peabody Museum, Harvard University.)

"Mexicanization" of Yucatán than on the results of their excavationary work. Committed most of all to restoring the large and glamorous structures that would impress visitors, this generation largely ignored (and even obliterated) the more prosaic ceramic evidence that could have helped to resolve these historical questions. Consequently, this group relied more heavily than any other, either before or after, on the striking parallels between the standing architectures of Tula and "Toltec Chichén" as the strongest (and for many of them seemingly irrefutable) material evidence of the veracity of their version of the pre-Columbian events.

This traditional view holds that "Toltec Chichén" was the epitome of a Postclassic Yucatecan era of cultural decadence and "Mexicanization," a city born of a major upsurge in militarism and political factionalism, a decentralization of religious authority, and, most relevant to the present discussion, sadly declining standards in art and architecture. In this spirit, the puzzlingly "non-Maya" look of "Toltec Chichén" architecture was typically explained as the result of a conquering Toltec minority who imposed the violent, imperialistic ideas and aspirations of their Central Mexican homeland (specifically Tula, Hidalgo) on a bullied labor force of Yucatán Maya craftsmen. Thus, "Toltec Chichén" was (and continues to be) described repeatedly as "predominantly Toltec [Tula-like] in design and inspiration, but executed in Maya technique."[214] Furthermore, similarly in accord with the traditional, pejorative evaluation of the Maya Postclassic (and clearly reflecting the value-laden paradigm of Maya-Mexican polarity), this union of Mexican ideals and Maya craftsmanship at "Toltec Chichén" was usually assessed during the Carnegie era as an aesthetic failure, an artistic bastard deserving of the same aspersions flung at Tula itself. Thus, "Toltec Chichén" architecture was conventionally deprecated as the brutal imposition of garish Mexican tastes, a stab in the back of the subtle and demure Puuc Maya style. In the phrasing of Ignacio Bernal, who takes lines directly from his critique of Tula and transfers them to Yucatán, the buildings of "Toltec Chichén" are "very spectacular . . . colorful but at the same time more superficial and emptier than those of the Classic [Maya] period; it is a *nouveau-riche* art suitable to the tastes of warriors who have lately achieved power."[215]

Nevertheless, while Tula art and architecture have almost no admirers, even within the Carnegie era, there was a considerable lobby of praise for "Toltec Chichén." This significant minority argued, contrary to the mainline defamation of the "Toltec-Maya" style but still within the traditional framework of the linear succession model of Yucatán culture history (that is, within the parameters of the old saga of the "Toltec Conquest" and "Mexicanization of Yucatán"), that "Toltec Chichén" actually represents a shot in the arm to a declining indigenous Maya style. According to this assessment, the more base but also more innovative Mexicans served as a catalyst (rather than a curse), providing an injection of energy and a refreshing antidote to the over-elaborate Puuc decoration of South Chichén. From this view, then, "Toltec Chichén" represents a happy synthesis of Tula's daring entrées into lighter construction, colonnaded halls, and unprecedentedly spacious interiors, paired for the first time with the superior craftsmanship of the Yucatán Maya. As Carlos Margain argued, "Toltec Chichén" must be appreciated as "a true fusion."[216]

Upon closer examination, however, the seemingly opposite alternatives in this debate actually emerge simply as parallel manifestations of the insidious paradigm of Maya-Mexican polarity. Whether scholars argue that the "Toltec Chichén" style arises from the Mexicans' vicious "stab in the back" of the gentle Maya or somewhat more generously, that the rambunctious Toltecs provided a much-needed catalytic "shot in the arm" to the urbane but somewhat lethargic Maya, the same set of basic presuppositions applies. In either case we witness what amounts to more creative manipulations of the old paradigm of Maya-Mexican polarity, more imaginal reflections on a hypothetical confrontation between two contradistinct types of American Indians, reflections on a collision of constructed images rather than historical peoples. The first option restates the notion of "Toltec Chichén" as an instance of "irreconcilable Maya-Mexican polarity" (or, at best, a coerced and unsuccessful synthesis), while the second option is a variation on the notion of "symbiotic polarity," wherein the serendipitous union of the very different but complimentary gifts of Maya and Mexican peoples issued in a measure of success that neither alone would have been able to achieve.[217] Both converse appraisals are, however, contingent on the facticity of the traditional model of a west-to-east Toltec "Mexicanization" of Yucatán — a historical eventuality that, in light of today's revisionist view of the pre-Columbian Maya, can by no means be taken for granted.

Maya masons and laborers at work on the Caracol in the early 1930s. Though located in the southern portion of the ruins, the Caracol, which has both characteristically Maya decorative elements and Tula-like serpent balustrades, was generally considered a "Toltec Maya" structure. (Carnegie Institution of Washington photo, courtesy of the Peabody Museum, Harvard University.)

Having dedicated themselves especially to piecing together a narrative sequence of pre-Columbian events that could account for the seemingly anomalous phenomenon of "Toltec Chichén," this prolific generation of traditional archaeologists (and ethnohistorians) produced a whole series of (re)construction scenarios (though virtually all of these historical scripts were conceived within the paradigm of Maya-Mexican polarity and the fabled "Toltec Conquest" of Yucatán). The subsequent "new," more process-oriented archaeologists, however, would take a quite different approach. This group largely (though not completely) rejects the quest after coherent storiological syntheses of onetime historical events in favor of retrieving more generalized pre-Hispanic sociocultural processes, for instance, urban settlement patterns and patterns of long-distance trade. Moreover, unlike their predecessors, this generation of scholars is largely denied excavationary access to the actual tourist-filled plaza of North Chichén, and, furthermore, they are far more suspicious (sometimes to the point of complete dismissal) of the viability of drawing any conclusions on the basis of the poetical ethnohistorical accounts of Itzá and Toltec adventurings, a strategy that had figured so largely in the construction of the traditional view. Accordingly, these archaeologists contribute to our understanding of Chichén Itzá not by more sophisticated excavations of the actual site (as happened in the case of Tula) but by widening the frame and by formulating a profoundly different picture both of the pre-Columbian Maya in general and of Late Classic and Postclassic Yucatán in particular.

The wider (and continuing) efforts of these Maya archaeologists foster, among other things, a tremendously greater appreciation for the cultural vitality of the previously maligned Postclassic Yucatán ambience and, moreover, an unprecedented appreciation of the peninsula's very considerable continuity with the great Classic Maya centers of the Southern Lowlands. In the context of that sweeping reconsideration, then, where North Chichén had long been classed as a weirdly non-Maya anomaly, the new vision of "Toltec Chichén" that emerges from this generation of Maya archaeologists is far less bizarre, less atypical, and more consonant with the revised image of the politically astute and fully urban pre-Columbian Maya. In fact, in a development that would have astounded their Carnegie predecessors, since the mid-1980s the emerging archaeological consensus is holding that Chichén Itzá in its entirety, including the so-called Gran Nivelación, was *not* the foreign-born product of roving Postclassic Toltec warriors after all. Instead, the whole site is now generally considered to have been a fundamentally indigenous Maya phenomenon, a *Classic Maya city* created by outward-looking, internationalizing Yucatán Maya (or perhaps Putun Maya). This reassessment almost completely disenfranchises the traditional assessment of both the historical origin and the essential content of the "Toltec Chichén" architectural program. If this generation of Mayanists has successfully dismantled the old formulations of Morley and Tozzer, they have, however, been much less successful in replacing those old historical hypotheses with similarly thoroughgoing alternatives. We stand, as it were, in the "post-paradigm pause" discussed in Chapter 1.[218]

Before proceeding to my own historical hypothesis, I should note also the major contribution of pre-Columbian art historians both to this general reassessment of Terminal Classic/Early Postclassic Yucatán and to current understandings of the relationship between Tula and Chichén Itzá.[219] Although art historians have not contributed a great deal to the most recent reconsiderations of Tula, perhaps because they are less fettered by the lack of excavationary access to the actual Yucatecan site, their contribution to the reassessment of "Toltec Chichén" has been even greater than that of their archaeological counterparts. Among the variegated contributions of art historians, the most important insight for this project (because it pushes outside of the standard, two-actor paradigm of Maya-Mexican polarity) is their recognition that the art and architecture of "Toltec Chichén" is far more broadly eclectic than previously presumed. Art historians have, in other words, been uniquely astute in helping us to see that Tula is but one of several sites with which "Toltec Chichén's" ritual-architectural program has strong affinities.

This realization that the old "Toltec-style-Maya-craftsmanship" explanation of North Chichén is far too simple, and that the monuments of this portion of the site actually participate in a very wide range of Mesoamerican artistic traditions — at the very least, Central Mexican, Oaxacan, Veracruzan, together with Southern and Northern Maya — has, however, been building over several decades. Even Tozzer, for instance, had acknowledged that "many of the resemblances found at Chichén Itzá seem to be far more widely distributed in Mexico than those associated definitively with the single site of Tula" (though he was not inclined to explore the ramifications of this wide sharing).[220] More than twenty years ago, Proskouriakoff likewise was arguing, on the basis of its stylistic diversity, that "Toltec Chichén" was the eclectic creation of an alliance of peoples drawn from several pre-Hispanic states.[221] Later George Kubler would build a controversial, though convincing, case that the builders of "Toltec Chichén," with deliberately synthesizing motives, had searched both the temporal and spatial reaches of Mesoamerica for historical models.[222] And, more recently, Arthur Miller and Clemency Coggins, on the basis of mural and iconographic evidence, both are arguing (albeit in quite different ways) that "Toltec Chichén" was the expression of a deliberate and sophisticated urge to integrate Maya and non-Maya peoples.[223] Each of these iconoclastic perspectives issuing from art history, which is really the most provocative strain of study at present, will figure prominently in the ensuing reassessment of "Toltec Chichén's" ritual-architectural events.

Chichén as Active Receptor: A Historical Hypothesis

There is, then, a glaring disparity between the stupendous resources and energy that have been expended on Chichén Itzá and our still-impoverished understanding of the site. Despite the ambitious initiatives of traditional archaeologists at "Toltec Chichén," together with the very considerable triumphs of their latter-day heirs and those of art history, the basic chronology of the buildings (let alone the succession of pre-Columbian peoples and events that transpired in and on those monumental structures) remains absolutely wadded. And, disappointingly, the morphologically comparative approach that I outlined in the previous chapters is not a particularly effective method for disentangling these historical circumstances. (Archaeologists and epigraphers are far more likely than historians of religions to settle those questions.) Nevertheless, sifting through the relevant literature on Tula and Chichén Itzá (and spending considerable time in hermeneutical dialogue with the monuments themselves) leads me to the endorsement of at least a minimal set of propositions regarding the *historical* phenomenon of "Toltec" Chichén Itzá and, particularly, the nature of its *historical* relatedness to Tula, Hidalgo — a working historical hypothesis if you will.

At present, the most likely candidates for both the material and conceptual basis of "Toltec Chichén" are the so-called Putun warrior-merchants (or, as Eric Thompson termed them, the Putun Itzá Maya).[224] A commercially adroit and highly mobile group, these "Mexicanized Maya" (less appropriately termed "Mayanized Mexicans") probably originated on the western Yucatán and interjacent Gulf Coast region of what is today Tabasco and Campeche.[225] The moving force behind "Toltec Chichén" was, in other words, not from Tula but, in all likelihood, a well-traveled contingent of indigenous Yucatecan Maya who had cultivated strong ties not only within the Maya zone but with Central Mexico as well. Moreover, by contrast to the Tula Toltecs' largely one-dimensional profile as expert warriors, these Putun Maya were, by all accounts, exceedingly proficient in trade as well as war. In fact, though Eric Thompson's extravagant claims for both the size and thorough integration of what he termed "the Putun empire" now seem seriously overstated, these Maya were, nonetheless, noteworthy for their commercial acumen and worldly wealth even more than for their military conquests. Their originality in their spheres of art, religion, and culture, while typically denigrated by modern scholars, was actually quite impressive as well.

The creators of "Toltec Chichén," then, according to this hypothesis, presented a very different sort of ethos and faced very different historical dilemmas than those of either South Chichén or Tula Grande. By contrast to the Maya builders of South Chichén, who enjoyed a relatively stable historical ambience (and, thus, were allowed to pursue a more relaxed, diversified, and fairly conservative ritual-architectural agenda), the Putun Maya were not nearly so content with the steady maintenance of the status quo. As regards their restlessness, their penchant for innovation, and their ambition, the Putun were more like the Toltecs (or even the Aztecs) than the Yucatecan Maya builders of the so-called Puuc Great Cities. Yet, by contrast to the always-embattled Tula Toltecs, who never enjoyed mercantile control over their military conquests, the Putun Maya, in the wake of declining Classic-period civilizations in both Central Mexico and the Southern Maya Lowlands, were able to parlay their strategic "in-between" geographic position and their trading expertise into an impressively international sphere of influence. Thus, where Toltec adventuring and control were largely restricted to Central Mexico, the more wandering exploits of the Putun Maya provided them with a genuinely cosmopolitan acquaintance with nearly the whole of the ancient Mesoamerican world. Moreover, where the Toltecs' most pressing problem was simply holding together their tenuous empire, the most urgent problem facing the Putun Maya, so it would seem, was accommodating and integrating the variegated peoples, traditions, and ideas that were increasingly coming under their sway.

It would appear, then, that the ritual-architectural programs of Tula Grande and "Toltec Chichén" (and, for that matter, Tenochtitlán) were similarly bold and innovative, and similarly encumbered by heavy informational burdens. All of these religio-civic architectural agenda shouldered a far heavier (or at least more single-minded) communicative burden than that of, for instance, South Chichén. Both the Toltecs and the Putun Maya (again like the Aztecs in this regard) endeavored to capitalize on the uniquely transformative potential of the human experience of art and ritual as a means of swaying and consolidating public opinion. In each case, ritual-architectural choreography and public ceremony were employed (however successfully or unsuccessfully) as perhaps *the* premier tool of stagecraft and propagandizing. The religio-political platforms of Tula Grande and "Toltec Chichén" were, however, dedicated to the promulgation of quite different messages. Unlike those of their Tula Toltec counterparts (and contrary to most conventional academic interpretations of "Toltec Chichén"), according to my hermeneutical reassessment, the ritual-architectural events of "Toltec Chichén" were *not* designed to intimidate and to warn subordinate groups of the dire consequences of resisting "Toltec-Maya" authority. Instead, I would wager that the first initiative in the ceremonial agenda of the Putun Maya, who enjoyed far greater worldly wealth and security than the Toltecs (though apparently no greater self-confidence), was to further their project of unification, that is, to synthesize and integrate the vastly different traditions and interests that had become entangled in this huge web of almost pan-Mesoamerican traveling and trading relations.

Nevertheless, accepting such a historical outline (if only provisionally) actually seems to intensify rather than mitigate the mystery of the similitude between Tula and Chichén Itzá. Why, if the Tula Toltecs and the Putun Maya had such a huge disparity in material resources, if they faced such drastically different historical dilemmas, and if they answered those challenges with such contrastive ritual-architectural initiatives, do the sumptuous plazas of Tula Grande and

"Toltec Chichén" look so much alike? How, given these profound differences at almost every level, can we account for the unmistakable formal resemblance between these two architectural configurations? In short, recent developments in Mesoamerican studies and the alternative historical scenarios that they imply do not provide an easy resolution to the question of Tula–Chichén Itzá similitude. They do, however, afford us a quite different starting point for addressing the old twin-city problem.

On the one hand, the old picture of the "Toltec Conquest" featuring the mean Mexicans vanquishing the gentle Maya and then replicating their Central Mexican capital in Yucatán no longer fits at all into this new frame. The notion of a somewhat softer and more prolonged Toltec domination of Yucatán, wherein Chichén Itzá was some sort of extension, or colonial outpost to the Tula Toltec empire, is also, at this point, unlikely in the extreme. And the reserve, east-to-west proposition (as espoused, for instance, by George Kubler) that Tula was a "frontier garrison" of Chichén Itzá is even less likely. On the other hand, the revamped image of the pre-Columbian Yucatecan Maya allows us to piece together an alternative story of "Toltec" Chichén Itzá quite apart from the old paradigm of Maya-Mexican polarity and without the glamour of a military, or even peaceful, "Toltec Conquest" of Yucatán.

According to this somewhat more prosaic (re)construction scenario, the destiny and shape of "Toltec Chichén" were controlled and choreographed from northern Yucatán by Yucatán Maya (probably so-called Putun Itzá Maya originally from the west coast of the peninsula, but certainly not by Central Mexican renegades). I would maintain, in other words, that the builders of La Gran Nivelación were neither "passive receptors" who had an east-rolling barrage of Tula Toltec attributes thrust upon them nor, reversing the direction of influence, the "active genitors" who exported the architectural forms and style of "Toltec Chichén" to Tula. More probably, endorsing a third option, the creators of "Toltec Chichén" were the "active receptors," the self-motivated Maya instigators of a west-to-east borrowing. The builders of the Castillo and the surrounding structures were, in all likelihood, energetic and well-endowed Maya acquisitors whose scouring search after models and pedigrees found, in the briefly florescent Tula, Hidalgo, precisely the sort of vigorous prototype they sought.

According to this version of the story (and foregrounding the widely eclectic character of the art and architecture of "Toltec Chichén"), Tula was, however, hardly the sole pattern for the Yucatecan capital. Tula would appear, instead, to be no more or less than the most appealing and prolific of a wide array of exemplars (or religio-artistic resources) on which the builders of "Toltec Chichén" drew. Furthermore, in this case, the ill-labeled "Mexicanization" of Yucatán emerges as a process of the indigenous Yucatecan Maya acting rather than being acted upon, of gathering into their cosmopolitan capital city allusions, especially — but not solely — to Central Mexican Tula. Like so many groups in pre-Columbian Mesoamerican history (quintessentially the Aztecs), the Putun Maya builders of "Toltec Chichén" were, it seems, a people in search of a pattern, an archetype, and a pedigree (or, in this case, almost a montage of pedigrees) to legitimate their project both in their own eyes and in the eyes of others. Accordingly, their special distinction among pre-Columbian groups derives not from the fabrication of roots (a religio-political tactic that any number of indigenous groups pursued both before and after the Putun Maya) but from the verve with which they capitalized on their itinerant familiarity with the reaches of Mesoamerica and the piecemeal, daringly eclectic manner in which

In North Chichén, a Tula-like Warrior Column in the colonnade adjacent to the Temple of the Warriors. Despite all the radical academic reassessments of the pre-Columbian Yucatán Maya in recent years, a special similitude between the iconography and architecture of Tula Grande and North Chichén remains unmistakable. (Photo by Lawrence G. Desmond.)

they fashioned their heritage and their viability as a synthetic whole.

Accepting this basic historical outline as a working hypothesis, and holding the analysis up to the level of ritual-architectural events (rather than presuming to have retrieved the once-and-for-all meanings of the buildings of Tula and Chichén Itzá), I endeavor in the following discussion to transcend the "deceptions in form," that is, to expose the way in which the notorious formal similitude has so long and so successfully camouflaged a more significant divergence between the religio-architectural priorities at the respective sites. Foreshadowing my alternative interpretive conclusions, the marked resemblance in architectures can be explained in terms of a kind of disjunction or (to avoid confusion with Panofsky's and Kubler's "principle of disjunction")[226] a "reduction" wherein similar formal elements come to occupy different positions, or play different roles, in the respective architectural events of Tula and "Toltec Chichén." In brief, I would contend that the hallmark sister-city parallels — serpent columns, atlantean statues, iconography of devouring jaguars and fearsome warriors — belonged in Tula Grande to the "back" half of those ritual-architectural events. At Tula, these graphic forms served as the bearers of a substantive and revolutionary message that was designed to alert the ritual participants to their practical responsibilities in relation to Tula Toltec leadership and hegemony. The nearly identical architectural forms, when incorporated afresh in "Toltec Chichén," have, in a sense, "dropped" (or been "reduced") from the status of components of variation and content to that of constituent elements in a remarkably elaborate, leading, or instigatory component. In short, the shared elements moved from the "back" position of Tula Grande's twofold architectural events to the "front" position in the events of "Toltec Chichén." Largely stripped of their intimidating content (a threatening message that "Toltec Chichén" needn't speak), the old Tula forms were integrated into an amazing admixture of instigative strategies that would begin, rather than complete, the ceremonial events of "Toltec Chichén."

This prim heuristic formulation (which is contingent on a very tentative historical hypothesis) is helpful insofar as it opens us to a quite novel interpretation of the sister-city resemblance. The following sections should demonstrate, however, that the actual, "on-the-ground" pre-Columbian ritual-architectural events of Tula Grande and "Toltec Chichén" were neither so predictable, nor was the distinction between them so neat.

The Rites of Xul: A Rhetorical Lens

Tula and "Toltec Chichén" were similarly enlivened and vexed by the problem of ethnic diversity, the challenge of respecting difference and of creating one from many. At Chichén Itzá, however, the times were considerably longer, the resources much greater, the origins of the contributors far more widely scattered, and the religio-architectural solutions, perhaps not surprisingly, exponentially more complex. Given these historical eventualities, it would appear that the ritual-architectural events of "Toltec Chichén" were dominated by the orchestration of (or at least the appearance of, or the plea for) unification, synthesis, and integration. Yet, I would argue that what was really remarkable about these events was not, after all, their unifying message (that is, the "back" half of these events), nor was it their decidedly theatrical ritual-architectural choreography (that is, their mode of presentation). Instead, what was most impressive, and most nearly singular, about the pre-Columbian ceremonial events of "Toltec Chichén" was the layering and weaving together of a remarkable variety of instigatory strategies that would get these events started (that is, their synthetic allurement, or their "front" halves).

To speed to the heart of these massive generalizations, I will focus on one building and one indigenous Maya ritual. I will, as a kind of rhetorical strategy, concenter my attention, as all who have entered the plaza of North Chichén for the past thousand years have done, first on the Castillo, the so-called Temple of Quetzalcoatl (or Kukulcán) and then enrich that encounter by reflecting on Bishop Landa's eyewitness description of a sixteenth-century Kukulcán festival — the *Chic Kaban* or rites of Xul — which he observed in Mani, a fairly important pre-Hispanic and colonial Yucatecan center some 70 kilometers south of Mérida (about 100 kilometers southwest of Chichén Itzá).[227] The hulkish Castillo pyramid, square-based, about 75 feet tall with four grand stairways to its crowning temple, provides a kind of crystallization of the whole "Toltec Chichén" ceremonial-architectural agenda; and Landa's account of the rites of Xul at Mani (an account that is unfortunately removed some 500 years and a considerable distance from the actual florescent "Toltec Chichén" context), nonetheless, provides the most explicit and detailed ethnohistorical account of the sort of ritual-architectural events for which this deceptively simple-looking pyramid presumably was originally intended.

In the context of his review of the Maya "months" and their respective festivals, virtually all of which are related to planting and harvest, Landa describes a five-day festival in honor of Kukulcán (the Feathered Serpent) in the month of Xul called the *Chic Kaban,* a festival that would appear to be a Maya version of the nearly pan-Mesoamerican New Fire Ceremony.[228] Landa notes that though this festival had previously been celebrated "throughout the land," it was decidedly atypical, "not like all the previous ones," first, because of the unusually intimate connection that the *Chic Kaban* had to a pyramid temple (the majority of these periodic rites were strictly open-air affairs) and, second, because of its nonagricultural, seemingly more political character.[229] While it is hardly a verbatim account of what actually happened centuries earlier at the thriving pre-Hispanic capital of Chichén Itzá, Landa's rendition of the colonial version of the rites of Xul does, nevertheless, direct our attention to the complex interplay of ritual-architectural priorities that would seem to have characterized the original pre-Hispanic Chichén Castillo event (or, more properly, set of events). Landa's account of the rites of Xul provides, in other words, a kind of rhetorical lens,[230] a provocative point of departure for my hermeneutical analysis both of the specific Castillo events and of the more general ritual-architectural program of "Toltec Chichén." Accordingly, the account deserves to be quoted in all its brevity:

> On the 16th of (the month) *Xul,* all the priests and lords assembled in Mani, and with them a large multitude from the towns, who came already prepared by their fasts and abstinences. On the evening of that day they went forth with a great procession of people, and with a large number of their comedians from the house of the lord, where they are assembled and went very quietly to the temple of Kukulcán, which they had previously properly adorned, and having arrived there, and making their prayers, they placed the banners on top of the temple, and they all spread out their idols below in the courtyard, each for himself, on leaves of trees, which he had for this purpose, and having kindled new fire, they began to burn their incense in many places and to make offerings of food cooked without salt or pepper or drinks made of their beans and the seeds of squashes. The lords and those who had fasted remained there without returning to their houses for five days and five nights of prayer, always burning copal and engaged in their offerings, and executing several sacred dances until the first day of *Yaxkin.* The comedians went during these five days among the principal houses, playing their pieces and collecting

The Castillo, in the early stages of the Mexican government's restoration project, which was completed in the 1930s. This structure, which has both Tula-like serpent columns at the entrance to its temple and huge serpent heads at the base of its stairways, is generally considered to have been dedicated to Quetzalcoatl-Kukulcán, the Feathered Serpent. The huge pyramid may have hosted pre-Columbian ritual-architectural events similar to those that Bishop Diego de Landa witnessed during the sixteenth century at a smaller "temple of Kukulcán" in Mani, a Yucatecan center some 100 kilometers southwest of Chichén Itzá. (Carnegie Institution of Washington photo, courtesy of the Peabody Museum, Harvard University.)

gifts which were given to them, and they carried the whole of them to the temple where, when the five days were ended and past, they divided the gifts among the lords, priests, and dancers, and they got together the banners and idols and returned to the house of the lords, and from there each one to his own house. They said and considered it as certain that Kukulcán came down from heaven on the last day of these (five days), and received their services, their vigils and offerings. They called this festival *Chic Kaban*.[231]

Even in this scant, anachronistic report, the post-contact pyramid rites of Xul at Mani typify and point up the essential and manifold priorities that would seem to have operated in the pre-Hispanic ceremonies at Chichén's Castillo and, in fact, in the ritual-architectural events of "Toltec Chichén" generally. With respect, for instance, to orientation and allurement, there is a strong possibility that these colonial Kukulcán rites of Xul were actually the vestige of a new year's ceremony (or New Fire ceremony), a possibility that is greatly enhanced directly by Landa's explicit reference to "kindling a new fire" and, somewhat more indirectly, by the intense cosmic-celestial referencing in the actual physical form of the Castillo (discussed momentarily).[232] This connection between the Castillo structure and the ritual celebration of the new year resonates with my assessment that the elaborate instigatory strategy of "Toltec Chichén" depended not only on displaying a wide oeuvre of eclectic architectural allusions (one sort of variation on the convention priority, I-B) but, likewise, on a carefully homologized and astronomical scheduling of ceremonies (an exercise of the homology and astronomy priorities, I-A and I-C).

The range and play of presentational priorities in Landa's account of the rites of Xul are similarly telling of the wider "Toltec Chichén" ritual-architectural program: there is the ubiquitous necessity of pre-performative sanctification of space in the special decoration of the pyramid and the purification of persons in the requisite fasting and abstinence (an expression of the sanctuary priority, III-D); there are individuated requests and petitionary offerings of food and copal to a Kukulcán deity that is understood to actually descend from the sky to receive those offerings (thus instantiating the propitiation priority, III-C); and, most unmistakably, the choreographic approach is inclusive and theatrical in the extreme, with a "large multitude" of residents and visitors treated to banners awave, lavish processions, and nonstop dancers and "comedians" (thus instantiating the theatre priority, III-A).[233] Moreover, with respect to the content of the rites of Xul (and thus perhaps of the pre-Hispanic ritual of "Toltec Chichén"), while they are ostensibly in honor of the mythological deity Kukulcán (the commemoration of divinity and of sacred history, priorities II-A and II-B), unlike the other, preponderantly agricultural monthly ceremonies that Landa describes, this Castillo event is proctored by "lords" rather than "priests," suggesting that this, like the bulk of "Toltec Chichén" ceremony, constituted a context for expressing civic and political as well as explicitly religious themes to the assembled host (thus instantiating in that case the politics priority, II-C).[234]

With this brief foreshadowing — a set of characterizations that, admittedly, is nearly general enough to apply to Tula (or to Tenochtitlán for that matter) as well as to "Toltec Chichén" — the remaining sections of the chapter pursue a more detailed hermeneutic of the specificity and uniqueness of "Toltec Chichén" ritual-architectural events. I will, of course, be paying particular attention to the discrepancies between these events and those of Tula and South Chichén.

Instigation: Doth Protest Too Much

While the architecture of "Toltec" Chichén Itzá has, over the years, engendered a host of superlatives (and expletives), I would hold that its greatest claim to singularity lies with its initiative in ritual-architectural allurement. "Toltec Chichén" stands supreme among Mesoamerican ceremonial centers for the diversity and ingenuity with which it pleads its legitimate order and beckons the committed participation of its audience. Not only did the Maya designers astutely site their capital directly adjacent to Yucatán's most esteemed natural feature — that is, the Sacred Cenote — they were also relentless in their dexterous unification of calendars, cosmologies, and built forms (thus instantiating the homology priority, I-A). They

Serpent head at the base of north stairway of the Castillo. This sculpture may find an ethnohistoric analogue in Bishop Landa's description of the sixteenth-century Kukulcán festival at Mani, in which he notes that the Maya "said and considered it as certain that Kukulcán [the Feathered Serpent] came down from heaven on the last of these (five days), and received their services, their vigils and offerings." (Photo by Lawrence G. Desmond.)

worked with equal diligence to exploit and incorporate celestial phenomena, particularly light and shadow (thus instantiating the astronomy priority, I-C). And, where the builders of Tula Grande cleverly wove together elements from a variety of traditions to engender the participation of its diverse constituency (thus instantiating one important variation on the convention priority, I-B), those of "Toltec Chichén" elaborated the same eclectic strategy but on a vastly higher and wider scale, synthesizing contributions from the reaches of Mesoamerican history and geography. Thus, via an ambitious multiplication, or layering of principles of order and allurement, not just one but all of the three generalized orientational priorities are magnificently evident.

This remarkable tapestry of conservative, instigative devices was balanced (in consonance with the general twofold pattern of ritual-architectural events) by a complementary component that was radical, daring, and new. Yet, according to my hypothesis — and this points to the special genius of "Toltec Chichén" architecture — the events of "Toltec Chichén" were, in a sense, "front heavy." These events were, it seems, more preoccupied (and more successful) with sucking, centripetalizing, and urging players into the ritual game than in redirecting them out with any message of revolutionary importance. In short, the allurement outstripped the content. The ritual-architectural program of "Toltec Chichén," viewed then in the most negative light, was an opportunistic, desperate attempt by the *nouveau riche* Putun warrior-merchants to anchor themselves in the unwelcoming, rocky Yucatán soil by appropriating the Sacred Cenote, expropriating the roots of their predecessors and contemporaries, and thus seducing their audience with what amounted to cosmo-astronomical gimmickry. Assessed, however, in the most positive light, "New Chichén" was the strongest and boldest of all pre-Columbian efforts to synthesize one eclectic whole from the "liquid rippling body" of ancient Mesoamerica.[235]

The Castillo, itself deeply layered with the three principal modes of proclaiming order and respectability (homology, astronomy, and convention, priorities I-A, I-C, and I-B), again is the appropriate point of departure for discussing the "starting" strategies of "Toltec Chichén" events. With respect to the first mode, the great Castillo, in fact, so meticulously homologizes architectural space and calendrical time as to provide a kind of didactic "text" for the space-time machinations of the northern Maya. Seemingly in fear of anything random, each of the four radially symmetrical stairways has ninety-one steps, which, together with the shared final step up to the temple, make 365, corresponding to the days of the solar year.[236] Each side of the pyramid has fifty-two niches or panels, equated to the fifty-two-year cycle. The body of the substructure has nine major stepped levels, presumably representing the nine levels of the Maya underworld, or a "nine-night calendar count," or, possibly, the notion of nine "hours" of the night;[237] and, because those nine tiers are divided by a stairway, there are eighteen sections on each side of the pyramid body, corresponding to the eighteen "months" in the indigenous calendar. Moreover, the four stairways themselves are correlated to a rotational cycle of four years that ended with the north stairway, the one that points directly toward the Sacred Cenote.[238] Delivering a final homologizing touch, the roof of the Castillo's temple was apparently once rimmed by twenty ornaments, which correlates with the Mesoamerican vigesimal (or base twenty) counting system.[239]

Furthermore, were these detailed cosmic referencings not enough, the perfectly symmetrical general conception of the Castillo exemplifies beautifully the notions of a cosmological-architectural center, "a pivot and four

The Castillo pyramid, sometimes described as an enormous stone calendar, provides perhaps the most meticulous set of unifications of space and time anywhere in pre-Columbian architecture. (Photo by Lawrence G. Desmond.)

quarters," a central *axis mundi, omphalos,* or sacred mountain, a symbolic anchoring hub for the spokes that penetrate out into the periphery of the capital city of Chichén Itzá and beyond.[240] Natural solar time, calendrical time, and mythical time, along with ritual-architectural space and political space, all coalesce in the amazingly self-conscious spatio-temporal arrangement of the Castillo. There are, in the whole history of sacred architecture, few more plenipotent representatives of Eliade's conception of "microcosmic" architecture (and, thus, of the homology priority, I-A) than "Toltec Chichén's" Castillo.[241]

This rigorous program of homologization may seem sufficient in itself to have provided pre-Columbian visitors to the City of the Sacred Well with compelling evidence of the capital's conformity to and involvement in the rhythms of the cosmos, and thus its worthiness of their respect. Nevertheless, the architects of "Toltec Chichén" worked with equal self-consciousness to weave "natural," celestial phenomena into their agenda of allurement (thus evincing at that point the astronomy priority, I-C). In addition to apparently orienting various plaza buildings toward the zenith sunset, the setting of the Pleiades, and the first appearance of Venus as the evening star at the beginning of the rainy season,[242] these Maya builders achieved their most famous (at least at this point) astro-architectural effect with the choreographed play of sunlight and shadow on the Castillo, a dramatic effect that was only belatedly recognized by modern observers.

For a long time the Castillo pyramid's atypical, 23.5 degrees east of north skew was explained as a roughly cardinal orientation, twisted slightly so that the most prominent, north stairway would point directly toward the Sacred Cenote. Yet, toward the middle of this century (once the Castillo had been (re)constructed by the Mexican government), it became apparent (several archaeologists and guides are still claiming credit for the initial discovery of this phenomenon[243]) that about an hour before sunset on the day of the vernal (or autumnal) equinox, the shadow cast by the nine main tiers of the pyramid substructure forms an undulating, "serpent-like" line along the balustrade of the Castillo's north stairway. As sunset approaches on this special day, the distinctive zigzag pattern of light and shadow becomes a sequence of seven well-formed isosceles triangles, stretched out corner-to-corner along the descent of the stairway. In the critical moments, all of the building is shadowed except for the chain of seven triangles and the giant carving of a serpent head at the base of the stair, which are brightly illuminated by the sun. The triangular swatches of light appear like a diamond-backed snake viewed from the side as it disembarks from the high Castillo temple and heads down toward the ground, an effect redoubled by the similarly illumined stone serpent head.[244] Over the span of some two hours on each March 20 (or September 20), as the sun sinks in the sky, causing the configuration of light and shadow to change, this massive "serpent of sunlight" slithers, as it were, down the Castillo's stairway, presumably off toward the Sacred Cenote — providing, then, a striking coincidence with Landa's account of the last day of the Xul rites when the Yucatecan Maya "said and considered it as certain that Kukulcán [the Feathered Serpent] came down from heaven . . . and received their services, their vigils and offerings."[245]

This magnificent, architecturally contrived "solar equinox hierophany" of light and shadow — the "Castillo equinox event," if you will — is not wholly unprecedented in Mesoamerican architecture. Luis Arochi, for instance, postulates a number of similar, somewhat more modest (and more contestable) astro-architectural effects even within the Castillo itself.[246] As a religio-astro-engineering coup, the serpent of light phenomenon, is, nonetheless, stunning. If the huge present-day audiences are impressed (as most but not all are), for pre-Columbian audiences, the affective power must have been tremendous. For them the spectacle may well have provided a vivid instantiation of, for example, the sort of spiritually illuminating experience described in Chapter 3 in relation to the epigrammatic pilgrim's transformative engagement with the pyramid. Yet, in the context of the present discussion of instigatory strategies (especially given the historical dilemma of the Putun Maya), the descending serpent could likewise be assessed, rather more harshly, as a colossal manipulation, an intriguingly ingenious gimmick, the somewhat crass architectural prestidigitation expected of a well-heeled society desperately begging for a hearing.[247] Moreover, if the serpent of light was a somewhat devious and contrived strategy of allurement, the entire preoccupation at "Toltec Chichén" with Quetzalcoatl/Kukulcán (a deity manifest particularly in snakes and Venus) might similarly represent (among other things) an opportunistic ploy to capitalize on two symbols that already had the deepest grounding and highest respect in Maya religion.[248]

Several days before and after each spring and fall equinox, the setting sun casts a zigzag, snake-like configuration of light and shadow along the north balustrade of the Castillo. For centuries prior to the (re)construction efforts of the Mexican government, the so-called serpent of light phenomenon would not have been visible. Now, however, the great plaza accommodates tens of thousands of visitors each spring who come to witness the ritual-architectural hierophany. (Photo by William M. Ferguson, courtesy of the University of Texas, Austin.)

In any case, it is certain that besides these intense programs of homologization (priority I-A) and astronomical alignment (priority I-C), the instigatory program of the Castillo, like that of "Toltec Chichén" generally, was further bolstered by a third sort of plea for serious consideration — namely, appeals to established and already well-respected architectural forms and configurations (a variation on the convention priority, I-B). The Maya architects (as I have noted repeatedly) capitalized on their wide familiarity with ancient Mesoamerica to assemble a daringly eclectic ensemble of allusions to the renowned pyramids and palaces of both the past and the contemporaneous present that would embellish still more their invitation to participate in, and to take seriously, the ritual-architectural events of "Toltec Chichén."

The Castillo itself, for instance, often noted for its uniqueness among Mesoamerican monuments, upon closer inspection, is actually a tour de force of architectural syncretism.[249] The exploitation of light and shadow on the Castillo, for instance, finds antecedents in the dynamic effects of the setting sun on the complex geometric facades of Mitla and Yagul in Oaxaca and, closer in time and space, on the mask-encrusted Codz-Pop at Kabah, and even on the

Puuc facades of South Chichén.[250] The fairly unusual radial symmetry of the Castillo (most Mesoamerican pyramids are bilaterally but not radially symmetrical) has typically been connected to the similarly quadrilateral pyramid E-VII Sub at Uaxactún in the Petén jungle, the oldest extant Mesoamerican pyramid (as much as a millennium older than the Castillo),[251] or, alternatively, there are also a number of nearly contemporaneous, four-sided monuments in northern Yucatán that could have served as patterns for the Castillo.[252] Moreover, it is very possible that the square form of the Castillo harkened to the low quadrangular platforms that were centered in the sunken plaza of Monte Albán, or in the Ciudadela of Teotihuacán, or (most likely of all) the Adoratorio platform in Tula Grande (though, in the case of the Castillo, that diminutive sort of square platform was stretched up like an accordion into monumental pyramidal proportions).[253] Furthermore, the nine-tiered body of the Castillo has earlier counterparts on an equally grand scale in Palenque's Temple of the Inscriptions and in Uxmal's Great Pyramid.[254] And the rectangular stone temple atop the huge Castillo substructure, essentially an elaboration on the basic prototypical Puuc range structure, is unmistakably eclectic with columns adorned by reliefs of Tula-Toltec style warriors supporting characteristically Maya corbelled vaulting.[255]

Thus, while this sort of backtracking of various Mesoamerican architectural elements, and discerning who copied whom (one of pre-Columbian art historians' principal preoccupations), is always uncertain, one could, nevertheless, continue in this fashion to generate a very long (if controversial) list of eclectic borrowings and imitations, not only in the Castillo but throughout the whole architectural configuration of "Toltec Chichén." A methodological caveat is, however, in order. Given my commitment to holding the interpretation up to the level of ritual-architectural events (rather than of buildings), I would resist in the strongest terms the danger of lapsing into the "noneventful" comparison of simply formal commonalities. Surveying possible borrowings is useful, but in the context of this discussion I insist that the stunning range of seemingly deliberate archaisms in the Castillo and throughout the rest of the plaza be appreciated *not* as the summation of the "Toltec Chichén" architectural project but, instead, as one of several major components in the elaborately crafted presentation of worldly proficiency and otherworldly credibility, a fashioning of irresistible allurement that constitutes the "front" or conservative component of the capital's ritual-architectural events. Moreover — to emphasize a point that has been too often neglected — this eclectic refashioning of foreign themes at "Toltec Chichén" (this sort of allurement via conventionality, priority I-B), while certainly demonstrating a special indebtedness to Tula, hardly confines itself to Central Mexican borrowings. La Gran Nivelación presented a genuinely cosmopolitan architecture, arguably the most cosmopolitan in Mesoamerican history. Thus, while one could amass an almost endless list of historical precedents for various "Toltec Chichén" architectural elements from across Mesoamerica, the most relevant cases for my purposes are those elements that have been generally presumed (however appropriately or inappropriately) to have been lifted (or imposed) directly from Tula, Hidalgo. In that regard, George Kubler is uniquely helpful.

Kubler, by his tireless effort to locate the individual works of pre-Columbian art with respect to their historical precedents and echoes, and by his iconoclastic conviction that the "Toltec Maya" style at Chichén Itzá represents a "renaissance of Classic Maya art" rather than a Central Mexican importation,[256] generates the longest list of "Toltec Chichén" archaisms that come from *other than* Tula, Hidalgo.[257] Kubler, in fact — and this is very important — proposes an indigenous Maya (or at least non-Toltec) precedent for virtually every one of the elements of "Toltec Chichén" architecture that has conventionally, even since Désiré Charnay, been presumed to have originated in Tula. Eight of his most important examples follow:[258]

1. The serpent columns, the most notorious of all Tula–Chichén Itzá parallels, could derive from the effigy columns of the Puuc region, principally Oxkintok (near Uxmal) instead of from Tula, and, in fact, the general plumed serpent element itself is preceded by magnificent Maya serpent images.[259]
2. The equally famous *chacmool* statues, since Charnay's era considered a definitive diagnostic of "Mexicanization" or "Toltecization," may originate in the Maya area rather than at Tula.[260]
3. The many little carytids or "atlantean" figures, which support tables and benches on their upstretched arms, represent, according to Kubler, a Classic Maya tradition of *bacabs* or "holders of the sky" rather than "Toltec" warriors; moreover, there are also ample precedents in Classic Maya architecture for the larger atlantean-type columns that support doorways and lintels around Chichén.[261]
4. Kubler provides a number of Maya antecedents for the jaguar throne in the inner building of the Castillo and similarly argues that the Tula-like reliefs of jaguars in procession also have Maya antecedents, particularly at Tikal.[262]
5. The intimidating and ubiquitous warrior figures at "Toltec Chichén," traditionally considered the very antithesis of the spirit of indigenous Maya art, actually have numerous precedents in the Southern Lowland Maya sites of Bonampak, Piedras Negras, and Yaxchilán.[263]
6. With respect to more properly architectonic forms, the round Caracol structure, typically attributed to the Central Mexican cult of Quetzalcoatl/Kukulcán, has associations with the Maya areas of the Petén, the Puuc, and even the styles of Río Bec and Xpuhil.[264]
7. Kubler holds that the profiles of the inner building of the Castillo, and the later and greater Castillo that was built over it, seem more like those of the Puuc period than those of the florescent period at Tula[265] and that "Toltec Chichén's" pyramid bodies with *tableros* (vertical panels that alternate with the sloping surfaces or *taluds*) are actually more like those of Teotihuacán, and even more like those of Monte Albán in Oaxaca, than they are like Tula Grande's.[266]
8. Kubler argues that the highly distinctive "Toltec Chichén" colonnades and the spacious interiors that they allow, considered by virtually everyone since Charnay to be copies of their very similar counterparts at Tula, actually find a more important precedent in the example of Late Classic Mitla in Oaxaca.[267]

Alberto Ruz, the most direct respondent to Kubler's heretical claims, does consent that some of the iconographic motifs shared by Tula and "Toltec Chichén" may have originated in the Maya zone, but, holding closer to the party line, rejects the Maya provenance of most of the other so-called Toltec features at Chichén Itzá.[268] However, in the context of the ensuing debate, which, thirty years later is not yet at rest, Ruz (like Kubler) furthers the case for a genuinely cosmopolitan "Toltec Chichén" by arguing that a number of the salient characteristics of its architecture issue from sources *other than* either Tula or the Classic Maya. (My reassessment can benefit greatly from the work of Kubler and Ruz without, however, fully endorsing either of their historical hypotheses.)[269] For instance, Kubler had already pointed to a number of influences at the Yucatán capital from Monte Albán and Mitla (both in Oaxaca), and Ruz considers that the controversial column form, so characteristic of

In North Chichén, *chacmool* at the entrance to the Temple of Warriors. Though the distinctive *chacmool* statues, which are uniquely prevalent at Tula and Chichén Itzá, were for decades considered among the most definitive signs of the "Mexicanization" of Yucatán, it is possible that this element originated in the Maya zone. (Photo by Lawrence G. Desmond.)

Tula and "Toltec Chichén," originated neither in Central Mexico nor the Maya area but rather in Oaxaca.[270] Ruz holds that the 17 degrees east of north orientation of the buildings at "Toltec Chichén," the *talud-tablero* articulation, and perhaps even the whole man-bird-serpent concept (that is, Quetzalcoatl/Kukulcán, the Feathered Serpent) were actually the direct legacy of Teotihuacán, not necessarily mediated through Tula.[271] From the Central Gulf Coast area to which Tula and "Toltec Chichén" were both indebted, Ruz finds a number of Huastecan traits in "Toltec Chichén."[272] And, more importantly, looking again for precedents in the interjacent Gulf Coast region, Ruz argues that the decapitation rites depicted in the reliefs of Chichén's Great Ball Court (by Tozzer's reckoning, symbolizing representations of the hostilities between Toltecs and Maya) and, in fact, the whole ball game complex, actually arose in the area of El Tajín, Veracruz, and then disseminated in both directions.[273]

Despite all these claims for the wider internationalism of "Toltec Chichén" (and there have been many more),[274] no one after Charnay, Kubler included, has been able to deny that by far the highest proportion of formal commonalities is between "Toltec Chichén"

On the Temple of the Warriors in North Chichén, Tula-like iconography and the *talud-tablero* style of Teotihuacán are integrated with more characteristically Maya architectural elements. While, at Tula, those violent iconographic depictions expressed a threatening message of intimidation, here at Chichén Itzá, the nearly identical images seem to have been part of an eclectic strategy of ritual-architectural allurement. (Photo by Lawrence G. Desmond.)

and Tula, Hidalgo. The parallels that the robust Frenchman noted so long ago — friezes of warriors and processions of jaguars, *chacmools,* carytids and atlanteans, giant colonnaded halls, and serpent columns — persist as unarguable testimony to a very special link between these two pre-Hispanic cities. The unending chase after the origins of "Toltec Chichén" art forms, if settling almost nothing else with certainty, has, however, successfully challenged the singularity and simplicity of Tula's role as the antecedent and counterpart to the great capital of Yucatán. At this point we can conclude with some assurance that Tula was not, after all, the sole prototype for "Toltec Chichén" but, instead, only the most important of several models or reservoirs of ritual-architectural imagery on which this remarkably ambitious project of borrowing and synthesis drew. The synthesizing project of the "Toltec Chichén" Maya architects was not in principle different from Tula Grande's own eclectic initiative (both are manifestations of the same sort of variation on the convention priority, I-B), although, with considerably greater resources and experience, the Maya were able to reach far wider for their patterns and to integrate them with far greater subtlety.[275]

Finally, to address the most obvious and almost assuredly the most effective instigatory strategy, in addition to all the homologized referencings (I-A), the celestial-architectural effects (I-C), and the eclectic religio-architectural allusions (I-B), the architects of "Toltec Chichén" delivered a coup de grâce in allurement by wedding themselves to the most religiously appealing ecological feature in the northern Maya area — the Sacred Cenote. The antiquity and extent of pre-Columbian veneration for and pilgrimage to the Sacred Cenote is another of these matters of great academic debate (to say the least).[276] Where some (like Tozzer, Brainerd, and Coe) hold that the Cenote cult was a relatively late (in their terms, "post-Mexicanization") phenomenon,[277] others (for instance, Ralph Roys, Eric Thompson, and now Clemency Coggins) consider that this uncanny circular sinkhole, an architectural feature honed by natural rather than human agencies, had been a highly revered pilgrimage destination well in advance of the construction of "Toltec Chichén."[278] Roys, for instance, concludes that pre-Columbian peoples had been traveling from all over the area, perhaps for centuries prior to the construction of the Castillo, to deposit their offerings in the murky, perpetually filling waters of the Cenote. Thus, he writes:

> Chichén Itzá was at one time not only the greatest and most powerful city in Yucatán, but it was a sacred city as well, a center of pilgrimage to which people flocked from every part of the peninsula and from foreign countries also to make offerings of gold, incense, copper, precious stones and human victims. The city owed its reputation for sanctity to its cenote, or natural well, which was believed to be inhabited by the gods and the spirits of the illustrious dead.[279]

According to this position, then (which I would accept with some qualifications), the resilient eco-hierophanic prestige of the Sacred Cenote both long preceded and far outlasted the comparatively ephemeral prime of Chichén Itzá as an important political capital.[280] (There are many accounts of colonial-era Maya pilgrimaging to the Sacred Cenote even after the associated buildings were thoroughly dilapidated.)[281] Yet, during the city's florescence, the plaza of "Toltec Chichén" was umbilically joined to the Sacred Cenote by a grand processional way, some 10 meters wide and 300 meters long, which extended from the principal stairway of the huge Castillo pyramid to the edge of the venerable well.

Thus, by tethering their plaza via this paved processional avenue to the Sacred Cenote (a maneuver like that which Victor Turner terms "pilgrimage structuration"),[282] the Putun Maya architects of "Toltec Chichén" — an affluent group with the power and mobility to choose freely where they located their inland capital — effected a masterful stroke of architectural allurement and, thereby, gained perhaps their greatest measure of appeal and legitimacy. Epitomizing the twofold pattern of familiarity and innovation that characterizes ritual-architectural events generally, the union of the esteemed old Cenote with the new, humanly constructed architectural forms of La Gran Nivelación was, among other things, an astute instigatorial maneuver. With the construction of the Castillo pyramid and its surrounding plaza nearly on the rim of the Sacred Cenote (and adjacent to "Old South Chichén"),[283] pilgrimage from the hinterlands of the Maya zone, apparently already a centuries-old obsession, now climaxed in a direct confrontation not only with the Sacred Well but also with the whole religio-civic arena of "Toltec Chichén." With this configuration of built and natural forms, the pilgrims were treated to (or forced into) a face-to-face confrontation with the imperial majesty of the new lords of Chichén Itzá and a realization that, like it or not, the new-fledged agenda of these sovereigns was

The naturally formed Sacred Cenote, which was fully integrated into North Chichén's wider ritual-architectural program, probably provided the city's most alluring and legitimating element. (Photo by Lawrence G. Desmond.)

inextricably bound up with the unfailing traditional power of the Sacred Cenote.

To summarize with respect to instigatory strategies — the most remarkable dimension of the ritual-architectural events of North Chichén — by the propitious siting of their capital alongside the renowned Cenote, and by the multiplication of principles of order, the Maya designers of "Toltec" Chichén Itzá called to attention the entire Mesoamerican world. And, if there was a flaw in this near-frenetic organizational self-consciousness, this onslaught against the random and the trifling, it was that it "protested too much." The layering and redundancy of allurements may have, in the end, signaled to visitors precisely the inconfidence that the Maya architects worked so hard to overcome. Their elaborations may have bespoken overcompensation and vulnerability, exactly the opposite of the effect that they had intended. The pre-Columbian reception of their efforts is particularly difficult to assess. It would seem, though, that where the events of Tula Grande coerced and demanded participation, and where those of South Chichén enticed with a more relaxed, refusable offer, the ritual-architectural agenda of "Toltec Chichén" begged for its hearing and pleaded to be taken seriously. The same air of insecurity, the same solicitation of respect (however successful or unsuccessful it may have been), in less remarkable ways, permeated the manner of presentation and the content of those events, issues to which the discussion now, more briefly, turns.

Presentation: Drama, Dance, and Procession

The choreographic strategy employed by the ritual-architectural designers of "Toltec Chichén," because it is largely one-dimensional and because it is so nearly parallel to that of Tula Grande, constitutes a far more straightforward matter than their elaborate layering of instigatory devices. In fact, it is in regard to their respective modes of ritual-architectural presentation that the plazas (and the ceremonial events) of Tula Grande and "Toltec Chichén" were most truly twins. Neither ceremonial space was designed to guide worshippers through esoteric reflections on the nature of life, death, and divinity. Neither even presumed to address the full range of their citizenry's religious lives. Instead, both were religio-civic arenas. Both architectural configurations worked indirectly to provide stage-like settings for events that were highly politicized, even propagandistic. And both were radically inclusive spaces designed to accommodate large crowds of spectators. Thus, in stark contrast to those of South Chichén, the ritual-architectural choreographers of Tula Grande and North Chichén embraced the theatrical mode of presentation (priority III-A) with a vigor that nearly smothered those of contemplation (III-B), propitiation (III-C), and sanctuary (III-D).

It is, moreover, primarily as a manifestation of this perfervor for inclusive, spectatorial rituals — for banner-waving, drum-pounding theatrics — that the general aspect of "Toltec Chichén" has for decades been judged (and condemned) as "non-Maya." The spacious layout of North Chichén is, in the eyes of most aficionados of the Southern Classic Maya, unappealing, somehow stark yet garish, reflecting a crassness that could only be explained, according to the standard view, by the unhealthy influence of Central Mexico. Morley, for instance, ever insistent upon a fundamental contradistinction between pre-Columbian Maya and Mexican peoples, accentuated the glaring discrepancy between the inward-looking, sheltering Maya courtyards and the openness of "Toltec Chichén," which has "no feeling of limitation or crowding of buildings."[284] Similarly and more recently, Davies echoes that polarizing view when he concludes that, in contrast to Petén Maya floridity and elaboration, "Toltec

Chichén" was "imbued with a spirit of austerity scarcely native to Yucatán . . . a stark contrast to early Maya styles."[285] And, in the same spirit, Muriel Porter Weaver counterpoises the meticulous accumulation of small geometric, abstract elements in Puuc Maya architecture against the unsubtle configuration of the "Toltec Chichén," where all attention was riveted on the "severe but simple" monolithic form of the Castillo, the grandeur of which was greatly enhanced by "the fact that it rises in lonely splendor from an immense clearing."[286] Thus, by contrast to the presumably more contemplative and individuated experience of Petén or Puuc Maya architecture, Weaver envisions immense pre-Hispanic crowds attending the rituals of North Chichén: "Thousands could have gathered on every side [of the Castillo] to share in the spectacle of music, fires and processionals and then to hear the voices of the gods."[287]

All of these somewhat condescending views of the stagy style of "Toltec Chichén" do, on the one hand, reflect the prejudices of the paradigm of Maya-Mexican polarity. Yet, on the other hand, the ease with which present-day assemblies of tens of thousands of visitors to the annual Castillo equinox event can gather on the east side of the pyramid to watch the descent of the serpent of light attests to the viability of Weaver's vision of huge crowds and histrionic spectacles.[288] La Gran Nivelación does, most certainly, constitute an abrupt departure from the ceremonial parameters of the Southern Maya cities and, even more, from the Puuc cities of west central Yucatán. At North Chichén all other presentational priorities, while not completely abandoned, ceded to that of theatric display (III-A).

In this rearrangement of presentational priorities that separated "Old" and "New Chichén," it was the contemplation mode (priority III-B) that seems to have suffered the most. The famed tradition of geometric and mask facades from Kabah and Uxmal, for instance, which had found so fertile a reception in South Chichén, was nearly snuffed out in the northern portion of the city. Unlike Tula, which is "singularly lacking in masks," there are numerous and conspicuous examples of the characteristic Puuc-style *chac* masks in "Toltec Chichén"[289] (particularly in the facade decoration of the Temple of the Warriors, the remodeled Caracol, and even the Castillo temple).[290] Yet, as ritual accoutrements, the function of these occasional Puuc-like masks would seem to have been largely reconfigured. In "Toltec Chichén" the ritual participants were no longer treated to facades of subtle complexity and mesmerizing repetition like those of Kabah's Codz-Pop and South Chichén's Iglesia — intricately decorative facades that could proctor a mandala-like meditation (and, thus, instantiate a deep concern for the contemplation priority, III-B). To the contrary, the long-snouted *chac* masks that do appear in North Chichén (for instance, at the corners of the Warriors Temple) were neatly interspersed with feather-collared serpent heads and warrior reliefs or, in some cases, tightly juxtaposed with other "non-Puuc" (or "Toltec") characteristics such as *chacmools,* atlantean figures, serpent columns, and colonnades.

Demonstrative of a phenomenon that happened again and again in the ritual-architectural design of "Toltec Chichén," the Puuc-style masks were in a sense "demoted" or "reduced" from the status of props for devotion (manifestations of the contemplation priority, III-B) to that of one among many eclectic instigatory touches (thus, in that case, playing as part of the strategy of allurement via conventionalization, priority I-B). Instead of being vehicles to spiritual insight, the geometric and mask elements served in a less-substantive role as tokens of the revered Puuc tradition, as signs of respectable continuity that had, nonetheless,

The "serpent of light" phenomenon, March 21, 1988. In recent years, each spring occurrence of this ritual-architectural hierophany has drawn thousands of visitors to the site, all of whom can be easily accommodated by the spacious plaza of North Chichén. (Photo by the author.)

been wrenched from their contemplative ritual contexts. In fact, epitomized by this demotion of the stone mosaic masks and other decorative elements that were borrowed from the Puuc style, the architects of the ritual-architectural program of "Toltec Chichén," generally speaking, seem to have been almost wholly uninterested in nurturing mystical or contemplative meditation of any sort (which is *not* to say, however, that self-motivated pre-Columbian persons of the proper inclination could not have found any number of artistic elements in this spectacular civic plaza capable of, after the fashion of Abbot Suger, "transporting them from the material to the immaterial").[291]

The propitiation mode (priority III-C) endured somewhat more strongly in the rearranged priorities of "Toltec Chichén" ceremony (though this resilience probably reflected the omnipresence of these sorts of concerns in virtually all Maya rituals rather than anything specific in the design agenda of the Putun Maya). With respect to evidence of these fairly generic propitiatory concerns, at least in Landa's account, the Xul festival, for instance, which culminated in the thanksgiving and petitioning of Kukulcán, if atypically political in nature, was, nonetheless (like virtually all Maya rites), connected and scheduled in relation to the annual agricultural cycle of planting and harvest.[292] In fact, the (re)construction scenarios of most of the early writers, which invariably imagine the principal pre-Columbian Castillo events as essentially first fruits ceremonies and occasions to "offer gifts to the gods," probably are correct at least at some level.[293] With respect to more specifically architectural manifestations of the propitiation priority (that is, circumstances in which the construction process itself may have been considered as offertory ritual), a number of the older buildings in South Chichén were apparently remodeled and elaborated according to the "Toltec" style (and perhaps "Toltec" priorities) in ways that were definitely transutilitarian and, thus, quite possibly instances of devotional construction.[294] Within the "Toltec Chichén" plaza itself, numerous instances of plastered-over reliefs and painted-over murals suggest periodic regenerations or "fresh starts" involving the deliberate destruction and (re)creation of works of art. And, demonstrating that sort of manifestation of the propitiation priority that effects a sense of periodic renewal by destroying and then (re)building, the Caracol, the Temple of the Little Heads, and the Temple of the Warriors (among other structures) all show the effects of what Tozzer terms the "pre-Columbian desire to mutilate," though there is no certain evidence that the defacements or rebuildings were carefully timed or religiously motivated.[295]

Furthermore, in relation to the propitiation mode, archaeologists found dedicatory caches in virtually every building in "Toltec Chichén" (though this also is the case in nearly all major pre-Columbian constructions). Slightly more remarkable are instances of intentionally buried sculpture — most dramatically, the unblemished *chacmool* figure that Le Plongeon, in 1875, found buried in the Platform of Venus and then proudly deemed "the greatest discovery ever made in American Archaeology."[296] But, perhaps the most vivid and irrefutable evidence of building as ritual propitiation in North Chichén (though this again exemplifies a nearly pan-Mesoamerican pattern) is provided by the two major constructions that were subsequently covered by later and larger structures, namely, the Temple of the Chac Mool, which lies buried beneath the Temple of the Warriors,[297] and the so-called Castillo-sub with its famous jaguar throne, which was covered over by the final Castillo.[298] As is often the case in Mesoamerica, neither buried structure was raped of precious sculpture or building materials (though some building elements do seem to have been reused elsewhere); instead, the old forms were carefully packed in and hermetically sealed under the later constructions, totally without human access, as though the entire buildings were intended as dedicatory caches that had been given over as offerings to some divine recipient.[299] Interesting and elaborate as all these "Toltec Chichén" variations on the propitiatory mode of construction and design are, it is all quite common fare among pre-Columbian building in Yucatán and elsewhere, hardly unique to the northern portion of Chichén Itzá.

Manifestations of the sanctuary mode in "Toltec Chichén" (that is, priority III-D), while somewhat more obvious, are equally unremarkable. Ruz, for instance, provides a detailed archaeological description of the construction and layout of an irregular polygonal wall that encircled and "protected" the entire sacred precinct of "Toltec Chichén."[300] A major feature that would change the visual aspect of La Gran Nivelación tremendously, this wall is now totally obliterated and strangely absent from almost all descriptive accounts of the site.[301] Besides this large-scale delineation of a sacred refuge, an exclusionary technique not unlike that of the *coatepantli* serpent walls at Tula and Tenochtitlán, there are two (or three) small buildings in "Toltec Chichén" that appear to have been vapor baths or sweat houses, presumably for preparatory purification rites (thus suggesting a somewhat different sort of manifestation of the sanctuary mode, priority III-D). The small shrine at the edge of the Sacred Cenote seems likewise to have been a sweat house for ritual cleansing.[302]

Moreover, reflecting the sanctuary priority (III-D) at the scale of rooms rather than whole structures, several buildings in North Chichén have the windowless, cell-like chambers that are so prevalent in South Chichén and throughout the Maya area.[303] Generally speaking, however, the airy aspect both of the whole plaza configuration and of the individual buildings of "Toltec Chichén," as every observer notes, is much more reminiscent of Tula Grande (or even Teotihuacán and Tenochtitlán) than of most Maya sites. The three-roomed enclosure atop the Castillo, for instance, is windowless and fairly small (like countless Puuc range structures), but, by capitalizing on the use of massive pillars, heavy sapote wooden beams, and three corbel vaults, this high temple was provided a more spacious interior than any in South Chichén. Kelemen is likely correct in his assessment that the change reflects not only a different style but different ritual priorities: "the temple at El Castillo offers a departure from the old. It is obvious that new conditions demanded greater interior space; the ritual was expanding, the cast becoming more numerous."[304] In the same vein, the nearby Temple of the Warriors, the twin to Tula's Temple of Tlahuizcalpantecuhtli, exploits the use of columns far more elaborately than the Castillo and, thus, in Vaillant's reckoning, becomes "the most important Central American example of a temple that afforded space for a congregation within its confines."[305] In sum, while there was not a complete abnegation of the sanctuary mode (III-D), "Toltec Chichén" is, nonetheless, as most critics have noted, exceptional among Maya centers for its "opening-up" and its revolutionary exploration of large interior spaces.

Modern scholars, particularly those still wedded to some version of the "Toltec Conquest" story, typically attribute these daring explorations of interior space in North Chichén to a breakthrough in roofing techniques that arose as the progeny of united Maya and Central Mexican engineering skills — as though the indigenous Maya had always wanted wide-open interiors but had to wait for the arrival of Mexicans to discover a means of achieving them (hardly a satisfactory explanation at this point). Approaching the problem of this indisputable transition in a more "eventful" fashion (and crediting the development to the efforts of indigenous Maya rather than to Mexican invaders), these unprecedentedly open spaces are, as Kelemen suggests, compelling evidence of a rearrangement of ritual-architectural priorities that favored spectatorial inclusion (the theatre priority, III-A) over cloistered and esoteric seclusion (sanctuary. priority III-D). In fact, I can close out this discussion of presentational modes by arguing that the new ascendancy of the theatric priority, vividly exemplified in both its stationary and processionary aspects, dominated the entire spatial order of "Toltec Chichén."

First, regarding stationary manifestations of this concern for ceremonial spectacle, the characteristically Central Mexican daises (like the Adoratorio at the center of Tula Grande), often identified explicitly as a "theatres," "stages," or "dance platforms," were multiplied and elaborated across "Toltec Chichén."[306] This basic tribunal element (as noted earlier) was apparently scissored into the sky to form the monumental Castillo, itself a huge stage of sorts, and at least three other major stage-like platforms were placed at the base of the pyramid: (1) the Venus Platform lies directly on the processional way between the Castillo and the Sacred Cenote; (2) the Platform of the Tigers

Architectural restoration of the Temple of the Warriors and Northwest Colonnade, by Dr. Kenneth G. Conant. This drawing was based on data at hand at the close of the 1926 field season, prior to excavation of the enormous colonnade known as the Hall of a Thousand Columns, which is adjacent to the south (or right) side of this structure. In that era, George Vaillant, besides emphasizing the heavy Central Mexican influences in this structure, considered that the atypical use of columns made this "the most important Central American example of a temple that afforded space for a congregation within its confines." Subsequent (and earlier) scholars have been dubious of that explicitly religious function. (Carnegie Institution of Washington photo, courtesy of the Peabody Museum, Harvard University.)

and Eagles, with feathered serpent balustrades and relief sculptures, which are virtually identical to those of Tula, lies slightly to the west; and (3) the Tzompantli, or Platform of the Skulls, an elongated version of the same basic element, is adjacent to the Great Ball Court.[307] Precisely what transpired on these tribunes is uncertain, though the third one supported a large skull rack like those known from Tula and Tenochtitlán, thus suggesting its association with public human sacrifice, and the first two were immortalized in Landa's explicit account of "two small stages of hewn stone, with four staircases, paved on the top, where they say that farces were represented, and comedies for the public."[308] Other scholars, particularly by analogy to the same-shaped Aztec "gladiator stones," suggest that these were stages for the more grim performance of mock combats wherein a captive was sacrificed by a warrior.[309] Whatever

The so-called Platform of Venus, viewed from the top of the Castillo. The somewhat overgrown path marks the formerly grand processional roadway to the Sacred Cenote. Daises or "dance platforms" of this sort in North Chichén, which are quite similar to the Adoratorio platform at the center of Tula Grande, probably served as stages for very public ritual-architectural events. (Photo by the author.)

transpired on these ceremonial rostrums, we can be sure that it was in full view of all who had entered the "Toltec Chichén" plaza.

Moreover, additional low tribunal platforms, in themselves eclectic monuments with *talud-tablero* profiles like Xochicalco and with unmistakably Tula-like reliefs, were positioned (after the fashion of Teotihuacán) along both sides of the grand processional way that leads from the main plaza of the Castillo to the Sacred Cenote.[310] Again accentuating the presumed extravagance and spectacle of the pre-Columbian ceremonials, Landa (who never actually witnessed such a performance at Chichén Itzá) describes this pathway as "very clear and ornamented, [along] which they went together with their accustomed devotion."[311] Lining this sacred avenue with dance stages (and thus juxtaposing stationary and mobile manifestations of the theatric priority, III-A), the Maya architects of "Toltec Chichén" redoubled the dramatic effect and assured that no stretch of northern Yucatán's extensive network of ceremonial roads was more unforgettable for visitors to the City of the Sacred Well than that last quarter-mile passage from the Castillo to the Sacred Cenote.[312]

The zealous enthusiasm for spectacular axial paths, majestic approaches, and ritual parading was hardly confined to this climactic Castillo-Cenote ambulatory route. Kubler, in fact, concludes on the basis of the layout of the architecture and the graphic art in the northern, "Toltec" portion of the city that "all life was ruled by fixed processions."[313] For instance, where scenes of motion and procession are rare in the art of South Chichén,[314] the friezes, walls, and benches of "Toltec Chichén" (even more than those of Tula, where such scenes are likewise very common) are veritably coated with depictions of elaborately decked animals, priests, and warriors, all marching in file. The largest procession scene (in the Lower Temple of the Jaguars) comprises some 114 figures arranged in seven lines, though Tozzer collects more than a dozen other major examples nearby.[315] Furthermore (and more "eventfully"), there is every indication from the lay of the stairs and avenues that the "Toltec Chichén" ceremonials themselves actually included similarly stately promenades. The arrangement of serpent columns, for instance, particularly in what seem to be the latest buildings (notably the Temple of the Warriors) suggests, at least to Kubler, not only an especial concern for "accenting a processional axis" but also that over the lifespan of "Toltec Chichén" the processional impulse was receiving ever greater elaboration.[316]

Even now, bereft of its polychromatic trappings and its musical accompaniment, its dancers and parades, the huge stadium-like plaza of the Castillo does not bespeak mystery and serenity like most Maya ruins. Rather, "Toltec Chichén" evokes a histrionic excitement and noise that all but drown out the more soft-spoken priorities of contemplation, propitiation, and sanctuary. With their vastly greater resources, and an incomparable performer in the Sacred Cenote, the Maya architects of North Chichén were able not only to imitate but to far exceed the theatric choreographic aspirations, the unsubtle ritual razzamatazz, of Toltec civic ceremony. Thus, where Tula Grande's and "Toltec Chichén's" strategies of instigation by eclecticism were roughly parallel, in manner of presentation, the ritual-architectural events of the sister cities attained their closest identity.

Looking ahead to the final sections of this hermeneutical reassessment, if the Maya architects of "Toltec Chichén" invoked an eclectic strategy of allurement not unlike that of Tula Grande, and if they relied on nearly identical modes of choreography — which accounts in large part for the formal similitude in the two architectures — it was with respect to the substantive content, that is, the central message of their ritual-architectural program that these Yucatecan designers made their most significant departure from the efforts of their Central Mexican counterparts.

Content: A Message of Unity

Once the Maya architects of "Toltec Chichén" had called to attention the entire ancient Mesoamerican world, what was it that they had to announce? Having choreographed with such energy and ingenuity a layered program of cosmic, astronomic, and conventional signs of worthiness to a hearing, what was it that the ritual-architectural events of "Toltec Chichén" had to say? What sorts of information were communicated, what sorts of meanings were transacted in the ritual-architectural dialogues with the Castillo, the Temple of the Warriors, and the rest? To what transformative messages were the assembled multitudes treated? What did they learn? And how were they changed?

The neat quartet of generalized commemorative priorities — divinity (II-A), sacred history (II-B), politics (II-C), and the dead (II-D) — is seriously overmatched by the subtle problem of the content of "Toltec Chichén's" architectural events. We can, nonetheless, rely on these four sets of informational concerns, first, to initiate the hermeneutical reassessment of the "back half" of the ritual-architectural events of North Chichén and then to introduce an alternative hypothesis regarding the central message that the Maya designers hoped to express to their world. I will argue in these final sections that, contrary to the entrenched old stereotypes of "Toltec" rape, pillage, and "secularization," and beneath all the swagger and extravagance of their ceremonial theatre, the architects of "Toltec Chichén" were *not* primarily concerned to issue a threat of martial supremacy. Rather, I hold that their principal initiative was the expression of a deep, simple, even humble message of unity, reconciliation, and synthesis.

In other words — and this may be the dimension of the Tula–Chichén Itzá problem where standard, pejorative assessments have most seriously short shrifted the Yucatán capital — in addition to whatever specific and highly diversified content that may have been at stake in any particular ceremonial occasion, there was, according to my reassessment, a kind of "root message," an essential, binding theme to which the ritual-architectural events of "Toltec Chichén" were consistently and faithfully dedicated. That consistent theme (whether it was ever successfully accepted or not) would seem to have been that all of the very heterogeneous peoples — Maya, Mexican, and otherwise — that had become entangled in the vast trading network of the Putun Maya did, after all, share a common human predicament, a common Mesoamerican human destiny. It was, in short, a message of reconciliation and accommodation rather than intimidation.

I can lay a foundation for this iconoclastic hypothesis by quickly surveying the spectrum of commemorative options. The conventional old story of the "Toltec Conquest of Yucatán" tells us that the bullying Mexicans responsible for "Toltec Chichén" were the bearers both of an unprecedentedly militaristic and totalitarian concept of urban authority and of a "secularized" outlook or, at best, a dark, quasireligious orientation that featured (along with their devotion to Quetzalcoatl/Kukulcán) human sacrifice, idolatry, and an unprecedented obsession with ritual death. Were we to accept this familiar (re)construction of the pre-Columbian events and personalities and translate it into my typological categories, we might then conclude, as any number of scholars have intimated, that the innovative ritual-architectural program of "Toltec Chichén" was dominated, unlike that of any previous Maya center, by the commemoration of temporal authority (politics, priority II-C) and by venerations of death (priority II-D). Extricating ourselves from the paradigm of Maya-Mexican polarity and adopting a more "eventful" hermeneutic, however, gives us pause to reconsider both these standard conclusions.

First, despite the grim reputation of "Toltec Chichén," the ritual-architectural commemoration of the dead would seem, ironically enough, to have been the least important of the four basic types of informational priorities. In many assessments, the infamous proliferation of both real and sculpted stone skulls on the Tzompantli, the graphic depiction of eagles and jaguars feasting on human bodies, the gruesome elaboration of decapitation in the Great Ball Court reliefs, and an unprecedented interest in human sacrifice by heart extraction have been considered the very essence of the "Toltec Chichén" artistic program.[317] Viewed from a more "eventful" frame of reference, however, assessing these artistic elements as components of larger ritual-architectural events, the necrotic images actually seem to have belonged to the conservative, "front" half of those occasions rather than to their informational dimension. These famously grisly images

Two detailed views of the Tzompantli, or skull rack, adjacent to the Great Ball Court. The famously grim iconography of warriors, jaguars, eagles, and skulls in North Chichén — another hallmark of Tula–Chichén Itzá similitude — may have served in this context as a conventionalized ritual-architectural instigatory device rather than as a threatening message of intimidation. (Photos by Lawrence G. Desmond.)

were, I would contend, eye-popping, complacency-smashing, instigatory hooks, and, as such, they surely did evoke a lurid fascination. Yet, even in their shockingly graphic presentation, the rife images of carnage, murder, and ritual sacrifice in "Toltec Chichén" (unlike the substantive role played by those elements at Tula Grande) were part of the incitement to listen rather than the message itself.

Moreover, with respect to other sorts of manifestations of the ritual-architectural commemoration of the dead, where South Chichén (and virtually all major Maya Lowland sites) had demonstrated a major fascination with specific royal ancestors and family histories, "Toltec Chichén," though seemingly in search of a legitimating pedigree, declined to participate (at least at a particularistic level) in the genealogical fervor. Proskouriakoff and Ruz, for instance, both lay great emphasis on the apparent uninterest among the designers of "Toltec Chichén" with glorifying specific historic individuals, whether in monumental tombs (as in the cases of Palenque or Mitla) or in iconography (after the fashion of Bonampak, Yaxchilán, and Piedras Negras).[318] While there are notable exceptions (particularly the so-called High Priest's Grave), the architects of "Toltec Chichén" were more concerned to commemorate classes of society, military orders, historical events, and theological concepts than specific individuals (deceased or otherwise) and their families.[319] The ritual-architectural commemoration of sacred history (priority II-B) and of conceptions of divinity (priority II-A), albeit in somewhat peculiar ways, would both seem to have been at least as important as the concern for the dead or death in any form.

The other most standard charge against the presumed non-Maya "Toltec Chichén" — that of the supposedly "secularizing" Toltecs — holds that its architecture and ceremony demonstrated an unprecedented and overbearing concern for the commemoration of temporal authority (politics, priority II-C). The belated appreciation of the profoundly political disposition of the pre-Columbian Maya in general largely deflates any claim to the uniqueness of "Toltec Chichén" in this regard. The old claim that the militant, opportunistic Toltecs "secularized" the preponderantly and explicitly "religious" ambience of the Yucatán Maya will no longer wash. Unarguably, however, La Gran Nivelación was an explicitly civic plaza, full of displays of worldly power, articulations of hierarchy, and justifications of politico-economic authority. Yet, here again, from a more "eventful" view, the Yucatán capital contrasted sharply with Tula Grande by refusing to exhaust itself in programmatic politics and in demands of allegiance and cooperation. Loosed from many of the quotidian pressures that forced the Tula Toltecs into a kind of hyper-pragmatism, the builders of "Toltec Chichén" could aspire to a transpolitical, genuinely religio-cultural integration. Thus, while "Toltec Chichén" may have been something of a garish mélange (perhaps even a menagerie) of borrowed elements, largely expropriated for their prestige, familiarity, and effectiveness as instigatory devices without great regard for the original contexts and meanings of those elements, in their new, northern Yucatán context, those old art forms were not so much emptied of meaning as reduced to a common Mesoamerican denominator and enlisted in an ambitious synthesis. The message of "Toltec Chichén's" ritual-architectural program was highly politicized, and the architects of this plaza were pragmatic and enterprising in the extreme, but it would be wrong to afford "Toltec Chichén" any special (or especially malefic) status on those grounds.

To move in a more constructive interpretive direction, I would hold alternatively that this ideal of unity — the most essential and consistent message of "Toltec Chichén's" ritual-architectural program — was articulated on three levels, roughly speaking: (1) unity in history, (2) unity in divinity, and (3) unity in cosmology. Briefly, the first level constituted a very special sort of exercise in the commemoration of sacred history (priority II-B) in which "Toltec Chichén's" profusion of murals and pictorial reliefs presented detailed renditions of recent military engagements between competitive Putun Maya factions, pictorial renditions that accentuated the eventual resolution of those conflicts. Together these murals and reliefs recounted (or perhaps invented) a kind of storiological foundation legend for the city, which explained to the participants in "Toltec Chichén" ritual that they were united by a shared history.

The second level involved an equally special sort of exercise in the ritual-architectural commemoration of divinity (priority II-A). This dimension of the unifying message was delivered in a program of iconography and architectonic statuary that marshaled the deity images of various Maya and Mexican traditions and then looped and bound them together with countless representations of the integrating mythic figure of Quetzalcoatl/Kukulcán, the Flying Serpent. In this case, "Toltec Chichén's" international ritual participants were apprised that they shared, if not a common, at least compatible conceptions of, divinity — broadly speaking, that they stood in commensurate relationships to the sacred. And, at the third and most elemental level (reverting to variations on the orientational priorities of homology and astronomy, I-A and I-C), the ritual-architectural designers of "Toltec Chichén" tapped into the pan-Mesoamerican fascination and anxiety over periodic regeneration and regularized relighting of the "New Fire" in order to accentuate a general consensus regarding conceptions of time, the universe, and the human condition. Thus, at Chichén Itzá, New Fire Ceremonialism, already familiar in some form to all of the constituencies, was lifted to unprecedented heights of stagecrafting and astro-architectural spectacle on the stairs of the Castillo. Via the elaboration of this shared indigenous tradition, the amalgamative audience of "Toltec Chichén" was in one more way reminded of (or challenged to accept) the base message that, as Mesoamericans, they all shared a common cosmology, a common cosmogony, and a common human transience.

This, I would wager, was the root message of the "Toltec Chichén" ritual-architecture agenda — common history, common divinity, and common cosmology. Though it may be a novel way of interpreting the great Yucatán capital, art historians Arthur Miller, George Kubler, and Clemency Coggins (each of whom concentrates on a somewhat different aspect of the Chichén Itzá evidence) all lend support to such a view (which is not, however, to presume that they would endorse that view). The final three subsections of this project adopt and extend their respective interpretations in order to explore the viability of this hypothesis that the first and most persistent initiative of the Maya architects of "Toltec Chichén" was, surprisingly enough, a proclamation of integration and unification.

Mural Evidence: Reconciliation Not Intimidation

North Chichén contains a wealth of highly detailed and finely executed murals, particularly in the Temple of the Warriors, in the Chac Mool Temple (which is buried beneath the Warriors Temple), and in the Upper and Lower Temples of the Jaguars. These paintings, which have no strong counterparts in South Chichén,[320] have, since the era of Stephens and Catherwood, typically been judged as much superior either to the architecture or the sculpture in the northern portion of the city.[321] For many modern critics, the murals constitute the

The Temple of the Jaguars, adjacent to the Great Ball Court. There are remnants of elaborate and highly detailed narrative murals in both the Upper Jaguars Temple, which faces the playing field, and the Lower Jaguars Temple, shown here with the life-size sculpted jaguar at its entrance. (Photo by Lawrence G. Desmond.)

sole redeeming feature of "Toltec Chichén's" otherwise unseemly artistic oeuvre and, for the hermeneut, this pictorial art at least seems to provide the most direct manifestation of the concern for ritual-architecturally commemorating sacred history (priority II-B). Ironically, what might first appear the most explicit, straightforward accountings of pre-Columbian "Toltec Chichén" history and, particularly, of the activities of the ill-understood Putun Itzá Maya, have, however, also been among the most controversial of evidences.

As early as the 1880s, Charnay, for instance, commented on the proliferation of the "Toltec" (or what he termed "High Plateau racial types") in the murals and reliefs of "Toltec Chichén";[322] and then, in consonance with his ethnohistorically based belief that the painters and builders of this plaza had an obsessive nostalgia for their Central Mexican homeland, he interpreted the narrative battle scenes at the Temple of the Bearded Man (adjacent to the Great Ball Court) as a commemorative depiction of the mythico-historical "victory [of Quetzalcoatl] over Tezcatlipoca in his football match which took place in Tula."[323] Tozzer, in a seminal paper in 1930, like Charnay, was particularly impressed by the apparent differences in physiognomy, costume, and paraphernalia between the various protagonists in the Chichén paintings.[324] Instead of quasihistorical events that took place in the Toltec capital,

Tozzer, however, considered that the murals provide a trustworthy historical rendering of the infamous "Toltec Conquest" of the Maya. He concluded that the murals in the Jaguar Temple depict a sequence of historical (not mythical) events with which he was already familiar from the ethnohistorical record: namely, the Mexican Toltec attack on Maya Chichén Itzá, the submission of the Maya, and the subsequent ceremonial acknowledgment of Toltec supremacy.[325] Moreover, he eventually interpreted the equally extensive murals in the Temple of the Warriors (which had not yet been excavated when he wrote his first article) in a very similar fashion, that is, as another fully historical pictorial record of the military and political subjugation of the Maya by the Toltecs. Thus, for Tozzer, these murals provided among the most (seemingly) certain evidence of the traditional "Mexicanization" scenario and the bi-ethnicity of Chichén Itzá.[326]

Perfectly consistent with the paradigm of Maya-Mexican polarity, Tozzer's interpretation, which continues to be reiterated by most guides at the site and by a few scholars,[327] generally prevailed until the early 1970s, when it was seriously challenged by Eric Thompson. Thompson, also struck by the apparently different ethnic types in the paintings, attacked Tozzer's "oversimplified" bi-ethnic classification of all the principals in the murals (and reliefs) as either "Toltec" or Maya, and argued instead that "there are surely more than two and maybe as many as five groups involved."[328] In Thompson's re-reading of the "Toltec Chichén" murals (which is an important component of his wider Putun hypothesis),[329] the protagonists are neither Central Mexicans nor Yucatán Maya; moreover, the site of their battles is "nowhere in the vicinity of Chichén Itzá."[330] Rather, Thompson argued that the combatants in the murals are all various factions of "Mexicanized Putun-Itzá" fighting among themselves along the Campeche-Tabasco Gulf Coast.[331] While Thompson won only a few full converts, his iconoclastic interpretations were sufficiently convincing to warn most scholars off of Tozzer's blunt two-party reading of the murals.

Arthur G. Miller, for instance, who has made the most thorough studies of these and other northern Yucatán murals, concurs with Thompson that these murals are not, as Tozzer had concluded, portrayals of a Toltec victory over the indigenous Maya of "Old Chichén Itzá" (a historical eventuality about which Miller is appropriately dubious).[332] Moreover, Miller agrees with Thompson that the paintings in "Toltec Chichén" are not simply generalized village and battle scenes. Instead, adopting a qualified version of Thompson's (re)construction scenario (and it is noteworthy that Miller's qualifications work, among other things, to mitigate the polarization of Maya and Mexican peoples to which Thompson was still attached), Miller argues that the murals are "quite specific visual records of Putun-Itzá history."[333] In that spirit, he contributes a raft of hypotheses about the particular settings and individuals involved.

For instance, having espoused a revised version of Thompson's Putun hypothesis (but having, for the most part, moved outside the paradigm of Maya-Mexican polarity), Miller holds that the important set of murals in the Temple of the Warriors depicts the raids and exploits of "Putun sea marauders" as they competed along the east coast Yucatán for control of highly prized long-distance trade and pilgrimage routes between the Mexican Highlands and the Maya Lowlands.[334] Similarly, Miller hypothesizes that the set of murals in the Upper Temple of the Jaguars depicts two separate episodes between the forces of two identifiable Putun-Itzá military leaders: "the Protagonist, Captain Serpent," and "the Antagonist, Captain Sun Disk."[335] He believes that the

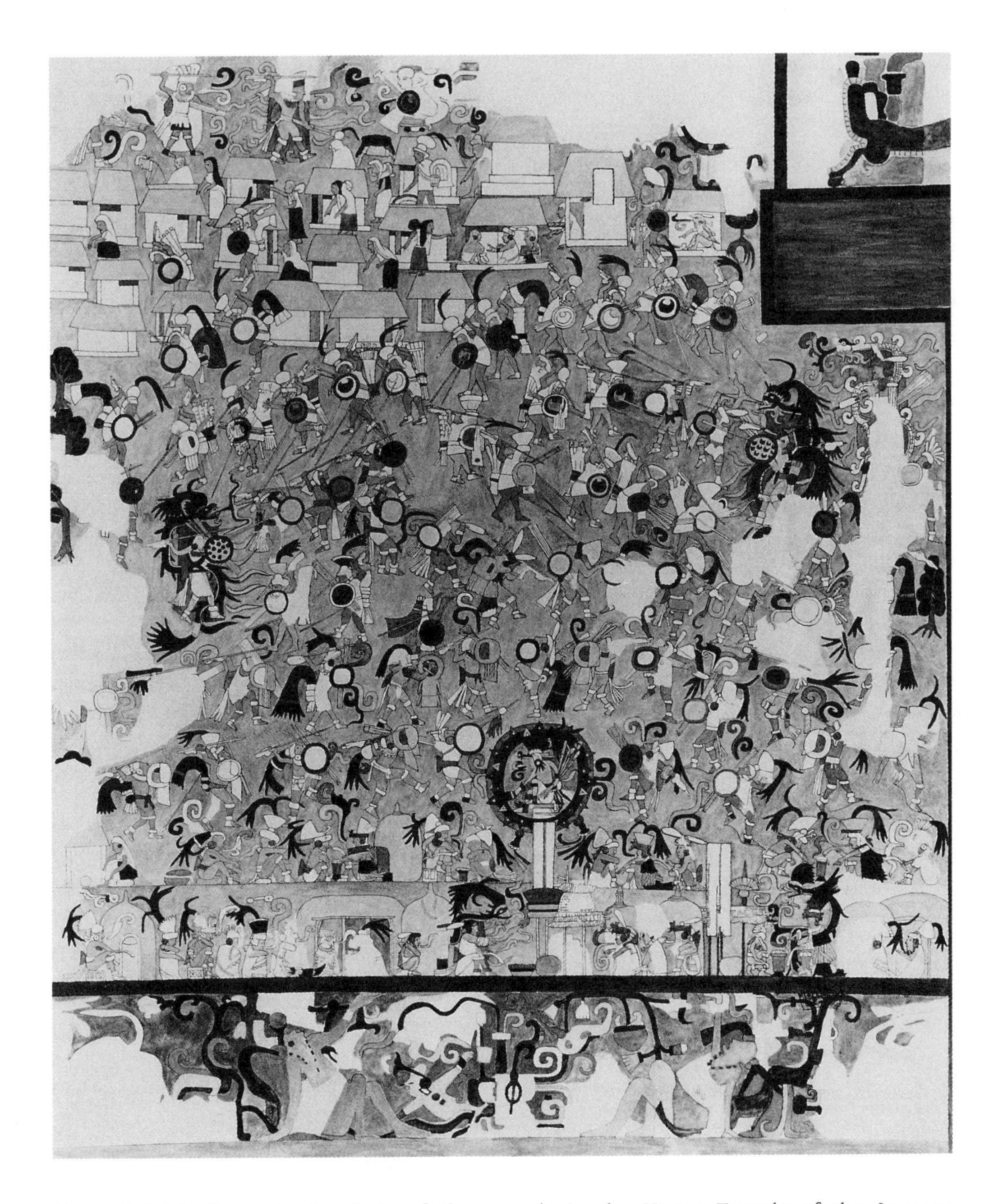

One of Adela Breton's drawings of the murals in the Upper Temple of the Jaguars, completed in 1902. Only scattered fragments of the original murals survive in situ today. Though Alfred Tozzer interpreted these painted images (and nearly all the pictorial remains in North Chichén) as historical renderings of the infamous Mexican Toltec attack on Yucatán Maya, more recent scholars have contested that reading. (From the City Museum, Bristol, England.)

first episode involves the attack on a village far from Chichén Itzá in Oaxaca, while the battle depicted in the second mural, based upon the terrain and the species of flora and fauna in the background of the paintings, appears to have been waged in the equally distant Petén rain forest. Yet, just as in the murals in the Warriors Temple, Miller believes that all of the combatants in these scenes are "rival Putun-Itzá factions" who were competing for access to resources and trade, this time inland, as they fought for the rich spoils of the Southern Maya Lowlands in an era when that area was experiencing an internal power vacuum, namely the so-called Southern Maya Collapse.[336]

Moreover — and this is particularly important for our understanding of the central message of "Toltec Chichén" — according to Miller's reading, each of these murals in the Upper Temple of the Jaguars conforms to a generally formulaic pattern: in each sequence, Captain Serpent vanquishes the other Putun-Itzá chieftain, Captain Sun Disk, and then consummates the victory with a magnificent display of military power and the ritual human sacrifice of members of the defeated forces. Yet, despite the obviously violent and extreme animosity between the various factions in the early going, the final events in the murals foreground signs of peace, capitulation, and conciliation on both sides. One lintel, for instance, depicts the victorious Captain Serpent facing his now-defeated old enemy, Sun Disk, in what Miller interprets as "a gesture of peace and friendship, perhaps a reference to the heavenly reconciliation of these two earthly enemies."[337] Thus, unlike the seemingly vengeful scenes on many southern Classic Maya stelae and lintels in which defeated warriors and captives are shown being stripped, bound, trampled, beheaded, or otherwise humiliated (most famously at Bonampak), the panels in Chichén's Temple of the Jaguars depict both chiefs, the winner and the loser, in equally large portraits with similarly magnificent regalia. The unusual prominence and respect with which the vanquished leader is represented, as Miller points up (and as I would emphasize even more strongly than he does), suggests that the principal theme was *not* intimidation (after the fashion of Tula iconography) but rather reconciliation.[338]

By nearly all estimates, from Charnay to Miller, the rich mural tradition of "Toltec Chichén" was committed to commemorating largely historical events, particularly military confrontations, in highly veristic (though likewise highly stylized) tones. Where exactly those battles took place is still subject to debate. Yet, by the interspersion of very specific martial engagements in their actual geographical contexts with more ethereal images from an otherworldly realm, these murals, so it would seem, depict at once the military and sacred history of this portion of the city. In other words, while the lines between myth and history are (as usual) not particularly clear, the Maya artists of "Toltec Chichén" seem to have been recording (and probably to a large extent inventing, or at least canonizing) one version of the events that had brought their capital into being. Moreover, the thoroughness and detail of their narrative documentary agendum, even given the lately reconfigured image of the pragmatic and politically minded pre-Columbian Maya, have only slim counterparts either in South Chichén or, for that matter, in the Maya area generally.[339]

Furthermore, because of its atypicality in the Maya zone, this preoccupation with the presumably historical adventurings of armies and men in the art of "Toltec Chichén" is not only among the most-cited "proofs" of the "Mexicanization" of Yucatán but also among the most obvious parallels to Tula, Hidalgo. If we continue to insist upon a more "eventful" approach, however, it becomes apparent that the Yucatecan program of martial painting and iconography actually had a very different conception from that of the Tula Toltecs. Where the notoriously graphic depictions of violent death and war in the art of Tula were intent on demonstrating an intimidating potential for destruction and conquest in very general terms — in

Abb. 185, 186. Ballspielplatz. Saal *E*. Mitte der Hinterwand. Krieger der III. und IV. Reihe. Nach Maudslay III, Pl. 49.

Murals in the Lower Temple of Jaguars. Instead of commemorative views of the notorious "Toltec Conquest" of the Yucatán Maya, as early investigators had theorized, these paintings may depict a conciliatory alliance between various competing Maya factions. (Alfred P. Maudslay, *Archaeology*.)

terms of a new concept of coercive authority — the combat scenes at "Toltec Chichén" (particularly in the murals) are more (quasi)historical and thus more narrative and much more specific. If we take a cue at this point from Miller's provocative interpretation, the "Toltec Chichén" murals, unlike anything extant at Tula, seem to have been dedicated to the exposition of a violent but also exceedingly specific foundation legend. The murals of "Toltec Chichén" would, in fact, seem to provide the city with a kind of urban cosmogony, a paradigmatic creation myth for the eclectic capital. The murals tell a legitimating story that does not ignore the endemic warfare between factionalized Putun Maya merchant-soldiers but puts (or at least attempts to put) those conflicts into the past and thus celebrates the present confederated truce. The story does not, in other words, try to cover over the awkward heterogeneity of contributors to and participants in "Toltec Chichén" but instead transforms that diversity into a virtue.

As paradigmatic sacred history (as a kind of seamless narrative blending of historical and quasihistorical, mythical events), the "Toltec Chichén" mural scenes carried a wealth of more highly particularistic messages. They articulated in no uncertain terms, for instance, appropriate standards of decorum before, during, and after battle, appropriate leadership as exemplified in the mighty "captains of the Itzá," appropriate class roles in a hierarchical society, as well as the appropriately dire consequences of resistance to Putun Maya authority. But the root message, the essential theme of the murals (and perhaps of the entire ceremonial complex), was one of reconciliation, integration, and synthesis of old enemies into a new mutually beneficial whole.

In sum, the murals (and Miller's mural-based hypothesis) provide more compelling evidence that "Toltec Chichén" arose not with the bashing and domination of one group by another but, rather more likely, as the consequence of a union of several more-or-less-equal Maya partners. The mural evidence suggests that the great "Toltec Chichén" plaza may well have been "founded" primarily as an architectural celebration of Chontal-Putun-Itzá Maya centralization, the manifestation of an "uneasy alliance" between long-warring merchant-warrior factions, a physical, hopeful sign of truce and cooperation. In Miller's own somewhat more tempered words, "[the Temple of the Warriors] and the other structures of Modified Florescent Period Chichén Itzá ['Toltec Chichén'] were built and decorated to commemorate and idealize earlier competition for important long-distance trade and pilgrimage routes from the Mexican Highlands to the Maya Lowlands."[340] Certainly the Maya's endeavor "to commemorate and idealize earlier competition" and to articulate a reconciliatory foundation legend for the city (which constituted, among other things, a very special manifestation of the commemoration of sacred history, priority II-B) cannot explain all of the buildings, or even all the military iconography in "Toltec Chichén." Yet, as the next sections show, the basic concern for compromise and mutual accommodation does seem to have pervaded a number of the other ritual-architectural realms as well.

Quetzalcoatl's Role: Serpent Column Synthesis

Since Charnay (and, in fact, since Landa and Sahagún), the story of Chichén Itzá, and particularly explanations of the Yucatán capital's remarkable resemblance to Tula, have been inextricably bound up with the Aztec traditions of Quetzalcoatl, the Feathered Serpent. More specifically, some version of the infamous mythical episode in which the chaste priest-king Topiltzin Quetzalcoatl is tricked and shamed by the dark Tezcatlipoca (the Smoking Mirror) and then forced to flee his paradisiacal city of Tollan in favor of "Tlapallan," a mysterious destination presumably in the direction of Yucatán, continues to be worked into nearly every storiological (re)construction of the founding of "Toltec" Chichén Itzá.[341] Of the dozens of variations that rely on the mythical exile of Quetzalcoatl to explain the similitude between Tula and North Chichén (most of which are expendable as accounts of historical events), the most rudimentary feature the beguiled god-king simply traveling with a small retinue of followers to Yucatán, where he attempts, with some success and probably at the expense of the indigenous Maya, to re-create his home city.

Without making any pretense to address the overabundance of controversial issues that are snarled up with the "Quetzalcoatl problem," we can reflect on the similar yet qualitatively different ways in which artistic representations of the Feathered Serpent, particularly in sculpture, contributed to the ritual-architectural agenda of both Tula and "Toltec Chichén." In both circumstances, the abundant Quetzalcoatl imagery represented variations on the commemoration of divinity (priority II-A) and, to a lesser extent, sacred

Quetzalcoatl, the mythological Feathered Serpent in his wind god aspect. Virtually every explanation of the similitude between Tula and Chichén Itzá has relied, in one way or another, on Aztec ethnohistorical traditions concerning the chaste priest-king Topiltzin Quetzalcoatl and his tragic exile from the paradisiacal city of Tollan. (Codex Magliabecchiano.)

history (priority II-B). Moreover, I am quite willing to accept the conventional assessment that the builders of "Toltec Chichén" patterned their formal representations of Quetzalcoatl (or Kukulcán, as the deity came to be known in Yucatán) directly after those in Tula Grande. Yet, if we concentrate especially on the most glamorous architectonic manifestations of the famous Plumed Snake — namely, the serpent columns — (and on the ceremonial occasions in which those snake columns were presumably featured), we are forced to reject the familiar presumption that a consistent conception of Quetzalcoatl made its way from Central

Mexico to Yucatán. To the contrary, I would maintain that, at Chichén Itzá, the imagery of the Feathered Serpent came to play a synthesizing, unifying role that, so it would seem, had never occurred to the Tula Toltecs.

Historian of religions Davíd Carrasco's provocative work on the symbolism of Quetzalcoatl in a whole series of "other Tollans" — that is, pre-Columbian ceremonial cities that patterned and legitimated themselves with respect to the mythic urban paradigm of Tollan (Tula and Chichén Itzá among them) — contributes both a problem and an important clue to the Feathered Serpent's synthesizing role in the ritual-architectural events of "Toltec Chichén."[342] On the one hand, Carrasco considers that, in Chichén Itzá as elsewhere in ancient Mesoamerica, Quetzalcoatl (or Kukulcán) stood for a "cosmological conception of sovereignty," that is, a kind of paradigmatic, thoroughly respectable religio-political leadership. Moreover, echoing the interpretation of Carlos Margain, Carrasco holds that "the Quetzalcoatl/Kukulcán Temple ['Toltec Chichén's' Castillo] was the supernatural source for the legitimation of military activity and the institutions of warfare."[343] These fairly general interpretive remarks on the Feathered Serpent's role at "Toltec Chichén," while not wholly inappropriate with respect to the Yucatán capital, might apply equally (or actually better) to the manifestations of Quetzalcoatl in the more martially minded ceremonial precincts of Tula and Tenochtitlán. In other words, while the Maya builders of La Gran Nivelación did have much in common with the Toltecs, and probably even more with the Aztecs, any intimation that "Toltec Chichén" was a fairly typical Central Mexican city simply relocated into the Maya zone, and that the imagery of Quetzalcoatl played essentially the same role there as in Tula, is, from my view, problematic.

On the other hand, Carrasco's work, albeit somewhat indirectly, provides a very useful clue as to perhaps the most important discrepancy between the respective roles of Quetzalcoatl at "Toltec Chichén" and Tula (or Tenochtitlán). That hint comes, somewhat surprisingly, not in his remarks on any of those cities but, instead, in the context of his nuanced discussion of yet a different "other Tollan," some 200 kilometers directly south of Tula, Hidalgo — namely, Xochicalco.[344] Except perhaps that both sites present equally daunting problems of historical (re)construction, the analogy between Xochicalco and "Toltec Chichén" may, at first, seem strained and unproductive. Xochicalco, one of several major centers that emerged in the chaotic period following Teotihuacán's decline and somewhat before Tula's florescence, lies in a mountainous portion of the present-day state of Morelos, while Chichén Itzá's lowland ambience is table-flat. Neither the individual buildings nor the general layout of Xochicalco bears any obvious formal resemblance to those of North Chichén (though they do share a number of isolated artistic elements, including similarly abundant feathered serpent imagery). No special historical or trading link between these two capitals has been firmly established.[345] In short, though Xochicalco was apparently partially contemporaneous with some rendition of "Toltec Chichén," scholars (including Carrasco) have found little reason to link these two sites.

Nevertheless, as Carrasco's analysis at least insinuates, there are very important morphological affinities. Xochicalco was perhaps the only center in Mesoamerica whose architecture could challenge La Gran Nivelación's claim to have been the most cosmopolitan of all pre-Columbian centers. Moreover — and this is where the analogy becomes particularly helpful for the present argument — if we compare the various "other Tollans" in terms of

Head at the base of a serpent column at the entrance to the Upper Temple of the Jaguars. Serpent columns and balustrades of varying shapes and sizes, usually in symmetrical pairs, are abundant throughout North Chichén Itzá. (Carnegie Institution of Washington photo, courtesy of the Peabody Museum, Harvard University.)

ritual-architectural events (rather than in terms of their formal appearances), it would appear that, of all the possibilities, Xochicalco provides the most illuminating parallel with respect to the way in which the imagery of flying snakes was appropriated and ingeniously incorporated into the ritual-architectural agenda of "Toltec Chichén." In fact, Carrasco's interpretive analysis suggests (though he never makes this claim explicit) that, by virtue of its highly eclectic nature and its dexterous manipulation of the Feathered Serpent imagery, it is Xochicalco (not Tenochtitlán or even Tula) that provides the closest Central Mexican counterpart to "Toltec Chichén." In both these cosmopolitan capitals, at least according to my hermeneutical reading, the Feathered Serpent came to work as a force for the unification of disparate, and probably somewhat antagonistic, peoples, religious traditions, and political interests.

Xochicalco was, like North Chichén, a site of intersecting and blended styles and concerns. It was, in Carrasco's estimate, "the peripheral capital of central Mesoamerica . . . a city of transition and eclectic creativity on the edge of two major cultural areas . . . a corridor for the movement of goods and ideas into and from the highlands."[346] Emphasizing Xochicalco's eclectic oeuvre, Carrasco hypothesizes that

> a mediation of foreign influences took place here. Various combinations of iconographic styles display a new level of integration of lowland and highland traditions. Contact and utilization of foreign designs by Xochicalco artisans is evident as Mayan, Teotihuacáno, Zapotec, Toltec, and Nahuan forms are woven together on stelae and temples. Such a reception and re-expression of different forms indicates the cosmopolitan and transitional nature of the city.[347]

Moreover, Carrasco considers that Xochicalco's so-called Temple of Quetzalcoatl (not unlike the Castillo at "Toltec Chichén") became the pivot and defining metaphor of the entire terraced complex by collecting iconographic elements from all of these areas and then, in a vividly literal fashion, lacing those elements together with the sinewy, undulating bodies of feathered serpents. In his words:

> just as Xochicalco makes some claim as a "peripheral capital" to have woven together historical periods and cultural traditions, so Quetzalcoatl's image on this temple supports and weaves together the *axis mundi* of this hilltop place, uniting not only the ceremonial precinct but also the emblems and symbols of other urban traditions. A kind of urban and spatial mediation is implied.[348]

Thus, where Carrasco (like most interpreters) tends to compare the Quetzalcoatl imagery of "Toltec Chichén" most directly with the artistic manifestations of the Plumed Serpent at Tula and Tenochtitlán, he actually provides a far stronger counterpart for the Maya appropriation of Quetzalcoatl in his astute analysis of Xochicalco. Again the architectonic forms deceive: the almost mirror-like formal similitude between the images of Quetzalcoatl at "Toltec Chichén" and those of Tula Grande notwithstanding, at the City of the Sacred Well, those snaky images were *not* primarily symbols of stately or even religious authority. Rather, I contend that the ubiquitous stone feathered serpents of North Chichén Itzá, like the slithering sutures in the iconography of Xochicalco's Temple of Quetzalcoatl, were principally binding elements in a self-conscious program of synthesis. In short, this religio-artistic essay at interweaving the heterogeneous (but preponderantly Maya) interests that had brought "Toltec Chichén" into being, a ritual-architectural agenda that was far more reminiscent of Xochicalco's than of the dauntingly militaristic ceremony of either the Tula Toltecs or the Aztecs, was the raison d'être of the Feathered Serpent in "Toltec Chichén."

Moreover, "Toltec Chichén's" pattern of serpentine synthesis is nowhere more evident than in the marvelously distinctive serpent columns. The quintessential expression of the Feathered Serpent in architecture, these columns (for instance, on the Temple of the Warriors) seem to capture the plumed, airborne snake in a downward flight from the sky, freezing him so that he appears to hang from the lintel by his tail while standing on his head.[349] The tail-waving serpent columns, which together with the highly distinctive *chacmools* have always been the loudest signals to some sort of special connection between Tula and Chichén Itzá, invariably appear as identical pairs that frame the entranceway to a major building.[350] Though limited almost exclusively to these two sites, the serpent column doorways, beginning with Sahagún's raves on the abundant snake portals at Tula, have always been prominent in the literature. Of some ten pairs that survive in North Chichén, besides the preeminent instance at the Temple of the Warriors, the Castillo, the Temple of the Jaguars, and the Osario (or the so-called High Priest's Grave) are also graced with especially magnificent examples.[351]

Temple of Quetzalcoatl at Xochicalco. Situated in the interjacent region between Highland and Lowland Mesoamerica, Xochicalco was, according to Davíd Carrasco, a transitional and highly eclectic capital city that integrated elements from both areas. At Xochicalco, as in North Chichén Itzá, the imagery of feathered snakes seems to have served to lace together iconographic and architectural elements borrowed from several Maya and Central Mexican regional styles. (Photos by Lawrence G. Desmond.)

Serpent columns at the entryway to the Warriors Building. Several pairs of these downflying sculpted snakes, which provide the quintessential architectonic expressions of Quetzalcoatl, the Feathered Serpent, remain intact in North Chichén. (Carnegie Institution of Washington photo, courtesy of Peabody Museum, Harvard University.)

There are, of course, countless creative interpretations of this seemingly paradoxical symbolic juxtaposition of the capability of flight with ground-hugging snakes. It is, however, George Kubler who provides the most provocative interpretation of these architectonic snake entrances as symbols of religio-political integration. Beginning with a vehement rejection of the stock designation of all the various "Toltec Chichén" serpent column buildings as "temples," Kubler insists instead on the strictly governmental function of these structures.[352] These buildings were, in his assessment, the "council chambers" of the "Toltec-Maya" government and, as such, participated in explicitly integrative architectural events of two sorts: as forums for closed council meetings inside (that is, the making of policy) and as focal points in more public, outdoor displays of authority (that is, the dissemination of policy).[353]

First, according to Kubler's intriguingly iconoclastic reading, the interior events or "council meetings" focused on the stone tables (variously termed "god-tables," "altar tables," or "atlantean platforms"), which are still found in several of "Toltec Chichén's" serpent column buildings.[354] Each of these platform tables is supported by a number of small stone men or "atlantean" figures (about 2.5 feet high), which are nearly identical to those found at Tula. All of them are basically the same, though each has somewhat individuated features and costumes. Kubler argues that these idiosyncratic platform bearers did not represent specific historical rulers; nor were they "Toltec" warriors (as, for instance, Tozzer had argued); and he is even more insistent that they were not conceived as deities or supernaturals. Instead, Kubler believes that the humanoid supports denoted "types of officers" or, perhaps, respective districts, towns, or lineages from the wide area under the control of the Yucatán capital. Moreover, he contends that the arrangement of the stone figures reflects a fastidious protocol of "seating according to rank," which was designed to showcase the relative strengths and weaknesses of the assembled council delegates. Furthermore, in perhaps the most risky portion of his hypothesis, Kubler makes the revolutionary suggestion that the assemblage of individuated atlantean statues under a single tabletop was intended as the architectonic metaphor for a "more humane," representative, almost democratic form of government that the "Toltecs" — perennially stereotyped as the arch-bullies of the pre-Hispanic world — had instituted in place of the earlier, more brutally totalitarian Maya polity.[355] In his own words, "[the art of North Chichén] may record the advent of a more humane polity than that of earlier Maya history . . . [and] these atlantean figures may portray *batabs* (agents) as representatives of the territorial rulers in Toltec-Maya government, who were appointed from among native Maya families."[356] Thus, the architectural events *inside* the serpent column buildings, at least in Kubler's vision, entailed sociopolitical integrations of the most deliberate sort, with representatives of several peripheral localities gathered at the shared center for the orchestration of a policy of common interest.

The other sort of "Toltec Chichén" serpent column events, the more public, *outside* events, which involved both vastly greater audiences and a more direct view of the sculpted snakes at the entryways, according to Kubler, had equally explicit integrative intentions. Emphasizing the prominent visibility and multiplication of the serpent columns in the plaza of the Castillo — several pairs of the flying snakes would have been grinning down on the crowd simultaneously from every direction — Kubler describes the Quetzalcoatl imagery (after the fashion of Carrasco and Margain) as an unmistakable "display of public authority."[357] Kubler, however, enriches this religio-political interpretation tremendously by recognizing, particularly at the Temple of the Warriors, what amounts to a Xochicalco-like, internationalizing juxtaposition of characteristically Highland Mexican images of authority (that is, the Plumed Serpent) with traditional Lowland Maya images of "the same concept of authority" (particularly *chac* masks). The desired goal of these completely public and highly politicized ceremonials thus was, as he sees it, deliberately integrative. The "Toltec Maya" designers endeavored "to state the same idea as it occurs in highland and lowland imagery."[358]

Once again, even if we accept Kubler's venturesome hypothesis, it is difficult to assess the extent to which the ritual-architectural designers of "Toltec Chichén" succeeded in convincing the heterogeneous audience of the fundamental compatibility of their more particularistic notions of legitimate authority. And, perhaps more importantly, we might object that Kubler's contention that the principal ceremonial initiative of North Chichén was an urge to integrate Highland and Lowland conceptions of rulership (though appropriately crediting indigenous Maya rather than invading Toltecs with the formative conception of the plaza) is simply a new and especially ingenious permutation of the insidious old paradigm of Maya-Mexican polarity (a version that leans in the

Atlantean altar inside the Temple of the Warriors. George Kubler argues, contrary to conventional interpretations, that these stone men, which have nearly identical counterparts at Tula, represent neither deities nor Toltec warriors. Instead, he hypothesizes that the humanoid supports denote "types of officers" or governmental agents, which served as representatives of the respective districts or towns that had come under the control of Chichén Itzá by the time this structure was completed. (Carnegie Institution of Washington photo, courtesy of Peabody Museum, Harvard University.)

direction of Eric Thompson's notion of symbiotic polarity rather than Tozzer's irreconcilable polarity).[359] Kubler's basic argument is, nonetheless, made more persuasive by several additional factors. First, he sees this urge toward the integration of respective Maya and Mexican themes manifested not only in the famous serpent columns and atlantean figures, but, moreover, in other media as well. He contends, for instance, that the same motive was at work in the relief sculpture on the Warriors Building, where recumbent human figures bearing staffs of rulership, a familiar element of the sculptural tradition of Maya royalty, were positioned immediately adjacent to carvings of eagles and jaguars that might have been plucked directly from the walls of Tula Grande. He describes this facade as, in other words, a deliberately eclectic configuration that instantiates (from the perspective of the Yucatán Maya) just the sort of productive juxtaposition of familiar and novel elements that is required to initiate a ritual-architectural event. And, regarding the content of such an event, as Kubler concludes, "this union of [Maya] human and [Mexican] animal figures also seems to state an ancient need to combine highland and lowland conceptions of rulership."[360]

Furthermore (and more directly relevant to the role of Quetzalcoatl/Kukulcán), while he concentrates on artistic expression of governmental authority (politics, priority II-C), Kubler's analysis likewise demonstrates that this self-conscious program of interweaving transcended the realm of strictly civic authority to foster more explicitly religious and mythological syntheses as well (thus, at that point, instantiating the commemoration of divinity and sacred history, priorities II-A and II-B). For instance, by adding horns to the head of the Feathered Serpent sculptures at the Warriors Building, one of the latest and most integrative structures, the architects of "Toltec Chichén," according to Kubler, depicted the imported Mexican figure of Quetzalcoatl/Kukulcán as subsuming (or embracing) rather than antagonizing the Maya's own horned lizard or iguana deity, Itzamná. In short, "the horned serpent-column heads at the Warriors [Building] convey the ideas of equivalent Kukulcán and Itzamná deities."[361] And, opposite the Warriors Temple, at the other end of the plaza of the Castillo, the Upper Jaguars Building likewise has a serpent column doorway, above which, employing a somewhat more prosaic integrative strategy, the North Chichén designers reproduced Puuc Maya-style spindles, Teotihuacán-style roundels, and other borrowed elements, all of which were framed and laced together by undulating serpents. Thus, despite lacking the bite and subtlety of tightly juxtaposed Maya and Mexican sculpted versions of the same theme that we see on the serpent columns, this self-conscious assemblage of far-flung images on the single facade of the Jaguar Building provides the closest Chichén parallel to Xochicalco's deliberately cosmopolitan Temple of Quetzalcoatl. This highly eclectic facade features, to use Kubler's phrasing, "a design bringing together elements of separate origin under the dominant theme of the undulant serpent bodies."[362]

By expanding on Carrasco's and Kubler's atypically "eventful" interpretations of the feathered serpent imagery at "Toltec" Chichén Itzá and elsewhere, we expose many "religiously significant" differences and few similarities between the respective ritual-architectural agenda of North Chichén and of Tula, Hidalgo. Reassessed in this fashion, the sculptural evidence, like the mural evidence, completely undermines any confidence that "Toltec Chichén" was the artistic expression of totalitarian brutality orchestrated by a band of Quetzalcoatl-led Central Mexicans. To the contrary, where the elaborate wall paintings of a "foundation legend" for the city feature reconciliation rather than intimidation, so too, the figure of Quetzalcoatl/Kukulcán (or of feathered serpents generally) seems to have been less a symbol of bullying conquest, or even of a dominant "Toltec" authority, than the spokesman for accommodation, compromise, and integration of disparate peoples and ideas. Moreover, even if the feathered snakes of "Toltec Chichén" do find their most exact *formal* parallels in Tula Grande, at the more significant level of ritual-architectural events, this Yucatecan agenda of serpentine synthesis finds a considerably stronger Central Mexican counterpart in Xochicalco than in either Tula or Tenochtitlán. Even if we agree with Kubler that this synthesizing agenda was primarily a pragmatic strategy of governmental control (and particularly if we accept his hypothesis that it reflected an unprecedented commitment to "humane democratization"), the substance of "Toltec Chichén's" religio-civic events — the central message — was profoundly different from that of the similarly public events at Tula Grande.

One more set of evidences, and one more daringly iconoclastic hypothesis — involving, in this case, the ambitious synchronization of Maya and Mexican calendars in one grand ritual-architectural Castillo event — reinforce still further my contention that the essential message of "Toltec Chichén's" architectural program was the synthesis of one from many.

Serpent columns at the entryway to the Warriors Building. George Kubler contends that this serpent column portal, and several others like it in North Chichén, served primarily as symbols of political and governmental integration. Kubler considers that the horns on this set of serpent columns reflect a deliberate attempt to synthesize the mythological Mexican figure of Quetzalcoatl with the horned lizard or iguana deity of the Maya, Itzamná. (Photo by William M. Ferguson, courtesy of the University of Texas, Austin.)

New Fire Integration: Toward a Summation

Relying especially on the iconography and hieroglyphic inscriptions, Clemency Coggins's fresh re-reading of the art history of "Toltec" Chichén Itzá largely circumvents the mural evidence and, moreover, casts serious doubt on the stock notion that the notorious serpent columns were intended to represent Quetzalcoatl/ Kukulcán.[363] Nonetheless, she arrives at conclusions parallel to those just presented insofar as she comes to understand Chichén Itzá as a pre-Columbian city that was impressive and distinctive, most of all, by virtue of its deliberately integrative, synthetic character. According to Coggins, in the wake of the "collapses" of Classic-period civilizations in both the Maya and Mexican areas, these two great strains joined forces and "deliberately conceived and founded ['Toltec Chichén'] as a cultural amalgam."[364]

Coggins's daring hypothesis, the latest and most provocative attempt to explain "Toltec Chichén" in terms of a "symbiotic Maya-Mexican polarity," will likely serve as the catalyst for a whole new round of debates about Chichén Itzá that is only just beginning.[365] Though presumably there was a preponderantly Yucatán Maya settlement at the site of the Sacred Cenote in the mid-Classic period, the pre-Hispanic events that are most important for Coggins's hypothesis began in the Late Classic era of Teotihuacán's decline. It is at that point, according to her reading of the evidence, that Mexicanized or "Toltec" groups (by which she means "all those peoples, whether superficially Mexican or Maya, who traced their ancestry and cultural traditions to Teotihuacán")[366] began to take a special interest in the site.[367] Pushing back the traditional date for the construction of the outer Castillo by more than a century,[368] Coggins pinpoints the "founding" of Chichén Itzá and the formal dedication of its central pyramid — the ritual inauguration of the site's ascendancy as a "Toltec" capital — in a spectacular New Fire Ceremony, which took place one March midnight in 830 C.E. This, according to Coggins, was the year of a remarkable coincidence in which the respective calendars of the Central Mexican and Maya areas closed out major blocks of time; specifically, it was the completion of the tenth Calendar Round of the 52-year Mexican cycle and of the Maya megacycle of nine *baktuns,* or cycles of 400 years.[369]

The completion of any Mesoamerican calendrical cycle was, by all accounts, an eschatological occasion of great anxiety, fear, and dread. Though the pre-Columbian Maya and Mexicans viewed these calendrical endings slightly differently (and operated with somewhat different schedules), they were similarly unconfident that the creation of another "new time" could be accepted as a foregone conclusion.[370] The simultaneous endings of these Mexican 52-year and Maya 400-year calendar rounds was, thus, timorously and additively cataclysmic. According to Coggins's hypothesis, however, via one marvelous feat of ritual preclusion, one spectacular ritual-architectural Castillo event — that is, the New Fire Ceremony of 830 C.E. at Chichén Itzá — the dire consequences of coetaneous Maya and Mexican age-endings were averted and the new synthetic "Toltec" capital of Yucatán was ushered into existence. To the extent that the ingenious ritual-architectural strategy succeeded, as Coggins apparently thinks it did, "there must have been great relief and jubilation over the continuation of the world, of time and of the usual ceremonial cycle after the end of the tenth *baktun.*"[371] Fear of the end was transformed into a new beginning. Calendars and cultures were unified and an era of "Toltec-Maya" Chichén hegemony initiated.

In addition to her careful iconographic and glyphic analyses, Coggins crafts this intriguing (re)construction scenario of calendrical-cultural

Aerial view of Chichén Itzá taken from a plane flown by Charles A. Lindbergh (probably in 1927). According to the novel hypothesis of Clemency Coggins, "Chichén Itzá was deliberately conceived as a cultural amalgam [that] served Mexican and Maya alike after the collapse of the two Classic period civilizations." She pinpoints the dedication of the great Castillo pyramid in a spectacularly integrative New Fire Ceremony, which was designed to mitigate the dire consequences of the simultaneous cyclic completion dates in both Maya and Mexican calendars. (Carnegie Institution of Washington photo, courtesy of the Peabody Museum, Harvard University.)

synthesis primarily on the basis of three lines of evidence. First, she analyzes the various astro-calendrical traditions of the Maya and Mexicans, which, while rich in idiosyncratic particulars, are all indebted to the cosmogonic pattern of cyclical creations and destructions; as she notes, all pre-Columbian Mesoamericans participated in the anticipatory terror that the present age could well be the last.[372] Second are the rich documentary, ethnohistorical records of Mesoamerican age-ending ceremonies, particularly Sahagún's detailed description of the Aztec New Fire Ceremony. According to this famous account, at the dreaded completion of each fifty two-year Calendar Round, the Aztecs embarked on an intricate series of ritual events that included completely extinguishing all fires in Tenochtitlán, then lighting or "drilling" a new fire literally in the chest of a human sacrificial victim, and then, subsequently, distributing that new fire throughout the darkened city until the entire Aztec metropolis had been relit from this single flame of renewal.[373] The third main sort of evidence on which Coggins relies is the material, archaeological remains of ritual accoutrements. Particularly important in this regard is her novel hypothesis that the distinctive *chacmool* statues, which are uniquely prevalent at Tula and Chichén Itzá, were intimately related to the same sort of New Fire Ceremonialism about which we learn in Sahagún's famous description.

This linkage of *chacmools* and New Fire Ceremonialism provides a new slant on a time-worn problem. These awkwardly postured humanoid *chacmool* figures, which traditionally were among the seemingly definitive signs of the "Toltecization" of Yucatán, have been interpreted as everything from the representations of kings, to divine messengers, to gods of drunkenness, to emblematic captives.[374] Coggins's highly original discussion, however, explains the peculiar recumbent posture of the *chacmools* and the dish-like object that each holds over its ribs by the fact that, in many cases, the "new fire" was drilled not literally inside the chest of a human sacrificial victim but, instead, upon a pyrite disk or "mirror" that was held over the chest of a captive warrior, or, in other cases, the chest of a stone *chacmool*. In other words, according to Coggins, the *chacmools* of Tula, "Toltec Chichén," and elsewhere (the Castillo, the Temple of the Warriors, the Chac Mool Temple, the Temple of the Little Tables, and the North Colonnade all have prominently sited *chacmools*[375]) represent "the noble captive warrior whose chest, or really epigastrium, served as a base for drilling the new fire at midnight."[376] Moreover, while Coggins considers that "it is likely that the Chac Mool form was created at Chichén Itzá since the most naturalistic ones are there,"[377] she traces the whole complex of pyrite mirrors and New Fire Ceremonialism to its original elaboration among the cult of the Pleiades in Teotihuacán.[378] But then, in a particularly convincing portion of her argument, she marshals evidence of the sweeping distribution of New Fire Ceremonialism at both Central Mexican and Maya sites — especially at Chichén Itzá, where, besides the unsurpassed number of *chacmools*, pyrite mirrors are prominent in the iconographic regalia of "Toltec" warriors and were found cached in several key buildings. New Fire Ceremonialism was, in other words, while taking a somewhat idiosyncratic form at the City of the Sacred Cenote, familiar to virtually all ancient Mesoamericans.

With this as background, Coggins describes a post-Teotihuacán, pan-Mesoamerican atmosphere of converging and multiplying anxieties as the ninth Maya *baktun* and the tenth Mexican Calendar Round tapered toward the same end point in 830 C.E. The tension, which was packed tighter still by the anticipation of several other cyclical celestial phenomena, could, according to Coggins's reading of the pre-Columbian mentality, be alleviated only by the staging of a spectacular, cooperative Maya-Mexican New Fire Ceremony.[379] Chichén Itzá, by its emplacement between the two political spheres, at a latitude affording astronomical viewing similar to that of Teotihuacán, and particularly because of its uncannily round and still body of water that was to serve as a "cosmic 'scrying' or divining vessel" — namely, the Sacred Cenote — was chosen as the most propitious site for this momentous and deliberately synthetic cycle-ending ritual.[380]

Continuing the saga of this remarkable ritual-architectural stratagem against world destruction, Coggins holds that the outer version of the Castillo was built specifically for this ceremonial occasion, that is, as a radially symmetrical "completion symbol" to commemorate the simultaneous endings of the Maya and

Reclining *chacmool* at the entrance to the Temple of the Warriors. According to Clemency Coggins, the *chacmool* statues in North Chichén, along with associated serpent columns and pyrite mirrors, probably belonged to a complex of New Fire Ceremonialism. She suggests that these *chacmools* may have served doubly in that ritual context, first as loci for drilling the new fire, and then as personifications of (or supports for) the actual heart sacrifices of human victims. (Photo by Lawrence G. Desmond.)

Mexican courts. The new pyramid was designed, according to Coggins, to provide an architectural context and support for the synergistic New Fire Ceremony that would, in one masterful stroke, vault the participants into the viridity of a new age and, not incidentally, inaugurate the new cosmopolitan capital of "Toltec" Chichén Itzá. In her own words, this spectacular ceremony of Castillo dedication in 830 C.E. "would have been an integrative event that would serve to unite all those of Toltec [by which she means Teotihuacánoid] affiliation and ancestry, including numerous Maya royal lineages, from throughout Southern Mesoamerica."[381] Furthermore, shifting at this point into a more emic mode of interpretation, Coggins is, it seems, quite confident that the grand ritual-architectural maneuver "worked." She writes: "When the New Fire was successfully rekindled at midnight [on the steps of the newly reconstructed Castillo] they ensured that the new cycle would follow, and that the New Sun would emerge from the nadir to which it had descended just as the Pleiades reached their nocturnal zenith and signaled the moment of fire-drilling."[382]

Coggins's wonderfully creative hypothesis, certain to enliven the discussion of "Toltec

The Sacred Cenote at Chichén Itzá. According to Clemency Coggins's intriguing hypothesis, the uncannily round shape and still water of the famous well made it an ideal "cosmic 'scrying,' or divining, vessel." She suggests that Chichén Itzá was selected as the site for a momentous and deliberately integrative Maya-Mexican New Fire Ceremony both because of its medial location and because of the uniquely appealing attributes of the Sacred Cenote. (Carnegie Institution of Washington photo, courtesy of the Peabody Museum, Harvard University.)

Chichén" for some years, is equally tantalizing and problematic. With respect to the old paradigm of Maya-Mexican polarity, her scenario, for all its innovation, has the suspiciously familiar ring of Eric Thompson's nimble (re)constructions of bi-ethnic, symbiotic complementarity.[383] To her credit, however, Coggins is not prey to the simplistic stereotypes of bullying Toltecs and benign Maya and, instead, implies a fairly equal partnership in "Toltec Chichén" (even if the primary impetus for the New Fire Ceremony did come from Central Mexican Teotihuacán). In her story, Maya and Mexican peoples shared in a common dilemma, namely, dread in anticipation of the impending endings of calendrical cycles and, thus, mounted a collaborative, mutually beneficial response. She provides, in other words, a picture of a largely unified and fully interactive ancient Mesoamerica rather than the old bow-tie-shaped model of largely disconnected Maya and Mexican regions. In fact, so similar are the concerns of all ancient Mesoamericans in this view that, if Chichén New Fire Ceremonialism was a genuine amalgam of Mexican and Maya interests, it is difficult to see the important respects in which it differs from the strictly Central Mexican version of the ceremony celebrated at Teotihuacán from which the basic analogy was drawn.[384]

With respect more specifically to the especial correspondence between the architectures of North Chichén and Tula Grande (a problem that Coggins addresses only indirectly), her (re)construction scenario depends heavily upon the reinterpretation of one of the banner indicators of the two cities' relatedness — that is, the *chacmool*. Even so, Coggins deprives Tula (and the historical Tula Toltecs) of any special prestige in relation to Chichén Itzá by: (1) finding only marginal evidence of New Fire Ceremonialism at Tula, Hidalgo; (2) virtually equating the "Toltec" dimension of Chichén Itzá with Teotihuacán (where, by the way, no *chacmools* have yet been found); and (3) thus, moving the crucial events at Chichén Itzá so far forward in time that it would have been impossible for the historical Toltecs of Tula to have played any important role whatever in the construction or formulation of the ritual-architectural plan of "Toltec Chichén."[385] Likewise, in regard to the historical issues, by moving the "founding" of "Toltec Chichén" right into the immediate wake of Teotihuacán's collapse, her interpretation seems to be riskily (though perhaps accurately) predicated on the total chronological overlap and single-minded unity of the southern and northern portions of Chichén Itzá. She declines to participate at all in the conventional notion that South and North Chichén correspond to an "Old" and "New Chichén" and, instead, launches an interpretation that draws equally on all sectors of the city. For instance, she takes most of her calendrical dates from the South Chichén inscriptions;[386] she suggests that "Kakupacal," subject of many of those inscriptions, rather than being a proper name, might denote a fire-drilling priestly role or title that could be translated as "Fire-His-Mirror;"[387] and, at times, she even implies the unlikely prospect that "Toltec Chichén" was actually built prior to (at least parts of) South Chichén.[388] Finally, in a more general vein, though perhaps most disturbingly, the whole amazing orchestration of cooperative synthesis in Mesoamerica's perilous hour of transition and fragmentation, "not long" after the collapse of Teotihuacán and the decline of the southern Maya cities, seems somehow to require an omniscient conductor who never appears.

On the other hand, Coggins's seemingly too-perfect-to-believe scenario of calendrical cooperation gains considerable plausibility in light of the version of pre-Columbian Yucatecan events that emerges from Munro Edmonson's (re)interpretation of *The Book of the Chilam Balam of Tizimin*.[389] *The Books of Chilam Balam,* which focus especially on the contestation between two native groups, had been foundational in Morley's, Tozzer's, and Thompson's enduring (re)constructions of the "Toltec Conquest" of Maya Chichén Itzá and of the subsequent "Mexicanization" of Yucatán.[390] These scholars, despite differing on the details, were in nearly unanimous agreement that the two principal native groups featured in these Maya texts were indigenous Yucatán Maya (who appeared to have authored these stories) and invading Central Mexicans, probably Toltecs. The version of the model of "irreconcilable polarity" espoused by scholars during the Carnegie Institution era, in fact, depended much more heavily on their readings of these quasihistorical colonial-period documents (particularly the *Chilam Balam of Chumayel*) than on any archaeological discovery. Edmonson's fresh and drastically different reading of the poetic Tizimin book, however, assesses both the native protagonists and antagonists as essentially Yucatán Maya — a major change to be sure. Yet, despite eliminating actual Central Mexicans from the pre-Hispanic drama,

Edmonson's (re)interpretation nonetheless reveals a Postclassic (or Terminal Classic) Yucatán ambience that was dominated, at least in the broad strokes, by the ongoing hostilities and then — after the fashion of Coggins's hypothesis of Maya-Mexican integration — the eventual accommodation between two peoples and two calendars. The eventual reconciliation in this case was, however, between two sets of Yucatán Maya contestants, which Edmonson identifies as the "Itzá" and the "Toltec Xiu."

For all its novelty, Edmonson's (re)construction provides, among other things, yet another much more detailed storiological explanation of "Toltec" Chichén Itzá as the product of a symbiotic Maya-Mexican polarity (or, actually, in this case, a symbiosis between largely non-Mexicanized Yucatán Maya and heavily Mexicanized Yucatán Maya). The first pre-Columbian party, the Itzá or, as he terms them, "Water Witches" (presumably the more strictly "Maya" component), was composed of a group of elite lineages who dominated the eastern half of the Yucatán Peninsula after the Classic period and who, like the Classic Maya, timed their important ceremonials with respect to *katun* transitions every 20 *tuns* (a *tun* is 360 days). The other major set of Yucatecan actors, the "Toltec Xiu," belonged to a similarly elite but considerably more "Mexicanized" group of Maya lineages who dominated western Yucatán and claimed an ancestral seat at "Tula" (that is, Tollan) itself.[391] Accordingly, Edmonson's "Toltec Xiu" (who, though ethnically Maya, would qualify as "Toltecs" by Coggins's embracing definition) adhered to a more typically Central Mexican cycle of 52-year Calendar Rounds that moved in and out of sync with the Itzá's characteristically Maya emphasis on *tun* and *katun* calendrical rituals.[392]

Moreover, Edmonson's (re)interpretation of *The Chilam Balam of Tizimin* demonstrates that the Itzá and Xiu fought over nothing so hard as the appropriate scheduling and location of the periodic "seating of the cycle," that is, the rotational ceremonial designation of a particular Yucatán center as the "cycle seat." To be designated as the seat of the cycle conferred on that city dynastic and religious primacy over the whole region for a period of 260 *tuns* (approximately 256 years), at the end of which "the primate city and its roads and idols were ritually destroyed, and a new cycle seat was established."[393] Given the dire urgency and apparently strict fidelity afforded this time-factored rotation of authority — it really does seem to have been *the* controlling fact in Terminal Classic and Postclassic Yucatán religion and polity — the possibility that the massive undertaking of rebuilding the huge Castillo and its glamorous plaza could have been the spatial, architectural counterpart to this compulsion for right ritual timing becomes imminently more plausible. From this view, then, the Castillo may very well have been, in Coggins's phrase, a "completion symbol," the dedication of which unified (or attempted to unify) calendrically and politically, if not the entirety of highland and lowland Mesoamerica, at least the entire Yucatán Peninsula.

Nevertheless, as a historical explanation for a suddenly ascendant "Toltec" Chichén Itzá, the New Fire hypothesis remains, at least for now, an intriguing unlikelihood, a provocative improbability, but one with important consequences.[394] Coming full circle to Landa's account of the Xul rites, the "rhetorical lens" that began this discussion of the ritual-architectural events of "Toltec Chichén," Coggins mentions, almost in passing, that the original cosmogonic drilling of the New Fire in the Castillo's dedication of 830 C.E. continued in perpetuity at Chichén Itzá in the form of the annual November Castillo festival of *Chic Kaban*, or, in other words, the fall occasion for the descent of the serpent of light and the Xul rites to Quetzalcoatl/Kukulcán.[395] Even toned to something considerably more modest than the prime motive for the initial "founding" of the "Toltec" capital of Chichén Itzá (which is Coggins's bold contention), the drilling of new fire on the Castillo in the rites of Xul each fall — a kind of annual version of the more far-spaced New Fire Ceremony — would have been a ritual-architectural event of great integrative significance. This annual celebration of new fire is, moreover, an event that might serve as an apt focus for summarizing the general pattern and character of the ritual-architectural program of "Toltec Chichén."

Among the most compelling dimensions of Coggins's discussion is her documentation of both the wide breadth and generally consistent logic of Mesoamerican New Fire Ceremonialism. Whether staged in the Central Mexican cities of Teotihuacán, Tula, and Xochicalco; in the Lowland Maya center of Becan; or in the Guatemalan sites of Kaminaljuyú and Zaculeu, the basic cosmological and ceremonial pattern was the same.[396] Whether celebrated in the humble context of the Chol Maya or the resplendent imperial capitals of Tenochtitlán and "Toltec Chichén,"[397] drilling the new fire conjoined a panicked ending and a pregnant beginning. The New Fire Ceremony in all its variations provided a vividly condensed metaphor for the pan-regional cosmogonic tradition of successive creations and destructions, an occasion for joy and relief but, simultaneously, a frightful reminder of the transience of the Mesoamerican human condition.

From the perspective of a hermeneutical historian of religions, it would appear that the choreographers of "Toltec Chichén" ritual tapped down through the particularistic traditions and idiosyncrasies of its city's far-flung constituency and grabbed hold of this root metaphor. They seized upon this piquant and shared anxiety that united Maya and Mexican, Itzá, Xiu, and Toltec, all together under the bond of "Mesoamerican" (to them, simply the bond of "human being"), and then fashioned it into their own characteristically spectacular presentation.[398] In the hands of the ritual-architectural designers of "Toltec Chichén," drilling the new fire at the Castillo thus became integrative not simply in the sense of homologizing and unifying architectural space, calendrical time, celestial phenomena, and sociopolitical organization (though it did all that). At a higher (or perhaps deeper) order of integration, providing the most vividly concentrated utterance of the fundamental message of North Chichén's ritual-architectural program, the New Fire Ceremony united (or attempted to unite) the disparate peoples of Mesoamerica by alerting them to, or reminding them of, their shared and inescapable human quandary. Where the murals of "Toltec Chichén" expressed to the people their mutual participation in the reconciliatory foundation legend of the city — one shared history — and where the sinewy, binding snakes, ubiquitous in the sculpture and iconography of North Chichén, expressed a fundamentally shared (or at least mutually compatible) conception of divinity, "Toltec Chichén's" adaptation of the New Fire Ceremony accentuated the essential continuity between Maya and Mexican cosmogonies and, accordingly, a basic continuity in the most fundamental aspects of human existence.

Invoking every conceivable strategy of allurement, the Castillo stage for the new fire rites of Xul was an old Teotihuacán-style dance platform jacked up to pyramidal monumentality, carved with an encyclopedic docket of astro-calendrical references, and laced with iconographic allusions to the Petén, Puuc, and Oaxacan, as well as the Central Mexican areas. Quetzalcoatl/Kukulcán, who had already been made quadruply present in paired serpent columns at the high temple's door and in giant serpent balustrades along the main stairway, came to life in the late afternoon as a descending beam of light on his way to the ever-beckoning Sacred Cenote. Yet, for all its trappings of fanfare and jubilation — its boisterous celebration of the ecstasy of a new year — the annual version of the New Fire Ceremony on the Castillo was simultaneously a quieting call to unity on the basis of a shared existential predicament, an admission of the less-than-foreverness of their empire and their world. The disparity between the superconfident instigatorial presentation and the nearly obsequious content was alarmingly paradoxical and tragically telling of the Mesoamerican human condition. Tugging, sucking, begging attention, the hollering pomp of "Toltec Chichén" ritual-architectural events, in the end, came forward with a sobering message of humility: we are, for all our differences, equally vulnerable to the turn of the ages. In the end, the designers of "Toltec Chichén" were compelled to admit: we of Chichén Itzá are different, but we are the same.

Notes

1. Thompson, *Rise and Fall of Maya Civilization,* 116–17.

2. Kubler, "Period, Style and Meaning," 22. Kubler is discussing the applicability of Erwin Panofsky's "principle of disjunction" to ancient Mesoamerican art and, particularly, warning against over-exuberant ethnographic analogy. I have alluded to the subtle and important relationship between Kubler's position and my own in regard to discontinuities between artistic forms and meanings at several points, but see especially n. 96 in Chapter 2.

3. For my working hypothesis about the historical relatedness of Tula and Chichén Itzá, see especially the final section of Chapter 1, "The Historical Problem Summarized," and the subsection of this chapter entitled "Chichén as Active Receptor: A Historical Hypothesis." I would emphasize again that solving this *historical* problem is *not* my primary goal.

4. Adolf E. Jensen, *Myth and Cult Among Primitive Peoples,* trans. Marianna Tax Choldin and Wolfgang Weissleder (Chicago: University of Chicago Press, 1963), 185. Jensen distinguishes the "basically affirmative attitude of the archaic cultivators toward the facts of existence" from his own cultural environment, wherein people rely on "a wealth of circumlocutions and euphemisms to avoid having to call a spade by spade."

5. See particularly Chapter 3 of this book on "The Universality of Hermeneutical Reflection."

6. See the Preface of this project for remarks on a small boy's experience in the cathedral of Cuernavaca, Morelos, Mexico.

7. Sahagún, *Florentine Codex,* 166. Attempts to correlate these colonial-period Aztec accounts of the fabulous architecture in the paradisiacal city of Tollan with the specific historical site of Tula, Hidalgo, are discussed momentarily in regard to "The Study of Tula: Five Voices."

8. Davies, *Toltecs Until the Fall of Tula,* 227, 340, 421–22, repeatedly emphasizes the credit due the Toltecs as the first to reconstruct order after a period of cultural collapse, even if they never succeeded in completing the structure. Coe, *Mexico,* 132, discusses the general ambience in which Tula arose and its architecture as a response to the "martial psychology of the age."

9. See Davies, *Toltecs Until the Fall of Tula,* 342, 470.

10. Ibid., 4.

11. See Diehl, *Tula,* 160; and Davies, *Toltecs Until the Fall of Tula,* 400.

12. Davies, ibid., 340–41, discusses the radical disparity in size between the Toltec and Aztec empires.

13. Davies, ibid., discusses "inherent imbalances" in Tula's power structure and particularly emphasizes the lack of commercial predominance. Ibid., 284–85.

14. See Charnay, *Ancient Cities,* chapters 3 and 4. Antonia García Cubas also undertook more modest investigations at Tula in the nineteenth century. See Diehl, *Tula,* 277.

15. Davies, *Toltecs Until the Fall of Tula,* 16 et seq., discusses the main ethnohistorical sources on Tula and the Toltecs. Davies stresses that the written sources deal with the beginning and, especially, the end of Tula, but provide almost no information for the middle period; moreover, those accounts of Tula's time of troubles almost hopelessly contradict one another. Ibid., 415.

16. Lawrence H. Feldman, "Tollan in Hidalgo: Native Accounts of the Central Mexican Tolteca," in

Studies of Ancient Tollan, ed. Diehl, 140, discusses the specific ethnohistorical references to the structure of Tollan (which he equates with Tula, Hidalgo). The most extended account is Sahagún's description of the "houses of Quetzalcoatl," quoted as an epigraph to this section.

17. Feldman, "Tollan in Hidalgo," 141–42, considers that these Aztec accounts of the Toltec buildings correspond literally to the site of Tula and, thus (albeit unconvincingly), attempts to plot the relative spatial position of the various structures from these verbal descriptions. Davies, *Toltecs Until the Fall of Tula,* 49–50, presents the interesting possibility that the so-called houses in Sahagún's account of Tollan could actually have been miniature size, resembling portable altars, and that "the place of worship of their priests" to which Sahagún alludes actually refers to rites in front of these altars rather than inside such structures.

18. Jiménez Moreno, "Tula y Toltecas según Fuentes Históricas." Davies, *Toltecs Until the Fall of Tula,* 40–41, has a concise summary of Jiménez Moreno's approach, particularly his reliance on place-names.

19. See Kirchhoff, "Quetzalcoatl, Huemac y el fin de Tula."

20. See Davies, *Toltecs Until the Fall of Tula;* and idem, *Toltec Heritage.*

21. It is worth noting in regard to the hermeneutics of suspicion and the (re)construction of Tula's most famous building — variously known as Pyramid B, the Temple of Quetzalcoatl, the Temple of Tlahuizcalpantecuhtli, the Temple of the Moon, and the Building of Atlanteans (that is, the structure that bears a close resemblance to the Temple of the Warriors at "Toltec" Chichén Itzá) — that Kubler, "Serpent and Atlantean Columns," 114, mentions in passing that "the present reconstruction of the building on Mound B probably follows the model of the Warriors building at Chichén more than any archaeological evidence at Tula."

22. The goals and methods of the "new archaeology," to which both Matos and Diehl adhere, were discussed in Chapter 2.

23. Diehl's volume, *Tula: The Toltec Capital of Ancient Mexico* (1983), synthesizes the results of the decade-long University of Missouri–Columbia Tula Archaeological Project; he explicates the UMC project's new archaeological style goals at 29–40.

24. Matos, *Proyecto Tula,* 1: 8, explicates the patently "new archaeological" goals of the INAH project at Tula with reference to "laws," "processes," "scientific method," and allusions to Gordon Childe, Willey and Phillips, and Julian Stewart. His introduction to the second volume of *Proyecto Tula* repeats many of the same ideas, and in the latest official tourist guide to Tula (1986), Matos once again campaigns for an appreciation of cultural processes and the nonelite areas of Tula; the contrast to the earlier INAH guide, written by Acosta, is telling of the major shift in orientation.

25. Matos, *Proyecto Tula,* 1: 12, defines the terms "micro area" and "macro area."

26. The Kubler-Ruz debate was discussed in Chapter 1 in regard to "Irreconcilable Polarity: Toltecs Versus Maya."

27. See, for example, Charnay, *Ancient Cities,* 107–8.

28. Séjourné, *Burning Water,* 83–84.

29. Weaver, *Aztecs, Maya, and Their Predecessors,* 212.

30. Bushnell, *Ancient Arts of the Americas,* 50–53.

31. Fernández, *A Guide to Mexican Art,* 17.

32. Coe, *Maya,* 141–42.

33. Waters, *Mexico Mystique,* 65, 80.

34. Thompson, *Rise and Fall of Maya Civilization,* 111, 114, 205.

35. Acosta, quoted by Diehl, *Tula,* 67.

36. Ibid., 67.

37. Davies, *Toltecs Until the Fall of Tula,* 213.

38. Covarrubias, *Indian Art of Mexico and Central America,* 273. Margain, "Pre-Columbian Architecture of Central Mexico," 76; Hester, *Introduction to Archaeology,* 408; and Terrance L. Stocker, "A Small Temple in the Tula Residential Zone," in *Studies in Ancient Tollan,* ed. Diehl, 29, are among the legion who follow Covarrubias's assessment of Tula architecture.

39. Fernández, *A Guide to Mexican Art,* 29, for instance, concludes that, even if Tula art and architecture are poor, they are "original in almost all aspects."

40. Robertson, *Pre-Columbian Architecture,* 38–39.

41. This fairly standard list of Tula innovations is repeated, for instance, by Weaver, *Aztecs, Maya, and Their Predecessors,* 202–13; von Hagen, *Aztec: Man and Tribe,* 142; and Diehl, *Tula,* 141.

42. Davies, *Toltecs Until the Fall of Tula,* 129.

43. Jorge Acosta, "Interpretación de algunos datos obtenidos en Tula relativos a la época Tolteca," *Revista Mexicana de Estudios Antropológicos* 14:2 (1956–57): 75–110.

44. Davies, *Toltecs Until the Fall of Tula,* 275, uses the expression "Golden Century of Tollan" in reference to the 1000–1100 C.E. florescence at Tula.

45. See Matos, "Tula Chronology: A Revision." This is largely a translation of his article in *Proyecto Tula,* ed. Matos, 1: 61–70, entitled "Excavaciones en la microárea: Tula Chico y la Plaza Charnay."

46. See Matos, "Tula Chronology: A Revision." The INAH and UMC Tula projects also extended Tula's chronology in the other direction by demonstrating significant habitation *after* its so-called collapse and a very prestigious role in the Aztec era.

47. Ibid., 177. Diehl, *Tula,* now believes that Tula was a minor village in Teotihuacán times.

48. This is the population estimate of the INAH study; Diehl, *Tula,* 43, would prefer to lower it by 40 or 50 percent.

49. Ibid., 58–60.

50. Matos, *Proyecto Tula,* 1: 62; there are actually three ball courts in Tula Chico.

51. Diehl, *Tula,* 43–45, summarizes the very close similarities between Tula Chico and Tula Grande without making reference to any significant differences.

52. Diehl, ibid., 43, 45, mentions the possibility that structures contemporaneous with Tula Chico may exist beneath the later Tula Grande building, but he does not pursue the idea.

53. Diehl, *Tula,* 290; and idem, *Tula,* 45–46, goes so far as to suggest, albeit unconvincingly, that the famed saga of Quetzalcoatl's demise at the hands of Tezcatlipoca may be a reference to the abandonment of Tula Chico in favor of Tula Grande.

54. Diehl, ibid., 45, continuing his speculation that the abandonment of Tula Chico could be representative of the suppression of a Quetzalcoatl faction by a Tezcatlipoca faction, suggests that the area was left unoccupied as a "visual warning to other political dissidents." Such a scenario is, at best, highly unlikely, especially given the predominance of Quetzalcoatl in Tula Grande.

55. I am not aware of anyone who has written specifically on the ramifications of the Tula Chico excavations for the Tula–Chichén Itzá issue. While these are archaeological-historical problems that lie somewhat outside the scope of this project and its largely nonhistorical, hermeneutical method, it would seem to me that with respect specifically to the Tula–Chichén Itzá problem (which has always been sustained by parallels between Tula Grande and "Toltec" Chichén Itzá) the greatest significance of the discovery of this anterior ceremonial precinct at Tula is the probability that the major elements that Tula and Chichén Itzá hold in common were present in Tula Chico, that is, more than a hundred years earlier than their manifestation in Tula Grande. In the ceaseless game of who-copied-whom, the revelations about Tula Chico, at the very least, disqualify the possibility of a "reverse" connection (such as Kubler presents), wherein Tula Grande was modeled directly after "Toltec" Chichén Itzá 800 miles to the east, when, instead, it seems fairly certain to be an elaboration of a prototype that is literally a stone's throw away. (The possibility remains that Tula Chico, rather than Tula Grande, was modeled after Chichén Itzá, but the older ceremonial plaza seems to be too early for that to be a viable possibility.) In short (and this seems to be entirely neglected in the literature) the phenomenon of Tula Chico emerges as more evidence for the mainline position that the forms that Tula and Chichén Itzá hold in common originated first as local developments in Central Mexico and then were somehow transferred to Yucatán. (In my opinion, though, contrary to the mainline position, those forms were self-consciously copied by the designers of "Toltec" Chichén Itzá and not carried there by any contingent from Tula.)

56. Davies, *Toltecs Until the Fall of Tula,* is singularly detailed in his treatment of these problems, but, as discussed in Chapter 1, sole reliance on his work is a dangerous practice.

57. Davies, ibid., 141, says, "the existence of two distinct migratory contingents no longer remains in doubt." Elsewhere (ibid., 176), Davies acknowledges a third major ethnic component, the Otomis, which may have been strong enough to give Tula a "tri-ethnic" rather than a "bi-ethnic" blend, but the Otomis are even harder to pin down. Diehl, *Tula,* 43, 48, 149, abstains on the precise times and circumstances of these migrations but insists that they should be viewed as "composite arrivals of countless small groups" rather than as monolithic population shifts.

58. See Davies, *Toltecs Until the Fall of Tula,* 162–63; and Diehl, *Tula,* 48–50, who concurs generally with Davies's assessment of the ethnic composition of Tula.

59. Ibid., 49–50. Diehl mentions precedents to the Toltec colonnaded hall at Alta Vista, Zacatecas, in the north of Mexico.

60. See Davies, *Toltecs Until the Fall of Tula,* 164, 167.

61. Ibid., 50.

62. Ibid., 167, 171. Also see ibid., 50–51. Moreover, Davies believes that the Nonoalca were originally responsible for the Quetzalcoatl cult at Tula. See ibid., 177.

63. Ibid., 177.

64. Ibid., 166.

65. See ibid., 380–90.

66. See ibid., 363–64, 408–9, for Davies's ideas about the respective departures of the Tolteca-Chichimeca and Nonoalca from the declining Tula. In Davies's (re)construction of Tula history, the whole issue of a Toltec diaspora in the final days of Tula is somewhat irrelevant to the Tula–Chichén Itzá problem because, by his reckoning, the important linkage between the two (he defers to Eric Thompson on the details) occurs during Tula's prime rather after its demise.

67. See ibid., 178–79. This generally accepted picture of Tula's career as a prolific synthesis of Tolteca-Chichimeca brawn and Nonoalca brains (which I too am provisionally willing to accept), in its broad strokes, looks suspiciously like the notion of "symbiotic polarity" (discussed in Chapter 1 in reference to "The Mexicanization of Yucatán"), wherein Eric Thompson explains "Toltec" Chichén Itzá as the fruit of fortuitous coalition between the materially well-endowed Putun Maya and the exiled but, nonetheless, prestigious Quetzalcoatl and his band of Tula Toltecs.

68. On the demise of Tula, Davies concludes: "In view of the failing by two ethnic groups to fully merge, times of dire stress would automatically bring old resentments to the fore. . . . In the final analysis, Tollan [that is, Tula] possessed too little unity, too few people and insufficient wealth to withstand the incursions from the north." Ibid., 391–92, 421.

69. By the "old religion" of ancestors and fertility I refer to that more ancient, pan-Mesoamerican stratum of religion that has been discussed by Johanna Broda, and at several points earlier in this book, particularly in regard to the architectural commemoration of the dead (priority II-D) and the propitiation priority (III-C). Diehl, *Tula,* 96, alludes to this dichotomy between a public and a private religion (which existed before, beside, and after the civic religion), but he does not elaborate. Excavations suggest that the residential areas of Tula did *not* undergo the same destruction that razed the public buildings. See Davies, *Toltecs Until the Fall of Tula,* 349.

70. Charnay, *Ancient Cities,* 90–91. Charnay did excavate two houses in Tula; see ibid., 104–9, for a discussion and ground plans.

71. See Diehl, *Tula,* 68 et seq. All these excavations of Tula Chico have since been filled in so that the visitor to Tula sees little more than rough spots in the desert at this point.

72. "Toltec Small Stone Construction" is the UMC project's term for a distinctive veneer of limestone fragments (or, in some cases, broken potsherds) laid in horizontal rows and covered with plaster. See Diehl, *Tula,* 72, 94. Such a *non*expedient construction technique suggests a ritual building, or an exercise of the propitiation priority (III-C), but it is even more noteworthy that this distinctive technique was employed in Tula Grande as well as in the domestic and neighborhood altars; the implications are discussed momentarily with respect to the "instigation" of Tula ritual-architectural events.

73. See Dan M. Healan, "Architectural Implications of Daily Life in Ancient Tollan, Hidalgo, Mexico," *World Archaeology* 9 (October 1977): 140–56, reprinted in *Ancient Mesoamerica,* ed. Graham, 315–30. (I will be citing page numbers from the reprinted version.) Healan, ibid., 324, makes a set of hypotheses about Tula social structure based on these residential excavations. Diehl, "Tula," 290; and idem, *Tula,* 90, agrees with Healan in the association of residential altars and ancestor worship.

74. See ibid., 72.

75. This is Diehl's conjecture as to the function of the broken figurines. See ibid., 106–8.

76. Settlement pattern studies of Tula by Mastache and Crespo of the INAH Proyecto Tula suggest a grid of large "neighborhoods" or barrios approximately 600 meters on a side with a concentration of large structures "that are probably temples" in one corner. See Guadalupe Mastache y Ana María Crespo, "La ocupacion prehispanica en el area de Tula, Hgo," in *Proyecto Tula,* ed. Matos, 1: 71–104; and Ana Maria Crespo Oviedo, "Uso del suelo y patron de poblamiento en el area de Tula, Hgo, in *Proyecto Tula,* ed. Matos, 2: 35–48. Healan of the UMC project likewise makes a set of hypotheses about Tula familial and neighborhood organization on the basis of the excavation of nonelite structures. See Dan M. Healan, "Residential Architecture at Tula," in *Studies of Ancient Tollan,* ed. Diehl, 16–24. Diehl, *Tula,* 92, 290, considers both studies and speculates that the Canal Locality Temple (excavated by the UMC project) was part of one of these neighborhood ritual

centers, specifically the "personal shrine for the worship of their own tutelary god."

77. Stocker directed the excavation of the small Canal Locality Temple in 1970. See Terrance L. Stocker, "A Small Temple in the Tula Residential Zone," in *Studies of Ancient Tollan,* ed. Diehl, 25–31. Diehl, "Tula," 286; and idem, "Tula," 72, summarizes the work.

78. *Chalchihuitls* is the Aztec term for circular emblems symbolizing water and its tutelary deity, Tlaloc. See ibid., 72.

79. I have discussed the characteristic Mesoamerican two-room temple plan in Chapter 3 in relation to the sanctuary priority (III-D).

80. The Corral Locality Structure is actually a rectangular block or complex of connected rooms rather than a single building; Margaret Mandeville did the excavation. Diehl, *Tula,* 286; and idem, *Tula,* 92–94, summarizes the results.

81. Diehl's account of the Corral Locality Structure (not to be confused with the much larger, circular, nearby "El Corral" temple excavated and restored by Acosta) is primarily a lament that more was not excavated; its close proximity to the large El Corral temple suggests an association, possibly as a domicile for priests or as a priestly school, but those are fairly empty guesses. See ibid., 93–95.

82. Broda, "Templo Mayor as Ritual Space," explores the evidence for this "old religion" in the offerings at the Templo Mayor.

83. Tedious Toltec Small Stone Construction, particularly because its time-consuming mosaic patterns are simply covered over by smooth plaster, could be an instance of "worshipful building" as discussed in Chapter 3 in reference to the propitiation priority (III-C). The suggestion by Stocker, "A Small Temple in the Tula Residential Zone," that the Canal Locality Temple was remodeled according to a calendrical schedule, moreover, implies the relevance of the homology priority (I-A).

84. See Gadamer, *Truth and Method,* 113, or the section on "The Mechanism of Architecture: Tradition and Instigation" in Chapter 3 of this project.

85. Carrasco, *Quetzalcoatl and the Irony of Empire,* 182–91, describes the amazing diversity of objects and elements from the distant and frontier provinces of the Aztec empire that were collected together in the Templo Mayor in terms of the "integration of peripheral places in the imperial center." The strategic integration of eclectic architectural elements at Chichén Itzá will be a major emphasis later in this chapter in relation to the content of the ritual-architectural events of "Toltec" Chichén Itzá.

86. In regard to the other orientational priorities that are typically responsible for instigating ritual-architectural events: there is apparently nothing in Tula that has captured the attention of archaeoastronomers except the 17 degrees east of north orientation, which is based not on alignments with the stars (astronomy, priority I-C) but on the imitation of Teotihuacán alignments (convention, priority I-B). However, with respect to homology (priority I-A), and specifically homologized polity, Kirchhoff has proposed a scheme wherein the Tula empire was constructed in a quadripartite fashion along symmetrical lines to the north, south, east, and west of the core city, and Davies gives examples of several Mesoamerican communities (perhaps including Tula) that seem to have been jointly ruled by four kings. All this is quite sketchy, but see Paul Kirchhoff, "Das Toltekenreich und sein Untergang," *Saeculim* 7:3 (1961): 251–52; discussed and elaborated by Davies, *Toltecs Until the Fall of Tula,* 292–94, 306. (Kirchhoff and Davies were writing before there had been any discernment of a consistent orientational scheme at Tula, so their suspicions about a homologized system of Toltec polity might actually be strengthened in light of recent macroarea archaeological studies.)

87. See Chapter 2.

88. The 17 degrees east of north orientation of Tula Grande is almost certainly a self-conscious imitation of Teotihuacán rather than a celestially derived alignment and, thus, demonstrates a convention priority orientation (I-B) rather than the astronomical alignment priority (I-C).

89. Carrasco, *Quetzalcoatl and the Irony of Empire,* 109, 126, for instance, considers that the famous feathered serpent imagery at Tula (and thus at Chichén Itzá) first arose at Teotihuacán. Davies, *Toltecs Until the Fall of Tula,* 212, suggests a Teotihuacán origin for the man-bird-serpent concept, which is prevalent both at Tula and Chichén Itzá. Kubler, "Serpent and Atlantean Columns," 110, similarly concurs that the "jaguar-serpent-bird compound" is originally of Teotihuacán origin.

90. Robertson, *Pre-Columbian Architecture,* 19–20, discusses the juxtaposition of the old Teotihuacán substructure and the new wood-roofed Toltec superstructure on the Temple of Tlahuizcalpantecuhtli (or Building B) at Tula Grande; he also notes

the difference between Teotihuacán's open avenues and Tula's closed arena.

91. Ruz, "Influencias Mayas en las tierres altas bajas del area Maya," argues that the column, a standard determinant of "Toltec" architecture (particularly at Chichén Itzá) does not originate in Tula, nor in the Maya zone, but rather in Oaxaca. Davies, *Toltecs Until the Fall of Tula,* 212, notes Ruz's opinion but, nonetheless, credits the colonnaded hall to the Tolteca-Chichimeca; see ibid., 49–50. Robertson, *Pre-Columbian Architecture,* 26, discusses the sense in which the Burnt Palace, Tula Grande's most elaborate colonnade, is different from the palace structures of Teotihuacán.

92. Davies, ibid., 208–337, cites Alfonso Caso and Barbo Dalgren as his authorities for parallels between the Mixtec-Zapotec region and Tula. Davies, ibid., 208, also considers that Xochicalco influenced Tula, but he does not specify how.

93. With respect to central Veracruz influences at Tula, Jorge Acosta, "La tercera temporada de exploraciónes en Tula, Hidalgo, 1941," *Revista Mexicana de Estudios Antropológicos* 6:1 (1944): 239–48, draws attention to certain reliefs in Tula Grande that reflect the influence of El Tajín; and Davies, *Toltecs Until the Fall of Tula,* 213, concurring with Acosta's observations, considers that the death cult of the ball game at Tula comes from El Tajín. However, the most important (and least understood) contribution from the Veracruz coastal area is made by the Huastecas. Explanations of the Huasteca component at Tula, never at all certain nor satisfactory, typically credit them with the large, circular El Corral temple, ostensibly dedicated to Quetzalcoatl in his manifestation as Ehecatl, the god of the wind (though all circular buildings in Mesoamerica are typically explained this way). The fact that this temple is located a good distance from the Tula Grande plaza is considered evidence that Huasteca religion influenced Tula but was accepted only at the edges, never integrated into the main center. See, for example, Richard Diehl y Lawrence Feldman, "Relaciónes entre la Huasteca y Tollan," in *Proyecto Tula,* ed. Matos, 1: 105–8.

94. See Davies, *Toltecs Until the Fall of Tula,* 212.

95. This particular Tula ball court and the Great Ball Court at Chichén Itzá, besides parallel sizes and shapes, also share a remarkably similar configuration of associated buildings, most notably *tzompantlis* (or skull racks) and a similar emplacement within their larger civic plazas (a configuration likewise shared by Tula Chico). See Matos, "Excavaciones en la microárea: Tula Chico y la Plaza Charnay."

96. There are pictures of ball game elements in the art of Teotihuacán, but, despite thorough reconnaissance of the area, as yet, no actual ball courts have been found there.

97. Diehl, *Tula,* 66, suggests that the Adoratorio is "a large version of the courtyard altars" and probably contained a high-status burial. Tozzer, *Chichén and Cenote,* 82, notes the close similarity between Tula's Adoratorio and "Toltec" Chichén Itzá's Mansolea I and III (more commonly known respectively as the Platform of the Eagles and Jaguars and the Venus Platform).

98. Though all the major public temples of Tula were looted and destroyed before the modern era, Diehl, *Tula,* 60, believes that they were probably square masonry buildings with two interior rooms, an antechamber, and an "inner sanctum." Coe, *Mexico,* 140, likewise re-creates Tula Grande's Temple of Tlahuizcalpantecuhtli according to this two-room plan.

99. Diehl, *Tula,* 60, argues that Sahagún's elaborate description of the Toltec temples (quoted above, as an epigraph for this section) "covered with coral, turquoise, red and white shells" may well be accurate. Also, Diehl, ibid., 72, notes that the distinctive Toltec Small Stone Construction that was used as a veneer in the domestic altars was also "frequently used on public and ceremonial buildings" (though precisely where in Tula Grande is unclear).

100. Weaver, *Aztecs, Maya, and Their Predecessors,* 209, is typical in her assumption that the human bodies that belong to the skulls held in the serpents' mouths in the *coatepantli* carvings have already been eaten. I am not, however, aware of anyone other than myself who has interpreted the *coatepantli* in terms of a juxtaposition of conservative and radical elements, that is, in terms of the twofold pattern of ritual-architectural events.

101. See, for instance, Heyden, "Caves, Gods and Myths," for remarks on a Mesoamerican cult of mountains and water. The massive pyramidal bases at Tula and elsewhere are often described as humanly constructed mountains or mountain-surrogates and, thus, similarly might be interpreted as conservative, instigatory elements.

102. Following its original manifestation at Tula, the *coatepantli* serpent wall became an integral element of the Central Mexican ceremonial precinct, repeated with greatest fidelity at Tenayuca and

Tenochtitlán (and possibly at "Toltec" Chichén Itzá, though nothing of the wall is any longer extant).

103. Stocker, "A Small Temple in the Tula Residential Zone," 29, suggests that Tula Grande was refurbished according to a calendrical schedule. In regard to ritual destruction and rebuilding (thus demonstrating conjoined propitiation and homology priorities, I-A and III-C), many scholars suggest that the 15-foot-high atlantean statues that, together with the serpent columns and pillars, were found, not in situ, but rather in a great trench dug in the north face of the Pyramid of Tlahuizcalpantecuhtli, had been ceremonially destroyed either by the inhabitants or invaders of Tula. See, for instance, Weaver, *Aztecs, Maya, and Their Predecessors,* 207–8. However, by contrast, Diehl, *Tula,* 63, says that great statues made their way into that trench in the context of unsuccessful attempts by Aztec looters to carry them off.

104. Acosta, "Interpretatión de algunos datos obtenidos en Tula relativos a la época Tolteca," 76.

105. Diehl, *Tula,* 64.

106. Robertson, *Pre-Columbian Architecture,* 38.

107. Two of the more appealing discussions of Quetzalcoatl at Tula — Carrasco, *Quetzalcoatl and the Irony of Empire;* and Davies, *Toltecs Until the Fall of Tula* — are diametrically opposed insofar as Carrasco focuses on the *continuity* between the Quetzalcoatl of Teotihuacán and the Quetzalcoatl of Tula (Tula is an "other Tollan" wherein the conception of Quetzalcoatl as a symbol of urban authority that first arose at Teotihuacán is espoused, perpetuated, and elaborated), while Davies emphasizes the *discontinuity* between Teotihuacán and Tula (the sense in which the Quetzalcoatl of Tula is part of a "new religion" that arises in the chaotic, post-Teotihuacán ambience). I am, at this particular point in my interpretation, more inclined to follow Davies and emphasize the extent to which Tula is a significant departure from Teotihuacán, a city with very different problems and, consequently, very different religio-architectural priorities.

108. Ignacio Marquina is apparently responsible for the initial identification of the figure on Pyramid B as Tlahuizcalpantecuhtli. See Carrasco, *Quetzalcoatl and the Irony of Empire,* 53.

109. See Robertson, *Pre-Columbian Architecture,* 29.

110. The narrative, veristic (and, presumably, historical) battle scenes on the walls of "Toltec" Chichén Itzá's Temple of the Chac Mool, Temple of the Warriors, and Temple of the Jaguars will be discussed later in this chapter, as will the identification of specific individuals in the hieroglyphs of South, or "Old Chichén."

111. The debate over the historical accuracy and applicability to Tula, Hidalgo, of the Toltec "king lists" in the Aztec documents (notably between Jiménez Moreno, "Tula y los Toltecas según las Fuentes Historicas"; and Kirchhoff, "Quetzalcoatl, Huemac y el fin de Tula") has been waged almost entirely on ethnohistorical grounds without specific reference to Tula architecture or archaeology.

112. Sahagún, *Florentine Codex,* bk. 10, 165–66.

113. Acosta found evidence of major Aztec looting in every building of Tula Grande, as did Diehl and Matos in all of the nonelite portions of Tula. See Diehl, *Tula,* 168, 292.

114. Broda, "Templo Mayor as Ritual Space," 50–51, discusses the excavation of processional reliefs on friezes along benches at the Templo Mayor, which are "almost identical to a similar side bench known from the Toltec capital of Tula." And a number of authors, for instance, Diehl, *Tula,* 168, believe that "most of the objects [looted from Tula] were ultimately reused in Tenochtitlán and other major Aztec cities." So far as I know, there is no sure archaeological evidence that the actual physical elements of Tula were transferred and re-incorporated elsewhere, but that is the implication.

115. Furthermore, methodologically speaking, both of these revalorative circumstances speak directly to the superabundance of pre-Columbian architectural forms.

116. By terming this "disjunctive revalorization" I want to suggest that it is a phenomenon related to but distinct from Kubler's and Panofsky's "principle of disjunction" (as discussed in Chapter 2 relative to "Ethnohistory: Ethnographic Analogy").

117. Morley, *Ancient Maya,* 1st ed., 325–26. Brainerd's revised edition of 1954 preserves this distinction between the two "halves" of Chichén Itzá though he tightens up the dates slightly (eighth to tenth centuries C.E. for the "pure Maya" half and eleventh to twelfth centuries C.E. for the "Mexicanized" half); Brainerd also changes Morley's term "Maya-Mexican" to "Toltec." See Morley/Brainerd, *Ancient Maya,* 285.

118. Lincoln, "Chronology of Chichén Itzá," 153.

119. See Thompson, *People of the Serpent,* 251. The uncertain origin of the Old Chichén/New Chichén distinction was discussed in Chapter 1 relative to

"Chichén Chronology: Empires and Overlaps"; see n. 231 in Chapter 1.

120. Tozzer's bi-ethnic scheme for Old South "Maya" Chichén and New North "Toltec" Chichén is already largely intact in his seminal discussion of the problem, "Maya and Toltec Figures at Chichén Itzá" (1930).

121. Tozzer, *Chichén and Cenote,* 24, explains his criteria (which are essentially formal) for including these five clusters of buildings among his "Chichén I" or "pure Yucatán Maya" group (what I am calling "South Chichén").

122. Willey, "External Influences on the Lowland Maya," 61, for instance, suggests that Tozzer's prestige and encyclopedic knowledge forestalled his contemporaries from challenging the basic scheme. Lincoln, "Chronology of Chichén Itzá," 150–55, makes a similar and more detailed assessment of Tozzer's overpowering influence.

123. Karl Ruppert, *Chichén Itzá: Architectural Notes and Plans,* Publication 595 (Washington: Carnegie Institution of Washington, 1951), fig. 151; reproduced as fig. 1 in Tozzer, *Chichén and Cenote.*

124. Lincoln, "Chronology of Chichén Itzá," 152–53. The other major cenote at Chichén Itzá, Cenote Xtoloc, the one that was apparently used as the more utilitarian water supply, does lie more near the center of the major constructions.

125. Ibid., 153–55. It is perhaps worth noting that Lincoln's correlation of North and South Chichén Itzá with, respectively, a "public" and a "private" sector at least intimates a dubiously sexist reading of the layout of the city in which the north "Toltec" portion of the city is conceived as somehow male (public) space while the south "Maya" portion is a female (private) space. I am not, however, aware of anyone who has raised that objection in print.

126. For early impressions of South Chichén see Stephens, *Incidents of Travel in Yucatán,* chapters 16, 17; Charnay, *Ancient Cities,* Chapter 18; Holmes, *Ancient Cities of Mexico,* 101–39; and Maudslay, *Archaeology,* 3: 1–43.

127. Thompson, *People of the Serpent,* 251, claims credit for the designations "Old" and "New Chichén," but my suspicion is that the idea is considerably older. See n. 119 in this chapter.

128. Tozzer, *Chichén and Cenote,* 190, comments on the concentration of the Carnegie's and the Mexican government's work in "Toltec" Chichén Itzá.

129. Bolles's original work on the Monjas was published in the Carnegie Institution Yearbooks of 1932–34, but the more thorough and final studies appear in John S. Bolles, *Las Monjas: A Major Pre-Mexican Architectural Complex at Chichén Itzá* (Norman: University of Oklahoma Press, 1977).

130. Tozzer, *Chichén and Cenote,* 190, credits Martin with the restoration of the Temple of the Three Lintels. Tozzer, ibid., 270, n. 18, enumerates the other buildings examined by the Carnegie Institution, many of which belong to South Chichén.

131. The fabulous Puuc-style facade decoration on the Iglesia and the Monjas (like its counterparts in Uxmal) has for centuries provided grist for imaginative speculations about the history, mythology, and beliefs of the ancient people of Chichén Itzá. Augustus Le Plongeon, *Sacred Mysteries Among the Mayas and Quiches: 11,500 Years Ago . . .* (New York: R. Macoy, 1886), 93–94, for instance, consonant with his opinion about the extreme antiquity of the ruins, considers that the long-nosed figures on the facade of the Iglesia (usually interpreted these days as Chaac, the Maya god of rain) were actually elephants or, more properly, prehistoric mastodons and that the iconography depicted "the act of worshipping the mastodon." Somewhat more appealingly, Le Plongeon also delivers an elaborate and actually stimulating interpretation of the adjacent facade on the east end of the Monjas as the commemoration of a Maya cosmogony (sacred history, priority II-B). He says, ibid., 72–73, that the oval motif in the center is "a luminous egg, emitting rays, and floating in the midst of the waters where it had been deposited by the Supreme Intelligence." Also see ibid., 112. See n. 190 of this chapter for several other interpretations of the same facade. (If newer, more well-tempered studies of the iconography of South Chichén are scarce, one need only stand there and listen to the freewheeling renditions of the tourist guides to be assured that the images are still superabundant with meanings.)

132. Landa, *Relación,* 177–84. Tozzer argues that the nature of Landa's description of Chichén Itzá implies that the southern portion of the city was entirely overgrown at that time. See Tozzer/Landa, 179, n. 943.

133. On the aborted Xui pilgrimage to the Sacred Cenote in 1536, often described as the episode that sealed the fate of the Yucatecans at the hands of the Spaniards, see Landa, *Relación,* 54–55.

134. See David H. Kelley, "Kakupacal and the Itzá," *Estudios de Cultura Maya* 8 (1968): 255–68; idem, *Deciphering the Maya Script* (Austin: University

of Texas Press, 1976); idem, "Notes on Puuc Inscriptions and History," in *The Puuc: New Perspectives,* ed. Mills; Michel Davoust, "Les premiers chefs Mayas de Chichén Itzá," *Mexicon* 2:2 (1980): 25–29; and Jeff Karl Kowalski, "Lords of the Northern Maya: Dynastic History in the Inscriptions of Uxmal and Chichén Itzá," *Expedition* 25:3 (1985): 50–60.

135. As noted earlier, the present work could go further than it does in integrating all the very important new epigraphical research.

136. Thompson, *Maya Archaeologist,* 21.

137. Pollock, *The Puuc,* repeatedly uses the term "Great Cities" to refer to Sayil, Kabah, and Uxmal. The data for this book were collected in the 1930s, though it was not published until 1980; accordingly, it belongs to the traditional archaeology strain and represents by far the most exhaustive descriptive account of the Puuc style.

138. Fray Antonio de Ciudad Real, quoted by Kelemen, *Medieval American Art,* 79–80.

139. Stephens, *Incidents of Travel in Yucatán,* 1: 237. Incidentally, Stephens's description of the effusive Puuc decoration as "an offering" is in consonance with my interpretation that this architecture primarily reflects the propitiation (III-C) and contemplation (III-B) priorities.

140. See, for instance, Pollock et al., *Mayapán, Yucatán, Mexico.*

141. Among the countless critics who provide very favorable assessments of Puuc architecture, see Zapata Alonso, *Guide to Puuc Region;* Coe, *Maya,* 106–10; Weaver, *Aztecs, Maya, and Their Predecessors,* 182–88; Kelemen, *Medieval American Art,* 74–82; Kubler, *Art and Architecture of Ancient America,* 233–43. The sole negative assessment of the Puuc considers that the exuberant decoration is overelaborate and cluttered; for instance, writing in 1927, Joyce, *Maya and Mexican Art,* 42, says, "in the later Maya period of Yucatán [that is, the Puuc], the art of sculpture showed a definite decline. . . . Elaboration and complexity of detail were carried to an extreme, luxuriance drowned dignity, and the grotesque took command."

142. Pollock, *The Puuc,* 589.

143. Pollock, ibid., 584–90, presents a tentative scheme for the chronological development of the Puuc architectural style beginning approximately 475 C.E. and ending sometime before 1000 C.E.

144. Tozzer, *Chichén and Cenote,* 24; and Thompson, *Maya Archaeologist,* 21, both articulate the conventional opinion that the Temple of the Three Lintels is the only purely Puuc building at Chichén Itzá.

145. In regard to the claim that the Puuc style is uniquely Maya, Tozzer, *Chichén and Cenote,* 165, notes a couple of Toltec elements at the Puuc sites of Kabah and Uxmal but concludes that "outside of Chichén, the Mexican or Toltec remains are few and far between." Morley/Brainerd, *Ancient Maya,* 293, emphasizes that Uxmal demonstrates almost no Mexican influence despite being in the region of great Mexican influence. Weaver, *Aztecs, Maya, and Their Predecessors,* 185; and von Hagen, *World of the Maya,* 158, are among the vast majority who follow Tozzer and Morley in stressing the purely Maya flavor of Puuc architecture.

146. See Kowalski, "Lords of the Northern Maya." These ideas are elaborated in Jeff Karl Kowalski, *The House of the Governor: A Maya Palace in Uxmal, Yucatán, Mexico* (Norman: University of Oklahoma Press, 1987).

147. Proskouriakoff, "Some Non-Classic Traits in the Sculpture of Yucatán."

148. Andrews IV, "Archaeology and Prehistory in the Northern Maya Lowlands," 309, 315.

149. Ball, "A Coordinate Approach to Northern Maya Prehistory," 86–87. Andrews and Robles, "Chichén Itzá and Coba," 64–65, follow Ball and reiterate this three-pronged origin for Puuc architecture. Davies, *Toltecs Until the Fall of Tula,* 131–32, also discusses the Toltec influences in Puuc architecture. Kubler, *Art and Architecture of Ancient America,* 233–45, is atypical in stressing a connection between Puuc and Oaxaca ritual-architecture; the formal (and typological) parallels between the two were discussed in Chapter 3 in regard to the contemplation priority, III-B.

150. Coe, *Maya,* 110; and Thompson, *Maya Archaeologist,* 20–21, both stress that South Chichén continued to use a type of block masonry rather than shift to the finely cut veneer masonry characteristic of the mainline Puuc. With respect to southern Maya influences at South Chichén, Tozzer, *Chichén and Cenote,* 23, 33, considers that the House of the Phalli and the east wing of the Monjas, "because of their plan and the heavy character of their stone walls and vaults," are related to the Late Classic of the Petén.

151. Spinden, *Study of Maya Art,* 97.

152. Pollock, *The Puuc,* 561–62, says that the east of north orientation of Puuc civic structures is "so consistently true that the occasional exception is

notable"; yet, he also notes that the extent of deviation from true north varies not only between sites but between structures at any one site.

153. See Ruppert, *Chichén Itzá: Architectural Notes and Plans,* fig. 151.

154. E. C. Krupp, "The Observatory of Kukulcán," *Griffith Observer* 41 (September 1977): 2–20, provides a controversial six-stage evolution of buildings and remodelings at the Caracol as well as the astronomical significance of this earliest, supposedly purely Maya phase. According to his scheme, even in its earliest construction phases (those that are typically considered "purely Maya"), the Caracol seems to have supported two small columns on a stylobate, or low pedestal, which facilitated certain celestial observations, thus signaling a significant concern for astronomical alignments. Ibid., 7. Also see Aveni, Anthony, Horst Hartung, and Sharon Gibbs, "The Caracol Tower at Chichén Itzá: Ancient Observatory," *Science* 18 (June 1975): 977–85.

155. John Carlson, personal communication.

156. See Aveni and Hartung, "Maya City Planning and the Calendar," 22–52, for a detailed discussion of astronomical alignments in Uxmal and other Puuc sites.

157. See, for instance, Milbrath, "Astronomical Images and Orientations in the Architecture of Chichén Itzá," which concentrates principally on the celestial alignments in the northern portion of the site.

158. Pollock, *The Puuc,* 562, for instance, concludes that more important than any axial orientation in the Puuc sites "seems to be the arrangement of groups of buildings so that they are facing a center." Spinden, *Study of Maya Art,* 97, 103, had come to essentially the same conclusion.

159. In other words, while South Chichén Itzá is significantly eclectic, unlike Tula (or "Toltec Chichén"), the pandering of imported images to a multi-ethnic constituency was *not* the essential strategy for drawing people into its ritual-architectural game.

160. I borrow this phrase from Pollock, *The Puuc,* 571.

161. Pollock, ibid., 567–70, summarizes the frequency and distribution of the manifold room plans in Puuc architecture, all basically variations on the simple rectilinear prototype.

162. See ibid., 567.

163. Alberto Ruz Lhuillier, *Chichén Itzá: Guia Oficial* (Mexico: Instituto Nacional de Antropología e Historia, n.d.), 42, makes this suggestion about the original plan of the Akab-Dzib.

164. Pollock, *The Puuc,* 567.

165. See Zapata Alonso, *Guide to Puuc Region,* 97–98.

166. Fewer Puuc buildings reduce the prototypical plan to simply one or two rooms, yet in South Chichén, both the Monjas Annex and the Iglesia do have single rectangular rooms. Pollock, *The Puuc,* 567, can point to only about a dozen single-room Puuc buildings. Tozzer, *Chichén and Cenote,* 73, comments on the presence of single-roomed structures in Chichén I (South Chichén) but their absence elsewhere at Chichén.

167. The Nunnery at Uxmal was a prime example in articulating the convention priority, I-B, in Chapter 3.

168. Pollock, *The Puuc,* 569, for instance, cites several Puuc building complexes that attain multistoried effects by building over natural slopes and artificial terrain, preeminently, the Cabalpak at Chacmultún, another major site in the Puuc hills, which attains complexity and differentiation in height by positioning relatively simple range forms behind and above one another up a terraced hillside.

169. Ibid., 576.

170. Zapata Alonzo, *Guide to Puuc Region,* 22, considers that the essential distinction between the Puuc and the Chenes style is that, where the latter decorates the entire building facade, the Puuc decoration is restricted to the upper portions. This fairly insignificant distinction is regularly reiterated (for instance, by the tourist guides at Chichén Itzá), but Pollock, *The Puuc,* presents many instances of Puuc decoration on lower facades.

171. Kubler, *Art and Architecture of Ancient America,* 234, actually considers this to be characteristic of the eastern Puuc area but less true of the west.

172. Pollock, *The Puuc,* 580, lists an almost endless array of geometric motifs found in Puuc decoration.

173. Kubler, *Art and Architecture of Ancient America,* 269. Similarly, Tozzer, *Chichén and Cenote,* 124, writes that these Puuc-style mask facades of South Chichén were "made up of fairly stable elements assembled together into a grotesque mosaic face." Spinden, *Study of Maya Art,* 127, considers the mask panels of the Chichén Monjas to be excellent instances of his concepts of "elimination" and "substitution," two elements of his "process of imaginative modification." For a discussion of Spinden's processes of imaginative modification,

see the section on "Organization by Tradition: Historical Continuity and Transformation" in Chapter 2 of this project.

174. Thompson, *Maya Archaeologist,* 21.

175. Ibid., 21.

176. See ibid.

177. See Lincoln, "Chronology of Chichén Itzá," 153–55.

178. See ibid., 155. Lincoln's argument for "total overlap" was discussed somewhat more fully in Chapter 1 with respect to "Chichén Chronology: Empires and Overlaps" and "The Historical Problem Summarized."

179. Lincoln, "Chronology of Chichén Itzá," 155.

180. See the section in Chapter 3 of this project entitled "Contemplation: Props for Devotion."

181. See the section in Chapter 3 of this project entitled "Propitiation: Building as Offering."

182. Both Spinden, *Study of Maya Art,* 97, 103; and Pollock, *The Puuc,* 564, note the absence in the Puuc area of the acropolis, amphitheatric plazas that are so typical of southern Maya cities.

183. See ibid., 565.

184. See ibid. on the frequency of centrally located, small masonry platforms in the Puuc area.

185. The same sort of concern for delimiting restricted-access precincts is similarly manifest on other scales of Puuc architectural design. For example, on a larger scale, the very impressive free-standing arches at Labná, Kabah, Uxmal, and Xculoc appear to have functioned, as Pollock among others has opined, like the Arc de Triomphe of Paris — to mark and formalize the entrance to a restricted precinct. See, for instance, Pollock, "Architecture of the Maya Lowlands," 412; or idem, *The Puuc,* 565. On a smaller scale, a hierarchical differentiation of sacred spaces is evident in the characteristic two-room range structure plan with an antechamber and an inner sanction which is usually slightly higher and slightly smaller than the outer room. See, for instance, ibid., 571.

186. Pollock, ibid., 579, alludes to the Puuc tendency to encircle entire buildings, not simply the front facade, with decoration.

187. Thompson, *Maya Archaeologist,* 22.

188. See especially Chapter 1 on "The General Problem: Maya-Mexican Interrelatedness" for a discussion of the rise and fall of the paradigm of Maya-Mexican polarity.

189. Zapata Alonzo, *Guide to Puuc Region,* 17, 98, expresses suspicion about the unreflective and automatic association of every Puuc mask with "Yum Chaac," the rain god. He believes that focusing on the diversity between the different masks will show that they represent several different deities. His cautionary words are well taken.

190. Maudslay, *Archaeology,* 3: 17, writing at the turn of the century, considered that this mask facade and doorway in the South Chichén Monjas represents an open mouth. In regard to the same facade, Spinden, *Study of Maya Art,* 127, disagrees and says that it represents the surviving elements of an older arrangement of three heads, one in front and two in profile. Tozzer, *Chichén and Cenote,* 12–13, considers that this Monjas doorway is a "degenerative form" of the open-mouth doorways of the Río Bec and Chenes areas. Augustus Le Plongeon's interpretation of this same facade as a representation of the Maya cosmogony was discussed in n. 131 of this chapter.

191. See "Divinity: Bodies, Abodes and Abstractions" in Chapter 3 of this project. The Copán Temple 22 ritual-architectural event was also a major example with respect to the astronomical alignment priority, I-C; see "Astronomy: The Power of Prediction," also in Chapter 3.

192. See Tozzer, *Chichén and Cenote,* 32, 167. Tozzer does, however, note a number of "naturalistic" designs in his Chichén I or Yucatán Maya phase (the epoch in which he believes that South Chichén was built). See ibid., 33, 94.

193. See Pollock, *The Puuc,* 573, 580.

194. "See Kelley, "Kakupacal and the Itzás"; idem, *Deciphering the Maya Script;* and idem, "Notes on Puuc Inscription and History." Kowalski, "Lords of the Northern Maya," provides a very helpful summary of what was known about the historical content of the inscriptions of Uxmal and Chichén Itzá prior to 1985; his own work has since superseded that summary. I have relied heavily on this article.

195. All fourteen of the glyphic designations of Kakupacal that Kelley has identified at Chichén Itzá are in association with "non-Toltec" (that is, South Chichén) buildings. See Kelley, "Notes on Puuc Inscriptions and History," 2. However, as of 1983, Wren and Schmidt were arguing that glyphs 21 and 22 on the "Great Ball Court Stone," a piece presumably from the very heart of "Toltec Chichén," which had been recently retrieved from a storeroom in the Museum of Anthropology in Mérida, "may tentatively be identified as an ideographic variant of the name Kakupacal." Linneas H. Wren, "The Great Ball

Court Stone From Chichén Itzá," Paper presented at the Mesa Redonda de Palenque, 1986. Also see Linneas Wren and Peter Schmidt, "A New Sculpture From the Great Ball Court at Chichén Itzá," Paper presented at the Annual Meeting of the Society for American Archaeology, Portland, Oregon, 1984. Coggins, "A New Sun at Chichén Itzá," 270, says, "In view of the temporal spread and textual associations of this compound [which Kelley has identified as Kakupacal, a specific Chichén ruler], it seems more likely to me that in its prehispanic role this glyphic compound was descriptive of a ritual act, or referred to a royal function rather than to a person."

196. Tozzer/Landa, 24, n. 129, collects some of the standard ethnographic references to Kakupacal, "the valorous Itzá captain."

197. See Kelley, "Kakupacal and the Itzá," for the original identification of Kakupacal; and idem, "Notes on Puuc History and Inscriptions," 8, for a discussion of these additional two glyphs that seem to signify something like "king of kings."

198. See Davoust, "Les premiers chefs Mayas de Chichén Itzá," for the list of ten specific Chichén "kings"; and Kelley, "Notes on Puuc History and Inscriptions," 5–7, for his discussion and qualified agreement with the list.

199. Kowalski, "Lords of the Northern Maya," 55, follows Kelley, "Notes on Puuc Inscriptions and History," in this dating of the South Chichén buildings.

200. See ibid., 11–12, for Kelley's opinion that the major buildings of South Chichén were constructed within an eighteen-year span; and, see Kowalski, "Lords of the Northern Maya," 59, for the notion of a series of dedicatory rituals.

201. Ibid., 59. In that spirit, one could perhaps generalize that the *southern* Maya merged the priority of the legitimation of temporal authority (politics, II-C) with that of the commemoration of sacred history (II-B), while the *northern* Maya merged the political priority (II-C) with that of the commemoration of ancestors (II-D). The actual situation is, however, considerably more complex than that, and the typological categories in this case may distort more than they illumine.

202. Landa, *Relación,* 178–79. Along with his eyewitness description of the plaza of North (or "Toltec") Chichén Itzá, Landa provides a plan drawing of the Castillo that is quite inaccurate in several respects. Tozzer/Landa, 178–79, nn. 933–43, discusses the discrepancies and reckons that Landa was writing from memory, considerably after his visit to the actual site.

203. See Landa, *Relación,* 21, quoted at the beginning of the Introduction to this project.

204. Edmonson, *The Ancient Future of the Itzá;* and idem, *Heaven Born Mérida and Its Destiny.*

205. See Gaspar Antonio Chi, *Relación Sobre las Costumbres de los Indios* (1582), MS. trans and notes by Ralph L. Roys, reprinted as Appendix C in Tozzer/Landa, *Relación,* 230–32; Tomas López Medel, *Relación* (1612), reprinted as Appendix B in Tozzer/Landa, *Relación,* 221–29; Bernardo de Lizana, *Historia de Yucatán: Devocionario de Nuestra Senora de Izamal y Conquista Espiritual,* 1633 (Mexico, D.F.: El Museo Nacional de Mexico, 1893); and López de Cogolludo, *Historia de Yucatán,* 1688, 3d ed.: 2 vols. (Mérida, 1867–68).

206. On the Le Plongeons' very extensive activities at Chichén Itzá, see, Desmond and Messenger, *A Dream of Maya: Augustus and Alice Le Plongeon in Nineteenth-Century Yucatán.*

207. See Charnay, *Ancient Cities,* 324–42. Charnay and all of the other early students of Chichén Itzá mentioned in this brief review have been addressed more fully in the first two chapters of this project.

208. Maudslay, *Archaeology,* 3: 35–36.

209. Thompson, *People of the Serpent,* 206–10, a major contributor to the early study of Chichén Itzá, admits to his considerable embellishment of the sources in (re)constructing the history of the site. For instance, regarding his use of Cogolludo, "a good old, but very dry chronicler," Thompson, ibid., 210, provides the following candid and telling admission: "I confess to having taken his skeleton and put a little flesh on it here and there, just to round out the form, and adding a little brown and red, just to give it color and pictorial effect, that is all."

210. Earl Morris headed the Carnegie Institution's excavation and (re)construction of the Temple of the Warriors. See Earl Morris, Jean Charlot, and Ann Axtel Morris, *The Temple of the Warriors at Chichén Itzá, Yucatán,* Publication 406 (Washington: Carnegie Institution of Washington, 1931). In the subsequent literature one finds nothing but praise for Morris's methods and results. See, for example, Alfred Kidder's epitaph for Morris, *American Antiquity* 22 (1957): 390–97; or Frans Blom's review of Morris's portion of *The Temple of the Warriors* in *Maya Research* 2 (April 1935): 203–15. (Blom is less enthusiastic about the rest of the publication.)

211. Tozzer, *Chichén and Cenote,* 190–91, recounts the names and accomplishments of the early Mexican archaeologists at Chichén Itzá.

212. Morley/Brainerd, *Ancient Maya,* 279.

213. The evolution of all these ideas was treated in greater detail in Chapter 1. Andrews V, "Dzibilchaltún," 335–36, has a concise summary of the "old view." Andrews IV, "Archaeology and Prehistory in the Northern Maya Lowlands," 386–93, a key figure in forming the traditional view, comments with suspicion on Chichén Itzá's singularity as "the only large post-Classic city known" (a suspicion that has since been confirmed).

214. Weaver, *Aztecs, Maya, and Their Predecessors,* 224. Morley/Brainerd, *Ancient Maya,* 379, extends this standard assessment of "Toltec" Chichén Itzá architecture as Mexican Toltec in style but Maya in technique to the ceramics of "Toltec Chichén" as well.

215. Bernal, *Mexican Wall Painting,* 21. Bernal does balance his assessment of "Toltec Chichén" art by admitting that "this [nouveau-riche quality] does not mean that some of its manifestations are not most successful." Ibid., 21. Among the most vehement detractors of the "Toltec Chichén" style, Thompson, *Rise and Fall of Maya Civilization,* 126–29 (and other places), comments on its shoddy construction and tastelessness; and Fernández, *A Guide to Mexican Art,* 21–22, is another to dispraise "Toltec Chichén" as "too bland," much inferior to Classic Maya art.

216. Margain, "Pre-Columbian Architecture of Central Mexico," 75. Similarly positive assessments of the "Toltec Chichén" style come from Davies, *Toltecs Until the Fall of Tula,* 214; Carrasco, *Quetzalcoatl and the Irony of Empire,* 140–46; Henderson, *World of the Ancient Maya,* 203, 214; and Wren, "Great Ball Court Stone," 15–16. Kelemen, *Medieval American Art,* 82, 88, takes a middle road, describing "Toltec Chichén" architecture as a "transition rather than a degeneration."

217. While all these ideas are, to varying degrees, manifestations of the paradigm of Maya-Mexican polarity, the situation is by no means straightforward. For instance, Eric Thompson, the most enthusiastic discussant of "Toltec" Chichén Itzá as the fortuitous product of a mutually beneficial symbiosis between Putun Maya and Tula Toltecs (see the section in Chapter 1 on "Symbiotic Polarity"), is among the most negative in his assessment of "Toltec Maya" architecture at Chichén Itzá.

218. Many present-day archaeologists (because they tend to take long-distance trade as the real key to late Yucatán history), with varying degrees of enthusiasm, concur that the Putun Maya were the strongest protagonists in a Terminal Classic/Early Postclassic era that saw *not* cultural decline but a wholesale reorientation in Maya society. Moreover, they concur that these Putun Maya were the primary force behind the spectacular architecture of "Toltec" Chichén Itzá. The most disturbing quirk in the current archaeological party line is the paradox that these Putun Maya protagonists (typically characterized as thoroughly pragmatic warrior-merchants who expertly exploited the commercial potential of their interjacent position at the Gulf Coast hinge between Highland Mexico and the Maya Lowlands but who were largely indifferent and inept in more artistic pursuits) are deemed the most likely builders (or at least financiers) of the spectacular architecture of "Toltec" Chichén Itzá. All these issues were addressed more thoroughly and more critically in Chapter 1.

219. Of course, all the recent advances in the decipherment of Maya glyphs, which have likewise issued largely for art history, have also been tremendously important in the revised image of the pre-Columbian Maya. See, for instance, Schele and Miller, *The Blood of Kings;* and Coe, *Breaking the Maya Code.*

220. Tozzer, *Chichén and Cenote,* 18.

221. Tatiana Proskouriakoff, "On Two Inscriptions at Chichén Itzá," in *Monographs and Papers in Maya Archaeology,* ed. William R. Bullard Jr. (Cambridge, Mass.: Peabody Museum, 1970). Also see Wren, "Great Ball Court Stone," 17.

222. See Kubler, "Chichén Itzá y Tula," 57; and idem, "Serpent and Atlantean Columns."

223. Arthur Miller's and Clemency Coggins's positions are both discussed at some length later in regard to the content of "Toltec Chichén" events.

224. See Thompson, *Maya History and Religion,* Chapter 1.

225. For more detailed remarks on the various opinions regarding the status and ethnic identity of the Itzá, see the section in Chapter 1 on "Symbiotic Polarity: Admixing Itzá."

226. For a discussion of Erwin Panofsky's "principle of disjunction" and George Kubler's application of that principle to Mesoamerican art history, see the section in Chapter 1 on "Ethnohistory: Ethnographic Analogy."

227. See Landa, *Relación,* 157–58. Mani is most well known as the site of Landa's famous *auto-da-çé,* an inquisition trial and torture of recently Christianized Indians who were accused of backsliding into the heathen practices. This is also the occasion in which the vast majority of pre-Columbian Maya books were supposedly burned. See Tozzer/Landa, 76–79, n. 340. The colonial church at Mani is still in use, but there is no standing pyramid there and, so far as I know, the site has never been the subject of a thoroughgoing archaeological study. Among the scores who cite Landa's account of the Kukulcán festival at Mani are Tozzer, *Chichén and Cenote,* 91; Weaver, *Aztecs, Maya, and Their Predecessors,* 226; and Henderson, *World of the Ancient Maya,* 209.

228. Landa, *Relación,* 157–58.

229. Landa's treatise mentions specifically only two pyramid temples dedicated to Kukulcán (the so-called Castillo of Chichén Itzá and the very similar Castillo of Mayapán). This account of the Chic Kaban, however, suggests a third Kukulcán temple at Mani (in any event, that is Tozzer's conclusion). See Tozzer/Landa, 158, n. 804. With respect to the atypicality of the Chic Kaban ceremony's special connection to a particular sort of monumental architecture, Tozzer, ibid., 163, n. 845, concludes that "few if any of the rituals described by Landa took place in the stone buildings known to archaeology." The only other festival described by Landa that resembles the Xul festival of Kukulcán in that regard is the one for the month of Pax; it also is five days long, takes place in a temple, has a political (nonagricultural) tone in which "lords" are more important than "priests," and involves (as do the rites of Xul) both heart sacrifice and explicit ritual destruction and renewal. See Landa, *Relación,* 146–47.

230. Davíd Carrasco, on several occasions, has described the Templo Mayor as a "lens" into the religious world of the Aztecs.

231. Landa, *Relación,* 158.

232. Tozzer/Landa, 158, n. 808, summarizes the suggestions of William Gates and Herbert Spinden that these rites of Xul were actually a new year's ceremony. The link between the Xul rites and the new year, or more specifically with the great Mesoamerican tradition of New Fire Ceremonialism, will become especially important in relation to Clemency Coggins's exciting hypothesis that the Castillo was built specifically to celebrate such a ceremony. See the final section of this chapter, "New Fire Integration: Toward a Summation."

233. Both in Landa's account of the Xul pyramid rites at Mani and generally with respect to "Toltec Chichén" ritual-architectural events, the contemplation priority (III-B), so vital in South Chichén, appears to be the least important of the generalized presentational priorities.

234. With respect to the content of Xul rites and "Toltec Chichén" events generally, the commemoration of the dead (priority II-D) is the most elusive category.

235. I used the phrase "liquid rippling body" earlier to refer to the extensive interrelatedness and unity of Mesoamerica as a whole.

236. Carlson, "A Geomantic Model," 179–87, provides one of the more thorough discussions of the symbolism of the Castillo. Waters, *Mexico Mystique,* 164–65; and Kelemen, *Medieval American Art,* 86, among dozens, present more brief discussions.

237. E. C. Krupp, "The Serpent Descending," *Griffith Observer* 46 (September 1982): 10–20.

238. See Carlson, "A Geomantic Model," 181, 184.

239. See Krupp, "Serpent Descending," 1.

240. Eliade, *Myth of the Eternal Return;* Wheatley, *Pivot of the Four Quarters;* and Carrasco, *Quetzalcoatl and the Irony of Empire,* all repeatedly discuss architectural *axis mundis,* and the categories of center and periphery in ways that are very relevant to the Castillo.

241. Similarly relevant to the homology priority (I-A), Carlson's expansive interpretation of the Castillo addresses the "cave-in-sacred-mountain character" and potential rebirth symbolism of the small grotto, womb-like temple that sits atop the Castillo's mountainous pyramidal base. Furthermore, comparing the Castillo to Mount Meru, Mesopotamian *ziggurats,* and Ch'omsong-dae of seventh-century Korea, Carlson considers that the great pyramid was not only a cosmologically designed "completion symbol" but also, being "geomantically located" in relation to other natural and constructed features at the site, was a potential participant in rites of augury and prediction. See Carlson, "A Geomantic Model," 179–85. His discussion is more provocative than precise on these issues but, nonetheless, very interesting.

242. See Mibrath, "Astronomical Images and Orientations in the Architecture of Chichén Itzá."

243. With respect to the ongoing controversy over who made the original "discovery" of the Castillo serpent of light phenomenon, José Díaz Bolio, *La Serpiente de Luz de Chichén Itzá* (Mérida: "El Mayab,"

1982), 5–9 (a small pamphlet that bears the bold subtitle, "por el descubridor del patron se pentino de las culturas precolombinas de America"), credits a worker on the reconstruction of the Castillo, Arcadio Salazar, with the initial discovery of the phenomenon in 1928. According to Díaz Bolio, Salazar told archaeologist Miguel Angel Fernández about it, and Fernández then published the first article in a magazine that no one remembers or can find. Díaz Bolio considers his own book, *La Serpiente Emplumada: Eje de Culturas* (Mérida, Yucatán: Registro de Cultura Yucateca, 1955), the first to address seriously the phenomenon. His angry remarks are addressed at Luis E. Arochi, whose very popular book, *La Pirámide de Kukulcán: Su Simbolismo Solar,* sexta ed. (Mexico: Panorama Editorial, S.A., 1987), originally published in the early 1970s, cites Díaz Bolio in the bibliography but does not give him any credit in the text. (At the 1988 Chichén Itzá vernal equinox event Arochi read from his book and was granted celebrity status, though one regularly hears other guides there claiming that they themselves actually had been the first to recognize it.) Krupp, "The Serpent Descending," 13, in a short but very helpful summary of the Castillo equinox event, adds more to the drama when he notes that Laura Gilpin, *Temples of Yucatán: A Camera Chronicle of Yucatán* (New York: n.p., 1948) has a picture of the light and shadow effect on the Castillo but does not mention the equinox. Certainly there is a great deal more to this drama of due recognition, but Jean-Jacques Rivard, "A Hierophany at Chichén Itzá," *Miscellaneous Series,* n. 26 (Greeley, Colo.: University of Northern Colorado, Museum of Anthropology, 1971), deserves credit for calling attention to the Castillo equinox event and for describing it as a "hierophany" with explicit reference to Eliade. Carlson, "A Geomantic Case," 187–89, summarizes Rivard's position (calling him "probably the first" to discuss the Chichén serpent of light).

244. Arochi, *Pirámide de Kukulcán,* 82–83, has pictures of several species of snakes that would, in profile, give this appearance of successive triangles. Incidentally, an interesting exercise of the priority of orientation according to abstract principles (I-B) is evident in the use of certain triangular and geometric shapes in the architecture of Chichén Itzá that mimic the designs on the backs of local snakes; a movie shown at the site explores this idea briefly, but I have never seen it in print.

245. Landa, *Relación,* 158. Tozzer's remarks on this widespread belief in the descent of the Feathered Serpent (see Tozzer/Landa, 143, n. 686) are particularly astute given that he was probably totally unaware of the light and shadow effect at the Castillo.

246. See Arochi, *Pirámide de Kukulcán.* Anthony Aveni, who holds perhaps the most authoritative opinion in these archaeoastronomical issues, is dubious about Arochi's work relative to the Castillo equinox phenomenon and, in fact, skeptical that the light and shadow effect itself is more than a marvelous, though unintentional, coincidence. Aveni, personal communication.

247. Coggins, "A New Sun at Chichén Itzá," 272–73, considers the descending serpent of light to be an element of the New Fire ceremony celebrated at Chichén Itzá. Her intriguing ideas are discussed more fully with respect to the content of the events of "Toltec Chichén," especially in "New Fire Integration: Toward a Summation."

248. Serpents and snakes are, of course, everywhere in Mesoamerican religion and, with respect to Venus, Aveni, "The Real Venus-Kukulcán," surveys the impressive number of ways in which Venus was incorporated into the architecture and religion of the Maya. Miller, "Maya and the Sea," 108, also discusses the Maya's capitalization on the intrinsic rebirth symbolism of Venus.

249. Pollock, "Architecture of the Maya Lowlands," 435, for instance, comments on the atypicality of the Castillo.

250. Kubler, *Art and Architecture in Ancient America,* 173, comments on the effects of light on the Mitla facades. Pearce, *View From the Temple,* 10, among others, notes the dynamic effects of the setting sun on the ornate Puuc facade of the Codz-Pop in Kabah.

251. Kelemen, *Medieval American Art,* 86–87; Kubler, "Design of Space in Maya Architecture," 517; and Robertson, *Pre-Columbian Architecture,* 22–23, 118, all consider the formal parallel between Uaxactún's pyramid E-VII Sub and the Chichén Itzá Castillo to be significant.

252. The Temple of the Seven Dolls at Dzibilchaltún, for instance, is radially symmetrical like the Castillo. Kelemen, *Medieval American Art,* 62, notes several four-sided pyramids at Tikal and describes the Castillo, erected some 400 years later, as "an interesting hark-back to this ancient type." And Kubler, "Serpent and Atlantean Columns," 108,

considers that the four-sided pyramid at Xkil (26 miles west of Chichén Itzá) is the most direct prototype for the Castillo's shape.

253. Robertson, *Pre-Columbian Architecture,* 41, for instance, notes the parallels between the low platforms of Monte Albán, Teotihuacán, and Tula and the high Castillo pyramid.

254. Zapata Alonzo, *Guide to Puuc Region,* 63, 67, surveys the distribution of the nine-tiered pyramidal form.

255. Weaver, *Aztecs, Maya, and Their Predecessors,* 225, among many, notes this close juxtaposition of characteristic "Toltec" and Maya forms in the Castillo temple.

256. Kubler's very appealing methodological approach was discussed in Chapter 2 with respect to "Organization by Tradition: Historical Continuity and Transformation." His iconoclastic ideas specifically with respect to the relationship between Tula and "Toltec Chichén" were reviewed in Chapter 1 in "Irreconcilable Polarity: Toltecs Versus Maya."

257. Kubler, "Tula y Chichén Itzá," 76–77, says (to paraphrase his Spanish) the "Maya-Toltec" architecture of Chichén Itzá appears now (1961) much more cosmopolitan and eclectic than the traditional comparison only with Tula permits. I am relying heavily on Kubler's work at this point *without,* however, accepting his historical hypothesis that Chichén Itzá was the original source and Tula was the receptor, "a frontier garrison," which was modeled after rather than for Chichén Itzá.

258. Davies, *Toltecs Until the Fall of Tula,* 202–17, in the context of his very helpful summary of the Kubler-Ruz debate, mentions some (but not all) of these themes. Tozzer, *Chichén and Cenote,* 180, lists the three principal indigenous Maya architectural traits that are traditionally considered to have persisted into "Toltec Chichén": (1) the Maya corbel vault, (2) the mask panel, and (3) a number of geometric and natural ornamental designs. Kubler's list is, of course, far longer.

259. Kubler, "Tula y Chichén Itzá," 66, 79. Davies, *Toltecs Until the Fall of Tula,* 205, takes particular exception with this claim, countering that, "frankly, it would seem that the somewhat pot-bellied figure in Oxkintok wearing feather dress constitutes a rather uncertain predecessor to the plumed-serpent columns [of Toltec Chichén]." I tend to agree with Davies on this point. Ruz, "Chichén Itzá y Tula," considers that the serpent columns of Chichén Itzá have *no* precedent in the Maya zone.

260. Kubler, "Tula y Chichén Itzá," 65, 79, remarks only briefly on the *chacmool* (at least in this article) but contends that it belongs thoroughly to the Maya tradition. Mary Ellen Miller, "A Re-examination of the Mesoamerican Chacmool," *Art Bulletin* 67 (March 1985): 7–17, has since conducted a far more thoroughgoing study of the *chacmool* figures and similarly advances the iconoclastic opinion that they originated in the Maya area.

261. Kubler, "Tula y Chichén Itzá," 65, notes that the sky bearers, while often full round statues in "Toltec Chichén," were usually represented in sculptured relief by the Classic Maya. On the larger atlantean columns, see ibid., 76. Tozzer/Landa, 137, n. 635. Thompson, *Maya History and Religion,* 277–79, among many, similarly connect Chichén's atlantean figures with the Maya tradition of *bacabs* or sky bearers.

262. Kubler, "Tula y Chichén Itzá," 64, cites sculptural representations of jaguar thrones (but not actual free-standing instances) at Tikal, Piedras Negras, Palenque, and Xultun, along with one actual throne at Uxmal.

263. Ibid., 79. Ruz, "Chichén Itzá y Tula," 214, following Proskouriakoff, counters that those southern Maya cases of warrior figures glorify specific individuals, but that in "Toltec Chichén" the warriors' figures are more impersonal and more numerous, glorifying an entire class of society (presumably as they do at Tula).

264. Kubler, "Tula y Chichén Itzá," 54.

265. Ibid., 45.

266. Ibid., 76.

267. Ibid. Besides these eight major points (which Kubler never enumerates as such), he also makes a number of less-significant insinuations about architectural borrowings from other than Tula.

268. Ruz, "Chichén Itzá y Tula," does agree with Kubler that the motif of a human head emerging from the mouth of a serpent (that is, the "face-in-the-serpent-mouth motif"), which is plentiful at both Tula and "Toltec Chichén," could likely have a Maya provenance.

269. To reiterate, I am siding with the historical hypotheses of *neither* Kubler nor Ruz but rather am benefitting from the work of both in documenting architectural archaisms at "Toltec Chichén" that come from *other than* Tula, Hidalgo.

270. See Ruz, "Influencias Mayas en las tierras altas y bajas," 234; cited by Davies, *Toltecs Until the Fall of Tula,* 212. Kubler, "Tula y Chichén Itzá," 55–

57, considers the Chac Mool Temple (the older, inner building beneath the Temple of Warriors) and the Castillo to be particularly indebted to Monte Albán. Similarly, with respect, Oaxacan influences, Kelemen, *Medieval American Art*, 85–86, finds important resemblances between the friezes on the Temple of the Jaguars and motifs at Monte Albán and between the articulation of stairs and terraces at the two sites.

271. See the summary of Ruz's position in Davies, *Toltecs Until the Fall of Tula*, 212.

272. Thompson, *Maya History and Religion*, 19, also calls attention to Huastecan (Central Gulf Coast) traits in "Toltec Chichén."

273. Like Ruz, Kubler, "Tula y Chichén Itzá," 70, considers that the reliefs in Chichén's Great Ball Court are indebted to El Tajín and the Veracruz region, but he does not elaborate. In that regard, also see Pasztory, "The Historical and Religious Significance of the Middle Classic Ballgame," discussed by Davies, *Toltecs Until the Fall of Tula*, 211–12. Others are currently arguing (in consonance with the growing consensus that "Toltec Chichén" is essentially an indigenous *Maya* phenomenon) that the Great Ball Court reliefs do *not* represent conflicts between the Maya and Toltec inhabitants of Chichén Itzá (as Tozzer claimed) but rather contain elements that could *all* be considered Maya in origin. See, for instance, Merle Greene Robertson, Edward Kurjack, and Ruben Maldenado C., "Ball Courts of the Northern Maya Lowlands," Paper presented at the Tucson symposium on the Native American Ball Game, 1985; and Wren, "Great Ball Court Stone," 9. I would argue that the prominent place of the ball game in "Toltec Chichén" is largely an instigatory strategy, much in the same way that the ball game functioned in Tula, Hidalgo; see the discussion earlier in the chapter on the instigation of Tula ritual-architectural events as "Coercion by Eclecticism."

274. For example, Piña Chan, *Chichén Itzá: La Ciudad de los Brujos del Agua*, 8–9, offering a considerably less-rigorous argument, recognizes influences in "Toltec Chichén" from Xochicalco, the Gulf Coast (especially El Tajín), the Pacific coast of Guatemala, and the Classic Maya Usumacinta area — all supposedly owing to the wanderings of a Quetzalcoatl cult that had originated in Xochicalco. As noted earlier, Tozzer, *Chichén and Cenote*, 18, also deserves credit for recognizing that "many of the resemblances found at Chichén Itzá seem to be far more widely distributed in Mexico than those definitively associated with the single site of Tula."

275. With respect to the comparison of Tula Grande's exercise of the strategy of instigation by eclecticism and "Toltec Chichén's" similar approach to allurement, I would venture that, where the architectural events of Tula Grande drew particularly on the traditions of resident Nonoalca and Tolteca-Chichimeca factions, "Toltec Chichén" seems to have borrowed from ancient and far-flung traditions whose direct progeny are not likely to have been among the actual citizenry of Chichén Itzá; in other words, at "Toltec Chichén" the general aspect of internationalism was probably more important than the enticement of special interest groups.

276. Regarding the considerable controversy over the antiquity of pre-Columbian pilgrimage to the Sacred Cenote, we can divide the multiplicity of opinions between two basic perspectives: one skeptical, which stresses the fairly recent and highly political nature of the pilgrimage phenomenon (for instance, Tozzer, Brainerd, and Coe), and the other more sympathetic, which tends to stress the great antiquity and specifically "religious" character of the phenomenon (for instance, Roys and Eric Thompson). See the next two notes for details.

277. Tozzer and Brainerd, representing a generally "skeptical" position (and basing their conclusions on the artifacts retrieved from the Sacred Cenote by Edward Thompson in the first decade of this century), challenged the ethnohistoric tradition of tremendous antiquity and contended instead that the bulk of the Cenote offerings belong to a fairly late period (Chichén III in Tozzer's scheme). They accounted for the very old and far-flung objects (some even from South America) that were dredged from the well by arguing that these were actually heirlooms acquired through trade and not the offerings of very ancient and distant pilgrims. See Tozzer, *Chichén and Cenote*, 18, 38, 84, 190–200, 196, 223. Consequently (epitomizing the paradigm of Maya-Mexican polarity), Tozzer and Brainerd both implied that Cenote worship was actually a quite late phenomenon, introduced by invading "Mexicans" as part of a foreign complex of idolatry and human sacrifice; in other words, that Cenote devotion was motivated more by trade and political opportunism (as one more occasion for intimidating ritual murder by the Toltecs) than by any specifically "religious" fascination with the Cenote. See especially Tozzer/Landa, 183, n. 956; and Tozzer, *Chichén and Cenote*, 186, 200. Coe, *Maya*, 131; and Benson, *Maya World*, 138, for instance, are among those

who generally follow Tozzer and Brainerd in suggesting that the Sacred Cenote was simply a utilitarian water hole in Classic times and only later became a ceremonial focus.

278. In contrast to Tozzer and Brainerd, Roys and Eric Thompson afforded Cenote veneration a greater age and a far more causative role in the historical development of Chichén Itzá. Roys (see a letter from Roys to Tozzer, quoted by Tozzer, *Chichén and Cenote,* 271, n. 2) argued that, where human sacrifice and throwing precious objects into the Sacred Cenote may be a later addendum of "the intrusive Mexicans" (now a suspect historical proposition at best), devotion to the Cenote was indeed indigenous and considerably older than Chichén's emergence as a politico-economic power. Furthermore, Roys's reading of the ethnohistorical accounts of Chichén's Cenote, particularly *The Chilam Balam of Chumayel,* convinced him of the intrinsically spiritual allure of the well. Thus he argues: "We cannot but believe that these foreign embassies, which traveled for weeks through tropical forests, swamps and waterless wastes to reach a far-off city in northeastern Yucatán, were motivated more by the religious veneration which its famous sanctuary enjoyed than by the political prestige which its rulers enjoyed in such a distant country." Ibid., 176. Also see ibid., 65, n. 4; 133, n. 7. Complementarily, Thompson, *Rise and Fall of Maya Civilization,* 113–14, contends that the Cenote cult was "in full swing before the Itzá arrived, but received fresh impetus under the Itzá." Moreover, Thompson, ibid., 133–35, argues "that the Mexicans chose Chichén Itzá as their principal city because the cenote cult had already given the center renown throughout Yucatán." The major problems in historical (re)construction aside, a number of scholars have followed Roys's and Thompson's nonreductive affirmation of the religious phenomenon of pilgrimage to the Sacred Cenote. See, for instance, Weaver, *Aztecs, Maya, and Their Predecessors,* 224–29; and Coggins, "New Fire at Chichén Itzá," 427, who, on the additional basis of artifacts recovered from the Cenote in the 1960s, concludes that the earliest ritual use of the Sacred Cenote apparently occurred toward the end of the eighth century. Also see *Cenote of Sacrifice,* ed. Coggins and Shane. The louder voice, however, issues from "new archaeologists" studying long-distance trade (the heirs to Tozzer and Brainerd in this regard), who, if ever more sensitive to the remarkable mobility of ancient Mesoamericans and to the pervasiveness of pre-Hispanic pilgrimage, invariably reduce religious pilgrimage to a side-effect of more determinative socioeconomic processes. See, for instance, Freidel and Sabloff, *Cozumel,* 185, who argue that "all [Mesoamerican long-distance] traders were in fact 'pilgrims' traveling under divine sanction for the ostensible purpose of visiting shrines and participating in festivals." Their discussion is exceedingly helpful in documenting the extent of pre-Hispanic pilgrimage, but their archaeological orientation invariably finds religious motives subservient to economic ones.

279. *Chilam Balam of Chumayel,* ed. Roys, 173. See the preceding note regarding Roys's position that the early pilgrims to Chichén Itzá were motivated primarily by the spiritual allure of the Sacred Cenote.

280. Despite the lack of specific information about the character of eco-architectural events at the Sacred Cenote in the era *before* "Toltec Chichén's" ascent, the general Mesoamerican enthusiasm for long-distance pilgrimage and fervid devotion to exotic natural features, particularly caves and water sources, ensures that Yucatán's most perfectly symmetrical cenote was always regarded as a very special place.

281. On colonial-era pilgrimage to the Sacred Cenote (particularly the aborted Xui pilgrimage of 1536), see, for instance, Tozzer, *Chichén and Cenote,* 61, 80–81, 185–86; Landa, *Relación,* 54–55; and Tozzer/Landa, 54–55, nn. 170–71.

282. Turner and Turner, *Image and Pilgrimage in Christian Culture,* define "pilgrimage structuration" in Weberian terms as the routinization and institutionalization of an ecstatic, "liminoid" sacred journey, the domestication of a salvific quest; see particularly ibid., 26, 171, 188, 196–201, 231–34. For a cross-cultural analogy to the way in which the Putun Maya apparently capitalized on the Sacred Cenote pilgrimage phenomenon, see Krautheimer, *Rome,* 87, regarding Gregory the Great's masterful exploitation of popular pilgrimage fervor to medieval Rome.

283. With respect to the siting of New "Toltec" North Chichén more or less adjacent to Old "Maya" South Chichén (assuming a "partial overlap" of the two portions of Chichén Itzá), there is an important sense in which the whole of South Chichén constitutes the "front" half, or conservative component, of the ritual-architectural events of Chichén Itzá while the great plaza of "Toltec Chichén" constitutes the

"back" half. Much more could be done with this line of interpretation.

284. Morley/Brainerd, *Ancient Maya*, 285.

285. Davies, *Toltecs Until the Fall of Tula*, 203.

286. Weaver, *Aztecs, Maya, and Their Predecessors*, 225.

287. Ibid., 225. With respect to the theatrical character of the Castillo, Kelemen, *Medieval American Art*, 87, waxes that "with its four similar sides the Castillo is the most dramatic building in Chichén Itzá. Its effect, however, is far beyond the theatrical; it was erected not for a passing night's entertainment, but for the eternal stage of Nature."

288. The attendance estimates in the local Yucatecan newspapers for the Castillo equinox event of 1988, for instance, ranged from 10,000 to 35,000 people.

289. Tozzer, *Chichén and Cenote*, 92, 124–25, discusses the limited resilience of the mosaic mask tradition in "Toltec Chichén" and the wholesale lack of masks in Tula.

290. Kubler, "Serpent and Atlantean Columns," 104, comments on the Puuc-style rain god masks on the Temple of the Warriors, as do Robertson, *Pre-Columbian Architecture*, 33; and Kelemen, *Medieval American Art*, 87.

291. See Chapter 3 on "Contemplation: Props for Devotion" for a discussion of Abbot Suger's notion of "anagogical illumination" via Gothic architecture.

292. See Landa, *Relación*, 157.

293. Willard, *The Lost Empires of the Itzáes and Mayas*, 17–24, for instance, presents an imaginative (re)construction of the pre-Hispanic Castillo event (based on the "old writers"), which amounts to a happy-go-lucky first fruits ceremony.

294. Tozzer, *Chichén and Cenote*, 34, 44, discusses the later "Toltec" remodelings of buildings in South Chichén, particularly at the Caracol, Monjas, Iglesia, and House of the Phalli; the lack of specific data, however, makes any hypothesis with respect to a shift in ritual priorities in this portion of the city highly conjectural.

295. Tozzer, *Chichén and Cenote*, 45, 259, n. 16, discusses "demolition by other than nature" in the Maya area generally and at Chichén Itzá specifically.

296. See Brunhouse, *In Search of the Maya*, 138–39.

297. The basic descriptive work on the Temple of the Chac Mool, which is buried beneath the Temple of the Warriors, is Morris, Charlot, and Morris, *Temple of the Warriors*. The chronology of this buried temple is much debated: Tozzer, *Chichén and Cenote*, 33, 182, considered the Chac Mool Temple to be early "Toltec" and the key evidence for distinguishing between his Chichén III-A and Chichén III-B phases; Thompson, *Maya Archaeologist*, 32–33, considered that the Chac Mool Temple was a "pre-Toltec," Itzá building (a historical eventuality that is not even possible in Tozzer's scheme); and Kubler, "Tula y Chichén Itzá," 47, places the Chac Mool Temple in his second period of "Maya-Toltec" influence, contemporary with the outer rather than the inner Castillo.

298. The identity of the builders and the chronology of the Castillo-sub are also highly debatable: Tozzer, *Chichén and Cenote*, 33–34, 93–94, repeatedly argued that the Castillo-sub was "transitional from Maya to Toltec"; Thompson, *Rise and Fall of Maya Civilization*, 119, emphasized the lack of feathered serpent imagery in the Castillo-sub (as opposed to the Castillo proper) and thus attributed the building to the first wave of Itzá (or Putun), who were without Tula Toltec or Quetzalcoatl/Kukulcán associations; and Kubler, "Tula y Chichén Itzá," 47, places the Castillo-sub in the first of his three "Toltec-Maya" stages at Chichén Itzá.

299. It is worth noting with respect to the offertory character of "Toltec Chichén" art and architecture that several of Chichén Itzá's most revered treasures were recovered from these intentionally sealed-up structures. For instance, Ann Axtell Morris, *Digging in Yucatán* (New York: Doubleday, 1931), 253–71, recounts her discovery of the superb turquoise mosaic serpent in the buried Chac Mool Temple; and Fernández, *Guide to Mexican Art*, 22, negative in his assessment of virtually all "Toltec Chichén" art and architecture, considers the Red Jaguar throne in the buried Castillo-sub to be a glowing exception, "tremendously moving in its expressive force."

300. Alberto Ruz Lhuillier, "Chichén-Itzá y Palenque, ciudades fortificadas," in *Homenaje al Doctor Alfonso Caso* (Mexico, D.F.: Imprenta Nuevo Mundo, S.A., 1951), 332–35, claims that all the older plans of Chichén Itzá show a double line around "Toltec Chichén" that signifies this wall; he is very confident that it had a real defensive purpose.

301. Weaver, *Aztecs, Maya, and Their Predecessors*, 224–25, taking her cue from Ruz, is one of the few to discuss in English this wall at Chichén Itzá.

302. See Tozzer, *Chichén and Cenote*, 82.

303. See ibid., 80.

304. Kelemen, *Medieval American Art,* 87.

305. Vaillant, *Artists and Craftsmen in Ancient Central America,* 29. He also emphasized the heavy Central Mexican influence on the Temple of the Warriors.

306. See Tozzer, *Chichén and Cenote,* 81–82, for a general review of the distribution of this sort of tribune, platform, or "theatre" in "Toltec Chichén" and elsewhere. Tozzer/Landa, 179, nn. 943, 944, gives a wealth of information about other Mesoamerican dance platforms.

307. These three platforms have been assigned an especially confusing number of different names over the years. The first has been variously known as the Venus Platform, the Platform (or Temple) of the Cones, the Tomb of the Chac Mool, and Mausoleum III; the second has been variously called the Platform (or Temple) of the Tigers and Eagles, the Platform of the Eagles, and Mausoleum I; and the third has been variously referred to as the *Tzompantli* (or skull rack), the Temple (or Wall) of the Skulls, and Mausoleum II.

308. Landa, *Relación,* 179. This is one of the most frequently quoted passages of Landa's manuscript.

309. For instance, Spinden, *Ancient Civilizations of Mexico,* 219, discusses gladiator stones or platforms; Waters, *Mexico Mystique,* 183, offers a Jungian interpretation of gladiatorial sacrifices; and Carmark, *Quiché Mayas of Utatlán,* 189–90, 285, discusses plaza platforms and mock battles among the Quiché Maya of the Southern Highlands.

310. Weaver, *Aztecs, Maya, and Their Predecessors,* 226, for instance, mentions the eclectic character of "Toltec Chichén's" dance platforms; and their specifically Central Mexican, "non-Maya" flavor is mentioned by everyone, for instance, Tozzer, *Chichén and Cenote,* 81. The platforms that had been positioned along the roadway from the plaza to the Sacred Cenote are now totally obliterated and (like the wall around the precinct) absent from nearly all descriptions of Chichén Itzá. For a discussion of them see ibid., 81, and Marquina, *Arquitectura Prehispánica,* 857.

311. Landa, *Relación,* 144. Similarly, Landa, ibid., 140, describes a ceremonial procession along a road that had been "cleaned and adorned with arches and greens." Tozzer, *Chichén and Cenote,* 212, discusses Landa's remarks on ceremonial processions and quotes the *Relación* of Tomas López (1612) in regard to a procession along the causeway from the Castillo to the Sacred Cenote, wherein the priests "went in procession with her [the victim to be sacrificed] by a paved causeway, all of slabs, which came to an end at a large and deep cenote which was there."

312. Deuel, *Conquistadors Without Swords,* 293–99, has a concise discussion of the history of the study of Yucatán's amazing network of *sacbes* (literally "white roads") or causeways.

313. Kubler, "Tula y Chichén Itzá," 67.

314. Spinden, *Study of Maya Art,* 26, comments on the lack of motion and procession in Maya art generally but its proliferation in "Toltec Chichén."

315. Tozzer, *Chichén and Cenote,* 163–64.

316. Kubler, "Serpent and Atlantean Columns," 104–5.

317. The whole issue of human sacrifice at Chichén Itzá is exceptionally complex, yet, suffice it to note that, despite the stock opinion that Tula Toltecs (or Itzá) imported large-scale human sacrifice (by heart extraction and otherwise) into an area where it was largely unprecedented, the actual representations of human sacrifice in Chichén Itzá art are surprisingly few. Tozzer, *Chichén and Cenote,* 128–29, enumerates the depictions of human sacrifice at Chichén Itzá; also see ibid., 202–22.

318. See Ruz, "Chichén Itzá y Tula," 214; and Davies, *Toltecs Until the Fall of Tula,* 206–7. Other, less rigorous accounts (for instance, Willard, *City of the Sacred Well,* 213) have stressed exactly the opposite, that is, the highly individualistic character of "Toltec Chichén" murals, friezes, and bas-reliefs. They are probably mistaken.

319. Arthur Miller's identification of specific individuals in the murals of "Toltec Chichén" (see Miller, "Captains of the Itzá," discussed later with respect to "Mural Evidence: Reconciliation and Intimidation") constitutes another important exception to the impersonal nature of this art.

320. There are some frescoes in South Chichén, notably in the Monjas and the Temple of the Owls. See, for instance, Morley/Brainerd, *Ancient Maya,* 399–404. Willard, *City of the Sacred Wall,* 230–31, considers that the mural in the Temple of the Owls tells "a complete story" about the birth of Kukulcán; no one is liable to agree with that opinion at this point.

321. See Catherwood, *Views of Ancient Monuments,* 130, for his rave review of the artistic quality of "Toltec Chichén" murals. Most later art historians share that flattering assessment of the

murals, particularly in contrast to their disapprobation of the "Toltec" architecture generally.

322. Charnay, *Ancient Cities,* 361–63.

323. Ibid. Note also that, with similar aplomb, Le Plongeon, *Sacred Mysteries of the Mayas and Quichés,* 77–82, interprets the "Toltec Chichén" murals as the commemorative retelling of the exploits of a founder king, Can (Serpent), his three sons, two daughters, and his bride, the apocryphal Queen Moo.

324. Tozzer, "Maya and Toltec Figures at Chichén Itzá."

325. Ibid.

326. D. E. Wray, "The Historical Significance of the Murals in the Temple of the Warriors, Chichén Itzá," *American Antiquity* 11 (1945): 25–27, concurs with Tozzer's 1930 interpretation of the murals in the Temple of the Jaguars as a historical account of the "Toltec Conquest" of the city, and then extends that interpretation to the murals in the Temple of the Warriors, which had been excavated in the interim; Wray, ibid., thus describes this second set of murals also as "a pictorial record of the political and military subjugation of the Maya by the Toltec." Tozzer later seconds that opinion in his own work; see Tozzer, *Chichén and Cenote,* 16, among many places.

327. Coe, *Maya,* 123, for instance (in this and other aspects of Chichén Itzá historical [re]construction), remains a holdout for Tozzer's position. Coe considers that the murals at the Temples of the Warriors and Jaguars are all depictions of a violent Toltec battle — the supposed conquest of Yucatán by Topiltzin Quetzalcoatl. (That would continue also to be the standard assessment of most guides and tourist literature at the site.)

328. Thompson, *Maya History and Religion,* 19.

329. For a discussion of Thompson's Putun hypothesis and its repercussions for the Tula–Chichén Itzá problem, see the section on "Symbiotic Polarity: Admixing Itzá" in Chapter 1 of this project.

330. Thompson, *Maya History and Religion,* 19.

331. As to possible precedents to Eric Thompson's work on these murals, Willard, *City of the Sacred Wall,* 214–17, writing in 1926, considered that the murals in the Temple of the Jaguars represented "Itzá dignitaries," a position that (with none of their rigor) may anticipate Thompson's (and Miller's) reassessment of the murals. Also, Eduard Seler, in 1898, had suggested that the bas-reliefs in the Temple of the Jaguars represented "fisher folk from the coast of the Olmeca in Tabasco." See Tozzer/Landa, 95, n. 415.

332. Miller has a whole series of articles addressing the murals of Chichén Itzá and the east coast of Yucatán. See particularly Arthur G. Miller, "'The Little Descent': Manifest Destiny From the East," *Actes du XLII Congrès International des Américanistes, Paris, 1976,* 8 (1979): 221–35; idem, "Captains of the Itzá"; and idem, "Maya and the Sea."

333. Miller, "The Little Descent," 233.

334. Ibid., 227–30.

335. Miller, "Captains of the Itzá." Kubler, "Serpent and Atlantean Columns," 106, contends that the murals inside the Temple of the Jaguars may correspond to the rising importance of Maya manuscript painting and (in general agreement with Miller) says that "these pictorial chronicles probably tell the deeds of the worthies and priests portrayed in low relief on the pilasters and columns throughout Chichén." Marvin Cohodas, "The Great Ball Court at Chichén Itzá, Yucatán, Mexico," Ph.D. diss., Columbia University, 1974, 237–45, taking a very different line, considers that the murals in the Temple of the Jaguars are more cosmological than literally historical, that they depict confrontations between opposed deities and celestial bodies rather than human factions. Adela Breton, who at the beginning of the century made colored renderings of these now largely destroyed murals in the Temple of the Jaguars (see Miller, "Captains of the Itzá," for reproductions of Breton's renderings), contributes the tantalizing detail that these narrative scenes were not the first decoration of the building. She says that underneath them are traces of "a kind of diaper pattern in red and blue" that could possibly represent a geometrical pattern. Adela Breton, "The Wall Paintings at Chichén Itzá," *Actes du XV Congrès International des Américanistes, Quebec, 1906,* 2 (1906): 166–67. Slim as this reference is, it does suggest (albeit very tentatively) a possible shift in typological priorities between the earlier and later ritual-architectural events at the Temple of the Jaguars.

336. See Miller, "The Little Descent," 231–33; and idem, "Maya and the Sea," 117–22. Miller changes his opinion somewhat over the course of these two articles (written respectively in 1976 and 1977). See ibid., 235, n. 6. Contrary to Miller's claim that the battle murals in the Upper Temple of the Jaguars recount events in Oaxaca, most archaeologists now believe that the "red hills" in those murals more likely depict the hills of the Bolonchen district of the

Puuc region, an area considerably closer to Chichén Itzá. See Andrews and Sabloff, "Classic to Postclassic," 451.

337. Miller, "Captains of the Itzá," 218.

338. In other words, Miller, ibid., 217–19, suggests that reconciliation is more important than intimidation in the mural portrayals of Putun Itzá adventuring, but I would emphasize that theme even more strongly than he does.

339. Tozzer/Landa, 33, n. 172, considered that Chichén Itzá was unique among Maya sites in the depiction of worldly events, "the only site where conquest is shown to any extent." That claim, issued in 1941, now seems overstated, particularly in light of the recent reassessment of the Maya as considerably more worldly, more political, more typically Mesoamerican than the old romantic stereotypes; nevertheless, there is something atypical in the way and the extent to which "Toltec Chichén" commemorates history.

340. Miller, "The Little Descent," 235. This portion of Miller's work depends particularly on his interpretation of the murals in the Upper Temple of the Jaguars. Wren, "Great Ball Court Stone," 10, summarizes Miller's interpretation of those murals as though Miller were arguing that they depict forays out from Chichén Itzá by Chichén-based troops down into southern Oaxaca and the Petén. That would seem to be a fairly serious misreading; I am contending (as I think Miller does) that the murals do *not* commemorate expansionist conquests out from the capital of Chichén Itzá (which would be more in the spirit of Tula) but, instead, episodes that had transpired earlier and that led to the "founding" of "Toltec Chichén."

341. More than a hundred years ago (1886) Le Plongeon, *Sacred Mysteries Among the Mayas and Quichés,* 108, for instance, was pontificating that because of the ubiquity of serpent images in "Toltec Chichén," the city "may indeed be called the 'city of serpents' par excellence."

342. See Carrasco, *Quetzalcoatl and the Irony of Empire,* Chapter 3.

343. Ibid., 143. The interpretations of Chichén Itzá's Castillo by Carrasco, ibid., 140–46; and Margain, "Pre-Columbian Architecture of Central Mexico," 71–72, also demonstrate extremely well the theatric manner of presentation and the inclusion of large crowds of spectators in the Castillo events (priority III-A).

344. See Carrasco, *Quetzalcoatl and the Irony of Empire,* 126–33.

345. Piña Chan, *Chichén Itzá: La Ciudad de los Brujos del Agua,* has an elaborate (if unconvincing) historical hypothesis that features the origin of the Quetzalcoatl cult in Xochicalco and its eventual arrival at Chichén Itzá. Coggins, "New Fire at Chichén Itzá," 463–64, introduces some iconographic evidence for historical contacts between Xochicalco and Chichén Itzá. Even so, I will be content for now with a *non*historical, morphological link between the two capitals.

346. Carrasco, *Quetzalcoatl and the Irony of Empire,* 126.

347. Ibid., 127.

348. Ibid., 131.

349. I steal here from the description of the serpent columns by Kubler, "Serpent and Atlantean Columns," 93. Note that this article, which is foundational for my discussion, is filled with intriguing ideas but is strangely unpolished and disjointed, particularly in comparison with most of Kubler's writings. Especially disconcerting is the way that Kubler interjects a generic sort of paragraph about Quetzalcoatl/Kukulcán (ibid., 93–94), but then makes no attempt to integrate the deity with his wider discussion of the serpent columns of Chichén Itzá; in other words, it is not at all clear whether he wants to identify the serpent columns with Quetzalcoatl or not. Also peculiar with respect to the historical (re)construction of events, elsewhere Kubler continues to maintain his iconoclastic position that the similitude between Tula and Chichén Itzá owes to a "reverse," east-to-west movement from the latter to the former, but this article seems to presume (without ever stating explicitly) the more conventional position that Chichén Itzá was originally a Maya city that experienced a major influx of Mexicans (or Toltecs).

350. Kubler, ibid., 108, discusses the typical configuration of "the serpent column buildings" and then, declining to call them "temples," hypothesizes a "public use as focal centers like council halls."

351. Kubler, ibid., 93, makes a survey of "all known examples of the serpent-column portal within the remains of their original settings." Besides the ten pairs of these columns at Chichén Itzá, he notes five examples extant at Mayapán and one at Tulum. Of the several sets of serpent columns that were once at Tula, only one remains in situ.

352. Consistent with his endeavor to locate Mesoamerican art forms with respect to their historical precedents and echoes, Kubler argues that the "Toltec-Maya" serpent column "replaces" earlier Maya serpent-mask doorways (ibid., 93) and that the atlantean and caryatid forms in Chichén Itzá "replace" the older Classic Maya imagery of bound captives beneath the feet of victorious rulers (ibid., 110). I find those historical claims the weakest part of his argument.

353. Kubler implies this distinction between two sorts of serpent column architectural events, but I am responsible for delineating them as such.

354. Eduard Seler called these platforms "god-tables," and Marvin Cohodas calls them "table-altars." Kubler, "Serpent and Atlantean Columns," 102, considers that the designation of these platforms as "altars" is "a modern misnomer based on a fancied resemblance to [a] place of sacrifice, as in Christian and Old World usage." Such "atlantean platforms," as Kubler prefers to call them, are extant in the Upper Jaguars Building, Warriors Building, Osario, Big Table Building, and Little Table Building, all of which are in North Chichén. (Note that Kubler also emphatically refuses to accept the typical designation of all these structures as "temples," opting instead for the more generic term "buildings.")

355. See ibid., 103–15. Kubler's contention that "Toltec-Maya" polity was "more humane" than the earlier Maya polity is based particularly on the absence at "Toltec Chichén" of the bound and captive figures that are so prominent in Classic Maya iconography.

356. Ibid., 103–15.

357. Ibid., 108.

358. Ibid., 104. Kubler does *not* (at least in this article) make the explicit comparison between the integrative programs of "Toltec Chichén" and Xochicalco.

359. See Chapter 1 of this project on the contrast between "irreconcilable Maya-Mexican polarity" and "symbiotic Maya-Mexican polarity."

360. Kubler, "Serpent and Atlantean Columns," 104. George Kubler, *Aspects of Classic Maya Rulership* (Washington, D.C.: 1977), 15–23, discusses a somewhat earlier exercise of this same need to integrate Mexican Highland and Maya Lowland conceptions of authority at Tikal.

361. Kubler, "Serpent and Atlantean Columns," 106. Kubler is speaking specifically of the west facade of the Upper Jaguars Building, which faces the Great Ball Court. The suggestion of a close parallel between this facade and Xochicalco's Temple of Quetzalcoatl is mine, not Kubler's.

362. Ibid., 104. Moreover, Kubler, ibid., 111–12, takes the notion of the serpent column itself as a symbol of integration even further, suggesting that its imagery was based on the seasonal symbolism of complementary Kukulcán (Feathered Serpent) and Xiuhcoatl (Fire Serpent), which stand respectively for the wet and dry seasons. Coggins, "New Fire at Chichén Itzá," 444, extends this seasonal interpretation even further, calling attention to the fact that in Yucatán both rattlesnake rattles and the Pleiades are referred to as *tzab*. Accordingly, Coggins believes that the serpent columns at "Toltec Chichén" could represent the transition from the rainy to the dry season — "one feathered serpent denotes the moment before and the other the moment after the Pleiades cross the zenith." Also, at a more basic level, Coggins, ibid., 5, calls into question the traditional assumption that "Toltec Chichén" feathered serpents are Quetzalcoatl/Kukulcán.

363. This section depends heavily on Clemency Coggins's two articles on New Fire Ceremonialism at Chichén Itzá: "New Fire at Chichén Itzá" (1987) and "A New Sun at Chichén Itzá" (1989). For her suspicions that the serpent columns do not represent Quetzalcoatl after all, see Coggins, "New Fire at Chichén Itzá," 444.

364. Ibid., 427.

365. The concept of "symbiotic polarity" was explored in Chapter 1 of this project. While Coggins's hypothesis is radically different from Eric Thompson's explanation of "Toltec Chichén" as the product of a mutually beneficial symbiosis between wayward Tula Toltecs and wealthy Putun Itzá, both interpretations belong to this variation on the notorious old paradigm of Maya-Mexican polarity.

366. Coggins, "A New Sun at Chichén Itzá," 260.

367. Coggins, "New Fire at Chichén Itzá," 441, writes, "This capital [of Chichén Itzá] was probably initially founded by Mexicanized Maya from the Puuc who at the disintegration of Teotihuacán joined with other 'Toltec' to create a sacred capital for religious, political and corporate reasons." She uses "Mexican" anachronistically "to designate the inhabitants of Central Mexico" (see ibid., 483, n. 2); and she uses "Toltec," actually the more embracing term in this case, to refer to "all those peoples, whether superficially Mexican or Maya, who traced their ancestry and cultural traditions to Teotihuacán" (see Coggins, "A New Sun at Chichén

Itzá," 260). The historical Toltecs of Tula, Hidalgo, play no special role in her interpretation, nor is the specific issue of Tula–Chichén Itzá similitude ever directly addressed.

368. See Tozzer, *Chichén and Cenote,* 41.

369. Regarding the rapid succession of calendrical and astronomical events in 830 C.E., see Coggins, "New Fire at Chichén Itzá," 426–41, 466–76; and idem, "A New Sun at Chichén Itzá," 272–73.

370. Coggins, ibid., 264–65, explains that the Mexican fear of cycle-ending years is well known; the Maya attribute a somewhat different astrological and apocalyptical significance to age-endings.

371. Ibid., 272.

372. Ibid., 264–65.

373. See Johanna Broda, "La fiesta Azteca del Fuego Nuevo y el culto de las Pleyades," in *Time and Space in Ancient American Cosmovision,* ed. Frank Tichy (Munich: Universität Erlangen-Nürnberg, Wilhelm Fink Verlag, 1982), 129–57.

374. The wildly diversified range of interpretations of the *chacmool* figure would constitute another full project in itself. Coggins, "New Fire at Chichén Itzá," 444–46, addresses the issue; and Miller, "A Re-examination of the Mesoamerican Chacmool," provides a fresh interpretation (1985) and considerable bibliography on *chacmools.* Also see Alfredo Cuéllar, *Texcatlzoncatl Esculturico: El Chacmool, el Dios Mesoamericano del Vino* (Mexico, 1981).

375. See Ruppert, *Chichén Itzá: Architectural Notes and Plans,* 166; or Miller, "A Re-examination of the Mesoamerican Chacmool," 9.

376. Coggins, "New Fire at Chichén Itzá," 444.

377. Ibid., 446.

378. It is somewhat problematic that Coggins sees the *chacmool* figures as all bound up with a complex of pyrite mirrors and New Fire Ceremonialism, which she traces back to Teotihuacán, but, as yet, there have been no *chacmools* found at Teotihuacán.

379. See Coggins, "A New Sun at Chichén Itzá," 272.

380. Coggins, "New Fire at Chichén Itzá," 441.

381. Ibid.

382. Coggins, "A New Sun at Chichén Itzá," 264.

383. See "Symbiotic Polarity: Admixing Itzá" in Chapter 1.

384. See, for instance, Coggins, "New Fire at Chichén Itzá," 448–60.

385. For the slim evidence of New Fire Ceremonialism at Tula, see Coggins, ibid., 466. While Coggins's emphasis is on Maya-Mexican synthesis, her own work implies that, rather than an equal partnership, the New Fire Ceremony at Chichén Itzá was considerably more Mexican (that is, Teotihuacáno) than Maya. She says, for instance, that the original occurrence was scheduled to coincide with the end of the Mexican tenth Calendar Round, some six months after the end of the Maya *bakun* nine, and she says that the "period of dominance by the highland Toltecs of Tula, Hidalgo," would eventually entail a "victory of the Mexican Calendar Round over the Long Count of the Lowland Maya." See Coggins, "A New Sun at Chichén Itzá," 272–73.

386. Kakupacal was discussed earlier in this chapter in regard to the content of the architectural events of South Chichén. Coggins, "New Fire at Chichén Itzá," 465, interprets Kakupacal as "Fire-His-Mirror." Elsewhere (idem, "A New Sun at Chichén Itzá," 271), she suggests that Kakupacal could be read as "Fire Shield."

387. This may be an unfairly literal reading of Coggins's brief remarks, but she does imply that "Toltec Chichén" (at least the Castillo) is actually older than many portions of South Chichén. For instance, she moves the construction/dedication of the Castillo back to 830 C.E. but continues to accept David Kelley's position that most of the hieroglyphic inscriptions in South Chichén were made between 869 and 884 C.E. See, for instance, Coggins, "A New Sun at Chichén Itzá," 261.

388. *The Ancient Future of the Itzá: The Book of Chilam Balam of Tizimin,* trans. and annotated by Munro S. Edmonson (Austin: University of Texas Press, 1982).

389. Ibid.

390. On Morley's and Tozzer's historical (re)construction of the "Toltec Conquest" of Chichén Itzá, see Chapter 1, "Chichén Chronology: Empires and Overlaps" and "The Tula–Chichén Connection: The 'Mexicanization' of Yucatán."

391. Edmonson, *Ancient Future of the Itzá,* xvi. By "Tula," Edmonson apparently intends the Tollan of tradition rather than the historical site of Tula, Hidalgo; see in Chapter 1, "Tula Chronology: Toltecs of Myth and History." Edmonson's "Itzá" and "Toltec Xiu" may perhaps be correlated with the competing "Putun Itzá warrior factions" to which Arthur Miller attributes the "founding" of "Toltec Chichén."

392. See Edmonson, *Ancient Future of the Itzá,* 48, n. 927.

393. Ibid., xvi.

394. I should stress one final time that the hermeneutical method that I am bringing to bear on these materials is *not* particularly well suited for resolving this sort of *historical* problem.

395. Alluding to Landa's description of the annual rites of Xul (see Landa, *Relación,* 158), Coggins, "A New Sun at Chichén Itzá," 272–73, explains that "for the Colonial Maya this (*Xul*) November festival was dedicated to Kukulcán or Quetzalcoatl. At this time the annual New Fire was drilled at the Castillo and feathered serpents descended to earth." The implication is that the serpent of light would be descending the Castillo during the November Xul rites; however, as I understand it, that is a phenomenon of the two equinoxes — March and September. A possible (but not likely) explanation comes in the suggestion of William Gates and Herbert Spinden that the Xul rites might possibly be a vestige of an older calendar. See Tozzer/Landa, 158, n. 808.

396. Coggins, "New Fire at Chichén Itzá," 446–66, surveys the evidence for the New Fire Ceremonialism in each of these cities. Becan, in Campeche, is a particularly interesting case because here, as at Chichén Itzá, Coggins (ibid., 461–62) sees a deliberate juxtaposition of Maya and Mexican symbolism.

397. In regard to the lighting of new fire in a humble village context, J. Eric S. Thompson, "Sixteenth and Seventeenth Century Reports on the Chol Mayas," *American Anthropologist* 40 (1938): 584–604; reprinted in *Ancient Mesoamerica,* ed. Graham, 205–20, describes "a special lighting ceremony" among the Chol Mayas that, while different, is very like the Mexican New Fire Ceremony. See particularly p. 212 of the reprinted version of Thompson's article. In regard to the lighting of new fire in a grander, urban context, specifically that of the Aztecs, see Broda, "La Fiesta Azteca del Fuego Nuevo"; and Davíd Carrasco, "Star Gatherers and Wobbling Suns: Astral Symbolism in the Aztec Tradition," *History of Religions* 26 (February 1987): 279–94. Weaver, *Aztecs, Maya, and Their Predecessors,* 106, gives a concise account of New Fire ceremonies in Tenochtitlán and elsewhere.

398. The appeal to the shared Mesoamerican anxiety about human intransience is, in a sense, the conservative, alluring component of these "Toltec Chichén" New Fire events that elicits the committed participation of the audience. Moreover, it is an appeal that transcends the dichotomy of Maya versus Mexican in favor of a more encompassing sensation of Mesoamerican unity.

Bibliography

Abercrombie, Stanley. *Architecture as Art.* New York: Van Nostrand Reinhold Company, 1984.

Acosta, Jorge. "Exploraciones en Tula, Hidalgo, 1940." *Revista Mexicana de Estudios Antropológicos* 4 (1940): 172–94.

———. "La tercera temporada de exploraciones en Tula, Hidalgo, 1941." *Revista Mexicana de Estudios Antropológicos* 6 (1944): 239–48.

———. "Interpretacion de algunos datos obtenidos en Tula relativos a la epoca Tolteca." *Revista Mexicana de Estudios Antropológicos* 14 (1956–57): 75–110.

Adams, Richard E.W. "Maya Archaeology 1958–1968: A Review." *Latin American Research Review* 4 (1969): 3–45.

———. *Prehistoric Mesoamerica.* Boston: Little, Brown and Co., 1977.

Adamson, David Grant. *The Ruins of Time: Four and a Half Centuries of Conquest and Discovery Among the Maya.* New York: Praeger, 1975.

Alberti, Leone Battista. *The Ten Books of Architecture.* Trans. James Leoni. Ed. Joseph Rykwert. London: Alec Tiranti Ltd., 1955.

Anders, F. *Das Pantheon der Maya.* Graz, Austria: Akademische Druck und Künstverlag, 1963.

Anderson, Arthur J.O., ed. *Morleyana: A Collection of Writings in Memoriam.* Sante Fe, N.M.: School of American Research and the Museum of New Mexico, 1950.

Andrews, Anthony P., and Fernando Robles C. "Chichén Itzá and Cobá: An Itzá-Maya Standoff in Early Postclasssic Yucatán." In *The Lowland Maya Postclassic.* Ed. Arlene F. Chase and Prudence M. Rice. Austin: University of Texas, 1985.

Andrews, E. Wyllys IV. "Archaeology and Prehistory in the Northern Maya Lowlands: An Introduction." In *Handbook of Middle American Indians: Archaeology of Southern Mesoamerica.* Vol. 2. Austin: University of Texas Press, 1965.

———. *Balankanche, Throne of the Tiger Priest.* Publication 32. New Orleans: Middle America Research Institute, 1970.

———. "Balankanche — Throne of the Tiger Priest." *Explorers Journal* 49 (1971).

———. "Dzibilchaltún." *Supplement to Handbook of Middle American Indians.* Vol. 1. Austin: University of Texas Press, 1981.

Andrews, E. Wyllys V, and Jeremy A. Sabloff. "Classic to Postclassic: A Summary Discussion." In *Late Lowland Maya Civilization: Classic to Postclassic.* Ed. Jeremy A. Sabloff and E. Wyllys Andrews V. Albuquerque: University of New Mexico Press, 1986.

———. Introduction to *Late Lowland Maya Civilization: Classic to Postclassic.* Ed. Jeremy A. Sabloff and E. Wyllys Andrews V. Albuquerque: University of New Mexico Press, 1986.

Andrews, George. *Maya Cities: Placemaking and Urbanization.* Norman: University of Oklahoma Press, 1975.

Anton, Ferdinand. *Art of the Maya.* Trans. Mary Whittell. London: Thames and Hudson, 1970.

Armillas, Pedro. "A Sequence of Cultural Development in Mesoamerica." In *A Reappraisal of Peruvian Archaeology.* Ed. Wendell C. Bennett. Menasha, Wis.: Society for American Archaeology, 1948.

———. "Teotihuacán, Tula y los Toltecas: Las culturas post-arcaicas y pre-Aztecas del centro de Mexico." *Revista de la Universidad Nacional de Argentina* 3 (1950): 37–70.

Arnheim, Rudolf. *The Power of the Center: A Study of Composition in the Visual Arts.* Berkeley: University of California Press, 1982.

Arochi, Luis E. *La Pirámide de Kukulcán: Su Simbiolismo Solar.* Mexico, D.F.: Panorama Editorial, 1987.

Aveni, Anthony F. *Skywatchers of Ancient Mexico.* Austin: University of Texas Press, 1980.

———. "Archaeoastronomy in the Maya Region: 1970–1980." In *Archaeoastronomy in the New World.* Ed. Anthony F. Aveni. Cambridge: Cambridge University Press, 1982.

———. "The Real Venus-Kukulcan in Maya Inscriptions and Alignments." Revised version of a paper presented at the Sixth Mesa Redonda de Palenque, June 1986.

———, ed. *Native American Astronomy.* Austin: University of Texas Press, 1977.

Aveni, Anthony F., and Sharon L. Gibbs. "On the Orientation of Pre-Columbian Buildings in Central Mexico." *American Antiquity* 42 (October 1976): 509–17.

Aveni, Anthony F.,and Horst Hartung. "Precision in the Layout of Maya Architecture." In *Ethnoastronomy and Archaeoastronomy in the American Tropics.* Ed. Anthony F. Aveni and Gary Urton. New York: New York Academy of Sciences, 1982.

———. *Maya City Planning and the Calendar.* Philadelphia: American Philosophical Society, 1986.

Aveni, Anthony F., Horst Hartung, and Sharon L. Gibbs. "The Caracol Tower at Chichén Itzá: Ancient Observatory." *Science* 18 (June 1975): 977–85.

Bachelard, Gaston. *The Poetics of Space.* Boston: Beacon Press, 1964.

Ball, Joseph W. "A Coordinate Approach to Northern Maya Prehistory: A.D. 700–1200." *American Antiquity* 39 (1974): 85–93.

———. "Ceramics, Culture History, and the Puuc Tradition: Some Alternative Possibilities." In *The Puuc: New Perspectives.* Ed. Lawrence Mills. Pella, Iowa: Central College, 1979.

———. "The 1977 Central College Symposium on Puuc Archaeology: A Summary View." In *The Puuc: New Perspectives.* Ed. Lawrence Mills. Pella, Iowa: Central College, 1979.

Barrera Vasquez, Alfredo, and Sylvanus G. Morley. *The Maya Chronicles.* Publication 585. Washington: Carnegie Institution of Washington, 1949.

Becker, Marshall Joseph. "Priests, Peasants and Ceremonial Centers: The Intellectual History of a Model." In *Maya Archaeology and Ethnohistory.* Ed. Norman Hammond and Gordon Willey. Austin: University of Texas Press, 1979.

Benson, Elizabeth P. *The Maya World.* New York: Thomas G. Crowell Company, 1967.

———. "Architecture as Metaphor." In *Fifth Palenque Round Table, 1983.* Vol. 7. Ed. Merle Green Robertson. San Francisco: Pre-Columbian Art Research Institute, 1985.

———, ed. *Mesoamerican Sites and World-Views: A Conference at Dumbarton Oaks, October 16–17, 1976.* Washington: Dumbarton Oaks, 1981.

Berkhofer, Robert F. *The White Man's Indian: Images of the American Indian From Columbus to the Present.* New York: Alfred A. Knopf, 1978.

Bernal, Ignacio. "Toynbee y Mesoamerican." *Estudios de la Cultura Nahuatl* 2 (1960): 43–58.

———. *Mexican Wall Paintings of the Maya and Aztec Period.* New York: New American Library of World Literature, 1963.

———. *3,000 Years of Art and Life in Mexico.* Trans. Carolyn B. Czitron. New York: Harry N. Abrams, 1968.

———. "Maya Antiquarians." In *Social Process in Maya Prehistory: Studies in Honour of Sir Eric Thompson.* Ed. Norman Hammond. London: Academic Press, 1977.

———. *A History of Mexican Archaeology.* London: Thames and Hudson, 1980.

Beyer, Hermann. *Studies on the Inscriptions of Chichén Itzá.* Publication 483. Washington: Carnegie Institution of Washington, 1937.

Bloomer, Kent C., and Charles W. Moore. *Body, Memory and Architecture.* New Haven: Yale University Press, 1977.

Blunt, Anthony, ed. *Baroque and Rococo Architecture and Decoration.* New York: Harper & Row, 1978.

Bolles, John S. *Las Monjas: A Major Pre-Mexican Architectural Complex at Chichén Itzá.* Norman: University of Oklahoma Press, 1977.

Borgeaud, Phillippe. "The Open Entrance to the Closed Palace of the King: The Greek Labyrinth in Context." *History of Religions* 14 (August 1974): 1–27.

de Borhegyi, Stephan F. *Pre-Columbian Ballgames: A Pan-Mesoamerican Tradition.* Contributions in Anthropology and History, no. 1. Milwaukee, Wis.: Milwaukee Public Museum, 1980.

Brainerd, George. Review of Sylvanus Morley, *The Ancient Maya. American Antiquity* 14 (1948): 133–36.

———. *The Maya Civilization.* Los Angeles: Southwest Museum, 1954.

———. *The Archaeological Ceramics of Yucatán.* University of California Anthropological Records, vol. 19. Berkeley: University of California Press, 1958.

Braunfels, Wolfgang. *Monasteries of Western Europe: The Architecture of the Orders.* Princeton, N.J.: Princeton University Press, 1972.

Breton, Adela. "The Wall Paintings of Chichén Itzá." *Actes du XV Congrès International des Américanistes, Quebec, 1906,* 2 (1906): 166–67.

———. "Preliminary Study of the North Building (Chamber C), Great Ball Court, Chichén Itzá, Yucatán." *Actes du XIX Congrès International des Américanistes, Washington, 1915* (1917): 187–94.

Brinton, Daniel G. *The Maya Chronicles.* Library of Aboriginal American Literature, no. 1. Philadelphia: D. G. Brinton, 1882.

———. "Were the Toltecs an Historic Nationality?" *American Philosophical Society, Proceedings* (Philadelphia) 24 (1887): 229–41.

———. *Essays of an Americanist.* Philadelphia: Porter and Coates, 1890.

Broda, Johanna. "Astronomy, *Cosmovision,* and Ideology in Pre-Hispanic Mesoamerica." In *Ethnoastronomy and Archaeoastronomy in the American Tropics.* Ed. Anthony F. Aveni and Gary Urton. New York: New York Academy of Sciences, 1982.

———. "Le fiesta Azteca del Fuego Nuevo y el culto de las Pleyades." In *Time and Space in Ancient American Cosmovision.* Ed. Frank Tichy. Munich: Universität Erlangen-Nurnberg; Wilhelm Fink Verlag, 1982.

———. "Templo Mayor as Ritual Space." In *The Great Temple of Tenochtitlán: Center and Periphery in the Aztec World.* Johanna Broda, Davíd Carrasco, and Eduardo Matos Moctezuma. Berkeley: University of California Press, 1987.

Brown, Kenneth L. "Postclassic Relationships Between the Highland and Lowland Maya." In *The Lowland Maya Postclassic.* Ed. Arlene F. Chase and Prudence M. Rice. Austin: University of Texas Press, 1985.

Brown, Peter Lancaster. *Megaliths, Myths, and Men: An Introduction to Astro-Archaeology.* New York: Taplinger Publishing Company, 1976.

Brundage, Burr Cartwright. *Two Earths, Two Heavens: An Essay Contrasting the Aztecs and the Incas.* Albuquerque: University of New Mexico Press, 1975.

———. *The Fifth Sun: Aztec Gods, Aztec World.* Austin: University of Texas Press, 1979.

Brunhouse, Robert L. *Sylvanus G. Morley and the World of the Ancient Maya.* Norman: University of Oklahoma Press, 1971.

———. *In Search of the Maya: The First Archaeologists.* Albuquerque: University of New Mexico Press, 1973.

———. *Pursuit of the Ancient Maya: Some Archaeologists of Yesterday.* Albuquerque: University of New Mexico Press, 1975.

Burl, Aubrey. *Rites of the Gods.* London: J. M. Dent and Sons, Ltd., 1981.

Bushnell, G.H.S. *Ancient Arts of the Americas.* New York: Praeger, 1965.

Carlson, John B. "A Geomantic Model for the Interpretation of Mesoamerican Sites: An Essay in Cross-Cultural Comparison." In *Mesoamerican Sites and World-Views.* Ed. Elizabeth Benson. Washington: Dumbarton Oaks, 1976.

———. "The Case of Geomantic Alignments of Pre-Columbian Mesoamerican Sites — The Maya." *Katunob: A Newsletter Bulletin on Mesoamerican Anthropology* 10 (June 1977): 67–88.

Carmack, Robert M. *The Quiché Mayas of Utatlán: The Evolution of a Highland Guatemala Kingdom.* Norman: University of Oklahoma Press, 1981.

Carrasco, Davíd. "City as Symbol in Aztec Thought: The Clue From the Codex Mendoza." *History of Religions* 20 (February 1981): 199–223.

———. "Templo Mayor: The Aztec Vision of Place." *Religion* 2 (1981): 275–97.

———. *Quetzalcoatl and the Irony of Empire: Myths and Prophesies in the Aztec Tradition.* Chicago: University of Chicago Press, 1982.

———. "Star Gatherers and Wobbling Suns: Astral Symbolism in the Aztec Tradition." *History of Religion* 26 (February 1987): 279–94.

———, ed. *The Imagination of Matter: Religion and Ecology in Mesoamerican Traditions.* B.A.R. International Series 515. Oxford, England: B.A.R., 1989.

Caso, Alfonso. "New World Culture History: Middle America." In *Anthropology Today.* Ed. Sol Tax. Chicago: University of Chicago Press, 1953.

Catherwood, Frederick. *The Views of Ancient Monuments of Central America, Chiapas and Yucatán.* London: Owen Jones, 1844.

———. Introduction to *The Views of Ancient Monuments of Central America, Chiapas and Yucatán.* In *Frederick Catherwood, Archt.* Victor Wolfgang von Hagen. New York: Oxford University Press, 1950.

Chadwick, Robert. "Native Pre-Aztec History of Central Mexico." In *Handbook of Middle American Indians: Archaeology of Northern Mesoamerica.* Vol. 11. Austin: University of Texas Press, 1971.

Chamberlain, Robert S. *The Conquest and Colonization of Yucatán 1517–1559.* Publication 582. Washington: Carnegie Institution of Washington, 1948.

Charnay, Désiré. *Cités et Ruines Américaines: Mitla, Palenque, Izamal, Chichén Itzá, Uxmal. Recueilliés et Photographiées par Désiré Charnay Avec un Texte par M. Viollet-le-Duc.* Paris: Gide, 1862–63.

———. *Les Anciennes Villes du Nouveau Monde. Voyages d'Explorations au Mexique et dans l'Amérique Centrale, par Désiré Charnay, 1857–1882.* Paris: Hachette, 1885.

———. *The Ancient Cities of the New World: Being Voyages and Explorations in Mexico and Central America From 1857–1882.* Trans. J. Gonine and Helen S. Conant. London: Chapman, 1887; New York: Harper Brothers, 1887.

Chase, Arlen F., and Diane Z. Chase. "Postclassic Temporal and Spatial Frames for the Lowland Maya: A Background." In *The Lowland Maya Postclassic.* Ed. Arlen F. Chase and Prudence M. Rice. Austin: University of Texas Press, 1985.

Chase, Arlen F., and Prudence M. Rice, eds. *The Lowland Maya Postclassic.* Austin: University of Texas Press, 1985.

Clendinnen, Inga. *Ambivalent Conquests: Maya and Spaniard in Yucatán 1517–1570.* Cambridge: Cambridge University Press, 1987.

Cline, Howard F. "Ethnohistory: A Progress Report on the *Handbook of Middle American Indians.*" *Hispanic American Historical Review* 50 (1960): 224–29.

———. "Guide to the Ethnohistorical Sources: A Progress Report." *Actes du XXXVI Congrès International des Américanistes, Spain, 1964,* 2 (1966): 133–43.

———. "Introduction: Reflections on Ethnohistory." In *Handbook of Middle American Indians: Guide to the Ethnographic Sources.* Vol. 12. Austin: University of Texas Press, 1972.

Clothey, Fred W. *Rhythm and Intent: Ritual Studies from South India.* Madras: Blackie and Son, Pvt Ltd., 1983.

Coe, Michael D. *The Maya Scribe and His World.* New York: Grolier Club, 1973.

———. "The Iconology of Olmec Art." In *The Iconography of Middle American Sculpture.* Ed. H. B. Nicholson. New York: Metropolitan Museum of Art, 1973.

———. *The Maya.* 3d ed. London: Thames and Hudson, 1984.

Coggins, Clemency C. "A Role for the Art Historian in an Era of New Archaeology." *Actes du XLII Congrès International des Américanistes, Paris, 1976* (1979): 315–19.

———. "A New Order and the Role of the Calendar: Some Characteristics of the Middle Classic Period at Tikal." In *Maya Archaeology and Ethnohistory.* Ed. Norman Hammond and Gordon Willey. Austin: University of Texas Press, 1979.

———. "The Shape of Time: Some Political Implications of a Four-Part Figure." *American Antiquity* 45 (October 1980): 727–39.

———. "The Zenith, the Mountain, the Center, and the Sea." In *Ethnoastronomy and Archaeostonomy in the American Tropics.* Ed. Anthony F. Aveni and Gary Urton. New York: New York Academy of Sciences, 1982.

———. "New Fire at Chichén Itzá." In *Memorias del Primer Coloquio Internacional de Mayistas, 5–10 de Agosto de 1985.* Mexico, D.F.: Universidad Nacional Autonoma de Mexico, 1987.

———. "A New Sun at Chichén Itzá." In *World Archaeoastronomy: Selected Papers From the 2nd Oxford International Conference on Archaeoastronomy Held at Mérida, Yucatán, Mexico 13–17 January 1986.* Ed. Anthony F. Aveni. Cambridge: Cambridge University Press, 1989.

Coggins, Clemency, and Orrin C. Shane III, eds. *Cenote of Sacrifice: Maya Treasures From the Sacred Well at Chichén Itzá.* Austin: University of Texas Press, 1984.

Cohadas, Marvin. *The Great Ball Court at Chichén Itzá, Yucatán, Mexico.* New York: Garland, 1978.

Cordy-Collins, Alana, ed. *Pre-Columbian Art History: Selected Readings.* Palo Alto, Calif.: Peek Publications, 1982.

Covarrubias, Miguel. *Indian Art of Mexico and Central America.* New York: Alfred A. Knopf, 1957.

Cowgill, George L. "Rulership and the Ciudadela: Political Inferences From Teotihuacán Architecture." In *Civilizations in the Ancient Americas: Essays in Honor of Gordon R. Willey.* Ed. Richard Leventhal and Alan L. Kolata. Albuquerque: University of New Mexico Press, and Cambridge: Peabody Museum of Archaeology and Ethnology, 1983.

Davies, Nigel. *The Toltecs Until the Fall of Tula.* Norman: University of Oklahoma Press, 1977.

———. *The Toltec Heritage: From the Fall of Tula to the Rise of Tenochtitlán.* Norman: University of Oklahoma Press, 1980.

Davis, Keith F. *Désiré Charnay: Expeditionary Photographer.* Albuquerque: University of New Mexico Press, 1981.

Davoust, Michel. "Les premiers chefs Mayas de Chichén Itzá." *Mexicon* 2:2 (1980): 25–29.

Desmond, Lawrence Gustave, and Phyllis Mauch Messenger. *A Dream of Maya: Augustus and Alice Le Plongeon in Nineteenth-Century Yucatán.* Albuquerque: University of New Mexico Press, 1988.

Deuel, Leo. *Conquistadors Without Swords: Archaeologists in the Americas.* New York: Schocken Books, 1967.

Diehl, Richard A. "Tula." In *Supplement to the Handbook of Middle American Indians.* Vol. 1. Austin: University of Texas Press, 1981.

———. *Tula: The Toltec Capital of Ancient Mexico.* London: Thames and Hudson, 1983.

Diehl, Richard A., ed. *Studies of Ancient Tollan: A Report of the University of Missouri-Columbia Tula Archaeological Project.* Columbia: University of Missouri, Columbia, 1974.

Diehl, Richard A., and Robert A. Benfer. "Tollan, the Toltec Capital." *Archaeology* 28 (1975): 112–24.

Diehl, Richard A., and J. T. Wynn. "Toltec Trade With Central America: New Light and Evidence." *Archaeology* 27 (1974): 182–87.

Durán, Fray Diego. *Book of the Gods and Rites and The Ancient Calendar.* Trans. and ed. Fernando Horcasitas and Doris Heyden. Norman: University of Oklahoma Press, 1971.

Dutton, B. P. "Tula of the Toltecs." *El Palacio* 62 (1955): 195–251.

———. "A Brief Discussion of Chichén Itzá." *El Palacio* 63 (1956): 202–32.

Ediger, Donald. *The Well of Sacrifice.* Garden City, N.J.: Doubleday, 1971.

Edmonson, Munro S., trans. and annotated. *The Ancient Future of the Itzá: The Book of Chilam Balam of Tizimin.* Austin: University of Texas Press, 1982.

———, trans. and annotated. *Heaven Born Merida and Its Destiny: The Book of Chilam Balam of Chumayel.* Austin: University of Texas Press, 1986.

Eliade, Mircea. *The Myth of the Eternal Return.* Trans. Willard R. Trask. Princeton, N.J.: Princeton University Press, 1954.

———. *Patterns in Comparative Religion.* Trans. Rosemary Sheed. New York: Meridian Books, 1967.

———. *A History of Religious Ideas.* Trans. Willard R. Trask. 3 vols. Chicago: University of Chicago Press, 1978–88.

Feldman, Lawrence H. "Tollan in Hidalgo: Native Accounts of the Central Mexican Tolteca." In *Studies of Ancient Tollan: A Report of the University of Missouri–Columbia Tula Archaeological Project.* Ed. Richard A. Diehl. Columbia: University of Missouri, Columbia, 1974.

Fenton, William. "The Training of Historical Ethnologists in America." *American Anthropologist* 54:3 (1952): 328–39.

Ferguson, William M., and Arthur H. Rohn. *Mesoamerica's Ancient Cities: Aerial Views of Precolumbian Ruins in Mexico, Guatemala, Belize, and Honduras.* Niwot, Colo.: University Press of Colorado, 1990.

Fernández, Justino. *A Guide to Mexican Art.* Trans. Joshua C. Taylor. Chicago: University of Chicago Press, 1969.

Flannery, Kent V. "Archaeological Systems Theory and Early Mesoamerica." In *Anthropological Archaeology in the Americas.* Ed. Betty J. Meggers. Washington: Anthropological Society of Washington, 1968.

Folan, William J. "The Cenote Sagrado of Chichén Itzá, Yucatán, Mexico, 1967–68: The Excavation, Plans and Preparations." *International Journal of Nautical Archaeology and Underwater Exploration* 3:2 (1974): 283–93.

Freidel, David A. "Cultural Areas and Interaction Spheres: Contrasting Approaches to the Emergence of Civilization in the Maya Lowlands." *American Antiquity* 44 (1979): 36–54.

———. "New Light on the Dark Age: A Summary of Major Themes." In *The Lowland Maya Postclassic.* Ed. Arlen F. Chase and Prudence M. Rice. Austin: University of Texas Press, 1985.

———. "Terminal Classic Lowland Maya: Successes, Failures, and Aftermaths." In *Late Lowland Maya Civilization: Classic to Postclassic.* Ed. Jeremy A. Sabloff and E. Wyllys Andrews V. Albuquerque: University of New Mexico Press, 1986.

Fry, Robert E. "Revitalization Movements Among the Postclassic Lowland Maya." In *The Lowland Maya Postclassic.* Ed. Arlen F. Chase and Prudence M. Rice. Austin: University of Texas Press, 1985.

Furst, Peter T. "The Olmec Were-Jaguar Motif in Light of Ethnographic Reality." In *Dumbarton Oaks Conference on the Olmec.* Washington: Dumbarton Oaks, 1968.

Fuson, Robert H. "The Orientation of Maya Ceremonial Centers." *Annals of the Association of American Geographers* 3 (1969): 494–511.

Gadamer, Hans-Georg. *Truth and Method.* Trans. W. Glen-Doepel. London: Sheed and Ward, 1975.

———. *Philosophical Hermeneutics.* Trans. and ed. David E. Linge. Berkeley: University of California Press, 1976.

———. *The Relevance of the Beautiful and Other Essays.* Trans. Nicholas Walker. Ed. Robert Bernasconi. Cambridge: Cambridge University Press, 1986.

Gallenkamp, Charles. *Maya: The Riddle and Rediscovery of a Lost Civilization.* 2d rev. ed. New York: Penguin Books, 1981.

Gann, Thomas. *Mystery Cities.* London: Duckworth, 1925.

———. *Glories of the Maya.* London: Duckworth, 1938.

———. *In an Unknown Land.* 1924. Reprint, Freeport, N.Y.: Books for Libraries Press, 1971.

Gendrop, Paul. "Dragon-Mouth Entrance: Zoomorphic Portals in the Architecture of Central Yucatán." In *Third Palenque Round Table, 1978.* Part 2. Ed. Merle Greene Robertson. Austin: University of Texas Press, 1980.

———. *Compendio de Arte Prehispanico.* Mexico, D.F.: Editorial Trillas, 1987.

Gendrop, Paul, and Doris Heyden. *Mesoamerican Architecture.* New York: Harry N. Abrams, 1974.

Gingerich, Willard. "Heidegger and the Aztecs: The Poetics of Knowing in Pre-Hispanic Nahuatl Poetry." In *Recovering the Word: Essays on Native American Literature.* Ed. Brian Swann and Arnold Krupat. Berkeley: University of California Press, 1987.

Gombrich, E. H. *Art and Illusion: A Study in the Psychology of Pictorial Representation.* Princeton, N.J.: Princeton University Press, 1972.

Gómez, Ermilo Abreu. *Canek: History and Legend of a Maya Hero.* Trans. Mario L. Davila and Carter Wilson. Berkeley: University of California Press, 1979.

Gordon, B. L. "Sacred Directions, Orientation and the Top of the Map." *History of Religions* 10 (February 1971): 211–27.

Graham, John A. *Ancient Mesoamerica: Selected Readings.* Palo Alto, Calif.: Peek Publications, 1981.

Grapard, Alan G. "Flying Mountains and Walkers of Emptiness: Towards a Definition of Sacred Space in Japanese Religion." *History of Religions* 20 (February 1982): 195–221.

Grieder, Terence. *Origins of Pre-Columbian Art.* Austin: University of Texas Press, 1982.

Guerra, Francisco. *The Pre-Columbian Mind.* New York: Seminar Press, 1971.

Gunn, Giles. *The Interpretation of Otherness: Literature, Religion and the American Imagination.* New York: Oxford University Press, 1979.

———. *The Culture of Criticism and the Criticism of Culture.* New York: Oxford University Press, 1987.

Hammond, Norman. *Ancient Maya Civilization.* New Brunswick, N.J.: Rutgers University Press, 1982.

———. "Lords of the Jungle: A Prosopography of Maya Archaeology." In *Civilizations in the Ancient Americas: Essays in Honor of Gordon R. Willey.* Ed. Richard M. Leventhal and Alan L. Kolata. Albuquerque: University of New Mexico Press, and Cambridge: Peabody Museum of Archaeology and Ethnology, 1983.

———. "Thrones of Blood." *Quarterly Review of Archaeology* 7 (June 1986): 8–10.

Hammond, Norman, ed. *Social Process in Maya Prehistory: Studies in Honour of Sir Eric Thompson.* London: Academic Press, 1977.

Hammond, Norman, and Gordon R. Willey, eds. *Maya Archaeology and Ethnohistory.* Austin: University of Texas Press, 1979.

Hanke, Lewis. *Aristotle and the American Indians.* Chicago: Henry Regenery Company, 1959.

———. *All Mankind Is One: A Study of the Disputation Between Bartolomé de las Casa and Juan Ginés de Sepulveda in 1550 on the Intellectual and Religious Capacity of the American Indian.* De Kalb: Northern Illinois University Press, 1974.

Hardoy, Jorge E. *Pre-Columbian Cities.* Trans. Judith Thorne. New York: Walker and Company, 1973.

Hartung, Horst. *Die Zeremonialzentren der Maya.* Graz, Austria: Akademische Druck-und Verlagsanstalt, 1971.

———. "Consideracíones sobre los trazos de centros ceremoniales Maya." *Actes du XXXVIII Congrès International des Américanistes, Stuttgart-Munich, 1968,* 4 (1972): 17–26.

———. "Ancient Maya Architecture and Planning: Possibilities and Limitations for Astronomical Studies." In *Native American Astronomy.* Ed. Anthony F. Aveni. Austin: University of Texas Press, 1977.

———. "Alignments in Architecture and Sculptures of Maya Center: Notes on Piedras Negras, Copan and Chichén Itzá." *Ibero-Amerikanische Archiv.* Neue Folge (Berlin: Colloquim Verlag Berlin, 1986): 223–40.

Haviland, William A. "A New Population Estimate for Tikal, Guatemala." *American Antiquity* 34 (1969): 429–33.

———. "Tikal, Guatemala and Mesoamerican Urbanism." *World Archaeology* 2 (1970): 186–98.

Hay, Clarence L., Ralph L. Linton, Samuel K. Lothrop, Harry L. Shapiro, and George C. Vaillant, eds. *The Maya and Their Neighbors.* New York: Appleton-Century, 1940.

Healan, Dan M. "Architectural Implications of Daily Life in Ancient Tollan, Hidalgo, Mexico." *World Archaeology* 9 (1977): 140–56.

———. "Architectural Implications of Daily Life in Ancient Tollan, Hidalgo, Mexico." In *Ancient Mesoamerica: Selected Readings.* Ed. John A. Graham. Palo Alto, Calif.: Peek Publications, 1981.

Henderson, John S. *The World of the Ancient Maya.* Ithaca, N.Y.: Cornell University Press, 1981.

Heyden, Doris. "An Interpretation of the Cave Underneath the Pyramid of the Sun in Teotihuacán, Mexico." *American Antiquity* 40 (April 1975): 131–47.

———. "Caves, Gods and Myths: World Views and Planning in Teotihuacán." In *Mesoamerican Sites and World-Views.* Ed. Elizabeth P. Benson. Washington: Dumbarton Oaks, 1981.

Holmes, William Henry. *Archaeological Studies Among the Ancient Cities of Mexico.* Chicago: Field Columbian Museum, 1895–97.

Hugh-Jones, Stephen. *The Palm and the Pleiades: Initiation and Cosmology in Northwest Amazonia.* Cambridge: Cambridge University Press, 1979.

Hurtado, E. D. "Return to the Sacred Cenote." *National Geographic* 120 (October 1961): 540–60.

Jakeman, M. Wells. *The Origin and History of the Maya.* Los Angeles: Research Publishing Co., 1945.

———. "The Identity of the Itzá." *American Antiquity* 12 (1946): 127–30.

Jauss, Hans Robert. "Literary History as a Challenge to Literary Theory." *New Literary History* 2 (Autumn 1970): 7–37.

Jencks, Charles, and George Baird, eds. *Meaning in Architecture.* New York: George Braziller, 1969.

Jiménez Moreno, Wiberto. "Tula y los Toltecas según las Fuentes Históricas." *Revista Mexicana de Estudio Antropológicos* 5 (1941): 79–83.

Johnsen, Harald, and Bjornar Olsen. "Hermeneutics and Archaeology: Philosophy and Contextual Archaeology." *American Antiquity* 57 (1992): 419–36.

Jones, Christopher, William R. Coe, and William A. Haviland. "Tikal: An Outline of Its Field Study (1956–1970) and a Project Bibliography." In *Supplement to the Handbook of Middle American Indians.* Vol. 1. Austin: University of Texas, 1981.

Jones, Lindsay. "The Hermeneutics of Sacred Architecture: A Reassessment of the Similitude Between Tula, Hidalgo and Chichén Itzá, Yucatán; Part I." *History of Religions* 32 (February 1993): 207–32.

———. "The Hermeneutics of Sacred Architecture: A Reassessment of the Similitude Between Tula, Hidalgo and Chichén Itzá, Yucatán; Part II." *History of Religions* 32 (May 1993): 315–42.

———. "Conquests of the Imagination: Maya-Mexican Polarity and the Story of Chichén Itzá, Yucatán." Unpublished manuscript.

Joyce, Thomas Athol. *Mexican Archaeology: An Introduction to the Archaeology of the Mexican and Maya Civilizations of Pre-Spanish America.* London: Philip Lee Warner, 1914.

———. *Maya and Mexican Art.* London: "The Studio" Ltd., 1927.

Katz, Friedrich. *The Ancient American Civilizations.* New York: Praeger Publishers, 1972.

Keen, Benjamin. *The Aztec Image in Western Thought.* New Brunswick, N.J.: Rutgers University Press, 1971.

Kelemen, Pál. *Medieval American Art.* New York: The Macmillan Company, 1943.

Kelley, David H. "Kakupacal and the Itzás." *Estudios de Cultura Maya* 8 (1968): 255–68.

———. *Deciphering the Maya Script.* Austin: University of Texas Press, 1976.

———. "Notes on Puuc Inscriptions and History." In *The Puuc: New Perspectives.* Ed. Lawrence Mills. Pella, Iowa: Central College, 1982.

Kidder, Alfred V. "A Program for Maya Research." *Hispanic American Historical Review* 17 (1937): 160–69.

———. "The Development of Maya Research." *Proceedings 2nd General Assembly, Pan American Institute of Geography and History, 1935* (1937): 218–25.

———. "Some Key Problems in New World Prehistory." In *Homenaje al Doctor Alfonso Caso.* Mexico, D.F.: Imprenta Nuevo Mundo, S.A., 1951.

———. "Earl Halsted Morris, 1889–1956." *American Antiquity* 22 (April 1957): 390–97.

———. "The Development of Maya Research." In *Alfred V. Kidder.* Richard B. Woodbury. New York: Columbia University Press, 1973.

Kirchhoff, Paul. "Mesoamerica." *Acta Americana* 1 (1943): 92–107.

———. "Quetzalcoatl, Huemac y el fin de Tula." *Cuadernos Americanos* 84 (1955): 163–96.

———. "Mesoamerica." In *Ancient Mesoamerica: Selected Readings.* Ed. John A. Graham. Palo Alto, Calif.: Peek Publications, 1981.

Klein, Cecelia F. "Woven Heaven, Tangled Earth: A Weaver's Paradigm of the Mesoamerican Cosmos." In *Ethnoastronomy and Archaeoastronomy in the American Tropics.* Ed. Anthony F. Aveni and Gary Urton. New York: New York Academy of Sciences, 1982.

———. "The Relation of Art History to Archaeology in the United States." In *Pre-Columbian Mesoamerica: Selected Readings.* Ed. Alana Cordy-Collins. Palo Alto, Calif.: Peek Publications, 1982.

Klemm, David E. *Hermeneutical Inquiry.* 2 vols. Atlanta: Scholars Press, 1986.

Kowalski, Jeff Karl. "Lords of the Northern Maya." *Expedition* 27 (1985): 50–60.

———. *The House of the Governor: A Maya Palace in Uxmal, Yucatán, Mexico.* Norman: University of Oklahoma Press, 1987.

Krochock, Ruth J. "The Hieroglyphic Inscriptions and Iconography of Temple of the Four Lintels and Related Monuments, Chichén Itzá, Yucatán, Mexico." Masters thesis, University of Texas at Austin, 1988.

Krupp, E. C. "The Observatory of Kukulcán." *Griffith Observer* 41 (September 1977): 2–20.

———. "The Serpent Descending." *Griffith Observer* 46 (September 1982): 11–21.

Kubler, George. "The Design of Space in Maya Architecture." In *Miscellanea Paul Rivet, Octogenario Dicata.* Mexico, 1958.

———. "On the Colonial Extinction of the Motifs of Pre-Columbian Art." In *Essays in Pre-Columbian Art and Archaeology.* Ed. Samuel K. Lothrop et al. Cambridge: Harvard University Press, 1961.

———. "Chichén Itzá y Tula." *Estudios de Cultura Maya* 1 (1961): 47–49.

———. *The Shape of Time: Remarks on the History of Things.* New Haven: Yale University Press, 1962.

———. "The Iconography of the Art of Teotihuacán." In *Studies in Pre-Columbian Art and Archaeology.* No. 4. Washington: Dumbarton Oaks, 1967.

———. "Period, Style and Meaning in Ancient American Art." *New Literary History* 1 (1970): 127–44.

———. "Science and Humanism Among Americanists." In *The Iconography of Middle America Sculpture.* Ignacio Bernal et al. New York: Metropolitan Museum of Art, 1973.

———. "History — or Anthropology — of Art?" *Critical Inquiry* 1 (June 1975): 757–67.

———. "Synopsis of the Meetings: Methodological Approaches." *Actes du XLII Congrès International des Américanistes, Paris, 1976,* 7 (1979): 283–89.

———. "Period, Style and Meaning in Ancient American Art." In *Ancient Mesoamerica, Selected Readings.* Ed. John A. Graham. Palo Alto, Calif.: Peek Publications, 1981.

———. "Serpent and Atlantean Columns: Symbols of Maya-Toltec Polity." *Journal of Society of Architectural Historians* 41 (May 1982): 93–115.

———. *The Art and Architecture of Ancient America.* 3d ed. New York: Penguin Books, 1984.

Landa, Diego de. *Relación de las Cosas de Yucatán.* Trans. and ed. Alfred M. Tozzer. Cambridge: Harvard University Press, 1941.

Le Plongeon, Augustus. *Sacred Mysteries Among the Mayas and Quichés.* New York: R. Macoy, 1856.

León-Portilla, Miguel. *Time and Reality in the Thought of the Maya.* Boston: Beacon Press, 1973.

Lewis, Oscar. *Tepoztlán: Village in Mexico.* New York: Holt, Rinehart and Winston, 1960.

Lincoln, Charles E. "Chichén Itzá: Clasico terminal o postclasico temprano?" *Boletín de la Escuela de Ciencias Antropológicas de la Universidad de Yucatán* 10 (1983): 3–29.

———. "The Chronology of Chichén Itzá: A Review of the Literature." In *Late Lowland Maya Civilization: Classic to Postclassic.* Ed. Jeremy A. Sabloff and E. Wyllys Andrews V. Albuquerque: University of New Mexico Press, 1986.

Linge, David E. "Introduction." In *Philosophical Hermeneutics.* Hans-Georg Gadamer. Trans. and ed. David E. Linge. Berkeley: University of California Press, 1976.

Linné, Sigvald. *The Art of Ancient America.* New York: Greystone Press, 1966.

Litvak King, Jaime. "En torno al problema de la definition de Mesoamerica." *Anales de Antropologia* 12 (1975): 171–95.

Lizana, Bernardo de. *Historia de Yucatán: Devocionario de Nuestra Señora de Izmal y Conquista Espiritual Impresa en 1633.* Reprint, Mexico, D.F.: Museo Nacional de Mexico, 1893.

Long, Charles. "The Study of Religion: Its Nature and Its Discourse." Inaugural Lecture of the Department of Religious Studies, University of Colorado, Boulder, October 7, 1980.

———. *Significations: Signs, Symbols, and Images in the Interpretation of Religion.* Philadelphia: Fortress Press, 1986.

López de Cogolludo, D. *Historia de Yucatán.* 2 vols. 3d ed. Mérida, Yucatán: n.p., 1867–68.

MacGowen, Kenneth. "The Orientation of Middle American Sites." *American Antiquity* 11 (1945): 118.

Magee, Susan F. *Mesoamerican Archaeology: A Guide to the Literature and Other Information Sources.* Austin: University of Texas Press, 1981.

Marcus, Joyce. "Territorial Organization of the Lowland Classic Maya." *Science* 180 (1973): 911–16.

———. "Archaeology and Religion: A Comparison of the Zapotec and Maya." *World Archaeology* 10 (1978): 172–91.

———. "Archaeology and Religion: A Comparison of the Zapotec and Maya." In *Ancient Mesoamerica: Selected Readings.* Ed. John A. Graham. Palo Alto, Calif.: Peek Publications, 1981.

Margain, Carlos R. "Pre-Columbian Architecture of Central Mexico." *Handbook of Middle American Indians: Archaeology of Northern Mesoamerica.* Vol. 10. Austin: University of Texas Press, 1971.

Marquina, Ignacio. *Architectura Prehispánica.* 2d ed. Mexico, D.F.: Instituto Nacional de Antropología e Historia, 1964.

Matos Moctezuma, Eduardo. *Proyecto Tula.* 2 vols. Mexico, D.F.: Instituto Nacional de Antropología e Historia, 1974, 1976.

———. "The Tula Chronology: A Revision." In *Middle Classic Mesoamerica: A.D. 400–700.* Ed. Esther Pasztory. New York: Columbia University Press, 1978.

Maudslay, Alfred P. "Archaeology." In *Biologia Centrali Americana.* Ed. Frederic Ducane Godman and Osbert Salvin. Vols. 1–4. London: Porter and Dulau, 1889–1902.

Meggers, Betty J. *Prehistoric Mesoamerica.* Chicago: Aldine, 1972.

Meyer, Jeffery F. "*Feng-Shui* of the Chinese City." *History of Religions* 18 (November 1978): 138–55.

Meyer, Leonard B. *Emotion and Meaning in Music.* Chicago: University of Chicago Press, 1956.

———. "Meaning in Music and Information Theory." *Journal of Aesthetics and Art Criticism* 15 (June 1957): 412–21.

———. "Some Remarks on Value and Greatness in Music." *Journal of Aesthetics and Art Criticism* 17 (June 1959): 486–500.

Milbrath, Susan. "Astronomical Images and Orientations in the Architecture of Chichén Itzá." In *New Directions in American Archaeoastronomy.* Ed. Anthony F. Aveni. Oxford: B.A.R. International Series 454, 1988.

———. "'Captains of the Itzá': Unpublished Mural Evidence From Chichén Itzá." In *Social Process in Maya Prehistory: Essays in Honour of Sir Eric Thompson.* Ed. Norman Hammond. London: Academic Press, 1977.

———. "The Maya and the Sea: Trade and Cult at Tancah and Tulum, Quintana Roo, Mexico." In *The Sea in the Pre-Columbian World.* Ed. Elizabeth P. Benson. Washington: Dumbarton Oaks, 1977.

———. "A Brief Outline of the Artistic Evidence for Classic Period Cultural Contact Between Maya Lowlands and Central Mexican Highlands." In *Middle Classic Mesoamerica: A.D. 400–700.* Ed. Esther Pasztory. New York: Columbia University Press, 1978.

———. "'The Little Descent': Manifest Destiny From the East." *Actes du XLII Congrès International des Américanistes, Paris, 1976,* 8 (1979): 221–35.

———. *Highland-Lowland Interaction in Mesoamerica: Interdisciplinary Approaches. A Conference at Dumbarton Oaks, October 18 and 19, 1980.* Washingon: Dumbarton Oaks Research Library and Collection, 1983.

Miller, Mary Ellen. "A Re-examination of the Mesoamerican Chacmool." *Art Bulletin* 67 (March 1985): 7–17.

———. "The Main Acropolis at Copán: Its Meaning and Function." In *Conference on the Southeast Maya Zone.* Ed. Gordon Willey and Elizabeth Boone. Washington: Dumbarton Oaks, in press.

Morley, Sylvanus G. *The Ancient Maya.* Stanford, Calif.: Stanford University Press, 1946, 1947.

———. *The Ancient Maya.* 3d ed. Rev. George W. Brainerd. Stanford, Calif.: Stanford University Press, 1956.

Morley, Sylvanus G., and George W. Brainerd. *The Ancient Maya.* 4th ed. Rev. Robert J. Sharer. Stanford, Calif.: Stanford University Press, 1983.

Morris, Ann Axtell. *Digging in Yucatán.* New York: Doubleday, 1931.

Morris, Earl H., Jean Charlot, and Ann Axtell Morris. *The Temple of the Warriors at Chichén Itzá, Yucatán.* 2 vols. Publication 406. Washington: Carnegie Institution of Washington, 1931.

Nicholson, Henry B. "Topiltzin Quetzalcoatl of Tollan: A Problem in Mesoamerican Ethnohistory." Ph.D. diss., Harvard University, 1957.

———. "Religion in Pre-Hispanic Mexico." In *Handbook of Middle American Indians: Archaeology of Northern Mesoamerica.* Vol. 10. Austin: University of Texas Press, 1971.

———. "Middle American Ethnohistory: An Overview." In *Handbook of Middle American Indians: Guide to the Ethnohistorical Sources.* Vol. 15. Austin: University of Texas Press, 1972.

———. Introduction. In *Origins of Religious Art and Iconography in Preclassic Mesoamerica.* Ed. H. B. Nicholson. Los Angeles: UCLA Latin American Center Publications, 1976.

———. "Preclassic Mesoamerican Iconography From the Perspective of the Postclassic: Problems in Interpretational Analysis." In *Origins of Religious Art and Iconography in Preclassic Mesoamerica.* Ed. H. B. Nicholson. Los Angeles: UCLA Latin American Center Publications, 1976.

Nitschke, Günter. "'Ma': The Japanese Sense of 'Place' in Old and New Architectural Planning." *Architectural Design* 36 (March 1966): 412–21.

Norberg-Schultz, Christian. *Intentions in Architecture.* Cambridge: Massachusetts Institute of Technology Press, 1965.

———. "Meaning in Architecture." In *Meaning in Architecture.* Ed. Charles Jencks and George Baird. New York: George Braziller, 1970.

———. *Meaning in Western Architecture.* New York: Rizzoli International Publications, 1975.

Nuttal, Zelia. *The Fundamental Principles of Old and New World Civilizations.* Cambridge, Mass.: Peabody Museum, 1901.

O'Gorman, Edmundo. *The Invention of America.* Bloomington: Indiana University Press, 1961.

Oliver, Paul, ed. *Shelter, Sign and Symbol.* Woodstock, N.Y.: Overlook Press, 1977.

Palacios, Enrique. "Teotihuacán, los Toltecas y Tula." *Revista Mexicana de Estudios Antropológicos* 5 (1941): 113–34.

Panofsky, Erwin. *Gothic Architecture and Scholasticism.* New York: Meridian Books, 1951.

Pasztory, Esther. "Masterpieces in Pre-Columbian Art." *Actes du XLII Congrès International des Américanistes, Paris, 1976,* 7 (1979): 377–90.

———, ed. *Middle Classic Mesoamerica A.D. 400–700.* New York: Columbia University Press, 1978.

Pearce, Kenneth. *The View From the Top of the Temple: Ancient Maya Civilization and Modern Maya Culture.* Albuquerque: University of New Mexico Press, 1984.

Pijoán, José. *Historia del Arte Precolumbino.* In *Summa Artis: História General del Arte,* Vol. 10. Barcelona, 1952.

Pilgrim, Richard B. "Intervals (*Ma*) in Space and Time: Foundations for a Religio-Aesthetic Paradigm in Japan." *History of Religions* 25 (1986): 255–77.

Piña Chan, Roman. "Exploracíon del Cenote de Chichén Itzá: 1967–68." *Boletin* 32 (June 1968).

———. *Informe Preliminar de la Reciente Exploración del Cenote Sagrado de Chichén Itzá.* Mexico, D.F.: Instituto Nacional de Antropología e Historia, 1970.

———. *Quetzalcoatl: Serpiente Emplumada.* Mexico, D.F.: Fondo Cultural Economica, 1977.

———. *Chichén Itzá: La Ciudad del los Brujos del Agua.* Mexico, D.F.: Fondo de Cultura Economica, 1980.

Pollock, H.E.D. *Round Structures of Aboriginal Middle America*. Publication 471. Washington: Carnegie Institution of Washington, 1936.

———. "Sources and Methods in the Study of Maya Architecture." In *The Maya and Their Neighbors*. Ed. Clarence L. Hay et al. New York: Appleton-Century, 1940.

———. "Architecture of the Maya Lowlands." In *Handbook of Middle American Indians: Archaeology of Southern Mesoamerica*. Vol. 2. Austin: University of Texas Press, 1965.

———. *The Puuc: An Architectural Survey of the Hill Country of Yucatán and Northern Campeche, Mexico*. Cambridge, Mass.: Peabody Museum, 1980.

Pollock, H.E.D., Ralph L. Roys, Tatiana Proskouriakoff, and A. Ledyard Smith. *Mayapán, Yucatán, Mexico*. Publication 619. Washington: Carnegie Institution of Washington, 1962.

Potter, David F. "Prehispanic Architecture and Sculpture in Central Yucatán." *American Antiquity* 41 (1976): 430–38.

Prescott, William H. *The History of the Conquest of Mexico*. New York: Harper and Brothers, 1843.

Price, Barbara J. "A Chronological Framework for Culture Development in Mesoamerica." In *The Valley of Mexico: Studies of Pre-Hispanic Ecology and Society*. Ed. Eric R. Wolf. Albuquerque: University of New Mexico Press, 1976.

Proskouriakoff, Tatiana. *A Study of Classic Maya Sculpture*. Publication 593. Washington: Carnegie Institution of Washington, 1950.

———. "Some Non-Classic Traits in the Sculpture of Yucatán." In *The Civilizations of Ancient America*. Ed. Sol Tax. Chicago: University of Chicago Press, 1951.

———. "Studies on Middle American Art." *Middle American Anthropology*. Social Science Monograph V. Washington: Pan American Union, 1958.

———. "Historical Implications of a Pattern of Dates at Piedras Negras, Guatemala." *American Antiquity* 25 (1960): 454–75.

———. *An Album of Maya Architecture*. Norman: University of Oklahoma Press, 1963.

———. "Historical Data in the Inscriptions of Yaxchilán. Part I." *Estudios de Cultura Maya* 3 (1963): 149–67.

———. "Historical Data in the Inscriptions of Yaxchilán. Part II." *Estudios de Cultura Maya* 4 (1964): 177–201.

———. "On Two Inscriptions at Chichén Itzá." In *Monographs and Papers in Maya Archaeology*. Ed. William R. Bullard Jr. Cambridge: Harvard University, 1970.

———. "Studies on Middle American Art." In *Anthropology and Art: Readings in Cross-Cultural Aesthetics*. Ed. Charlotte M. Otten. Austin: University of Texas Press, 1971.

Ragon, Michel. *The Space of Death: A Study of Funerary Architecture, Decoration, and Urbanism*. Charlottesville: University Press of Virginia, 1981.

Rathje, William L. "The Origin and Development of Lowland Classic Maya Civilization." *American Antiquity* 36 (1971): 275–85.

———, et al. "Trade and Power in Post-Classic Yucatán: Initial Observations." In *Mesoamerican Archaeology: New Approaches*. Austin: University of Texas Press, 1974.

Recinos, Adrián, trans. *Popol Vuh: The Sacred Book of the Quiché Maya*. Trans. Delia Goetz and Sylvanus G. Morley. Norman: University of Oklahoma Press, 1950.

———, and Delia Goetz, trans. *The Annals of the Cakchiquels*. Norman: University of Oklahoma Press, 1953.

Redfield, Robert. *Folk Culture of Yucatán*. Chicago: University of Chicago Press, 1941.

———. *A Village That Chose Progress: Chan Kom Revisited*. Chicago: University of Chicago Press, 1950.

Redfield, Robert, and Alfonso Villa Rojas. *Chan Kom: A Maya Village*. Chicago: University of Chicago Press, 1934.

Réville, Albert. *The Native Religions of Mexico and Peru*. New York: Charles Scribner's Sons, 1884.

Rivard, Jean-Jacques. "A Hierophany at Chichén Itzá." *Miscellaneous Series*. No. 26. Greeley: University of Northern Colorado, 1971.

Robertson, Donald. *Pre-Columbian Architecture*. New York: George Braziller, 1963.

———. "Anthropology, Archaeology and the History of Art." In *Codex Wauchope: A Tribute Roll, Human Mosaic*. Ed. Mario Giardino et al. New Orleans: Tulane University Press, 1978.

Roys, Lawrence. *The Engineering Knowledge of the Maya.* Publication 436. Washington: Carnegie Institution of Washington, 1934.

Roys, Ralph L. *The Political Geography of the Yucatán Maya.* Publication 613. Washington: Carnegie Institution of Washington, 1957.

———. *The Book of Chilam Balam of Chumayel.* Norman: University of Oklahoma Press, 1967.

———, trans. and ed. *The Book of Chilam Balam of Chumayel.* Publication 438. Washington: Carnegie Institution of Washington, 1933.

Rudofsky, Bernard. *The Prodigious Builders.* New York: Harcourt Brace Jovanovich, 1977.

Ruppert, Karl. *The Caracol at Chichén Itzá, Yucatán, Mexico.* Publication 454. Washington: Carnegie Institution of Washington, 1935.

———. *The Mercado, Chichén Itzá, Yucatán.* Publication 546. Washington: Carnegie Institution of Washington, 1943.

———. *Chichén Itzá: Architectural Notes and Plans.* Publication 595. Washington: Carnegie Institution of Washington, 1952.

Ruskin, John. *The Seven Lamps of Architecture.* 1849. Reprint, New York: Noonday Press, 1971.

Ruz Lhuillier, Alberto. *Guia Arqueologia de Tula.* Mexico, D.F.: Ateneo Nacional de Ciencias y Artes de Mexico, 1945.

———. "Chichén Itzá y Palenque, ciudades fortifacados." *Homenaje al don Alfonso Caso.* Mexico, D.F.: Imprenta Nuevo Mundo, S.A., 1951.

———. "Chichén Itzá y Tula: Commentaries a un Ensayo." *Estudios de Cultura Maya* 2 (1962): 205–20.

———. "Influencias Mexicanas sobre los Mayas." In *Desarrolo Cultural de los Mayas.* Ed. Evon Z. Vogt and Alberto Ruz Lhuillier. Mexico, D.F.: Universidad Nacional Autonoma de Mexico, 1964.

Sabloff, Jeremy A., and E. Wyllys Andrews V, eds. *Late Lowland Maya Civilization: Classic to Postclassic.* Albuquerque: University of New Mexico Press, 1986.

Sabloff, Jeremy A., and C. C. Lamberg-Karlovsky, eds. *Ancient Civilization and Trade.* Albuquerque: University of New Mexico Press, 1975.

Sahagún, Fray Bernardino de. *The Florentine Codex: General History of the Things of New Spain.* Trans. and ed. Arthur J.O. Anderson and Charles Dibble. 12 vols. Sante Fe, N.M.: School of American Research and University of Utah, 1950–69.

Sanders, William T., and Barbara J. Price. *Mesoamerica: The Evolution of a Civilization.* New York: Random House, 1968.

Satterthwaite, Linton. "An Unusual Type of Building in the Maya Old Empire." *Maya Research* 3 (January 1930): 62–73.

———. "Notes on the Work of the Fourth and Fifth University Expeditions to Piedras Negras, Petén, Guatemala." *Maya Research* 3 (January 1936): 74–91.

Schavelzon, Daniel. "Temples, Caves, or Monsters? Notes on Zoomorphic Facades in Pre-Hispanic Architecture." In *Third Palenque Round Table, 1978.* Part 2. Ed. Merle Greene Robertson. Austin: University of Texas Press, 1980.

Schele, Linda. "Sacred Site and World-View at Palenque." In *Mesoamerican Sites and World-Views.* Ed. Elizabeth P. Benson. Washington: Dumbarton Oaks, 1981.

———, and Mary Ellen Miller. *The Blood of Kings: Dynasty and Ritual in Maya Art.* Ft. Worth, Texas: Kimbell Art Museum, 1986.

Schellhas, Paul. "Fifty Years of Maya Research." *Maya Research* 3 (April 1936): 129–39.

Scholes, F. V., and R. L. Roys. *The Maya Chontal Indians of Acalan-Tixchel: A Contribution to the History and Ethnography of the Yucatán Peninsula.* Publication 560. Washington: Carnegie Institution of Washington, 1948.

Scholes, F. V., R. L. Roys, and E. B. Adams. "History of the Maya Area." *Carnegie Institution of Washington Yearbook* 44 (1945): 177–83.

Schuman, Malcolm K. "Archaeology and Ethnohistory: The Case of the Lowland Maya." *Ethnohistory* 24 (Winter 1977): 1–18.

Schwerin, Karl H. "The Future of Ethnohistory." *Ethnohistory* 23 (Fall 1976): 323–41.

Scully, Vincent. *The Earth, the Temple and the Gods: Greek Sacred Architecture.* New Haven: Yale University Press, 1962.

Séjourné, Laurette. *Burning Water: Thought and Religion in Ancient Mexico.* Berkeley, Calif.: Shambhala, 1976.

Sharp, Rosemary. "Architecture as Inter-elite Communication in Preconquest Oaxaca, Veracruz, and Yucatán." In *Middle Classic Mesoamerica, A.D. 400–700*. Ed. Esther Pasztory. New York: Columbia University Press, 1978.

Sidrys, Raymond. "Megalithic Architecture and Sculpture of the Ancient Maya." In *Papers on the Economy and Architecture of the Ancient Maya*. Ed. Raymond Sidrys. Los Angeles: UCLA Institute of Archaeology, 1978.

Simpson, Leslie Byrd. *Many Mexicos*. 4th rev. ed. Berkeley: University of California Press, 1969.

Smith, A. Ledyard. "Architecture of the Guatemalan Highlands. In *Handbook of Middle American Indians: Archaeology of Southern Mesoamerica*. Vol. 2. Austin: University of Texas Press, 1965.

Smith, Jonathan Z. "The Influence of Symbols Upon Social Change." *Worship* 44 (October 1970): 457–74.

———. *Map Is Not Territory: Studies in the History of Religions*. Leiden, Netherlands: E. J. Brill, 1978.

Soundara Rajan, K. V. *Invitation to Indian Architecture*. New Delhi: Arnold-Heinemann, 1984.

Soustelle, Jacques. *The Four Suns*. New York: Grossman, 1971.

Spinden, Herbert J. *A Study of Maya Art: Its Subject Matter and Historical Development*. Cambridge, Mass.: Peabody Museum, 1913.

———. *Ancient Civilization of Mexico and Central America*. Handbook Series no. 3. New York: American Museum of Natural History, 1917.

———. *Maya Art and Civilization*. Indian Hills, Colo.: Falcon's Wing Press, 1957.

———. "Alfred Marston Tozzer (1877–1954)." *National Academy of Sciences, Biographical Memoirs* 30 (1957): 383–97.

———. *A Study of Maya Art: Its Subject Matter and Historical Development*. Intro. and bib. J. Eric S. Thompson. New York: Dover Publications, 1975.

Stedman, Raymond William. *Shadows of the Indian: Stereotypes in American Culture*. Norman: University of Oklahoma Press, 1982.

Stephens, John Lloyd. *Incidents of Travel in Central America, Chiapas and Yucatán*. 2 vols. New York: Harper and Brothers, 1841.

———. *Incidents of Travel in Yucatán*. 2 vols. New York: Harper and Brothers, 1843.

———. *Incidents of Travel in Yucatán*. 2 vols. New York: Dover Publications, 1963.

———. *Incidents of Travel in Central America, Chiapas and Yucatán*. 2 vols. New York: Dover Publications, 1969.

Stewart, Julian. "The Direct Historical Approach to Archaeology." *American Antiquity* 38 (1942): 195–99.

Stierlin, Henri. *Living Architecture: Mayan*. Fribourg, Switzerland: Olbourne Book Co., Lts., 1964.

Strong, William Duncan. Review of Sylvanus G. Morley, *The Ancient Maya*. *American Anthropologist* 49 (1947): 640–45.

Sturtevant, William, C. "Anthropology, History, and Ethnohistory." *Ethnohistory* 13 (1966): 1–57.

Suger, Abbot. *On the Abbey Church of St. Denis and Its Art Treasures*. Ed. and trans. Erwin Panofsky. Princeton, N.J.: Princeton University Press, 1979.

Sullivan, Lawrence E. "Astral Myths Rise Again: Interpreting Religious Astronomy." *Criterion* 22 (Winter 1983): 12–17.

Taylor, Walter W. *A Study of Archaeology*. Memoir Series, no. 69. Menasha, Wis.: American Anthropological Association, 1948.

———. "Clyde Kluckhohn and American Archaeology." In *Culture and Life: Essays in Honor of Clyde Kluckhohn*. Ed. Walter W. Taylor, John L. Fischer, and Evon Z. Vogt. Carbondale: Southern Illinois University Press, 1973.

Thompson, Edward H. *People of the Serpent*. Boston: Houghton Mifflin Co., 1932.

———. *The High Priest's Grave: Chichén Itzá, Yucatán, Mexico*. Intro. J. Eric Thompson. Chicago: Field Museum of Natural History, 1938.

———. *People of the Serpent*. New York: Capricorn Books, 1960.

Thompson, J. Eric S. "A New Method of Deciphering Yucatecan Dates With Special Reference to Chichén Itzá." In *Contributions to American Archaeology 22*. Publication 483. Washington: Carnegie Institution of Washington, 1937.

———. "Archaeological Problems of the Lowland Maya." In *The Maya and Their Neighbors*. Ed. Clarence L. Hay et al. New York: Appleton-Century, 1940.

———. "A Coordination of the History of Chichén Itzá With Ceramic Sequences in Central Mexico." *Revista Mexicana de Estudios Antropológicos* 5 (1941): 97–111.

———. "A Survey of the Northern Maya Area." *American Antiquity* 11 (1945): 2–24.

———. Review of Sylvanus G. Morley, *The Ancient Maya. New Mexico Quarterly Review* 17 (1947): 503–4.

———. *The Rise and Fall of Maya Civilization.* Norman: University of Oklahoma Press, 1954.

———. Review of Alfred M. Tozzer, *Chichén Itzá and Its Cenote of Sacrifice. American Journal of Archaeology* 63 (1959): 119–20.

———. *Maya Archaeologist.* Norman: University of Oklahoma Press, 1963.

———. *Maya History and Religion.* Norman: University of Oklahoma Press, 1970.

Tichy, Frank. "Order and Relationship of Space and Time in Mesoamerica: Myth or Reality." In *Mesoamerican Sites and World-Views.* Ed. Elizabeth P. Benson. Washington: Dumbarton Oaks, 1976.

Todorov, Tzvetan. *The Conquest of America: The Question of the Other.* Trans. Richard Howard. New York: Harper and Row, 1985.

Toscano, Salvador. *Arte Precolombino de Mexico y de la America Central.* Mexico, D.F.: Universidad Nacional Autonoma de México, 1944.

Totten, George O. *Maya Architecture.* Washington: Maya Press, 1926.

Townsend, Richard F. *State and Cosmos in the Art of Tenochtitlán.* Studies in Pre-Columbian Art and Archaeology, no. 20. Washington: Dumbarton Oaks, 1979.

———. "Pyramid and Sacred Mountain." In *Ethnoastronomy and Archaeoastronomy in the American Tropics.* Ed. Anthony Aveni and Gary Urton. New York: New York Academy of Sciences, 1982.

———. "Coronation at Tenochtitlán." In *The Imagination of Matter: Religion and Ecology in Mesoamerican Traditions.* Ed. David Carrasco. B.A.R. International Series 515. Oxford: B.A.R., 1989.

Tozzer, Alfred M. "The Toltec Architect of Chichén Itzá." In *American Indian Life.* Ed. Elsie Clews Parson. New York: B. W. Huebsch, 1922.

———. "Architecture and Romance." *Saturday Review of Literature* (19 June 1926): 862.

———. "Maya and Toltec Figures at Chichén Itzá." *Actes du XIII Congrès International des Américanistes, New York, 1928* (1930): 155–64.

———. "Maya Research." *Maya Research* 1 (1934): 3–19.

———. *Chichén Itzá and Its Cenote of Sacrifice: A Comparative Study of Contemporaneous Maya and Toltec.* Memoirs of the Peabody Museum, vols. 11 and 12. Cambridge: Harvard University, 1957.

———, trans. and ed. *Landa's Relación de las Cosas de Yucatán.* Papers of the Peabody Museum of Archaeology and Ethnography, vol. 10. Cambridge: Harvard University, 1941.

Troike, Nancy P. "Fundamental Changes in the Interpretation of the Mixtec Codices." *American Antiquity* 43 (1978): 553–68.

———. "Fundamental Changes in the Interpretation of the Mixtec Codices." In *Ancient Mesoamerica: Selected Readings.* Ed. John A. Graham. Palo Alto, Calif.: Peek Publications, 1981.

Tuan, Yi-Fu. *Space and Place: The Perspective of Experience.* Minneapolis: University of Minnesota Press, 1977.

Tucci, Giuseppe. *The Theory and Practice of the Mandala.* Trans. Alan Houghton Brodrick. London: Rider and Co., 1961.

Turner, Victor. "The Center Out There: Pilgrim's Goal." *History of Religions* 12 (February 1973): 191–215.

———, and Edith Turner. *Image and Pilgrimage in Christian Culture.* New York: Columbia University Press, 1978.

Vaillant, George C. *Artists and Craftsmen in Ancient Central America.* New York: American Museum of National History, 1935.

———. *The Aztecs of Mexico: Origin, Rise and Fall of the Aztec Nation.* New York: Doubleday, Duran and Co., 1944.

———. *The Aztecs of Mexico: Origin, Rise and Fall of the Aztec Nation.* 2d ed. Rev. Suzannah B. Vaillant. New York: Doubleday, Duran and Co., 1962.

Van der Leeuw, Gerardus. *Sacred and Profane Beauty: The Holy in Art.* New York: Holt, Rinehart and Winston, 1963.

Vasquez, Juan A. "The Religions of Mexico and of Central and South America." In *A Reader's Guide to the Great Religions.* Ed. Charles J. Adams. New York: Free Press, 1977.

Vásquez, Irene Sosa. *Images of the Unspoke Maya: Silence and Discourse Concerning the New World Classic Maya Culture.* Ph.D. diss., Duke University, 1982.

Ventur, Pierre. *Maya Ethnohistorian: The Ralph L. Roys Papers.* Nashville: Vanderbilt University, 1978.

Vitruvius. *The Ten Books of Architecture.* Trans. Morris Hicky Morgan. New York: Dover Publications, 1960.

Vogt, Evon Z. "Some Aspects of the Sacred Geography of Highland Chiapas." In *Mesoamerican Sites and World-Views.* Ed. Elizabeth P. Benson. Washington: Dumbarton Oaks, 1981.

von Hagen, Victor Wolfgang. *Maya Explorer: John Lloyd Stephens and the Lost Cities of Central America and Yucatán.* Norman: University of Oklahoma Press, 1948.

———. *Frederick Catherwood, Archt.* New York: Oxford University Press, 1950.

———. *World of the Maya.* New York: New American Library, 1960.

Von Simson, Otto. *The Gothic Cathedral: Origins of the Medieval Concept of Order.* Princeton, N.J.: Princeton University Press, 1956.

Wach, Joachim. *The Sociology of Religion.* Chicago: University of Chicago Press, 1944.

———. *Types of Religious Experience: Christian and Non-Christian.* Chicago: University of Chicago Press, 1951.

———. *The Comparative Study of Religions.* Ed. Joseph M. Kitagawa. New York: Columbia University Press, 1958.

———. *Introduction to the History of Religions.* Ed. Joseph M. Kitagawa and Gregory D. Alles. New York: Macmillan Publishing Company, 1988.

Wauchope, Robert. *Lost Tribes and Sunken Continents: Myth and Method in the Study of American Indians.* Chicago: University of Chicago Press, 1962.

———, ed. *They Found Buried Cities: Exploration and Excavation in the American Tropics.* Chicago: University of Chicago Press, 1965.

Weaver, Muriel Porter. *The Aztecs, Maya, and Their Predecessors.* New York: Seminar Press, 1972.

Westheim, Paul. *The Art of Ancient Mexico.* Garden City, N.J.: Anchor Books, 1965.

Wheatley, Paul. *The Pivot of the Four Quarters: A Preliminary Enquiry Into the Origins and Character of the Ancient Chinese City.* Chicago: Aldine, 1971.

Willard, Theodore A. *The City of the Sacred Well.* New York: Century, 1926.

———. *The Lost Empires of the Itzáes and Mayas.* Glendale, Calif.: Arthur H. Clark, 1933.

Willey, Gordon R. *An Introduction to American Archaeology.* 2 vols. Englewood Cliffs, N.J.: Prentice Hall, 1966.

———. "Alfred Vincent Kidder." *National Academy of Science, Biographical Memoirs* 39 (1967): 293–322.

———. "Mesoamerican Art and Iconography and the Integrity of the Mesoamerican Ideological System." In *The Iconography of Middle American Sculpture.* Ignacio Bernal et al. New York: Metropolitan Museum of Art, 1973.

———. "External Influences on the Lowland Maya: 1940 and 1975 Perspectives." In *Social Process in Maya Prehistory: Studies in Honour of Sir Eric Thompson.* Ed. Norman Hammond. London: Academic Press, 1977.

———. "Recent Researches and Perspectives in Mesoamerican Archaeology: An Introductory Commentary." *Supplement to Handbook of Middle American Indians.* Vol. 1. Austin: University of Texas Press, 1981.

Willey, Gordon R., Gordon Ekholm, and Rene Millon. "The Patterns of Farming Life and Civilization." In *Handbook of Middle American Indians: Natural Environment and Early Cultures,* Vol. 1. Austin: University of Texas Press, 1964.

Willey, Gordon R., and Philip Phillips. *Method and Theory in American Archaeology.* Chicago: University of Chicago Press, 1958.

Willey, Gordon R., and Jeremy A. Sabloff. *A History of American Archaeology.* 2d ed. San Francisco: W. H. Fremont and Co., 1980.

Wittkower, Rudolph. *Architectural Principles in the Age of Humanism.* New York: W. W. Norton and Co., 1971.

Wolf, Eric. *Sons of the Shaking Earth.* Chicago: University of Chicago Press, 1959.

Wolfe, Tom. *From Bauhaus to Our House.* New York: Pocket Books, 1981.

Woodall, J. Ned. *An Introduction to Modern Archaeology.* Cambridge, Mass.: Schenkman, 1972.

Woodbury, Richard B. *Alfred V. Kidder.* New York: Columbia University Press, 1973.

Woodward, Hiram W. "Borobudur and the Mirrorlike Mind." *Archaeology* 34 (November-December 1981): 40–47.

Wray, Donald E. "The Historical Significance of the Murals in the Temple of the Warriors, Chichén Itzá." *American Antiquity* 11 (1945): 25–27.

Wren, Linnea A. "The Great Ball Court Stone From Chichén Itzá." Paper presented at the Mesa Redonda de Palenque, 1986.

Wren, Linnea A., and Peter Schmidt. "A New Sculpture From the Great Ball Court at Chichén Itzá." Paper presented at the Annual Meeting of the Society for American Archaeology, Portland, Oregon, 1984.

Yadeún Angulo, Juan. *El Estado y la Ciudad: El Caso de Tula, Hgo.* Mexico, D.F.: Instituto Nacional de Antropología e Historia, 1975.

Zapata Alonzo, Gualberto. *Guide to Puuc Region: Uxmal, Kabah, Xlapak, Sayil, Labná.* Mérida, Yucatán: Dante, n.d.

Zimmerman, Charlotte. "The Hermeneutics of the Maya Cult of the Cross." *Numen* 12 (April 1965): 139–59.

Zuidema, R. T. *The Ceque System of Cuzco: The Social Organization of the Capital of the Inca.* Leiden, Netherlands: Brill, 1964.

———. "The Inca Calendar." In *Native American Astronomy.* Ed. Anthony F. Aveni. Austin: University of Texas Press, 1971.

Index